Germany
A New Social and Economic History

General Editors: Sheilagh Ogilvie and Bob Scribner

Already published

VOLUME I: 1450–1630
Edited by Bob Scribner

VOLUME II: 1630–1800
Edited by Sheilagh Ogilvie

In preparation

VOLUME III: SINCE 1800
Edited by Sheilagh Ogilvie and Richard Overy

GERMANY

A New Social and Economic History

Volume 2
1630–1800

Edited by Sheilagh Ogilvie

Lecturer in the Faculty of Economics and Politics and
Fellow of Trinity College, University of Cambridge

A member of the Hodder Headline Group
LONDON • NEW YORK • SYDNEY • AUCKLAND

First published in Great Britain in 1996 by
Arnold, a member of the Hodder Headline group,
338 Euston Road, London NW1 3BH
175 Fifth Avenue, New York, NY 10010

Distributed exclusively in the USA by
St Martin's Press Inc.,
175 Fifth Avenue,
New York, NY 10010

British Library Cataloguing in Publication Data
A catalogue entry for this book is available from the British Library

Library of Congress Cataloging-in-Publication Data
Germany : a new social and economic history / edited by Bob Scribner.
 p. cm.
Includes bibliographical references and index.
Contents: Vol. 1. 1450–1630
ISBN 0–340–51332–2. — ISBN 0–340–65217–9
 1. Germany—Social conditions. 2. Germany—Economic conditions.
I. Scribner, Robert W.
HN445.G472 1995
306'.0943—dc20

95-17543
CIP

ISBN 0 340 51395 0 (Hb)
ISBN 0 340 65216 0 (Pb)

Typeset in 10/12pt Sabon by Anneset, Weston-super-Mare, Avon
Printed and bound in Great Britain by J W Arrowsmith Ltd, Bristol

Contents

List of Figures and Tables   vii
Overview of Contents of Volumes I and II   ix
General Preface   xi
Preface to Volumes I and II   xiii
Acknowledgements   xv
Abbreviations   xvi

1. Social and Economic Landscapes   JÖRN SIEGLERSCHMIDT   1
2. Population Change and the Economy   ERNEST BENZ   39
3. Agriculture and Agrarian Society   HEIDE WUNDER   63
4. Trade   PETER KRIEDTE   100
5. Social Structure   OLAF MÖRKE   134
6. Learned Men and Merchants: The Growth of the *Bürgertum*
   ROBERT VON FRIEDEBURG and WOLFGANG MAGER   164
7. The Growth of the Modern State   PAUL MÜNCH   196
8. War, Economy, and Society   BERNHARD STIER and
   WOLFGANG VON HIPPEL   233
9. The Beginnings of Industrialization   SHEILAGH OGILVIE   263
10. Confession as a Social and Economic Factor
    KASPAR VON GREYERZ   309
11. Daily Life, Consumption, and Material Culture
    ERNST SCHUBERT   350
12. Poverty and Poor Relief   ROBERT JÜTTE   377

General Index   405
Index of Modern Authors   416

Figures and Tables

Figures

1.1 The Holy Roman Empire around 1550   3
1.2 Distribution and location of hammer mills (manufacturing iron) during the middle ages in the Upper Palatinate   6
1.3 Geographical distribution of agricultural yields (dry matter product) on the basis of crop results 1910–13 and 1936/37   10
1.4 Relation between crop and average humidity 1909–13   11
1.5a Forest area at the beginning of the middle ages in Bohemia and Saxony   13
1.5b Forest area in Bohemia and Saxony today   14
1.6 Desertion of settlements during the later middle ages   15
1.7 Viniculture in Germany since the middle ages   18
1.8 Size and location of German towns above 500 inhabitants around 1700   27
1.9 Size and location of German towns above 500 inhabitants around 1800   28
1.10 Population density in Germany around 1800   29
3.1 Payments by peasants and recipients of these payments, before the peasant emancipation in Germany   72–3
4.1 Hamburg's trading fleet, 1765–1800   118
4.2 Arrival of ships in Bremen, 1755–1800   119
4.3 The Leipzig fairs, 1763–1800   121
9.1 Map of the Holy Roman Empire of the German Nation after 1742 (excluding Austrian Lands)   272
12.1 The decline in the purchasing power of the wages of building workers (masons and carpenters) in selected German cities, 1401–1850 (day wages in kilograms of grain)   381
12.2 Decline of economic assets in case of widowhood in early modern Lemgo, c. 1500   383
12.3 The causes of poverty in Würzburg (1791) and Cologne (1798) (percentage of poor families)   385
12.4 Expenditure on public poor-relief in selected German towns, 1528–1720   399

Tables

4.1   Prussia's balance of trade, 1795–6   112
4.2   The merchant fleets of Hamburg, Bremen, and Lübeck in
      July 1786   119
9.1   German industrial regions, *c.* 1800: a provisional survey   270–1
12.1 Disease conditions of foreign recipients of alms in Lower
      Saxony in the seventeenth and eighteenth centuries   379
12.2 The structure of poor households in a German and an
      English town in the sixteenth century   382
12.3 The sex ratio of poor-relief recipients   382
12.4 Distribution of poverty among male citizens in major
      occupational groups (percentage of poor-relief recipients)   384
12.5 'Fiscal poor' in early modern German tax records   386
12.6 Poor-relief recipients in selected German towns   388
12.7 Distribution of charitable legacies in Münster, 1530–1618   397

Contents of Volumes I and II

Volume I: 1450–1630, edited by Bob Scribner

1. Economic Landscapes   TOM SCOTT
2. The Population of Late Medieval and Early Modern Germany CHRISTIAN PFISTER
3. The Agrarian Economy 1300–1600   WERNER RÖSENER
4. Consumption and Demand   ULF DIRLMEIER and GERHARD FOUQUET
5. The Urban Network of Early Modern Germany   TOM SCOTT and BOB SCRIBNER
6. Markets and Marketing, Town and Country   ROLF KIEßLING
7. The Nature of Early Capitalism   WILLIAM J. WRIGHT
8. Gender and the Worlds of Work   MERRY E. WIESNER
9. German Social Structure, 1300–1600   CHRISTOPHER R. FRIEDRICHS
10. The Social and Economic Role of Institutions   THOMAS A. BRADY JR
11. Communities and the Nature of Power   BOB SCRIBNER
12. Daily Life in Late Medieval and Early Modern Germany   ROBERT JÜTTE
13. The Structure of Belief: Confessionalism and Society, 1500–1600 R. PO-CHIA HSIA

Volume II: 1630–1800, edited by Sheilagh Ogilvie

1. Social and Economic Landscapes   JÖRN SIEGLERSCHMIDT
2. Population Change and the Economy   ERNEST BENZ
3. Agriculture and Agrarian Society   HEIDE WUNDER
4. Trade   PETER KRIEDTE
5. Social Structure   OLAF MÖRKE
6. Learned Men and Merchants: The Growth of the *Bürgertum* ROBERT VON FRIEDEBURG and WOLFGANG MAGER
7. The Growth of the Modern State   PAUL MÜNCH
8. War, Economy, and Society   BERNHARD STIER and WOLFGANG VON HIPPEL
9. The Beginnings of Industrialization   SHEILAGH OGILVIE
10. Confession as a Social and Economic Factor   KASPAR VON GREYERZ
11. Daily Life, Consumption, and Material Culture   ERNST SCHUBERT
12. Poverty and Poor Relief   ROBERT JÜTTE

General Preface

There has long been no adequate or modern social and economic history of Germany, despite a proud tradition of Germanophone scholarship in the field since the nineteenth century, especially on the traditional themes of economic history (trade, capitalism, craft production, agriculture). In part this has been the result of the scope and complexity of the German-speaking world, whose diverse developments over the centuries have made it no less difficult to produce overviews of its political history. To complicate the problem, there have been striking new advances in several fields of history over the past generation – historical demography and family structure; the history of disease, diet, and nutrition; material culture and daily life; and climate and ecology as historical factors. There have been new approaches to the history of social structure, work, forms of production, and the relationships between town and country, while awareness of the importance of gender has radically altered our historical perspectives. There has also been a considerable interpretative reorientation. The *Annales* paradigm, with its emphasis on long-term structures and the material basis of culture and society, brought about a revolution in French historiography, but its general approach was only slowly received in German scholarship, the more so since its implicit demand for an *histoire totale* radically called into question the more compartmentalized approach of traditional social and economic history. All these developments explain why the project of a general social and economic history of Germany has become a formidable task beyond the capabilities of any one scholar.

There has been, however, a growing volume of new work in many specialist fields which makes possible a collective attempt at a synthesis suitable for use by teachers, students, and general readers. Some recent scholarship has taken the form of traditional economic history, building on and incorporating the work of the great pioneers, while a great deal of it has also been inspired by the *Annales* school. In some areas, older approaches have been cross-fertilized with the new, as in the case of agricultural history, which has profited from recent work on climatology and ecology. Newer fields of research such as demography have changed some of our commonplace generalizations, or opened up new material to historical scrutiny, as in the case of daily life. The range of expertise and coverage required to make the best use of this scholarship demands a team of authors, each of whom is a specialist scholar, summarizing, and generalizing from, the most recent research in a number of major topics. The themes of each chapter have been chosen for attention because they either encompass structures fundamental to the development of economy and society, such as population, agriculture, consumption, trade, or industry; or else they present a significant development within a given period (early capitalism, poverty and poor-relief, confessionalization). It is the aim of the work as a whole to keep in view the long-term development of economy and society in Germany, while directing attention to characteristic features of a given century or phase of socioeconomic development.

Preface to Volumes 1 and 2

The period covered by the first two volumes is that of the later middle ages and early modern centuries, from *c.* 1300 to 1800. The history of these centuries can most suitably be conceived of as a *longue durée*, involving a period of contraction (1300–1450) followed by one of expansion (1450–1600), succeeded by another period of contraction (1600–1700) and incipient recovery (1700–1800). By treating this extended period as a unity, it will be possible to gain an overview of long-term structural developments in demography, agriculture, manufacture, consumption, and so on, while examining their interaction with the characteristic social formations of the medieval and early modern periods up to the eve of industrialization. However, each volume has its own distinctive focus. That of Volume I is the late medieval 'crises' – those associated with plague, population decline, economic contraction, and the 'crisis of feudalism' – and the age of the Reformation, with its characteristic themes of early capitalism, religious and social upheaval, and growing secular control of the church. Although this volume concentrates its attention more narrowly on the period 1450–*c.* 1630, it is necessary to survey some developments back to 1300 in order to gain a better appreciation of their scope and complexity. The focus of Volume II is the dislocation caused by renewed contraction and economic crisis, the impact of the Thirty Years War, the beginnings of industrialization, integration into world colonial markets, mercantilism and cameralism, and the growth of bureaucratic absolutist states. Where appropriate, German developments have been situated within a wider context of European developments.

Rather than merely repeating the same themes in both volumes for different chronological periods, each has a slightly different emphasis with complementary themes. Thus, discussion of urban networks, social and economic institutions, the nature of communities, and the socioeconomic features of gender relations are discussed in Volume I, but provide a background for Volume II. Analysis of the impact of warfare, of long-distance trade, of the growth of the middle classes and of the intervention of the state in economy and society demands special attention in Volume II. Although these themes are not absent in Volume I, the generalizations derived from the later period have applicability for the overall chronological span of the two volumes. Within each volume there has inevitably been some overlap of subject-matter, as individual authors trace the ramifications of their themes. Thus many issues are discussed from varying angles in two or three chapters, and a comprehensive grasp is made possible through the index and by comparison between chapters.

Acknowledgements

The editor wishes to thank the Centre for History and Economics at King's College, Cambridge, and the Pew Trust, for research support in 1994–5 during the final editing of this volume. The editor also wishes to thank the Ellen McArthur Fund, Cambridge University, for generous support to enable the drawing of maps and figures in this volume.

Abbreviations

AHR	American Historical Review
ARG	Archiv für Reformationsgeschichte
BdLG	Blätter für deutsche Landesgeschichte
CEH	Central European History
EcHR	Economic History Review
fl.	florins, gulden
GG	Geschichte und Gesellschaft
HansGbl	Hansische Geschichtsblätter
HessJbLG	Hessisches Jahrbuch für Landesgeschichte
HZ	Historische Zeitschrift
Jb	Jahrbuch
JbfränkLF	Jahrbuch für fränkische Landesforschung
JbGFeudalismus	Jahrbuch für Geschichte des Feudalismus
JbRegG	Jahrbuch für Regionalgeschichte
JbWG	Jahrbuch für Wirtschaftsgeschichte
JEEH	Journal of European Economic History
JMH	Journal of Modern History
MPIG	Max-Planck-Institut für Geschichte
P & P	Past and Present
SchweizZG	Schweizerische Zeitschrift für Geschichte
SVRG	Schriften des Vereins für Reformationsgeschichte
VSWG	Vierteljahrschrift für Sozial- und Wirtschaftsgeschichte
ZAgrarGAgrarSoz	Zeitschrift für Agrargeschichte und Agrarsoziologie
ZAGV	Zeitschrift des Aachener Geschichtsvereins
ZBLG	Zeitschrift für bayerische Landesgeschichte
ZGO	Zeitschrift für die Geschichte des Oberrheins
ZHF	Zeitchrift für historische Forschung
ZKG	Zeitschrift für Kirchengeschichte
ZRG KA	Zeitschrift für Rechtsgeschichte, Kanonische Abteilung
ZWLG	Zeitschrift für württembergische Landesgeschichte

1

Social and Economic Landscapes

JÖRN SIEGLERSCHMIDT

> There is a chaos that arises from doubt and despair, a parasite upon order when it reminds us of the temporal nature of all human ordering, even though occasionally it may fructify order. (August Lösch, 1940)[1]

The current view is that the modern period began with the European colonization of the world. Whereas the old, or first world – before the discovery of the new, second world – had the Mediterranean as its centre, now the centre of gravity of European economic life shifted northwards to the Atlantic. This was an extraordinarily significant turning-point, yet it is of little use in demarcating the medieval from the modern period. There are continuities which are too strong, and which are only interrupted around 1800. The middle ages, invented by the humanists, created a tradition which marked European society into the nineteenth century. Only the scientific and technical revolution of the nineteenth century created a discontinuity as deep-reaching as the Neolithic revolution. Technical domination of nature led to a standardization of life and landscape to an extent never before experienced. One expression of this homogenization was an increasing centralization of power, people, and resources. Developments of this sort do not take place within the space of a few years: the first beginnings of the scientific and technical revolution made themselves apparent as early as the fourteenth century, but it only triumphed as the dominant pattern of thought in the twentieth century. There were gaps and overlaps not just in chronology, but also in space: even in the nineteenth century the differences between the rapidly expanding industrial areas and those regions still primarily determined by agriculture were still clearly to be seen. Viewed as a whole, however, fundamental changes took place between 1750 and 1850, changes in culture and in nature, closely linked with one another, with man as the intermediary. This chapter will first discuss their continuities in early modern Europe up to the enormous discontinuity which set in around 1800. Then it will describe in turn the various important changes in the landscape and geographical structure of Germany during this period.

Where was Germany in 1500? Johannes Cochlaeus, in his *Brevis Germaniae descriptio* of 1512, circumscribed its frontiers as follows:

> Germany's borders. I believe that no region in Europe extends further than Germany... It is enclosed in the south by Italy and Dalmatia [Yugoslavia]; in the east by Hungary and Poland; in the north by the Baltic and the North Sea; and in the west by France and the English Channel.[2]

What Cochlaeus was describing were not political frontiers in the modern sense, dividing sovereign states from one another. Nor were they linguistic frontiers, since substantial parts of the area he described lay west of the Rhine, east of the Elbe, or south of the Alps, and cannot be regarded as part of the German linguistic area. Rather, he was describing the spatial extent of the Holy Roman Empire of the German Nation (shown in Fig. 1.1).[3] As late as 1667, Samuel von Pufendorf described the Holy Roman Empire as a 'somewhat irregular body similar to a monster'. In doing so, he was seeking to draw attention to the extraordinary development of constitutional law in Germany, where, unlike elsewhere in Europe, a solely reigning monarchy had not developed. Pufendorf regarded the limited degree of power enjoyed by the Emperor as irregular, since a centre of power was lacking. The Empire, with its separate sovereign powers, loosely linked together by the Imperial constitution, was thus for him a monster, a freak.[4] To define the frontiers of this monster in terms of constitutional law is hardly possible.[5] And geographically, too, it is hard to pin down what Germany was supposed to consist of.

The Empire's lack of a centre was the expression of a constitutional situation which gave the family and the (occupational) corporate group decisive social weight. Coupled with rights of government which adhered to the land (*feudum*), this situation is referred to as the 'feudal constitution', and it only reached an end in the nineteenth century, when the French Revolution generated a political model for the abolition of the feudal state, and defeat by Napoleon forced German territories to undertake political reforms. Germany owed Napoleon not only the dissolution of the Holy Roman Empire, but also the formation for the first time of territorial closed states, and – to a considerable extent – the abolition of corporative intermediary powers. This resulted in a fundamental reshaping of the political map, which in turn reflected the upheaval in constitutional law.

Previously, the largest German territory, like the smallest domain of a Free Imperial Knight, was operated as the enterprise of one noble family. The dynasty and its interests took priority over everything else. Marriage relations, inheritance, and inheritance conflicts between rival noble clans often resulted in changes in government, and not infrequently caused long-

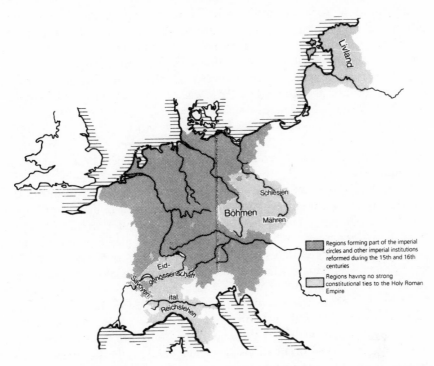

Fig. 1.1 The Holy Roman Empire around 1550 (*Source*: Rabe *Reich und Glaubensspaltung*)

lasting military conflicts. The policy of the Habsburg Emperor was also dynastic in nature, and thus often difficult to sell as an imperial one.[6] The power of the prince, which was constrained only by a few basic laws, was limited by numerous corporative privileges: parliaments, guilds, monasteries, clans, and corporations constituted corporate groups, membership of which was defined by birth or occupational estate, and which either directly shared in the exercise of power, or prevented important governmental rights, such as rights of jurisdiction, from being completely effectual almost anywhere.[7] Thus the constitutional and governmental structure of the Holy Roman Empire continued to be splintered.

In the pre-modern period, therefore, the exercise of power was fragmented. Beginning in the fourteenth century, and increasingly from the seventeenth century on, there were attempts to create territorially closed states by bundling together various governmental rights. This was less successful in the long-settled regions in the South and West of the Empire than in the North and the East. But despite all the signs of an increasing density of government, despite the measurement of territories and the definition of their frontiers which increasingly set in during the eighteenth century, a constitution still prevailed which was characterized by numerous graduated rights of government – the feudal, corporative constitution. Despite the beginnings of an imperial patriotism, there also developed a patriotism in the territories, one defined by regional origins and the ruling dynasty. Although Cochlaeus did speak of territorial gains for Germany beyond the Rhine, usually it was of the Franconian, Alemannic,[8] or even Prussian nation that he spoke.[9] The princes sought to further local patriotism, since it suited their ambitions as territorial rulers.[10] Only in the course of the nationalist infatuations of the nineteenth and twentieth centuries were the territorial conflicts of the medieval period redefined into national ones.

More decisive for the development of a collective identity, from the sixteenth century on, was religious confession (discussed in detail in Chapter 10 of this volume). In terms of constitutional law, confession brought something new, because it could not be shared. The principle of shared property and governmental rights was no longer tenable. Confession made clear governmental boundaries necessary.[11] But confession also had additional social effects: the spread of writing and literacy took place more rapidly in Protestant territories. It is also known that confession had effects on the shape of family life and on family planning.[12]

The tying of social life to the region was only broken by corporative ties: some industrial occupations (e.g. merchants, millers, paper-makers), academics (scholars and professors), and social groups such as nobles, but also thieves, beggars, and vagrants, had internal corporate links across regions.[13] The basis for social and economic life in the pre-modern period was the family and the household, which has been labelled by Otto Brunner the 'ganzes Haus' ('whole household').[14] Here, too, the divorce between workplace and family which took place in the nineteenth century created new spatial patterns in social and economic life.

The 'ganzes Haus' also shaped economic attitudes: economic activity was orientated not around calculations of profit, but rather around a livelihood suitable to one's estate in society. During the nineteenth century a new pattern of economic thought – quantitative, calculating – was gradually disseminated in almost all areas of social life. This revolution is made clear by the definition of the tasks of agriculture by Albrecht Daniel Thaer (1752–1828): '§1. Agriculture is an industry whose purpose is, through production (and sometimes also through further processing), to create profit or earn money from vegetable and animal substances.'[15] It was not only in agriculture and industry that considerable time had to pass before this style of economic thinking prevailed in the nineteenth century. Thus it was not only the sciences which were changed by the introduction of controlled experiment, calculation, and consistent quantification. It is important to remain conscious of these social and cultural principles of pre-modern society in assessing changes in the social and economic landscape.

A second fundamental difference between the pre-modern period and the nineteenth and twentieth centuries lay in the dependence of human beings on nature. As with the cultural differences just discussed, here too there arises a whole range of separate perspectives.

In a society which derives its subsistence mainly from work in agriculture, weather plays an extraordinarily important role. This was even more the case because the yield of the harvest was much more dependent than it is nowadays upon climate and soil. Despite the recognition by agricultural science even in the pre-modern period that properly selected seed led to better harvests, purposeful breeding did not take place. This was also the case with the breeding of animals. The deliberate breeding of domestic animals with the intention of increasing economically exploitable yields did not begin before the middle of the eighteenth century. The numerous provincial breeds, despite the fact that they were found only in specific regions, were by no means always adapted to natural conditions. For this reason, and also because for the most part there was a lack of sufficient fodder, the yields from animal husbandry were generally poor. Horse-breeding was a limited exception, because it was also important for military purposes. To achieve better results from cultivation, what was lacking was not only knowledge but also, often, money and labour. This is shown by the many examples of intensive farming carried out as early as the sixteenth century in the proximity of towns or orientated toward export.[16] One consequence of dependence on nature was a wide regional variation in yields, over both short and long distances. To wrest more from nature did not become a consistently pursued aim until the agrarian reformers of the eighteenth century. It is important to recall that the furtherance of 'national culture' at that period had nothing to do with the furthering of the so-called fine arts, but rather with the furthering of agriculture.

Industrial production, too, was highly dependent on natural preconditions. First, there was the question of energy provision, the precondition for any kind of processing or transformation of materials. The most important potential sources of energy in the pre-modern period were natural forms of energy, water-power above all, wind-power to a much lesser extent. Muscle-power played a significant role in transportation, which was just as important for the manufacturing of goods as it was for their distribution and consumption. It should not be surprising that enterprises dependent on water-power were strung along the river-courses and brooks like pearls on a string (as can be seen in Figure 1.2).[17] For those manufacturing processes which required thermal energy – especially the smelting and processing of metal, glass-making, and salt production – wood was the necessary precondition; turf and hard coal played no role worth mentioning. Wood and energy were so important that even raw materials which were hard to transport were laboriously brought to the energy sources. It must be stressed that for agriculture, as for industry, solar energy was the basic motor. Energy from fossil raw materials (coal, oil, and natural gas) played no role before the nineteenth century. Early industrialization still

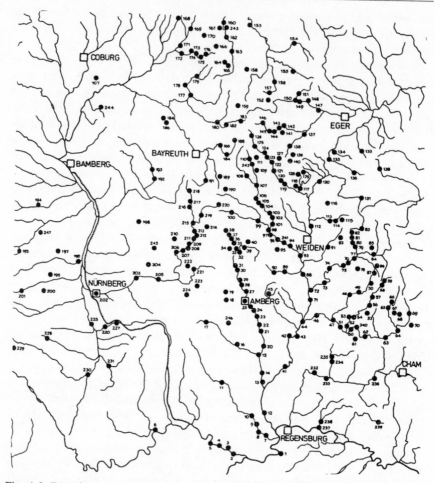

Fig. 1.2 Distribution and location of hammer mills (manufacturing iron) during the middle ages in the Upper Palatinate (*Source*: Lutz, *Eisenhämmer und Hüttenwerke*, p. 286)

relied completely on natural energy and growing raw materials. Only from the mid-nineteenth century on was wood gradually displaced by iron as a building material, and by hard coal as an energy source. Even after this date, water-power, now better utilized because of turbines, remained the motor of industrial development in many regions. Industrial location thus remained tied to water, even when an industry did not rely on substantial amounts of water for production itself, as did paper-making and tanning. But human beings themselves were also more dependent on nature than in the nineteenth century. On one hand, this dependence arose from the fluctuating nature of the agricultural yields which were necessary for feeding people. A majority of people almost always had too little to eat, especially too little protein and fat, and were undernourished over long periods.[18]

This already made them much more vulnerable to infections. In addition, not only nutrition but also housing and clothing were largely insufficient, houses were too damp and – because of the lack of fuel – too cold, and clothing too meagre. Furthermore, the hygiene situation was intolerable. Water supplies and sewage disposal were often not kept sufficiently separate. Bacteria, viruses, and other micro-organisms had better opportunities to multiply in dwellings that were seldom cleaned, in clothes that were infrequently changed, and on bodies that were little washed. The average life expectancy was very low, not least because of high infant mortality. Dependence on nature meant risks to survival. Here, too, the nineteenth century created changes in the direction of a more secure life, even if secured only against the monsters of nature.

In conclusion, it must be emphasized that the pre-modern world was highly variegated in a large number of wide-ranging areas of life: clothing, house-building, nutrition, language, confession, government, law, currency, measures, weights, prices, wages, vegetation, fauna, soil quality, energy, and raw material supplies. Better knowledge of the circumstances and technical domination of nature, as well as the primacy of economic rationality, reduced this variety, homogenized the landscape, and, increasingly, equalized living situations. In exchange for this, people obtained greater security in life. This, too, was due to developments which took place after 1800.

In terms of its natural setting, Germany can hardly be demarcated from its neighbouring regions. Certainly the Mittelgebirge and the Alps form natural frontiers, but they share geological and climatic characteristics with neighbouring areas such as eastern central France and Bohemia. Northern Germany is geologically and climatically part of a belt of land which stretches from northern France through The Netherlands up to the Weichsel, becoming broader from west to east; east of the Elbe, the influence of the continental climate (hot, dry summers and wet, cold winters) increases. As far as temperatures are concerned, it appears that in the warmer months temperatures declined from south to north, but in winter they declined from west to east. Around 1900 the average yearly temperature lay between 6 and 12 degrees Celsius.[19] The volume of precipitation was first of all clearly determined by differences in altitude. In the Mittelgebirgen (Eifel, Hunsrück, Westerwald, Rothaargebirge) and the Alps, the average annual volume of precipitation was substantially higher than in the rest of Germany. In Germany as a whole, precipitation was highest in the summer; it was only in the higher points of the Eifel, the Hunsrück, the Vosges, the Black Forest, the Rhone, and the Harz that precipitation was highest in December. However, the seasons of lowest precipitation varied: up to the Elbe and the Main, it was lowest in April, while east and south of these rivers it was lowest in February. The eastern part of Germany up to about the river Elbe, with the exception of the higher-altitude South-East (Saxony and Silesia), had less precipitation than the West and South.[20]

This very rough climatic division of Germany, based on average values from the period around 1900, overlays a much more differentiated smaller-scale subdivision, which depended on local factors in a variety of ways. Whether such a rough division can also claim to be valid for earlier periods, back to the middle ages, must remain an open question. It is certainly the case that climate could show significant variations, not only from year to year but also over greater periods of time. Thus in the period between 1550 and 1850, the climate west and south of the Elbe may also have been more continental in character: that is, warm and dry summers accompanied by cold and wet winters.[21] However, such statements are subject to a variety of uncertainties.

On the other hand, it is certain that long stretches of years during the period from 1550 to 1850 were colder and, in the summer, wetter than in the twentieth century. With few exceptions, the first half of the sixteenth century was climatically favoured, i.e. as warm as, or even warmer than, comparable periods of the present century. Although some summers were too dry, in general the weather during this period favoured agricultural yields. Only the winters were really cold and too dry.[22] From the middle of the sixteenth century on, winters were already becoming clearly colder, and summers were also cooling down and becoming, for the most part, substantially wetter: not a good precondition for a rich harvest. The beginning of the seventeenth century was marked by warmer and drier weather, but by about 1620 this had already given way to a period of late onset of spring, and wetter and colder summer and autumn months. The years from c. 1635 to the end of the seventeenth century were characterized by dryness. From about 1685 on, there began a period during which the climate was among the worst experienced until the present day: both winters and summers were colder than average, and summers and autumns were also too wet for the harvest to succeed. It is not surprising, therefore, that one of the most terrible pan-European famines took place in exactly this period (in 1695). The beginning of the eighteenth century brought a comparative warming up, and also weather which tended to improve harvest yields. From about 1730 on there began a period of continental climate, which lasted until the beginning of the nineteenth century: cold and dry winters were followed by cool springs, which passed into wet and warm summer months, and these were followed by autumn months which were sometimes already quite wintry. Although the eighteenth century was characterized by better weather conditions than the seventeenth century, in this century, too, climatic anomalies led to poor harvests and thus to difficulties in the food supply. However, even the famine period 1771–2 was less far-reaching than that of the end of the seventeenth century. In earlier times, as nowadays, contemporaries remembered extraordinary weather events for a long time, especially when they were accompanied by low agricultural yields. Thus the winters of 1572–3, 1683–5, 1694–5, 1708–9, and 1740–1 – especially the last of these, when as late as May frost damaged the wine grapes on Lake Constance and elsewhere – counted among the coldest between 1350 and 1850. In Central Europe, the waterways froze.[23] Spring months that were too cold were harmful for the growth of vegetation, especially when they were accompanied by too much precipitation, as in 1705, 1742, 1770, and 1771. Too much moisture during the harvest period reduced yields, especially for the green fodder which was necessary for ensuring milk yields in winter. The last two decades of the seventeenth century stand out not only for cold, but also for wet summers.[24] Storms, even hail, had only local effects. By contrast, floods – such as the great floods of 1682 and 1784 – remained long in the memories of those affected by them.[25]

The weather also played an especially important role in influencing short-term fluctuations in agricultural yields, not only annual but also seasonal ones, corresponding to the various phases of growth of crops. A summer that was too wet, which made the grain sprout, could turn a harvest initially expected to be good into a poor one. Wet grain also suffered very high losses in storage. Plants were affected by the different influences of the weather in extremely various ways: some, such as wine grapes, were generally sensitive; others, such as spelt, much less so. Meadows, too, had varying yields, which influenced not only the milk yields of cows during the winter months, but also the draught capacities of animals. If animals died or had to be slaughtered in an emergency because of lack of fodder, this not only further limited the food supply, but also reduced draught capacities. Since in the period before 1850 these were irreplaceable, further areas of life were affected: transportation was less possible, and the cultivation of the fields could also suffer.

Of long-term significance for agricultural yields was location: the quality of the soil and its altitude. In this context, the direct relationship between yields and weather must also be considered. The distribution of annual precipitation across Germany was (and is) very uneven. In the Mittelgebirge and the foothills of the Alps, rain was especially frequent, while northern Germany and large areas of Germany south of the Mosel and Main received rather little. Depending on location – e.g. whether it was a very steep slope or a broad, open area – water and wind could also diminish the soil. In the same way, certain high-altitude localities were, because of soil or more particularly sunlight, especially sought after: vine-growing required sunlight and an exposed position where the soil quickly absorbed the warmth and held it. Besides altitude, the quality of the soil was unquestionably of great significance. In Germany there were very few areas – according to surveys of soil quality carried out in the first half of the twentieth century – which permitted only a single agricultural use, or even none at all: the only examples were high hills and the lime and clay soils of the karstic areas of the Franconian and Swabian Jura. Otherwise, Germany was distinguished by soils which could be used in a wide variety of ways.[26] A survey of the fertility of the soil, taking account of numerous environ-

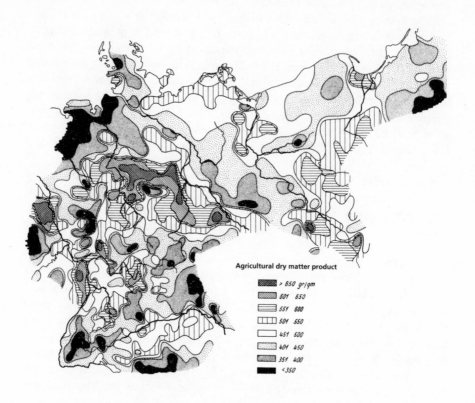

Agricultural dry matter product

- ■■■ > 650 gr/qm
- 601 650
- 551 600
- 501 550
- 451 500
- 401 450
- 351 400
- < 350

Fig. 1.3 Geographical distribution of agricultural yields (dry matter product) on the basis of crop results 1910–13 and 1936/37

mental influences (see Fig. 1.3),[27] shows above-average yields for northern Mecklenburg and Pomerania, the Middle and Lower Rhine, the Neckar and Main regions, the wide belt from the Cologne Embayment through the upper Weser region to that of the Saale and Upper Elbe, the lower Oder, Silesia, and West Prussia. In the Austrian lands it was especially parts of Bohemia and Moravia and Lower Austria where yields were above average. Admittedly, the areas of actual agrarian surplus lay in Galicia, Hungary, and Krain. Less favoured were north-west Germany, broad expanses of the Mittelgebirge north of the Danube, the areas between the Elbe and Oder (and thus especially the Mark of Brandenburg), and north-east Germany. In the Mittelgebirge, the North-West, and the North-East, too-frequent precipitation in particular had a harmful effect on the harvest, while in the other low-yield areas the culprit was dryness (see Figure 1.4).[28]

Finally, altitude was decisive for harvest yields. Arable land, meadows, and wooded areas all had different sensitivities to altitude. Here, soil quality also certainly played a role. The sand and marl soils which are found

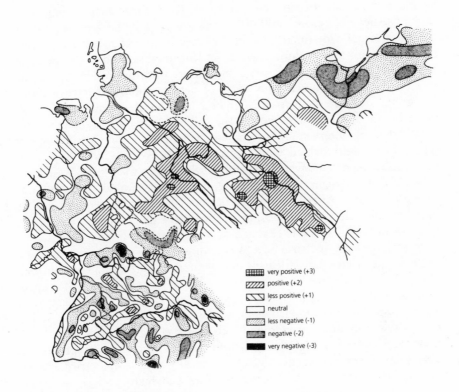

very positive (+3)	
positive (+2)	
less positive (+1)	
neutral	
less negative (-1)	
negative (-2)	
very negative (-3)	

Fig. 1.4 Relation between crop and average humidity 1909–13 (*Source*: Filzer, *Grundlagen des Pflanzenertrages*, p. 96)

more frequently in lower altitudes provided poor conditions for high yields. But it was the climatic situation, influenced by altitude, that was decisive. It emerges that the highest yields for grain were generated at an altitude of 400 metres, while root vegetables flourished best up to *c.* 500 metres. Forests had highest yields at between 500 and 600 metres, although the oak passed its optimum yield at as low as 300 metres, fir and beech at 400 metres, and spruce at above 500 metres. Just as for forests, so also for meadows, yields could still be good at altitudes of 600 to 700 metres.[29]

Corresponding to climatic and soil conditions, vegetation in Central Europe was also highly variegated, and changed substantially over time. Geographically, the distribution of plants and animals was (and is) determined by weather, altitude, water supply, and quality of soil. Human beings, too, were influenced in their settlement by these geographical and physical conditions. The effects of human beings on the environment have increased with the passage of time; but the extent to which they had an impact on geographical and physical conditions in the period before 1800 should not be under-estimated. However, the historical development of human settlement before 1800 did not follow a linear progression: rather, phases of settlement (in the twelfth, sixteenth, and eighteenth centuries) alternated with phases during which settlements disappeared (in the fourteenth and seventeenth centuries), and phases of afforestation and extensive cultivation alternated with those of deforestation and intensification of agriculture. Forests in particular had (and have) considerable importance for the local climate and for the soil and water situation.[30]

Without the intervention of human beings, most of Central Europe would have been covered with forest (see Figures 1.5a and 1.5b).[31] The most widespread trees were oak and beech, and in the North-West birch as well. Only at higher altitudes were spruce to be found, and on sandy soils pine as well. After continual settlement began in the Neolithic period, but especially after the expansion of settlement in the high middle ages, this natural landscape was changed in many ways by human beings.

Forest coverage, in particular, was a direct indication of increasing or decreasing capacity for settlement and economic utilization. The considerable population decline of the fourteenth century put an end to the expansion period of the high middle ages: many areas of settlement were abandoned. Forests expanded again at the cost of cultivated areas. Admittedly, these were areas of marginal soils which could only provide a livelihood in times of need. Deserted lands are evidence of the process of abandonment of settlements, which was regionally highly varied. People moved into areas with favourable weather and high-quality soil, where land was only ever abandoned for short periods. In this process, an extensification of cultivation took place (see Fig. 1.6).[32] Toward the end of the fifteenth century, and especially after the mid-sixteenth century, a renewed phase of expansion began, which was interrupted for a good 50 years by the plague during the Thirty Years War, but which after the war was enduringly furthered by the state. Abandonment of settlements such as had taken place in the fourteenth century occurred to a much lesser extent in the seventeenth century.

One consequence of population growth, especially in the eighteenth century, was increasing arable cultivation of forested areas and moorland. Forested areas contracted, probably reaching their low point in the first half of the nineteenth century; by 1900 many deforested areas had already been reforested (see Fig. 1.6).[33] Around 1800, approximately one quarter of the total area of Germany was covered in forest.[34] By this time substantial changes in the forested area had already occurred. An early example of rational forest cultivation is provided by the rural area of Nuremberg as early as the later middle ages: iron smelting and silver mining required large amounts of wood, which could be generated more quickly with coniferous forests, with their copious mass yields.[35] Wood was the only raw material which provided thermal energy. Only in a few areas such as

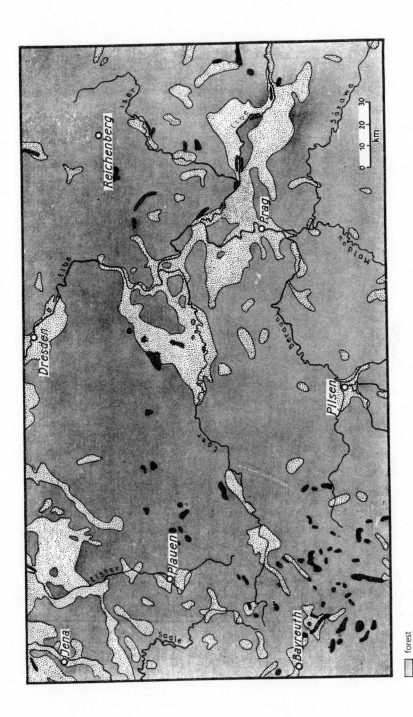

Fig. 1.5a Forest area at the beginning of the middle ages in Bohemia and Saxony (*Source:* Fels, *Der wirtschaftende Mensch*, p. 148)

forest

marsh

prehistoric settlements

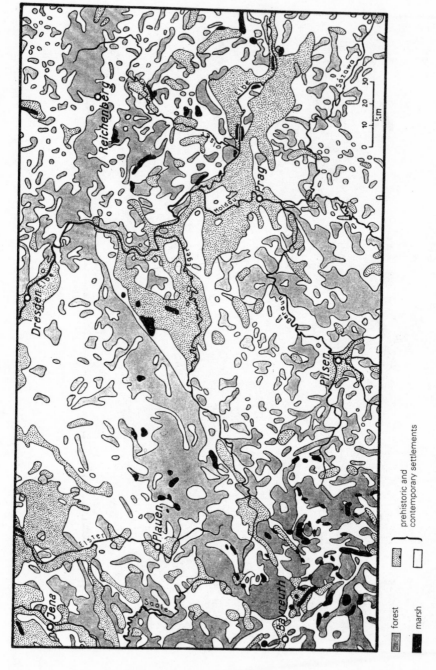

Fig. 1.5b Forest area in Bohemia and Saxony today (*Source:* Fels, *Der wirtschaftende Mensch*, p. 149)

forest

marsh

prehistoric and
contemporary settlements

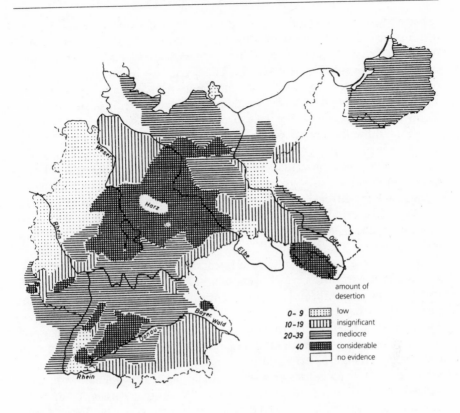

amount of
desertion

0- 9 low
10-19 insignificant
20-39 mediocre
40 considerable
no evidence

Fig. 1.6 Desertion of settlements during the later middle ages (*Source*: Abel, *Landwirtschaft*, p. 113)

Westphalia was wood replaced by turf or hard coal.[36] The energy gained from wood was necessary for domestic hearths and many industrial processes: metal-smelting, glass-making, and salt production, to name only the most important. Wood was also indispensable as a working material for producing tools, for building houses, and for constructing ships and other means of transportation. Given such enormous demand, governments had to establish a properly regulated cultivation of forests if they wanted to ensure wood supplies in the long term. The simplest way to do this was to replace the deciduous forests which predominated in Germany with coniferous forests; this afforestation policy continued into the nineteenth century, and is responsible for the present appearance of German forests.[37] Damage to forests therefore occurred wherever the relevant industries were located: in the Thuringian forest, the Harz, the Upper Palatinate, Saxony, the Siegerland, Lüneburg, Reichenhall, Carinthia, and Styria.[38] The best known example is the Lüneburg Heath, which owes its existence to the saltworks in Lüneburg: the wood requirements of this industry thinned out the forest to such an extent that heath invaded the deforested areas. The expansion of sheep-keeping in the seventeenth century and the subsequent turf manuring then prevented any reafforestation in the longer term.[39] Although by 1800 complaints about wood scarcity had become widespread, the production of salt in Lüneburg, for example, was never restricted by lack of wood.[40] The complaints heard everywhere thus cannot be generalized; only where production was restricted can one speak of wood scarcity. At least the fact that wood supplies were undoubtedly becoming difficult in some places created the incentive increasingly to seek to remedy this scarcity through a rational cultivation of forests from the eighteenth century onwards. As a consequence of state forests policies, deciduous or mixed forests were displaced by coniferous forests in many areas. Thus the Black Forest, for example, took on its present appearance only in this period. The extent to which such deforestation and reafforestation changed local weather and water supplies has not yet been investigated.

The cultivation of the soil also influenced the landscape in many ways. In this, the urbanization which went hand in hand with population growth (between the eleventh and the fourteenth centuries, in the sixteenth century, and in the eighteenth century) was of equally decisive importance. There arose a relationship of mutual supplementation between town and country, not only over small distances, but also through close links between larger regions: highly developed industrial areas became reliant on importing foodstuffs. Even before precise investigations of this phenomenon were carried out in more recent studies,[41] it was known that Russia, Poland, the Baltic area, and Prussia delivered wheat to markets in The Netherlands, England, Sweden, and in emergency years also France and Italy.[42] The dependence of the Silesians on Polish grain, the Lower Austrians on Hungarian grain, and the Swiss on Baden and Württemberg grain were also mentioned.[43] The Netherlands was supplied from Westphalia, and France partially from the Rhine area. Long-distance dependencies were not the rule, however, in an era of long and difficult transportation routes. Instead, it was customary for industrially developed areas, or areas under-supplied because of natural disadvantages, to lie in quite close proximity to those which delivered the missing food supplies.

The main bread grain in Germany was rye, and this remained so into the twentieth century. Only in south-west Germany, the Alsace, and northern Switzerland did winter spelt predominate; this was a variety of wheat which was probably a legacy of the ancient Roman period.[44] In the summer fields, oats and barley predominated, oats especially as a fodder grain; in some localities in the eighteenth century barley was increasingly cultivated for malting, i.e. for brewing beer. Wheat only began to be cultivated frequently in the nineteenth century, because it was more demanding in terms of soil and weather, and was especially vulnerable to attacks of mould when the summer was too wet.[45] Of local importance on sandy soils with low nutrient supplies were millet and buckwheat. Both were sown late in the year. Buckwheat was especially sensitive to cold. Only in the sixteenth and seventeenth centuries did maize come to Central Europe. It could only be cultivated in areas with a favourable climate, such as the Upper Rhine valley, the Neckar region, Styria, the Tyrol, and Moravia.[46] Peas, beans, and vetch were cultivated almost everywhere, lentils only in scattered locations. Pulses were mostly grown as animal fodder, but in crisis periods could also replace grain, and in some localities were sown, harvested, milled, and baked together with grain. Mixed grains of this sort can be found more frequently in south-west Germany in the sixteenth and seventeenth centuries. Among root crops (such as potatoes and turnips), only the white turnip (*brassica rapa rapa*) was already known and widespread in the sixteenth century. The potato was intensively cultivated in Central Europe only toward the end of the eighteenth century,[47] its cultivation being promoted in Prussia after the famine of 1771–2. Elsewhere, for example in Swabia, potatoes were reserved for animals. Before 1800, vegetable growing was unimportant in both quantity and contribution to nutrition. By contrast, fruit, especially dried fruit for winter, could be important for nutrition, which was otherwise rather one-sided.

Exercising greater impact on the landscape also, because of their effects on industry, were the trade plants and specialized crops: flax and hemp, chicory, tobacco, hops, and wine-grapes. Hemp, a raw material for rope and coarse textiles for everyday use, was increasingly cultivated in Baden, Württemberg, Westphalia, Hesse, Darmstadt, Lüneburg, and Moravia. As with flax, the hemp plant could also be used for obtaining oil. Flax, a raw material used, like wool and cotton, for making finer textiles, thrived best in Silesia, Westphalia, Braunschweig, Hannover, Upper Austria, Styria, and Bohemia; however, it was still remarked in 1800 that in none of these areas did it attain the fineness and length of the Flemish flax.[48] Chicory was cultivated primarily as a coffee substitute in the eighteenth century, with the main centres in northern Württemberg, Braunschweig, Magdeburg, around Vienna, and in Bohemia and Moravia.[49] Like other plants originating overseas, tobacco attained only local significance, in Baden, the Rhineland, Electoral Hesse, Hannover, and Brandenburg, with declining quality.[50] Hops thrived best in Bohemia, Braunschweig, the Rezatkreis of Bavaria, and Prussian Saxony.[51] Wine-grapes, as a specialized crop, required favourable weather and soil conditions, as did tobacco. As a consequence of the deterioration in the climate from the end of the sixteenth century on, vine cultivation shifted southward (see Figure 1.7). While in the sixteenth century wine growing was still to be found north of the fiftieth parallel, after 1600 it moved back to the areas still known today: the Rhine, Neckar, Main, and Moselle areas, the Upper Saale and Upper Elbe areas, northern Silesia, the Tyrol, Styria, Bohemia, Moravia, and Carinthia. These wines were, however, almost exclusively produced for domestic consumption.[52] Like the edible chestnut, wine-grapes had also come to Central Europe with the Romans. Finally, other important plants used were the oil plants, nuts for eating and for oils, and the dye plants madder (red), woad (blue), and weld (yellow). Woad was cultivated primarily in Thuringia, Saxony and around Preßburg (Bratislava), weld in Bohemia, Lower Austria, Baden, and Silesia, and madder or 'dyer's red' in Baden, in Silesia, and around Meissau.

It must be pointed out that despite the diversity of the vegetation, which still included plants growing in the wild, a grain monoculture predominated in Central Europe before 1800. This grain monoculture was characterized by quite low average yields, generally less than 10 decitonnes per hectare (dt/ha). Only in the eighteenth century were there many examples of average yields over 10 dt/ha prevailing for longer periods. In this context it must be recalled that the known examples of yields were generally not for ordinary peasant farms, but rather for farms with better-than-average farming practices. The basic problem of agriculture before 1800 was lack of manure, a fact not unknown to contemporaries. But it was only in the eighteenth century that an essential defect was pointed out: the

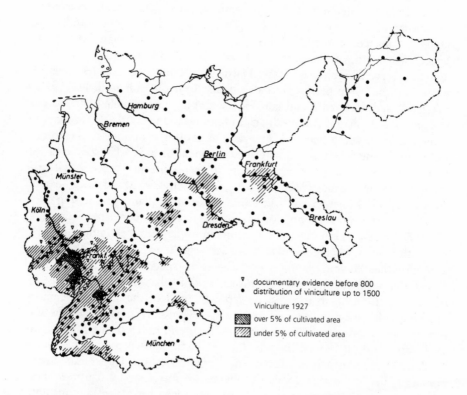

Fig. 1.7 Viniculture in Germany since the middle ages (*Source*: Abel, *Landwirtschaft*, p. 130)

expansion of arable fields, because of higher food needs, at the cost of woods and meadows. Phases of extensification in agriculture are recognizable by the expansion of meadows, such as took place almost everywhere in Central Europe after 1650. The expansion of meadows not only led to increased animal husbandry and larger amounts of manure, but in the second half of the eighteenth century, further innovations were added: the planting of fallow land with nitrogen-fixing plants, better care of meadows, and stall feeding of animals. The latter was usual in winter, but only almost year-round stall feeding enables exploitation of all the manure. It was only through practices such as this that it was possible to make up the lack of manure, although it was only from the end of the eighteenth century that this led to a decisive improvement in yields.[53] Intensive grain cultivation, especially in areas of agrarian surplus with several times as much arable field area as meadows, necessarily led to falling yields in the longer term, unless cultivation practices were changed and care taken to obtain enough manure.

In Central Europe in the later middle ages, the three-field system began to prevail as the most widespread system of cultivation. As villages emerged, they developed an outward appearance whose traces can be seen into the twentieth century. Especially in the areas of earliest settlement in southern and western areas of Central Europe, villages had irregular ground plans, with gardens and other intensively cultivated areas in direct proximity to the houses. This inner sector of the village was separated from the rest of the field area of the village by a fence. The arable area was divided into the typical narrow strips, which were in turn collected into blocks, the so-called *Gewanne* (furlongs). From a certain number of furlongs a *Zelge* was formed, which was collectively cultivated by the peasants in the framework of the three-field rotation. Within and surrounding the field area of the village lay, finally, the pastures, the woods, and the seldom-cultivated meadow areas. Because of their low productivity, these were only used as arable land at longer time intervals. Otherwise they lay fallow or served as pasture. It was the woods and the less fertile parts of the territory of the village that belonged to the commons, which all citizens of the village were permitted to use. In the areas east of the Elbe which were only settled by Germans from the eleventh century on, it was more usual to find village ground plans which were more regular, with a corresponding distribution of the field area of the village. But in the areas of older settlement (for example, northern Austria, Bavaria, and Franconia) as well, similar forms of village arose as the landscape was brought under cultivation.[54]

Settlement and soil use changed according to the movement of population. The rural sub-strata of cottagers (variously called *Seldner, Tagelöhner, Tauner, Kötter, Gärtner, Häusler, Insten,* and *Heuerlinge*), which began to expand again from the fifteenth century on, contributed to an increasing density of settlement in villages, but also to their enlargement. On the North Sea, additional land was won through endykement, and land already long under cultivation was secured. The large feudal noble estates emerging in northern and eastern Germany had an enduring impact on the landscape, with a large-scale distribution of the village field area. Only the abandonment of settlements during the Thirty Years War led to an accelerated expansion of large feudal noble estates at the cost of the peasants, and these estates became a distinctive component of the agrarian landscape into the twentieth century.[55] The period of expansion in the sixteenth century was ended by the Thirty Years War. In the eighteenth century, the extension of the land was further pursued. The most enduring intervention in the landscape was in Brandenburg-Prussia, through the draining of the Havelländer Luch in 1719–24 for Dutch settlers, of the middle and lower Oderbruch in 1747–53, and of the Netzebruch and Warthebruch in 1765–86, in order to obtain new land for agricultural use. As a consequence of settlement by religious refugees beginning at the end of the seventeenth century in Brandenburg-Prussia, Hesse, Württemberg, and the Palatinate, there arose schematic ground plans for settlement, such as were also usual for planned settlements.

More important for the development of the agrarian landscape, however, was the beginning of a major change in land utilization in the eighteenth century. Admittedly, many measures had large-scale effects only in the nineteenth century when the law concerning use of the soil and property-holding relations was profoundly changed. In 1800, the three-field system still clearly predominated in grain-growing zones.[56] But this system of cultivation was already in the process of dissolution. On fallow land, fodder plants, 'foundation' (nitrogen-fixing) plants such as lucerne, sainfoin, and clover, and the newly introduced potato were being cultivated. The improvement in cultivation and the increase in manuring now also made it possible to make use of the outer areas of the village territory, which until then had scarcely been cultivated at all. At the same time, with so-called *Verkoppelung* in Schleswig-Holstein and *Vereinödung* in Swabia – both of them forms of enclosure, i.e. of rationalization and consolidation of scattered holdings, sometimes involving dissolution of common lands – there arose forms of cultivation which allowed individual peasants more room to make their own decisions. Only in this way could a proper crop rotation arise. It must be emphasized that the three-field system provided a certain amount of insurance against unfavourable meteorological influences: thus winter corn that had been damaged by cold and snow could be ploughed under in the spring and replaced by a new sowing. But it also created legal obstacles which hindered potentially better uses of the land: the recipients of taxes and dues always paid close attention to make sure that they suffered no disadvantage from any change in cultivation. Thus many large feudal landlords in Holsatia followed Count Rantzau in distributing demesne land to peasants only when it emerged that this could actually increase their own revenues.[57]

The development of the agrarian landscape before 1850 was necessarily orientated towards providing the basic requirements for human survival. These consisted almost completely of the re-growing of raw materials. Any expansion in provisioning implied an expansion in the amount of land cultivated (an extension of the land), or a greater intensity of cultivation of existing land. It also always implied intervention in the landscape, making an impact on vegetation which had previously grown naturally. Farming and forestry had changed the landscape so enduringly by 1800 that there were hardly any areas still to be found which could have counted as natural landscape, unchanged by human beings. This process continued on a massive scale in the nineteenth century, since it was in this particular period that fallow lands, and other areas previously only very little cultivated, began to be utilized. The twentieth century then brought ubiquitous human intervention, through air pollutants and effects on climate.

Like the plant world, the animal world was also influenced by human beings. The expansion in the cultivated landscape could be seen especially clearly in the fact that by 1800 the number of large wild animals had declined substantially. Individual species, such as the brown bear, were still to be found in remote areas in 1800: in the Alps, the Sudetenland, the Erzgebirge, and Carpathia. Wolf and lynx were still frequently found in the Mittelgebirge, East Prussia, and Posen.[58] By 1800, aurochs and elk had for centuries been absent from Germany, although they could still be found in scattered locations in Galicia and Transylvania (Central Rumania). The ibex had apparently been largely eradicated from the Alps and was only to be found at very high altitudes. Chamois were still to be seen everywhere. Fur animals such as fox, badger, marten, polecat, and weasel could also still be found everywhere. Wolves, like other beasts of prey, could also still sometimes be threats to human beings. The density of settlement played a role in this, since wolves reappeared after 1650 in the area around Lake Constance, although they had not been seen there for a long time. Beaver were encountered – in the Harz and in the Alps – infrequently. In the forests there was no lack of game that could be hunted, even if some hunters at the beginning of the nineteenth century looked back nostalgically to the old days, when game still had equal rights with human beings.[59] There were large numbers of game birds: while the bustard was only to be found in central and southern Germany, other varieties (hazel hen, partridge, grey hen, capercaillie, quail, wild duck, snipe, and smaller game birds) were found everywhere and could become pests for farmers. The golden eagle nested in the Alps, as did some vultures, other birds of prey, owls, and varieties of raven everywhere. The waterways were very rich in fish. In the large rivers and freshwater lakes there were salmon, European salmon trout, electric eel, sheathfish, pike, carp, perch, Prussian carp, zander, and other white fish. Crayfish, too, were present in large numbers. In the Baltic and the North Sea, there were conger eel, klipfish, haddock, cod, plaice, turbot, mackerel, herring, and shrimp.

There were many varieties of tame animals. Horses, cattle, and sheep were already bred on a large scale before 1800. Horses were required in large numbers for military purposes and judged by their endurance and draught capacities. With cattle, in addition to draught capacity, meat quality and milk yield were decisive. While in northern Germany East Frisian cattle (widespread in East Frisia, Oldenburg, and Holstein) were sought after because of their productivity, in the Alpine area the Swiss breed predominated. The East Frisian cattle distinguished themselves by their stoutness and the fat content of their milk, similar to the Swiss cattle; the cattle breed originating in Styria was known for the heaviness of the oxen and the tastiness of the meat. Although the German provincial breeds were not so productive as these, there were areas such as Hohenlohe and Braunschweig which were known for cattle breeding. Hohenlohe oxen were exported in large quantities as far away as to France. Especially beginning in the eighteenth century, the quality of sheep was improved through the introduction of Spanish merinos, with their much superior wool. As a result, by 1800 the German provincial breed hardly existed any more. The pig was the most widespread slaughter animal in Bavaria, Westphalia, Hannover, Braunschweig, Mecklenburg, and Pomerania, but looked meagre in comparison to the modern pig. Nevertheless, in Westphalia a pig could become as heavy as five hundredweight. The provincial breeds of pig, which varied a great deal from one locality to another, predominated. The populations of the other animals used by humans (goats and fowl) were not yet unified through breeding.[60]

In the pre-industrial economy, animals were important in many respects, indeed essential for life: first as draught animals and means of transportation; then as providers of meat and milk which could alleviate the notorious lack of protein and fat in nutrition before 1850; as providers of other basic materials such as leather, wool, and oil; and finally, as sources of the manure which was a necessary precondition for the increase in yields which took place beginning in the second half of the eighteenth century. Animal husbandry in the past did not influence the landscape very much: but the use of woods as pasture for pigs and cattle brought in its train particular forms of growth (high forest or low forest);[61] and developments in the landscape such as in the Lüneburg Heath and on the Swabian Jura also arose through sheep pasturing.

Human beings had a greater impact on the landscape through settlement and industrial activity, even though in Central Europe the damage before 1800 appears rather inconsiderable in comparison to the nineteenth and twentieth centuries.[62] This was especially the case because in earlier times environmental harm had consequences which were only local, and which were perceptible through the senses to all. Nevertheless, the burdens and damage perceived by contemporaries should not be underestimated.

Three-quarters of the people in Central Europe lived immediately from agriculture. Industrial and commercial activities were also directly dependent on agriculture to a considerable degree. In addition to these, there were the numerous industries necessary for satisfying daily needs, forms of work which could not be carried out by a member of one's own household. Such industries were to be found everywhere: milling, baking, butchering, smithing, potting, weaving, rope-making, shoemaking, carpentry, joinery. These trades existed in every village; indeed, in some settlement conditions they even existed on every farm. Thus in the areas of dispersed settlement in the Mittelgebirge and the Alps many farms operated their own water mills. Nevertheless, there were regions in Central Europe in which particular industries had become very concentrated (as is discussed in detail in Chapter 9 of this volume). To a considerable extent this was determined by the availability of raw materials and energy. Three things are important for evaluating the location of industry.

For one thing, towns played an important role in organizing the distribution of raw materials, the provision of capital, and the distribution of finished or half-finished wares. Especially in the putting-out textile industries, there developed a close relationship between town and hinterland. Such dense industrial areas in the vicinity of towns could have direct effects on the settlement and social structure of villages, as is shown by the example of Ulm. There, 'Seldner' (cottagers) found work in the textile industry, but in the seventeenth and eighteenth centuries first had to struggle for their places in the village. The village social structure was completely changed by purchases of land and incorporation of cottagers into the community.[63]

Secondly, transportation opportunities were of considerable importance for the location of industry. Mass products were only transported when water transportation routes were available, or when the profits from arbitrage were sufficiently high. Grain in particular came under this heading. But good transportability could also be decisive for textiles.

Finally, the incidence of raw materials and energy could be decisive for the choice of industrial location, especially in metal-working. It should not therefore be surprising that in Central Europe there was a clear division between the North-East and the South-West, in which the Elbe formed a rough dividing line. The Mittelgebirge and the Alpine area were rich in raw materials (metals) and energy (water-power and wood). This dividing line is clearly recognizable in the differing densities of population.

It is not clear to what extent the tradition of the early-settled areas – in contrast to the areas only settled by Germans since the eleventh century – played a role. The influence of the settlement tradition can only be excluded when an industrial location shows obvious natural advantages.

Central Europe counts as especially rich in treasures of the earth. Among metals, it is especially rich in silver, tin, copper, lead, zinc (hemimorphite), and iron, which was suited to a high degree for further processing into steel.[64] Iron production amounted to some 2,000,000 tonnes in 1800, most of it in Prussia (a total of 117,000 tonnes); in Silesia, 20,000 tonnes were produced; in Westerwald, Mark, and Westphalia 33,000 tonnes; and in the Lower Rhine area (Eifel, Hunsrück, Saar, and Ardenen) 25,000 tonnes. Significant mining regions were also to be found in Styria (15,000 tonnes) and Bohemia (50,000 tonnes). Minor deposits were exploited in the Upper Palatinate, the Palatinate, and Upper Bavaria (16,000 tonnes), in the Harz (6,000 tonnes), in the Braunschweig region (5,000 tonnes), in Württemberg (15,000 tonnes), in the Black Forest (1,000 tonnes), and in the Erzgebirge. In the hilly mining regions, there were sufficient supplies of wood and water-power for further processing of the iron as well. After being mined, therefore, the iron was smelted on the spot and coarsely transformed in forges. There were such centres of iron processing in Carinthia, the Tyrol, Styria, Bohemia, Upper and Lower Austria (almost 750 forges in 1800), Saxony (60), the Upper Palatinate (45), and above all in the Rhineland and Westphalia (some 850 in Solingen, in the duchy of Berg, Remscheid, Altena, Iserlohn, Lüdenscheid, and Siegen) and Prussian Silesia (some 120 forges). It is clear that the centres of iron processing (especially wire-making, tin forges, scythe forges, needle-making and weapon production) were generally to be found in immediate proximity to fuel sources because of energy requirements. Thus the largest number of scythe and sickle smiths were found in Styria (60 scythe forges), Remscheid (16 scythe forges with an annual output of 400,000 scythes and sickles), Altena, and Lüdenscheid (37 scythe forges). In Altena 60 million needles were produced annually, and Solingen was the centre of blade, knife, and scissors production, where 650 tonnes of iron and steel were processed annually around 1800. There were wire mills in Styria (14), Carinthia (149), the Upper Palatinate and the Fichtelgebirge (69), and in the Sauerland of Mark.[65] Admittedly, iron processing took place not only in these regions, which had already specialized in it for a long time, but also elsewhere: even in East and West Prussia, as well as in many other places in Germany, bog iron ore was found. As in Wasseralfingen in Württemberg, even smaller ore deposits could, with the associated processing workshops, have a long tradition (since the fourteenth century), and could also leave their marks on small areas. Finally, there was the specialized production of firearms in Essen, Burg, Suhl, Spandau, and Potsdam, where more than 20,000 guns were produced annually. Iron products (scythes, sickles, knives, fish-hooks, farm tools, and needles) found markets all over Europe.[66]

Metals other than iron, especially silver and copper, were mined and processed to a significant extent only in Saxony and the Harz (Hannover). There were zinc (hemimorphite) deposits in the area around Aachen and in Silesia in particular. Zinc was used mainly for the production of tin for roof coverings. Mineral coal was introduced for smelting as early as 1790. Otherwise, zinc was a basic material for the dyeing industry, for example in the Rhineland.[67] Also, in combination with copper, it yielded alloyed brass, from which vessels and mountings were made. Lead was mined in significant amounts around Aachen, in the Harz, in Silesia (Tarnowitz), in Karinthia, in Styria, and in Upper Austria, a total of some 9,000 to 10,000 tonnes. It was in demand because lead was used in the processes for producing silver (copper liquation), ceramic glazes, house roofs, pipes, glass edging, and bullets.[68]

One indispensable raw material for daily life was salt, which in Germany was mainly obtained from brine and not through mining. The largest quantities of salt were produced in Bavaria (in Reichenhall, Traunstein, Rosenheim, and Berchtesgaden a total of 25,000 tonnes), in Electoral Hesse (12,000 tonnes), in Braunschweig-Lüneburg, especially in Lüneburg itself (15,000 tonnes), in Prussian Saxony (especially Schönenbeck and Halle, at 45,000 tonnes), in Westphalia (Königsborn, Neusalzwerk, Werl, and Westerkotten, at 9,800 tonnes), in Württemberg (at 5,500 tonnes), and in the territory of Salzburg, the Salzkammergut.

For smelting and reduction processes, wood was required not only for fuel, but also for building (in mining) or as packing material (for salt). In the eighteenth century there was an increasing awareness that wood was not available in infinite quantities; from as early as the sixteenth century, mineral coal was mined for fuel. At the end of the seventeenth century a Brandenburg bureaucrat described mineral coal deposits as *silva subterranea* (subterranean forest).[69] Mineral coal was introduced both for household hearths and for industrial purposes. As a result, in 1800 the quantities mined were already substantial: in Mark 181,000 tonnes (around Hörde), around Aachen 108,000 tonnes, on the Mosel and the Saar 67,000 tonnes, in Silesia 146,000 tonnes, in the Harz 230,000 tonnes, and in Bohemia 23,000 tonnes. Mineral coal was also mined in smaller quantities in other areas, such as the Palatinate. Gaspari explicitly emphasized that in Westphalia mineral coal was indispensible as a wood surrogate because there were too few forests.[70] In Brandenburg, Pomerania, West and East Prussia, and elsewhere in Central Europe, turf was used as a fuel. The burning of mineral coal had especially harmful effects on the air, as had already been shown by the example of England since the middle ages.[71]

By far the most important industry before 1800 was textile production. This sector provided livelihoods for the next largest number of people after agriculture, whether in the preparation of the raw materials, in the further processing, or in the distribution of the finished wares, even when only as a by-employment. Ahead of all other processed fibres in Central Europe into the nineteenth century was flax, which was made into linen. From the fifteenth century on, cotton played an important role in the Swabian textile industry as a component of fustian, a mixed cloth made from linen and cotton. Both the raw material and the process had come to Germany from Italy, which obtained cotton from the Mediterranean region. Wool textile production was less significant, since here most of the raw material had to be imported; however, it increased in importance up to 1800. Only in the eighteenth century was sheep-breeding decisively promoted with a view to wool quality, so that by 1800 raw wool was even being exported. In 1800, wool textile production was concentrated in the territory ruled by Aachen, in Silesia with a total of some 7,000 looms, in Kurmark and Neumark with the same number, in Bohemia with 16 woollen manufactories and six worsted manufactories, for which 7,000 workers are supposed to have been employed, in Moravia with some 10,000 looms, and in the Linz area with 25,000 workers. Cotton textile production was most strongly represented in Brandenburg around Berlin and Potsdam (4,700 looms), in Silesia (5,000), in Bohemia, in Moravia (almost 6,000), and in Lower Austria (almost 7,000).

Linen production was linked to the main areas in which the raw material was cultivated. Flax requires a moderate, moist climate. The main areas of European flax cultivation, which also exported to Central Europe, lay in eastern Europe (the Baltic states and Russia).[72] In Central Europe, the areas of cultivation which provided the largest quantities of flax lay especially in the Voralpenland and in the Bavarian Forest, apart from that (and especially intensely) in Silesia, then in East Prussia,[73] and finally in Vorarlberg, the Inntal, the Pustertal, Bohemia, Moravia, and on the Carpathian border. In Central Europe, linen cloths were mostly produced in coarse qualities, and sold mainly to the Mediterranean region and overseas.[74] For selling linen, controlling quality and marking the wares were of decisive importance. It was for these reasons that Bielefeld achieved its significance as the centre of the Ravensberg region, one of the main locations of linen cloth production. In the area of Hesse in 1800 there were some 6,000 looms in operation, in the Weser and Leine areas 2,000. By contrast, in Prussian Silesia and Lusatia there were more than 400,000 looms in operation, in Bohemia with its 65,000 linen weavers substantially more, in Moravia more than 25,000 looms, and in Upper Austria another 12,500.[75] Swabia, with its major centres of Ulm and Augsburg still one of the most significant regions for linen and fustian production in the sixteenth century, was hardly worth mentioning any more by 1800, in comparison to the neighbouring north Swiss areas (St. Gallen and Zürich).

Of largely local significance were paper production, glass production, and tobacco and chicory processing. Paper production, for reasons to do with raw materials, was to be found mostly in proximity to textile producing areas. Paper mills were to be found in large numbers in Silesia, Bohemia, Moravia, Brandenburg, East and West Prussia, Saxony, Württemberg, Baden, and Upper and Lower Austria. For glass-making, fuel for heating and processing was the decisive location factor. The glass works of Bohemia and the Bavarian Forest were especially famous. Tobacco and chicory were processed from the eighteenth century on, in locations determined by the centres of tobacco cultivation in Baden, Franconia, the Upper Weser area, and Brandenburg, and the centres of chicory cultivation in northern Baden, northern Württemberg, and Sachsen–Anhalt. Worth mentioning, finally, were the gold and silver processing of Vienna and

Schwabach, the making of clocks in Vienna (in 1800 some 100,000 pocket watches annually) and the Black Forest (at the end of the eighteenth century some 107,000 wooden clocks annually), wooden toys in Bohemia, scientific instruments in Munich, Augsburg, Nuremberg, and Fürth, porcelain in Meissen, Vienna, and Berlin, and finally printed matter in Saxony (Dresden and Leipzig).

The West and South of Central Europe were already industrially highly developed before 1500. By 1300, many towns had already been founded, and even after the post-1350 population decline these areas continued to develop.[76] In 1500, this early settlement was still reflected in the distribution of the larger towns: in addition to the concentration of settlement in The Netherlands, there was a zone of dense urban settlement stretching from the Lower Rhine across southern Lower Saxony and northern Hesse

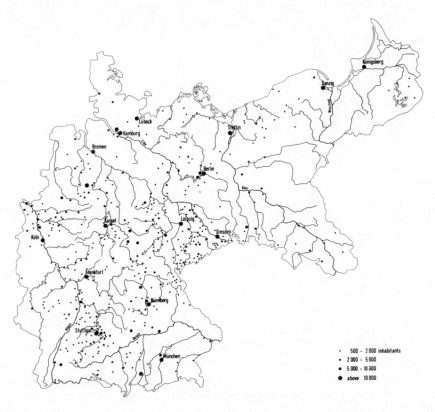

Fig. 1.8 Size and location of German towns above 500 inhabitants around 1700 (*Source*: E. Keyser and H. Stoob, eds, *Deutsches Städtebuch. Handbuch Städtischer Geschichte* (5 vols, Stuttgart/Berlin, 1939–1974); design: B. Übel; drawing: C. Branner)

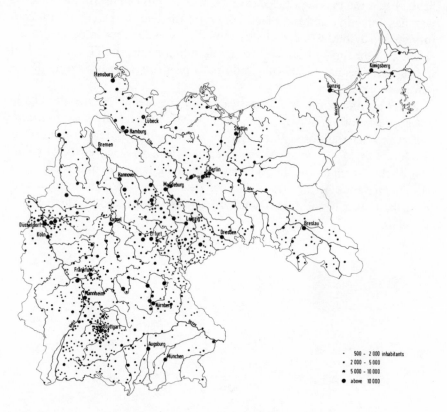

Fig. 1.9 Size and location of German towns above 500 inhabitants around 1800 (*Source*: Keyser and Stoob, *Deutsches Städtebuch*; design: B. Übel; drawing: C. Branner)

and Saxony to Upper Silesia. The rest of western and southern Central Europe was also covered with numerous towns, especially along the great river courses (the Rhine, Main, Neckar, and Danube). Northern and south-eastern Central Europe were, with few exceptions (such as the Hanse cities, Prague, and Vienna) much less densely settled.

It is worth mentioning that these concentrations of settlement largely corresponded to those areas which offered favourable conditions for agricultural production. Thus there were long continuities of settlement, and its distribution endured until around 1800 (see Figures 1.8–1.10).[77] While in western and southern Central Europe the density of population was between average (around 45 inhabitants per square kilometre) and above average (50–150 inhabitants per square kilometre in large cities such as Vienna, Hamburg, Bremen, Frankfurt, and even more in Berlin), north of the Mittelgebirge it was considerably lower, even though there was no lack of large cities. The low density of population found in large expanses of

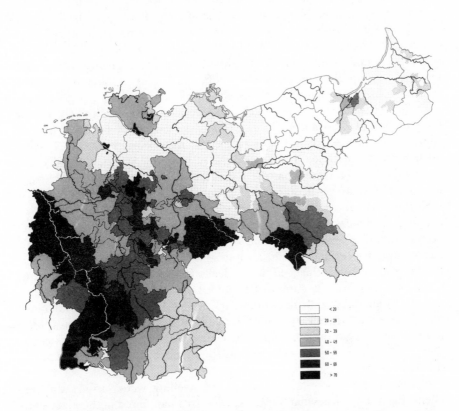

Fig. 1.10 Population density in Germany around 1800 (*Source*: Gaspari, Hassel and Cannabich, *Handbuch*; design: J. Sieglerschmidt; drawing: C. Branner)

northern Germany (except for Holstein and parts of Frisia) could otherwise only be found in scattered areas of the Alps (the Oberinnviertel, the Pustertal in the Tyrol, Bruck, Judenburg in Styria, and Villach in Carinthia), that is, under especially unfavourable settlement conditions. What is astonishing is the continuity of settlement, despite many small-scale changes: the decisive factor was favourable conditions for agriculture, which provided not only foodstuffs but also industrial raw materials. Without suitable climatic conditions, even good soils would not provide significant yields. The catchment basins of the Rhine, Main, Neckar, and Danube were fertile areas for cultivation, where plants flourished which did so nowhere else in Central Europe: for example, maize, chestnuts and figs. The main areas for growing wine-grapes also lay there. Similarly, the West and South of Central Europe were more suited to be industrial locations, since their supplies of raw materials and fuels were much richer. There was thus a noticeable correspondence between well-developed industries and high density of population, as in Jülich-Cleve-Berg, the Lower Rhine, south Lower Saxony, Rhine Hesse, the Neckar region, Saxony, and Bohemia.[78] In the more agrarian regions, only areas which specialized in animal husbandry stood out for high population density: Holstein and East Frisia.

Over this underlying great continuity of settlement, a great deal changed in detail during the period before 1800, more than is often recognized today. People's lives were full of insecurity, and death was a constant presence. Illness could mean the end of secured social existence, and the beginning of restless vagrancy. On one hand, there was a large variety of supra-local social relationships which came into being through marriage. Such marriage circles did not customarily extend very far, generally less than a day's walk away from the individual's home community. In particular industries or particular social groups, social relationships could be larger in scale. In occupations such as paper-making, milling, and tavern-keeping, marriages were contracted not within the village but within the occupation. The upper bourgeoisie of the towns and the nobility also contracted supra-local social relationships. Not only social estate and occupation but also age influenced the tendency to travel: both journeymen and scholars were normally supposed to look beyond their local horizons and become acquainted with new things in strange places. This sort of more or less enforced travelling shaded into the various forms of educational journey or young noble's 'grand tour' which began to arise in the sixteenth century.[79] Voluntary journeys were also undertaken to attain salvation, in the form of pilgrimages.

Occasions for less voluntary kinds of travelling were various and frequent. Even the journeyman's travels, widely romanticized in the nineteenth century, were by no means felt to be pleasant experiences. In many ways material compulsion, indeed survival itself, lay behind the travels of journeymen, seasonal workers, peddlers, musicians, actors, tramps, beggars, and rogues.[80] This already large group of people without fixed dwelling also contained not a few individuals who lacked social security, for instance because they were unemployed, and were therefore seeking a living in a nearby or distant town. The numbers of such people increased extraordinarily in crisis periods of famine, pestilence, and war. Towns appeared to offer better protection and better provision. When better times returned, industrial localities and regions returned to their former state more rapidly than other areas, which required considerably longer to recover.[81] In addition to the journeys caused by poverty, age, season, and the beginnings of tourism in the eighteenth century, there were also the transportation trades and the merchants (who were also frequently on the move for occupational reasons).

The roads on which these numerous people moved were already recorded on maps in 1500. However, even the great overland roads marked on maps at that time were generally lower in quality than present-day field roads and woodland roads. They lacked firm foundations: depending on soil quality and on weather, travellers had to struggle through sand dunes and muddy marshes. Naturally, on such roads it was impossible to move large loads over long stretches. Even the gentry preferred to travel on horseback until well into the eighteenth century, and it was only at that date that coaches began to appear. A two-axle cart harnessed with two draught animals could transport up to two tonnes. A one-axle cart drawn by one draught animal still managed a good tonne. In steep tracts of land, freight mules or sumpter mules were required, each of which could carry up to half a tonne. The speed of these forms of transportation amounted to some 30 kilometres per day, on straight and high quality roads perhaps even 40 kilometres, and for urgent loads even as much as 50 kilometres a day. Since the frequency of transportation of people and goods was quite low, it is not surprising that the authorities did not direct a great deal of attention to maintaining roads and bridges. Instead, fear of foreign soldiers could sometimes be greater than the desire for trade to flourish. Good roads operated as gates for invasion by foreign armies, which could bring enormous devastation. As a consequence, expanding these roads, as became customary in France from the seventeenth century onwards, often did not seem desirable.

The roads connecting settlements were maintained by the inhabitants of the villages. Admittedly, the authorities were responsible for security on the roads, but it was not until 1670 that the Imperial Diet issued an edict instructing road inspectors also to monitor whether the roads were passable.[82] Artificial roads, i.e. roads with a firm foundation, began to be built in Central Europe only in the second half of the eighteenth century. However, this did not prevent important roads from being extended even before this period. Thus in swampy tracts of country in north-west Germany, embankments and plank roads were laid down from the eleventh century on. The Alps, which in the middle ages were the most difficult barrier for Central Europeans on the road to the centre of their world, the Mediterranean, could be crossed on many roads, mostly with freight animals, the so-called sumpter mules. However, these could be loaded only with a maximum of 200 kilograms. Wagons, by contrast, were able to move more than half a tonne of usable freight in hilly tracts of country, as long as the necessary draught animals were available. In the Tyrol, therefore, the mountain passes were already extended in the fifteenth century. In this process, explosives were used as early as the end of the fifteenth century to make the road over the Brenner Pass to Bozen (Bolzano) passable for wagons at all times.[83] As with bridges, so, too, expensive pieces of construction such as these were carried out in expectation of money revenues. Only in the course of the growth of the absolutist state after the Thirty Years War did road-building come to be viewed as a task of governmental administration, to help promote economic development. In this, governments paid attention primarily to the post roads. By 1800, at least the largest overland routes were mostly in good condition.

However, little is known about currents of traffic. Road-building techniques and means of transportation are well researched, but what volumes of wares were moved on which roads in how much time are matters that have been investigated very little. Only where customs registers provide more detailed information about the number of people, animals, and wares passing through annually is it possible to estimate trends in traffic. Thus around 1500 some 5,000 tonnes of wares were transported across the Brenner annually, which was admittedly one of the main passes in Central Europe. By the eighteenth century, this volume had increased more than twofold.[84] Nevertheless, the density of traffic remained extraordinarily low: some 200 freight wagons and freight animals passed through the Brenner on days which were especially rich in traffic; in 1734, for example, the main period for traffic was the winter months. Land routes were thus not well suited for traffic in mass wares. Consequently, only very valuable or easily transported wares were moved for longer distances over land.

Considerably better suited for the transportation of mass goods were waterways: rivers, lakes, and the sea. Artificial water routes began to be built in Prussia more intensively in the eighteenth century: the Holstein Canal (built between 1777 and 1784), which connected the Baltic with the North Sea via the Eider; the Plauen Canal, which shortened the route from the Havel to the Elbe; the Finow Canal, connecting the Havel and the Oder; the Friedrich Wilhelm Canal, which opened the route from the Havel to the Oder; and the Papenburg Canal, which connected the Fehn colonies to the Ems and thence to the North Sea.[85] Additional canals were also built in Prussia. One was the Bromberg Canal, constructed in 1772–5, which connected the Oder and the Weichsel and could be travelled by 30-tonne ships. By the beginning of the nineteenth century, some 600 ships used this connection. The Finow Canal was travelled by 5,600 barges of different loading capacities at this period. The number of ships travelling through the Eider Canal was 453 in 1785, but had reached 1,072 by 1789.[86] The building of canals improved transportation options in Prussia. However, there were also – as elsewhere in Germany – canal projects which were not completed, such as the Rhine Canal which was supposed to connect the Maas and the Rhine.[87] In comparison with England or France, in Central Europe very few canals were built. This was another manifestation of the distinct Central European development path toward industrialization, because the late beginning of the industrialization process coincided with the first steps into the railway age. In Bavaria as late as the nineteenth century there was a debate about the advantages of railway expansion over canal expansion.[88] Canals and rivers were the routes for transportation of mass goods. Without the railway, Central Europe would today probably be covered with a network of canals.

The size of ships was determined by the state of the river: thus on the upper course of the Rhine from Basel to Mainz, ships had a freight capacity of only 50 tonne whereas, from Mainz on, they carried between 75 and 150 tonnes. Then from Cologne the ships travelling up to the Rhine estuary reached the loading capacity of the smaller varieties of ship capable of sea travel: some 200 tonnes. The rivers neighbouring on the Rhine and the Danube were capable of carrying only much smaller ships, many of them with a capacity of less than 15 tonnes. As on the rivers, so also in the river estuaries, transportation was made more difficult by the shallowness of the water. As a consequence, the types of ship most common in the Baltic and North Sea – such as the *Fluitschip*, which became common from the sixteenth century – had very low draught, with carrying capacities of between 200 and 1,000 tonnes. To travel upstream on the river, ships had to be rowed or towed, which, for a ship of 150 tonnes, required 10 or 12 horses. On the Rhine, beginning at Speier, human beings had to pull the ships. For the same load, about ten times as many human beings as horses were required. Also characteristic of the Rhine and the Danube were the numerous wood rafts, which were also partly used for freight transportation.[89]

Although there was potential for expansion, freight traffic remained rather limited in the period before 1800. As a consequence, despite these supra-regional, indeed continental, economic relationships, economic spaces remained rather small. This increased regional differences in prices, wages, and thus living circumstances. Only the railway enabled economic spaces to converge, and contributed – at least on a national scale – to a widespread equalizing of living circumstances. The acceleration of the exchange of wares then contributed to economic growth, which in the course of the nineteenth century enabled Central Europe to become an industrial region which offered, to a substantially increased population – despite all tendencies towards crises – more social and economic security than had ever been the case in the preceding period.

Notes

1   August Lösch, *The Economics of Location* (New Haven/London, 1967), p. 220. The original study was published in 1940. Lösch (1906–45) was one of the German scholars – besides Johann Heinrich von Thünen (1783–1850) and Walter Christaller (1893–1969) – who strongly influenced locational analysis in human geography. Lösch died shortly after the Second World War. He was one of the few German scholars who refused to submit to a scholarly career during the period of the National Socialist régime. Surveys of the historical geography – some would prefer to term it the environmental history – of Germany are not very common: see R. Kötzschke, 'Quellen und Grundbegriffe der Historischen Geographie Deutschlands und seiner Nachbarländer', in A. Meister, *Grundriss der Geschichtswissenschaft zur Einführung in das Studium der deutschen Geschichte des Mittelalters und der Neuzeit* (Leipzig/Berlin,

1906), 1/1, pp. 397–449; recently I. Mieck, 'Wirtschaft und Gesellschaft Europas von 1650–1850', in *Handbuch der europäischen Wirtschafts- und Sozialgeschichte*, 4 (Stuttgart, 1993), pp. 1–119; H. Jäger, 'Zur Geschichte der deutschen Kulturlandschaften', *Geographische Zeitschrift*, 51 (1963), pp. 90–143; H. Jäger, *Entwicklungsprobleme europäischer Kulturlandschaften. Eine Einführung* (Darmstadt, 1987); H. G. Steinberg, 'Zeitgenössische Veröffentlichungen als Quelle für Übersichtskarten der Gewerbeverteilung in Deutschland zu Beginn des 19. Jahrhunderts', in G. Franz, ed., *Stadt-Land-Beziehungen und Zentralität als Problem der historischen Raumforschung* (Hannover, 1974), pp. 325–42.

2 'Germaniae fines. Credo equidem nullam in Europa latiorem esse regionem Germania... Clauditur a meridie Italia et Dalmatia, ab oriente Hungaria et Polonia, a septentrione Mari Baltheo Magnoque Oceano, ab occidente vero Gallia Marique Britannico'; in K. Langosch, ed., *Johannes Cochlaeus, Brevis Germaniae descriptio (1512)* (Darmstadt, 1969), pp. 64–7.

3 Fig. 1.1 is from H. Rabe, *Reich und Glaubensspaltung. Deutschland 1500–1600* (München, 1989), pp. 515f.

4 Severinus de Monzambano (Samuel von Pufendorf), *De statu imperii Gemanici* (Weimar, 1910), pp. 126f.: 'Nihil ergo aliud restat quam, ut dicamus, Germaniam esse irregulare aliquot corpus et monstro simile, siquidem ad regulas scientiae civilis exigatur, quod lapsu temporum per socordem facilitatem Caesarum, ambitionem Principum, turbulentiam Sacerdotum ex regno regulari in tam male concinnatam formam est provolutum, ut neque regnum etiam limitatum amplius sit, licet exteriora simulacra tale quid prae se ferant, neque exacte corpus aliquod aut systema plurium civitatum foedere nexarum, sed potius aliquid inter haec duo fluctuans'; see H. Conrad, 'Recht und Verfassung in der Zeit Maria Theresias. Aus den Erziehungsvorträgen für den Erzherzog Joseph', in H. H. Hofmann, ed., *Die Entstehung des modernen souveränen Staates* (Köln/Berlin, 1967), pp. 228–43, here p. 241.

5 Rabe, *Reich und Glaubensspaltung*, pp. 11f.

6 *Ibid.*, pp. 18f.

7 O. G. Oexle, 'Die mittelalterliche Zunft als Forschungsproblem', in *BdLG* 118 (1982), pp. 1–44; O. G. Oexle, 'Stand, Klasse I-VI', in O. Brunner, W. Conze, and R. Koselleck, eds., *Geschichtliche Grundbegriffe, Historisches Lexikon der politisch-sozialen Sprache in Deutschland* (Stuttgart, 1989), vi. pp. 155–200.

8 F. L. Brunn, *Tabellarisches Lehrbuch der neuesten Geographie und Statistik* ...(Basel, 1786), p. I; but Brunn also speaks of the fact that Germans, Lithuanians, and Poles live in Prussia (p. XXII); he finds, despite the variety of the Germans, German loyalty worthy of remark; and he writes that 'although they are accused of having too great a desire to imitate foreigners, one must also not ignore the fact that no people is so zealous to make their own the good that is to be found in foreign nationalities' (p. XXII).

9 A. C. Gaspari, G. Hassel, and J. G. F. Cannabich, *Vollständiges Handbuch der Erdbeschreibung*, 1/III (Weimar, 1819), p. 29; D. Dann, 'Begriffe und Typen des Nationalen in der frühen Neuzeit', in B. Giesen, ed., *Nationale und kulturelle Identität. Studien zur Entwicklung des kollektiven Bewußtseins in der Neuzeit* (Frankfurt am Main, 1991), pp. 56–73.

10 P. Münch, 'Die Obrigkeit im Vaterstand – Zu Definition und Kritik des "Landesvaters" während der frühen Neuzeit', *Daphnis*, 11 (1982), pp. 15–40.

11 J. Sieglerschmidt, *Territorialstaat und Kirchenregiment: Studien zur Rechtsdogmatik des Kirchenpatronatsrechts im 15. und 16. Jahrhundert* (Cologne/Vienna, 1987), pp. 154–67, 282–4.

12 T. Robisheaux, *Rural Society and the Search for Order in Early Modern Ger-*

many (Cambridge, 1989); H.-C. Rublack, 'Konfession als demographischer Faktor?', in H. Molitor, H. Rabe, and H.-C. Rublack, eds, *Festgabe für E. W. Zeeden zum 60. Geburtstag am 14. Mai 1976* (Münster, 1976), pp. 62–96.

13 E. Schubert, *Arme Leute, Bettler und Gauner in Franken des 18. Jahrhunderts* (Neustadt a. d. Aisch, 1983).

14 O. Brunner, 'Das "ganze Haus" und die alteuropäische Ökonomik', in O. Brunner, *Neue Wege der Verfassungs- und Sozialgeschichte* (2nd edn., Göttingen, 1968), pp. 103–27.

15 Albrecht Daniel Thaer, *The Principles of Agriculture*, 1 (London, 1844), p. 1; first published as *Grundsätze der rationellen Landwirtschaft*, vol. 1 (Berlin, 1809).

16 R. Berthold, 'Entwicklungstendenzen der spätfeudalen Getreidewirtschaft in Deutschland', in *JbWG* Sonderband [special issue] (1982), pp. 7–134; R. Berthold, 'Die statistische Erfassung der Bodennutzung im Spätfeudalismus', *JbWG* Sonderband [special issue] (1981), pp. 7–134.

17 Source for Fig. 1.2: W. v. Stromer, 'Gewerbereviere und Protoindustrien in Spätmittelalter und Frühneuzeit', in H. Pohl, ed., *Gewerbe- und Industrielandschaften vom Spätmittelalter bis ins 20. Jahrhundert* (Stuttgart, 1986), p. 85; J. Lutz, 'Die ehemaligen Eisenhämmer und Hüttenwerke und die Waldentwicklung im nordöstlichen Bayern', *Mitteilungen aus Forstwirtschaft und Forstwissenschaft*, 12 (1941), pp. 277–94.

18 H.-J. Teuteberg and G. Wiegelmann, *Der Wandel der Nahrungsgewohnheiten unter dem Einfluß der Industrialisierung* (Göttingen, 1972); H.-J. Teuteberg and G. Wiegelmann, *Unsere tägliche Kost. Geschichte und regionale Prägung* (Münster, 1986); see H. J. Teuteberg, ed., *European Food History. A Research Review* (London, 1992).

19 G. Hellmann, G. v. Elsner, H. Henze, and K. Knoch, *Klima-Atlas von Deutschland* (Berlin, 1921), fol. 1–13.

20 *Ibid.*, fol. 48–63.

21 R. Glaser, *Klimarekonstruktion für Mainfranken, Bauland und Odenwald anhand direkter und indirekter Witterungsdaten seit 1500* (Stuttgart/New York, 1991), p. 117; C. Pfister, *Klimageschichte der Schweiz 1525–1860. Das Klima der Schweiz von 1525 bis 1860 und seine Bedeutung in der Geschichte von Bevölkerung und Landwirtschaft* (2 vols, 3rd edn, Bern/Stuttgart, 1988), here i. pp. 130f.; H. Flohn, *Das Problem der Klimaänderungen in Vergangenheit und Zukunft* (Darmstadt, 1985); W. Lauer and P. Frankenberg, *Zur Rekonstruktion des Klimas im Bereich der Rheinpfalz seit Mitte des 16. Jahrhunderts mit Hilfe von Zeitreihen der Weinquantität und Weinqualität* (Stuttgart/New York, 1986).

22 Glaser, *Klimarekonstruktion*, pp. 110–16; Pfister, *Klimageschichte*, i. pp. 110–31.

23 Glaser, *Klimarekonstruktion*, p. 115.

24 Pfister, *Klimageschichte*, i. pp. 127f.; Glaser, *Klimarekonstruktion*, pp. 111f.

25 *Ibid.*, pp. 114, 116; M. Jakubowski-Tiessen, *Sturmflut 1717 – die Bewältigung einer Naturkatastrophe in der Frühen Neuzeit* (München, 1992).

26 E. Otremba, 'Gunst und Ungunst der Landesnatur für die Landwirtschaft im Gebiet der Bundesrepublik Deutschland', in E. Otremba, ed., *Atlas der deutschen Agrarlandschaft* (Wiesbaden, 1968), i. fol. 1.

27 P. Filzer, *Die natürlichen Grundlagen des Pflanzenertrages in Mitteleuropa* (Stuttgart, 1951), pp. 28f.

28 *Ibid.*, p. 96.

29 *Ibid.*, 113–26, especially based on examples from Württemberg and Upper Bavaria.

30 E. Fels, *Der wirtschaftende Mensch als Gestalter der Erde* (Stuttgart, 1954),

pp. 118ff.

31 Figs 1.5a and 1.5b: Fels, *Der wirtschaftende Mensch*, pp. 148f.; D. Dengler, *Karte der Wald- und Holzartenverteilung in Deutschland* (Berlin, 1937); J. Allmann, *Der Wald in der frühen Neuzeit. Eine mentalitäts- und sozialgeschichtliche Untersuchung am Beispiel des Pfälzer Raumes, 1500–1800* (Berlin, 1989).

32 M. Born, *Die Entwicklung der deutschen Agrarlandschaft* (2nd edn, Darmstadt, 1980), pp. 67–71; W. Abel, *Geschichte der deutschen Landwirtschaft vom frühen Mittelalter bis zum 19. Jahrhundert* (3rd edn, Stuttgart, 1978), pp. 112–22.

33 M. Williams, 'Forests', in B. L. Turner, ed., *The Earth as Transformed by Human Action: Global and Regional Changes in the Biosphere over the Past 300 Years* (Cambridge, 1990), pp. 179–202.

34 Gaspari, Hassel, and Cannabich, *Handbuch*, 1/2, 1/3, and 1/4.

35 Stromer, 'Gewerbereviere', pp. 82f.

36 Gaspari, Hassel, and Cannabich, *Handbuch*, 1/3, p. 46.

37 K. Fehn, 'Wirtschaftsentwicklung und Umweltbeeinflussung in Mitteleuropa aus historisch-geographischer Sicht', in H. Kellenbenz, ed., *Wirtschaftsentwicklung und Umweltbeeinflussung (14.–20. Jahrhundert)* (Wiesbaden, 1982), pp. 277–92; R.-J. Gleitsmann, 'Der Einfluß der Montanwirtschaft auf die Waldentwicklung Mitteleuropas. Stand und Aufgaben der Forschung', in W. Kroker and E. Westermann, eds, *Montanwirtschaft Mitteleuropas vom 12. bis 17. Jahrhundert. Stand, Wege und Aufgaben der Forschung* (Bochum, 1984), pp. 24–39.

38 Gleitsmann, 'Einfluß', pp. 31f.

39 Fehn, 'Wirtschaftsentwicklung', p. 282; J. G. Krünitz, *Oeconomisch-technologische Encyclopädie, oder allgemeines System der Staats-, Stadt-, Haus- und Landwirthschaft und der Kunstgeschichte in alphabetischer Ordnung* (252 vols, Berlin, 1773–1858; repr. Hildesheim, 1982), cxiii. p. 148.

40 H. Witthöft, 'Produktion, Handel, Energie, Transport und das Wachstum der Lüneburger Saline 1200 bis 1800 – Methoden und Ergebnisse', in H. Kellenbenz, ed., *Wirtschaftliches Wachstum, Energie und Verkehr vom Mittelalter bis ins 19. Jahrhundert* (Stuttgart, 1978), pp. 29–54, p. 37; Williams, 'Forests'; Gleitsmann, 'Einfluß'; Fehn, 'Wirtschaftsentwicklung'; Stromer, 'Gewerbereviere'; Allmann, *Wald*.

41 N. S. B. Gras, *The Evolution of the English Corn Market from the 12th to the 18th Century* (London, 1915); W. Achilles, 'Getreidepreise und Getreidehandelsbeziehungen europäischer Räume im 16. und 17. Jahrhundert', *ZAgrarGAgrarSoz*, 7 (1950), pp. 32–55; J. Vögele, 'Die Struktur des Einzugsbereiches des Stockacher Wochenmarktes in der Mitte des 18. Jahrhunderts', *Schriften des Vereins für die Geschichte des Bodensees*, 102 (1984), pp. 163–73; F. Göttmann, *Getreidemarkt am Bodensee. Raum–Wirtschaft–Politik–Gesellschaft (1650–1810)* (St. Katharinen, 1991).

42 Gaspari, Hassel, and Cannabich, *Handbuch*, 1/3, p. 65.

43 *Ibid.*, 1/4, p. 39.

44 U. Körber-Grohne, *Nutzpflanzen in Deutschland, Kulturgeschichte mit Biologie* (Stuttgart, 1987), pp. 74f.; T. H. Engelbrecht, *Die Feldfrüchte des Deutschen Reiches in ihrer geographischen Verbreitung. Erster Teil* (Berlin, 1928), pp. 8f., Map 5, pp. 7f., Map 1; T. H. Engelbrecht, *Die Landbauzonen der außertropischen Länder*, 3: *Atlas* (Berlin, 1899).

45 Pfister, *Klimageschichte*, ii. p. 50.

46 Körber-Grohne, *Nutzpflanzen*, pp. 88f.; Engelbrecht, *Feldfrüchte*, p. 10, Map 11; Gaspari, Hassel, and Cannabich, *Handbuch*, 1/2, p. 62, and 1/4, p. 39.

47 Körber-Grohne, *Nutzpflanzen*, pp. 141–4.

48 *Ibid.*, pp. 372–5, 385–7; Engelbrecht, *Feldfrüchte*, p. 12, Map 24; Gaspari, Hassel, and Cannabich, *Handbuch*, 1/4, pp. 22f.
49 Körber-Grohne, *Nutzpflanzen*, p. 292; Gaspari, Hassel, and Cannabich, *Handbuch*, 1/4, p. 23; Engelbrecht, *Feldfrüchte*, p. 12, Map 23.
50 *Ibid.*; Gaspari, Hassel, and Cannabich, *Handbuch*, 1/4, p. 22.
51 *Ibid.*; Engelbrecht, *Feldfrüchte*, p. 12, Map 25.
52 Abel, *Geschichte der deutschen Landwirtschaft*, pp. 129f., see Fig. 1.7; Gaspari, Hassel, and Cannabich, *Handbuch*, 1/2, pp. 64f., and 1/4, p. 21.
53 R. Berthold, 'Enwicklungstendenzen der spätfeudalen Getreidewirtschaft in Deutschland', *JbWG* Sonderband [special issue], (1981), pp. 7–134; Pfister, *Klimageschichte*, ii. pp. 84f., 115.
54 Born, *Entwicklung*, pp. 50f.
55 *Ibid.*, pp. 89f.
56 Gaspari, Hassel, and Cannabich, *Handbuch*, 1/2, p. 80, 1/3, pp. 34f., and 1/4, pp. 37f.
57 Born, *Entwicklung*, p. 102.
58 Gaspari, Hassel, and Cannabich, *Handbuch*, 1/2, pp. 60f., 1/3, pp. 17f., and 1/4, pp. 18f.
59 Gaspari, Hassel, and Cannabich, *Handbuch*, 1/4, p. 18.
60 *Ibid.*, 1/2, pp. 58f., 1/3, pp. 16f., and 1/4, pp. 16f.
61 Fehn, 'Wirtschaftsentwicklung', p. 281.
62 *Ibid.*, pp. 279ff.
63 H. Grees, *Ländliche Unterschichten und ländliche Siedlung in Ostschwaben* (Tübingen, 1975).
64 Gaspari, Hassel, and Cannabich, *Handbuch*, 1/4, p. 50.
65 Stromer, 'Gewerbereviere', p. 87.
66 Gaspari, Hassel, and Cannabich, *Handbuch*, 1/2, pp. 67ff., 94ff.; 1/3, pp. 40ff.; 1/4, pp. 49ff., 120ff., 355ff., 436ff., 589ff.; 1/5, pp. 11ff., 125ff., 220ff., 434ff.
67 J. Radkau, *Technik in Deutschland. Vom 18. Jahrhundert bis zur Gegenwart* (Frankfurt am Main, 1989), p. 76f.
68 U. Troitzsch, 'Technischer Wandel in Staat und Gesellschaft zwischen 1600 und 1750', in A. Paulinyi and U. Troitzsch, eds, *Mechanisierung und Maschinisierung 1600 bis 1840* (Berlin, 1991), pp. 9–267, here 69f.
69 R. P. Sieferle, *Der unterirdische Wald. Energiekrise und industrielle Revolution* (München, 1982).
70 Gaspari, Hassel, and Cannabich, *Handbuch*, 1/3, p. 25.
71 Troitzsch, 'Technischer Wandel', pp. 31f.; P. Brimblecombe, *The Big Smoke. A History of Air Pollution since Medieval Times* (London, 1987).
72 Engelbrecht, *Landbauzonen*, Map 21; Körber-Grohne, *Nutzpflanzen*, p. 369.
73 Engelbrecht, *Feldfrüchte*, Map 24.
74 F.-W. Henning, *Handbuch der Wirtschafts- und Sozialgeschichte Deutschlands* (Paderborn, 1991), i. p. 639.
75 See n. 66.
76 H. Stoob, ed., *Die Stadt. Gestalt und Wandel bis zum industriellen Zeitalter* (Cologne, 1979), p. 155.
77 E. Keyser and H. Stoob, eds, *Deutsches Städtebuch. Handbuch städtischer Geschichte* (5 vols, Stuttgart/Berlin, 1939–1974).
78 See K.-H. Kaufhold, 'Gewerbelandschaften in der frühen Neuzeit (1650–1800)', in H. Pohl, ed., *Gewerbe- und Industrielandschaften vom Spätmittelalter bis ins 20. Jahrhundert* (Stuttgart, 1986), pp. 112–202, here 171–3.
79 P. S. Brenner, ed., *Der Reisebericht. Die Entwicklung einer Gattung in der deutschen Literatur* (Frankfurt am Main, 1989).
80 Schubert, *Arme Leute*; S. Kullen, *Der Einfluß der Reichsritterschaft auf die*

Kulturlandschaft im Mittleren Neckarland (Tübingen, 1967).

81 M. P. Gutmann, *War and Rural Life in the Early Modern Low Countries* (Assen, 1980); R. Brosig, 'Die Pest als Krisenzeit. Die Bevölkerung des Hegaus im Dreißigjährigen Krieg', in F. Göttmann and J. Sieglerschmidt, eds, *Vermischtes zur neueren Sozial-, Bevölkerungs- und Wirtschaftsgeschichte des Bodenseeraums. Horst Rabe zum Sechzigsten* (Konstanz, 1990), pp. 46–74.

82 F. Bruns and H. Weczerka, *Hansische Handelsstraßen* (Cologne/Graz, 1967), pp. 35–122; U. Troitzsch, 'Die technikgeschichtliche Entwicklung der Verkehrsmittel und der Einfluß auf die Gestaltung der Kulturlandschaft', *Siedlungsforschung*, 4 (1986), pp. 127–43; H. J. Teuteberg, 'Zur Bedeutung und Methodik verkehrsgeschichtlicher Forschung', in *Verkehrsgeschichtlicher Workshop* (Bergisch Gladbach, 1992), pp. 3–41; U. Lindgren, *Alpenübergänge von Bayern nach Italien 1500–1850* (Munich, 1986); U. Troitzsch, 'Die technikgeschichtliche Entwicklung der Verkehrsmittel und der Einfluß auf die Gestaltung der Kulturlandschaft', *Siedlungsforschung*, 4 (1986), pp. 127–43.

83 Lindgren, *Alpenübergänge*, p. 114.

84 *Ibid.*, pp. 177f.

85 Gaspari, Hassel, and Cannabich, *Handbuch*, 1/4, pp. 14f.

86 H. Kellenbenz, 'Landverkehr, Fluß- und Seeschiffahrt im europäischen Handel (Spätmittelalter bis Anfang des 19. Jahrhunderts)', in *Les grandes voies maritimes dans le monde (XVe–XIXe siècles)* (Paris, 1965), pp. 67–174, here p. 149.

87 Gaspari, Hassel, and Cannabich, *Handbuch*, 1/3, pp. 13f.

88 Radkau, *Technik*, p. 73.

89 Gaspari, Hassel, and Cannabich, *Handbuch*, 1/4, pp. 62–4; one horse was reckoned to be necessary to draw 2.5 tonnes on the Danube at times of ordinary water height.

Translated by Sheilagh Ogilvie.

2

Population Change and the Economy

ERNEST BENZ

Early modern demographic and economic trends in the German lands fell broadly into two patterns. The first pattern, in many areas characteristic of most of the seventeenth century, was one of dislocation. Specific regularities in production and reproduction were overridden by general disturbances, the most prominent being warfare. Later, in areas where external disruptions had subsided, the underlying regularities asserted themselves. For much of the eighteenth century, they generated a second pattern in which both population and economy displayed greater stability.

Stability did not mean uniformity. Especially in peacetime there were wide variations, geographically and socially. Inheritance customs and infant feeding practices produced dramatic regional contrasts in economic and family life. Yet these variations formed part and parcel of a coherent demographic and economic system built around entry into marriage. Social rules regarding family formation were flexible, allowing differentiation in response to economic opportunities and personal circumstances. In the German territories, as elsewhere in western Europe, there was considerable scope for individual differences within overall social norms.

Nor did stability imply stagnation. Almost everywhere, birth-rates exceeded death-rates in normal times. In peacetime, especially in the eighteenth century, the population rose steadily, reaching the highest levels attained in the German lands to that point. At first much of this growth simply made up for the heavy losses of the first half of the seventeenth century. By the early 1700s, overall population had returned to roughly the level of a century earlier. Then, the number of German-speakers increased by about half as much again over the next hundred years.[1]

In numerous separate local contexts, rising population encouraged economic development, particularly the intensification of agriculture. Some artisan crafts also underwent change, expanding their markets and incorporating new techniques. In boom times the social and cultural patterns associated with these trades spread to wider parts of the population. Yet this too involved no fundamental reorganization of society.

To be sure, these trends could not continue indefinitely. Eventually the population would grow beyond the ability of the early modern economy to cope in conventional ways. However, that crisis began to be acute only at the very end of this period. For much of the eighteenth century, German populations and German economies sustained a solid advance.

The municipal framework

For most German speakers, the borders of their particular population and economy were determined by local institutions. The loose structure of the Holy Roman Empire lent importance to regional powers and even to municipal governments. Society was built on the norm of the citizen, an adult male inhabitant of a defined territory. Within that legal and geographical area, he enjoyed specific privileges, as did his wife or widow, sons, and daughters. In many rural areas established citizens and their families made up a majority of the population. Even in towns, a substantial portion of the population enjoyed full citizenship. In any case, the model of the citizen determined equally the status of non-citizens, who dwelt on the margins of the settled communities.

The importance of locality was reinforced by its coincidence with institutional structures. Often the borders of the municipality coincided with those of the parish, guild authority, and the domains of the lord. In larger states, such as Prussia, lordship carried with it legal jurisdiction over cases of local importance. In the South-West, a single municipality might be a petty state in its own right and its lord as full a sovereign as the Holy Roman Empire admitted. In each case the overlap of municipal citizens with political subjects reinforced the local character of politics, and indeed of life in general.

As corporate bodies, municipalities exploited their legal standing to pursue local interests. They fought lengthy court battles against economic, political, and religious overlords, and against other municipalities. These struggles forged citizenries, making them a social as well as a legal reality. The inhabitants of a municipality felt solidarity with one another and with it, their *Heimat*. A *Heimat* was a special homey place, a familiar set of buildings, an integrated network of institutions, legal rights, and responsibilities, personal and political histories. To be a citizen was to have a *Heimat*, a place where one belonged and a base from which to exert leverage on the outside world.[2]

Across the municipal frontier, loyalties and identities were different. The people there heard different churchbells, perhaps followed different religions, were accredited by different guilds, supplied different markets, obeyed different authorities, employed different weights and measures, spoke a different dialect, paid different dues and taxes into different coffers. To be a citizen carried with it a range of distinct rights and obligations, a range that typified and defined the *Heimat*.

Individuals built their lives within this municipal framework, for the most part reinforcing it, defining it even when they resisted. Sons and daughters of citizens generally wed within the municipality, and then resided in a house there. When they looked beyond the local scene for mates, it was seldom farther than the next village or town. Even then a branch of the family typically returned to the ancestral home in the next generation.

Inheritance followed the lines of kinship, creating a concentrated nest of ties within the municipality, with only a few trails straggling beyond it. Inheritance was particularly important in an economy that grew only slowly at the best of times. Newly created wealth formed a thin crust on an economic pie that had been baked and sliced long before. At any given point, the vast bulk of wealth took the form of land, shops, offices, dues, and rights to control them that had existed for many lifetimes. Effective access to wealth therefore depended on family ties. Because these were overwhelmingly local, economic enterprise was likewise generally local.

Slow growth and patterns of inheritance were not the only reasons the economy displayed a local focus. Without cheap land transport, the resources available were local. The uses to which they were put were determined by local demand. In response to vagaries of weather and soil, custom and calculation, Reformation and Counter-Reformation, regional and even local patterns dominated population and economy.

The diversity of experience within the German territories makes it appropriate to examine these peculiarities close up, in their local context. So, too, does the unusual importance of municipal institutions. As it happens, the vital records are also organized for local history. To begin with, the parish registers of baptisms or births, weddings, and deaths were kept by local church officials.[3] They record events in the lives of their parishioners almost exclusively.

The parish registers can be exploited for population studies through the technique of family reconstitution.[4] Family reconstitution reconstructs the history of a couple by linking the register entry for its wedding to the entries for the spouses' births and deaths, and to the records of the births and deaths of their children. This information makes it possible to calculate, for instance, the age of the mother at the birth of each of the children. From this information in turn, one may calculate the frequency with which this woman and others of the same age gave birth, or got married, or died. Family reconstitution makes it possible to study population history at the grass roots, looking directly at the individuals who made that history.

Family reconstitution is a particularly attractive avenue of enquiry into German population history. To begin with, historians need not start from scratch, as they do in France or Britain, for example. Genealogists have re-constituted the families for quite a few locations and published the results as collective genealogies, or *Ortssippenbücher*.[5] These works reproduce the contents of the parish registers, reorganized into individual family histories. The demographer may then apply statistical calculations to those histories, taking advantage of the extensive preparatory labours of the genealogist.[6]

The framework of the *Ortssippenbuch* can be justified on scholarly grounds as well as practical ones. The fundamental context of economic rand family life was the municipality. By making available data on popula-tion organized in just such units, the local genealogies direct attention to this key arena of economic and personal decision-making. Ironically, the form of the investigation once more reflects and reinforces the municipal structure. The records were initially compiled on a local basis, in accor-dance with church organization and the realities of daily life. They were worked into *Ortssippenbücher* out of local pride and a conviction that the *Heimat* mattered. In exploiting these sources, contemporary historians en-deavour to recapture those local realities and highlight them for new gen-erations.

A time of troubles

The capturing of realities, local or otherwise, is extremely difficult at the outset of this period. Parish record keeping does not become reliable until well into the seventeenth century in most areas. Where registers do begin in the sixteenth century, they often become unusable in subsequent years, es-pecially during the Thirty Years War (1618–48).

This deterioration is a manifestation of the unsettled times. Threats of war, famine, and disease scattered the population. Civilians sought refuge in fortified towns or garrisoned camps, or simply fled. Deaths and births occurring among fugitives were reported in places of exile abroad, or not reported at all. The ministers, priests, and rabbis responsible for maintain-ing records sometimes fled themselves. At other times, the parish registers would be sent abroad for safe keeping, and updated only haphazardly upon their return. Church books remaining on the local scene risked destruction through vandalism or fire.

These conditions were most prevalent from 1618 to 1648, but they by no means disappeared in the second half of the century. In the West, the cam-paigns of Louis XIV disrupted life on both sides of the Rhine until the Treaty of Utrecht (1713). In the North-East, lasting peace returned only after Rus-sia displaced Sweden as a great power in the Great Northern War (1700–21). For a century, then, reliable and complete vital records are scarce.

Historians are left to make what they can of the fragments that have been preserved. Perhaps influenced by the state of the records, they make out a fragmentary reality behind them. That is to say, what appears in the disrupted sources is a dislocated economy and society. This condition is particularly evident in its fundamental unit: the splintered family.[7]

In its most straightforward form, dislocation meant death. Battle casualties marked only the beginning of the heightened mortality of wartime. Armies requisitioned crops and animals with little thought for the fates of their former proprietors. Troops marching and counter-marching spread diseases such as dysentery and typhus in their wake, and there remained the danger of plague. Refugees likewise carried epidemics with them, and the survivors presented their hosts with extra mouths to feed. The hardships of flight and exile took their toll on everyone, pressing especially heavily on the vulnerable aged, pregnant, and infants. Overall losses ran to a third or more during the Thirty Years War.[8]

The boost to the death-rate was particularly significant among adults. Seventeenth-century marriages were more apt to be interrupted by the death of one partner at a time when the wife was still capable of bearing children. The foregone fertility[9] was to some extent compensated for by rapid remarriage. Widowers typically remarried within months of bereavement. Widows under thirty were rather slower to choose a new spouse, with about half waiting more than 2 years. Older widows were least apt to remarry, but their decisions are less relevant either to fertility or to family structure.[10]

Higher death-rates sometimes meant repeated remarriage, especially for men. Even where only one party had been widowed previously, remarriage often bridged a wide age gap. A third of couples differed in age by more than 5 years. Markedly older husbands were twice as common as markedly older wives.[11]

At the same time as it threw together generations of adults, remarriage assembled in a single household children from different beds. Occasionally, a succession of remarriages left children to be brought up by a couple neither member of which was their biological parent. Complicated emotional and economic links were created by inheritance rights that tied parts of each generation together against the rest of the household.[12]

These developments weakened family ties already shaken by political turmoil and geographic mobility. As makeshift ports in a storm, many households did not offer the emotional refuge possible in more permanent arrangements.[13] Brief unions between spouses with divergent interests, a heavy death-toll among stepchildren towards whom parents felt ambivalent, constant movement in and out of the household by lodgers, apprentices, and distant relatives, all left the family a convenient association of emotional strangers. Without an enduring base, deep sentiments were less often engendered and sustained.

Economies likewise splintered under the impact of war. Disruption of

trade routes, volatility of prices, and insecurity of property vitiated efficiency and undercut planning. Whether in transit or in place, supplies were
in constant danger of requisition or pillage. Where the fortunes of war
brought acute crises, the prices of staples such as grain soared. Yet without
vehicles, buildings, herds, stores, and the other capital stocks that had been
destroyed, producers were in no position to meet this demand.

Where dramatic hardship temporarily passed, the outlines of a radically
different economy could be made out.[14] With population reduced well below pre-war levels, the terms of trade between land and labour altered. Living standards rose. With more land available at lower prices, smallholders
were able to supply their households more amply. A reduced population
meant less demand, at least for foodstuffs, and so prices of basic commodities fell. At the same time, a smaller population allowed wage-earners
to bargain harder. They held their nominal earnings above the depressed
prices, thereby increasing real wages.

Similar shifts took place in the terms of trade between agriculture and industry, as well as within them. With population pressure reduced, a more
variegated economy emerged. Demand for meat by the affluent was met by
more extensive use of land, no longer pressed to produced cereals for an
abundant population. Arable land was turned over to grazing. At the same
time manufactured goods – and above all textiles – found new markets,
providing more lucrative employment for artisans in both town and country.

East of the Elbe, serfs were unable to take full advantage of these opportunities, owing to the extra-economic compulsion to which they were
subject. Caught under tighter political and legal controls, serfs lacked opportunities and incentives. Whatever gains they could make in purely economic terms were apt to be skimmed off by their overlords. Moreover, the
lords dictated agricultural organization and technique over large tracts of
land. They preferred tried and true methods of exploitation, such as using
serf labour to cultivate grain for export through the Baltic Sea to urban centres in western Europe.[15]

In the relatively free West, peasants and townspeople benefited more substantially from the new possibilities. Thanks to the social balance of power
created by their previous struggles, westerners enjoyed greater freedom to
experiment economically.[16] More important, they had won a share in any
gains those experiments might produce. Yet in the seventeenth century,
these advantages were as much prospective as real. As long as large-scale
warfare loomed, neither population nor economy could reach a settled
state. East and West, the desires and hopes of common folk were constrained, indeed frustrated, by the power politics of their superiors.

Paradoxically, the German lands may have enjoyed greater unity during
the seventeenth century time of troubles than during the less arduous eighteenth century. In the 1600s the tumult of war, the virulence of disease, and
the severity of climate overrode local customs and personal plans, consign-

ing masses of the population to similar stringent conditions. Differences between Catholic and Protestant, between partible and impartible inheritance, between farming and manufacturing, between old and young brides, between prudent and imprudent husbandry, came to naught in the face of the onslaught. War and hardship created an artificial uniformity of condition within the German lands.

With peace, these previously insignificant distinctions gained importance, heralding the heyday of local diversity. During the respite from the wild sledgehammer blows directed from the top of the social scale, the lower orders seized opportunities to construct their own worlds over the long term. Not everyone was granted a choice in this construction, nor were all contributions equally skilful. Yet the range of interests and traditions represented was sufficient to produce a flourishing variety of economic and demographic experiments.

Impartible inheritance

One of the original characteristics of the early modern European economy was the flexibility with which it operated. Individuals, couples, households, and communities made decisions for their own reasons. The parameters of their decisions might be set by custom or law, but within that framework differentiation was encouraged. To be sure, certain choices limited others and the range of choice was not equally wide everywhere. In particular, rules of inheritance determined to a great extent how much initiative was left to individuals. For instance, rural communities practising impartible inheritance displayed less variety than their counterparts in regions where inheritances were split.

Under impartible inheritance, landed property was considered an unbreakable block, under the control of a single proprietor. The holding outlasted the proprietor, for it remained a unit regardless of death or sale. This unitary conception of the holding reinforced patriarchal tendencies by restricting the roles that individuals might play. The proprietors were almost always male, reinforcing already sharp distinctions in economic position by gender. Women appeared auxiliary to a social and economic unit that was defined in terms of a leading male. Females typically married into that unit, residing in a house and working on land identified with their husbands long before the wedding.

The children, too, were clearly subordinate to the father. They grew up in his house, on his land, eating his food, and using his tools. They remained completely subject to him until achieving full adulthood. Even that transition rested under the father's control, for full adulthood required control of an independent homestead, and the patriarch controlled the only one available. Even the son, eldest or youngest, marked as heir had no effective leverage over his fate in this crucial respect. Other sons were weaker still, to say nothing of the inferior position of daughters.

In regions where impartible inheritance was the rule, the crucial demographic and economic event was the rare transfer of the holding between generations. The death or retirement of a patriarch opened a place in the adult world to his lone heir. Constituting that place were the economic resources necessary to support a family. Until they were in hand, the heir was in no position to wed or to reproduce. The passing on of the holding therefore typically coincided with the wedding of the heir.

The former patriarch, if he still survived, retired to a cottage or upstairs apartment. A written contract protected him against egregious mistreatment by his successor, but in other respects the heir was now full master of the house.[17] He might draw on the labour of his own siblings or house the siblings of his parents, but these sojourners in his domain lay clearly under his authority. Brothers and sisters not in the direct line of succession had to rest content with this inferior standing for their entire lives, deprived of access to wealth and sex. Unless they were lucky enough to wed into another equally hierarchical household, their only alternative was to emigrate.

Impartibility often accompanied a peculiar set of social and economic arrangements to which it was adapted. As long-established units, holdings were consolidated and clearly marked off from one another. They tended to be larger than in areas of partible inheritance.[18] These large consolidated holdings were worked extensively, sometimes because of poor soil, sometimes because of the nature of local production (for instance, raising livestock for dairy products). The dwelling was located within the holding and was therefore separated from those of other villagers. When villagers did meet, it was on a basis of equality between households, with citizenship limited to the patriarchs. The isolation of farmsteads and the rigidity of the social structure made many regions of impartibility into stolid backwaters.

Within such a framework, growth took place through the multiplication of essentially similar units. Patriarchal households might expand quantitatively, but they resisted qualitative change. Even quantitative expansion took a direct, straightforward form. Because existing properties could not be divided, expansion required new land to be brought under cultivation. Such clearances were possible immediately following population drops, as in the seventeenth century. Once those losses had been made good, however, municipalities quickly came up against foreign borders, unsuitable soil, or lands reserved for special use. Cutting into woodland or fishery or pasture made no economic sense in the long run. Thus, municipalities made up of unbreakable holdings sooner or later became rigid structures incapable of further development.

It was this rigidity that then compelled the non-favoured siblings to seek their fortunes elsewhere or bear the full weight of their increasing numbers on static resources used in a fixed way. In the absence of new products or new techniques, and the new social structures that might accompany them, those who did not inherit were condemned to vanish from the scene. Their lines would die out if they remained at home under forced celibacy, and their only alternative was to leave. As the eighteenth century progressed, areas of impartible inheritance generated a steady flow of emigrants.

The emigrants often joined the streams of religious refugees and colonists headed east. Pioneers settled on the frontiers in Hungary, Poland, and even the Crimea. Mercenaries, most notoriously from Switzerland but also from other German lands, sought employment with French, Prussian, and British armies.

Many migrants eschewed the hardships of pioneering or campaigning, and moved only as far as the urban centres of their regions. Often they found themselves in a familiar environment. Life in small towns was much like life in large villages. Local concerns dominated politics; agriculture dominated the economy. Artisans produced tools, apparel, buildings, food, and drink, but their livelihoods and wealth were still determined by their landholdings.

Only in larger cities did a distinct economy emerge. There a more substantial population led by an affluent and educated élite supported greater diversity of occupation. Urban guilds wielded considerable power over municipal governments. Under guild influence, each municipality arrayed protectionist barriers against competition. Exorbitant fees effectively prevented outsiders from setting up shop. On the other hand, only nominal fees were charged to sons of guild masters or to new husbands of widows of guild masters.

By capping the number of masters and prescribing traditional techniques, guild regulations prevented the multiplication of urban livelihoods even more rigorously than nature fixed the number of agricultural enterprises in the countryside. Both in standard crafts and in more exotic fields such as fishing and innkeeping, opportunities for advancement were strictly contained. Large numbers of townspeople were stalled at the level of journeymen, making lifelong careers of what was for others a brief transition.

Towns drew female immigrants in disproportionate numbers. They worked as domestic servants, usually remaining celibate throughout their lives. Like their less numerous male counterparts, these women swelled urban mortality rolls, while contributing nothing to fertility. The entry into towns of these adults accentuated the less favourable balance of births to deaths that characterized the unsanitary early modern city. Under these artificial conditions, deaths outnumbered births, yet cities continued to grow. The surplus of deaths was in fact a mark of the attractiveness of city life.[19]

With their great economic inequalities, defined social roles, and high proportion of celibates, cities in some respects resembled villages under impartible inheritance. To be sure, the diverse and concentrated urban environment offered more extensive possibilities for growth in the long term. Yet in the absence of industrialization, that potential was not realized.

German cities were administrative or mercantile centres, not hotbeds of industrial production. Indeed, at all times, townspeople constituted a small minority of the German population. Throughout the early modern era, economic developments in the countryside were more significant.

Partible inheritance

The most lively sections of that countryside were those under partible inheritance. Splitting property each generation stimulated innovations, qualitative as well as quantitative.[20] In many places, sons shared equally in the inheritance from their parents, with portions set aside as dowries for daughters. In other areas, a daughter's portion, whether treated as dowry or as inheritance, was in every respect equal to a son's. These economic realities had important consequences for social structure, not least for the standing of women.[21]

Patterns of settlement differed notably. In place of isolated farmhouses scattered at wide intervals along winding roads, peasants practising partible inheritance favoured nucleated villages. Within a traditional area of settlement, all houses and outbuildings were clustered together. People lived next door and across the street from families they encountered every day in numerous capacities. Visiting shops, transacting business at the village hall, attending church, gossiping, haggling at market, and performing chores brought villagers into shared public realms that incubated solidarity.

The layout of a nucleated village reinforced local identity. The dwellings belonging to a single municipality were adjacent, and well apart from those of other municipalities. Moreover, that cluster or nucleus could be recognized at a distance by its outstanding features, such as the church steeple and perhaps the roof of the town hall. Walking the same streets and sharing the same forums enhanced villagers' sense of community. Finally, they trudged to work on the same paths, and laboured side by side.

That labour took place in the fields that stretched around the area of settlement. Each field was divided into strips rather than enclosed blocks. A villager might hold dozens of strips, located in widely distant parts of the municipality. The inconvenience of working these parcels separately, or of having to co-operate with others in the exploitation of an entire field, was partly outweighed by the smoothness with which parcellization fitted partible inheritance. Holdings consisting of numerous distinct parcels were easily split, not only at the death of the proprietor, but also one piece at a time as the proprietor aged.

Because property did not come in unbreakable blocks, both economic and family life were considerably more dynamic under partible inheritance. The transition to adulthood, for instance, was not an all-or-nothing shift that took place once and for all. Rather, it was a process, marked by piece-meal acquisition of greater rights and responsibilities.[22] Partible inheritance distributed property rights more widely within society. It also set up more extended and complex interactions among claimants. In place of the uniform, one-to-one bond of father to son under impartible inheritance, partibility connected each individual to siblings, spouse, in-laws, and parents or step-parents by a skein of relations of differing weight.

Particularly noteworthy is that women were full players in this game. When it came to accumulating the critical mass of wealth necessary to maintain a new household, the female line was as apt to be crucial as the male line. The lands or shop on which a couple began its independent economic career might as easily be the property of the bride as of the groom. The chance that the wife would continue to live in the home in which she had been raised, and to which she welcomed her groom as an outsider, was vastly increased. On average, the wife brought as much to the newly established economic partnership as her husband did. Women reared within a system that assigned them shares of valued resources equal to those of their brothers and sweethearts were more assertive. Their inheritances provided material bases from which to defend their own interests.

Thus, even if the only difference between partible and impartible inheritance had been the presence of female heirs and female benefactors, the system would have had far-reaching social consequences. However, the practice of partible inheritance also spread wealth across society. Each couple stood to inherit from four parents: the groom's mother as well as his father, and the bride's father and mother. Rather than wait on the final decision of a lone patriarch as their counterparts in other regions did, a couple could receive sufficient resources to set up on its own from any of these four sources. Barriers to marriage were thus far lower than in regions of impartible inheritance.

The wider distribution of wealth was also apparent from the other side of the transaction. The death of one member of the older generation scattered property over a range of heirs, including the children of this and previous marriages, and perhaps even stepchildren. If those direct heirs had already wed or died, property devolved still farther, to spouses or grandchildren. Even adolescents found their standing altered as they received further instalments towards their eventual holdings. They and their sweethearts, or suitors, could track their progress towards full adulthood. Whereas death was of limited interest under impartible inheritance, involving only a single heir and that only when the death struck a patriarch, each death under partible inheritance concerned the interests of a large group. The population was held together more strongly and in more intricate ways.

A further intricacy arose from the fact that property transfers did not have to wait on death. Nor did they require a full abdication by the previous generation. Rather, property passed easily between generations in pieces, representing advances on inheritance. Other devices for sharing property across generations were also more common under partible inheritance. Finally, ties within each generation were stronger, as bands of siblings united or competed over holdings they only partly controlled.[23]

These economic ties were matched on the social level, where a stronger communal life prevailed. Compelled to co-operate within the family, over inheritances, and outside it, to farm the divided fields, peasants took advantage of other collectivities to advance their self-interests. Moreover, they did so as relative equals, against a background in which siblings differed little in wealth, and in which resources attached to women as directly as to men. All children of citizens were citizens, and possessed, moreover, a concrete stake in the community in the form of their inheritance. They were therefore less apt to emigrate.

Instead, they remained in the municipality, residing in the homes of their parents or partners, or building new homes of their own. There were limits to this process, set by the boundaries between settlement and field, but those limits were not encountered as soon as they had been in regions of impartible inheritance. Instead of being exported, surplus population built up within the original municipality. Moreover, it was hard to spot the surplus, which consisted of economic and juridical equals rather than subordinate, disinherited outcasts.

Perhaps because of the flexibility and intricacy built into their economic dealings, peasants living under partible inheritance showed greater willingness to adjust qualitatively to meet population pressure as the eighteenth century wore on. Having to feed an increasing number of mouths from fragmenting holdings, they intensified their agricultural practices. The problem of surabundant population was transformed into the solution of demand for more labour.[24]

One classic solution was the transformation of the open three-field system. Perpetually resting a third of the arable, while reserving large areas for inefficient grazing, could not feed a growing population. Peasants began planting a wider variety of crops in the officially fallow field: clover, lucerne, beans, peas, lentils, rapeseed, poppyseeds, maize. In addition, smallholders turned increasingly to cash crops. Hemp, flax, market vegetables, and chicory generated high returns from small specialized plots. The new crops and crop rotations required much more labour, in the form of hoeing or processing, for example, but that labour was available, especially from women, to whom gender stereotypes assigned these tasks.[25]

Converting grazing land to arable made economic sense as part of a series of interlocking revisions to agricultural organization. Banished from the formerly common pastures, livestock were now fed in stalls within the area of settlement. Their fodder was grown on specialized tracts, often in neighbouring municipalities or on land unsuitable for other crops. Retaining the animals in one spot meant that their owner could collect manure and utilize it as fertilizer immediately and effectively. The qualitative changes of specialization produced higher output more reliably. By reducing the frequency of harvest failures, the new agriculture kept pace with the growing population, at least until the end of the eighteenth century.

The prudential check

However, even increased food production could not mask all the economic consequences of population growth. Except perhaps during the most acute crises, the German countryside was overpopulated in a technical sense. Marginal returns fell off sharply with increased labour. Smallholders received far less in return for their final hour of work on their plots than they did for their first hour. To be sure, additional labour did produce some extra output, and the gain was all to the good when labour was freely available from subordinate family members. However, there was little incentive to seek out further labour, which could have only very slight benefit when applied to most holdings.

These considerations grew ever stronger as the population rose in the eighteenth century. Land and its controllers exerted more and more leverage over labour and its controllers. Because land was scarce and labour abundant, the prices of the two commodities followed opposite courses. Peasants were prepared to pay high prices for land to be worked by idle hands within the family. Under those conditions, labour from outside the family could not command a favourable price. Thus, as the eighteenth century progressed, strains within the peasant population tightened. Rising population meant higher demand for agricultural products, a demand which the new agriculture met successfully and profitably. At the same time, rising population meant less demand for labour, threatening immiseration of the poorer elements in rural society.

These economic trends can be traced in the movements of age at marriage. Because marriage and procreation required the previous accumulation of sufficient resources to support a household independently, access to marriage varied with wealth. The children of the rich stood to inherit more, all other things being equal. Moreover, their parents could live well even after passing along sufficient assets to enable their offspring to make good matches.

On the other hand, poor parents required the support of their entire holdings well into old age, and might cling to them right to the grave. Their children therefore had to wait longer to inherit. Even then, they received less. From a purely economic standpoint, the children of the poor had little to attract a partner.[26]

These economic considerations became important because of the flexibility built into the European marriage pattern.[27] German-speakers, like most other west Europeans, chose both their spouses and the time of their weddings. Marriage did not follow automatically and closely on puberty in the late teens,[28] but was often delayed for a decade or more. In their early and even mid-twenties, large percentages of women and men remained single. They entered marriage only gradually, through individual decisions rather than as a massed cohort.

These decisions were not completely voluntary. In many cases, the poor were forced to be flexible – forced, that is, to postpone weddings or to forgo marriage altogether. Custom and law prevented the formation of unions that would be unable to support themselves at an acceptable standard of living. These rules had little impact on affluent citizens, whose inheritances, in hand or in prospect, guaranteed a comfortable livelihood. The offspring of solid proprietors, innkeepers, merchants, tax collectors, millers, brewers, and the like faced few economic barriers to marriage and so wed in their early twenties, and occasionally even younger.

By contrast, the children of day-labourers, masons, pedlars, and other humble citizens were compelled to wait several years longer. These postponements were especially lengthy in hard times. As population pressure built up over the eighteenth century, the economic opportunities of the poor became more and more restricted. Their ages at marriage gradually rose, opening a wider social gap.

With time these trends shut wider and wider segments of the population out of marriage for longer and longer periods. Indeed, in the 1800s over-population would alter the personal destinies of most of the population. Still, in the eighteenth century those pressures remained less acute. The poor might wait longer to wed, but they were eventually able to do so. More-over, the postponements imposed by the better-off on the less fortunate were not strikingly out of line with norms the poor themselves shared. By linking marriage to possession of resources sufficient to sustain a house-hold, the system kept population and economy in rough balance.

This responsiveness of marriage to economic conditions provided a pru-dential Malthusian check on population growth.[29] To begin with, repro-duction was limited to marriage for the most part, meaning that population was controlled by restricting access to marriage rather than childbearing within it. By contrast, childbearing outside marriage was minimized. Births out of wedlock came to just 1 or 2 per cent of all births in normal times. Illegitimacy rates were rather higher in regions of impartible inheritance, where weddings were rarer.[30] Locked out of marriage, non-inheriting sib-lings could not regularize sexual liaisons.

The frequency of births out of wedlock varied chronologically as well as geographically. Wartime brought to the local community an influx of un-wed soldiers subject to loose discipline. Armed men far from home were given to sexual harassment and outright rape. In the absence of social pressures to wed their victims, soldiers left behind unwed mothers when they marched on.[31] Nor were soldiers the only men to take advantage of unsettled times.

The impact of irregular unions was all the greater when marital fertility was disrupted, as it was during the seventeenth century. The number of legitimate births fell at the same time as more children were born out of wedlock. Combining these statistical effects doubled the illegitimacy rate to around 4 per cent at the height of trouble. The rate then subsided for much of the 1700s, only to rise once more as the eighteenth century drew to a close.[32]

On one level, this rise reflected the renewal of large-scale warfare in the wake of the French Revolution of 1789. Once again parts of the German lands became battlefields and campgrounds, and once again those territories saw an increase in births out of wedlock. However, there were also new elements present in the 1790s that would subsequently lift illegitimacy to much higher peaks in the nineteenth century. According to one view, the increased frequency of sexual intercourse among the unmarried was due to new norms of self-gratification and secular fulfilment.[33]

A less dramatic interpretation suggests conflicts among old norms. As population pressure grew, the marriage prospects of the poor shrank further. The gentle rise in age at marriage left more unmarried women at risk of childbearing. As more were exposed to temptation and opportunity, more succumbed. Moreover, those who became pregnant found that it was not as easy as it had once been to legitimize offspring by a wedding before or after their births. In restricting access to marriage, economic forces, communal authorities, and parents drove illegitimacy rates upward.

However, the full impact of these policies was reserved for a later period.[34] In the seventeenth and eighteenth centuries, sex was successfully confined to marriage for the most part. Adolescents remained chaste during the decade that elapsed between the time they became capable of having children and the time society permitted them to do so. German populations had broken the link between puberty and marriage that obtained outside Europe. However, marriage, sex, and procreation remained tied together. Getting married meant starting a family, with nine brides in ten pregnant within a year of their weddings.[35] After that, pregnancies continued until the wife became biologically incapable of childbearing.

In other words, early modern German populations were characterized by natural fertility.[36] In technical terms, natural fertility means that the pattern of decline in birth rates as wives age matches the pattern of decline in couples' fecundity, their propensity to produce children. The number of actual births falls off in the same proportion as the number of potential births. By contrast, family limitation in the strict sense refers to deviations from natural fertility in which fertility drops more substantially with age than fecundity does. Couples stop bearing children at ages at which they could have continued. Natural fertility may be either high[37] or low;[38] what makes it natural is that the course of fertility is not a deliberate contrivance by the couple. Historically, widespread massive conscious contraception has coincided with family limitation.

Although Genevan and French populations show the first signs of family limitation in the seventeenth and eighteenth centuries,[39] the practice had not yet spread across the Rhine. Whether a German couple continued to have further children or stopped did not depend on how many children it already had. Instead, stopping was essentially involuntary. The average woman whose marriage endured until after menopause gave birth for the last time around age 40.[40] With biology fixing the end of the period of childbearing, family size depended on the age at which the wife began reproducing. This in turn was determined by the age at which she wed.[41] The prudential check on entry into marriage was thus the primary means of controlling fertility.

The feedback between people and resources mediated by inheritance evened out swings in population.[42] When mortality increased, the property set free by the dead provided new opportunities to the living. Unwed couples took advantage of those opportunities to finalize commitments, wed, and begin bearing children. The new arrivals offset the previous loss. Conversely, a decrease in adult mortality forced the young to wait longer before they received property and began to reproduce. Controlling access to marriage thus prevented fertility from running too far ahead of mortality.

This Malthusian fertility control linked populations to their economies in a straightforward way. Because access to marriage varied with economic circumstances, overall population responded to economic changes. As depression reduced opportunities to earn a living, marriages were postponed and population tended to decline. Conversely, when the economy grew, livelihoods and marriages were created, stimulating population growth. These coincident cycles of economic and demographic growth or economic and demographic decline could be observed both in long waves over centuries and in short cycles between harvest years.[43]

In good times, people wed young, but in hard times, marriage came late. This was especially true for brides, whose ages swung more widely than grooms'. Under natural fertility, adjusting the bride's age influenced family size directly. Each two-year postponement of the wedding reduced eventual family size by about one child. An average age at marriage of 26 rather than 20 meant bearing six children instead of nine. Still later weddings cut the number even lower.

This logic was especially compelling among the poor, who bore the brunt of postponements. While the very affluent might wed young and produce families of eight, the very poor waited, sometimes into their thirties, and raised smaller broods of three or four. Among the goods money brought its possessors were companionship, sex, and parenthood. Yet in regions of partible inheritance it was not always an advantage to come from a large family. Where differences in wealth were slight, the few children of the poor might find themselves on an equal footing with the numerous offspring of their wealthier neighbours. In that sense, the prudential check tended to head off misery.

A dramatic confirmation of the importance of the prudential check can be found in manufacturing regions. Agricultural areas, even under partible inheritance, were characterized by moderate population growth. Because that growth was sustained over the eighteenth century, the long-term rise was substantial, amounting in many places to a doubling or tripling before the population levelled off in the nineteenth century. However, a full unleashing of human prolific power required a marked lowering of the age at marriage. That phenomenon took place only where economic opportunities were expanding rapidly, allowing youthful couples to meet, wed, and procreate.

Just such conditions have been found in some regions dominated by textile manufacturing, where the population boomed in the eighteenth century.[44] As a trade, weaving was not always subject to the constraints that limited the expansion of farming and guild crafts. A market stood prepared to absorb a vastly increased output of textiles. Merchant capitalists developed putting-out systems to link potential producers to that market.

Textile manufacture accommodated itself to rural conditions and rustics accommodated themselves to it. Households living from weaving demanded little space. Cheap, easily erected shacks could multiply within the area once occupied by a single farmstead. Siblings excluded from landownership by impartible inheritance could set up on their own now that alternative livelihoods beckoned in manufacturing. Finally, large families were less burdensome in fields where women and children produced alongside their menfolk.

By expanding this peculiar sort of economic opportunity, textile manufacturing could sometimes permit a sharp rise in population. Couples found it easy to enter the trade and set up households of their own. Their earnings were not extensive, but they were available right from the outset of their career. Instead of gradually building up a holding as their farming cousins might, young weavers could enjoy their full income in their earliest days of employment.[45]

Moreover, that income came in cash, a scarce resource. Textile workers found themselves enmeshed in a money economy. If they suffered misery when their trade periodically underwent recession, good times allowed them to enjoy a flashy life with what they regarded as easy money. The style of life and its quantitative expansion distinguished entire communities and specific groups within those larger units. Population grew rapidly within particular lineages, producing a substantial measure of inbreeding.[46]

Nevertheless, these changes did not mean a fundamental alteration in economic or social life. Within the eighteenth century, manufacturing was limited to particular areas and groups. Their numbers might be rising quickly, but they had begun from such a small base that their absolute impact remained slight. Moreover, the overall continental economy was not sharing in the industrial revolution under way in Britain. Cottage industry meant a quantitative multiplication of essentially stable social formations, not the dynamic introduction of qualitatively different social relations.

In the absence of shared traditions of individualism and empiricism in economics and politics, or of an abundance of coal to which to apply them, German economies were in no position to industrialize.[47] Without an industrial revolution, they could not break out of the deceptively stable early modern patterns. That escape had to wait on the arrival of innovations such as liberalism and industrialism from Britain, or radicalism and contraception from France.

Regional diversity

Instead of experiencing an industrial boom, the German lands entered the nineteenth century displaying geographic variations of long standing. Within the European marriage pattern, populations adjusted to local conditions, from new economic opportunities to prevailing cultural norms regarding child care. Because the system worked by manipulating entry into marriage, the ages of brides and grooms provide a convenient index of population and economy.

In the West, in areas where landholdings were divided, marriage was becoming less accessible, but overcrowding did not yet pinch the majority of the population. The average bride was in her mid-twenties. After the wedding, she could anticipate carrying five or six pregnancies to term before reaching menopause. Deaths in the womb and in infancy cut the number of children she reared to four. Mortality in adolescence and permanent celibacy reduced still further the number who reproduced in their turn. The most effective means of preventing infant deaths was extensive breastfeeding, as practised in the North-West, in Frisia for example. There, no more than one in six died in the first year of life.[48]

Some idea of the importance of breastfeeding can be gained by comparing the North-West with the South-East. In large parts of Bavaria, the Tyrol, Bohemia, and Saxony, breastfeeding was rare or perfunctory.[49] This south-eastern cultural tradition influenced mortality directly and fertility indirectly. Infants deprived of mothers' milk died twice as frequently, with a third or more not living to see their first birthdays. Like the lower rates in the North-West, these figures remained essentially constant right into the nineteenth century. There was no sign of a sustained drop in infant mortality, much less of the decline in fertility it is sometimes supposed to set in train. What reductions in mortality did take place were confined to adulthood, as the crises of the seventeenth century receded into memory.

Even as the adult population built up, fertility continued unremitting. High marital fertility rates were especially characteristic of the South-East. Mothers who did not nurse a surviving child resumed ovulating sooner and became pregnant more rapidly. They produced offspring every year and a half, while those who did breastfeed might wait two-and-a-half years between children.[50]

Under natural fertility, these differences were not a function of preferred family sizes. The contraceptive effects of prolonged breastfeeding were incidental, applying equally after every birth. Mothers showed no clear signs of attempting to slow the flow of births in response to the number, sex, or fate of their previous offspring.[51] In regions where breastfeeding was frowned upon, women avoided it for all their children; in regions where it was customary, they practised it with all their children; in regions such as the South-West where an intermediate schedule of nursing was common, it too was general for all offspring within a single family.

Married women who did not breastfeed could expect to produce more children, and to see more of them die as infants. Regions where breastfeeding was rare displayed much higher infant mortality than the North-West, and their fertility was higher still. At extensive cost in biological and emotional wear and tear, such regions could generate rapid population growth.[52] Where a booming economy supported large families, and especially where women were valued more for their earnings than for childrearing, that was just what happened. Couples wed young and reproduced fast, faster than their offspring died. The survivors joined their parents in the work-force at a young age, and quickly followed in their footsteps by leaving home to set up their own precocious and, soon, crowded households.

However, outside exceptional manufacturing communities, most German economies could not sustain such a pace. Despite its short birth intervals, this was true of much of the South-East. With marital fertility out of control, the only way to hold population within bounds was to choke off entry into marriage. Thus, the Bavarian regions where breastfeeding was not practised featured higher ages at marriage. Brides averaged about 28 in contrast to the 25 or less registered in East Frisia.[53] By postponing entry into marriage, Bavarian villagers held the number of surviving family members at roughly the same level as elsewhere. Older marriage and higher infant mortality counterbalanced rapid reproduction.[54]

In other regions advanced ages at marriage were a response to economic conditions rather than demographic ones. The Alps featured many older brides and grooms, who might not enter marriage until around 30.[55] This state of affairs meshed with impartible inheritance and extensive agriculture to create another stable social pattern.

The opposite extreme could be found in the Far East. German-speakers carried the European marriage pattern into regions where postponement of marriage was uncommon.[56] However, in adapting to their surroundings, the immigrants often took on the characteristics of previous residents. Lords who viewed population as a personal resource encouraged early and fruitful marriage among their serfs and tenants. Where settlers in the East retained their freedom, there was sometimes abundant land, and hence livelihoods were easily accessible. Under those conditions, marrying young made sense within the European marriage pattern.

Indeed, the flexibility of that pattern provides one of the few unifying features of early modern German populations. The sliding Malthusian scale for assessing economic prospects allowed for variation across time, space, and wealth. German-speakers created their own local societies within the loose political framework of the Holy Roman Empire, acknowledging both natural and artificial conditions even as they transformed them. Manipulating entry into marriage adjusted population to suit the prevalence of disease and hunger. The same mechanisms permitted flexible responses to economic opportunities, whether in agricultural fields long ploughed or in newly fashioned manufacturing pursuits. Likewise, exercising prudential checks on marriage sustained peculiar traditions of inheritance, household structure, and infant feeding. The flexibility of the European marriage pattern generated the stability characteristic of the otherwise diverse early modern German populations and economies.

Yet that stability was to prove only temporary. The system coped with the depopulation of the Thirty Years War and the depredations attendant on subsequent conflicts. It likewise accommodated the sustained population growth of the eighteenth century, though under increasing strain. Yet in the nineteenth century, the accumulated demographic momentum fractured the system. The creation of economic opportunities no longer kept pace with the accelerating population. Lacking mechanisms for substantially reducing fertility or massively generating prosperity, the old system was doomed. Its death throes and the struggles to replace it would transform not only German economies and populations, but also German politics and societies.

Notes

1   Paul Bairoch, Jean Batou, and Pierre Chèvre, *La population des villes européennes* (Geneva, 1988), p. 297; Herbert Moller, 'Introduction', in Herbert Moller, ed., *Population Movements in Modern European History* (New York, 1964), pp. 5–6. Summarizing more recent estimates, Christian Pfister, *Bevölkerungsgeschichte und historische Demographie 1500–1800* (Munich, 1994), p. 10, indicates a population for Germany excluding Habsburg lands and Switzerland of 16 million in 1600, 14 million in 1700, and 22 million in 1800. In any case, absolute totals were less important than local trends.

2   Mack Walker, *German Home Towns* (Ithaca, NY 1971); Jerome Blum, 'The European Village as Community: Origins and Functions', *Agricultural History*, 45 (1971), pp. 157–78; Celia Applegate, *A Nation of Provincials: The German Idea of Heimat* (Berkeley, 1990), pp. 1–14.

3　Systematic official records on Jews and other minorities usually begin after this period. For an example of their use, see Alice Goldstein, 'Some Demographic Characteristics of Village Jews in Germany: Nonnenweier, 1800–1931', in Paul Ritterband, ed., *Modern Jewish Fertility* (Leiden, 1981), pp. 112–43.

4　Michel Fleury and Louis Henry, *Nouveau manuel de dépouillement et d'exploitation de l'état civil ancien* (Paris, 1985); E. A. Wrigley, 'Family Reconstitution', in E. A. Wrigley, ed., *An Introduction to English Historical Demography* (London, 1966), pp. 96–159.

5　Arthur Imhof, *Einführung in die Historische Demographie* (Munich, 1977), pp. 18–35, 101–7; John Knodel, 'Ortssippenbücher als Daten für die historische Demographie', *GG* 1 (1975), pp. 288–324 (see also the other articles in that issue); John Knodel and Edward Shorter, 'The Reliability of Family Reconstitution Data in German Village Genealogies (Ortssippenbücher)', *Annales de Démographie Historique* (1976), pp. 115–54; Ernest Benz, 'The Completeness and Reliability of the OSBs', Appendix A to 'Fertility in Three Baden Villages, 1650–1900' (Ph.D. dissertation, Univ. of Toronto, 1987), pp. 485–517. Many remarks not specifically footnoted draw on this unpublished work.

6　Works exploiting *Ortssippenbücher* include Jacques Houdaille, 'Quelques résultats sur la démographie de trois villages d'Allemagne de 1750 à 1829', *Population*, 25 (1970), pp. 649–54; Jacques Houdaille, 'La Population de Remmesweiler en Sarre aux XVIIIᵉ et XIXᵉ siècles', *Population*, 25 (1970), pp. 1183–92; Arthur Imhof, ed., *Historische Demographie als Sozialgeschichte* (Darmstadt, 1975); John Knodel, *Demographic Behavior in the Past* (Cambridge, 1988); and Benz, 'Three Baden Villages'. Robert Lee, *Population Growth, Economic Development and Social Change in Bavaria 1750–1850* (New York, 1977), Peter Zschunke, *Konfession und Alltag in Oppenheim* (Wiesbaden, 1984), and David Sabean's forthcoming volumes on Neckarhausen in Württemberg rely upon their own family reconstitutions.

7　On 'la famille en miettes', see Micheline Baulant, 'The Scattered Family: Another Aspect of Seventeenth-Century Demography', in Robert Forster and Orest Ranum, eds, *Family and Society* (Baltimore, 1976), pp. 104–16.

8　Günther Franz, *Der Dreissigjährige Krieg und das deutsche Volk* (3rd edn, Stuttgart, 1961). Pfister, *Bevölkerungsgeschichte*, pp. 10 and 74, suggests even heavier losses in little Germany, with the population cut from about 17 million in 1618 to 10 million in 1650.

9　David Levine, *Reproducing Families* (Cambridge, 1987), p. 79, pp. 75–93.

10　John Knodel and Katherine Lynch, 'The Decline of Remarriage: Evidence From German Village Populations in the Eighteenth and Nineteenth Centuries', *Journal of Family History*, 10 (1985), pp. 34–59; Arthur Imhof, 'Remarriage in Rural Populations and in Urban Middle and Upper Strata in Germany from the Sixteenth to the Twentieth Century', in Jacques Dupâquier, Etienne Hélin, Peter Laslett, Massimo Livi-Bacci, and Solvi Sogner, eds, *Marriage and Remarriage in Populations of the Past* (New York, 1981), pp. 335–46.

11　Knodel, *Demographic Behavior*, pp. 137–41.

12　Martine Segalen, 'Mentalité populaire et remariage en Europe occidentale', in Dupâquier *et al.*, eds, *Marriage and Remarriage*, pp. 67–77.

13　Edward Shorter, *The Making of the Modern Family* (New York, 1975), pp. 22–39.

14　Wilhelm Abel, *Agrarian Fluctuations in Europe From the Thirteenth to the Twentieth Centuries* (London, 1980), pp. 154–219; Thomas Robisheaux, *Rural Society and the Search for Order in Early Modern Germany* (Cambridge, 1989), pp. 248–54.

15　Eric Hobsbawm, 'The General Crisis of the European Economy in the 17th

Century', *P&P* 5 (1954), pp. 43–50.

16 Robert Brenner, 'Agrarian Class Structure and Economic Development in Pre-Industrial Europe', *P&P* 70 (1976), pp. 52–60.

17 Lutz Berkner, 'The Stem Family and the Developmental Cycle of the Peasant Household: An Eighteenth-Century Austrian Example', *AHR* 67 (1972), pp. 398–418; Lutz Berkner, 'Peasant Household Organization and Demographic Change in Lower Saxony (1689–1766)', in Ronald Lee, ed., *Population Patterns in the Past* (New York, 1977), pp. 53–69; Hermann Rebel, *Peasant Classes: The Bureaucratization of Property and Family Relations under Early Habsburg Absolutism 1511–1636* (Princeton, 1983), esp. pp. 170–98.

18 For examples from a later period see Hermann Schubnell, *Der Kinderreichtum bei Bauern und Arbeitern* (Freiburg, 1941), pp. 32, 45.

19 Allan Sharlin, 'Natural Decrease in Early Modern Cities: A Reconsideration', *P&P* 79 (1978), pp. 126–38.

20 Lutz Berkner, 'Inheritance, Land Tenure and Peasant Family Structure: A German Regional Comparison', in Jack Goody, Joan Thirsk, and Edward Thompson, eds, *Family and Inheritance* (Cambridge, 1976), pp. 71–95; Lutz Berkner and Franklin Mendels, 'Inheritance Systems, Family Structure, and Demographic Patterns in Western Europe, 1799–1900', in Charles Tilly, ed., *Historical Studies of Changing Fertility* (Princeton, 1978), pp. 209–23.

21 Jack Goody, 'Inheritance, Property and Women: Some Comparative Considerations', in Jack Goody *et al.*, eds, *Family and Inheritance*, pp. 10–36.

22 David Sabean, *Property, Production, and Family in Neckarhausen 1700–1870* (Cambridge, 1990), esp. pp. 16, 183–207, and 300–20.

23 David Sabean, 'Young Bees in an Empty Hive: Relations between Brothers-in-Law in a South German village around 1800', in Hans Medick and David Sabean, eds, *Interest and Emotion* (Cambridge, 1984), pp. 171–86.

24 On the logic, see Ester Boserup, *The Conditions of Agricultural Growth* (Chicago, 1965).

25 David Sabean, 'Small Peasant Agriculture in Germany at the Beginning of the Nineteenth Century: Changing Work Patterns', *Peasant Studies*, 7 (1978), pp. 218–24; Robert Lee, 'The Impact of Agrarian Change on Women's Work and Child Care in Early-Nineteenth-Century Prussia', in John Fout, ed., *German Women In the Nineteenth Century* (New York, 1984), pp. 234–55.

26 On considerations that went into making marriages, compare Hans Medick and David Sabean, 'Interest and Emotion in Family and Kinship Studies: A Critique of Social History and Anthropology', in Medick and Sabean, eds, *Interest and Emotion*, pp. 9–27.

27 John Hajnal, 'European Marriage Patterns in Perspective', in David Glass and David Eversley, eds, *Population in History* (London, 1965), pp. 101–43; John Hajnal, 'Two Kinds of Pre-Industrial Household Formation System', *Population and Development Review*, 8 (1982), pp. 449–94.

28 Gaston Backmann, 'Die beschleunigte Entwicklung der Jugend', *Acta Anatomica*, 4 (1948), pp. 421–80; D. Hofmann and T. Soergel, 'Untersuchungen über das Menarchen- und Menopausenalter', *Geburtshilfe und Frauenheilkunde*, 32 (1972), pp. 969–77.

29 Thomas Malthus, *An Essay on the Principle of Population and A Summary View of the Principle of Population* (Harmondsworth, 1976), p. 250.

30 Robert Lee, 'Bastardy and the Socioeconomic Structure of South Germany', *Journal of Interdisciplinary History*, 7 (1977), pp. 403–25; Edward Shorter, 'Bastardy in South Germany: A Comment', *Journal of Interdisciplinary History*, 8 (1978), pp. 459–69.

31 Compare Lee, *Bavaria*, p. 299, and Pfister, *Bevölkerungsgeschichte*, p. 89.

32 Edward Shorter, 'Illegitimacy, Sexual Revolution, and Social Change in Modern Europe', *Journal of Interdisciplinary History*, 2 (1971), pp. 237–72; *Modern Family*, pp. 79–108.

33 Edward Shorter, 'Capitalism, Culture, and Sexuality: Some Competing Models', *Social Science Quarterly*, 53 (1972), pp. 338–56; Michael Phayer, 'Lower Class Morality: The Case of Bavaria', *Journal of Social History*, 8 (1974), pp. 79–95; Michael Phayer, *Sexual Liberation and Religion in Nineteenth-Century Europe* (London, 1979).

34 At this later period, they would be exercised especially harshly against non-citizens, resident aliens imposed on municipalities by state bureaucracies. By contrast, before 1800 lords often willingly sold marriage licenses to itinerant non-citizens, seeing in them a source of revenue rather than a burden on the public purse.

35 Compare Knodel, *Demographic Behavior*, pp. 272–81.

36 For this concept, see Louis Henry, 'Some Data on Natural Fertility', *Eugenics Quarterly*, 8 (1961), pp. 81–91; Louis Henry, 'Concepts actuels et résultats empiriques sur la fécondité naturelle', in *International Population Conference, Mexico 1977* (Liège, 1977), pp. 5–15; and Chris Wilson, Jim Oeppen, and Mike Pardoe, 'What is Natural Fertility? The Modelling of a Concept', *Population Index*, 54 (1988), pp. 4–20.

37 Joseph Eaton and Albert Mayer, 'The Social Biology of Very High Fertility Among the Hutterites: The Demography of a Unique Population', *Human Biology*, 25 (1953), p. 206–64.

38 Nancy Howell, *Demography of the Dobe !Kung* (New York, 1979), pp. 117–211.

39 Louis Henry, *Anciennes familles genevoises* (Paris, 1956); Louis Henry and Jacques Houdaille, 'Fécondité des mariages dans le quart nord-ouest de la France de 1670 à 1829', *Population*, 28 (1973), pp. 873–924.

40 John Knodel, 'Natural Fertility in Pre-Industrial Germany', *Population Studies*, 32 (1978), pp. 481–510; John Knodel, *The Decline of Fertility in Germany, 1871–1939* (Princeton, 1974), p. 49.

41 As it happens, age at marriage exerts a slight positive influence on age at last birth under natural fertility. Younger brides have older grooms on average, and the ardour of late marriers is at any given age fresher. Controlling for age at marriage can thus dissolve apparent signs of family limitation. See e.g. Zschunke, *Oppenheim*, p. 211.

42 G. Ohlin, 'Mortality, Marriage, and Growth in Pre-Industrial Populations', *Population Studies*, 14 (1961), pp. 190–7.

43 Such short cycles were of course intensified by the fact that women who did not give birth in a given year, because they were separated from their husbands, or infecund due to famine, or for any other reason, were typically available to give birth in the next year.

44 Rudolf Braun, *Industrialisierung und Volksleben* (Zurich, 1960); Hans Medick, 'Village Spinning Bees: Sexual Culture and Free Time among Rural Youth in Early Modern Germany', in Medick and Sabean, eds, *Interest and Emotion*, pp. 317–39; Peter Kriedte, Hans Medick, and Jürgen Schlumbohm, *Industrialization before Industrialization: Rural Industry in the Genesis of Capitalism* (Cambridge, 1981).

45 Charles Tilly, 'Demographic Origins of the European Proletariat', in David Levine, ed., *Proletarianization and Family History* (Orlando, Fla, 1984), pp. 42–3.

46 Volkmar Weiss, 'Die Verwendung von Familiennamenhäufigkeiten zur Schätzung des genetischen Verwandtschafts', *Mitteilungen der Deutschen*

Gesellschaft für Bevölkerungswissenschaft, 55 (1978), pp. 1–16.

47 E. A. Wrigley, *Continuity, Chance and Change* (Cambridge, 1988); Levine, *Reproducing Families*, p. 97. See also David Levine's forthcoming work on early modernizations, which reiterates the importance of Britain's peculiar path.

48 Knodel, *Demographic Behavior*, p. 44.

49 Hallie Kintner, 'Trends and Regional Differences in Breastfeeding in Germany from 1871 to 1937', *Journal of Family History*, 10 (1985), pp. 163–82; John Knodel and Etienne van de Walle, 'Breast Feeding, Fertility and Infant Mortality: An Analysis of some Early German Data', *Population Studies*, 21 (1967), pp. 109–31; John Knodel and Hallie Kintner, 'The Impact of Breast Feeding on the Biometric Analysis of Infant Mortality', *Demography*, 14 (1977), pp. 391–409.

50 Knodel, *Demographic Behavior*, pp. 545–9.

51 John Knodel and Susan De Vos, 'Preferences for the Sex of Offspring and Demographic Behavior in Eighteenth- and Nineteenth-Century Germany: An Examination of Evidence from Village Genealogies', *Journal of Family History*, 5 (1980), pp. 145–66; Knodel, *Demographic Behavior*, pp. 76–101.

52 These conditions are reminiscent of the high-pressure demographic régime described in E. A. Wrigley and Roger Schofield, *The Population History of England, 1541–1871* (Cambridge, 1981), pp. 450–3.

53 Knodel, *Demographic Behavior*, pp. 121–6.

54 *Ibid.*, pp. 353–67.

55 Robert Netting, *Balancing on an Alp* (Cambridge, 1981), pp. 133–40.

56 Rudolf Andorka and Sander Balazs-Kovács, 'The Social Demography of Hungarian Villages in the Eighteenth and Nineteenth Centuries (with Special Attention to Sárpilis, 1792–1804)', *Journal of Family History*, 11 (1986), pp. 169–92.

3

Agriculture and Agrarian Society

HEIDE WUNDER

Questions and methodological problems

The cultivation of the land in the early modern period is nowadays as a matter of course referred to as the 'agrarian sector', and is analysed using the tools of modern economics.[1] However, there are problems with this use of the modern concept 'agrarian sector', since to its very end the Holy Roman Empire largely had the character of an *agrarian society*. The division of labour between town and country did not change the fact that the whole economy essentially relied on the output of the land, its bringing to market, and its further processing. Not only were landlords supported by the output of peasant cultivation, but also the main revenues of most German territorial states derived from agricultural output. Thus the terminological equation of *agriculture in the agrarian society* of the early modern period with the *agricultural sector* of the nineteenth and twentieth centuries obscures fundamental differences between pre-industrial economies and the national economies of the industrial age – differences in forms of production and their distribution, and in the moral standards relevant to economic transactions.

In the early modern period the exploitation of the soil and inland waters produced not only foodstuffs, but also raw materials for industrial processing, and animals as mobile energy sources. In the nineteenth century, by contrast, the focus of cultivation shifted to growing foodstuffs and specific raw materials, especially wood. The energy requirements of households, crafts, and industries were increasingly satisfied using coal and electricity, and many raw materials were imported from overseas or replaced by chemical products. Thus in the nineteenth century there arose a new division of labour between town and country, in which rural agricultural production actually began to comprise the agrarian sector to a considerable extent. In

1800, the endpoint of this chapter, this process was still in its initial stages in comparison with England, the great model for 'rational agriculture'. Even so, important changes can be detected in German agriculture from 1600 on: an intensified commercialization and rationalization of production, and diversification and increases in yields.

This chapter will trace the structural changes in agriculture between 1600 and 1800. An introductory section discusses several conceptual and methodological issues which pose challenges for the exposition. A second section describes important features of the early modern agrarian economy, which either do not appear at all, or do so only in distorted form, in linear accounts of the 'agrarian sector' from the point of view of modern economics.[2] A third section describes the relationship between the agrarian system (*Agrarverfassung*) and socio-economic change. A final section discusses the beginning of agrarian reforms in the later eighteenth century.

Conceptual problems

The history of agriculture in agrarian society encompasses numerous actors, social groups, and institutionalized relationships: peasants and rural substrata in the countryside; noble, ecclesiastical, and bourgeois landlords; rulers; and towns and their inhabitants, urban citizens and the urban substrata – to name only the most important. Institutionalized relationships included not only agrarian systems and markets, but also households and communities. This opens up a large number and variety of perspectives, options for negotiation, and experiences, which cannot be reduced to a single common denominator: grain prices were evaluated differently by producers and buyers, a crisis of the nobility by no means meant the same as a crisis of the peasantry, and peasant indebtedness cannot be used as a straightforward indicator that the peasants were in a difficult situation, but rather, on the contrary, it may be a sign of their creditworthiness.

It is therefore important to analyse empirical findings in the appropriate context, and also to make one's own perspective explicit, since this plays an important role in deciding which contexts are selected, which questions are posed, and which long-term connections are drawn between the past and the present day. German agrarian history is a good example of this. In the five-volume *Deutsche Agrargeschichte* ('German Agrarian History'), an attempt is made to do justice to this complexity, in that 'the agrarian system', 'agriculture', and 'the peasantry', and thus the institutional, the economic, and the social aspect, is each allocated its own volume.[3] By contrast, the historiography of the former German Democratic Republic derived the criteria and concepts for its *Deutsche Agrargeschichte des Spätfeudalismus*

('German Agrarian History under Late Feudalism') from Marxism-Leninism.[4] The two most recent surveys of the history of German rural society in the early modern period follow new paths: Werner Troßbach combines the approaches of social history and institutional history, while Walter Achilles consistently uses an economic approach.[5] Troßbach provides the first documentation in any general survey of the change in perspectives in recent research on agriculture under the influence of anthropology. In his work, as in that of David Sabean, Rainer Beck, Thomas Robisheaux, Rudolf Schlögl, Jon Mathieu, and Albert Schnyder-Burghartz, the perspectives specific to peasant economic activity are placed at centre stage.[6] The different rationalities of lords and peasants are clearly distinguished: for peasants, risk-minimization lies at the centre of economic activity – even sometimes preventing their seeking unrestricted independence[7] – while for the lords, it is profit-maximization. This has led to a significant widening of theoretical approaches: alongside modern theories about the transformation of rural society in the early modern period, there have appeared 'indigenous' theories originating with the ideas of the peasants themselves.

Methodological problems

The early modern period belongs largely to the pre-statistical age, so the basis for econometric studies is extremely limited.[8] Such surviving material as does permit statistical analysis originates in landlords' accounts, customs registers, price schedules for grain, cattle, and cash crops (mainly from towns), the business books of merchants, and the records of state grain storehouses. However, there are no production statistics corresponding to modern standards. The earliest surviving set of peasant's accounts dates only from the eighteenth century. Although it enables important glimpses into peasant economic activity, it is not well suited to statistical purposes.[9] Thus peasant economic activity in the early modern period must be observed almost exclusively from the perspectives of landlords, states, and towns. The perspectives of peasants emerge from the voluminous records produced by peasant legal cases, but these contain not so much quantifiable information as qualitative attitudes about what was endurable and what was not, what was just and what was unjust, and what peasants viewed as an appropriate standard of living.

Because of this state of affairs as far as documentation is concerned, economic historians have portrayed agriculture in a very restricted way, from the perspective of rents and dues, and grain and cattle markets. Thus Wilhelm Abel based his model for calculating the output of peasant farms and the food needs of peasant households on grain and cattle.[10] Although this unquestionably added to knowledge, the use of grain prices as the standard measure neglects important aspects of peasant production for both consumption and sale: buckwheat and millet (basic foodstuffs in areas such as Franconia and Westphalia);[11] cabbage (mentioned by Abel only as an export, not as an essential component of consumption);[12] garden produce such as apples, pears, and plums (which made up the 'small tithe' received by the local pastor in many localities);[13] chestnuts; and products of the 'gathering economy' such as sloes, hazelnuts, and bilberries (included in peasant dues in the county of Sayn-Wittgenstein).[14] It is thus important to connect agricultural history more closely than hitherto with the history of nutrition, in order to bring into view 'agriculture' as a whole, not merely that portion of it which was involved in supra-regional trade and which thus appears in the traditional sources of economic history.[15]

There are other problems with making grain prices the standard measure for all calculations. On the basis of the wage-price scissors which opened up in the sixteenth century, Abel developed his thesis of 'mass poverty and hunger crises' in the early modern period. His evaluation of the wages of craft journeymen in terms of rye prices undoubtedly enabled insights into an important aspect of economic life in medium-sized and large towns, but it was representative neither of all towns, nor of all of society in the Holy Roman Empire. To assess the performance of agriculture between *c.* 1600 and *c.* 1800, it is equally important to examine the nutritional situation in the countryside, where by far the majority of people still lived.

The framework: climate, land, population, and transportation

Among the factors which influenced the cultivation of the land in the seventeenth and eighteenth centuries, the climatic deterioration which is often termed the 'Little Ice Age' stands in first place (as discussed in Chapter 1 of the present volume). Sixteenth- and seventeenth-century chroniclers report long winters, late frosts, rainy summers, and plagues of mice and locusts which damaged the output of the fields.[16] Dendrochronological studies confirm that from the second half of the sixteenth century on there was a decline in average temperatures, which noticeably worsened the conditions for cultivating grain, wine-grapes, and fruit, especially in regions of marginal agriculture. The effects of this climatic deterioration have hitherto come to light particularly in studies of the persecution of witches, while regional studies are still exceptions.[17]

What about the land used in agriculture? It is estimated that, in 1800, 55.5 per cent of the land in Germany was under cultivation, 25 per cent was forest, and 19.5 per cent consisted of settlements and wasteland.[18] These figures already include the land gains from the improvements made in the eighteenth century, and thus provide only an approximate idea of magnitudes in 1600. The relationship between arable fields, pastures, and meadows was not static: arable fields could be expanded by clearing, draining, and endykement, transformed into pastureland, or abandoned once more to forest. The size of the arable area alone does not permit any adequate statement to be made about the condition of agriculture. The quality of soil on arable fields differed widely, and was affected by the type of crops grown on them; crop rotations led to an exchange between arable cultivation and fallow (which, like stubble fields, was used to pasture cattle in this period). Similarly, parts of forests were brought into the agricultural land area: for pig fattening, leaf fodder, and animal straw. In the 'Wooden Age', the demands of agriculture thus competed in the forest with the demands of households and industries; there was increasing need for wood as fuel, building material, and a source of wood products (as discussed in Chapter 1).

The significance of climate and land for arable cultivation and cattle-raising depended fundamentally on the number of people that had to be fed and provided with raw materials. Measuring the absolute size of the population is not sufficient; it is much more a question of the distribution of people between town and country and between agriculture and industry, of the number of wage-workers without access to land, and of the standard of nourishment of various social groups.

Until the middle of the nineteenth century, the majority of Germans lived in villages, hamlets, or single farms. In Germany, unlike The Netherlands, the period of town foundations which began in the eleventh century did not continue, in the form of urbanization, into the early modern period. It is thought that Germany had some 3,000 towns in this period, and the Holy Roman Empire as a whole had between 3,500 and 4,000.[19] The number of towns increased only very little before the end of the eighteenth century, but medieval industrial towns and trading towns were restructured into princely capitals and garrison towns,[20] and many smaller towns saw an increase in population in the seventeenth and eighteenth centuries.[21] Between the sixteenth century and the mid-eighteenth century, some 18 to 30 per cent of the population lived in towns, depending on region. Only in the Mark of Brandenburg was it almost 50 per cent, because of Berlin.

This did not mean that the urban population was exclusively active in industry and trade, or that the rural population was exclusively occupied with cultivating fields and raising cattle. In the many smaller towns, the cultivation of the citizens' landed property and the exploitation of the town's pastures and woods for grazing and foraging of animals were part of the urban *Nahrung* ('livelihood', but literally 'nourishment') in a double sense:[22] that is, they represented a source of nutrition as well as of income. The output of towns' agricultural and pastoral lands, and of the gardens in and around the towns, was primarily intended for urban consumption,[23] although town citizens also cultivated grapes for wine (which was largely sold) and flax (which they mostly processed themselves). A common feature of such small towns was that their citizens supplied part of their food needs either themselves or by buying from neighbours. These *Ackerbürgerstädte* (literally 'field citizen towns') were thus not unlike large villages. This is certainly the case as far as the size of their populations is concerned, although the craft and industrial sector was much more important in towns than in villages.[24]

The larger towns and even the big cities also had *Ackerbürger* ('field citizens'), who farmed like peasants, but many ordinary town citizens also possessed land in the countryside around the town.[25] In the later middle ages many towns had obtained control over the surrounding villages, even if they had not altogether established their own rural political territories; and they exercised intensive influence over the economic exploitation of these villages. Towns in central and eastern Germany had been granted areas of land at their foundation; until the fifteenth century, these were cultivated by peasants in 'town villages', and then in the course of the 'crisis of the fourteenth century' increasingly by the town citizens themselves.[26] The opportunities which the markets of larger towns brought for the profitable exploitation of the surrounding land were being recognized from the later middle ages on.[27]

This meant that towns were not exclusively dependent for food on the countryside. The role played in urban incomes by cultivation of the fields and raising of cattle depended on the size of the town, its economic structure, the population which had to be provisioned, and the changing situation of the economy. The size of the population was not identical to the number of citizens and their household members, and urban population growth was due mainly to the growth in wage-dependent groups lacking landed property. In a sense, the soldiers of the standing armies also belonged to the non-citizen urban strata, although their food was mainly provided from the prince's grain storehouses.[28] By contrast, the provisioning of the state bureaucracy followed an older pattern: in addition to a money income, they received a variety of payments in kind and rights of usufruct over land (as discussed in Chapter 6 of this volume).

We must picture 'the countryside' as being just as differentiated as 'the town'. For agriculture the main social stratum was the peasants, who were subdivided into various groups according to property ownership and legal rights. Many villages also contained craftsmen working for local needs. From about 1700 on, however, the largest population group in the countryside was the rural substratum: almost everywhere in Germany from the sixteenth century on, there was an increase in the population of smallholders, who did not own enough land for a livelihood, and were thus dependent on finding earnings in day-labouring, casual work, or proto-industry.[29] That is, a continually increasing number of rural people were unable themselves to grow the food they needed, and instead had to resort to grain purchases. This meant that the demand for growth in agricultural production emanated not just from the towns, but also from expanding rural requirements. However, this model does not apply to all regions: the numerous smallholders on many central and eastern German estates received wage payments in kind, making them unimportant as a source of demand.

In estimating the magnitude of agrarian production, therefore, not only peasant farms but also smallholdings and the output of urban farming areas must be taken into account. In the early modern period, the 'agrarian sector' consisted of a variety of groups of producers which were located for the most part in the countryside, but were also found, although to a lesser extent, in towns and their rural political territories. The structure of demand was equally complex: in addition to the towns and the territorial rulers (through their standing armies), there was also the demand of the rural land-poor and landless. But economic and social relationships were even more complex: neither the magnitude of production nor its distribution can be grasped solely in terms of the goods mediated through markets. Rather, exchange relationships among individual households, and distribution patterns within the large manorial estates, must also be included in our calculations,[30] since they were just as important as the exchange process between households and markets. These other exchange relationships were distinct from market relationships, in that not only were goods exchanged for money, but also labour for products (as part of the wage), and labour for labour. However, even though the household economy was the central unit of economic activity in the early modern period, households were not self-sufficient, but rather were based on mutual dependence: they were linked with one another through a network of governmental, economic, social, and ritual relations, and institutionally connected through kinship, the local community, landlords, rulers, the market, and the church.

Another important factor for agriculture was transportation. The poor condition of the roads was a matter of complaint for contemporaries, who pointed out how dependent was transportation (particularly of mass goods, such as iron and grain) on accessibility by water. Structures of transportation underwent only minor changes in the early modern period (as discussed in Chapters 1 and 4 of this volume). The canal system was extended, and special care was given to maintaining the great pass routes over the Alps to Italy. However, the condition of most large roads was dependent on military needs, the deliberate extension of roads began only in the eighteenth century, and maintenance of the vast majority of roads linking villages and small towns was the responsibility of the communities. Not only was the condition of the roads and waterways an obstacle to trade and traffic, but also the numerous customs barriers used by the privileged to improve their revenues accounted for a considerable share of 'transport costs'.[31]

A transportation industry with specialized occupational groups had already developed in the medieval cities, and it expanded in the early modern period, but was not as large as might be expected. This was because of the agrarian labour system, which organized a substantial portion of labour provision in the economy via the services demanded by landlords from peasants. Everywhere in Germany, peasants had to deliver dues in kind to landlords, and peasant draught animals were requisitioned for the transportation of landlords' revenues in kind to market, and for bringing them in from distant possessions.[32] Similarly, peasants' draught animals were used for landlords' journeys, official journeys, and in wartime. A large, although not yet calculated, portion of transportation services thus took place within the manorial economy.

These transportation services not only consumed the peasants' own time, but also that of their working animals. Agriculture was thus affected by the problems of pre-industrial transportation in a variety of ways. The crucial source of energy, namely animals used for riding, draught, and freight, were bred not only by peasants and landlords, but also by smallholders, and represented a not insignificant source of income. Territorial rulers, too, began to set up studs to satisfy military needs. The dependence of lords on draught animals in particular is shown in the requirement that peasants keep a particular number of horses or oxen, which had to be available for the landlord's use, especially on the demesne. Yet draught animals offered additional income to peasants.[33] They provided additional energy on roads with steep slopes,[34] and also provided transportation services for supplying rural industries with inputs and for bringing the output to market.[35]

The radius which could be reached using peasant draught services was generally limited to a day's journey. Thus these services were too restricted for supra-regional traffic, or could be implemented only with considerable organizational costs. For supra-regional trade, therefore, professional transportation arose very early on, although this involved substantial costs (as described in Chapter 4). In the cattle trade, very long distances could be covered with comparative ease, since the animals could transport themselves, albeit with some weight loss.[36] The grain trade, by contrast, was limited by transportation costs, especially in inland regions. For the transportation of grain the waterways were particularly important. But it was difficult to move large quantities upstream on the river, since ships mostly had to be pulled by animals and manpower. However, an analysis of customs payments on the middle Weser river in the sixteenth and at the beginning of the seventeenth century shows that, despite these additional costs, in times of rising prices it was actually more profitable to ship grain upstream on the Weser to Hesse than downstream.[37] Even overland transport must have been worthwhile under particular conditions, especially in periods of rising prices[38] and in wartime.[39]

Given the high costs of transporting grain, it was an enormous advantage for large and medium-sized towns if they were situated on navigable rivers. Towns devised various strategies to ensure food supplies, not only in 'normal' times but also during periods of rising prices. As early as the later middle ages, citizens were compelled to set aside adequate stores for their households. Magistrates also tried to force the surrounding countryside to sell in the town market, for example by prohibiting 'forestalling' in the countryside and by setting up purchasing prerogatives over grain and cattle.[40] They also often established cornhouses (where urban grain was stored) and storehouses (for provisioning the poor).[41]

The question of transportation thus cannot be answered solely in terms of roads, rivers, and canals, or of animals used for riding, draught, and freight. The labour services of peasants to their landlords, and the mobility of the poorest members of the rural and urban populations, also comprised important parts of the pre-industrial pattern of traffic and transportation, in which there existed no 'infrastructure' distinct from the institutionalized network of human relationships.

The agrarian system and social change

The agrarian system

The dependence of the whole of early modern German society on the output of the land was expressed in a variety of regulations directed at controlling its use and distributing the output of peasant labour. This meant that the market was not the dominant institution for organizing production and distribution. Instead, most transfers took place through legally defined relationships between lords and peasants: the church demanded tithes; landlords and feudal lords claimed annual dues, labour services, and payments on change of ownership; jurisdictional lords demanded labour services and fines in cases of delicts; and territorial lords claimed peasant labour services and taxes for general purposes. Peasants were forced to produce according to these societal demands. Closely connected with the distribution of peasant output was the influence exerted by landlords on what their peasant subjects produced. Through dues in kind, landlords prescribed the crops which were to be cultivated on the land owing such payments. The market-orientation of the landlords is shown in their favouring of 'saleable' grains as dues. Where the landlord demanded dues in the form of fixed money payments, peasants had to sell their crops. The multiplicity of rights to enjoy a share of peasant output, and the multiplicity of those who held these rights (including peasant communities and community officials), is illustrated in Fig. 3.1.

However, the societal allocation of peasant output was not only an expression of landlord power. Rather, the indispensability of the peasants meant that they themselves helped to shape their economic and social position. This is shown not only by the German Peasants' War (1524–6),

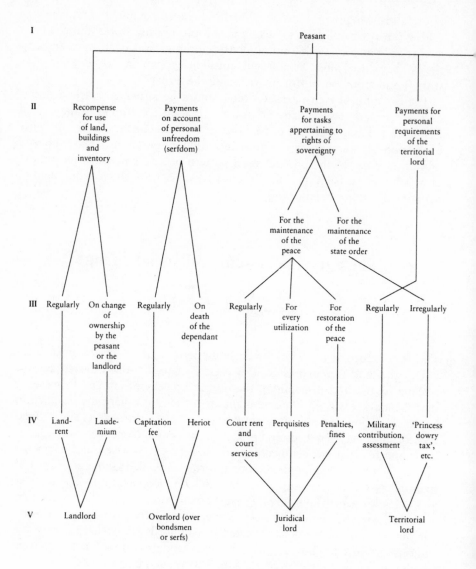

I   Peasant

II

Recompense for use of land, buildings and inventory

Payments on account of personal unfreedom (serfdom)

Payments for tasks appertaining to rights of sovereignty

Payments for personal requirements of the territorial lord

For the maintenance of the peace

For the maintenance of the state order

III

Regularly — On change of ownership by the peasant or the landlord

Regularly — On death of the dependant

Regularly — For every utilization — For restoration of the peace

Regularly — Irregularly

IV

Land-rent — Laude-mium

Capitation fee — Heriot

Court rent and court services — Perquisites — Penalties, fines

Military contribution, assessment — 'Princess dowry tax', etc.

V

Landlord

Overlord (over bondsmen or serfs)

Juridical lord

Territorial lord

Fig. 3.1 Payments by peasants and recipients of these payments, before the peasant emancipation in Germany (*Source*: Friedrich-Wilhelm Henning, *Der vorindustrielle Deutschland, 800 bis 1800* (Paderborn, 1974), pp. 256f)

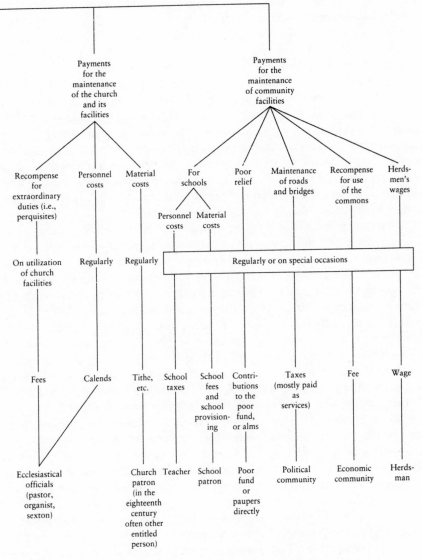

	Payments for the maintenance of the church and its facilities			Payments for the maintenance of community facilities				
Recompense for extraordinary duties (i.e., perquisites)	Personnel costs	Material costs	For schools	Poor relief	Maintenance of roads and bridges	Recompense for use of the commons	Herdsmen's wages
			Personnel costs / Material costs					
On utilization of church facilities	Regularly	Regularly	Regularly or on special occasions					
Fees	Calends	Tithe, etc.	School taxes	School fees and school provisioning	Contributions to the poor fund, or alms	Taxes (mostly paid as services)	Fee	Wage
Ecclesiastical officials (pastor, organist, sexton)		Church patron (in the eighteenth century often other entitled person)	Teacher	School patron	Poor fund or paupers directly	Political community	Economic community	Herdsman

Legend:
I.   Person required to make payment.
II. Justification or purpose of the payment.
III. Point of time at which the payment made.
IV. General terms used to designate the payment.
V.   Recipient of the payment.

but also by the peasant resistance which persisted throughout the early modern period. Peasants' own influence on their socio-economic position was based firstly on the local power of disposition they exercised over land, labour, and property within the framework of their village communities, and secondly on their legally defined relationships with the lords, through which they could pursue their rights up to the highest Imperial courts.[42] One of the lords' major problems was to maintain accurate information about the land and its taxable capacities on the local level.[43] Both individual peasant households and peasant communities constituted barriers to lords' obtaining such information. Although individual interests led to many conflicts among peasant households, especially concerning cultivation, the most important arable cultivation system, the three-field method, was also a source of solidarity against intervention by the landlord. This was increased by the fact that in many German regions the commons continued to be used by both lord and peasants, and landlords' sheep herds had rights of pasturage on stubble and fallow fields.

By the 'agrarian system' (*Agrarverfassung*), I refer both to peasant–landlord relations and to the various systems regulating the use of land which formed part of the communally organized legal relationships among the peasants.[44] Both systems of relationships had developed since the high middle ages in the course of the shift of agriculture towards grain growing, the shift of property relationships towards manorialism, and the shift of the peasant community towards greater independence. In most German regions both systems of relationships remained in operation until the agrarian reforms which took place at the end of the eighteenth century and during the nineteenth century. The regulation of peasant–landlord relationships (through tithes, tenancy, serfdom, and jurisdiction) was abolished in all German states after the Revolution of 1848; in parts of Prussia, however, the police powers of the great estate-owners – and thus the position of the landowning nobility as local lords – survived: the regulations governing servants, for example, remained in force as late as the end of the First World War. The dissolution of the old system of land use and the individualization of peasant cultivation was only completed in most German states toward the end of the nineteenth century.[45]

A distinction must be drawn between my broad concept of the 'agrarian system' (*Agrarverfassung*), by which I refer to the whole structure of rural social power relations, and the concept of the 'agrarian system' as developed by agrarian historians and worked out into a typology by Friedrich Lütge. This typology is based on the structure of rents (with the associated burdens on the peasants), dependency relations ('freedom' and 'unfreedom' from serfdom), and peasant rights of ownership. Based on the different combinations of these three criteria in different German regions, Lütge developed a typology of agrarian systems for central, north-western, western, south-western, and south-eastern Germany; for the early modern period this typology is subordinated to the great dualism between the old German

Grundherrschaft in the West and the *Gutsherrschaft* found east of the Elbe.[46] *Grundherrschaft* is the name given to manorial systems, mainly in western German regions, characterized by little or no demesne farming, weak ties of serfdom between peasants and lords, rents payable in money or kind, relatively few labour services, and comparatively free disposition by peasants of landholdings. *Gutsherrschaft* is the name given to manorial systems, mainly in eastern German regions, characterized by large demesne farms, strong restrictions of serfdom on the rural population, labour services as well as money rents, and strong landlord controls on peasant property transmission and many other aspects of peasant life.

Apart from the fact that Lütge's typology is incomplete for important regions (such as Hesse and Franconia) because of lack of research, and 'a special development of a very unique sort' is claimed for Frisia, Lütge himself has pointed out difficulties in maintaining his strict distinction between *Grundherrschaft* and *Gutsherrschaft*. Serfdom and landlord demesne farms with peasant services were to be found not only east of the Elbe, but also in many parts of Saxony, Franconia, Westphalia, and Bavaria,[47] where both peasant labour services and the classic link between rights of serfdom, landlordship, and jurisdiction can be observed. However, the main problem is that differences in agrarian systems have been invoked as being responsible for far-reaching political consequences, in particular for developments in Prussia. This political interpretation was widely accepted in international scholarship, especially after the end of the Second World War under the banner of the Cold War.[48] After the end of the East–West confrontation, more critical and differentiated studies may find greater resonance than hitherto.[49] An important new challenge in European history is to refrain from taking the Atlantic economy as the standard, and instead to develop continental models for Central and eastern Central Europe, as historians from these areas have long demanded.[50] An important concept in this context is that of 'Wirtschaftsherrschaft' – 'economic dominion' – a concept already used successfully in discussing the large estates of Bavaria's nobility.[51]

In evaluating the different forms of rent and patterns of peasant ownership, a number of problems arise. First, in analysing the structure of peasant rents, it is important to assess the implications of the distinction between rents in kind, in money, and in labour. Money rents have been associated with the highest degree of freedom, while labour rents have been seen as an expression of the greatest unfreedom. Such evaluations lay behind the liberal economic views of the nineteenth century; but early modern German peasants did not necessarily evaluate the market as implying 'freedom'. They reacted quite ambivalently to offers to commute labour services to money payments, because they realistically judged that money dues implied that their dependence on the market would become permanent, while demands for labour services fluctuated substantially.[52] Given their dependence on nature, dependence on the price fluctuations of the market appeared to them to be even more threatening in many ways than requisitions on their resources by the landlords. The rationality of peasant economic activity thus followed its own rules: unlike the profit-maximization of the lords, peasant rationality was fundamentally orientated toward risk-minimization.[53] While even in the early modern period the market functioned ruthlessly according to the laws of supply and demand, peasants could in difficult years appeal to their lords for support. Fixed money payments were advantageous for the peasant in periods of high grain prices when this was part of an agrarian boom, but not in periods of high prices caused by bad harvests, when peasants were generally not in a position to bring anything to the market. When grain prices were low because of good harvests, it was difficult for peasants to come up with money payments, while for landlords the sale of grain was still profitable since they could supply large quantities to the market. No linear process of increasing, irreversible monetarization of rents can be traced in Germany: rather, there was a change from rents in kind to rents in money and back again, which could be brought about both by lords and by peasants, in the respective interests of each and according to their respective bargaining positions.[54] Payments in kind remained in existence as a part of landlords' revenues in Germany until the agrarian reforms.[55]

Labour services were linked either to the land or to the person of the serf; the quantity owed was either specified or unspecified; they applied to men and to women; and they related to a multiplicity of forms of work in manor house, farmyard, field, forest, and far beyond. Peasant services were also demanded by jurisdictional lords and territorial lords in return for 'protection and defence' and for maintaining the peace: 'Landesscharwerk' (corvée for the territorial state) could be very significant, as could services owed to landlords and jurisidictional lords.

Peasant burdens varied from one feudal domain to another, and from one territory to another; they also depended on historical period and agrarian conjuncture, making them difficult to reduce to a common denominator. Their magnitude depended decisively on whether they could be utilized for cultivating a landlord's demesne farm, for hunting, or for commercial purposes. In all of these questions, calculations were quite strict: when the services of the peasants were not needed, or when using them was more expensive than employing free servants, they were temporarily or permanently transmuted to money payments.[56] This was also the case with corvée for the territorial state: in Bavaria it was transmuted to a money payment as early as the end of the Thirty Years War.[57]

The significance of peasant labour services also depended on the demographic situation: if labour was scarce, they played a greater role than in times of population growth such as the second third of the eighteenth century. Compulsory work by peasants' children as servants to landlords, which was introduced in the sixteenth and seventeenth centuries in areas such as Bavaria[58] and the Mark of Brandenburg, disappeared in the eighteenth century. However, they were retained in principle, probably as a cushion against any future return to labour scarcity. As a result peasants remained 'unfree', even when they enjoyed a comparatively advantageous economic position.

When considering forms of ownership a distinction must be drawn between inheritable tenancies, long-term property rights, and short-term property rights.[59] (Sharecropping played only a minor role in Germany in the early modern period.) The decisive difference between long-term and short-term property rights was that the former permitted peasants to alienate or mortgage land (with the agreement of the landlord), while short-term contracts meant that landlords had the possibility of changing the conditions of landholding at short intervals in response to the economic situation. In periods of population scarcity, peasants could also profit from such contracts.[60]

To forms of ownership must be added inheritance customs, which dictated whether one child inherited the farm or whether the property was divided up among all children. The impartible or partible transmission of property had great importance in peasant life planning, since it affected the provision made for children and their future social status. For landlords, it was mainly important because they had to ensure that peasant inheritance strategies did not reduce productivity. Which inheritance law was most advantageous for peasants or for landlords could not be laid down categorically, but rather depended on local and regional economic characteristics.[61]

The burdens on peasants arising out of the various payments and services they owed are extraordinarily difficult to calculate. The share of output comprised by payments to landlords has been estimated at between 20 and 40 per cent.[62] In this estimate, however, there remains a big unknown, namely the total output of the peasant economy, which (for the reasons discussed at the beginning of this chapter) cannot be calculated using econometric methods. To obtain an idea of peasants' economic position in each rural economy, therefore, it is necessary to resort to indirect indicators such as house-building or credit-worthiness.[63]

Debates about the German agrarian system and the emancipation of the peasants have obscured the fact that in the eighteenth century a core component of the agrarian system, the relationship between landlord and peasant, no longer applied to more than a part of rural society. It applied only to peasants in the narrow sense, while landless rural people were only bound by it when labour was scarce. This situation can be seen very clearly in East Prussia where, as population grew, it became cheaper for landlords to exploit their demesne lands using a small number of full-time labourers and a larger number of 'free servants', who only had to be engaged for the period of peak work between the ploughing in the spring and the harvest in August, and who then had to work out for themselves ways of surviving the winter. The 'freedom' of these men and women was the precondition for profitable economic operation, since the landlord was no longer obliged to support them in hard times.

Social change

The various types of agrarian and land utilization system did not make up an inflexible institutional framework which survived unchanged from the middle ages to the nineteenth century. Rather, they were flexible enough to open up room for manœuvre for their participants in response to the economic, political, and social changes which took place from the fifteenth century on. Landlords welcomed the intensification of agriculture through cash crops (woad, madder, flax and hemp, hops, vegetables and fruit, tobacco), since their peasants could then bear higher rents and dues. There was also flexibility in the economic and social status of peasants, who could buy themselves free from obligations to the landlords and obtain freedom from serfdom and inheritable ownership rights when they found themselves in a good bargaining position. When this was not the case, the position of peasants also could deteriorate, as is shown by the rise and spread of 'hereditary serfdom' (*Erbuntertänigkeit*) in central and eastern Germany.

The agrarian system also permitted the integration of the growing smallholding groups and rural sub-strata, although to some extent this involved coercion by landlords against the resistance of peasant communities.[64] The agrarian system even permitted structural changes in relations between peasant and landlord and between landlord and territorial lord. The Peasants' War of 1524–6 in central, south-western, and western Germany was a sign of the importance of such structural changes. Despite their defeat in 1526, the peasants were in many ways able to secure their economic and legal position by means of *Agrarverfassungsverträge* ('contracts concerning the agrarian system'), and they subsequently remained an important factor in politics.[65] Between the Peasants' War and the agrarian reforms, peasant resistance continued, and research on it has opened important perspectives on the process of early modern state-building.

LANDLORDS AND TERRITORIAL LORDS: CHANGES IN THE ECONOMY OF DOMINATION

Beginning in the fifteenth century, there arose a powerful competitor against landlords in the appropriation of peasant output: the territorial lords. In the middle ages, taxes were not levied regularly by territorial lords, but the necessity of defending Christendom against the Turks, the desire to further the true faith, and their own dynastic interests, in wars, and above all the Thirty Years War with its military 'contributions', led to an enormous rise and entrenchment of taxes.[66] The peasants were especially important for landlords and state, because they had to bear the highest burdens (much more, for instance, than the urban citizens). Thus it was in the interests of both landlords and state to maintain the economic capacity of the peasants. A first measure to guarantee this was the prohibition against dividing farms which was instituted in many territories.[67]

In seeking to expand the early modern state and to enhance landlords' position, territorial lords and landlords resorted to parts of the medieval repertoire of rights of lordship. Thus in the German South-West, serfdom was an important tool for the territorialization of lordship between the fifteenth and seventeenth centuries, but it was not very well suited for increasing revenues.[68] Because payments to landlords were more or less fixed and thus could not be increased in line with the land rents obtainable during the agrarian boom of the sixteenth century, many landlords got into economic difficulties.[69] By contrast, due to the enormous demand for land, the various forms of peasant property rights could very effectively be shaped so as to increase landlords' revenues, for instance through levying 'laudemia', payments to landlords when property changed hands.[70]

Noble landlords therefore sought new sources of revenues.[71] They were not totally free in their own choice of activities, since they were prohibited, for instance, from operating as merchants. However, new revenues suited to their social status could be obtained through military service and entry into state service; in addition, depending on the geographical features and market links of their possessions, the size of their domains, and the obligations of their subjects, nobles could obtain economic benefits through their rights of lordship over land and people. Successful strategies included the expansion of demesne farming to produce marketable surpluses of grain or cattle; the settlement of smallholders (who were obliged to make payments to the landlord and represented a labour force potential); the commercial exploitation of landlords' forests (through sales of wood and wood products) and fishponds;[72] and the expansion of prerogative rights (*Bannrechte*) over the rural market, especially for mills, breweries, and taverns. In addition, landlords often asserted rights of prior purchase over grain which their subjects desired to bring to the market, so that in addition to their own production they could also appropriate the market quota of their subjects.

Given this highly differentiated state of affairs, it is questionable whether the 'agrarian dualism' of *Gutsherrschaft* (the manorial system east of the Elbe) and *Grundherrschaft* (that west of the Elbe) is sufficient to do justice to the changes in the manorial economy in Germany in this period.[73] The concept of 'economic dominion' is an attempt at taking into account regional developments in Austria and Bavaria. Another useful conceptual differentiation has been proposed by Herbert Knittler, who advocates applying the term 'demesne economy' (*Eigenwirtschaft*) not only to agrarian activities in the narrowest sense, but also to other ways of exploiting landed property.[74] This reduces the emphasis placed on the link between market-orientated agrarian production and landlords' enforcement of peasant labour services, and shifts attention to the role of labour services in other fields of the landlords' economy and to the burdens these services implied for the peasants. These conceptual insights are used in the following account of the demesne economy and peasant services in the various parts of Germany.

In the second half of the sixteenth century, landlords (including territorial lords in their manorial possessions), spurred on by the rising demand for grain, began to expand demesne farms and establish new ones. They no longer granted waste lands to peasants but rather to smallholders; they bought out peasant holdings; or they expelled peasants in order to create new demesne farms.[75] Just as important as appropriation of land was recruitment of labour and draught animals; in the first phase of demesne expansion in the sixteenth and the beginning of the seventeenth century, both were secured through the labour dues of the dependent peasants.[76] Sometimes the new demesne farms were enclosed holdings (for example, when they were established on former wasteland), but sometimes the demesne land was intermingled with peasant land. The main area in which demesne farms expanded was central and eastern Germany and eastern Holstein; however, there are many examples of demesne farms in north-western, central, and southern Germany (such as the Weser basin, southern Lower Saxony, Hesse, and Franconia[77]), which still largely await detailed study.[78]

A new phase of establishment and expansion of demesnes began after the Thirty Years War, which had caused large population losses and had created abandoned lands in both southern and central and north-eastern and eastern Germany. In many parts of central and eastern Germany, landlords forced the remaining peasants to take on higher dues and labour services. In the resettlement of the abandoned territories south of the Baltic, peasants were unable to obtain good conditions because most of them had no property of their own. In this way, the landlords secured not only peasant labour services for their demesne farms, but also the possibility (created by disadvantageous peasant property rights) of altering the obligations of the peasants in line with their own needs. However, they only obtained these new powers through the territorial lords' recognizing peasant unfreedom ('serfdom', the binding of the peasants to the land). This had already taken place in 1577 in the Duchy of Prussia, in 1614 in Holstein, and in 1616 in Pomerania; Lower Lusatia followed in 1651, the Mark Brandenburg in 1653, and Mecklenburg in 1654. Thus *Gutsherrschaft* attained its full expression only after the Thirty Years War. Moreover, it varied a great deal: the *Gutsherrschaft* of the nobility was distinct from that of territorial lords, ecclesiastical institutions, and towns. There were also enormous differences between the large feudal landlords and the so-called 'cabbage Junkers' in the severity with which seigneurial demands could be put into practice. Given the labour scarcity in the various parts of Prussia, peasants who possessed property of their own could obtain free status and operate independently. Thus for the Uckermark, which is regarded as the core area of the most severe serfdom, Lieselott Enders has recently shown how landlords on the one hand reinvoked the old Westphalian law of serfdom in order to achieve the subjection of the peasants who were already settled in the area, but on the other hand introduced limited-term tenancies, which opened up considerable freedom for manœuvre for new tenants.[79]

Similarly, in a number of western German territories new efforts to establish *Gutswirtschaft* can be observed after the Thirty Years War. In the Wetterau (north of Frankfurt am Main) the Free Imperial Knight Philipp Ludwig von Franckenstein expanded his demesne economy in Ockstadt, which in 1666 evoked complaints by the peasants: they had to perform labour services on the lord's own fields and in his vegetable and hop gardens, use their own draught animals to fetch the grain rents paid by tenants in distant villages, and transport wood and clay for the lord's brickworks and salt for his cattle; women had to wash the laundry; widows had to weed the lord's pleasure garden; and peasants' children had to work for the landlord as servants.[80] Another example is provided by the county of Sayn-Wittgenstein, where in 1721–35 the territorial lord Count August, who had previously been in Brandenburg service, deliberately transplanted Brandenburg-style *Gutsherrschaft*.[81] The revitalization of serfdom was legitimized by appealing to documents of the sixteenth century, and was put into operation with military force and Prussian advisers. The peasants' vigorous resistance could not prevent their ultimate defeat, to which they reacted – like the east-Elbian peasants – with passive resistance.[82]

In large areas of Germany, the landlords' demesne economy had no importance for their revenues. Nevertheless, in these territories peasant labour services played a large role in the commercial exploitation of landlords' possessions. Hunting services (which ministered to the lifestyle appropriate to the social status of the nobility) were a large burden on peasant time in many areas of western and southern Germany. In addition, there was the damage to the fields caused by game, reason enough for the many revolts.[83] The economic dynamic of 'petrified *Grundherrschaft*' was shown in other activities: for instance, in the large noble estates of Bavaria, it was expressed in the settlement of craftsmen and others dependent on wage work, resulting in a new form of 'economic dominion'.[84] In other territories, smallholdings were granted in order to settle domestic-industrial producers; these developments are discussed in Chapter 9 of this volume.

The regional distribution and combination of the various forms of noble *Grundherrschaft* and *Gutsherrschaft* in early modern Germany was the expression both of the political power-relations between territorial lords and nobility, and of the economic options open to nobility and peasants in the territory in question. This is shown by a glance at Frisia, where the so-called 'marsh farmers' took part, like the landlords, in agrarian exporting, while the 'sand peasants', who were bound to the landlords, did not.[85] The centrality of this argument is shown by a comparison between Lower Saxon and east-Elbian peasants: the latter could not take part in grain exporting, because the revenues obtainable from the quantity they could bring to market were too small.[86] The applicability of this interpretation of the market opportunities of east-Elbian peasants is shown by recent research on the Uckermark, where in the eighteenth century, in a time of rising agrarian prices, peasants with limited-term tenancies successfully appeared on the Baltic market.[87]

In the dynamic of the manorial economy, the territorial lords of medium-sized and larger territories exercised an important influence on rural relations of domination. When landlords attempted to expand their interests at the cost of the peasants, the political strength of the territorial lord decided whether he could put a brake on these attempts. This is shown by the policies of *Bauernschutz* ('peasant protection') practised by many larger German territorial lords. Moreover, the domain policies of territorial lords were orientated toward state finances, which often required measures contradicting the interests of the great landlords. In Prussia as early as the beginning of the eighteenth century, the attempt was made to transform the royal demesnes into hereditary tenancies, although without success. In many ways, the situation of the royal peasants was better than those of the 'private' peasants, with the result that the nobility frequently complained because their peasants ran away from them.[88] The situation was different in the many small territories, where the territorial lord was frequently also the sole landlord.[89] In the Wetterau, many peasant movements from the sixteenth to the eighteenth century were directed against the expansion of landlords' incomes both through new taxes and through the imposition of new labour services. In such areas, 'peasant protection' was guaranteed not by the Free Imperial Knight as 'territorial lord', but rather by the Imperial courts, to which the peasants turned.[90]

POPULATION, SETTLEMENT, AND ECONOMIC AND SOCIAL DIFFERENTIATION

The growth of population in Germany from the middle of the fifteenth century up to the Thirty Years War, the enormous population losses caused by the war, demographic recovery, and the renewed population growth from the second third of the eighteenth century on (discussed in detail in Chapter 2 of this volume) all represented a key factor in German agriculture.

Land which had been abandoned in the fourteenth century was resettled in the course of the sixteenth century. Around 1600, the potential for new peasant settlements had been exhausted in most regions of Germany, with the result that the growing numbers of rural inhabitants had to be content with smallholdings. This explains why the population losses and abandoned settlements caused by the Thirty Years War and the 'Reunion Wars' of the second half of the seventeenth century were so soon filled: they were settled by the non-inheriting children of peasants and by land-poor groups from the region itself, and by immigrants from areas which had not been demographically affected by the war or from areas of religious persecution. The same was true of the devastating consequences of the plague in East Prussia (1708–10), which were made good partly by the indigenous Lithuanians, and partly by Protestants expelled from Salzburg in 1732.[91]

The increased population growth of the eighteenth century provided a stimulus for expansion of agriculturally exploitable areas in the German interior and on the North Sea coasts. Improvements of large areas of moorland and low-lying plain were furthered by the state: in Brandenburg the great Havelländer Luch in 1719–24, the Oderbruch in 1747–53, the Netzbruch in 1763–9, and to some extent the Warthebruch (completed in 1786);[92] in Bavaria the Donaumoos; and in East Frisia the fens. Less spectacular, but just as important, were the many local efforts made by peasants and landlords to reclaim uncultivated land in order to expand fields, pastures, and meadows.[93] But these undertakings were insufficient to secure an adequate economic basis for the growing rural population, since the land could not be expanded to keep pace with demand. As a result, newly gained land was strictly rationed: besides a few full peasant holdings, it was mainly smallholdings which arose, orientated not around a peasant existence but rather around industrial activity.

Population growth intensified the economic and social differentiation of rural society which had begun in the later middle ages. In the fifteenth and sixteenth centuries, and to some extent after the Thirty Years War, landlords and territorial lords focused on bringing about a re-occupation of peasant farms. Once this was achieved, the interests of peasants and lords diverged: peasants sought to provide for their descendants, while landlords and territorial lords wanted to maintain the productivity of farms. Where agricultural conditions and landlords' interests permitted, peasants could provide for their children through partible inheritance, as in parts of the Rheinland and Württemberg.[94] In areas in which farms passed undivided to a single child, non-inheriting heirs were compensated with a portion, with which they might marry into a peasant farm, set up house on a smallholding, or go into a town and train in a craft. Non-inheriting daughters, even more than sons, faced the likelihood of downward mobility: in Westphalia, they provided the recruitment source for a portion of the cottagers who settled on full peasant holdings in return for rent payments and labour services.[95] In other territories, it was the landlords who created smallholdings, which seldom offered more than the basis for nourishing the holder himself;[96] even in order to generate the payments they owed to the landlord, such smallholders had to resort to additional sources of income from agrarian and/or industrial activity. Not only the demesne farms, but also the holdings of the larger peasants required the day-labour of men and women for the work peaks in spring and during the harvest. There were complaints about labour scarcity not only after the Thirty Years War but also quite frequently in periods of population growth: obviously people were disinclined to go into service, which meant entering into dependency. In this, not only in absolute labour scarcity, lay the grounds for the compulsory services of peasant children in central and north-eastern Germany, Bavaria, and Westphalia.

Smallholdings created for a growing rural population the possibility of earning a living from work in agriculture, crafts, and industry. There were great differences in the legal and economic status of smallholders: thus in the large estates of the Bavarian nobility, some of the cottagers were 'free', and their economic position varied greatly from region to region.[97] The cottagers ('Heuerlinge') in Westphalia were also personally free, but their dependency on the owners of the farms on which they lived was considerable. In regions characterized by *Gutswirtschaft* cottagers were mostly serfs, and constituted a permanently available, dependent class of rural workers. In East Prussia, Silesia, and Brandenburg, they had the status of 'married servants'.[98] In the eighteenth century, these land-poor groups were joined by the totally landless *Einlieger*, who lived with peasants on a rental basis, or on the smallest size of holding, and depended exclusively on wages.[99]

By the beginning of the eighteenth century a broad stratum of smallholders and landless people had arisen, recruited mainly from its own ranks, while the peasants on large and medium-sized holdings remained constant in number, and thus became a minority.[100] The unequal distribution of land and usufruct rights among the peasants, the land-poor, and the landless was based on an artificial scarcity of land created by the landlords and territorial lords.[101] It implied an unequal distribution of life chances, very different standards of nourishment for the different strata of the rural population, and unquestionably a fundamental social injustice. In retrospect, however, there remains the question of what other form of survival there could have been in the early modern agrarian society for the growing population: an equal distribution of the usable agrarian area to all interested parties would have rapidly surpassed the limits of land partibility, and would have prevented the production of any marketed surplus for feeding the urban population.

Commercialization and intensification of agriculture

In the countryside, as well as the towns, an increasing number of people were forced to buy grain for bread. From this perspective, the labourers on the great eastern German feudal estates who were paid in kind were comparatively well-secured, but they generated no stimulus for the market. By contrast, in proto-industrial regions the local market for agrarian goods profited from the demand of the domestic-industrial population. There was considerable variety among the different regions of Germany. However, in general it can be stated that in the catchment area of the North Sea and the Baltic, there was a strong demand for grain and cattle not only from the

German interior, but also from foreign markets, so that in periods of high prices exports of bread grain or their use for beer production was prohibited. In parts of central and southern Germany, substantial demand emanated from the dense network of towns and from exchange between different production regions. But this demand did not necessarily bring about the commercialization and intensification of agriculture; these were viewed very differently by landlords, peasants, and smallholders.

For landlords, market relations had been very important since the high middle ages. Both in agrarian booms and in periods of low prices their market behaviour was directed at increasing the share of output sold on the market. To achieve this, they made use of strategies of appropriation (new measurements of peasant land and implementation of rights of prior purchase on peasant grain) and of new forms of production on both the arable and pastoral demesnes. Enclosed demesnes which did not lie interspersed with peasant fields already represented progress in rational farming. The performance of demesne farms engaging in arable production depended on the labour power, draught animals, and working tools of the dependent peasants being available at comparatively low cost, so that a high proportion of output could be sold on the market. But there were also other demesne farms which were cultivated using tenants and servants, such as the farms of the territorial lord in the County of Sayn-Wittgenstein, which devoted themselves to intensive pastoral production for the market from the late sixteenth century on.[102] In Schleswig-Holstein, demesnes engaged in fattening of oxen between *c.* 1600 and *c.* 1700, and then, with the rise in grain prices, shifted to rye cultivation and dairy farming for butter and cheese production. But despite enormous efforts, only a few landlords were able to intensify cultivation. Careful working and manuring of the demesne fields was envisaged, but with the labour services of reluctant peasants this could not be achieved. For this reason, attempts were made at an early date to transmute peasant services into money payments, and to farm using servant labour. A further commercialization strategy was for landlords to expand their sheep herds in response to rising wool prices. For this, landlords could make use of their rights of pasture on the commons and the fallow fields of the peasants; this led to numerous conflicts with peasant communities, which wanted to exploit the fallow themselves in the summertime. Nevertheless, through cross-breeding with introduced Spanish merino sheep, a beginning was made in improving wool quality.

Whether peasants appeared on the market depended on the characteristics of the land rent and the tax burden, and on local fluctuations in output. A 'commercialization from above' occurred, in the form of a tendency toward a transmutation of labour services and dues in kind into money payments; as we have seen, the peasants did not necessarily view this positively.[103] Indeed, it is questionable whether it is appropriate to use the term 'commercialization' to describe this enforced move toward the market. However, it may be assumed that it accustomed peasants to market opera-

tions. Market relations only created an incentive for peasants to become involved in the market when not only the landlords but they themselves profited from them, as was the case in the North Sea marshes, in the Alte Land
near Hamburg, or in the Knoblauchland near Nuremberg. By contrast,
where those enjoying institutional rights over peasant production were in a
position to participate directly in any increase in peasant output, market relations did not necessarily create any incentive for peasants to increase production. This was the case, for example, where tithes were levied in kind or
where, as in Westphalia, the landlord demanded a fixed share in the inheritance when property changed hands.

Commercialization arose more often in those sectors of peasant production which were not fully included in the regime of payments to the landlord, or where there were monitoring problems in the levying of payments.
Examples were the keeping of small animals and fowl and the cultivation
of vegetables, herbs, and fruit; these were all areas of production in which
women's work dominated. Income from sales of such products was very important, because they represented some of the few opportunities peasants
possessed for obtaining cash. In general, the intensification of agriculture
among peasants appears to have occurred mainly in sectors included either
not at all or only marginally in the rent system: this was the case of sowing the fallow with flax in summertime, growing legumes, cabbage, and tobacco, improving pastures, and carefully preparing and manuring gardens.
In many villages, there were larger or smaller areas of land which lay outside the rent-owing land, and which were by all accounts looked after much
more carefully than the fields.[104] Nevertheless, there are also scattered examples of rationalization on ordinary peasant land. Thus in Schleswig-Holstein from the sixteenth century on the commons began to be enclosed,
enabling them then to be used with little outlay to fatten Lübeck oxen. The
rationalization of peasant farms in the Allgäu from the sixteenth century on
can also be seen in this light: land was enclosed and the distance travelled
to work in the fields became shorter.

Finally, immigrants from western Europe operated as middlemen for new
crops such as tobacco, potatoes, and certain varieties of fruit, and provided
a model for careful cultivation. But they, too, confronted obstacles. Frederick William I of Prussia wanted to introduce 'Magdeburg-style' farming into
Prussian Lithuania, but failed despite the assistance of immigrants from
Salzburg. This was because of the region's water supply, which could not
be regulated in such a way as to make intensive agriculture possible until
the second half of the nineteenth century.

For the smallholders, the only strategy at their disposal for working their
land more intensively was to invest more labour. Through this and better
manuring, however, they achieved higher yields than the peasants did on
their fields.[105] They also made considerable efforts to keep animals, more
for sale than for their own use, since scarcity of fodder largely precluded
keeping more than one animal alive over the winter. Such intensification of

land use by smallholders is not included in the calculations of economic historians; smallholder households tend to appear only as a source of labour and demand for foodstuffs.

A further area of intensification was in the market-orientated gardening economy around the larger cities, in which older traditions were continued and innovations were introduced. This can be seen extraordinarily well in the Knoblauchsland near Nuremberg, and in the countryside around Erfurt. Not only was there a reorientation to new crops such as hops and tobacco but also careful breeding of seeds, which were exported into all countries of the world.

To sum up: commercialization and intensification of agriculture occurred only to a limited extent in arable cultivation and cattle raising, although these were important for large landlords in both eastern and western Germany. But for most of rural society, it was a question either of securing a narrow basis for survival through intensive processing of the soil on smallholdings, or of intensifying those sectors of production which were largely removed from the grasp of the landlords.

Agrarian society in transition: the reforms of the eighteenth century

Most of the research on German rural society in the eighteenth century has concentrated on the question of the extent to which conditions arose which explain the effectiveness of the French Revolution in Germany and the dominance of the 'Prussian path' into modernity. This has led to the impression that political, economic, and social change in Germany were similar to the situation in France. Counter to this view, it must be pointed out that although the German nobility, like the French nobility, came under fire from bourgeois enlightened critics, this had no radical consequences for its social position. This is confirmed by the very gradual progress of the German agrarian reforms, which stretched out over the whole nineteenth century. Thus the Prussian reforms, so frequently abbreviated to 'peasant emancipation', did not mark the end of 'feudal' agrarian society; the turning-point was not reached until the middle of the nineteenth century.[106] Nevertheless, the eighteenth century did see an intensification of economic, social, and political developments in Germany which accelerated the transformation of agrarian society.

The growth of population and industry in Germany from about 1700 on (and especially after about 1750) stimulated agriculture through a constantly rising demand for grain and raw materials, causing an expansion in internal markets. External markets also expanded because the populations of western European countries were also growing, increasing the possibilities of exporting German grain.

Peasants and landlords profited from this growing demand in different ways, owing to the structural features of the agrarian systems which have already been discussed. Landlords reacted by transforming pastures into arable fields in order to increase grain production. On the English model, they first shifted over to improved three-field systems and later to more complicated crop rotations, thereby increasing both yields and soil fertility. They also introduced cultivation of fodder vegetables and stall feeding, enabling more animals to be kept and more manure to be produced, which in turn improved the fields. Unlike in the sixteenth and seventeenth centuries, when agricultural innovations were introduced through importing skilled foreigners, in the second half of the eighteenth century English agriculture was itself taken under observation and attempts were made to transfer it to Germany.[107]

Peasants, by contrast, did not enjoy such flexibility in cultivation, since in most regions the payments they owed to landlords bound them into maintaining a particular field system. Instead, they pursued two strategies: first, they increasingly used the fallow fields in summertime to grow raw materials (flax, madder, tobacco, hops) and marketable foodstuffs (legumes, cabbages, and turnips). This improved the soil, thereby increasing the output of ordinary peasant cultivation.[108] Secondly, in the second half of the eighteenth century many regions saw division of the commons, largely among the peasants with usufruct rights over them, but also between peasants and landlords; the growing numbers of land-poor were generally excluded. But this was only possible if the landlords co-operated. In Prussia and Schleswig-Holstein, royal domains provided the model for such co-operation.[109] In Prussia, the attempt was also made to enclose peasant fields, although this succeeded only in the nineteenth century. On the whole, the majority of peasants continued to cultivate under field systems which greatly limited the individual peasant's freedom of decision. This helps explain why innovations (which also always involved risks) emanated primarily from landlords, who could deliberately follow their own interests, and was the case both for the large estates of the nobility in eastern Germany and for the domains belonging to territorial lords in central, northern, and eastern Germany.

In Brandenburg-Prussia from 1712 on, the royal domains were no longer managed by noble administrators, but rather by tenants of bourgeois origins. Many noble estates were also held in tenancy. These tenants, who had to pay substantial rents, had a great interest in cultivating as profitably as possible, and thus were especially interested in innovations, turning into the main agents of agricultural progress.[110] Although tenants on noble farms and those on the domains of territorial lords were confronted with the same demographic developments, they possessed very different capacities to react to them. Until about 1700 there was still considerable labour scarcity, but as the population grew the supply of labour rose, so that it was no longer necessarily economical to use the coerced labour-services of peasants and smallholders. Very precise calculations were made of what could be achieved using the reluctant and by no means costless labour-services of subject peasants as compared with employing 'free' servants and day-labourers.[111] Unlike in Mecklenburg, where aristocratic estates (which were again expanded in the first half of the eighteenth century) were cultivated mainly with unfree labour,[112] in East Prussia as early as the first half of the eighteenth century a number of landlords decided that it was more profitable to work their demesne farms with free servants.[113] This meant that dependent peasants and smallholders on a number of feudal estates gained the opportunity to buy themselves free from serfdom. Some feudal landlords went so far as to separate their land from that of their peasants, in order to be able to cultivate in unhindered fashion. On the whole, however, scepticism about innovations in the labour system was widespread among noble landlords, suggesting that the Brandenburg-Prussian nobles (most of whom owned comparatively small areas of land) had too little capital to obtain labour on the market. This is confirmed by the criteria used in valuing estates, which focused much less on the size of the land area than on the number of subject peasants owing labour services to the estate. Estate-owners likewise tended to avoid taking the risk of capitalizing their entitlements from the peasants; and even where a landlord did so, he always reserved the right to return to the old state of affairs.

Before the move toward setting up tenancies (*Generalpacht*) on Prussian domains in 1712, attempts were made to utilize the domains more efficiently: the domain land was supposed to be divided up and granted to peasants in inheritable tenancies, and the labour services were supposed to be largely abolished.[114] However, this project did not succeed. Attempts were also made (in 1719–23) to abolish serfdom on the royal domains, but these also remained ineffectual, since the emancipated peasants continued to be subject to the old burdens attached to their holdings. Progress in this direction was only achieved in the last third of the eighteenth century.[115] It was not only in Prussia that the first guiding steps in the direction of 'peasant emancipation' were undertaken on the royal domains, but also in territories such as Baden in 1783 and Schleswig-Holstein in 1805.[116] However, changes in landlord–peasant relations as far-reaching as those in Hannover, where the personal services of peasants were abolished on the domains, were the exception before the end of the eighteenth century.

Although in the eighteenth century there was only limited development in German agriculture, the century has gone down in the annals of agricultural history as an age of progress. Part of the explanation resides in the agrarian boom of its second half, part in the new opportunities to obtain agrarian credit in Prussia with the consequent speculation in estates, and part in the fact that agriculture had become a central object of Prussian and Austrian cameralist thinking. The bureaucratization of domination over the peasants (control through annual economic registers, new measurement and statistical descriptions of the land) which had already begun in the sixteenth century attained its culmination in the eighteenth century with the 'art' of domain administration, and began to be studied as part of the university discipline of 'cameralistics'.[117] But although the innovations of the sixteenth and seventeenth centuries benefited the domains of the territorial lords, measures to improve the peasants' economy could only be implemented in the eighteenth century, when the absolutist state had at its disposal agents on the local level in the form of local pastors and discharged soldiers provided for as village schoolteachers.

In the age of enlightened absolutism, the cameralistic thinking of the bureaucrats was combined with the ideas of the Enlightenment and the new sciences. At the university of Königsberg the philosopher Kraus proclaimed Adam Smith's moral philosophy, and the Berlin Academy of Sciences offered prizes for solutions to urgent problems in agriculture.[118] Agricultural associations were established, in which adminstrative bureaucrats and estate-owners debated ways of furthering agriculture.[119] The peasants, too, were supposed to be included in the process of enlightenment. Bourgeois authors wrote numerous treatises advocating progress and seeking to influence the peasants, who were viewed as being superstitious and conservative. More successful than these 'enlighteners of the peasants', however, were the many rural pastors who, as trusted members of the community, not only preached but also persuaded by their example; and even the peasants' own experience in manorial labour services could achieve more than the rhetoric of the 'enlighteners of the peasants' or the measures of government bureaucrats.[120] Nevertheless, model farms such as those set up by the Prussian monarch Frederick II, by Thünen in Prussia, by Schubart von Kleefeld in Saxony, and by Thaer in Hannover, appear also to have wielded some influence.

In the last third of the eighteenth century, therefore, on the eve of the French Revolution, it is possible to identify initiatives by state bureaucrats, landlords, and peasants which aimed at the optimization of their own interests but which, at the same time, were directed toward bringing about fundamental changes in rural relations of domination. Many German states began to institute reforms of the agrarian system in their domains, particularly to abolish serfdom, which was the focus of enlightened criticism and promised important stimuli for the development of peasants into 'economic and political citizens'. In this way, personal unfreedom was transformed into freedom, and the dues associated with it (especially compulsory service of serfs' children as servants) were abolished without recompense. However, the positive consequences for the peasants which had been hoped for did not materialize; indeed, to some extent the peasants even opposed such measures, because they meant a loss of support in times of crisis.

A different view must be taken of the capitalization of landlords' rights over their peasants, which had already occurred for the peasants of territorial lords in areas such as Bavaria in the second half of the seventeenth century, but now encompassed additional groups. Although a separation and rationalization of peasant and manorial land began to take place and there were moves toward division and individual exploitation of the commons, the actual relations of domination in rural society, the relationship between landlord and peasant, remained largely untouched. 'Individualization' of economic activity applied mainly to the landlords; for most peasants, the realm of free decision remained limited, since landlords' rights still intervened in their time and labour budgets and restricted free decisions in arable and pastoral production. Moreover, there was a lack of credit for peasants with poor rights of ownership who had to obtain the landlord's consent before they could take out a loan. What did begin to manifest itself in the last third of the eighteenth century was a 'rural class society' (to use the phrase of J. Mooser), which involved not only the traditional opposition between lord and peasant but also a common opposition by both lords and peasants against smallholders and rural labourers. These social oppositions were strengthened by the agrarian reforms, and were accentuated in the nineteenth century by the state-implemented dissolution of peasant–landlord relations.

Notes

1 Walter Achilles, *Landwirtschaft in der Frühen Neuzeit* (Munich, 1991), p. 5; Karl-Heinrich Kaufhold, 'Landwirtschaft, Fischerei und Forstwirtschaft', in *Handbuch der europäischen Wirtschafts- und Sozialgeschichte* (4 vols, Stuttgart, 1993), iv. pp. 557–65. See, by contrast, Friedrich-Wilhelm Henning, *Landwirtschaft und ländliche Gesellschaft in Deutschland*, i. *800 bis 1750* (Paderborn, 1977), and Edith Ennen and Walter Janssen, *Deutsche Agrargeschichte. Vom Neolithikum bis zur Schwelle des Industriezeitalters* (Wiesbaden, 1979).

2 Toni Pierenkemper, 'Agrarsektor in der vorindustriellen Gesellschaft. Einige Anmerkungen zur preußischen Entwicklung, 1815–1830, aus produktionstheoretischer Sicht', *Zeitschrift für Agrargesellschaft und Agrarsoziologie*, 37 (1989), pp. 168–86.

3 Günther Franz, ed., *Deutsche Agrargeschichte* (5 vols, Stuttgart, 1967–72); see the critical review on this by Hans Rosenberg, 'Deutsche Agrargeschichte in alter und neuer Sicht', in Hans Rosenberg, ed., *Probleme der deutschen Sozialgeschichte* (Frankfurt am Main, 1969), pp. 1–147.

4 Hartmut Harnisch and Gerhard Heitz, eds, *Deutsche Agrargeschichte des Spätfeudalismus* (Berlin, GDR, 1986).

5 Werner Troßbach, *Bauern. 1648–1806* (Munich, 1993); Achilles, *Landwirtschaft*.

6 Werner Troßbach, *Soziale Bewegung und politische Erfahrung. Bäuerlicher Protest in hessischen Territorien 1648–1806* (Weingarten, 1987); David Warren Sabean, *Property, Production, and Family in Neckarhausen,*

1700–1870 (Cambridge, 1990); Rainer Beck, *Unterfinning. Ländliche Welt vor Anbruch der Moderne* (München, 1993); Thomas Robisheaux, *Rural Society and the Search for Order in Early Modern Germany* (Cambridge, 1989); Rudolf Schlögl, *Bauern, Krieg und Krise. Oberbayerische Bauernwirtschaft und frühmoderner Staat im 17. Jahrhundert* (Göttingen, 1988); Jon Mathieu, *Bauern und Bären. Eine Geschichte des Unterengadins von 1650–1800* (Chur, 1987); Jon Mathieu, *Eine Agrargeschichte der inneren Alpen. Graubünden, Tessin, Wallis, 1500–1800* (Zürich, 1992); Albert Schnyder-Burghartz, *Alltag und Lebensformen auf der Basler Landschaft um 1700. Vorindustrielle, ländliche Kultur und Gesellschaft aus mikrohistorischer Perspektive – Bretzwill und das obere Waldenburger Amt von 1690–1750* (Liestal, 1992).

7   Schlögl, *Bauern.*

8   Since statistics only emerged in the early modern period, there are great difficulties in measuring the performance of agriculture. Our knowledge about it is fragmentary, and relies on individual findings – on local and regional examples – which document selected aspects, depending on the focus of interest. Thus seigneurial rent registers list the large number of peasant dues in money, kind, and services. Church accounts list the revenues owing for tithe payments or tithes in kind, and the payments made by members of the community to support the pastor, the church, and the poor. The proceedings of parliaments reveal the increasing regularity with which subjects were burdened with taxes, and tax registers show how these taxes were actually levied. In towns, the prices for the most important sorts of grain were recorded, grain was deliberately warehoused, and the citizenry was urged to maintain stores. Account-books of large and small merchant-houses provide information about the volumes of grain which they sold, their suppliers, and their customers. Marriage, inheritance and sales contracts, and auction minutes for peasant farms and lords' estates, provide an insight into yields. Not least, important information is contained in retirement contracts.

9   Jan Peters, Hartmut Harnisch, and Lieselott Enders, eds, *Märkische Bauerntagebücher des 18. und 19. Jahrhunderts. Selbstzeugnisse von Milchviehbauern aus Neuholland* (Weimar, 1989); Helmut Ottenjann and Günter Wiegelmann, eds, *Alte Tagebücher und Anschreibebücher. Quellen zum Alltag der ländlichen Bevölkerung in Nordwesteuropa* (Münster, 1982).

10   Wilhelm Abel, *Geschichte der deutschen Landwirtschaft vom frühen Mittelalter bis zum 19. Jahrhundert* (3rd edn, Stuttgart, 1978).

11   Hildegard Weiß, *Stadt- und Landkreis Bamberg* (München, 1974), p. 74.

12   Beck, *Unterfinning,* pp. 189f.

13   'Bericht des Pfarrers Nikolaus Moterus über die Plünderung von Roßdorf am 2./3. November 1621', in Fritz Herrmann, ed., *Aus tiefer Not. Hessische Briefe und Berichte aus der Zeit des Dreißigjährigen Krieges* (Friedberg, 1916), pp. 27–37; see also 'Gesuch des Pfarrers Mag. Joh. Georg Kommerell in Gronau bei Bensheim a. d. B. an den Grafen Georg Albrecht zu Erbach um Unterstützung. Juni 1637', *Ibid.*, pp. 159–61; Horst Schöck, *Plieningen. Ein Dorf lebt nicht vom Kraut allein* (Stuttgart, 1988), p. 15.

14   Werner Troßbach, 'Widerstand als Normalfall: Bauernunruhen in der Grafschaft Sayn-Wittgenstein-Wittgenstein 1696–1806', *Westfälische Zeitschrift,* 135 (1985), pp. 25–111, p. 97; see also the importance of berry-collection in the Lüneburger Heide in Stefan Brakensiek, *Agrarreform und ländliche Gesellschaft. Die Privatisierung der Marken in Nordwestdeutschland 1750–1850* (Paderborn, 1991), p. 196.

15   Hans J. Teuteberg and Günter Wiegelmann, *Der Wandel der Nahrungsge-wohnheiten unter dem Einfluß der Industrialisierung* (Göttingen, 1972).

16   See Margit Ksoll, *Die wirtschaftlichen Verhältnisse des bayerischen Adels 1600–1679. Dargestellt an den Familien Törring-Jettenbach, Törring zum Stain sowie Haslangkreit und Haslang zu Hohenkammer* (Munich, 1986), p. 158.

17   Christian Pfister, *Das Klima der Schweiz von 1525–1860 und seine Bedeu-tung in der Geschichte der Bevölkerung und Landwirtschaft*, i (2nd edn, Bern, 1985); Helmut Hildebrandt and Martin Gudd, 'Getreidebau, Miß-ernten und Witterung im südwestlichen unteren Vogelsberg und dem an-grenzenden Vorland während des 16. und frühen 17. Jahrhunderts', *Archiv für hessische Geschichte und Altertumskunde*, NS 49 (1991), pp. 85–145.

18   Rudolf Berthold, 'Wachstumsprobleme der landwirtschaftlichen Nutzfläche im Spätfeudalismus (zirka 1500 bis 1800)', *Deutsche Agrargeschichte des Spätfeudalismus*, 6 (1986), pp. 58–75, p. 61.

19   Klaus Gerteis, *Die deutschen Städte in der Frühen Neuzeit. Zur Vorgeschichte der 'bürgerlichen Welt'* (Darmstadt, 1986), pp. 52–64. See also Erich Keyer and Heinz Stoob, eds, *Deutsche Städtebuch* (11 vols, Stuttgart, 1939–74); Eberhard Isenmann, *Die deutsche Stadt im Spätmittelalter 1250–1500. Stadtgestalt, Recht, Stadtregiment, Kirche, Gesellschaft, Wirtschaft* (Stuttgart, 1988), pp. 31f.

20   *Probleme der frühneuzeitlichen Stadt, vorzüglich der Haupt- und Residen-zstädte. Referate und Aussprachen auf der 30. Arbeitstagung des Instituts für geschichtliche Landeskunde der Rheinlande an der Universität Bonn in Verbindung mit der 9. Arbeitstagung des Arbeitskreises für landschaftliche deutsche Städteforschung vom 27.-29. März 1972 in Bonn*, compiled by Edith Ennen and Manfred van Rey (Bonn, 1973), pp. 168–212.

21   Volker Press, ed., *Städtewesen und Merkantilismus in Mitteleuropa* (Cologne, 1983); Helga Schultz, 'Kleinstädte im 17. und 18. Jahrhundert', *JbRegG* 14 (1987), pp. 209–17.

22   Klaus-Joachim Lorenzen-Schmidt, *Die Sozial- und Wirtschaftsstruktur schleswig-holsteinischer Landesstädte zwischen 1500 und 1550* (Neu-münster, 1980), pp. 147–52; Gerhard Fouquet, 'Stadt, Herrschaft und Terri-torium – Ritterschaftliche Kleinstädte Südwestdeutschlands an der Wende vom Mittelalter zur Neuzeit', *ZGO* 141 (1993), pp. 70–120.

23   Ulrich Willerding, 'Ernährung, Gartenbau und Landwirtschaft im Bereich der Stadt,' in Cord Meckseper, ed., *Stadt im Wandel. Kunst und Literatur in Norddeutschland 1150–1650. Ausstellungskatalog* (Stuttgart-Bad Cannstadt, 1985), iii. pp. 569–605, p. 573.

24   Klaus Greve and Kersten Krüger, 'Steuerstaat und Sozialstruktur – Finanz-soziologische Auswertung der hessischen Katasterbeschreibungen für Wald-kappel 1744 und Herleshausen 1748', *GG* 8 (1982), pp. 295–323; see by contrast Fouquet, 'Stadt'.

25   Erich Gaenschalz, 'Die Nahrungsmittelpolitik der Stadt Erfurt bis zum Jahre 1664,' (Ph.D. dissertation, Univ. of Breslau, 1928); Heinrich Rüthing, *Höxter um 1500. Analyse einer Stadtgesellschaft* (Paderborn, 1986).

26   Walter Kuhn, 'Die Stadtdörfer der mittelalterlichen Ostsiedlung', *Zeitschrift für Ostforschung*, 20 (1971), pp. 1–69; Wilhelm Krimpenfort, *Der Grundbe-sitz der Landstädte des Herzogtums Preußen. Geschichte, Wirtschaft, Recht, Sozialordnung* (Marburg/Lahn, 1979).

27   Franz Irsigler, 'Groß- und Kleinbesitz im westlichen Deutschland vom 13. bis 18. Jahrhundert: Versuch einer Typologie', in Péter Gunst and Tamás Hoff-mann, eds, *Grand Domaine et petites exploitations en Europe au moyen age et dans les temps modernes. Rapport nationaux* (Budapest, 1982), 33–59;

Weiß, *Bamberg*; Fritz Schnelbögl, *Die wirtschaftliche Bedeutung ihres Landgebietes für die Reichsstadt Nürnberg in den Grundzügen dargestellt, Beiträge zur Wirtschaftsgeschichte Nürnbergs herausgegeben vom Stadtarchiv Nürnberg* (Nürnberg, 1967), i. pp. 261–317, pp. 263–5.

28 Wilhelm Naudé, *Die Getreidehandelspolitik der Europäischen Staaten vom 13. bis zum 18. Jahrhundert* (Berlin, 1896); Wilhelm Naudé and Gustav Schmoller, *Die Getreidehandelspolitik und Kriegsmagazinverwaltung Brandenburg-Preußens bis 1740* (Berlin, 1901).

29 Examples of casual work are gathering herbs, keeping bees, and raising birds. On proto-industry, see Chapter 9 of this volume.

30 See Michael North, *Die Amtswirtschaften von Osterode und Soldau. Vergleichende Untersuchungen zur Wirtschaft im frühmodernen Staat am Beispiel des Herzogtums Preußen in der zweiten Hälfte des 16. und in der ersten Hälfte des 17. Jahrhunderts* (Berlin, 1982).

31 Bernd Roeck, *Bäcker, Brot und Getreide in Augsburg. Zur Geschichte des Bäckerhandwerks und zur Versorgungspolitik der Reichsstadt im Zeitalter des Dreißigjährigen Krieges* (Sigmaringen, 1987), pp. 90–6.

32 Wolfgang von Hippel, *Die Bauernbefreiung im Königreich Württemberg* (Boppard am Rhein, 1977), i. p. 189.

33 Beck, *Unterfinning*, pp. 543–5.

34 Troßbach, 'Widerstand', pp. 96f.

35 Schnelbögl, *Bedeutung*.

36 Ekkehard Westermann, ed., *Internationaler Ochsenhandel (1350–1750), Akten des 7th International Economic History Congress Edinburgh 1978* (Stuttgart, 1979).

37 Petra Möller, 'Beobachtungen zum Getreidehandel im Weserraum', in *Der Weserraum zwischen 1550 und 1650. Gesellschaft, Wirtschaft und Kultur in der Frühen Neuzeit* (Marburg, 1992), pp. 115–41.

38 Gaenschalz, 'Nahrungsmittelpolitik', p. 28.

39 Heinrich Schnee, 'Madame Kaulla. Deutschlands bedeutendste Hoffaktorin und ihre Familie. 1739–1809', in *Lebensbilder aus Schwaben und Franken*, 9 (Stuttgart, 1964), pp. 84–104, p. 89.

40 Rolf Kießling, 'Das Umlandgefüge ostschwäbischer Städte vom 14. bis zur Mitte des 16. Jahrhunderts', in Hans K. Schulze, ed., *Städtisches Um- und Hinterland in vorindustrieller Zeit*, (Cologne/Vienna, 1985), pp. 32–60; Roeck, *Bäcker*.

41 Gaenschalz, 'Nahrungsmittelpolitik', pp. 37–40.

42 Troßbach, *Bewegung*.

43 Lieselott Enders, *Die Uckermark. Geschichte einer kurmärkischen Landschaft vom 12. bis zum 18. Jahrhundert* (Weimar, 1992), p. 47; Karl Baumgarten and Ulrich Bentzien, *Hof und Wirtschaft der Ribnitzer Bauern* (Berlin, 1963).

44 Heide Wunder, *Die bäuerliche Gemeinde in Deutschland* (Göttingen, 1986).

45 Christof Dipper, *Die Bauernbefreiung in Deutschland 1790–1850* (Stuttgart, 1980). In areas on the left bank of the Rhine, the *Flurzwang* (community regulation of field utilization) survived into the twentieth century: Hermann Kellenbenz, 'Wirtschafts- und Sozialentwicklung der nördlichen Rheinlande seit 1815', in Franz Petri and Georg Droege, eds, *Rheinische Geschichte* (Düsseldorf, 1979), iii. pp. 31f.

46 Friedrich Lütge, *Geschichte der deutschen Agrarverfassung vom frühen Mittelalter bis zum 19. Jahrhundert* (2nd edn, Stuttgart, 1967).

47 Werner Troßbach, '"Südwestdeutsche Leibeigenschaft" in der Frühen Neuzeit – eine Bagatelle?', *GG* 7 (1981), pp. 69–90.

48 Heide Wunder, 'Das Selbstverständliche "denken". Ein Vorschlag zur vergleichenden Analyse ländlicher Gesellschaften in der Frühen Neuzeit, ausgehend vom "Modell ostelbische Gutsherrschaft"', in Jan Peters, ed., *Gutsherrschaft als soziales Modell. Vergleichende Betrachtungen zur Funktionsweise frühneuzeitlicher Agrargesellschaften* (München, 1995), pp. 23–49.

49 Enders, *Uckermark*; Peters, *Gutsherrschaft*.

50 Jerzy Topolski, 'Sixteenth-Century Poland and the Turning Point in European Economic Development', in J. K. Fedorowicz *et al.*, eds, *A Republic of Nobles: Studies in Polish History to 1864* (Cambridge, 1982), pp. 74–90.

51 Eckart Schremmer, 'Agrarverfassung und Wirtschaftsstruktur. Die südostdeutsche Hofmark – eine Wirtschaftsherrschaft?', *ZAgrarGAgrarSoz* 20 (1972), pp. 42–65.

52 Schlögl, *Bauern*, pp. 174f.

53 *Ibid.*, p. 32.

54 For the fifteenth and sixteenth centuries, see Sigrid Schmitt, *Territorialstaat und Gemeinde im kurpfälzischen Amt Alzey* (Stuttgart, 1992), p. 184f.

55 Hans Lerch, *Hessische Agrargeschichte des 17. und 18. Jahrhunderts* (Hersfeld, 1926), pp. 30–7.

56 Ksoll, *Verhältnisse*, pp. 37f, 157.

57 Rudolf Schlögl, 'Zwischen Krieg und Krise. Situation und Entwicklung der bayerischen Bauernwirtschaft im 17. Jahrhundert,' *ZAgrarGAgrarSoz* 40 (1992), pp. 133–67, p. 145; Renate Blickle, 'Scharwerk in Bayern. Fronarbeit und Untertänigkeit in der Frühen Neuzeit', *GG* 17 (1991), pp. 407–33.

58 Blickle, 'Scharwerk', pp. 419–21.

59 Friedrich Lütge, *Die mitteldeutsche Grundherrschaft und ihre Auflösung* (2nd edn, extensively revised, Stuttgart, 1957), pp. 56–101; on Bavaria: Schlögl, *Bauern*, pp. 165–9; Beck, *Unterfinning*, pp. 400–25.

60 Schlögl, *Bauern*, p. 269.

61 Schmitt, *Territorialstaat*, pp. 177–89.

62 Friedrich-Wilhelm Henning, *Abgaben und Dienste der Bauern im 18. Jahrhundert* (Stuttgart, 1969); Achilles, *Landwirtschaft*, pp. 28–41; von Hippel, *Bauernbefreiung*, i. pp. 290–304.

63 Willi A. Boelcke, 'Der Agrarkredit in deutschen Territorien vom Mittelalter bis Anfang des 18. Jahrhunderts', in Michael North, ed., *Kredit im spätmittttelalterlichen und frühneuzeitlichen Europa* (Cologne/Vienna, 1991), pp. 193–213; Schlögl, *Bauern*, pp. 319–342; Beck, *Unterfinning*, pp. 460–72.

64 See e.g. Rudolf Endres, 'Sozialer Wandel in Franken und Bayern auf der Grundlage der Dorfordnungen', in Ernst Hinrichs and Günter Wiegelmann, eds, *Sozialer und kultureller Wandel in der ländlichen Welt des 18. Jahrhunderts* (Wolfenbüttel, 1982), pp. 212–27.

65 Peter Blickle, *Unruhen in der ständischen Gesellschaft 1300–1800* (Munich, 1988).

66 Schlögl, *Bauern*, pp. 198–261; v. Hippel, *Bauernbefreiung*, i. pp. 228–51; Schmitt, *Territorialstaat*, pp. 139–56; Beck, *Unterfinning*, pp. 472–504.

67 e.g. in Braunschweig-Wolfenbüttel in 1597: see Diedrich Saalfeld, *Bauernwirtschaft und Gutsbetrieb in der vorindustriellen Zeit* (Stuttgart, 1960), p. 17.

68 Claudia Ulbrich, *Leibherrschaft am Oberrhein im Spätmittelalter* (Göttingen, 1979); Schmitt, *Territorialstaat*.

69 Heiner Haan, 'Prosperität und Dreißigjähriger Krieg', *GG* 7 (1981), pp. 91–118; Ksoll, *Verhältnisse*, p. 36.

70 Stephan Kellner, *Die Hofmarken Jettenbach und Aschau in der frühen Neuzeit* (München, 1986), pp. 62–7; Schlögl, *Bauern*, pp. 169–71, 180f.

71   Rudolf Endres, *Adel in der Frühen Neuzeit* (München, 1993), pp. 37–46.

72   See e.g. Michael North, 'Die frühneuzeitliche Gutswirtschaft in Schleswig-Holstein. Forschungsüberblick und Entwicklungsfaktoren', *BdLG* 126 (1990), pp. 223–42, p. 231; Willi Boelcke, *Verfassungswandel und Wirtschaftsstruktur. Die mittelalterliche und neuzeitliche Territorialgeschichte ostmitteldeutscher Adelsherrschaften als Beispiel* (Würzburg, 1969).

73   Holm Sundhausen, 'Der Wandel in der osteuropäischen Agrarverfassung während der frühen Neuzeit. Ein Beitrag zur Divergenz der Entwicklungswege von Ost- und Westeuropa', *Südost-Forschungen*, 49 (1990), pp. 15–56.

74   Herbert Knittler, 'Adelige Grundherrschaft im Übergang. Überlegungen zum Verhältnis von Adel und Wirtschaft in Niederösterreich um 1600', in Grete Klingenstein and Heinrich Lutz, eds, *Spezialforschung und Gesamtgeschichte. Beispiele und Methodenfragen zur Geschichte der frühen Neuzeit* (Munich, 1982), pp. 84–111; Herbert Knittler, 'Einkommensstruktur niederösterreichischer Adelsherrschaften', in Rudolf Endres, ed., *Adel in der Frühneuzeit. Ein regionaler Vergleich* (Cologne/Vienna, 1991), pp. 99–118; see also András Vári, 'Der handelsmonopolisierende Grossgrundbesitz und seine sozialgeschichtlichen Auswirkungen im 18.-19. Jahrhundert', in Sándor Gyimesi, ed., *Der Binnenhandel und die wirtschaftliche Entwicklung* (Budapest, 1989), pp. 273–91.

75   See e.g. Werner Wied, 'Das Hofgut Saßmannshausen und die ihm angeschlossenen gewerblichen Betriebe', in Eberhard Bauer and Werner Wied, eds, *Saßmannshausen. Ein Dorf im Wittgensteiner Land* (Laasphe, 1975), pp. 78–157; Jürgen Schlumbohm, *Lebensläufe, Familien, Höfe. Die Bauern und Heuerleute des Osnabrückischen Kirchspiels Belm in proto-industrieller Zeit, 1650–1860* (Göttingen, 1994), p. 57.

76   Dagmar Kerschbaumer, 'Wiederbesiedlung im braunschweigisch-wolfenbüttelschen "Weserdistrikt" im 16. Jahrhundert', in *Der Weserraum zwischen 1500 und 1650. Gesellschaft, Wirtschaft und Kultur in der Frühen Neuzeit* (Marburg, 1993), pp. 61–91.

77   Kerschbaumer, 'Wiederbesiedlung', pp. 68f; J. Soenke, 'Die Weserrenaissance', in *Führer zu vor- und frühgeschichtlichen Denkmälern*, (Mainz, 1966), iv. pp. 65–73, p. 65; Saalfeld, *Bauernwirtschaft*, pp. 23–31; Hugo Brunner, 'Rittergüter und Gutsbezirke im ehemaligen Kurhessen', *Jahrbücher für Nationalökonomie und Statistik* III. Folge 60 (1920), pp. 50–72; Lerch, *Agrargeschichte*, pp. 38–58; Martin Born, *Wandlung und Beharrung ländlicher Siedlung und bäuerlicher Wirtschaft. Untersuchungen zur frühneuzeitlichen Kulturlandschaft im Schwalmgebiet* (Marburg, 1961), who repeatedly refers to such efforts, e.g. pp. 75f, 105f; Martin Born, *Studien zur spätmittelalterlichen und neuzeitlichen Siedlungsentwicklung in Nordhessen*, (Marburg/Lahn, 1970), pp. 17–19; Troßbach, *Bauernbewegung*, pp. 105–20; Hellmuth Gensicke, *Landesgeschichte des Westerwaldes* (Wiesbaden, 1958), p. 348 on the principality of Nassau-Hadamar.

78   For some approaches, see Troßbach, '"Südwestdeutsche Leibeigenschaft"'.

79   Enders, *Uckermark*, pp. 387, 443f.

80   Troßbach, *Bauernbewegungen*, pp. 106–8.

81   Troßbach, 'Widerstand'.

82   For this reason, Sayn-Wittgenstein is an important case to contrast with the theses of Robert Brenner concerning the role of peasant resistance. See also Manfred von Boetticher, '"Nordwestdeutsche Grundherrschaft" zwischen

Frühkapitalismus und Refeudalisierung', *BdLG* 122 (1986), pp. 207–28, and North, 'Gutswirtschaft', p. 226.

83 Klaus Gerteis, 'Regionale Bauernrevolten zwischen Bauernkrieg und Französischer Revolution', *ZHF* 6 (1979), pp. 37–61.

84 Schremmer, *Agrarverfassung*; Schlögl, 'Krieg'; Ksoll, *Verhältnisse*, pp. 39, 42f; see also Hermann Grees, *Ländliche Unterschichten und ländliche Siedlungen in Ostschwaben* (Tübingen, 1975).

85 Friedrich Swart, *Zur friesischen Agrargeschichte* (Leipzig, 1910).

86 Boetticher, '"Nordwestdeutscher Grundherrschaft"'.

87 Enders, *Uckermark*, pp. 487–97.

88 Rudolf Lehmann, ed., *Quellen zur Lage der Privatbauern in der Niederlausitz im Zeitalter des Absolutismus* (East Berlin, 1957).

89 See e.g. Robisheaux, *Rural Society*.

90 Troßbach, *Bauernbewegungen*.

91 Mack Walker, *The Salzburg Transaction: Expulsion and Redemption in Eighteenth-Century Germany* (Ithaca, NY, 1992); Heide Wunder, 'Siedlung und Bevölkerung im Ordensstaaat, Herzogtum und Königreich Preußen (13.-18. Jahrhundert)', in Hans Rothe, ed., *Ostdeutsche Geschichts- und Kulturlandschaften*, ii. *Ost- und Westpreußen* (Köln/Wien, 1987), pp. 67–98.

92 Ingrid Mittenzwei and Erika Herzfeld, *Brandenburg-Preußen 1648–1789. Das Zeitalter des Absolutismus in Text und Bild* (3rd edn, Berlin, 1990), pp. 298f, 360f.

93 Ksoll, *Verhältnisse*, p. 137; Kerschbaumer, *Wiederbesiedlung*, pp. 69–71.

94 Barthel Huppertz, *Räume und Schichten bäuerlicher Kulturformen in Deutschland. Ein Beitrag zur Deutschen Bauerngeschichte* (Bonn, 1939), pp. 25–63; Sabean, *Property*, pp. 247–58; Clemens Zimmermann, '"Behörigen Orthen angezeigt". Kindsmörderinnen in der ländlichen Gesellschaft Württembergs, 1581–1792', *Medizingeschichte*, 10 (1991), pp. 67–102.

95 Josef Mooser, *Ländliche Klassengesellschaft 1770–1848. Bauern und Unterschichten, Landwirtschaft und Gewerbe im östlichen Westfalen* (Göttingen, 1984), pp. 246–66; Schlumbohm, *Lebensläufe*, esp. pp. 539–620; Alwin Hanschmidt, 'Das 18. Jahrhundert', in Wilhelm Kohl, ed., *Westfälische Geschichte*, i. p. 660.

96 See esp. Hartmut Heller, *Die Peuplierungspolitik der Reichsritterschaft als sozialgeographischer Faktor im Steigerwald* (Erlangen, 1971).

97 Beck, *Unterfinning*, pp. 220–43; Schlögl, 'Krieg'; Grees, *Unterschichten*.

98 Enders, *Uckermark*, e.g. pp. 177f.

99 Jan Peters, 'Ostelbische Landarmut – Sozialökonomisches über landlose und landarme Agrarproduzenten im Spätfeudalismus', in Harnisch and Heitz, eds, *Agrargeschichte*, pp. 213–45; on the 'Inleuten' (inmates) in Bavaria see Walter Hartinger, 'Bayerisches Dienstbotenleben auf dem Land vom 16. bis 18. Jahrhundert', *Zeitschrift für bayrische Landesgeschichte*, 38 (1975), pp. 598–638, p. 600.

100 Achilles, *Landwirtschaft*, p. 58; see on this Dietrich Saalfeld, 'Stellung und Differenzierung der ländlichen Bevölkerung Nordwestdeutschlands in der Ständegesellschaft', in Hinrichs and Wiegelmann, eds, *Wandel*, pp. 229–251, esp. the tables; for Franconia and Bavaria, see Endres, 'Wandel'; on East Prussia see Heide Wunder, 'Sozialer und kultureller Wandel in der ländlichen Welt des 18. Jahrhunderts – Überlegungen am Beispiel von "Bauer und Religion" (unter besonderer Berücksichtigung Ostpreußens)', in Hinrichs and Wiegelmann, eds, *Wandel*, pp. 43–63, p. 53.

101 Alois Hahn, 'Soziologische Aspekte der Knappheit', *Kölner Zeitschrift für Soziologie und Sozialpsychologie*, Sonderheft 28 (1987), pp. 119–32.

102   Wied, 'Hofgut'; Troßbach, 'Widerstand', pp. 33–6.

103   North, 'Gutswirtschaft', p. 238.

104   Karl Siegfried Bader, *Rechtsformen und Schichten der Liegenschaftsnutzung im mittelalterlichen Dorf* (Vienna, 1973), pp. 92–126; Karl F. Helleiner, 'Peunten und Sonderkulturen in Nieder- und Oberösterreich', in Ingomar Bog, Günter Franz, Karl-Heinrich Kaufhold, Hermann Kellenbenz, and Wolfgang Zorn, eds, *Wirtschaftliche und soziale Strukturen im saekularen Wandel, Festschrift für Wilhelm Abel zum 70. Geburtstag* (Hannover, 1974), i. pp. 131–42.

105   Schlögl, 'Krieg', p. 143.

106   Reinhart Koselleck, *Preußen zwischen Reform und Revolution. Allgemeines Landrecht, Verwaltung und soziale Bewegung von 1797–1848* (Stuttgart, 1967); Barbara Vogel, ed., *Preußische Reformen 1807–1820* (Königstein/Ts., 1980); Dipper, *Bauernbefreiung*; Hanna Schissler, *Preußische Agrargesellschaft im Wandel. Wirtschaftliche, gesellschaftliche und politische Transformationsprozesse von 1763 bis 1847* (Göttingen, 1978); Toni Pierenkemper, ed., *Landwirtschaft und industrielle Entwicklung. Zur ökonomischen Bedeutung von Bauernbefreiung, Agrarreform und Agrarrevolution* (Stuttgart, 1989); Winfried Speitkamp, 'Agrarreform in der Restauration. Planungen zur kurhessischen Agrarverfassung 1814–1819', *HessJbLG* 36 (1986), pp. 183–246; Ulrich Hagenah, 'Ländliche Gesellschaft im Wandel zwischen 1750 und 1850 – das Beispiel Hannover', *Jahrbuch für Niedersächsische Landesgeschichte*, 57 (1985), pp. 161–206; Christine Zeile, 'Zur Grundentlastung in Baden 1819 bis 1848', *ZGO* 139 (1991), pp. 199–238; Brakensiek, *Agrarreform*; Mooser, *Ländliche Klassengesellschaft*.

107   Otto Ulbricht, *Englische Landwirtschaft in Kurhannover in der zweiten Hälfte des 18. Jahrhunderts. Ansätze zu einer historischen Diffusionsforschung* (Berlin, 1980).

108   Hans-Heinrich Müller, 'Bäuerliche Rittergutspachtungen im Cottbuser Kreise in der zweiten Hälfte des 18. Jahrunderts', *Letopis, Reihe B*, 11 (1964), pp. 29–54; Hartmut Harnisch, 'Peasants and Markets: The Background to the Agrarian Reforms in Feudal Prussia East of the Elbe', in Richard J. Evans and W. R. Lee, eds, *The German Peasantry: Conflict and Community in Rural Society from the Eighteenth to the Twentieth Centuries* (London, 1986), pp. 37–70.

109   Wolfgang Prange, *Die Anfänge der großen Agrarreformen in Schleswig-Holstein bis um 1771* (Neumünster, 1971).

110   Hans-Heinrich Müller, 'Bauern und Pächter im alten Preußen', *JbWG* (1966), pp. 259–77; Hans-Heinrich Müller, 'Domänen und Domänenpächter in Brandenburg-Preußen im 18. Jahrhundert', *JbWG* (1965/4), pp. 152–92; Hans-Heinrich Müller, *Märkische Landwirtschaft vor den Agrarreformen von 1807* (Potsdam, 1967); James Leonard Roth, 'The East Prussian Domaenenpaechter in the Eighteenth Century: A Study of Collective Social Mobility' (Ph.D. disseration, Univ. of Berkeley, 1979).

111   On Schleswig-Holstein, see North, *Amtswirtschaften*, pp. 239f; Günther Franz, ed., *Quellen zur Geschichte des deutschen Bauernstandes in der Neuzeit* (Darmstadt, 1976), pp. 312–15.

112   Friedrich Mager, *Geschichte des Bauertums und der Bodenkultur im Lande Mecklenburg* (Berlin, 1955).

113   Robert Stein, *Die Umwandlung der Agrarverfassung Ostpreußens durch die Agrarreform des neunzehnten Jahrhunderts* (Jena, 1918), i. pp. 358–61; Hartmut Harnisch, *Die Herrschaft Beitzenburg. Untersuchungen zur Entwicklung der sozialökonomischen Struktur ländlicher Gebiete in der Mark Brandenburg vom 14. bis zum 19. Jahrhundert* (Weimar, 1968), pp. 169–77.

114 August Skalweit, *Die ostpreußische Domänenverwaltung unter Friedrich Wilhelm I. und das Retablissement Litauens* (Leipzig, 1906).

115 Johannes Ziekursch, *Hundert Jahre schlesischer Agrargeschichte. Vom Hubertusburger Frieden bis zum Abschluß der Bauernbefreiung* (Breslau, 1915).

116 Heiner Wulfert, 'Die Agrarreformen in Schleswig-Holstein von 1765 bis zum Ende des 19. Jahrhunderts', *Zeitschrift für Geschichtswissenschaft*, 34 (1986), pp. 40–6; Hans-Heinrich Müller, 'Der agrarische Fortschritt und die Bauern in Brandenburg vor den Reformen von 1807', in Harnisch and Heitz, *Deutsche Agrargeschichte*, pp. 186–212; Clemens Zimmermann, *Reformen in der bäuerlichen Gesellschaft. Studien zum aufgeklärten Absolutismus in der Markgrafschaft Baden 1750–1790* (Ostfildern, 1983).

117 Ingrid Mittenzwei, 'Die Agrarfrage und der Kameralismus', in Harnisch and Heitz, eds, *Deutsche Agrargeschichte*, pp. 146–85.

118 Hans-Heinrich Müller, *Akademie und Wirtschaft im 18. Jahrhundert. Agrarökonomische Preisaufgaben und Preisschriften der Preußischen Akademie der Wissenschaften (Versuch, Tendenzen und Überblick)* (Berlin, 1975).

119 Gertrud Schröder-Lembke, 'Oeconomische Gesellschaften im 18. Jahrhundert', *ZAgrarGAgrarSoz* 38 (1990), pp. 15–23; Ludwig Deike, *Die Entstehung der Celler Landwirtschaftsgesellschaft*, compiled by Ilse Deike and Carl-Hans Hauptmeyer (Hannover, 1994).

120 Ludolf Kuchenbuch, '"Säuisches Wirthschaften" auf dem Land als Problem der Volksaufklärung', *Jahrbuch für Volkskunde*, 10 (1987), pp. 27–42; Walter Achilles, 'Bauernaufklärung und sozio-ökonomischer Fortschritt (1770–1830)', *ZAgrarGAgrarSoz* 41 (1993), pp. 174–89; Klaus Herrmann and Harald Winkel, eds, *Vom 'belehrten' Bauern – Kommunikation und Information in der Landwirtschaft vom Bauernkalender bis zur EDV* (St. Katharinen, 1992).

Translated by Sheilagh Ogilvie.

|4|

Trade

PETER KRIEDTE

Domestic commerce and foreign trade: general preconditions

'In the pre-stages of capitalist society, trade dominated industry; in modern society, it is the other way around.'[1] This quotation from Marx illustrates the fundamental importance of trade in the pre-modern period. At the same time, it makes clear that it would be an abbreviation of historical reality if an analysis of this trade restricted itself to foreign trade and neglected domestic commerce. Trade – and with it commercial capital – mediates between the two extremes, producers and consumers, often through numerous intermediaries. It is trade which first transforms products – whether finished products, half-finished products, raw materials, or fuels – into wares, by creating markets in which they can be sold.

A highly developed trade is linked to the validity of the market principle. This principle, however, only gradually broke a path for itself. To the peasant economy it was at first still largely 'peripheral' (in the term used by P. Bohannan and G. Dalton)[2] since this economy produced primarily 'use values' and not 'exchange values'. Only a small proportion of the gross yield of the peasant economy was sold on the market. There was greater acceptance of the market principle in the towns, at least in the larger ones. However, these were no more than small enclaves in an environment which was determined by peasant agriculture. As a consequence, any structural expansion of trade was linked to two preconditions. First, the self-sufficient unit of peasant production had to be broken open. It could only become a relevant participant in market activity if it opened itself up to specialization: whether as a supplier of agricultural products (as discussed in Chapter 3) or as a supplier of the products of rural industry (discussed in Chapter 9), in either case replacing the production of industrial or agricultural goods for its own needs. And secondly, the urban sector had to grow substantially if a significant stimulus for the market principle to prevail were to emanate from it.

A thrust toward commercialization (an issue hardly even investigated as yet) can be detected in the eighteenth century at the earliest.[3] Several factors were simultaneously at work, leading the economy out of the setback brought by the seventeenth century. Gradually, agrarian regions with a structural surplus of foodstuffs were assigned to other regions with a structural deficit. This required a specialization and commercialization of agrarian production in the first type of region. At the same time, in the wake of proto-industrialization, social strata emerged which, as they lost access to land, became increasingly dependent on the market and its imponderabilities. The urban population – defined as the number of people living in towns with at least 10,000 inhabitants – increased, according to the calculations of Jan de Vries, from *c.* 714,000 to *c.* 1.353 million in this period; but as a percentage of the total population the urban population increased only from *c.* 4.8 per cent to *c.* 5.5 per cent.[4] Germany thus remained far behind The Netherlands and England.

Two factors in particular unfavourably affected the position of German states with respect to foreign trade. First, linked with Europe's reaching out overseas, the economic centre of gravity of the Continent shifted to the North-West. In particular, with the replacement of Antwerp by Amsterdam as the most important trading centre in Europe from the end of the 1560s on, Central Europe fell increasingly behind. The currents of trade would in future be concentrated in Amsterdam and increasingly, from the end of the seventeenth century, in London and the French Atlantic ports. Secondly, the German states did not participate in commercial and colonial expansion overseas. As a consequence, their foreign trade had to do without the growth stimulus which emanated in particular from the 'new colonialism' of the seventeenth century, based on the plantation economy and colonies of settlers. At best, Central Europe participated indirectly, via Hamburg in particular, in the import and export trade with America, Asia, and Africa; the same was true for the entrepôt trade and the slave trade.

It is only with difficulty that we can distinguish between domestic and foreign trade. Describing French trade in the seventeenth and eighteenth centuries, Pierre Léon and Charles Carrière have spoken of an 'organic whole which was carried forward by the same growth impulse'.[5] For the German area, with its large number of state entities, it is even more difficult to draw a separation between the two, since a considerable proportion of that which falls under the rubric of *foreign* trade from the point of view of individual states should be counted as *domestic* trade when looking at the world of German states as a whole. Viewed from this standpoint, in all probability considerably less than 20 per cent of the total volume of German trade would be counted as foreign trade (for France foreign trade has been estimated at between 20 and 25 per cent of total trade).[6] Nevertheless, its significance must not be underestimated. Although it was not an 'engine of growth', it was certainly a 'handmaiden of growth', in the terminology used by I. B. Kravis. The internal market was often so limited that the only resort was, as W. Hofmann put it, the 'appropriation of foreign purchasing power'.[7]

Transportation routes, means of transportation, and networks of communication

Paths and roads were for the most part narrow and difficult to travel by. Their course was dictated by the terrain through which they led; there would have been no intervention in the terrain for the purpose of making way for the road. In flat terrain, the roads followed the courses of rivers, while in mountainous regions they followed the hillocks, ridges, and mountains. Their condition was in most cases understandably poor. A report on the roads in the Duchy of Braunschweig-Wolfenbüttel dating from 1681 noted a large number of 'very bottomless and bad places'. The maintenance of a road was the responsibility of the communities which it touched upon. These often lacked not only money but also good intentions: every cart that got stuck and every broken axle brought employment and money into the village in question.[8] Governments initially tried to regulate the condition of the roads through a flood of mandates and instructions, but without overwhelming success. Only when they accustomed themselves to the idea of taking the building of roads into their own hands did matters noticeably change. The building and maintenance of roads became an important point in the programme of mercantilism. The Austrian cameralist J. von Sonnenfels asserted 'that the state must itself take care of road building'.[9] In Bavaria, the expansion of trade-roads into metalled highways was pushed forward particularly under Maximilian III Joseph (1745–77). For the period around 1770, metalled roads were estimated to comprise c. 60 to 80 per cent of the total length of Bavarian highways. Prussia did not keep pace with this. Frederick II neglected road building because he feared it would further the transit trade, of which he was suspicious. Only from the end of the 1780s onward did Prussia begin building highways.[10] By the turn of the eighteenth into the nineteenth century, a clear South-North gradient, and also a no less noticeable West-East gradient, had developed within the German road network.

The worse the condition of the roads, the greater the importance of the canal network. These were used upstream as far as was at all possible. Roads often only provided the link between two canals. At the beginning of the eighteenth century, as a rule one 'took one's road by water, because it is much more comfortable and also does not cost so much'. In Bavaria in 1778, the average freight rate per hundredweight and kilometre was 0.7

Kreuzer by land, compared with 0.5 *Kreuzer* upstream on the Danube and 0.3 *Kreuzer* downstream.[11] Particularly with mass commodities such as grain, the advantages of water transport made a large difference in costs. It is therefore not surprising that governments, even before they turned to extending the roads, had many smaller rivers made navigable, and had canals built. The best-known canals from this period are the Müllroser Kanal of 1662–9, which established a link between the Oder and the Spree rivers, and the Schleswig-Holsteinische Kanal of 1774–84, which connected the North Sea with the Baltic via the Eider, and was passable even for ocean-going ships. In 1780, after sixteen locks had been constructed, it was finally possible to undertake boat traffic on the Ruhr. The further extension of the canal system in Mark Brandenburg in the eighteenth century led to the rise of a canal network orientated around Berlin which was among the best in Europe.[12]

Many of the projects pursued in this period quite swiftly revealed themselves to be not very promising, in so far as they could be brought to completion. Thus on the Oker, which had been made navigable by the officials of the Duchy of Braunschweig-Wolfenbüttel from 1741, ship traffic had already been abandoned again by 1775. The building of the canal which was supposed to connect Kassel with the Weser – partly by using the flow of the river Diemel, at the mouth of which the city of Karlshafen had been deliberately founded in 1699 – was abandoned in 1730.[13] Although it is undeniable that the efforts of governments to extend the waterways – except for in Mark Brandenburg – were not very successful, this does not alter the great importance which these had for domestic trade. Only the forced extension of the road network from the beginning of the nineteenth century, and the building of railways from the 1840s, made the waterways less important.

Means of transportation changed only very slowly. This was true especially for freight vehicles. Nevertheless, it appears that the weight of freight they could carry did increase to a not inconsiderable extent in the course of the eighteenth century. In passenger traffic, among the more elevated social strata coaches gradually prevailed from the seventeenth century on. Passenger posts came later; only toward the end of the eighteenth century did the post coach replace the post cart. Still, for one Russian traveller in 1789 the Prussian 'post calèches' were 'nothing more than long freight carts, with two seats, lacking straps or springs'.[14] The ships which plied the inland waterways varied very widely indeed. They ranged from narrow, flat skiffs up to wide, heavy barges. Every river, and sometimes (as on the Rhine) every section of a river, had its peculiarities.[15] Among oceangoing ships, the Dutch 'fluitschips' increasingly gained the upper hand from the beginning of the seventeenth century on. Imitated for the first time in Lübeck as early as 1617, they decisively influenced shipbuilding in the Hanseatic cities until the first decades of the nineteenth century. On the coastal waterways, but also in the trade between Hamburg and The Netherlands, a large number of smaller types of ship predominated, such as tjalks, smacks, and so-called 'Schniggen'.[16] Overland freight traffic lay for the most part in the hands of peasant freight carriers. For these, the carrying trade was a by-employment. Since they derived a significant portion of their livelihood from agriculture, they could supply transportation services more cheaply than full-time freight carriers. In so far as specialized transportation firms arose as, for example, in Frankfurt, Cologne, and Lüneburg, they initially remained reliant on peasant freight carriers, unless they provided themselves with their own freight wagons. At the end of the eighteenth century in localities which were favourably located for traffic there were not a few full-time carriers.[17] River-ship transportion was mostly carried out by small boatmen who were often organized into guilds. Bruno Kuske described the Cologne 'Börtschiffer' (shore boatmen) as 'craftsmen on the water'. Only in overseas ship transportation did regular shipping companies gradually arise.[18]

The condition of the roads and of the means of transportation placed limits on how fast the circulation not only of goods but also of information and people could accelerate, and these limits could be overcome only with difficulty. When to this were added fluctuations in the weather, such as severe rainfall or snowfall, traffic could break down completely. Staple privileges such as those of Cologne and Magdeburg and the exaction of customs fees further slowed the circulation of goods, especially when these meant that merchants travelled longer distances to circumvent such centres. All of this corresponded to a sense of time which was very different from ours. It is thus possible to understand why the average speed of traffic increased only very slowly, and why it continued to be characterized by a great deal of unreliability.

Transportation costs were substantial. Depending on weight and volume, shipping goods between Pirna and Hamburg in 1671–4 increased the price to customers by between 4 per cent (for tobacco) and 273 per cent (for millstones). For linen it was 11 per cent and for millet it was 22 per cent of the price to customers. More than 60 per cent of these freight costs consisted of the customs fees which had to be paid at the approximately 35 customs posts between Pirna and Hamburg. Transporting a gigantic wood boom whose value was estimated at 650,000 *Gulden* between Mannheim and Holland in 1782 cost 120,000 *Gulden*; here again, approximately half the sum consisted of customs charges.[19] However, the inflation of transportation costs by the exploitative practices of territorial powers should not be over-emphasized; they were heavy, but only infrequently prohibitive. Whether freight costs decreased in the course of the eighteenth century, as in some cases in France, is questionable. More probably, there was a 'quasi-stability of tariffs', in the words of P. Léon and C. Carrière, or sometimes even a rise.[20]

From the seventeenth century on, communication networks became considerably more dense. In this, an essential if not decisive role was played by the expansion of the postal system, first the horse post and later, beginning in the eighteenth century, the carriage post also, which as well as passengers also frequently carried letters and other items. The Imperial post, operated by the family Thurn und Taxis (ennobled in 1512), developed from a purely point-to-point postal system into one which covered entire areas. Once it began to confront competition from the postal organizations of individual territories after the end of the Thirty Years War, the postal network increased even more in density. Admittedly, in the eighteenth century the speed of the post did not increase any further, but its density continued to rise. In the South-West the length of the stretches travelled by the Imperial post doubled between 1730 and 1803; and its frequency also increased substantially. Around 1700, the post departed from Frankfurt to cover the more important routes twice a week; by 1750 it was already once a day.[21] The second half of the eighteenth century saw the emergence of special communication media: in addition to the books on commerce for merchants handed down from the past, there appeared appropriate reference works, such as Johann Christian Gädike's 'Fabriken- und Manufakturen-Addreß-Lexikon' ('Dictionary of Factory and Manufactory Addresses') in 1799, and above all specialized newspapers. Of these the *Handlungs-Zeitung* ('Trade Newspaper'), appearing in Gotha between 1784 and 1799 and edited by Johann Adolph Hildt, was especially important.[22]

Localities, agents, and means of trade

The ancient and customary locations at which trade was transacted were weekly markets, annual markets, and trade fairs. Here supply and demand intersected; here sellers and buyers met one another. While at weekly markets and annual markets the retail trade dominated, at trade fairs merchants met with merchants. Weekly markets, annual markets, and trade fairs took place at fixed locations and times, and for this reason could be easily controlled by the state authorities. The state had an interest in the maintenance of this fixed system, since it enabled it to exact fees and taxes, and to monitor weights, measures, and not least, prices.[23]

Weekly markets generally took place once or twice a week. They were held in cities and market towns and less frequently in villages as well, although only in cases in which a village had in the mean time grown to take on the functions of a market centre or a town. In 1794, Upper and Lower Bavaria possessed 37 urban markets and 90 market centres. This amounted to one market centre for every 7,300 inhabitants. Weekly markets primarily served to provide towns and cities with foodstuffs; in this

sense, they were the expression of a town-orientated division of labour between town and country. The larger the town, the larger the number of
weekly markets. In Braunschweig in 1765 there were weekly markets at five
different locations together with their neighbouring streets. Not only peasants and cottagers of the surrounding area sold at these markets, but also
almost all the craftsmen of the town. Sometimes there developed a clear
rank-ordering of the different weekly markets. In Hamburg the 'Höpfen-
markt' put all other weekly markets in the shade. As the number of markets increased, so too did specialization. In Augsburg, where 1,609 markets
took place at 20 different locations, small animals were sold in the Kitzen-
markt, textiles in the Steingasse, and hay, straw, and coal in the
Heumarkt.[24]

Annual markets – in western Europe they counted among the trade
fairs – took place once or twice a year, and often lasted for several days.
Their numbers appear to have been increasing. Thus the number of
localities in the Duchy of Braunschweig-Wolfenbüttel with annual markets
increased from fifteen in 1694 to twenty-nine in 1803. Some annual
markets were purely for small wares, others purely for animals; some were
for both at once. The selection of goods offered at the annual markets
was from the beginning much greater than at the weekly markets, except
for those in larger towns and cities. At the Nicolaus annual market in
Wolfenbüttel in 1748, 54 different crafts and trades were represented by
the 187 stalls. This meant that annual markets were much less strictly
regulated than were weekly markets. As a general rule, foreign craftsmen and shopkeepers were admitted. At the annual market in Helmstedt
in 1764, there were 21 shoemakers from Schöningen and 30 from
Braunschweig.[25] Although we still know little about annual markets, they
may well have played an important role in the establishment of the market
principle. The animal markets could sometimes take on gigantic dimensions. At the Cologne annual market, which took place in the autumn,
6,000 to 7,000 oxen are supposed to have been traded at the turn of the
seventeenth century. In the two centuries that followed, their numbers
declined considerably. Animal markets also lined the great oxen routes from
Jutland and eastern Central Europe to Central and western Europe. Markets are mentioned as taking place in Husum, Wedel, Brieg, Zerbst, and
Buttstädt.[26]

The transition from annual market to fair was a fluid one, and indeed it
can be shown that the fairs had, as a general rule, developed out of annual
markets. Leipzig and Frankfurt an der Oder are good examples of this. In
contrast to annual markets, what was characteristic for fairs, as the 'most
important form of inter-local trade organization', was the 'trade between
merchant and merchant', in the words of Max Weber. The objects of trade
at the fairs were 'goods that were present'. Trade with 'samples and patterns' was initially resisted, and began to gain in significance only from the
second half of the eighteenth century onward. Equipped with important

trade privileges and a special fair law and fair court, the trade-fair cities were able to attract trade to themselves. Some fairs had no more than regional significance. This was the case for the fairs of Nördlingen and Naumburg, less so for those of Frankfurt an der Oder (from *c.* 1635) and Braunschweig (from 1681). The two leading trade-fair centres were Frankfurt am Main and Leipzig. Frankfurt was initially far more important, but from the turn of the eighteenth century Leipzig, based on its role as intermediary between West and East, was able to catch up with Frankfurt and surpass it.[27]

Specialized markets were responsible for providing industry with raw materials, especially with linen yarn and wool. In industries in which the 'Kaufsystem' (a system in which the merchants bought the products from the producers) predominated, as in the linen industry, markets played an important role in the selling of the finished or half-finished product; for it was at markets that contact was established between weaver and trader. While the linen-cloth markets which were to be found in the small towns of the Silesian Riesengebirge were to a great extent left to the free play of the different forces – and were gradually sucked dry by the linen-cloth collectors – the east Westphalian linen-cloth markets were more strictly regulated. Here state inspection facilities, which were compulsory, intervened between producer and merchant.[28]

The regulated system which had prevailed until this period found its highest expression in the 'staple and warehousing obligation' by which many towns sought to secure a monopoly over trade and traffic. Their aim, in addition to securing provisions of foodstuffs and raw materials, was to concentrate trade and traffic in the town while excluding all foreigners, and to reserve the middleman trade for their own citizens. Although the staple and warehousing obligation had had a real function in the period when the cities were first flowering, in the early modern period it was increasingly a resort for towns which saw themselves threatened with decline. The more Cologne's own trade slumped, the greater was its interest in maintaining its staple privileges. An established fiscal interest also played a role. The Cologne wholesale markets and public department stores such as the Gürzenich, which at the same time functioned as a staple centre, grew to serve trade less and less, and instead served to control and register the stream of goods. The various taxes and fees imposed on incoming goods were in fact by far the most important revenue source for the city. Lübeck sought to assist its own trade by prohibiting the 'transit carriage' of foreign wares from 1605–6 on. The city insisted that foreign merchants who brought goods into Lübeck sell them to Lübeck merchants; only then was re-exporting them permitted. By doing this Lübeck involved itself in serious conflicts, particularly with Hamburg, for whose Baltic trade Lübeck was an important point of entry, especially when the land route was selected for the stretch between Hamburg and Lübeck. Only in 1728, after long negotiations, did Lübeck come round. Other towns were able to maintain their staple rights, often in the reduced form of a transport monopoly, until the end of the eighteenth century.[29]

To the 'true markets', especially the weekly and yearly ones, there grew up serious sources of competition: 'resident retailing' (in the phrase of W. Sombart) which was undergoing increasing expansion; and peddling, which was developing rapidly. Craftsmen were among the first to have their own shops. The shopkeepers went one step further: they sold as middlemen between producer and consumer, although generally still only foreign goods; and 'resident retailing' grew by leaps and bounds from the seventeenth century on. At the end of the eighteenth century Justus Möser opined, not without exaggeration, that the shopkeepers had

> increased threefold and the craftsmen lost less than half.... And can one conceive of anything which the shopkeeper does not now trade in, either secretly or publicly? Does he not watch out for all opportunities and crazes, in order to introduce something new, wonderful and foreign?

In Upper and Lower Bavaria in 1771 there were almost as many merchants as bakers. In Silesia, as in other eastern territories, the village tavern, the 'Kretscham', for the most part took on the function of a general shop; and in 1787 there were 3.8 tavern-keepers and shopkeepers for every 1,000 inhabitants.[30] Admittedly, in general the density of shops remained far behind that achieved in this period in England.[31] Selling practices were in the process of being revolutionized. In the larger cities, shopkeepers began to place advertisements in local newspapers. Along with this, in place of the rather passive economic behaviour they had hitherto practised, they adopted an explicit sales strategy which went straight for the potential customer and solicited him to buy.[32]

The peddling trade developed no less dynamically than the resident retailing trade. All the prohibitions against it achieved very little. The selling of small iron goods, glass-wares, clocks, textiles, and even overseas imports, was for the most part in the hands of peddlers. In the 'Göttingischen Ausruff' ('Göttingen Cry') of 1744 can be found copper etchings of twenty-six different travelling traders. Itinerant clock traders, 'one pack of clocks on the back and another under the arm, banging at a little bell', distributed Black Forest clocks across all of Europe.[33] Entire villages, such as Recke, Mettingen, Schapen, and Hopsten, villages north of Münster in which originated the so-called 'Tödden' (hawkers, etymologically related to the English verb 'to toddle'), dedicated themselves to a far-reaching itinerant trade, whose corner-points in this case were The Netherlands in the West and the frontiers of the Prussian monarchy in the East. Among itinerant traders an important role was played by foreigners, especially Savoyards and Italians from the area of the Upper Italian lakes. For Jews, peddling not infrequently offered the only opportunity of earning a small living.[34] It was the peddlers who first created any market at all for many goods. Justus Möser, already cited above, concluded his 'Complaint against the pack carriers' with the words: 'In short, the pack carrier is the fashion carrier of the farmer's wife, and tempts her into things she would never have thought of without him.'[35]

Merchants, too, sought to keep pace with this development. In 1804 the Prussian inspector of ship traffic in Hamburg remarked:

> that no European merchant, unless he is a retail trader, concerns himself with trivialities so much as the Bremen merchant. A whole army of travelling merchants' servants flood the greatest part of Germany and, not content with inciting the smallest market hamlet and in it the smallest shopkeeper or the sizeable consumer to place orders, they go almost from village to village, sell to preachers and tavern keepers smaller goods down to one-sixteenth of a hundredweight, fine spices to one-sixteenth of a pound, wine to one-sixteenth of an anker; yea, they push their mischief so far that they have communion wine as a rubric on their price list, although it is the lowest quality of this drink.[36]

The wholesale trade reveals a more ambivalent picture, in which stubborn tendencies from the past co-existed with developments which seem to point more to the future, making it difficult to draw up a balance sheet. Commerce at trade fairs continued to be quite significant. Many industries which were organized into a putting-out system marketed their products at the spring and autumn fairs. However, there are a few indications that they were losing share in the volume of trade to the wholesale trade which took place outside the trade fairs. Although the success of the Leipzig fairs may at first sight seem to contradict this, it must be recalled that they owed their rise to a specific constellation of factors: their position at the intersection between western Europe and western Central Europe on one hand and eastern Central Europe and eastern Europe on the other; and their mediating of economic exchange with a less-developed economic zone, for which the organization of trade in the form of commerce at trade fairs was very well suited.[37]

Sombart and, following him, Braudel sought to show that the wholesale trade took on the form of a depot trade. Storehouses and warehouses, in other words depots, are supposed to have become the 'centre-point and focus of all trade'; goods were 'brought to the depot in order to be traded, i.e. transformed from wares into money'. The storehouses and warehouses which the merchants maintained in particular locations are supposed to have 'represented something equivalent to a perpetual trade fair at this location'.[38] An alternative to the depot trade, which also amounted to installing permanent markets, was the establishment of consignment warehouses. The merchant in question avoided setting up his own depot; instead, he gave his goods to a foreign merchant on commission. The latter in turn sold them in his own name but to the account of the other merchant in exchange for a fee. This way of organizing trade emanated from Italy in the sixteenth century, and spread from Antwerp throughout Europe, with Cologne specializing in the commission trade from the seventeenth century onward. The glass- and clock-trading associations of the Black Forest, by contrast, kept to the organizational model of the depot trade.[39] Admittedly, development was at first primarily in the direction of the commission trade. Its importance resided above all in the fact that it opened up to smaller-scale merchants the opportunity of expanding their bases.

No less important was a general tendency which also led to a deregulation of the trading system: the rise of a group of middlemen and small traders, who operated between the small producers and the wholesale trade. They may not have been so numerous in Germany as in England, but we meet them repeatedly in the documents. The Upper German merchant houses already employed factors, for instance in purchasing linen in eastern Central Germany. Some of the linen collectors we encounter in the Silesian linen-weaving villages were such middlemen; the Hirschberg linen merchants made use of them to buy up village linen. Several of these linen collectors practised the linen trade 'al grosso' and thereby undermined the trade of the mountain towns which insisted on their market privileges. It was not so very different on the Swabian Jura, where the rural weaver-merchants drained trade away from the privileged Urach linen-trading company.[40]

The organizational structure of the wholesale trade changed, in that the large – and therefore relatively inflexible – trading companies, with their wide and specialized networks of agents, declined considerably in importance. In the process, it became much more open. Indications of this development are provided by the expanding commission trade, and the shareholding shipping which must be mentioned alongside it. The dominant form of enterprise was the one-man business and the unincorporated firm in the form of a general partnership, whether a pure family company or one which included outside members.[41] In shipping companies, joint ownerships played a large role. Joint owners of ships held so-called 'ship shares' in the ships of other shippers (from 1780 to 1820 in Hamburg, these were generally shares of one sixteenth or one eighth). Thus in the eight smaller ships of the Hamburg shipper Pieter Eldert, forty co-shippers held shares in 1790.[42] If putters-out followed a 'policy of diversification', as S. D. Chapman put it, this was no less the case for wholesale merchants. In general, the wholesale trade lacked almost any sort of specialization.[43] Trade on one's own account took place side by side with trade on commission; the two were generally closely connected with one another. Not infrequently, banking, insurance, and shipping business were included as well. Greater risks in one field were insured against by lower risks in another – all of which were typical features of a merchant capitalism which had to operate in an environment characterized by numerous insecurities.

Trade in any relatively developed form relies on money as a general mediator of exchanges. However, the general validity of money in Central Europe was restricted because of the competition which reigned there between a multiplicity of currency-issuing governments, mints, and currency systems. Minting associations, minting conventions, and Imperial currency ordinances sought to control and direct this multiplicity, but with limited success. Devaluation of the money of account was general, as in other European countries (the great exception was England), although it must be pointed out that these inflationary tendencies gradually weakened in the course of time. In contrast to this long-term devaluation of the monetary system, the comparatively short-term inflationary periods of the *Kipper- und Wipperzeit* at the beginning of the Thirty Years War (1618–23), the so-called 'Second or Small *Kipper- und Wipperzeit*' of 1667–90, and the currency debasements for the purposes of war-financing in Prussia (and Saxony) during the Seven Years War, had substantial repercussions on economic processes.[44]

According to an old proverb, credit is the 'soul of trade'. Trade was kept going by a whole cascade of loans. Sales loans already played a substantial role at the lowest level: the small shopkeeper had to provide loans to his customers if he wanted to further his business. Wholesalers who also operated on the side as retailers provided loans to their customers as well. The Munich grocer Angelo Sabbatini had paper-makers, dyers, chocolate-makers, confectioners and surgeons as debtors. He had debts receivable amounting to 26,074 *Gulden* in 1792, compared to debts payable totalling 34,683 *Gulden*.[45] In trade between one merchant and another, the bill of exchange more and more dominated the field. After the bill of exchange became negotiable, through endorsement, it functioned as the means of payment *par excellence*. As a paper between one person and another, it expressed, as Charles Carrière aptly wrote, 'the aversion of the merchant to any form of anonymous capitalism'.[46]

Urban banks, such as the Hamburgische Bank founded in 1619 and the Nuremberger Banco Publico founded in 1621 – both orientated towards the model of the Amsterdam Wisselbank – already functioned as important clearing centres, while at trade fairs most payment transactions still took place according to the method of the 'Skontration', whereby credits and debits were reckoned up against one another without the use of cash. With the rise of private banks from the end of the seventeenth century on, this declined in importance. In the eighteenth century private banks, such as the Bankhaus Gebrüder Bethmann in Frankfurt (to name the outstanding example) took on central functions in supra-regional payment transactions. The customer network of this bank reached as far as The Netherlands, Switzerland, and France; however, its clear focus was the areas of Frankfurt, Cologne, and Saxony.[47]

Objects, directions, and centres of trade

Domestic trade within the territories of individual German states is impossible to quantify. It can only be said with anything approaching secure probability that trade in agricultural products occupied the first rank, even though only a relatively small share of agrarian production left internal circulation within the peasant economy and was put onto the market. According to the model of Johann Heinrich von Thünen, around a town lay several concentric circles, organized according to the principle of declining intensity with increasing distance from the market. In the first circle, that of the 'free economy', horticulture is practised, in the second arboriculture, then arable production with crop rotation, pastoral production on enclosed pastures, three-field cultivation, and in the sixth and last circle animal husbandry. The reality of the seventeenth and eighteenth centuries did not always follow this model, but in general it came quite close. In Cologne, vegetables were cultivated immediately in front of the walls. The city's grain store was the Lower Rhine plain. In crisis years, the distance from the place of procurement became substantially greater; thus in 1693 considerable quantities of grain had to be purchased in The Netherlands. Until the mid-

Table 4.1 Prussia's balance of trade, 1795–6[a]

	Exports		Imports	
	abs.	%	abs.	%
Foodstuffs	6.46	12.5	6.37	11.9
of which grain	4.72	9.2	2.90	5.4
Beverages	1.19	2.3	3.47	6.5
Colonial goods	3.85	7.5	8.10	15.2
Raw materials, auxiliary				
materials, and fuels	3.34	6.5	7.43	13.9
of which for weaving	0.63	1.2	3.18	6.0
Industrial products	36.34	70.5	27.49	51.5
of which textiles	25.52	49.5	15.47	29.0
Other	0.39	0.8	0.49	0.9
Sub-total	51.57	100.0	53.34	100.0
Balance (deficit)	1.77	–	–	–
Total	53.34	–	53.34	–

[a]In millions of *Taler*; including transit goods.
Note: abs.: absolute value.
Percentages may not add up precisely to 100 because of rounding.
Source: P. Behre, *Geschichte der Statistik in Brandenburg-Preußen bis zur Gründung des Königlichen Statistischen Bureaus* (Berlin, 1905), pp. 356–57, and additionally Kaufhold, 'Schwerpunkte', pp. 245–7.

dle of the seventeenth century, oxen were driven to the Cologne markets primarily from Friesland and the Weser marshes; after this, the markets for procurement apparently shifted to the South.[48] Not only other large cities such as Frankfurt, Augsburg, and Nuremberg, but also whole regions were dependent for provisions of foodstuffs on neighbouring regions. The densely populated Bergisch Land, neighbouring on Cologne, and the similarly densely settled Silesian hilly zone were examples of such subsidy regions. The end destinations of trade in agricultural products point to those localities and regions which had structural deficits.

Only in one case does a Thünen ring extend beyond the external borders of the individual German states: in the breeding of oxen. Oxen were driven westward from Denmark and Schleswig, Red Russia (western Ukraine with Lwów), and the Ukraine, as well as from Hungary. While the export of oxen from Denmark and Hungary declined from the seventeenth century on, the export trade from Red Russia and the Ukraine increased until the first partition of Poland (from 40,000 head in the second half of the sixteenth century to between 80,000 and 90,000 in the eighteenth century). It should be noted that the oxen trade was to some extent one of transit. More than half of the oxen from Denmark were brought across the Elbe into The Netherlands.[49] The situation in the grain trade was unlike that in the oxen trade. Here, Germany belonged among the exporting countries and only to a limited extent among the importing countries; it imported grain above all in times of food provision crises. Regions in which exportable surpluses were generated were especially the territories east of the Elbe in which, from the sixteenth century on, *Grundherrschaft* (a manorial system with quite weak seigneurial controls) had been transformed into *Gutsherrschaft* (a manorial system with very strong ones). For the years between 1560 and 1620 the grain exports of the Mark Brandenburg in good years have been estimated at between 10,000 and 15,000 tonnes. From the eighteenth century on, the centre of Prussian grain exports shifted further eastwards: Königsberg, which according to the Sund customs register exported an average of 10,400 tonnes of rye and wheat to western Europe between 1562 and 1619, increased its exports to *c.* 54,400 tonnes in the years 1784–95.[50] The Prussian import and export tables which survive for 1795–6 show an export surplus of 1.8 million *Taler*'s worth of grain (see Table 4.1). Besides The Netherlands, England rose to be the main purchaser of German grain at the end of the eighteenth century. Additional grain exports went above all to the Alpine countries. Thus at the end of the eighteenth century Bavaria sold significant quantities of grain to Austria, and the areas north of the Rhine did so to eastern Switzerland. Among the importing countries was Silesia, which was dependent on grain imports from Poland.[51]

Even though industrial goods made up a small share of domestic trade, they were nevertheless very important in foreign trade, at least at the end of the eighteenth century. Admittedly, in absolute terms the bulk of industrial products was probably sold on the domestic market. At the turn of the seventeenth century Germany already possessed an array of significant industrial centres. Among them were the mining regions in the Upper Palatinate, the Harz, and the Erzgebirge (Ore Mountains); the centres of small iron goods production in Nuremberg, the Grafschaft Mark, and the Bergisches Land; and the textile centres in Augsburg and Upper Swabia, Cologne, eastern Central Germany, and Silesia. Almost all of these were hard hit by the Thirty Years War and the crisis of the seventeenth century. In the second half of the seventeenth century there began a long-lasting reconstruction of industrial locations which resulted in a new prosperity. The old industrial exporting cities, with only a few exceptions such as Augsburg, fell behind; the countryside forcibly pushed itself forward as the location of production. Here and in small towns new industrial agglomerations arose.[52] The production of industrial goods expanded substantially, especially from the middle of the eighteenth century on; and a large proportion of these was sold on the domestic market. With the deregulation of trade there arose new channels of sales for them, which enabled a rapid growth of the new industrial centres. Möser's 'Packenträger' ('pack carriers'), who 'seduced' male servants and maidservants into buying 'unnecessary frivolities' such as silk neckerchiefs, silver buckles, 'prettily mounted pipe bowls', lace, and trimmings, can be seen as emblems of this new alliance between production and marketing.[53] The structures of industrial commodity-production and trade involved in this upheaval entered into a dynamic relationship with one another which furthered change.

In some industries, substantial proportions of production were exported. The export ratio was especially high in the linen industry. In Silesia in 1791–2 it amounted to *c.* 75.5 per cent.[54] In many other similarly dense linen-producing areas the export ratio may have been just as high. In the meantime, the Atlantic economic area had become the most important selling-market for the Central European linen industry. In 1787, C. L. P. Hüpeden described the Hessian linen-cloth trade as the 'main channel through which Spanish gold and silver flow into our coffers'. Between 1748–9 and 1789–90, 75.6 per cent of Silesian linen exports went to western Europe and overseas.[55] In the sixteenth century and at the beginning of the seventeenth a large proportion of German (and especially south German) linen was still being exported to southern Europe. For south German linen, the markets of southern Europe remained important in the eighteenth century as well, while the linen of East Westphalia, Hessia, Upper Lusatia, and Silesia became increasingly orientated to the Atlantic economic area. Merchants from England and The Netherlands, who appeared in eastern central Germany from the end of the sixteenth century onwards as buyers of linen cloth and linen yarn, had been the forerunners in opening up these selling-markets.[56] In other industries, the export ratio may have sometimes been equally high; however, as a rule they did not show such a strong orientation toward the Atlantic economic area. Thus favoured selling areas for the fine-woollen-cloth industry and the silk industry were eastern Central Europe and eastern Europe.

Industrial exports per capita of the population at the end of the eighteenth century varied greatly across regions. They were at their highest in the West and at their lowest in the East (except for Silesia). For example, in the Duchy of Berg the per capita value of industrial exports was more than 11 *Taler*, in the Grafschaft of Ravensberg nearly 10 *Taler*, and in East Prussia and Pomerania, by contrast, only 0.2 *Taler*. In Bavaria it was very low, as well, at 0.2 *Taler*. Industrial goods as a proportion of total foreign trade also fluctuated substantially. In Prussia in 1795–6 industrial goods made up 70.5 per cent of exports and 51.2 per cent of imports. In Bavaria, by contrast, at the end of the century, industrial goods were only between 7 and 7.3 per cent of exports (no figures are available for imports).[57]

In Prussia, industrial exports were dominated by textiles (which accounted for 70.2 per cent of the total), and among these once again by linen (with 55.1 per cent). In 1802, Silesia, with 45.9 per cent, generated nearly half the exports of industrial products; then followed the central provinces with 29.9 per cent, the western provinces (excluding the areas west of the Rhine) with 20.6 per cent, and the eastern provinces with 3.6 per cent. The relatively favourable figures for Prussian foreign trade at the end of the eighteenth century should not deceive us, however, concerning their weaknesses. The high share represented by textiles, and by linen in particular, necessarily made it very vulnerable to crises in a period in which England was entering factory industrialization and, closely related to this, linen was confronting the rapid growth of its rival and substitute, cotton.[58]

Industrial products also played a significant role in imports, in 1795–6 making up 56.3 per cent of imports for Prussia. The countries of origin for imports into Germany lay primarily in southern, western, and north-western Europe. While Italy fell increasingly behind from the seventeenth century on, France was able to catch up. From that point on, it was no longer Italy but France which was the main supplier of silk goods. English woollens had been reaching Central Europe in growing numbers from the later middle ages on. Although initially this trade lay mainly in the hands of Hanseatic merchants, from the sixteenth century on it was increasingly monopolized by the Merchant Adventurers: in addition, these were able to establish themselves firmly on the German North Sea coast from 1564 on. From 1611 on, Hamburg was the main port of entry for imports of English woollen cloth into Central Europe, remaining so long after the fall of the monopoly of the Merchant Adventurers.[59]

In Prussia in 1795–6 the positive balance of 8.9 million *Taler* of industrial products was counterbalanced by a negative balance of 4.1 million *Taler* of raw materials, auxiliary materials and fuels (see Table 4.1). This was a sign of the favourable development of industrial production and was, in some ways, a consequence of it. It can be postulated that the balance of foreign trade for Germany as a whole was also negative in respect of these resources. It is difficult to say how this foreign trade balance had developed from the beginning of the seventeenth century with respect to these two sums. But since in the sixteenth century exports of metals (which come under the heading 'raw materials') are known to have been very important, we may speculate that between then and the late eighteenth century there was a shift toward a more positive trade balance on industrial products and a less positive trade balance on raw materials. However, the danger of underestimating exports of raw materials even in the eighteenth century is shown by the exports of wood from the hinterland of the Rhine into The Netherlands, which was organized on a large scale by Dutch wood traders.[60]

In the meantime, trade in colonial produce had come to occupy an important position in the balance of trade, especially since, in addition to spices (especially pepper), sugar, tobacco, tea, coffee, and cocoa had appeared. At the end of the sixteenth century, more than half of the volume of spices was temporarily once again coming to Central Europe via the caravan routes, the cities on the coast of the eastern Mediterranean, and Venice, and not via the Cape route. But as early as the first decade of the seventeenth century, with the rise of the Dutch and English East India Companies, the land trade had conclusively triumphed.[61] From then on, spices arrived into German territories via The Netherlands and the ports on the North Sea and Baltic coast. It was also here that sugar, tobacco, tea, coffee, and cocoa, imports of which greatly increased from the middle of the eighteenth century on, found their most important ports of entry into the markets of Central Europe. By the end of the eighteenth century, colonial produce made up a substantial share of total imports: in Bavaria in the second half of the century it was *c.* 18 per cent, in Prussia in 1795–6 it was *c.* 15 per cent (here excluding colonial produce in processed form; see Table 4.1).

Only estimates are available for the total size of the export trade. For the period around 1800 Hermann Kellenbenz estimates it at more than 223 million Prussian current *Taler*. Considering that German foreign trade has been estimated at 282 million *Taler* in 1830, the export trade may have amounted to between 230 and 250 million *Taler* in 1800.[62] This is *c.* 10 *Taler* per head of population – a modest amount when one compares the German states with the British Isles, but a considerable sum when one takes into account that Germany, unlike Britain, was not a maritime power.

With the shift in the direction of trade, the trading centres also changed in location. Augsburg and Nuremberg, the centres of south German trading capital in the sixteenth century, were still very important trading centres at the beginning of the seventeenth century. The importance of Nuremberg is shown by its great colonies of merchants from Italy and The Netherlands. In 1621–4, the former accounted for 13.9 per cent and the latter for 7.7 per cent of the volume of trade carried out via the Nürnberger Banco Publico. This had an average value of 8.95 million *Taler* over these three years, making it considerably greater than that carried out via the Hamburg bank (with 6.54 million *Taler* in 1619). The most important trade goods were metalwares and textiles. The financial handling of Nuremberg's trade took place via Amsterdam, Venice, and Hamburg.[63] Only in the course of the Thirty Years War did a severe slump take place; in Augsburg the sum of taxes paid by merchants fell from 18,680 *Gulden* (in 1618) to 3,056 *Gulden* (in 1646). After the end of the war, both towns were able to benefit from the outstanding position they had occupied just before the war began, although without ever again reattaining it. Augsburg developed into the most important centre of money and exchange in southern Germany after Frankfurt. In 1781, Friedrich Nicolai wrote of Augsburg: 'It does on a small scale what Holland does on a large scale: it keeps the accounts for neighbouring countries, especially for Austria, Swabia, and parts of Switzerland and Italy.'[64] Its long-distance trade also remained significant. Nuremberg's function as mediator between West and East, North and South still survived even after the end of the Thirty Years War, which was advantageous to its commission trade. Moreover, it also continued to have a substantial trade of its own: in 1720–41 its trade with Italy was not much less sizeable than that of Augsburg.[65] The significance of Cologne as a trading centre somewhat increased after the rise of Amsterdam as the switching centre of world trade, but its own trade slumped in the face of over-mighty Dutch competition. From the second half of the seventeenth century on, the Cologne merchants were pushed out of the trade with England. For Holland, Cologne became the most important centre for buying and selling goods upstream on the Rhine. For the Cologne merchants, there remained only the commission trade and the transport trade.[66]

Frankfurt owed its rise to become the leading German centre of trade at the turn of the seventeenth century to the mass immigration of exiles from The Netherlands from the end of the 1560s on. Within a few years, they turned Frankfurt not only into a thriving industrial centre, but also into the most important centre of trading, trade fairs, and money in Central Europe. Many merchants from Antwerp were among them. In the words of A. Dietz, Frankfurt was transformed into a 'small Antwerp'. Until *c.* 1630 its trade fairs maintained themselves at a level which was apparently never again attained.[67] After the end of the Thirty Years War, Leipzig increasingly made itself felt as a competitor. When, in 1710, conflict arose between Frankfurt and Leipzig over the timing of the spring trade fairs in both cities, it emerged that the Leipzig fairs had in the meantime become 'far more important and considerable'; in the end, after years of conflict, Frankfurt had to come round. Although Leipzig's own trade remained behind that of Frankfurt, the trade at its fairs put that of Frankfurt increasingly into the shade. As the 'gate to the East', Leipzig attracted a large share of the exports from western and Central Europe to eastern Central and eastern

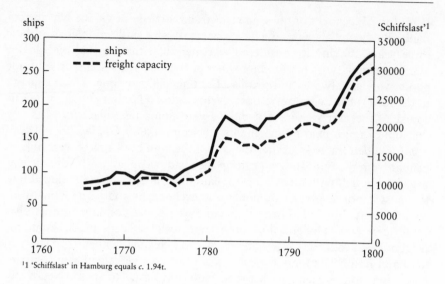

Fig. 4.1 Hamburg's trading fleet, 1765–1800 (*Source*: Kresse, Materialien, p. 67)

Europe, and of the imports from this area to Central and western Europe. Manufactured goods from Germany, especially Saxony, as well as from France and England, were exchanged for smoked goods and other raw materials from the East. Among the visitors to the Leipzig fairs in the second half of the eighteenth century, those from Poland and Lithuania comprised the largest group after those from Saxony. In third place followed Hamburg – an indication of how closely the rises of the two cities were linked with one another. Not without justification was Hamburg referred to as the port of Leipzig. The 'Elbe line' entered into competition with the Rhine line.[68]

At the beginning of the seventeenth century, Lübeck, the head of the Hanseatic League, was still the most important German maritime trading centre. In 1595, its fleet, with 253 ships and a freight capacity of *c.* 9,000 *Last* (1 *Schiffslast* in Hamburg was equal to approximately 1.94 tonnes), was still the largest among the Hanseatic cities. Between the mid-1490s and 1580 its trade had more than tripled. Admittedly, the monopoly position of the Hanseatic League was already a thing of the past. All attempts to prevent the decline of the Hanseatic League through defending its inherited trading privileges abroad and maintaining its regulation of trade were in vain. This did not, however, mean that Lübeck's share in the Baltic trade, especially that of the Baltic ports, was not still quite significant.[69]

Hamburg reacted to the changes in international trade much more flexibly than did Lübeck. Desiring 'to become a free trading city', in 1567 it permitted the Merchant Adventurers to settle there, initially for 10 years. In 1611 there followed further privileges. The town council behaved similarly accommodatingly towards other foreigners, especially towards exiles from

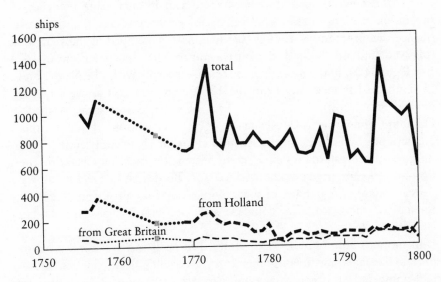

Fig. 4.2 Arrival of ships in Bremen, 1755–1800 (*Source*: von Witzendorff, 'Beiträge', p. 387)

Table 4.2 The merchant fleets of Hamburg, Bremen, and Lübeck in July 1786

	Ships	Freight capacity[a]	
		absolute	%
Hamburg	213	46,724	48.3
Bremen	158	33,400	34.5
Lübeck	109[b]	16,580	17.1
Total	480	96,704	100.0

[a] In French tonnes (1 French tonne = 0.979 metric tonnes).
[b] Of which 18 (with a capacity of 2,530 French tonnes) u..ær Russian flags.
Source: P. Jeannin, 'Die Hansestädte im europäischen Handel des 18. Jahrhunderts', *Hansische Geschichtsblätter*, 89 (1971), p. 55.

The Netherlands and Sephardic Jews from Portugal. This foreigner-friendly policy contributed considerably to its initially seeming that Hamburg would be able to emerge as the heir of Antwerp, 'florentissimum emporium totius Germaniae'.[70] But Amsterdam, thanks to its more favourable geographical position and better framework conditions, surpassed it. This did not prevent the trade of Hamburg from continuing to expand, not least with the northern Netherlands. Its trading fleet, which in 1600 was still smaller than that of Lübeck, expanded by 1674 to 309 ships with a freight capacity of

23,822 *Last*, while that of Lübeck stagnated. Its increasing tendency to favour, on grounds of risk, ships sailing under foreign flags, had the consequence that Hamburg's trading fleet temporarily slumped in the years that followed, and only in the 1790s once again attained the dimensions of 1674 (see Figure 4.1). In the meantime, its trade, especially with The Netherlands, England, and France, and from the 1780s with America as well, had expanded enormously. In the boom year of 1795, 3,589 ships berthed in Hamburg (this was a consequence of the occupation of the northern Netherlands by France). In the second half of the eighteenth century, Hamburg rose, at Amsterdam's expense, to become the most important destination for re-exports of colonial produce from Bordeaux: in 1783 it had a 21 per cent share of re-exports of sugar, 46 per cent for coffee, and 25 per cent for indigo; only with sugar could Amsterdam, with 27 per cent, maintain its primacy.[71]

In the meantime, Bremen had established itself as the second most important German maritime trading centre. Its trading fleet, which in 1594–5 had numbered 88 ocean ships with a freight capacity of 2,466 *Last*, consisted in 1702 of 71 ocean ships with a freight capacity of 4,675 *Last*. By 1786 it had expanded to *c.* 158 ships with a freight capacity of *c.* 16,350 *Last*. In the second half of the 1790s, an average of 1,097 ships berthed in Bremen (see Fig. 4.2); and in the 1780s it entered into direct traffic with North America and the West Indies. The trade in colonial produce, especially in coffee – 18 per cent of the coffee re-exported from Bordeaux in 1783 went to Bremen – increased enormously.[72]

Comparing the three cities, it seems sensible to begin with the size of their trading fleets (see Table 4.2). Considering the fact that Hamburg merchants frequently made use of ships travelling under foreign flags to transport their goods, however, it would be too hasty to jump to conclusions about the trade of each city based on its number of ships. Instead, Pierre Jeannin, on the basis of careful investigations, has estimated that in the second half of the eighteenth century Hamburg had between a 67 and a 71 per cent share of the trade of the three cities, Bremen between 21 and 27 per cent, and Lübeck *c.* 7 per cent, figures which make clear the steep rise of Hamburg and the decline of Lübeck. This indicates that the trade between West and East was no longer the primary one for these three cities, with the possible exception of Lübeck. In the meantime, they had come to function as ports for Central Europe, and as such established the connection to the Atlantic economic area and the capitalist world system which was in the process of coming into being.[73]

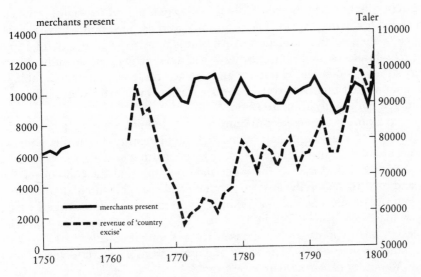

Fig. 4.3 The Leipzig fairs, 1763–1800 (*Source*: Hasse, *Geschichte*, p. 245; Reinhold, *Polen/Zitauen*, p. 173)

Trends and fluctuations; intervention of the state authorities

Although it is certain that trade moved parallel to economic development in general, it is very difficult to show this in detail. This is especially the case for the seventeenth and the first half of the eighteenth century. There is considerable debate about the point at which the upswing of the 'long' sixteenth century ended: whether as early as the turn of the seventeenth century, around 1619–22, or only in the middle of the century. There is no less debate about whether the Thirty Years War should be viewed as economically 'exogenous' or 'endogenous'. The only thing which is undeniable is that it was among the factors which enduringly intensified the secular downswing of the economy.[74] That the volume of trade declined in the seventeenth century in both quantity and value was rendered likely by the decline in population alone, which amounted to as much as 25 per cent between 1600 and 1650. Unfortunately, we possess only a very few pieces of direct evidence for such a decline. The volume of grain traded at the Cologne grain markets had already declined in the sixteenth century, although this intensified only from the 1580s on; however, from 1680–5 on it rose once more. The international exchange of agricultural products, however, declined. The average amount of grain annually exported from the Baltic area declined, too, from 68,500 *Last* (in 1600–49), to 55,800 (in 1650–99), to 31,800 (in 1700–49), with one *Last* of rye being approximately equal to 2.19 tonnes. Only in the second half of the eighteenth century did it rise once again. The oxen trade also declined noticeably. The decline of the fustian production of Augsburg from 466,412 pieces (in 1609) to 67,041 pieces (in 1646) must have had aggravating repercussions on the city's trade.[75] While in Hamburg and Bremen trade was apparently able to maintain itself relatively well, Lübeck's freight traffic with western Europe suffered enduringly from 1635 on.[76]

At the turn of the eighteenth century a new long-term upswing began, accelerating in the second half of the eighteenth century. From this point in time, at latest, it also included trade. The population growth, the expansion of agriculture and that of the industrial economy, and the consequent demand for raw materials, auxiliary inputs, and fuels, all stimulated it. Only a few figures are known. The number of merchants present at the Leipzig fairs increased from 6,296 in 1750 to 11,738 in 1800 (see Fig. 4.3). The Silesian linen export trade increased from 3.5 million *Taler* in 1748–9 to 5.9 million in 1789–90. The value of exports from northern Germany into the Admiralty of Amsterdam rose from 3.4 million *Gulden* in 1750 to 5.1 million in 1793, and the value of imports rose from 5.3 to 7.6 million *Gulden*. In 1793, the trade of Germany (excluding northern Germany) with the Admiralty of Amsterdam was, at 34.4 million *Gulden*, more than double that of 1750 (at 16.5 million *Gulden*). Exports from Germany to England and Wales climbed from 0.6 million pounds sterling in 1701–5 to 2.1 million in 1796–1800, imports increased from 0.9 to 9.5 million pounds (in both cases in official prices); and growth in the wake of the revolutionary wars in the 1790s was especially rapid (between 1786–90 and 1795–1800, exports increased by *c.* 333 per cent and imports *c.* 549 per cent).[77]

In each case, the secular trends obscured a large number of relatively short-term conjunctures and crises. The causes of these were many and varied. Crises of insufficient agrarian production led to those of insufficient industrial consumption, and could severely impair trade in industrial products as a consequence. A change in customs policy could also have effects on trade. The customs war which Prussia waged against Saxony from 1740 on, under the slogan 'The Saxons shall be persecuted and their wares shall encounter difficulties on entry' (in the words of Friedrich II), damaged trade at the Leipzig fairs, but in the end revealed itself to be a failure. Wars could bring trade to a total standstill: the outbreak of the War of the Spanish Succession, for example, threw Hamburg into a severe crisis. The Silesian linen-cloth trade was repeatedly and severely hit by military events.[78] Authentic 'trade goods crises', in the phrase of M. Bouniatian – crises, that is, of an essentially endogenous nature, the distinguishing characteristic of which was a massive devaluation of the stock of wares after a large rise in prices had taken place in a preceding boom period – were relatively infrequent. The crisis of 1763, centred in Amsterdam, Hamburg, and Berlin, can be regarded as being at least partly of this kind, even though it can be traced back primarily to the strain on credit during the Seven Years War. The crisis of 1799, the 'great trade entanglement', as the contemporary Hamburg economist Johann Georg Büsch termed it, approached being a real 'trade goods crisis', in which prices for colonial produce fell after having previously risen strongly. In Hamburg in September and October of that year more than 100 merchant houses went bankrupt.[79]

The crisis of the seventeenth century and the destruction caused by the Thirty Years War became the starting-point for attempts by the state authorities to intervene in economic life and thereby to encourage development of the forces of production, not least with a view to the state's own financial requirements. In the eighteenth century this policy found its highpoint in cameralism, the German version of mercantilism.[80] In addition to extending the material infrastructure (such as canals and roads) and intervening directly in the economic process (through establishing manufactories, for example), a high priority was assigned to foreign trade policy. Friedrich II of Prussia wrote in his political testament of 1752: 'The foundation of commerce and of manufactures is to prevent money from getting out, and to make it come back in.' This maxim, whose hard core was the fetish for a positive balance of trade, led to a whole array of measures: these ranged from levying customs charges to import prohibitions against particular wares on one hand, and on the other to the establishment of export industries, coupled with production or export premiums, and export prohibitions on particular raw materials; and the transit trade was made considerably more difficult in order to prevent smuggling of foreign industrial products.[81]

Other states, such as Saxony, which were less backward than Prussia in their economic development, pursued a much more moderate policy. The chairman of the Saxon 'Restaurationskommission' ('restoration commission') (1762–3), Thomas von Fritsch, held views which approached not 'ordinances or policy arrangements', but rather 'a great deal of competition', and met the great Leipzig trading merchants, who insisted on the 'undamaged freedom of trade'.[82] Admittedly, when one casts a glance at the other German states, representatives of a liberal trade policy were still in a minority. Only the 'revolution from above', which was set off by the French Revolution, brought a change. State policies toward trade and external economic relationships, which had established themselves as a counter-force to the deregulation of trade which had been the operative tendency at a lower level, took on a less dirigiste form. How strong the counter-pressures had already been for a long time was shown after the end of the Seven Years War, when Frederick II finally had to give up his plans for monopolizing particular branches of trade.[83] The social basis of state interventionism faltered in the face of an economic upturn which favoured traders and merchants.

Conclusion: the role of trade in the transitional phase

Marx ascribed to trade an effect which 'was more or less to dissolve ... the ways in which production was previously organized'. In which direction it developed, however, was very much an open question. What was of imminent significance here was, in particular, how trade behaved toward production, whether it penetrated into the sphere of production and seized it, and the direction in which production itself developed: whether it did indeed arrive at the 'capitalization' which Marx apostrophized as 'revolutionary'.[84] Both can be observed in the period discussed here, but this is not the place for a detailed analysis of the reorganization of industrial commodity production.

Looking at trade in the narrow sense of the word, leaving out its relationships with the sphere of production, it is unmistakably clear not only that its quantitative dimensions changed, but also that it was in the process of entering qualitatively into a new phase. The restructuring of industrial commodity production encountered in trade, and especially in retailing, an opposite number which was undergoing enormous upheaval and encouraging the triumph of the market principle. The incarnations of this upheaval were the resident shopkeepers and the travelling peddlers. This led to the rise of a constellation of phenomena which further advanced the changes in both industry and trade and at the same time secured them. Although the deregulation of trade was sometimes thwarted by increasing state interventionism, the latter was not able to prevail enduringly, nor was it able to keep the process of change on a path which it alone controlled.

Even if the trading fleets of individual German states were vanishingly small – according to an account of 1786–7, they made up only 3.7 per cent of total European tonnage[85] – this did not prevent the domestic economies of these states from meanwhile becoming linked, via Amsterdam and the North Sea ports, with the Atlantic economic area, and from participating in the growth impulses which emanated from it. The preconditions were laid for Germany's becoming one of the metropolises of the capitalist world system at some point in the future.

Admittedly, if one concentrates only on the factors which had implications beyond the eighteenth century, one will not do justice to the transitional nature of the two centuries discussed here. Their distinguishing characteristic was precisely the co-existence of old and new, of the retarding and the progressive. This can be observed in almost every field. One of the permanent limits on the economy of the *ancien régime*, in the words of F. Braudel, was undoubtedly the slowness and limited efficiency of transportation. This lastingly affected both trade and the time-sense of those participating in it. In this crucial area, changes took place only very slowly. The fixing of trade to particular places and times, and to prescribed norms such as that of sufficient provision, did loosen, but by no means did they fully disappear. Not infrequently, the state authorities replaced the local control network, which was becoming fragile, with new forms of control which constricted trade no less. Although trade unquestionably expanded, it is equally certain that it everywhere encountered limits.

Notes

For the production of the figures, I would like to think Birgitt Sippel.

1 K. Marx, *Das Kapital* (3 vols, Berlin, 1964–1968), iii. p. 342.
2 P. Bohannan and G. Dalton, 'Introduction', in P. Bohannan and G. Dalton, eds, *Markets in Africa* (Evanston, Ill., 1962), pp. 2, 7–9, 12.
3 On England, see J. Thirsk, *Economic Policy and Projects: The Development of a Consumer Society in Early Modern England* (London, 1978); N. Mc-Kendrick, J. Brewer, and J. H. Plumb, *The Birth of a Consumer Society: The Commercialization of Eighteenth-Century England* (London, 1982).
4 J. de Vries, *European Urbanization, 1500–1800* (London, 1984), pp. 30, 39.
5 P. Léon and C. Carrière, 'L'appel des marchés', in F. Braudel and E. Labrousse, eds, *Histoire économique et sociale de la France* (4 vols, Paris, 1970–1980), iii. p. 164.
6 *Ibid.*, p. 180; on England see J. A. Chartres, *Internal Trade in England, 1500–1700* (London, 1977), p. 10.
7 I. B. Kravis, 'Trade as a Handmaiden of Growth: Similiarities between the Nineteenth and Twentieth Centuries', *Economic Journal*, 80 (1970), pp. 850–72; W. Hofmann, *Europa-Markt und Wettbewerb* (Berlin, 1959), p. 10. On what follows, see W. Sombart, *Der moderne Kapitalismus* (3rd edn Munich/Leipzig, 1919), ii. 1; F. Braudel, *Civilisation matérielle, économie et capitalisme, XVe–XVIIIe siècle* (Paris, 1979), i and ii; H. Aubin and W. Zorn, eds, *Handbuch der deutschen Wirtschafts- und Sozialgeschichte* (Stuttgart, 1971), i; H. Kellenbenz, *Deutsche Wirtschaftsgeschichte* (München, 1977), i; F.-W. Henning, *Handbuch der Wirtschafts- und Sozialgeschichte Deutschlands* (Paderborn, 1991), i; C. Dipper, *Deutsche Geschichte 1648–1789* (Frankfurt, 1991), pp. 168–83. For bibliography, see Dahlmann-Waitz, *Quellenkunde zur deutschen Geschichte. Bibliographie der Quellen und Literatur zur deutschen Geschichte* (Stuttgart, 1992), vii. sections 297, 298, 333, and 334.
8 P. Albrecht, *Die Förderung des Landesausbaues im Herzogtum Braunschweig-Wolfenbüttel im Spiegel der Verwaltungsakten des 18. Jahrhunderts (1671–1806)* (Braunschweig, 1980), p. 36; E. Schremmer, *Die Wirtschaft Bayerns. Vom hohen Mittelalter bis zur Industrialisierung. Bergbau, Gewerbe, Handel* (Munich, 1970), p. 574.
9 Quoted from H. Knittler, 'Das Verkehrswesen als Ausgangspunkt einer staatlichen Infrastrukturpolitik', in H. Matis, ed., *Von der Glückseligkeit des Staates. Staat, Wirtschaft und Gesellschaft in Österreich im Zeitalter des aufgeklärten Absolutismus* (Berlin, 1981), p. 141.
10 Schremmer, *Bayern*, pp. 575–6; B. Schultze, 'Die Anfänge des norddeutschen

Kunststraßenbaus', *BdLG* 84 (1938), pp. 220–6; on Württemberg see R. Walter, *Die Kommerzialisierung von Landwirtschaft und Gewerbe in Württemberg (1750–1850)* (St. Katharinen, 1990), pp. 57–9.

11 E. J. Häberle, 'Zur Bestimmung der Wirksamkeit merkantilistischer Außenwirtschaftspolitik. Eine elastizitätstheoretische Hypothese am Beispiel der bayerischen Zahlungsbilanzstatistik von 1765 bis 1799', *VSWG* 62 (1975), pp. 164–5; for details, Walter, *Kommerzialisierung*, pp. 67–71, 76–8; quotation from K. Beyrer, *Die Postkutschenreise* (Tübingen, 1985), p. 164.

12 K.-H. Manegold, 'Technik, Handelspolitik und Gesamtstaat. Brandenburgische Kanalbauten im 17. Jahrhundert', *Technikgeschichte*, 37 (1970), pp. 122–9; C. Degn, 'Die Herzogtümer im Gesamtstaat 1773–1830', in O. Klose, ed., *Geschichte Schleswig-Holsteins* (Neumünster, 1960), vi. pp. 199–204; W. Kliche, 'Die Schiffahrt auf der Ruhr und Lippe im achtzehnten Jahrhundert', *Zeitschrift des Bergischen Geschichtsvereins*, 37 (1904), pp. 1–178; F.-W. Henning, 'Standorte und Spezialisierung des Handels und des Transportwesens in der Mark Brandenburg um 1800', *Scripta Mercaturae*, 5 (1971), p. 33.

13 Albrecht, *Landesausbau*, pp. 46–54; F.-A. Kadell, *Die Hugenotten in Hessen-Kassel* (Darmstadt/Marburg, 1980), pp. 246–7, 262–3.

14 A. Dietz, *Frankfurter Handelsgeschichte* (4 vols, Frankfurt, 1910–1925), iii. p. 335; quotation from Beyrer, *Postkutschenreise*, p. 77.

15 B. Kuske, 'Die Rheinschiffahrt zwischen Köln und Düsseldorf vom 17. bis 19. Jahrhundert', *Beiträge zur Geschichte des Niederrheins*, 20 (1905), pp. 317–18; on the Main, see Dietz, *Handelsgeschichte*, iii. pp. 302–3; on the Elbe, see E. Mai, 'Die Magdeburger Elbschiffahrt im 18. Jahrhundert', in *Magdeburgs Wirtschaftsleben in der Vergangenheit* (Magdeburg, 1925), i. pp. 680–86.

16 B. Hagedorn, *Die Entwicklung der wichtigsten Schiffstypen bis ins 19. Jahrhunderts* (Berlin, 1914), pp. 114–22; K.-F. Olechnowitz, *Der Schiffbau der hansischen Spätzeit. Eine Untersuchung zur Sozial- und Wirtschaftsgeschichte der Hanse* (Weimar, 1960), pp. 12–14; F. Röhlk, *Schiffahrt und Handel zwischen Hamburg und den Niederlanden in der zweiten Hälfte des 18. und zu Beginn des 19. Jahrhunderts* (2 vols, Wiesbaden, 1973), i. p. 46.

17 Schremmer, *Bayern*, pp. 674–8; Dietz, *Handelsgeschichte*, iii. pp. 333–4; D. Ebeling, *Bürgertum und Pöbel. Wirtschaft und Gesellschaft Kölns im 18. Jahrhundert* (Cologne/Vienna, 1987), pp. 66–7, 76; H. Witthöft, 'Die Lüneburger Spedition. Zur Entwicklung des Warenverkehrs im Einzugsbereich von Hamburg und Lübeck', in K.-H. Manegold, ed., *Wissenschaft, Wirtschaft und Technik. Studien zur Geschichte. W. Treue zum 60. Geburtstag* (Munich, 1969), pp. 147–56; Henning, 'Standorte', pp. 176–7.

18 Kuske, 'Rheinschiffahrt', p. 341; W. Kresse, *Materialien zur Geschichte der Hamburger Handelsflotte 1765–1823* (Hamburg, 1966), pp. 38–52. See also T. Brück, *Korporationen der Schiffer und Bootsleute. Untersuchungen zu ihrer Entwicklung in Seestädten an der Nord- und Ostseeküste vom Ende des 15. bis zum Ende des 17. Jahrhunderts* (Weimar, 1994).

19 K. Blaschke, 'Elbschiffahrt und Elbzölle im 17. Jahrhundert', *HansGbl* 82 (1964), pp. 42–54; D. Ebeling, 'Rohstofferschließung im europäischen Handelssystem der frühen Neuzeit am Beispiel des rheinisch-niederländischen Holzhandels im 17./18. Jahrhundert', *Rheinische Vierteljahrsblätter*, 52 (1988), pp. 169–70.

20 Léon and Carrière, 'Appel', p. 180; Schremmer, *Bayern*, pp. 676–7, and Häberle, 'Bestimmung', pp. 164–7; see R. Walter, 'Merkantilistische Handelshemmnisse (im territorialen Vergleich) am Beispiel eines territorial relativ zersplitterten Gebietes', in H. Pohl, ed., *Die Auswirkung von Zöllen und an-*

deren Handelshemmnissen auf Wirtschaft und Gesellschaft vom Mittelalter bis zur Gegenwart (Stuttgart, 1987), pp. 93–101.

21 K. Gerteis, 'Das "Postkutschenzeitalter". Bedingungen der Kommunikation im 18. Jahrhundert', *Aufklärung*, 4 (1989), pp. 57–66; W. Behringer, *Thurn und Taxis. Die Geschichte ihrer Post und ihrer Unternehmen* (München, 1990), pp. 74–6, 95–8, 125–6. See also his research report in W. Behringer, 'Bausteine zu einer Geschichte der Kommunikation. Eine Sammelrezension zum Postjubiläum', *ZHF* 21 (1994), pp. 92–112.

22 J. Hoock and P. Jeannin, *Ars Mercatoria. Eine analytische Bibliographie*, ii: *1600–1700* (Paderborn, 1993); J. Kirchner, *Die Zeitschriften des deutschen Sprachgebietes bis 1900* (Stuttgart, 1969), i. pp. 152–60.

23 As an example, see T. Fox and P. Hertner, 'Marburg als Marktort im 18. Jahrhundert: Ein Beispiel für Stadt-Umland-Beziehungen im vorindustriellen Zeitalter', in E. Dettmering and R. Grenz, eds, *Marburger Geschichte. Rückblick auf die Stadtgeschichte in Einzelbeiträgen* (Marburg, 1980), pp. 323–44.

24 Schremmer, *Bayern*, pp. 608, 612–14; Albrecht, *Landesausbau*, p. 435; E. von Lehe, *Die Märkte Hamburgs von den Anfängen bis in die Neuzeit* (1st edn, 1911; Wiesbaden, 1966), p. 75; B. Roeck, *Bäcker, Brot und Getreide in Augsburg. Zur Geschichte des Bäckerhandwerks und zur Versorgungspolitik der Reichsstadt im Zeitalter des Dreißigjährigen Krieges* (Sigmaringen, 1987), p. 58. On Württemberg see Walter, *Kommerzialisierung*, pp. 92–6.

25 Albrecht, *Landesausbau*, pp. 428–33; on the Hamburger yearly markets, see von Lehe, *Märkte*, pp. 57–63.

26 W. P. Feldenkirchen, 'Der Handel der Stadt Köln im 18. Jahrhundert (1700–1814)', (Ph.D. dissertation, Univ. of Bonn, 1975), pp. 117–22; H. Wiese and J. Bölts, *Rinderhandel und Rinderhaltung im nordwesteuropäischen Küstengebiet vom 15. bis zum 19. Jahrhundert* (Stuttgart, 1966), pp. 35–9; E. Westermann, 'Forschungsaufgaben des internationalen Ochsenhandels aus mitteleuropäischer Sicht', in E. Westermann, ed., *Internationaler Ochsenhandel (1350–1750)* (Stuttgart, 1979), pp. 261–8.

27 M. Weber, *Wirtschaftsgeschichte. Abriß der universalen Sozial- und Wirtschaftsgeschichte* (Berlin, 1981), pp. 195–6, as well as Albrecht, *Landesausbau*, pp. 386–8; N. Brübach, *Die Reichsmessen von Frankfurt am Main, Leipzig und Braunschweig (14.-18. Jahrhundert)* (Stuttgart, 1994), pp. 65–390, 391–514; E. Hasse, *Geschichte der Leipziger Messen* (Leipzig, 1885), pp. 66–72; Dietz, *Handelsgeschichte*, i. pp. 90–93, and P. Beyer, 'Leipzig und Frankfurt am Main. Leipzigs Aufstieg zur ersten deutschen Messestadt', *JbRegG* 2 (1967), pp. 62–86; Walter, *Kommerzialisierung*, pp. 97–100.

28 S. Kühn, *Der Hirschberger Leinwand- und Schleierhandel von 1648–1806* (Breslau, 1938), pp. 24–32; J. Mooser, *Ländliche Klassengesellschaft 1770–1748. Bauern und Unterschichten, Landwirtschaft und Gewerbe im östlichen Westfalen* (Göttingen, 1984), p. 67–71; A. Flügel, *Kaufleute und Manufakturen in Bielefeld. Sozialer Wandel und wirtschaftliche Entwicklung im proto-industriellen Leinengewerbe von 1680 bis 1850* (Bielefeld, 1993), pp. 61–70.

29 O. Gönnenwein, *Das Stapel- und Niederlagerecht* (Weimar, 1939), pp. 187–230, 357–362 and *passim*; Feldenkirchen, *Handel*, pp. 22–6; C. Graf von Looz-Corswarem, *Das Finanzwesen der Stadt Cologne im 18. Jahrhundert. Beitrag zur Verwaltungsgeschichte einer Reichsstadt* (Cologne, 1978), p. 65–9, 102–11; E. Baasch, 'Die "Durchfuhr" in Lübeck. Ein Beitrag zur Geschichte der lübischen Handelspolitik im 17. und 18. Jahrhundert', *HansGbl* 13 (1907), pp. 109–52.

30 On the competition faced by the privileged markets on account of the rise of so-called 'Winkelmärkte' ('corner markets'), see, based on the example of the

grain trade, F. Göttmann, *Getreidemarkt am Bodensee. Raum – Wirtschaft – Politik – Gesellschaft (1650–1810)* (St. Katharinen, 1991), pp. 17–77.

31   J. Möser, *Sämtliche Werke* (Oldenburg, 1943), iv. pp. 26–7; Schremmer, *Bayern*, p. 595; J. Janczak, ed., *Śląsk w końcu XVIII wieku [Schlesien am Ende des 18. Jahrhunderts]*, 2 vols (Wrocław, 1976–1984), i. 2, p. 106, and ii. 2, p. 38; additionally, Albrecht, *Landesausbau*, pp. 396–428; W. Merkle, *Gewerbe und Handel der Stadt Ulm am Übergang der Reichsstadt an Bayern im Jahre 1802 und an das Königreich Württemberg im Jahre 1810* (St. Katharinen, 1988), pp. 173–94; on England see H.-C. Mui and L. H. Mui, *Shops and Shopkeeping in Eighteenth-Century England* (London, 1989), pp. 29–45.

32   H. Homburg, 'Warenanzeigen und Kundenwerbung in den "Leipziger Zeitungen" 1750–1800. Aspekte der inneren Marktbildung und der Kommerzialisierung des Alltagslebens', in D. Petzina, ed., *Zur Geschichte der Ökonomik der Privathaushalte* (Berlin, 1991), pp. 109–31.

33   G. D. Heumann, *Der Göttingische Ausruff von 1744*, ed. R. W. Brednich (Göttingen, 1987); on this widespread type of picture, see K. F. Beall, *Kaufrufe und Straßenhändler. Cries and Itinerant Trades. Eine Bibliographie. A Bibliography* (Hamburg, 1975).

34   H. Kahlert, *300 Jahre Schwarzwälder Uhrenindustrie* (Gernsbach, 1986), pp. 82–97, p. 83, also for the quotation; W. Reininghaus, 'Die Tödden und der Wanderhandel im 17. bis 19. Jahrhundert. Recker Beispiele', *Beiträge zur Geschichte der Gemeinde Recke*, 1 (1990), pp. 76–90; J. Augel, *Italienische Einwanderung und Wirtschaftstätigkeit in rheinischen Städten des 17. und 18. Jahrhunderts* (Bonn, 1971), pp. 189–205; see also the collected volume, W. Reininghaus, ed., *Wanderhandel in Europa* (Dortmund, 1993). A fundamental work is L. Fontaine, *Histoire du colportage en Europe, XVe–XIXe siècle* (Paris, 1993).

35   Möser, *Werke*, iv. p. 187.

36   E. Baasch, ed., *Quellen zur Geschichte von Hamburgs Handel und Schiffahrt im 17., 18. und 19. Jahrhundert* (Hamburg, 1910), p. 240, and concerning this L. Beutin, *Der deutsche Seehandel im Mittelmeergebiet bis zu den napoleonischen Kriegen* (Neumünster, 1933), pp. 86–7.

37   Braudel, *Civilisation*, ii. pp. 74–5; P. Jeannin, 'The Sea-borne and the Overland Trade Routes of Northern Europe in the XVIth and XVIIth Centuries', *JEEH* 11 (1982), p. 54; for France, pointing out some limitations, D. Margairaz, *Foires et marchés dans la France préindustrielle* (Paris, 1988), pp. 8–9, 101–39; on Leipzig, J. Reinhold, *Polen/Litauen auf den Leipziger Messen des 18. Jahrhunderts* (Weimar, 1971), pp. 3–27; Brübach, *Reichsmessen*, pp. 464–74.

38   Sombart, *Kapitalismus*, ii. pp. 488–93, and Braudel, *Civilisation*, ii. pp. 75–8.

39   G. Aubin and A. Kunze, *Leinenerzeugung und Leinenabsatz im östlichen Mitteldeutschland zur Zeit der Zunftkäufe. Ein Beitrag zur industriellen Kolonisation des deutschen Ostens* (Stuttgart, 1940), pp. 255–60; Ebeling, *Bürgertum*, pp. 66–7; E. Gothein, *Wirtschaftsgeschichte des Schwarzwaldes und der angrenzenden Landschaften* (Strasbourg, 1892) i. pp. 847–51, 855–63.

40   G. Seibold, *Die Viatis und Peller. Beiträge zur Geschichte ihrer Handelsgesellschaft* (Cologne/Vienna, 1977), pp. 321–58; Kühn, *Leinwand- und Schleierhandel*, pp. 25–32; H. Medick, 'Privilegiertes Handelskapital und "kleine Industrie". Produktion und Produktionsverhältnisse im Leinengewerbe des altwürttembergischen Oberamts Urach im 18. Jahrhundert', *Archiv für Sozialgeschichte*, 23 (1983), pp. 267–310.

41   H. Kellenbenz, *Unternehmerkräfte im Hamburger Spanien- und Portugalhandel 1590–1625* (Hamburg, 1954), pp. 327–8; G. S. Gramulla, *Handelsbeziehungen Kölner Kaufleute zwischen 1500 und 1650* (Cologne/Vienna, 1972), pp. 387–93; C. Meyer-Stoll, *Die lübeckische Kaufmannschaft des 17.*

Jahrhunderts unter wirtschafts- und sozialgeschichtlichen Aspekten (Frankfurt/Bern, 1989), pp. 114–15. The proportion of one-man businesses was 80.3 per cent in Nuremberg in 1621/24 and 92.0 per cent in Hamburg in 1619; that of family companies was 12.4 per cent and 5.4 per cent respectively; and that of companies which included non-family members was 7.0 per cent and 2.6 per cent respectively. Admittedly, the share of family companies in the turnover sold through the relevant banks was substantially higher: 31.1 per cent and 15.7 per cent respectively; that of companies which included non-family members was 20.9 per cent and 7.3 per cent respectively; and one-man businesses accounted for 47.4 per cent and 77.0 per cent respectively. See L. F. Peters, *Der Handel Nürnbergs am Anfang des Dreißigjährigen Krieges. Strukturkomponenten, Unternehmen und Unternehmer* (Stuttgart, 1994), pp. 78–88.

42 Kresse, *Materialien*, pp. 38, 40; for the period around 1600, in which merchant shippers still predominated, see Kellenbenz, *Unternehmerkräfte*, pp. 313–16.

43 Kellenbenz, *Unternehmerkräfte*, pp. 323–6; M. Reißmann, *Die hamburgische Kaufmannschaft des 17. Jahrhunderts in sozialgeschichtlicher Sicht* (Hamburg, 1975), pp. 91–4, 126; Meyer-Stoll, *Kaufmannschaft*, pp. 109–11; R. Prange, *Die bremische Kaufmannschaft des 16. und 17. Jahrhunderts in sozialgeschichtlicher Betrachtung* (Bremen, 1963), pp. 44–5.

44 E. Schremmer, 'Über "stabiles Geld". Eine wirtschaftshistorische Sicht', in E. Schremmer, ed., *Geld und Währung vom 16. Jahrhundert bis zur Gegenwart* (Stuttgart, 1993), pp. 10–19; R. Metz, *Geld, Währung und Preisentwicklung. Der Niederrheinraum im europäischen Vergleich 1350–1800* (Frankfurt, 1990), pp. 31–41, 95–199, 261–99. On German monetary history, see esp. H. Rittmann, *Deutsche Geldgeschichte 1484–1914* (Munich, 1975); in addition, see B. Sprenger, *Das Geld der Deutschen. Geldgeschichte Deutschlands von den Anfängen bis zur Gegenwart* (Paderborn, 1991); see also M. North, *Das Geld und seine Geschichte. Vom Mittelalter bis zur Gegenwart* (Munich, 1994), pp. 101–7, 126–8 (here also additional bibliographical references). On exchange relationships, see J. Schneider, O. Schwarzer, and P. Schnelzer, *Statistik der Geld- und Wechselkurse in Deutschland und im Ostseeraum (18. und 19. Jahrhundert)* (St. Katharinen, 1993); additionally, M. A. Denzel, ed., *Europäische Wechselkurse vor 1620* (Stuttgart, 1995); J. Schneider, O. Schwarzer, and M. A. Denzel, eds, *Europäische Wechselkurse im 17. Jahrhundert* (Stuttgart, 1994); J. Schneider, O. Schwarzer, F. Zellfelder, and M. A. Denzel, eds, *Geld und Währungen in Europa im 18. Jahrhundert* (Stuttgart, 1992); J. Schneider, O. Schwarzer, and Friedrich Zellfelder, eds, *Europäische und nordamerikanische Devisenkurse 1777–1914* (3 vols, Stuttgart, 1991); M. A. Denzel, ed., *Geld- und Wechselkurse der deutschen Messeplätze Leipzig und Braunschweig (18. Jahrhundert bis 1823)* (Stuttgart, 1994).

45 M. Edlin-Thième, *Studien zur Geschichte des Münchner Handelsstandes im 18. Jahrhundert* (Stuttgart, 1969), pp. 87, 122–3.

46 See, *inter alia*, Gramulla, *Handelsbeziehungen*, pp. 396–8; in general, M. A. Denzel, *La Practica Della Cambiatura. Europäischer Zahlungsverkehr vom 14. bis zum 17. Jahrhundert* (Stuttgart, 1994), *passim* and (for the seventeenth century) pp. 397–482; on the limited role of the bill of exchange at the beginning of the seventeenth century, see Peters, *Handel*, pp. 114–23; the quotation is from C. Carrière, *Négociants marseillais au XVIIIe siècle. Contribution à l'étude des économies maritimes* (Marseille, 1973), p. 874.

47 E. Klein, *Von den Anfängen bis zum Ende des Alten Reiches, 1806* (Deutsche Bankengeschichte vol. 1) (Frankfurt, 1982), pp. 166–92, 245–83; Brübach, *Reichsmessen*, pp. 281–340; F. Zellfelder, *Das Kundennetz des Bankhauses Gebrüder Bethmann (1738–1816)* (Stuttgart, 1994), pp. 25–37, 138–42; on the

history of the stock exchanges, see H. Pohl, ed., *Deutsche Börsengeschichte* (Frankfurt, 1992), pp. 13–132.

48   H. Pohl *et al.*, 'Wirtschaftsgeschichte Kölns im 18. und beginnenden 19. Jahrhundert', in H. Kellenbenz, ed., *Zwei Jahrtausende Kölner Wirtschaft* (2 vols., Cologne, 1975), ii. p. 44; Feldenkirchen, *Handel*, p. 97; S. Gramulla, 'Wirtschaftsgeschichte Kölns im 17. Jahrhundert', in Kellenbenz, ed., *Kölner Wirtschaft*, i. pp. 459, 461; Wiese and Bölts, *Rinderhandel*, p. 33.

49   Wiese and Bölts, *Rinderhandel*, pp. 55–78; E. L. Petersen, 'Production and Trade in Oxen 1450–1750: Denmark', in Westermann, ed., *Ochsenhandel*, pp. 144–6; I. N. Kiss, 'Die Bedeutung der ungarischen Viehzucht für Ungarn und Mitteleuropa vom 16. bis zum 18. Jahrhundert', in Westermann, ed., *Ochsenhandel*, pp. 108–9; J. Baszanowski, 'Ochsenzuchtgebiete und Ochsenausfuhr aus Polen vom 16. bis zum 18. Jahrhundert', in Westermann, ed., *Ochsenhandel*, pp. 130–3.

50   H. Harnisch, 'Die Gutsherrschaft in Brandenburg. Ergebnisse und Probleme', *JbWG* 4 (1969), p. 123; W. S. Unger, 'De sonttabellen', *Tijdschrift voor geschiedenis*, 41 (1926), pp. 154–5; H. C. Johansen, *Shipping and Trade between the Baltic area and Western Europe 1784–95* (Odense, 1983), p. 104.

51   M. Kutz, *Deutschlands Außenhandel von der Französischen Revolution bis zur Gründung des Zollvereins* (Wiesbaden, 1974), pp. 40–1; Schremmer, *Bayern*, p. 647; Göttmann, *Getreidemarkt*, pp. 194–201, 253–61, 332–8, 358–62; W. Naudé and A. Skalweit, *Die Getreidehandelspolitik und Kriegsmagazinverwaltung Preußens 1740–1756* (Berlin, 1910), p. 64.

52   See the survey in Kellenbenz, *Wirtschaftsgeschichte*, i. pp. 247–57, 327–40 and W. Zorn, 'Schwerpunkte der deutschen Ausfuhrindustrie im 18. Jahrhundert', *Jahrbücher für Nationalökonomie und Statistik*, 173 (1961), pp. 427–45. On the process as such, see P. Kriedte, H. Medick, and J. Schlumbohm, *Industrialization before Industrialization: Rural Industry in the Genesis of Capitalism* (Cambridge, 1981), pp. 21–3, and P. Kriedte, 'Die Stadt im Prozeß der europäischen Proto-Industrialisierung', *Die alte Stadt*, 9 (1982), pp. 19–51.

53   Möser, *Werke*, iv. pp. 185–7.

54   The basis for these and the following figures is the region in question, not the totality of the individual German states: thus the exports for Silesia, for example, also include goods sold into other Prussian provinces.

55   C. L. P. Hüpeden, 'Vom Leinenhandel in Hessen', in *A. L. Schlözer, Staats-Anzeigen*, 41 (1789), p. 3; 'Nachweisung, wie viel leinene Ware von 1748/9 bis 1789/90 in Schlesien, und zwar in beyden Cammer-Departements außer Landes versandt worden', *Schlesische Provinzialblätter*, 31 (1800), pp. 9–12; Kriedte, Medick, and Schlumbohm, *Industrialization*, p. 36.

56   Aubin and Kunze, *Leinenerzeugung*, pp. 2–3, 137–9, 172–3; W. Zorn, 'Schwerpunkte', pp. 427–31.

57   F.-W. Henning, 'Die Wirtschaftsstruktur mitteleuropäischer Gebiete an der Wende zum 19. Jahrhundert unter besonderer Berücksichtigung des gewerblichen Bereichs', in W. Fischer, ed., *Beiträge zu Wirtschaftswachstum und Wirtschaftsstruktur im 16. und 19. Jahrhundert* (Berlin, 1971), pp. 118–21; Schremmer, *Bayern*, pp. 649–51 and Table 1.

58   Table 4.1 and K.-H. Kaufhold, 'Schwerpunkte des preußischen Exportgewerbes um 1800', in F. Matis and J. Riedmann, eds, *Exportgewerbe und Außenhandel vor der Industriellen Revolution. Festschrift für G. Zwanowetz anläßlich der Vollendung des 65. Geburtstages* (Innsbruck, 1984), pp. 245–6, 249. The crisis which early set in in Prussian and German foreign trade had as a consequence that around 1830 only *c.* 22 per cent of German exports consisted of finished goods (Kutz, *Außenhandel*, p. 366).

59   S. Ciriacono, 'Silk Manufacturing in France and Italy: Two Models

Compared', *JEEH* 10 (1981), pp. 167–99; C. Pallach, *Materielle Kultur und Mentalitäten im 18. Jahrhundert. Wirtschaftliche Entwicklung und politisch-sozialer Funktionswandel des Luxus in Frankreich und im Alten Reich am Ende des Ancien Régime* (München, 1987), pp. 31–40; W.-R. Baumann, *The Merchant Adventurers and the Continental Cloth-Trade (1560s–1620s)* (Berlin/New York, 1990), pp. 7–18, 137–43, 205–16, 309–15.

60   Ebeling, 'Rohstofferschließung', pp. 160–70; D. Ebeling, *Der Holländer-Holzhandel in den Rheinlanden. Zu den Handelsbeziehungen zwischen den Niederlanden und dem westlichen Deutschland im 17. und 18. Jahrhundert* (Stuttgart, 1992), pp. 72–95; for the 16th cent., see the discussion in R. Gascon, *Grand commerce et vie urbaine au XVIᵉ siècle. Lyon et ses marchands (environs de 1520–environs de 1580)* (Paris, 1971), p. 121.

61   N. Steensgard, *The Asian Trade Revolution of the Seventeenth Century: The East India Companies and the Decline of the Caravan Trade* (Chicago, 1973), pp. 155–64, and in addition, C. H. H. Wake, 'The Changing Pattern of Europe's Pepper and Spice Imports, ca. 1400–1700', *JEEH* 8 (1979), pp. 386–7, 394–5; P. Kriedte, 'Vom Großhändler zum Detaillisten. Der Handel mit "Kolonialwaren" im 17. und 18. Jahrhundert', *JbWG* 1(1994), pp. 19–31; Schremmer, *Bayern*, pp. 651–2.

62   H. Kellenbenz, 'Der deutsche Außenhandel gegen Ausgang des 18. Jahrhunderts', in F. Lütge, ed., *Die wirtschaftliche Situation in Deutschland und Österreich um die Wende vom 18. zum 19. Jahrhundert* (Stuttgart, 1964), p. 53; Kutz, *Außenhandel*, p. 364.

63   Peters, *Handel*, pp. 64–6, 89–107, 111–23.

64   B. Roeck, *Eine Stadt in Krieg und Frieden. Studien zur Geschichte der Reichsstadt Augsburg zwischen Kalenderstreit und Parität* (Göttingen, 1989), p. 941; W. Zorn, *Handels- und Industriegeschichte Bayerisch-Schwabens. Wirtschafts-, Sozial- und Kulturgeschichte des schwäbischen Unternehmertums* (Augsburg, 1961), pp. 14–70; P. Fassl, 'Wirtschaft, Handel und Sozialstruktur 1648–1806', in G. Gottlieb *et al.*, eds, *Geschichte der Stadt Augsburg von der Römerzeit bis zur Gegenwart* (Stuttgart, 1984), pp. 470–2, here also the quotation.

65   S. Gramulla, 'Nürnberger Kaufleute im Italienhandel zwischen 1720 und 1740', *Mitteilungen des Vereins für Geschichte der Stadt Nürnberg*, 73 (1986), pp. 131–7.

66   Gramulla, 'Wirtschaftsgeschichte', pp. 473–6; Pohl *et al.*, 'Wirtschaftsgeschichte', pp. 72–96.

67   H. Schilling, *Niederländische Exulanten im 16. Jahrhundert. Ihre Stellung im Sozialgefüge und im religiösen Leben deutscher und englischer Städte* (Gütersloh, 1972), pp. 52–9; Dietz, *Handelsgeschichte*, i. pp. 68–101, ii. pp. 11–73; Brübach, *Reichsmessen*, pp. 221–9.

68   Beyer, 'Leipzig', pp. 62–80; Brübach, *Reichsmessen*, pp. 464–73, 487–514; Reinhold, *Polen/Litauen*, pp. 10–27 and *passim*; K.-F. Olechnowitz, *Handel und Seeschiffahrt der späten Hanse* (Weimar, 1965), p. 119; Dietz, *Handelsgeschichte*, ii. p. 274.

69   P. Jeannin, 'Le commerce de Lubeck aux environs de 1580', *Annales E.S.C.*, 16 (1961), p. 52; P. Jeannin, *Trade*, pp. 45–7; E. Harder-Gersdorf, 'Lübeck, Danzig und Riga. Ein Beitrag zur Frage der Handelskonjunktur im Ostseeraum am Ende des 17. Jahrhunderts', *HansGbl* 96 (1978), pp. 124–38; P. Dollinger, *Die Hanse* (Stuttgart, 1966), pp. 444–68; K. Fritze, J. Schildhauer, and W. Stark, *Die Geschichte der Hanse* (Berlin, 1974), pp. 213–21.

70   R. Ehrenberg, *Hamburg und England im Zeitalter der Königin Elisabeth* (Jena, 1896), pp. 76–100, 113–30, and 226–30; Schilling, *Exulanten*, pp. 77–79; H. Kellenbenz, *Sephardim an der unteren Elbe. Ihre wirtschaftliche und politische*

Bedeutung vom Ende des 16. bis zum Beginn des 18. Jahrhunderts (Wiesbaden, 1958), pp. 25–45, 104–55; H. Kellenbenz, 'Der Pfeffermarkt um 1600 und die Hansestädte', *HansGbl* 74 (1956), pp. 35–6; J. I. Israel, *Dutch Primacy in World Trade, 1585–1740* (Oxford, 1989), pp. 33–4.

71   P. Jeannin, 'Zur Geschichte der Hamburger Handelsflotte am Ende des 17. Jahrhunderts. Eine Schiffsliste von 1674', *Zeitschrift des Vereins für hamburgische Geschichte*, 57 (1971), p. 71; Kresse, *Materialien*, p. 67; Röhlk, *Schiffahrt*, i. pp. 46–8, 54–72; H. Pohl, *Die Beziehungen Hamburgs zu Spanien und dem spanischen Amerika in der Zeit von 1740 bis 1806* (Wiesbaden, 1963), pp. 114–22, 235–62, 310; P. Butel, *Les négociants bordelais, l'Europe et les Iles au XVIIIᵉ siècle* (Paris, 1974), pp. 48–50, 64–7; L. Becker, *Die Geschichte des Hamburger Zuckerhandels (Von seinen Anfängen bis zum Weltkrieg)* (Rostock, 1933), pp. 5–69.

72   H. Müller, 'Untersuchungen zur bremischen Reederei im 17. Jahrhundert', *Bremisches Jahrbuch*, 53 (1975), pp. 94, 127–8, 134; H. J. von Witzendorff, 'Beiträge zur bremischen Handelsgeschichte in der zweiten Hälfte des 18. Jahrhunderts', *Bremisches Jahrbuch*, 43 (1951), p. 387; Butel, *Négociants*, p. 50; H. Müller, 'Aus den Anfängen des Kaffeehandels an der Weser', in D. Brosius *et al.*, eds, *Geschichte in der Region. Zum 65. Geburtstag von Heinrich Schmidt* (Hannover, 1993), pp. 292, 295–6.

73   Jeannin, 'Hansestädte', pp. 56–8, 72–3 (here recalculated).

74   H. Haan, 'Prosperität und Dreißigjähriger Krieg', *GG* 7 (1981), pp. 91–118; P. Kriedte, *Peasants, Landlords and Merchant Capitalists: Europe and the World Economy, 1500–1800* (Leamington Spa, 1983), pp. 91–9.

75   D. Ebeling and F. Irsigler, eds, *Getreideumsatz, Getreide- und Brotpreise in Köln 1368–1797* (2 vols, Cologne/Vienna, 1976), i. pp. xlvi–liii, 666–89; J. A. Faber, 'The Decline of the Baltic Grain Trade in the Second Half of the Seventeenth Century', *Acta Historiae Neerlandica*, 1 (1966), p. 118; Roeck, *Bäcker*, pp. 79, 243.

76   W. Vogel, 'Handelskonjunkturen und Wirtschaftskrisen in ihrer Auswirkung auf den Seehandel der Hansestädte 1560–1806', *HansGbl* 74 (1956), pp. 59–60; W. Vogel, 'Beiträge zur Statistik der deutschen Seeschiffahrt im 17. und 18. Jahrhundert', *HansGbl* 53 (1928), pp. 135–7, 141–4; H. J. von Witzendorff, 'Bremens Handel im 16. und 17. Jahrhundert', *Bremisches Jahrbuch*, 44 (1955), pp. 130–6; on the decline of the Bremen trading fleet in the second half of the 17th cent., see Müller, 'Untersuchungen', pp. 111–33.

77   Reinhold, *Polen/Litauen*, p. 173; Reinhold, 'Nachweisung', pp. 9–12; Röhlk, *Schiffahrt*, i. pp. 168–83; J. de Vries, *De economische achteruitgang der Republiek in de achttiende eeuw* (Leiden, 1968), p. 38; E. Boody Schumpeter, *English Overseas Trade Statistics 1697–1808* (Oxford, 1960), pp. 17–18.

78   Kriedte, Medick, and Schlumbohm, *Industrialization*, pp. 117–25; Reinhold, *Polen/Litauen*, pp. 51–64; Vogel, 'Handelskonjunkturen', pp. 60, 63; Kühn, *Leinwand- und Schleierhandel*, pp. 51–6.

79   M. Bouniatian, *Wirtschaftskrisen und Überkapitalisation. Eine Untersuchung über die Erscheinungsformen und Ursachen der periodischen Wirtschaftskrisen* (Munich, 1908), pp. 30–7; Kriedte, Medick, and Schlumbohm, *Industrialization*, pp. 121–2; W. Abel, *Hungerkrisen im vorindustriellen Europa. Versuch einer Synopsis* (Hamburg/Berlin, 1974), pp. 198, 263–4; S. Skalweit, *Die Berliner Wirtschaftskrise von 1763 und ihre Hintergründe* (Stuttgart/Berlin, 1937), pp. 28–75; W. O. Henderson, 'The Berlin Commercial Crisis of 1763', *EcHR* 2nd ser. 15 (1962–3), pp. 89–102; J. G. Büsch, *Geschichtliche Beurtheilung der großen Handelsverwirrung im Jahre 1799* (Hamburg, 1858), pp. 1–91; von Witzendorff, 'Beiträge', pp. 372–4.

80   See D. C. Coleman, ed., *Revisions in Mercantilism* (London, 1969); P. Deyon,

Le mercantilisme (Paris, 1969); L. Magnusson, *Mercantilism: The Shaping of an Economic Language* (London, 1994); on the regulation of the grain trade, which dated back to earlier periods, see Göttmann, *Getreidemarkt*, pp. 78–165.

81   G. B. Volz, ed., *Die politischen Testamente Friedrichs des Großen* (Berlin, 1920), p. 24; H. Krüger, *Zur Geschichte der Manufakturen und der Manufakturarbeiter in Preußen. Die mittleren Provinzen in der zweiten Hälfte des 18. Jahrhunderts* (Berlin, 1958), pp. 92–111; I. Mittenzwei, *Preußen nach dem Siebenjährigen Krieg. Auseinandersetzungen zwischen Bürgertum und Staat um die Wirtschaftspolitik* (Berlin, 1979), pp. 102–126.

82   Reinhold, *Polen/Litauen*, pp. 56–7; H. Schlechte, ed., *Die Staatsreform im Kursachsen 1762–1763. Quellen zum kursächsischen Rétablissement nach dem Siebenjährigen Kriege* (Berlin, 1958), pp. 38–42, 190.

83   Mittenzwei, *Preußen*, pp. 14–51.

84   Marx, *Kapital* iii. pp. 344, 347.

85   R. Romano, 'Per una valutazione della flotta mercantile europea alla fine del secolo XVIII', *Studi in onore di A. Fanfani* (Milano, 1962), v. p. 578.

Translated by Sheilagh Ogilvie.

5

Social structure

OLAF MÖRKE

Analysing changes in social structure in the early modern period means identifying the factors which determined the concrete shape of coexistence among people. The individual is part of a multiplicity of groups which belong together because of their common position in a concrete political and social context, whose outline the historian distils out of the complexity of the context of life. Two main fields lie at the focus of our attention, each of which interests us in itself, but the relationship between which also illuminates essential features specific to the early modern period: they are the economy and politics. The autonomy of social and cultural institutions such as the church, which nowadays we take for granted, did not yet exist. A spectacular example of this is provided by the unity between the policies of the early modern state on one hand and ecclesiastical and confessional developments on the other. Indeed, this becomes a symbol of the first large sub-period during the time-span we are interested in, that of the 'confessional age'.[1] From the later middle ages on, the political primacy of the territorial state began to prevail against social groups and structures still characterized by strong elements of self-organization. In the latter, the 'corporative' component held equal rights with the 'political' or 'governmental' component – indeed, in theory, even greater rights: from the village community, through the citizenries of the small towns and large cities, right up to the Empire itself, as a 'corporative legal union based on history and religion',[2] a community of the temporal and ecclesiastical princes and lords, as well as – to a lesser extent – the Free Imperial Cities. The increasing dominance of the 'governmental' component in the self-image of this political and social organization fundamentally touched upon the whole internal framework of society, and thus on social structure. This change, which found its expression in the early modern growth of the state, came about to a considerable extent in the sixteenth and seventeenth centuries.[3]

Characteristic of the social organization of the *ancien régime* is the close interlocking between these two fields of economy and politics, which is much more evident in Germany than, for example, in England. Guilds and corporations, as politically sanctioned organizational elements in both economy and everyday coexistence, were still dominant in structuring the social shape of German towns for much of the eighteenth century, and survived into the nineteenth century. In the German countryside, the economic organization of agrarian society was fundamentally shaped by the political and legal relationships between peasants and landlords. These, too, changed fundamentally only at the beginning of the nineteenth century. In addition, there was a feature specific to the political shape of the Holy Roman Empire of the German Nation, which was partly responsible for the heterogeneity in the relationship within German social structure between economic factors on one hand and political and legal factors on the other: this was the fragmentation of Germany into hundreds of territories.[4] The structural particularism of the Empire made it more possible for certain social structures to survive; the intentionally interventionist policy of the early modern state was just as much responsible for the shape of these social structures as was the apparent internal dynamic of economic and social processes, if not even more so.

The pronounced political fragmentation of the Empire, and the relationship between economic development and the purposive policies of the early modern state, will repeatedly interest us in this chapter as the key elements in social change. They mark out the framework for a change in social structure accomplished within the boundaries of a society of corporate orders or social estates.

This concept must first be explained. A society organized on the principle of 'corporate orders' or 'social estates' is divided hierarchically into legally and socially exclusive groups according to social origins. 'A social estate was distinguished by specific behavioural norms, a corporate honour, and a specific corporate culture.'[5] Contemporaries saw society as essentially divided into three or four social estates: the nobility, sub-divided into the higher and lower nobility; the clergy, although after the Reformation this was a fully valid social estate only in the Catholic territories; the urban citizen; and the peasant inhabitant of the countryside. These divisions document an idea of society which is found in pre-modern Europe more widely: that of an immobile hierarchy, in which each social estate was assigned a firmly defined social function. Admittedly, social practice fundamentally collided with this static picture, permitting processes of restructuring which undermined the system of social estates and dissolved it from within.

Nevertheless, the idea of a stable society organized into social estates determined the political constitution of the Empire until its end in 1806. Meetings of the estates – the Imperial Diet on the level of the Empire (meeting permanently from 1663 on), and the territorial diets in the territories – retained their importance as one component of a dual political system, whose other component consisted of a 'monocratic' element: the Emperor in the Empire and the princes in the territories. A distinction was drawn between the 'governing estates' – the princes in the Empire, the nobility in the territories, the 'patriciate'[6] in the towns – and the 'governed estates'. In practice, however, in the period of interest to us, this 'dualism between the monocratic holders of governmental authority and the estates of government'[7] became fundamentally differentiated. On the level of the Empire, the increasing constitutional strength of the territorial princes led the 'social estates' component to become increasingly dominant over the 'monocratic' component. In this way, Germany differed fundamentally from the centralized state pattern of its great neighbour and political rival, France. But it also differed, just as fundamentally, from the political structure of England, where the parliamentary delegates were not, as in Germany, representatives of independent states within a loose Imperial union whose cohesion was increasingly threatened in the late seventeenth and eighteenth centuries by the internecine rivalry among the larger German territories.[8]

Quite the opposite development took place inside a number of the German territories themselves. The influence of the diets, and thus of the nobility as the territorial 'governing estate', declined in favour of an expanding princely power. This led to fundamental changes in the composition of the territorial political élites. These will be of interest to us because, although in principle society continued to be structured according to social estates, the transformation which accompanied the growth of the early modern state in Germany was so deep-reaching that it became less and less possible to maintain the basic principle of the existence of social estates, the immutability of the social status into which the individual was born. In a long-term process, a social climate was created which made this change appear acceptable to contemporaries. These changes penetrated all levels of the political and social constitution, from the political élites, through the relationships between people working in agriculture and industry, down to what has been described as the rise of the modern family. Long-term evolution became the hallmark of social change in Germany.

At latest in the eighteenth century, an ever-increasing portion of the population could no longer be classified within the schema of social estates. A basic problem in evaluating this process is the question of whether it led to the development of a 'class society'. In a class society, social hierarchy is no longer manifested in legally fixed distinctions between social estates. Individuals similar as far as their natural rights are concerned attain their place in the hierarchy of the class society through their position in the economic process. For Marxist theory, as is well-known, command over the means of production is the key criterion for locating a social group in the class hierarchy. This principle is supposed to have attained its greatest extent only in the antagonism between the proletarian, who possesses solely his own labour power, and the capitalist, who has exclusive power over the means of production: that is, in 'capitalism'. For 'pre-capitalist' social formations, this concept encounters definitional difficulties, because in such social formations no economic or social group is completely divorced from access to or ownership of the means of production. A more flexible concept of classes, better suited for analyzing social development in the early modern period, was sketched out by Max Weber.[9] We will pull out one core aspect of his very broadly conceived concept of class, which views social differentiation as arising from differences in opportunities to exploit property on the market. This can take place through possession not only of material goods, but also of special skills for which there exists a market demand.[10] This assigns a high valuation to non-material goods, such as competence in legal studies or technical expertise, which the early modern state needed for setting up its administration and improving national technical and economic infrastructure. Indeed, precisely in this area, a social system predominantly organized according to social estates manifests massive strains. This will be discussed in greater detail presently. Here let us first of all emphasize the following: in a class society, the ability to perform on the market rather than the privileges of birth determine the social position of an individual or a group. The complete development of a class society, however, ultimately depends on the prevalence of modern capitalistic market relationships:

> The market's capacities for social organization show that in the new 'economic society', the economic system, which has differentiated itself out, tends to predominate.... To designate pre-industrial social strata, it is therefore desirable to retain a special term, such as that of the social estate, since it provides a reminder of the altogether different social circumstances prevailing in a period in which the economy was more firmly than at any later period bound into a socio-cultural context, instead of being subordinated to society in the form of market society.[11]

This provides a definition of the two poles of social estate and class, between which social change oscillated from the sixteenth century to the end of the eighteenth.

The concrete developments in early modern German society structure will be described on the basis of this conceptual framework. The hierarchy of social estates, which until long into the early modern period – to some extent until well into the nineteenth century – was recognized as the natural organizational criterion for social relations, serves as a point of departure for the argument. Through the division of the Empire into a multiplicity of territories varying greatly in size, constitution, and economic structure, the apparently very simple ideal schema of this hierarchy became highly differentiated. The simultaneous co-existence of a variety of forms and stages of development in political, social, and economic constitutions is a hallmark of German development. In this chapter, however, it will only be possible to make a first approach to discussing them.

However, several large spatial areas can be distinguished whose different structures were based on medieval traditions. First of all there were the

German areas east of the Elbe, which only moved into the field of force of the Empire and the cultural sphere of central and western Europe in the course of the colonization movement of the high middle ages. These areas included the core lands of the later Brandenburg-Prussian state, one of the European great powers of the eighteenth century. With *Gutswirtschaft* (the eastern German manorial system, characterized by strong landlord powers, large demesne farms, peasant labour-services, and strong bonds of serfdom), this relatively thinly settled area which was lacking in larger towns developed an agrarian constitution fundamentally distinct from *Grundherrschaft* (the western German manorial system, characterized by much weaker landlord powers, insignificant demesne farming, money rents rather than labour services, and weak or non-existent bonds of serfdom); this distinction is discussed in detail in Chapter 3.

The East and North-East of the Empire shared basic traits of state structure with the North-West. These areas were characterized by the presence of large princely territorial states, although in the West lay the archbishopric of Cologne and the prince-bishopric of Münster, two of the most important ecclesiastical territories of the Empire.[12] The cities in these areas of the Empire belonged to the territorial states, with the exception of a very few Free and Imperial Cities such as Lübeck, Hamburg, Bremen, and Dortmund. However, several of the larger territorial cities, such as the main Welfian centres of Lüneburg, Braunschweig, and Göttingen, were in the sixteenth century still the type of autonomous territorial city in which the citizens themselves guided the city's destiny, largely free from princely influence.[13] Like the Imperial Cities, the autonomous territorial cities were also run by a traditional type of urban *Bürger* (burgher, citizen), for whom the urban freedom of the later middle ages stood at the top of the collective scale of values.[14] The pressure exerted by princes on the autonomy of these cities from the sixteenth century on ultimately led to their integration into the early modern state in the seventeenth and eighteenth centuries, which forced the self-image of their citizens to begin to change. These once-autonomous territorial cities played an important role in the relocation of the political and social position of the former 'urban' citizen as a 'territorial' citizen.

Characteristic of the political and social shape of southern Germany was its anachronistic small-scale nature. The overwhelming majority of the Imperial Cities lay in this region, from Augsburg, the trading and banking metropolis of the sixteenth century, to Bopfingen, which in 1800 had all of 2,000 inhabitants, and Buchau am Federsee, the smallest Imperial City of Upper Swabia. An additional relic of late-medieval 'state organization' was represented by the many small territories of Free Imperial Knights, subject directly to the Emperor, in the Swabian-Franconian and Middle Rhine areas.[15] What linked most of the Imperial Cities with the Free Imperial Knightage was their orientation around one of the two traditional components of the Old Empire, the monarchical power of the Emperor. Along with the latter, however, they fell behind in political development in the course of the sixteenth and seventeenth centuries. The territories of the Imperial Cities and of the Free Imperial Knights could not develop into foci of social change, but instead became an example of backwardness. Nevertheless, even in the eighteenth century they remained an important component of the political and social reality of Germany. But one of the most important territories of the Empire, Bavaria, also lay in the South; until the mid-eighteenth century, Bavaria was sometimes in a position to play an autonomous political role alongside its great neighbour, Austria and the Imperial House of Habsburg, one repeatedly characterized by political reliance on the classic opponent of the Habsburgs, the French king. Even though Bavaria's attempt to act as a great power in the Empire alongside the Habsburgs and Brandenburg-Prussia ultimately failed wretchedly, nevertheless Bavaria experienced the dynamic growth of the early modern state in the seventeenth century as did hardly any other German territory. From the second half of the seventeenth century on, Bavarian economic policy manifested distinct mercantilist features, and an efficient governmental administration secured the country for the interventionist policies of princely absolutism.[16]

The nobility

The division of the Empire into clearly distinct political and social spaces, which has been briefly described here, influenced the extent and nature of social change. This is emphasized by the concentration into the German South of the Free Imperial Knights and other lords subject directly to the Emperor. They represented a type of nobility which was a relic of a notion of the Empire based on personal relations of dependency between feudal lord and vassal, dating from the high and later middle ages. As retainers of the Emperor in the sixteenth century, they still constituted an important counter-pole to the expanding claims of the larger territorial states to exercise political dominance in the Empire. In the seventeenth century, they provided a large proportion of the Habsburg bureaucracy. A very small proportion of the Imperial minor nobility accomplished the leap into the ranks of the powerful Imperial princes through gaining sovereignty over one or more of the Catholic ecclesiastical territories as bishops or archbishops. Thus the Franconian family of Free Imperial Knights, the Schönborns, provided archbishops of Mainz, Würzburg, and Bamberg from the mid-seventeenth until the mid-eighteenth century, thereby rising into the ranks of the most influential princes of the Empire.[17] But this was hardly more than an arabesque in the complicated lattice-work formed by the political and social importance of the minor nobility in early modern Germany. In so far as it did not manage to make the transition to leadership of an ecclesiastical territory or into the Habsburg administration, it led a marginalized existence until the end of the Old Empire, without any significance for the process of social change.

A similar transition was also undergone by considerable portions of the nobility not immediately subject to the Emperor in the large territories, into the service of the early modern state, or of the princely territorial lord as its personal incarnation. The regional lower nobility, as an autonomous political power below the level of the territorial state (which was becoming centralized in the power of the princes), became just as marginalized as did large portions of the Free Imperial minor nobility in the course of the seventeenth and eighteenth centuries. However, they did have one opportunity: that of transition into the ranks of the higher clergy, where – for instance, in a cathedral chapter – they might become a powerful social estate in an ecclesiastical territory.[18]

The unity of the nobility as a 'governing estate', which still survived in political and social practice and above all in ideology at the beginning of the early modern period in the late fifteenth and in the sixteenth century, was dissolved in the seventeenth and eighteenth centuries. Its shift, on one hand, into the service of the House of Habsburg which represented the Empire as a whole, and on the other into the service of the great territorial lords, was a sign of a fundamental process of social change, which severed most of the nobility from their unified social estate, integrating them into a changed political and social system as a 'functional élite'.

One characteristic of this system was the changed function of the prince. In the larger temporal territories he seceded from the community of his fellow members of the social estate of the nobility, and became 'ruler' over a state whose population groups, although they continued to be differentiated from one another according to the criteria typical of social estates, namely descent, reputation, and heterogeneous legal position, were involved in a process of equalization *vis-à-vis* the prince: they were increasingly becoming elements in a unified mass of subjects. Admittedly, it was well into the nineteenth century before this process reached its culmination. However, the fact that it was already strongly in progress in the seventeenth century is an important indication of the gradual path, below the level of the revolutions undergone by other European countries, by which social change was accomplished in Germany. The functional integration of the nobility into the territorial state enabled it to survive and retain its privileged position in Germany until well into the nineteenth century; indeed, until the beginning of the twentieth.

In this context it is useful to survey the development of the noble estate in Brandenburg-Prussia; not because this state was typical of early modern German territories, but because of its long-term political success. Its development into a European great power in the eighteenth century has already been mentioned. Beyond this, political and social structures developed there which in the nineteenth century left their imprint on a Germany which was to develop into an authoritarian nation-state created in 1871 through a 'revolution from above'.[19] 'Revolution from above' is also the key phrase characterizing the political and social development of the Brandenburg-Prussian state in the eighteenth century under its king, Friedrich II.[20] This development involved a redefinition of the role of the nobility, which was turned into a functional élite for the territorial state, although in Brandenburg-Prussia it also retained some of the functions of a 'governing estate'. However, the exercise of government was now only possible in consensus with a concept of the state as a whole. Thus the local and district administrations were made the responsibility of the nobility. In addition, the Junkers were allowed to govern their villages and estate districts according to their own lights and largely free of princely state intervention. This was an important legal precondition for the development of the *Gutswirtschaft* (noble demesne economy) which characterized the agrarian structure of Germany east of the Elbe. Unlike previously, however, the new legal and political power of the local nobility was not legitimized by autonomous authority, but rather derived from consensus with the princely state. Thus the rural nobility in Brandenburg Prussia was able to retain the traditional mentality of the 'governing estate', to feel itself, through its key position in the military and administration, to be the favoured agent of the state, and in this way to distinguish itself from the other social estates. However, this did not diminish the primacy of monarchical power, and it was no longer possible to speak of a dualism between the 'monocratic' component and the 'corporative' component as a distinguishing feature of the political structure. This disempowerment of the nobility as a largely autonomous governing estate at the same time as it was privileged as a new key group in the administration of the state and the military, to all intents and purposes as the Prussian functional élite, is described by historians as the 'Prussian compromise with the nobility'.[21]

Of decisive importance for the economic and social position not only of the Prussian but also the German nobility in the eighteenth century was their mental distance as a social estate from the bourgeois groups, who made it impossible for the nobility to be economically active except in agriculture. This corresponded to the general tendency of a policy of the early modern state that had been becoming clearer since the late sixteenth century, which aimed to strengthen the social and legal barriers between the different social estates, and thereby to control the challenge posed by increasing economic and social differentiation.[22] Guaranteeing or extending privileges in agriculture, the economic sector in which the nobility traditionally secured its livelihood and its social estate, was the legal and political means through which tendencies toward social differentiation and loss of influence were supposed to be stemmed. This tendency to increase legal privileges for the nobility was especially pronounced in Brandenburg-Prussia, but also prevailed in principle in the other parts of the Empire. It included freeing the nobility from taxation, restricting sales of landed property, and prohibiting the subdivision of knightly estates. However, the Prussian 'Allgemeine Landrecht' (General National Law Code) of 1794, a work of legal reform which attempted to do justice to the demands of a changing economic and social system without being compelled to question the organization of society into social estates, shows the ambivalence of such attempts at the end of the *ancien régime*. This code defined the nobility unambiguously as the first social estate of the state. More than other groups, the nobility retained genuine rights as a social estate, 'but it was at the same time more "étatized" than ... the others'.[23] The integration of the nobility into the state entrenched a tendency which, despite all increases in the privileges of the nobility as a social estate, levelled out differentiations between social estates and permitted them to become obsolete when faced with the power of the state. This was the tendency toward the transformation of a segmented society of social estates into a society of state citizens. 'A state citizenry was attained only in the sense of equal subjecthood under the head of state.'[24]

The position of the nobility as the privileged social estate within the state increasingly came under pressure from rising bourgeois groups between the eighteenth and the nineteenth century. 'In both areas, in state service and in landed property, bourgeois forces put pressure on the position of the nobility.'[25] In the countryside it was frequently bourgeois tenants on the royal domains who stole a march on the owners of knightly estates, who were often deeply indebted. They became 'agents of a future agrarian capitalism'.[26] It was also they who introduced a disruptive element into the top level of the hierarchy of social estates, which was now no longer firmly ordained.

The nobility was the privileged estate not just in Prussia, of course, but also in the other parts of Germany. However, in areas of southern Germany such as Bavaria and Franconia extensive noble landed property never played an important role. The combination of landed property and governmental functions which characterized the east-Elbian *Gutswirtschaft* (noble demesne economy) did not in general prevail in the South and the West. The Prussian 'compromise with the nobility', which led the nobility to accept being bound into the centralized band of officials of the early modern territorial state, found its functional equivalent in the other territorial states – Saxony, Bavaria, Austria, and the ecclesiastical Electorates – in the princely court of the eighteenth century. For one thing, the princely court and the prince himself represented the political power of the early modern state *vis-à-vis* its subjects. For another, the nobility was bound into the social network of the court and simultaneously domesticated by it.[27] Compared with the incursion of the Brandenburg-Prussian nobility into the key areas of state penetration of society, those of the military and the bureaucracy, integrating the nobility into the state via the court seems archaic. In the pattern followed in Brandenburg-Prussia, in addition to privileged membership in an élite social estate, a performance criterion was also clearly in effect as a necessary condition for maintaining the élite function. Administrative or military competence served the growth of a state structure whose basic pattern survived throughout the entire nineteenth century. The 'unproductive' courtier, by contrast, remained a valid social model only under the *ancien régime*. However, in Prussia, not to mention in other German territories, the 'progressive' aspect of the nobility as a performance-orientated functional élite was counteracted by the fact that in the end the nobility remained imprisoned within the boundaries of social estate. On one hand this protected it, but on the other it was an obstacle on its path into capitalist market society. The prohibition against engaging in industrial production and distribution remained in existence until the end of the Old Empire. Its abolition appears not yet to have corresponded to the subjective interest of the nobility in the eighteenth century.

This was the decisive difference between Germany and England in the development of the nobility. In Germany, despite all its internal differentiation and its fundamental change in function within the framework of the early modern state, the nobility basically remained within the boundaries imposed on it by the traditional social structure of corporate orders. It was unable to develop into a class in the sense defined above. The English development is probably the clearest example of an alternative path of social change for the nobility. It was based on a relationship between the nobility (initially also a governmental élite) and the monarchy (as the embodiment of central political power) which from the later middle ages on was already quite different from that in Germany. As early as the end of the fifteenth century, the Wars of the Roses created the basis for a political and social system in which the high nobility, with their tendency toward particularism, could only still play a political role within the nation-state as a whole, and in which the monarch was bound into a rational bureaucratic apparatus which was 'freed from the personal activity of either king or entourage'.[28] When social and economic conditions changed, the nobility was no longer able (or required) to set itself apart as the 'governing estate' or distinguish itself from other social strata by strengthening barriers between social estates, and this created the preconditions for the much greater social adaptability of the English nobility than the German. The early completion of 'nation-building' in Great Britain[29] was thus functionally connected with the opening up of the English nobility, in a society which, of course, still had boundaries between social estates, but which had already developed market-determined classes early on. The massive penetration of market relations into agriculture, beginning at latest in the early seventeenth century, was the second important component in this adaptability of the English nobility compared to the German. Schröder has summarized its implications concisely:

> The early development of market- and profit-oriented 'landlords' and 'tenants', the dominance of a gentry and aristocracy which did not

exclusively box itself off, but rather was linked with other groups of the population and branches of the economy, ultimately created in England a social structure and an ambiance which were at least not injurious to change, first in the area of commerce and then in the industrial sector itself.[30]

The interplay of those two factors – the nobility's early loss of status as an autonomous 'governing estate' at the same time as it was integrated into the political and social system of a nation-state, and the opportunity to obtain new sources of material revenue in a market-orientated economic system – made it more possible both to dismantle barriers between social estates and to develop an open mind toward economic and social innovations. What distinguished England so fundamentally from Germany was, among other things, the adaptation to gradual structural change in England, compared to the necessity of a half-hearted 'revolution from above' in the large German territories, even if it was one which permitted the nobility to survive as a social estate.

The nobility in France followed a third path. The opposition of regional magnates to royal central power was only finally broken down one-and-a-half centuries later than in England, after defeat in the Fronde in 1653. The Estates General met in 1614 for the last time before the Revolution, and the possibility of traditional representation by the estates disappeared. An integration into political decision-making through parliament, as in England, was even less conceivable. French absolutism became characterized by the binding of a majority of the nobility to the royal court. Norbert Elias describes this as a closed social system, with the figure of the king at its centre.[31] The highly personalized nature of French absolutism, in which the court nobility were merely satellites heightening the brilliance of the king, contained no developmental perspectives for the nobility leading beyond absolutism. Both the landed nobility and the *noblesse de robe*, the nobility of office which had issued out of the bourgeoisie, were subjected to forms of supervision by the royal administration under Louis XIV which made it impossible for them to violate the boundaries of their social estate.[32] Even the creation of a nobility of office merely meant a differentiation of the noble estate for fiscal reasons. Furthermore, unlike in England, in France the economic preconditions were lacking for the nobility to adapt to structures other than those of social estate. Admittedly, France survived as the great European power in the late seventeenth and early eighteenth centuries not least through the political neutralization of its nobility by means of the monopolization of power in the court.

The English path remained, as we have seen, closed to the German nobility, and the adoption of the French model of the court nobility at several German princely courts was merely an imitation of a social symptom. There remained the unbridgeable difference in size. A German princely state could not measure up to the French absolutist state. However, they both had in common a redefinition of the nobility within a reshaped system of social estates, although in Germany this achieved much greater stability, and survived beyond the end of the eighteenth century. Whether a contributory cause of this was a particular pattern of development on the part of the bourgeoisie is investigated in the next section.

The bourgeoisie

Compared to the approximately 1 per cent of the population of Germany made up by the nobility around 1800, the 24 per cent made up by the inhabitants of towns, somewhat undifferentiatedly termed 'Bürger' (burghers, town citizens)[33] were quantitatively important. However, when the towns are described 'as centres of social change' in the eighteenth century,[34] it was not because of the growing size of the urban population, since in relative terms it increased only very little after 1500. In this, as also in the share of the nobility in the population, Germany followed a Europe-wide trend.[35] The potential for social change must thus be sought in qualitative changes in bourgeois existence. The question with which this chapter began, about the transition from a society primarily structured according to social estates to·one determined by membership in 'classes', must now be considered in connection with the development of the bourgeoisie (a group examined in detail in Chapter 6).

In analysing the development of the nobility, we have already seen that an important criterion of change for a social group is the function taken on by this group in the social constellation as a whole. The thesis has been advanced that 'essential steps' were taken in the eighteenth century 'on the path from the stratificatory to the functional differentiation of society'; and that this took place especially in the towns.[36] What does this mean? First of all, functional differentiation presumes that all social groups are integrated into an overall social system and are indissolubly connected with one another as elements within it. One's function exercised in that connection, and not in the hierarchy of relatively autonomous social estates, becomes the dominant criterion for determining one's place in society. With the nobility we saw that the changed shape of the early modern state played a major role in relocating that group in the social spectrum. However, it also became clear that this alone was not sufficient for the nobility to transcend the barriers imposed by the dominance of social estates.

For the development of the bourgeoisie as well, the changes which occurred in politics and the state, within the structures of the Empire, played an important role. The binding of the bourgeoisie to the town in the late medieval period, which remained in being within the legal structure of the

Empire until well into the nineteenth century, is a mark of the tenacity of the traditional hierarchy of social estates.[37] The debate which arose in the eighteenth century concerning the state *Bürger* (citizen) who was supposed to enjoy legal equality within the state, and who then in the nineteenth century was supposed to become the hallmark of the 'modern' state, made use of the functional criterion which was now becoming dominant in social differentiation. What counted was no longer the juristically codified differences between social estates, but the function of the individual in a society in which social differentiation was determined, to a greater extent than ever before, by his or her position within the economic process. The possibility of a unified federation of subjects – manifested, for example, in the Prussian General National Law Code – marked an important station on the path toward this basic precondition for modern society.

The urban *Bürgertum* (bourgeoisie, citizenry) of the later middle ages and the early modern period, however, represented only a portion of the urban population, namely those possessing *Bürgerrecht* (citizenship) in the community. Only this guaranteed participation in the rights and obligations of the band of citizens united by oath.[38] Citizenship divided urban residents into three large groups differing in both legal status and social estate: full citizens, inhabitants with lesser rights, and a fluctuating number of people without rights.[39] Around 1800, only 10 to 12 per cent of the urban population possessed citizenship.[40] The growth of sub-citizen strata became a long-term feature of the early modern period. This process increasingly pushed to absurdity the traditional notion of the town as a corporation of equals, which had been the ideal characterizing the phase of town foundations between the twelfth and the fourteenth centuries. It showed that the corporate and hierarchical nature of town society strengthened rather than weakened between the sixteenth and the eighteenth centuries. However, the rise of this urban society was characterized by an element which infiltrated the traditional privileging of social estates through birth. This was work as craftsman or merchant, an economic criterion which connected the *Bürger* to one another:

> For the first time, merchants and craftsmen rose enduringly into the leading strata! ... Rational earning of a livelihood, building, arts, university, scientific thinking, in general the secularized interpretative model of the bourgeois understanding of the world, all the way up to the Enlightenment, found a home mainly in towns. Without the town of the *Bürger*, complete with the energies it set free and preserved, the triumphal progress of European capitalism is hardly imaginable.[41]

Despite the advancing differentiation which, in the face of the disruptive developments which occurred from the late sixteenth century on, manifested itself in apparently petrified barriers between social estates, the ideal basis of the urban community remained the 'General Weal', to which all members of the community of citizens were supposed to feel allegiance.[42]

The material basis for social position within the community of citizens was ultimately economic success in trade and industry. The combination of these two elements eased social permeability between the two main groups of the town citizenry: those who participated in political power in the town – the political élite – on one hand, and those who were excluded from it on the other. In many places until well into the seventeenth century conflicts within towns repeatedly forced political élites to open up to 'homines novi' (new men).[43] Even when they primarily involved conflicts within the élite, these disputes led to a relatively widespread readiness to accept changes in the social and political structure as the result of economic changes. In the town, the system of social estates was in principle more open than that in non-urban areas of society.

However, there were differences in the structure and social mobility of political élites in the various regions of the Empire and the various types of town, such as the Imperial Cities of the South and the autonomous territorial cities of the North. Especially in the large Imperial Cities of southern Germany, and above all in Nuremberg and Augsburg which until well into the sixteenth century had been economic centres of world significance, the seventeenth and eighteenth centuries saw a loss of social dynamism in the ranks of the political élite. Equally responsible for this were changes in the European economy and in the political shape of the Empire. The shift of economic dynamism from Central Europe and the Mediterranean basin to north-west Europe and the Atlantic area deprived these cities of much of their importance as banking and trading centres. This was undoubtedly an important reason for the strengthening of the social profile of the bourgeoisie and for the unchallenged oligarchization of the political élite in these cities.[44] The outlook of the bourgeoisie of the Imperial Cities, concentrated on itself and its own traditions, was not transcended. Until the end of the Old Empire, the Imperial Cities of the South remained strongholds of the corporative principle of social estates. Impulses toward bursting this narrow corporative framework can be observed only where that perspective was challenged: in the cities which succeeded in forming connections with the Atlantic economy, and in the larger territorial cities. In the latter, the capital cities once again played a special role.

Hamburg and Frankfurt, although both Imperial Cities, were among the urban communes which owed their economic rise beginning in the seventeenth century to the attraction of the Atlantic area – Hamburg as an intermediary between East and West, and Frankfurt as a relay for trade between the centre of the European continent and the North-West.[45] Hamburg's social constitution was distinguished by a measure of openness which far exceeded that of the oligarchies of the south German Imperial Cities: 'It was divided not least according to occupational performance, which was essentially co-determined by occupational position and social rank, in addition to membership by birth in city council families.'[46] Especially jurists, which to some extent came from petty-bourgeois or immigrant families, rose in the seventeenth century into important functions in the city council and the administration. They broke through the boundaries of the traditional élites as defined by social estate, which even in Hamburg were still quite high but which, unlike in Nuremberg and Augsburg, turned out to be surmountable. Another contributory factor was the demographic dynamic of migration, which influenced the social profile and the policy of the Hanseatic city until the end of the Old Empire. The multi-confessionality and 'multi-nationality' of the indigenous and immigrant population groups – Lutherans, Catholics, Calvinists, and Sephardic Jews – created initial moves toward breaking down the corporate order, whose maintenance was ultimately dependent on the continuity of group structures handed down from the past.[47] To begin with, admittedly, this did not yet lead toward class structures, although their beginnings can be found in Hamburg at the end of the eighteenth century, when the growth of non-guilded textile industries and sugar refineries brought into being a new type of entrepreneur and a new labour-force which in 1800 already numbered between 6,000 and 10,000.[48] The two forms of organization, that of social estates and that of classes, existed side by side.

Wherever there was an absence of the central precondition for organizing society according to social estates, namely stability in the constellation of social groups over long periods, the society of corporate orders was challenged. For the system of social estates survived because of the legal privileges and the prestige which each group had obtained in the past. The rise of new élites through economic success, and the formation of new groups which exceeded the admission capacities of the social corporations, the guilds, and dynastic associations, repeatedly compelled the corporate organization of urban society to be formed anew. But as soon as influential new groups no longer identified themselves with the traditional system of urban norms its integration capacities became exhausted.

In this process, the transition from urban *Bürger* (citizen) to territorial *Bürger* marked a decisive break.[49] This is especially clear in a number of the larger territorial cities, especially the princely capitals. The territorial *Bürger* had given up his identification with the town and its corporative structure. He had formed economic and social connections which were no longer characterized by the guild, the principle of the 'bürgerliche Nahrung' (the bourgeois livelihood),[50] the concern for urban autonomy, and the striving for participation in urban government through council membership. The new framework in which he now moved had been marked out by the early modern territorial state. Thus he was not troubled even by the attempts of territorial princes to set aside urban autonomy in favour of the political integration of the town into the territory, which had been taking place with increasing success from the sixteenth century on.[51] This new type of *Bürger* embodied the urban bourgeois variant of the princely subject, the importance of whom, as an important step on the path toward the state *Bürger*, has already been discussed above. We encounter him as a bourgeois office-holder in the princely administration, who played an important part in the development of territorial government in the seventeenth and eighteenth century, and as an entrepreneur producing for the market outside guild regulations, as a putter-out or manufactory-operator. For this new group of 'economic *Bürger*' the territorial state played a twofold function. Firstly, new kinds of business concern often required legal protection by the state against traditional industrial institutions. Secondly, in the larger princely capitals of the eighteenth century markets for luxuries expanded because of demand from the princely court. The military demanded the products of ironworks and textile industries. In Berlin, the 'most dynamic of German capital cities', at the end of the eighteenth century,

> only a fifth of the population still belonged to the two classical sectors, craft industry and trade. By contrast, the number of manufactory workers and those in one way or another linked to the dynastic princely state was quite high. ... The Prussian capital city developed into a central place characterized by a close interpenetration between state and city: the administrative élites and the military ... were superimposed over the pattern which had dominated urban life for centuries: traditional industry, trade, and *Ackerbürgertum* ['the field-bourgeoisie', urban citizens who also cultivated some land].[52]

However, cities such as Hamburg and Berlin, and the array of other large capital and territorial German cities which followed a similar development, were still merely isolated 'development islands'. Additional examples of the 'development islands' in which in which this new type of *Bürger* arose were provided by those cities and small towns in the West of Germany in which religious refugees established flourishing putting-out networks, especially in textiles but also in metalworking.[53] In almost all cities characterized by heightened economic and social dynamism, exiles constituted a ferment of change.[54] Such cities saw a dissolution of the corporate structures of urban society by the end of the eighteenth century; and political factors, namely the growth of the early modern state, clearly played an important role in this process. However, these processes did not take place throughout the urban milieu. We have already pointed out the deep abyss which existed between this pattern and the obstinately backward corporate orientation of the Imperial Cities. But the great mass of small towns also persisted in self-sufficient navel-gazing. Mack Walker described life in the typical town of less than 10,000 inhabitants in the Old Empire as an existence without movement or change: 'stability, like separateness, was a condition of its existence and part of its definition'.[55] In such towns, the corporate consciousness of social estates remained for the time being unbroken.

However, urban life everywhere in Germany was infiltrated by the crisis of traditional crafts and thus of the core of the urban middle strata, a crisis which became virulent toward the end of the eighteenth century.[56] Frequently, traditional crafts were no longer in a position to maintain them-

selves against unguilded forms of industry. They made up a profoundly conservative element, which held fast to the corporate organization of society
into social estates in order to resist sinking down into the growing mass of
the urban substrata. Urban poverty increased: in the seventeenth century,
an average of 30 to 40 per cent of the urban population was counted among
the poor, but by the eighteenth century this had as a rule risen to more than
50 per cent. But its structural change deserves attention even more than its
growth. The traditional 'paupers' were joined, 'through constant immigration from the countryside, by day-labourers and manufactory workers, hod
carriers and helpers, the lowest bureaucrats and urban clerks, discharged
soldiers and invalids, and not least the growing army of servants'.[57] Even if
a 'working class' cannot be spoken of in the eighteenth century, this development proclaimed the dissolution of the corporate order of social estates.
The lower strata became fragmented into numerous sub-groups. The wage
workers among them made up a tiny group of perhaps 100,000 people in
the Empire as a whole at the end of the eighteenth century. It was out of
the broad reservoir of all these groups that the rapidly increasing number
of early industrial wage-workers was recruited in the nineteenth century. 'In
this, the fundamental dichotomy of modern market society signalled itself
ever more unmistakably.'[58]

On the other side of the social spectrum, out of the new bourgeois groups
there grew that type of *Bürger* which until well into the twentieth century
is supposed to have been characteristic of the self-image of the German
Bûrgertum (bourgeoisie), and indeed of the social profile of German *Bürgerlichkeit* ('middle-class-ness') as a whole: the 'educated *Bürger*'. He appeared side-by-side with the 'entrepreneurial *Bürger*', the 'bourgeois',
although because of the comparatively late industrial development of Germany in the nineteenth century the latter left much less of a stamp on the
mentality and culture of the German bourgeoisie than the former. The 'educated *Bürger*' developed out of those bourgeois groups whose rise was so
closedly linked to the growth of the state: the princely officials, the bureaucrats of government administration, the jurists, the professors, the
clergy.[59] In Germany, he exercised an enduring influence on the self-image
of the modern *Bürgertum*, indeed on the cultural stamp of the nation as a
whole, to a greater extent than anywhere else in Europe.[60] The traditional
corporate order of social estates was broken down by this group, in so far
as its members no longer derived their social status from privilege of birth,
but rather from the abilities obtained through education, which they placed
in the service of the state. On one hand, in its identity as the new performance and functional élite, the 'educated *Bürgertum*' surmounted the
old organization of society. On the other hand, for example in Prussia until the mid-nineteenth century, they were assigned a special legal position
which placed them alongside the nobility in the social hierarchy of prestige,
and thus located them above the 'economic *Bürgertum*' of the new
'bourgeoisie'.[61] This gave renewed effectiveness to certain elements of the

corporate organization of society into social estates, although in changed form; but the performance and capabilities of this group on the labour market within the expanding state apparatus determined their status as a 'class', in the sense defined above. The simultaneous coexistence of social estate side-by-side with class still remained the decisive characteristic of the German *Bürgertum* in the nineteenth century.

Likewise, it was these sections of the *Bürgertum*, those that no longer shared the 'church-tower' perspectives of traditional town society, which consciously relinquished corporate barriers between social estates, both in their practical dealings and in their theoretical views. However, it was only a very small minority of the total population which, by doing so, situated itself at the forefront of conscious change.

Rural society

The quantitative inner lining of this transformation process did not develop primarily in the towns, however. For this, the urban population made up too small a share of the total population. At the end of the Old Empire, 75 per cent of people still lived in the countryside. The ratio between urban and rural population had shifted in favour of the towns only to a trivial extent since 1500. However, the structure of the rural population itself had changed fundamentally in the three centuries between 1500 and 1800. Around 1500, 60 per cent of this group consisted of the owners of farms, the actual peasants; by 1800, it had fallen to 35 per cent. That is, in the course of the eighteenth century, the peasants became a minority in the rural population. In the same period, the land-poor and altogether propertyless rural inhabitants, groups which were also internally subdivided in a variety of ways, expanded from 20 per cent of the rural population to 40 per cent. The corresponding figures for Europe as a whole reveal that the German development was particularly polarized. In Europe, farm-owners declined 'only' from 53 to 43 per cent, while the land-poor and propertyless increased merely from 25 to 35 per cent of the rural population.[62]

Only in England was the transformation possibly more fundamental. There the 'yeomanry' or independent peasantry, still numerous in the last decades of the seventeenth century, had largely disappeared by the second half of the eighteenth century, giving way to a tenant peasantry which produced for the market.[63] In France, by contrast, the traditional agrarian constitution, in which common lands continued to play a central role in subsistence and in which there was only a very small and primitive system of market-orientated large tenancies, essentially remained in being until the Revolution. This was a tradition, however, which increasingly revealed its susceptibility to crises. The poor economic position of most of the French peasants also resulted from the fact that in the eighteenth century they owned only about 35 per cent of the land directly, while the clergy held 10 per cent, the nobility 20 per cent, and the bourgeoisie 30 per cent. This they partly worked themselves, and partly granted to small tenants on extraordinarily unfavourable conditions.[64] The peasants also found themselves subjected to intensified attempts on the part of the seigneurs to reactivate feudal rights which had for the most part become dormant; this was one reason among others for demands that restrictions on rural property rights be abolished, demands which became ever louder in the period leading up to the Revolution.[65]

The market-orientation which had become the decisive hallmark of the English agrarian structure also characterized agrarian developments in many parts of Germany. This chapter has already discussed its connection with the role of the nobility, especially in the development of *Gutswirtschaft* (the noble demesne economy) east of the Elbe. *Gutswirtschaft* became incorporated into an international division of labour which turned eastern Central Europe – and thus also Germany east of the Elbe – into the grain supplier of the West. This development set in as early as the fifteenth century. Admittedly, in the second half of the seventeenth century there was a temporary diminution in the attractiveness of distant markets. However, after the Thirty Years War noble agrarian entrepreneurs found themselves in a relatively favourable situation, since they were in a position to buy up abandoned land cheaply. The worsening in the rights of peasants, and the increase in the powers of the nobility over the rural population on their estates, created the economic and political basis for the boom enjoyed by the east-Elbian knightly estates in the last third of the eighteenth century.[66] The political and social consequences this had for eastern Germany, which found its expression in the special position of the nobility in the Prussian state until well into the nineteenth century, have been analysed above in the discussion of the Prussian 'compromise with the nobility'. They cemented the dividing line between the agrarian systems of Germany east and west of the Elbe.

The agrarian economy in the West had also for a long time orientated itself to the market. However, here the peasant produced mainly for local and regional needs, and his dependency on general economic trends confirms the fact that he was linked into general social and economic developments. Social change manifested itself as an integrated system. The countryside could not uncouple itself from developments either in the towns or in the international context. The upward demographic trend of the late fifteenth and sixteenth centuries favoured an agrarian upswing during the sixteenth century. However, this had different effects on town and countryside. In the towns, rising grain prices at the same time as stagnation in industrial prices and declining purchasing power of urban industrial wages led to an expansion in the urban substrata and a crisis in traditional urban social relations. This development not only was a precondition for the ultimate establishment of *Gutswirtschaft* in eastern Germany, but also opened up favourable development opportunities for peasant agriculture in the North, South, and South-West of Germany.[67] At the same time, however, population pressure ensured that by no means all rural inhabitants profited from the upward trend in agrarian prices. From the beginning of the sixteenth century on, arable land became scarce. Far from all of those who had once originated in the peasant milieu could now be provided with farms. For them, the rural industries which had already arisen in the later middle ages, and were now expanding further, offered new but rather meagre earning opportunities. Upper Germany, Saxony, the Rhineland, and Westphalia in particular developed into centres of this form of economic organization, which is thought not to have fitted easily into the tradition system of social estates.[68] For one thing, it infiltrated the guild-organized urban industries, especially in the key sector of textile production. For another, it led to social differentiation across broad expanses of rural Germany. Groups in peasant society located below or outside the corporate order of social estates increased in size.

The seventeenth century, indeed the entire period up to 1750, has been described by various authors as an 'age of crises'.[69] This, too, relates to the social transformation which was gaining sway and becoming apparent in the restratification of the rural population. But first it must be realized that, despite the increasing dominance of *Gutswirtschaft* in the east-Elbian area and the increase in the land-poverty of the rural sub-strata, even in the eighteenth century agriculture remained overwhelmingly structured by peasant farms. Despite the enormous regional variety in property rights, a majority of peasants owned inheritable holdings. This made the German social estate of the peasantry fundamentally different from both the English and the French tenantries, who often had to work without any legal security.[70]

Rural development in Germany was characterized not by a worsening in the legal situation of peasant ownership as a whole, which was above all restricted to the East, but rather a redistribution in rural population structure, away from groups with full peasant holdings and toward those for whom agriculture no longer represented the sole or even the main basis for subsistence. It must be stressed that this rural structural transformation was characterized by an all-encompassing social differentiation of village society. In the course of this differentiation during the eighteenth century, the peasants became a minority in the village population. Besides the 'full peasants' and 'half peasants', who lived (often rather poorly) from agricultural production, there were three large groups within the sub-peasant stratum.[71] First, there were the smallholders who worked a piece of often low-value land, but were dependent on by-employments. Second, there were the landless, which included both the cottagers, who still owned their own huts, and those who had to live in the houses of others. The third group was made up of the servants, who worked for board and lodging, and at best very low

wages, on peasant farms and landlords' demesnes. In Saxony in 1550 peasants still made up 49.5 per cent of the total. By 1750 their share had fallen
to 24.6 per cent; 38.5 per cent of the rural population consisted of land-
poor or landless cottagers and so-called 'Insten', who no longer even possessed their own dwellings. Similar and to some extent even more dramatic
figures are provided by Wehler for southern Germany, Lower Saxony, Brandenburg-Prussia, and Silesia. 'In all German countrysides at the end of the
eighteenth century' village society had 'apparently slid into a condition of
irreversible disintegration.'[72]

The division of labour between town and countryside was no longer
merely one between agrarian and industrial production: it was in the areas
with dense rural industry that the economic integration between town and
village became stronger. This must also have had consequences for the position assigned to the countryside in the regulatory policies of the early
modern state. The first successful beginnings of policies of 'Bauernschutz'
(peasant protection) by the territorial lords aimed to maintain the independent peasant as a taxpayer and a basis for recruitment into the standing
army of the territory. On the royal domains in Brandenburg-Prussia, the serf
status of the peasants was abolished in 1719–23. Attempts to improve the
legal position of peasants outside the royal domains also followed under
Friedrich II. In 1783, serfdom was abolished in the Margraviate of Baden,
and at the turn of the nineteenth century in Schleswig-Holstein. In Hannover, from 1753 on, dues in kind payable to the territorial lord were transmuted into money payments.[73] The most dedicated attempts at 'peasant
protection', however, were undertaken in Austria under Maria Theresia and
Joseph II. In practice, admittedly, even they remained only fragmentary.[74]
The state interest in the peasantry is a sign of the advancing integration of
previously separate social estates into a general undifferentiated group of
state subjects. The countryside, too, was subjected to and affected by territorial state regulation.

Marginal social groups

The demands on the regulatory powers of the state were also increased by
the growth in those population groups which both fell completely outside
the corporate order of social estates and could not be integrated into the
new branches of the economy: the vagrants and beggars, the 'people on the
roads'.[75] For Bavaria in 1750, it is estimated that some 8 per cent of the total population was on the move at any one time. Toward the end of the century this had actually risen to around 10 per cent. In other regions this
proportion was, if anything, even higher. Half of these were individuals who

lived on the roads permanently, while the other half were temporarily under way in the search for work and a new home.

The state sought to overcome this problem through compulsory incorporation of these people into the work process, through using them in road- and canal-building projects and in the drainage of moors. Government and state pressure was intensified, through the establishment of poorhouses and workhouses, without solving the problem. It is estimated that in the eighteenth century there were as many as 250 beggars for every 1,000 inhabitants in the ecclesiastical territories of Germany.[76] In Protestant areas, the poverty problem manifested itself hardly differently.[77] To create new earning opportunities for this surplus population would have required a fundamental transformation in the structure of the economy. However, in the eighteeenth century manufactories and putting-out industries were far from being sufficiently widespread to be able to take in the mass of the uprooted. The traditional economy, in which the urban guilded industries were still the most important factor and the boundaries between social estates handed down from the past were still observed had, by the end of the Old Empire, run up against its structural limits, and had, indeed, gone beyond them. Mass poverty emerged strikingly as a structural problem, reflected in the first half of the nineteenth century as a fact under the keyword 'pauperism',[78] and in theory in the beginnings of political economy by Karl Marx and Friedrich Engels.

Toward the end of the eighteenth century an ever-greater portion of the population no longer fitted into the traditional constitution of society, both at the upper end of the scale with the new bourgeois groups and at the lower end with the sub-peasant groups, domestic workers, and vagrants. This was the result of a long-term process of transformation, whose first signs had already become apparent toward the end of the sixteenth century in the shape of disruptive change in the economic and social system. Its effects manifested themselves not only in the economic constitution and the corporate order of social estates, but penetrated the whole spectrum of human life, including the organization of everyday life. This, too, showed itself to be a function of the corporate order of social estates. Coexistence took place to a considerable extent within the domestic community, within what was understood – both at the beginning of the seventeenth century and at the beginning of the nineteenth, although with fundamentally different substantive content – as constituting the 'family'. The transformation in the concept of the family and family structure is the area in which the macro-level and the micro-level of social transformation are connected.

'Ganzes Haus' and family

The concepts of the 'ganzes Haus' on one hand and the 'bourgeois family' on the other stand for this process of transformation. The 'ganzes Haus' (literally the 'whole house') means the family as a living community and a production commmunity, consisting not only of the married couple and its children, but also of the 'Hausgenossen' ('house-fellows' or inmates of the house) as a whole, the journeymen and servants, with the 'Hausvater' ('house-father') at the head.[79] The house as a production community, however, was closely linked to economic forms handed down from the past: craft production within a guild framework in the town, and the peasant economy in the countryside. The structure of the 'ganzes Haus' and the role of the 'house-father' was as much reflected in the shape of the princely house and the role of the territorial lord as it was in the house of the guild master. From the sixteenth century on, this ideal found expression in the so-called 'Hausväterliteratur' ('house-father literature'), with its practical instructions for the economy of the 'ganzes Haus', for the bringing up of children, and for the co-residence of all members of the 'familia'. Only from the end of the eighteenth century on was the unity of the family as a living community and an economic community dissolved in literary texts, as well.[80] The further development of the theoretical and literary concern with family and economy on the eve of the end of the Old Empire points to developments which were at first only hinted at in the reality of co-residence. The family as a private area of life, an emotional community, distinct from the economic community, was fully developed in theoretical thinking only during the first half of the nineteenth century, and found its real-life shape in the 'bourgeois family' of this period.[81]

Admittedly, even in the seventeenth and eighteenth centuries the 'ganzes Haus' was merely a theoretical construct, which sought to bring reality into definitional harmony with the structures of a corporate order of social estates, orientated around the norms of the noble and princely house. However, it has been shown that the reality of urban guilded and rural peasant households manifested a degree of differentiation not wholly reconcilable with this construct. There was no unified or obligatory pre-modern family form.[82] The noble family as a living community and a production community was a phenomenon of the middle ages. The idea of the 'ganzes Haus' was, however, transferred to the public and political role of the nobility:

> The centre of gravity of noble family life consisted of its economic and political authority over its 'territorium'; to secure and extend this authority required the public representation of the house, and the organization and fostering of political and social contacts.... The rise of a private sphere and of more intensive personal emotional relations was here ... structurally not favoured.[83]

The guilded bourgeois 'Hausgemeinschaft' (literally 'house-community'), in which the 'ganzes Haus' still manifested itself in a relatively pure form, lost its character as the exclusive form of life of urban society because of the economic and social developments of the early modern period. The same was the case for the peasant family. Domestic workers in 'proto-industry' in town and countryside manifested a family form which lay between the 'ganzes Haus' and the 'proletarian family' of the nineteenth century. Although it still fulfilled production functions, it did not bring in any additional labour-power besides the married couple and the children: 'Loss of economic independence, monotony of work, small families, and a tendency toward individualization of marital relations, already point ... toward the proletarian family.'[84] The bourgeois family as a private residential and emotional community, with its norm-creating character for the nineteenth and twentieth centuries, found its first beginnings in the new bourgeois groups which were breaking down the traditional pattern of the old urban bourgeoisie of corporate social estates: the functional agents of the state, the Protestant clergy, and the new entrepreneurs, the putters-out and the manufactory-operators.[85] However, as we have seen, these new social forms were still phenomena developing on the margin of the traditional social spectrum; in the eighteenth century they were still far from typical, and they would not become so until after 1800. However, the last decades of the eighteenth century do show some signs of accelerated social transformation.

Social transformation as a long-term phenomenon

It was not short-term eruptive and revolutionary transformations, therefore, nor acute crises in political and social structures, which led to fundamental changes in the German social system and its political and institutional superstructure. Rather, the political and institutional framework of the Old Empire apparently manifested considerable flexibility in the face of the challenges posed by the process of social transformation. With its multiplicity of manifestations, between the authority of the absolutist prince and that authority which still very much relied on regional corporate élites, with the instrumental framework of the early modern state, the old structure was for a considerable time able to integrate changing social structures into the framework of the early modern princely state. This tendency is clear enough in the example of Brandenburg-Prussia with its General National Law Code, but also in the reforms observed in many other German territories. On the other hand, however, the traditional system of social estates remained stubbornly and strikingly dominant in comparison to England and the France of the 1789 Revolution. Eighteenth-century Germany was able to generate merely the first beginnings of a new understanding of the political and social role of the bourgeoisie: this was because the 'church-tower' perspective of the corporate guilded notability of the old bourgeoisie of social estates had been relinquished only by a few new bourgeois groups which still stood on the margins of the political and social spectrum. Furthermore, it was not primarily the new 'economic *Bürger*', the manufactory-operators and putters-out, who were assigned this new role, but rather those *Bürger* who continued in a very close relationship with the (admittedly changing) institutions of the princely state – bureaucrats, professors, clerics. It was these who gave their stamp to the climate of political and social opinion in the last decades of the eighteenth century.

The impulses toward economic transformation turned out to be not yet strong enough, in the early eighteenth century, for the corporate system of guilds and social estates in the towns and the agrarian constitutions of *Grundherrschaft* and *Gutsherrschaft* in the countryside to lose their economic basis. These dissolved only gradually:

> It was characteristic of the new consciousness of the age after the end of the eighteenth century that their own period was seen not only as an end or a beginning, but rather as a period of transition. In this, the German reception of the French Revolution was unquestionably different at first from the experience of those who participated in it directly, who initially emphasized it as an absolutely new beginning.[86]

This subjective sense of transition is consistent with the findings of historians concerning objective social developments. Social transformation certainly accelerated toward the end of the Old Empire. This was spectacularly demonstrated by the structural transformation of formerly peasant-dominated village society into a differentiated social formation with an ever-growing proportion of non-peasant and sub-peasant groups. In its place, however, no dominant new economic structures had yet appeared, structures to which a society organized into social estates (along with its political and administrative superstructure) would no longer be able to react in a way inherent to the system. Furthermore, the processes of transformation which have been sketched out in this chapter began as early as the end of the sixteenth century: the 'crisis of the 1590s'[87] and the 'crisis of the seventeenth century' are their key phrases. These very long-term pressures within the framework of the traditional social and economic system made it possible for the political system to react successfully, through developing a regulatory armament specific to the early modern polity. Its adaptive capacity was only to become exhausted in the course of a long transitional phase which began at the end of the eighteenth century.

Notes

1 H. Klueting, *Das Konfessionelle Zeitalter, 1525–1648* (Stuttgart, 1989); contains numerous additional bibliographical references.
2 H.-U. Wehler, *Deutsche Gesellschaftsgeschichte* (Munich, 1987), i. p. 47. A fundamental work on corporate groups and political sovereignty in medieval and early modern Europe is D. Gerhard, *Old Europe: A Study of Continuity, 1000–1800* (New York, 1981).
3 On the early modern princely state, see H. Boldt, *Deutsche Verfassungsgeschichte*, i: *Von den Anfängen bis zum Ende des älteren deutschen Reiches 1806* (Munich, 1984), pp. 149–246; H. Schilling, *Aufbruch und Krise. Deutschland 1517–1648* (Berlin, 1988), pp. 317–49.
4 G. Oestreich, 'Verfassungsgeschichte vom Ende des Mittelalters bis zum Ende des alten Reiches', in Herbert Grundmann, ed., *Gebhardt – Handbuch der deutschen Geschichte* (9th edn, Stuttgart, 1970), ii. pp. 361–436, esp. pp. 389–90, 394–6.
5 H. Möller, *Fürstenstaat oder Bürgernation. Deutschland 1763–1815* (Berlin, 1989), p. 94.
6 On the problem of the patriciate, see, e.g. I. Bátori, 'Das Patriziat der deutschen Stadt', *Zeitschrift für Stadtgeschichte, Stadtsoziologie und Denkmalpflege*, 2 (1975), pp. 1–30.
7 Wehler, *Gesellschaftsgeschichte*, i. p. 41.
8 H. Schilling, *Höfe und Allianzen. Deutschland 1648–1763* (Berlin, 1989), *passim*, esp. pp. 148–97, 271–302.
9 The argument here essentially follows that in Wehler, *Gesellschaftsgeschichte*, i. pp. 127–39.
10 M. Weber, *Wirtschaft und Gesellschaft* (5th edn, Tübingen, 1972), pp. 177–80.
11 Wehler, *Gesellschaftsgeschichte*, i. p. 135.
12 On the ecclesiastical territories, see P. Moraw and V. Press, article 'Fürstentümer, geistliche', in *Theologische Realenzyklopädie*, II (Berlin, 1983), pp. 711–19.
13 O. Mörke, *Rat und Bürger in der Reformation. Soziale Gruppen und kirchlicher Wandel in den welfischen Hansestädten Lüneburg, Braunschweig und Göttingen* (Hildesheim, 1983).
14 H.-C. Rublack, 'Political and Social Norms in Urban Communities in the Holy Roman Empire', in Kaspar von Greyerz, ed., *Religion, Politics and Social Protest* (London, 1984), pp. 24–60.
15 On the Free Imperial Knighthood, see V. Press, *Kaiser Karl V., König Ferdinand und die Entstehung der Reichsritterschaft* (Wiesbaden, 1980); V. Press, 'Adel, Reich und Reformation', in Wolfgang J. Mommsen, ed., *The Urban Classes, the Nobility and the Reformation* (Stuttgart, 1979), pp. 330–83.
16 On Bavaria, see Schilling, *Höfe und Allianzen*, pp. 183–8.
17 On the Schönborn family, see Schilling, *Höfe und Allianzen*, pp. 178–9.
18 G. Rauch, 'Das Mainzer Domkapitel in der Neuzeit. Zur Verfassung und Selbstverständnis einer adeligen geistlichen Gemeinschaft', *Zeitschrift der Savigny-Stiftung für Rechtsgeschichte, Kanonistische Abteilung*, 92 (1975), pp. 161–227; 93 (1976), pp. 194–278; 94 (1977), pp. 132–279.
19 H.-U. Wehler, *Das Deutsche Kaiserreich 1871–1918* (Göttingen, 1973), pp. 33–40.
20 L. Gall, *Bürgertum in Deutschland* (Berlin, 1989), p. 76; Wehler, *Gesellschaftsgeschichte*, i. pp. 57–8.

21 For a thorough discussion of the compromise with the nobility, see Schilling, *Höfe und Allianzen*, pp. 404–14; on the development of the nobility in Brandenburg-Prussia, see R. Endres, *Adel in der frühen Neuzeit* (Munich, 1993), pp. 23–32; on the 'Gutswirtschaft', see F. Mathis, *Die deutsche Wirtschaft im 16. Jahrhundert* (Munich, 1992), pp. 112–15; W. Trossbach, *Bauern 1648–1806* (Munich, 1993), pp. 6–12.

22 This policy found its codified expression in state ordinances regulating dress and social estate: see L. C. Eisenbart, *Kleiderordnungen der deutschen Städte zwischen 1350 und 1700* (Göttingen, 1962), esp. p. 103. The *Reichspolizeiordnung* (Imperial Regulatory Ordinance) of 1577 can be found in H. Duchhardt, ed., *Quellen zur Verfassungsentwicklung des Heiligen Römischen Reiches Deutscher Nation* (Darmstadt, 1983), pp. 120–34.

23 R. Koselleck, *Preußen zwischen Reform und Revolution. Allgemeines Landrecht, Verwaltung und soziale Bewegung von 1791 bis 1848* (Stuttgart, 1975), p. 80.

24 *Ibid.*, p. 56.

25 *Ibid.*, p. 81.

26 Wehler, *Gesellschaftsgeschichte*, i. p. 86.

27 H. C. Ehalt, *Ausdrucksformen absolutistischer Herrschaft. Der Wiener Hof im 17. und 18. Jahrhundert* (Munich, 1980); J. Freiherr von Kruedener, *Die Rolle des Hofes im Absolutismus* (Stuttgart, 1973); A. Winterling, *Der Hof der Kurfürsten von Köln. 1688–1794* (Bonn, 1986). Fundamental to all of these studies of courts is N. Elias, *Die höfische Gesellschaft. Untersuchungen zur Soziologie des Königtums und der höfischen Aristokratie* (Darmstadt, 1969).

28 G. R. Elton, *England under the Tudors 1485–1603* (2nd edn, London, 1974), p. 181.

29 On this, with numerous bibliographical references, see H.-C. Schröder, 'Die neuere englische Geschichte im Lichte einiger Modernisierungstheoreme', in Reinhart Koselleck, ed., *Studien zum Beginn der modernen Welt* (Stuttgart, 1977), pp. 30–65, pp. 45–6.

30 *Ibid.*, p. 45.

31 Elias, *Höfische Gesellschaft*.

32 R. Mandrou, *Staatsräson und Vernunft, 1649–1775* (Frankfurt am Main, 1975), pp. 40–3; R. Briggs, *Early Modern France 1560–1715* (Oxford, 1977), pp. 61–5.

33 Möller, *Fürstenstaat*, pp. 99–100.

34 M. Dinges, 'Die Ehre als Thema der Stadtgeschichte. Eine Semantik im Übergang vom Ancien Régime zur Moderne', *ZHF* 16 (1989), pp. 409–40, p. 411; for further reading on the early modern German town, see H. Schilling, *Die Stadt in der frühen Neuzeit* (Munich, 1993).

35 Möller, *Fürstenstaat*, p. 100. Around 1500, the proportion of the population living in towns was about 20 per cent.

36 Dinges, 'Ehre', pp. 410–11.

37 On the development of the concept of the *Bürger*, see M. Riedel, 'Bürger, Staatsbürger, Bürgertum', in O. Brunner, W. Conze, and R. Koselleck, eds, *Geschichtliche Grundbegriffe. Historisches Lexikon zur politisch-sozialen Sprache in Deutschland* (Stuttgart, 1972), i. pp. 672–725.

38 W. Ebel, *Der Bürgereid als Geltungsgrund und Gestaltungsprinzip des deutschen mittelalterlichen Stadtrechts* (Weimar, 1958); E. Isenmann, *Die deutsche Stadt im Spätmittelalter* (Stuttgart, 1988), pp. 93–7.

39 Wehler, *Gesellschaftsgeschichte*, i. pp. 182–3.

40 Möller, *Fürstenstaat*, p. 107.

41 Wehler, *Gesellschaftsgeschichte*, i. p. 179.

42 Rublack, 'Political and Social Norms'; O. Mörke, 'Die städtische Gemeinde im mittleren Deutschland (1300–1800)', in P. Blickle, ed., *Landgemeinde und Stadtgemeinde in Mitteleuropa* (Munich, 1991), pp. 289–308, pp. 296–8.

43 See, with more detailed bibliographical references, C. R. Friedrichs, 'Citizens or Subjects? Urban Conflict in Early Modern Germany', in M. Usher Chrisman and O. Gründler, eds, *Social Groups and Religious Ideas in the Sixteenth Century* (Kalamazoo, Ill., 1978), pp. 46–58; C. R. Friedrichs, 'German Town Revolts and the Seventeenth-Century Crisis', *Renaissance and Modern Studies*, 26 (1982), pp. 27–51; O. Mörke, 'Der "Konflikt" als Kategorie städtischer Sozialgeschichte der Reformationszeit', in Bernhard Diestelkamp, ed., *Beiträge zum spätmittelalterlichen Städtewesen* (Cologne, 1982), pp. 144–61.

44 In general, see C. R. Friedrichs, 'The Swiss and German City-States', in Robert Griffeth and Carol G. Thomas, eds, *The City-State in Five Cultures* (Santa Barbara, 1981), pp. 109–42. For a case study of the petrification of a Free Imperial City, see I. Bátori, *Die Reichsstadt Augsburg im 18. Jahrhundert. Verfassung, Finanzen und Reformversuche* (Göttingen, 1969).

45 H. Böhme, *Frankfurt und Hamburg. Des deutschen Reiches Silber- und Goldloch und die allerenglischste Stadt des Kontinents* (Frankfurt am Main, 1968); G. L. Soliday, *A Community in Conflict. Frankfurt Society in the Seventeenth and Early Eighteenth Centuries* (Hannover, NH, 1974).

46 Möller, *Fürstenstaat*, pp. 121–2.

47 J. Whaley, *Religious Toleration and Social Change in Hamburg 1529–1819* (Cambridge, 1985).

48 F. Kopitzsch, 'Hamburg zwischen Hauptrezeß und Franzosenzeit', in Wilhelm Rausch, ed., *Die Städte Mitteleuropas im 17. und 18. Jahrhundert* (Linz a. d. Donau, 1981), pp. 181–210, p. 198.

49 See, with an extensive bibiliography, H. Schilling, 'Wandlungs- und Differenzierungsprozesse innerhalb der bürgerlichen Oberschichten West- und Nordwestdeutschlands im 16. und 17. Jahrhundert', in Marian Biskup and Klaus Zernack, eds, *Schichtung und Entwicklung der Gesellschaft in Polen und Deutschland im 16. und 17. Jahrhundert* (Wiesbaden, 1983), pp. 121–73.

50 On the principle of *Nahrung* (livelihood) as the basis for the guild economy, see Isenmann, *Die deutsche Stadt*, pp. 313, 395–6.

51 O. Mörke, 'Der gewollte Weg in Richtung "Untertan". Ökonomische und politische Eliten in Braunschweig, Lüneburg und Göttingen vom 15. bis ins 17. Jahrhundert', in Heinz Schilling and Herman Diederiks, eds, *Bürgerliche Eliten in den Niederlanden und in Nordwestdeutschland* (Cologne, 1985), pp. 111–33; L. Wiese-Schorn, 'Von der autonomen zur beauftragten Selbstverwaltung. Die Integration der deutschen Stadt in den Territorialstaat am Beispiel der Verwaltungsgeschichte von Osnabrück und Göttingen in der frühen Neuzeit', *Osnabrücker Mitteilungen*, 82 (1976), pp. 29–59.

52 Möller, *Fürstenstaat*, pp. 118–9; H. Schultz, *Berlin 1650–1800. Sozialgeschichte einer Residenz* (Berlin, 1987).

53 Schilling, 'Wandlungs- und Differenzierungsprozesse', pp. 159–65.

54 H. Schilling, 'Innovation through Migration: The Settlements of Calvinistic Netherlanders in Sixteenth- and Seventeenth-Century Central and Western Europe', *Histoire sociale – Social History*, 16 (1983), pp. 7–33.

55 M. Walker, *German Home Towns: Community, State, and General Estate 1648–1871* (Ithaca, NY, 1971), p. 5.

56 M. Stürmer, ed., *Herbst des Alten Handwerks* (Munich, 1979).

57 Wehler, *Gesellschaftsgeschichte*, i. p. 193.

58 *Ibid.*, p. 201.

59 On the clergy, see L. Schorn-Schütte, 'Die Geistlichen vor der Revolution', in Helmut Berding, Etienne François, and Hans-Peter Ullmann, eds, *Deutschland*

und Frankreich im Zeitalter der Französischen Revolution (Frankfurt am Main, 1989), pp. 216–44.

60 On the 'educated *Bürgertum*', see U. Frevert, '"Tatenarm und gedankenvoll"? Bürgertum in Deutschland 1780–1820', in Helmut Berding, Etienne François, and Hans-Peter Ullmann, eds, *Deutschland und Frankreich im Zeitalter der Französischen Revolution* (Frankfurt am Main, 1989), pp. 263–92; W. Ruppert, *Bürgerlicher Wandel. Die Geburt der modernen deutschen Gesellschaft im 18. Jahrhundert* (Frankfurt am Main, 1984); R. Vierhaus, 'Bildung', in O. Brunner, W. Conze, and R. Koselleck, eds, *Geschichtliche Grundbegriffe. Historisches Lexikon zur politisch-sozialen Sprache in Deutschland* (Stuttgart, 1972), i. pp. 508–51; Wehler, *Gesellschaftsgeschichte*, i. pp. 210–7.

61 Koselleck, *Preußen*, pp. 90–1.

62 Möller, *Fürstenstaat*, p. 100.

63 T. S. Ashton, *An Economic History of England: The Eighteenth Century* (London, 1961), pp. 30–48; J. Kulischer, *Allgemeine Wirtschaftsgeschichte des Mittelalters und der Neuzeit* (München, 1971), ii. pp. 61–72.

64 Möller, *Fürstenstaat*, p. 146–7, referring to E. Weis, 'Ergebnisse eines Vergleichs der grundherrschaftlichen Strukturen Deutschlands und Frankreichs vom 13. bis zum Ausgang des 18. Jahrhunderts', *Vierteljahrschrift für Sozial- und Wirtschaftsgeschichte*, 57 (1970), pp. 1–14.

65 Briggs, *France*, pp. 35–43; Kulischer, *Wirtschaftsgeschichte*, ii. pp. 72–87.

66 Wehler, *Gesellschaftsgeschichte*, i. pp. 73–4, with, in n. 18, numerous references to more detailed literature.

67 W. Abel, 'Landwirtschaft 1500–1648', in Hermann Aubin and Wolfgang Zorn, eds, *Handbuch der deutschen Wirtschafts- und Sozialgeschichte* (Stuttgart, 1971), i. pp. 391–405.

68 Schilling, *Aufbruch und Krise*, pp. 57–8.

69 M. Hroch and J. Petřán, *Das 17. Jahrhundert – Krise der Feudalgesellschaft?* (Hamburg, 1981); J. de Vries, *The Economy of Europe in an Age of Crisis, 1600–1750* (Cambridge, 1976).

70 Möller, *Fürstenstaat*, p. 147.

71 Wehler, *Gesellschaftsgeschichte*, i. pp. 170–4.

72 *Ibid.*, p. 172.

73 W. Treue, 'Wirtschaft, Gesellschaft und Technik in Deutschland vom 16. bis zum 18. Jahrhundert', in Grundmann, ed., *Gebhardt – Handbuch*, ii. pp. 437–545, pp. 515–7; on 'Bauernschutz', see Trossbach, *Bauern*, pp. 11, 18, 114.

74 Möller, *Fürstenstaat*, pp. 160–4.

75 C. Küther, *Menschen auf der Straße. Vagierende Unterschichten in Bayern, Franken und Schwaben in der zweiten Hälfte des 18. Jahrhunderts* (Göttingen, 1983); B. Roeck, *Außenseiter, Randgruppen, Minderheiten. Fremde im Deutschland der frühen Neuzeit* (Göttingen, 1993), pp. 66–80.

76 F. Lütge, *Deutsche Sozial- und Wirtschaftsgeschichte* (Berlin, 1952), p. 274; R. Endres, 'Das Armenproblem im Zeitalter des Absolutismus', in Franklin Kopitzsch, ed., *Aufklärung, Absolutismus und Bürgertum in Deutschland* (Munich, 1976), pp. 220–41, p. 223.

77 Möller, *Fürstenstaat*, p. 109.

78 W. Abel, *Massenarmut und Hungerkrisen im vorindustriellen Deutschland* Göttingen, 1972), pp. 58–61.

79 A fundamental work is O. Brunner, 'Das "Ganze Haus" und die alteuropäische "Ökonomik"', in O. Brunner, *Neue Wege der Verfassungs- und Sozialgeschichte* (Göttingen, 1968), pp. 103–27; on the 'ganzes Haus' in the urban context, see B. Roeck, *Lebenswelt und Kultur des Bürgertums in der*

frühen Neuzeit (Munich, 1991), p. 14; in the rural context, see Trossbach, *Bauern*, pp. 88–101.

80   D. Schwab, 'Familie', in O. Brunner, W. Conze, and R. Koselleck, eds, *Geschichtliche Grundbegriffe. Historisches Lexikon zur politisch-sozialen Sprache in Deutschland* (Stuttgart, 1975), ii. pp. 253–301.

81   *Ibid.*, pp. 287–99.

82   H. Rosenbaum, ed., *Seminar: Familie und Gesellschaftsstruktur* (Frankfurt am Main, 1978), p. 23.

83   H. Rosenbaum, *Formen der Familie. Untersuchungen zum Zusammenhang von Familienverhältnissen, Sozialstruktur und sozialem Wandel in der deutschen Gesellschaft des 19. Jahrhunderts* (Frankfurt am Main, 1982), pp. 19–20.

84   *Ibid.*, p. 21.

85   *Ibid.*, pp. 251–309; additionally, M. Mitterauer and R. Sieder, *Vom Patriarchat zur Partnerschaft. Zum Strukturwandel der Familie* (München, 1977).

86   R. Koselleck, '"Neuzeit". Zur Semantik moderner Bewegungsbegriffe', in R. Koselleck, ed., *Studien zum Beginn der modernen Welt* (Stuttgart, 1977), pp. 264–99, p. 285.

87   P. Clark, ed., *The European Crisis of the 1590s* (London, 1985).

Translated by Sheilagh Ogilvie.

|6|

Learned Men and Merchants: The Growth of the Bürgertum

ROBERT VON FRIEDEBURG AND WOLFGANG MAGER

Definitions and concepts

The history of the *Bürgertum* (middle classes) in Germany between the Peace of Westphalia and the end of the Old Empire confronts a terminological difficulty which conceals within it a conceptual problem. German research has concentrated mainly on the concept of the *Bürgertum*, even though this arose only in the nineteenth century. Graduates of the universities and other institutions of higher education were merged together with the merchants and industrial entrepreneurs into a social group described as the *Bürgertum* only from the second third of the nineteenth century on – indeed, the terms *Bildungsbürgertum* (educated middle classes) and *Wirtschaftsbürgertum* (economic middle classes) became current only in the twentieth century.

Admittedly, the word *Bürger* – which corresponds, etymologically, to the English word 'burgher' – was already current during the early modern period. The article on *Bürger* in the 'Economic Encyclopaedia, or General System of State, Town, Household and Agricultural Economy', edited in 1787 by Johann Georg Krünitz, documents the meanings of *Bürger* which were current in Germany up to the eve of the French Revolution.[1] The article begins with the traditional usages of *Bürger*: first, in the classical Aristotelian sense, meaning 'member of a state'; second, as an antonym to 'sovereign prince', meaning 'permanent subject', conforming to Jean Bodin's definition of *citoyen*; third, in relation to the 'specific civil society, which we call the town', as when the term 'burgher' is used to designate 'town inhabitant' or 'town inhabitant with citizenship'. Then the article lists two more recent definitions of 'Bürger' which anticipate to some extent the meanings of *Wirtschaftsbürger* (economic *Bürger*) and *Bildungsbürger* (educated *Bürger*): first, 'person of bourgeois estate', meaning 'a person who practises only an urban livelihood, which is therefore specifically called a bourgeois livelihood... even when he lives in the countryside'; and second, a person who is 'non-noble by birth, and does not belong to those of noble blood', but who 'on account of his learned and honourable services, especially in holding offices' is regarded as 'belonging to the honourable and respected people' – Krünitz regarded these non-noble ecclesiastical and temporal of-fice-holders as being similar to the *noblesse de robe*. These terms – *Bürger-tum* and *Bürger* – have no precise equivalents in English, and will therefore be retained in the original German in this chapter.

During the early modern period, the precursors of the 'educated *Bürger*' and the 'economic *Bürger*' were clearly distinguished from one another: the educated *Bürger* consisted of the university-trained 'learned men' who served in state, town, or church offices and in the professions – including the 'learned of name', i.e. private scholars without office or profession. Be-cause they had studied at university they enjoyed a special social standing. The aura of distinction enjoyed by the 'learned men' was partly owing to the fact that, like the nobles, they saw their destiny as serving the general good. They regarded their remuneration not as payment for work per-formed, but rather as honoraria or gratifications, whose magnitude was left to the goodwill and capacities of the paying party. For both reasons, they were situated, in the hierarchy of honour, above the precursors of the eco-nomic *Bürger*, who consisted of merchants, including putters-out and man-ufactory entrepreneurs. In contrast to the 'learned men', the merchants were not university-trained, depending for their livelihoods on business earnings.

However, in the course of the eighteenth century they increasingly rose to equal the learned men in standing and honour. This was due to the secular upswing in trade and industry in the age of the Enlightenment.[2] After the ravages caused by the Thirty Years War were made good and its population losses replaced during the first half of the eighteenth century, the second part of the century saw a continual increase in population. This brought in its wake a rise in food prices which lasted until 1816. From the middle of the eighteenth century onward, this rise in agrarian prices created lasting stimuli to growth in agricultural production. The demand by the expand-ing agrarian sector for household goods and working tools in turn stimu-lated industrial production. Trade and industry also profited from the growing overseas demand for goods, first for luxury needs and soon also for simple ones: after the end of the War of the Spanish Succession, transat-lantic trade rapidly expanded, and the 'modern world-system' (in the phrase of Immanuel Wallerstein) opened up expanding market opportunities, not only for western and central European exporters, but also for 'rusticalized industry' (in the phrase of Werner Sombart) or 'proto-industry' (in that of Franklin Mendels); this sort of industry is discussed in greater detail in Chapter 9. This was the context in which Hamburg experienced its comet-like rise to trade, shipping, and financial centre of European standing.

This upswing in trade and industry greatly increased the economic power and the social standing of the great merchants. A contributory factor was that many merchants engaged in 'putting-out', not only to urban export craftsmen (as they had since the later middle ages), but also, to a much greater extent than in earlier centuries, to domestic-industrial producers in proto-industries. In addition, merchants were increasingly becoming manufactory entrepreneurs in the expanding coal, iron, and steel industries, and in other 'proto-factories', to use the term coined by Hermann Freudenberger and Fritz Redlich. The entrepreneurial decisions of wholesale merchants, putters-out, and manufactory owners were often of considerable financial and social – indeed sometimes even political – importance, and some of their business relationships spanned continents. Consequently, contemporaries did not hesitate to attribute to the more important figures among these entrepreneurs in trade, transport, banking, and large-scale industry (whether centralized or decentralized) a social rank approaching that of the 'learned men' and the well-off nobles.

Admittedly, merchants not infrequently had the reputation of engaging in 'frauds, lies and other vices' – at any rate, this was how they were described by Johann Michael von Loen in his treatise *Der Adel* ('The Nobility') published in 1752. In addition, the risks inherent in doing business meant that they were always threatened with the danger 'of nothing being left of all their goods except their sins alone'.[3] On the other hand, the rising social esteem accorded to merchants from the middle of the eighteenth century on is reflected by the fact that first in France,[4] but soon in Germany as well,[5] a lively debate arose about whether nobles should be able to conduct wholesale commercial operations without loss of social status.[6] Carl Günther Ludovici, who in 1752–6 brought together the commercial wisdom of his day in his widely read five-volume reference work entitled 'The Published Academy of Merchants: Or Complete Merchant's Dictionary, from which All Businesses and Industries, with All Their Advantages, and the Way of Practising Them, Can Be Learned', significantly stated that in Germany 'retail trade' 'inarguably lost the nobleman his nobility'. On the other hand, although old nobles of knightly status, enjoying exclusive rights of admission to cathedral chapters, could not conduct 'a great and important trade' without losing their high rank, the 'common nobleman' could. It was well known that 'in great trading centres, old noble families and members of the patriciate still continue their trading business'; besides, 'every year, merchants *qua* merchants are honoured by the Emperor along with the nobility and knightage'.[7]

The social revalorization of merchant activity in the age of the Enlightenment was reflected not least in the fact that in many places the great merchants, putters-out, and manufactory owners became active in patriotic associations, reading circles, freemasons' lodges, and other voluntary associations, side by side with university graduates and noblemen.

An indication of the growing standing of the merchants, and also of the larger market-orientated agrarian producers, is provided by the work of the Prussian pedagogue and school reformer, Friedrich Gabriel Resewitz, published in Copenhagen in 1773 under the title 'The Upbringing of the *Bürger* to the Use of a Healthy Mind, and to Publicly Beneficial Activity'. The author divided the 'livelihood-earning *Bürger*'[8] into two major subgroups: on one hand, the 'peasants and craftsmen',[9] or the 'lower estate', who are 'effectual for the general well-being only through the use of their hands and by means of mechanical performance of learned habits';[10] and on the other hand, 'the higher estate of the livelihood-earning *Bürger*', namely 'merchants, artists,[11] ship-owners, manufactory-owners, larger agriculturalists, whether they are noble or not, and all other persons who engage in substantial livelihood-earning businesses', and work 'not only with their hands, but also with their heads'.[12] The destiny of this sort of *Bürger* is to serve the general well-being, 'primarily through the enlightenment and activity of his mind, through the development of his talents, and through the clever use of his genius'.[13] 'Where this social estate, which is justifiably termed the well-bred ('gesittet') among the livelihood-earning *Bürger*', does not yet flourish, and instead persists in following 'old habitudes and a learned routine', 'there is only little progress in the improvement of the people'.[14] Through the activity of the 'well-bred *Bürger*', 'the well-being of the country must be improved, livelihoods increased, the lower estate employed, good arts diffused, mores and modes of thought improved and made more general, and the nation given a new upward impetus toward perfection'.[15] By characterizing the 'well-bred *Bürger*' – the 'skilled artists, intelligent merchants, clever agriculturalists'[16] – as 'honourable *Bürger*',[17] Résewitz placed these representatives of the rising economic *Bürgertum* close to the 'learned men of profession',[18] that is to say to the precursors of the educated *Bürgertum*.

Admittedly, since the economic *Bürger* earned their livelihoods, for the time being their social standing remained below that of the university graduates, and certainly below that of the nobles. This had the consequence that once they had achieved wealth they were keen to set their sons – or at least their younger sons, in so far as these were not going to inherit from the parents – on the path to university study, and they tended to arrange marriages for their (highly endowered) daughters with (impoverished) nobles. In this way, the wealth acquired in business opened up state, urban, and ecclesiastical careers, or sealed social elevation through the acquisition of land – the culminating achievement was to take over a knightly estate. In the age of the Enlightenment, learned men and merchants thus increasingly merged together, as the 'well-bred social estate'.[19]

Pursuing this definition of a specific 'well-bred social estate' of learned men and merchants, this chapter will first examine what is known from empirical research concerning university-graduated officials and pastors as models for the learned men. It will then survey the research on merchants, putters-out, and manufactory owners, as models for the entrepreneurs. Finally, it will explore empirical studies of the urban *Bürger* (burgher) as the etymological source for the German term *Bürgertum*. At the end of the chapter, the following question will be posed: how, in the course of the nineteenth century, did the transition take place from the previous conception of the *Bürgertum* as a 'well-bred social estate' (*gesitteter Stand*), divided essentially into the two factions of 'learned men' and merchants, to the new conception of *Bürgertum* which merged educated *Bürger* and economic *Bürger* together into an all-encompassing social formation?

Learned men

The 'learned men' who served as state, urban, or ecclesiastical officials, and the academics practising free occupations or professions, enjoyed a special social standing in early modern times which placed them in proximity to the nobility and the distinguished urban patricians. Admittedly, during the seventeenth and eighteenth centuries, the sons of the latter two groups also increasingly began to spend a portion of their education at universities. Nevertheless, the nobles all, and the patricians for the most part, viewed an academic degree as beneath their dignities.

The high standing of the university-trained scholar in the Germany of the *ancien régime* was based primarily on his having graduated to become a licentiate and doctor of jurisprudence, theology, or medicine, or at least on his having obtained a Master's degree at a faculty of arts. In Germany, where in the age of the Enlightenment the universities formed highly esteemed centres of cultural life, the aura of 'learnedness' (*eruditio*) gave the scholar access to the *Res Publica Litteraria* (republic of letters),[20] which elevated the learned men far above the burghers of the 'German Home Towns'.[21] While the spatial and spiritual horizons of the latter often extended hardly further than the walls of the home town and its catchment area, studying at a university – generally far from home – and undertaking the educational tour (*peregrinatio academica*) which often followed endowed the young scholar with knowledge of the world, laid a basis for his personal or epistolary acquaintance with academics and *hommes de lettres* all over Europe, and enabled him, especially when he became a member of learned societies and academies, to appear to be a citizen of a cosmopolitan republic of learned men.

A substantial contribution to the high social standing of the German learned man of the Old Empire was made by the fact that in the age of the Enlightenment scholars increasingly appropriated the model of the 'man of the world' sketched out first by Christian Weise and later by Christian Thomasius.[22] In this way, they sought to refute the widespread prejudice which held that the universities brought forth only 'pedants', with the result that 'through study' the learned man 'becomes unskilled' in 'serving the republic usefully in both wartime and peacetime'.[23] To oppose this, the university graduates made efforts to manifest a 'gallant', i.e. practised, demeanour, 'according to the manners and laws of decorum passed down by the customs of polite persons of the world',[24] and to conduct themselves as 'true politicians'.[25] In this way, 'by means of a courageous ingeniousness combined with a well-practised judiciousness' they aimed to become apt for filling public offices and thus, like persons of noble estate, 'to further the outward happiness of themselves and others in a fitting way'.[26]

In doing so, they moved up into proximity with the noble power-élites, whose undisputed qualification for the leading positions in government, diplomacy, administration, and military service relied not so much on knowledge provided through education as on their polite manners. Admittedly, the nobles kept to themselves in the court, and the patricians kept to themselves in their drinking-halls and dancing-halls, excluding bourgeois persons from the rituals of formal invitation and counter-invitation, and thus also from social intercourse. But on the other hand many nobles belonged to the 'republic of letters' and were placed on an equal footing with bourgeois colleagues in the performance of the business of office; and this favoured – although for the most part only sporadically – private contacts between the two groups. For example, the legal councillor (*Syndicus*) to the noble estate of the prince bishopric of Osnabrück and at the same time secretary (*Konsulent*) to the Privy Council of the territory, Justus Möser, during his annual spa sojourn in Bad Pyrmont – that is, in a space outside his social estate – frequented noble social circles,[27] and Werther (in Johann Wolfgang von Goethe's novel *The Sorrows of Young Werther*, published in 1774) was in the habit of private intercourse with the Count of C. On the other hand, Werther had to absent himself from the noble company when the count's guests of noble birth gathered one evening at his residence (Second Book, Letter of 15 March 1772), and Möser avoided noble company in Osnabrück in order to avoid giving rise to compromising situations.

Learned jurists

The rise of the 'learned men' in the seventeenth and eighteenth centuries was substantially owing to the jurists, who were increasingly being educated to become not just experts in their own speciality, but also men of the world. At the reformed German universities such as Halle (founded in 1694) and Göttingen (founded in 1737), and at the old German universities which were reformed on the same pattern, teaching was provided not only in legal studies but also in cameralistics and political science, and efforts were made to rid the future state officials graduating from these institutions of the 'pedantry' of the *Schul-Fuchs*[28] (lit. 'school fox', meaning pedant), and to guide them into the style of life of the 'gallant' and the 'politician'.[29] The bourgeois jurists rose to become the load-bearing pillars of the administrative staffs of the German territorial states, which in 1648 obtained *ius superioritatis*, i.e. a far-reaching territorial sovereignty, and then greatly developed the institutions of state administration.

Historical research on the university-trained officials of the Empire and the German territories therefore stands in the shadow of the history of the territorial state.[30] As a consequence, apart from a few studies which investigate the princes' legally trained commoners in the context of investigating the territorial state in the age of the Reformation,[31] only a few works of social history focus on the legally trained officials of the late seventeenth century and the eighteenth century.[32] The discussion that follows is therefore based on analysis of available examples.

However, the point of departure in such a discussion remains the growing importance of the territorial state and of Imperial institutions such as the *Reichshofrat* (Imperial Aulic Council) and the *Reichskammergericht* (Imperial Chamber Court), since in the course of the sixteenth century these enormously intensified their demand for legally trained specialists.[33] From the mid-sixteenth century on, out of the very small number of legally trained officials for each individual territory there developed associations of families which were related to one another through kinship, and which for generations supplied legally trained officials to council positions and ultimately also to the middle and lower positions of the state administration in their territories of origin; to this extent, the jurists of the Empire were internally stratified according to territory. In the course of the sixteenth century these associations of jurists became quasi-exclusive territorial social estates, *vis-à-vis* both the town citizens and other territories. Then, from the seventeenth century on, they were increasingly joined by the nobility in the competition for council positions, since the latter were likewise beginning to pursue university studies in faculties of law.[34] Until the end of the eighteenth century, the distinction in social estates between noble and non-noble councillors persisted in the central government; this was the case, for instance, both in the central administration of the Calvinist Landgraviate of Hessen-Kassel, and in those of the (Catholic) ecclesiastical principalities of north-west Germany. However, in Kassel, for example, the bourgeois councillors held some two-thirds of the positions in the council.[35] The number of jurists and their positions grew as a consequence of the growing importance of territorial state administration as a reservoir of positions. However, this group could not have been further from comprising a more-or-less closed 'profession' throughout the Empire such as was formed by the barristers and lawyers of the London Inns of Court.

Instead, by the middle of the seventeenth century, a new social grouping had arisen within each German territory in the shape of the jurists and other university-educated princely officials. Through their special 'Gerichtsstand' (the privilege, in case of legal proceedings, of being tried directly by the prince instead of by other princely officials) and their personal link with the territorial lord, they belonged to the band of officials serving a particular territorial prince. They were sharply distinguished, both formally and legally, but also socially through marriage and social intercourse, from the nobility of the parliamentary estates and from the urban citizens eligible for town-council positions, not to mention from the urban guilded craftsmen. As a consequence of their dependence on service with their own territorial lord, these associations of families had little contact with those in other territories. The confessional divide between the associations of officials in Catholic, Calvinist, and Lutheran territories was in any case never crossed. Confessionally, the leading councillors followed the situation in the territory in which they held their appointments.

Given this background, there arises the question of the extent to which the dictionaries' idealized vision of a well-bred social estate of leaders, which was neither internally stratified along territorial lines nor externally demarcated strongly from the nobility, actually came into being as a social reality in the Old Empire by the end of the eighteenth century. Did this 'corporate world of jurists' slide into crisis because the study of law lost its corporate privilege, because in the spirit of the Enlightenment the territorial state increasingly relied on specialist examinations rather than on recommendations through family ties?[36] Or did the direct path 'from social estate to occupation'[37] simply not exist, even for jurists? Were there tendencies toward an (at least partial) de-territorialization of bureaucracies, toward a relativization of the barriers of social estate between bourgeois councillors and nobility? Did the Enlightenment, from the beginning of the eighteenth century, operate less as a path toward occupation and professionalization in the twentieth-century sense than as the advocate of an unchanged society of orders in the eighteenth-century sense, in which the study of law merged the educated social estates together into a well-bred social estate displaying civilized manners and having its own specific honourable status and code of behaviour? With these questions in mind, let us trace the destinies of those who emerged from university studies in law during the eighteenth century.

The demand for jurists and the number of graduates of legal faculties rose steeply from the second half of the seventeenth century on. The Electorate of Brandenburg alone increased the number of positions for university-trained jurists in the Privy Council, the Supreme Court, the Consistory, the two Treasurer's Offices, and the Exchequer from 60 in the mid-seventeenth century to more than 140 by the beginning of the eighteenth. In all the different parts of the country taken together, the demand for jurists rose from just 170 in 1641 to more than 200 in the 1660s.[38] In the Free Imperial City of Frankfurt am Main, although the number of positions did not increase, from the 1730s on they were filled less and less by members

of the patriciate and increasingly by bourgeois jurists. Looking only at the
180 members of the Frankfurt city council in the period 1727–1806, 53
were jurists, forty of them bourgeois. The number of jurists graduating
from universities in the Empire increased from an average of just over fifty
per decade around the middle of the seventeenth century to more than 200
in the 1670s. It fell again to around 150 in the 1690s, but in the first decade
of the eighteenth century grew to about 300, and until the 1760s remained
at between 150 and 200 graduates per decade. In the three following
decades the average slumped to around 100 per decade. Assuming gradua-
tion in the mid-twenties, and a career in office of about four decades, there
would have been fewer than 1,000 university-trained jurists in the Empire
in 1740.[39] Considering the multiplicity of sovereign estates in the Old Empire which were subject directly to the Emperor and had a potential demand
for legal advice – there were about 2,000 corporations, towns, knights,
counts, princes, and electors, subject directly to the Emperor – this number
is probably an underestimate. The difference may be attributable to the fact
that, as previously, many offices were held by jurists who had not graduated from universities.

From studies of the Free Imperial Cities of Frankfurt, Cologne, Speyer, and
Wetzlar, and of the territorial cities of Göttingen, Koblenz, and Karlsruhe,
the following provisional conclusions can be drawn concerning the activity
of jurists in town councils or in urban service. To the extent that towns, too,
had to overcome increasingly broad and complex administrative challenges
during the eighteenth century, they also required an increasing volume of ex-
pert knowledge and administrative experience. The practice of administration by amateurs, which had been handed down from the past, was scarcely
suited for this. As a consequence, the town magistracies were increasingly
transformed into agencies of academically educated specialists, who followed
careers and were remunerated accordingly. In so far as council members from
the ranks of the patriciate like those in Frankfurt am Main, or from the ranks
of the merchants such as in Cologne remained active in the city administration, they were transformed into full-time (and also well-paid) amateurs, who
in the everyday business of administration were backed up by legal experts,
such as legal councillors (*Syndici*). As a consequence, the magistracy regarded
itself as holding administrative authority over the burghers. Examples of the
governmental self-image of town-council members can be instanced for many
German cities in the eighteenth century. When in 1769 the guilded citizens of
Koblenz complained to the Elector about the financial conduct of the magistracy, the town council defended itself, strikingly, against such a 'respect-
forgetting passing-over of [the burghers'] proper authorities', characterized
the conduct of the citizenry as an act of presumption by the 'subordinated'
against the 'authorities', and demanded obedience:

> What sort of disorder would arise in a state if the proper authorities
> had to pay heed to the vengeful calumniations of their unruly

subalterns! Through their base desires, our subordinates arouse the suspicion that they are actually going so far as to dispute rendering their superiors due obedience and proper respect.[40]

In the administration of German towns in the eighteenth century, therefore, jurists – but also graduates of the faculties of arts and medicine – rose to become academically educated office-holders, and formed the governmental authorities, whether under the supervision of the prince in the territorial towns, or under only the weak supervision of the Emperor, or under no supervision at all, in the Free Imperial Cities.

On the basis of a study of 599 law students born in the Free Imperial City of Frankfurt, a number of statements can be made about the origins, places of study, and later careers of the graduates. Of the 277 fathers of these law graduates whose occupations could be found out, 46 were members of the Frankfurt town council – that is, members of the Frankfurt citizenry who were eligible for council membership – and 58 were members of some government administration, whether on a superior (34), middle (13), or lower level. Of these fathers of law graduates, 68 came from trade and industry; 60 more were jurists outside the field of administration; and eighteen were pastors. Urban patriciate, government administration, legal practice, and trade and industry were the four main fields of origin of the jurists born in Frankfurt.[41] Compared to the jurists born outside a large Free Imperial City, the Frankfurt jurists had a pattern of origins in which the urban patriciate and trade or industry played an especially significant role. Among the leading councillors of Bavaria at the beginning of the eighteenth century, a majority had fathers who were jurists and councillors.[42] In the Lutheran and Calvinist Landgraviates of Hessen-Kassel and Hessen-Darmstadt, councillors were also recruited from councillor families – Carl von Moser, son of the well-known Johann Jakob Moser, even believed that he had detected just a single association of families.[43] In Hessen-Kassel, Bavaria, the north-west German ecclesiastical principalities, and the Ernestine territories of Saxony, appointments to vacated council positions and to positions as local district officials (discussed in greater detail below) were also regulated within the associations of office-holding families which had already established themselves before the beginning of the eighteenth century. Legal studies at a university were a necessary but not sufficient condition for rising into the desired position in the service of a territorial lord.[44]

Of the 599 Frankfurt jurists mentioned above, only 182 themselves found positions in the administration (108 in the higher administration, seventy-one at the middle level, and three at the lower level). Nevertheless, 112 became members of the city council, like many of their fathers – a path which was specific to the sons of the Frankfurt patriciate and cannot be generalized to apply to jurists from families of the territorial bureaucracies. Only ten of the Frankfurt jurists found positions in the church or in universities, and only 13 with the military; only eight became merchants or practised an industry, five became notaries, 11 became judges outside the administration, and 19 remained legal councillors (*Syndici*); while 253, almost half of the 599 jurists, remained simple 'Advocaten' (lawyers).[45]

The university study of law was in any case frequently followed by employment as a lawyer or judge in the patrimonial courts of the lower nobility of the region in question, for a transitional period, as a way of obtaining practical experience. As a consequence of the poor salary-outlook in such positions, however, this was hardly a substitute for rising into a career in territorial service, for which familial relationships were once again a precondition. In Hessen-Kassel, furthermore, the Territorial and Criminal Court in Kassel, and the association of the lawyers admitted into the government and the courts in Kassel, were the decisive career channels for making the leap into central administration for those who did not want to end their careers as district bureaucrats.[46]

For a career outside one's own territory or outside the dominion of one's own Free Imperial City, an academic degree alone was in any case not sufficient. Such a career came into question only for those few jurists who gained supra-regional reputations through publications. For the bulk of graduates, gaining an office in their territory of origin was the only possibility of leading a life befitting their social estate. In the ecclesiastical principalities of north-west Germany, however, from the very outset university-educated bourgeois jurists did not come into question, because the nobility dominated; however, they did come into question for positions as judges and bureaucrats for the preparation of decisions at the middle level. Bourgeois jurists also found positions as legal councillors (*Syndici*) with cathedral chapters, *Domkellnereien* (cathedral offices collecting dues from the peasant subjects and organizing the demesne), baronies, and more important cities, in such positions as *Amtsrentenmeister* (prince's officials collecting feudal dues), *Gografen* (stewards presiding over local courts), *Hofkammerräte* (prince's councillors), *Stadtschreiber*, and *Prokuratsschreiber* (different ranks of clerk).[47] In a Free Imperial City such as Frankfurt am Main, among 23 village mayors in the seventeenth and eighteenth centuries there were 17 jurists who had graduated from university; and six more of the village mayors had studied law, even though they had not graduated with a degree. Among the 15 town clerks, the ratio between legally trained men with a degree and those without was seven to four, for the 20 council clerks it was 12 to 13, and for the 11 legal court clerks it was five to two.[48] In the Landgraviate of Hessen-Kassel, the kinship network, which can be shown to have existed as early as the sixteenth century, also extended from the early eighteenth century to the officials serving the territorial lord in the local districts.[49] Most of the jurists entering legal studies began their university studies between the ages of 17 and 20 years, and obtained their academic degrees between the ages of 22 and 26. In addition to the approximately 20 offices of the Landgraviate which were filled by legally trained men serving the prince on the local or district level, in the Kassel court in the second half of the eighteenth century there were only nineteen *Assessoren* (men at the entrance rank into the hierarchy of councillors of the central government) and higher-level village mayors. The overwhelming majority of these judges, however, themselves originated from bureaucrat families in Kassel. The bulk of the legally trained men serving the prince on the local or district level in the Hessian small towns never advanced beyond this position.[50]

The revenues of the ordinary German territorial state consisted to a significant extent of the dues in cash and kind which the peasant subjects owed the prince as 'Grund-, Leib-, Zehnt- und Gerichtsherr' (literally, 'landlord, feudal lord, tithe lord and juridical lord'). It is not inappropriate to think of a middling German territorial state as one huge manor, with a number of stewards dispersed over the territory collecting the rents in cash and kind from the peasants. Each territory was sub-divided into a number of districts, referred to using different terms in different territories. Very often, such a district was called an 'Amt' (literally 'office'). Each *Amt* consisted, as in Hessen-Kassel, of one or two small towns, often with fewer than 2,000 inhabitants each, and a dozen or so villages. Each *Amt* had two main 'servants of the prince' assigned to it. One of them was responsible mainly for the collection of the feudal dues in cash and kind from the inhabitants, and was not as a general rule academically trained. He was often called the 'Rentmeister' (literally, 'rent-master'), derived from 'Rente', a general term referring to the various dues owed by the subject peasants. The other 'servant of the prince' on the district level was responsible for the administration of justice in the *Amt* and, at least in the eighteenth century, was nearly always trained in law at a university. He was the local head of the *Amt*, and was called the 'Amtmann' (a possible English equivalent is the title of 'bailiff').

Both the *Rentmeister* and the *Amtmann* received some of their salaries in the form of cash from the prince, but often only a minor part. A very important part of their salaries remained the right to collect a certain proportion of the dues owed by the peasant subjects. This proportion was generally fixed and was clearly defined in the 'Bestallung', the written contract drawn up between the prince and his official. Moreover, the *Amtmann* had the right to collect further payments, in cash or kind, for administering justice – payments from subject peasants who came to him to have their cases tried. This part of his income was called 'Sporteln' (perquisites). Most *Amtmänner* enjoyed a fairly wide degree of autonomy in deciding how much they would levy as perquisites from the subjects.

To sum up, the nature of many of the small and middling principalities in Germany can be compared to that of a big manorial estate. Agrarian revenues formed the core element of public finances. Each district within each territory, and the administration of that district, was supported directly from the agrarian revenues of the subject peasant population. It was thus possible for some districts to be wealthy and others poor. A term which can be used to describe this sort of economic independence of each separate district is 'Eigenwirtschaft' (manorial economy), referring to the manorial nature of the financing of each district.

As a consequence, agrarian benefits continued to make up a significant proportion of the remuneration received by legally trained men serving the prince on the local or district level. The 'manorial economy' of the district and its administration still played a central role in providing for the office-holder. This also indirectly included the fees which could be levied from the district's subjects for the performance of particular administrative tasks – the so-called 'Sporteln' or perquisites. These ways of providing for the office-holder are evidence of the traditional character of the conduct of office at this middle level. Incidentally, such offices were also important as a source of provision in old age. Those succeeding to an office, before taking it over frequently had to submit to conditions requiring that they support their predecessors materially with its revenues. A middle-level office, just like the living of a pastor, was viewed as a resource which was expected to be made use of, in the framework of perquisites and benefits in kind; there was no material alternative to the exploitation of these benefits.

Given this background, how is the character of jurists as part of a well-bred social estate, equipped with a specific academic honour on the level of the Empire, to be assessed? On one hand, through the mutual stratification of various associations of families with different spheres of influence and placement opportunities for their descendants, the jurists remained socially splintered into innumerable small territorial groups. Each of these groups remained oriented around its own territorial lord, who at least in the medium-sized and smaller territories often personally knew his officials in the local district and central administrations, and appointed them personally. This reflected the patrimonial character of many of the German polities subject directly to the Emperor. The ordinary Hessian jurist studied at one of the territorial universities, Marburg or Gießen. In the eighteenth century the Frankfurt jurists also moved in here. However, studying at several universities which were distant from one's own territory was by no means the rule.[51]

On the other hand, these associations of families were linked to one another through intermarriage and self-recruitment. Student friendships were maintained over entire lifetimes, and broke through barriers, especially the barriers between different associations of families, and to some extent also those between different territorial states.[52] Even in Hesse the group consciousness of the jurists was strong enough, toward the end of the eighteenth century, to provide protection from reprisals by the infuriated territorial prince against those officials who had collected money for one of their fellows – a lawyer – imprisoned in 1789–90 on account of alleged revolutionary activities.[53] The Margrave of Baden even found that his room for manœuvre was noticeably restricted by the jurists in his council and their arguments against his policies.[54] Not in the rural towns of the local district officials, but certainly in the capital cities of the territorial lords, the number of educated men ultimately became large enough to enable the emergence of an educated society.[55] Admittedly, as the example of Kassel makes apparent, within the central administration the sharp distinction between bourgeois and noble councillors remained the rule.[56] From the second half of the eighteenth century on, however, there was increasing intermarriage between the leading bureaucrats and the resident nobility in this territory. Thus 12 per cent of the Lower Hessian nobility of the birth cohort of 1700–49, and 24 per cent of the birth cohort of 1750–99, married bourgeois women.[57] In the Electorate of Bavaria, as well, bourgeois academic councillors began to merge with noble office-holders within the circle of leading bureaucrats.[58] In the sense that they formed territorial bureaucratic patriciates which maintained themselves until the end of the eighteenth century, and to some extent intermarried with the nobility, the highest legally trained jurists became part of a social estate which conceived of itself under the banner of the Enlightenment as 'well-bred', even though at the same time each territorial faction of this estate remained strongly oriented toward its own particular territory. Thus a multiplicity of territorial social estates was formed, rather than a single social estate throughout the Empire.

Pastors[59]

Studies of German pastors have long regarded the Protestant parsonage as the cradle of the bourgeoisie. For the seventeenth and eighteenth centuries, such studies draw attention to the increasing intermarriage between the pastors and the temporal bureaucracy, and the growing self-recruitment of the pastors. The history of ideas emphasizes the resistance of the clerical estate to the Enlightenment and to the relativization of confessional boundaries. For the historians of each German territory, the pastors were above all the executive organs of the absolutist state – as court preachers, superintendents, and members of territorial governments and urban authorities, in which they definitively occupied a leading position.[60] Their position as a social estate of their own was relativized by the increasing definition of their tasks in directions that were supposed to further the public good as conceived by government policy. According to this view they were no longer representatives of a social estate of their own while not yet being members of the new social estate of well-bred *Bürgerlichkeit* – 'middle-class-ness' – in the Old Empire.[61] This view has not been altogether superseded. The eighteenth-century territorial state actually did in many ways aim at the integration of pastors into its band of serving officials; and the Protestant clergy actually did see its confessional self-confidence and its social standing endangered by the crisis of the clerical estate.[62]

However, the pastors were not fully integrated into the temporal apparatus of serving officials, neither can they be viewed as the lowest stratum of leaders within the absolutist territorial state. While their integration into the bourgeoisie of the nineteenth century has since been disputed,[63] more recent research from the perspective of social history points out the growing interpenetration between the pastors and the temporal academic bureaucrats. In terms of the history of ideas, the opposition between academic theology and the Enlightenment has been relativized by pointing to the importance of the theological Enlightenment, particularly the emerging pastoral theology. For the new self-image of the pastors, this was a significant element in their special role as members of the well-bred and educated social estate.[64] Let us begin by examining the social interpenetration between the pastors and the non-ecclesiastical bureaucrats.

In the seventeenth century, the need for new pastors was so great that they could not be recruited wholly from their own ranks. Instead, *homines novi* – new men – streamed into the Protestant clergy, especially from the ranks of the well-off urban citizenry. In Württemberg as late as 1800 two-fifths of pastors came from the 40 towns of the country, while the approximately 480 rural communities provided as many as three-fifths of the total. In the course of the eighteenth century self-recruitment had increased without leading to a complete closing-off of the ranks of the pastors. In the Duchy of Braunschweig and the Landgraviate of Hessen-Kassel between 1685 and 1750, 30 to 40 per cent of fathers of pastors were themselves pastors, and 12 to 15 per cent were bureaucrats in urban or princely service. Among the fathers of pastors and their wives, and among pastors' sons and sons-in-law, peasants and craftsmen no longer played more than a very minor role (in total less than 4 per cent). However, up to the mid-eighteenth century, between 30 and 40 per cent of fathers of pastors and their wives were recruited from the higher clergy, from the middle- and lower-level territorial administration, from trade, and from the ranks of the apothecaries. From the mid-eighteenth century on, however, self-recruitment increased, and there was a growing exchange with the middle- and higher-level territorial bureaucracy, which was as a rule also academically – i.e. legally – educated. The office of pastor turned out to be a 'platform occupation' from which the sons of pastors set their sights on rising into the higher clergy (such as superintendents or court preachers) or the ranks of the university-trained men serving the prince on the local and district level.[65] With regard to the origins, marriage patterns, and aims of pastors' sons, there was a close connection with the university-trained men serving the prince on the local and district level and academically educated apothecaries and better-off merchants. However, there was hardly any connection with labouring peasants and even less with urban crafts.

Up to the last third of the seventeenth century studying at a faculty of arts was sufficient for obtaining a rural parish if one was nominated to it. After this, however, the seminary ethos and the view that this group should receive a proper academic education increasingly gained ground.[66] One aim of the reform of academic education was that the pastor should be prepared for the task of 'bringing up' the populace, as part of an all-encompassing regulatory and utilitarian care. The theological Enlightenment, by contrast, developed its own programme. In it, a new importance was attached to the sermon, the sacraments, pastoral theology, and mastery of Greek for the purposes of biblical exegesis.[67] In many respects, the theological Enlightenment broke with dogmatic views of orthodoxy: it sought to combine eclectic methods, a Wolffian system, and Pietist inwardness, and it brought about a 'reorientation of theology toward the perspectives of the enlightened and pious subject'. But this also contributed to increasing the general agreement that university studies should be made more scholarly, which in turn emphasized the character of the clergy as a well-bred social estate similar to the others.[68]

Of course, it must be stressed that the meagre provisioning of the overwhelming bulk of rural livings, and the exceptionally heterogeneous interests of many rural pastors with regard to a more scholarly education, set narrow limits on the realization of this ideal.[69] The complaints of the pastors about the diminished standing of the clerical estate which arose at latest by the beginning of the eighteenth century, and the movements seeking to transform this group into a special group of teachers for the state,[70] cannot be denied. But this could not alter the vision of pastors as a special subgroup within the academically educated well-bred social estate, participating in the honourable status and code of behaviour of that estate, a vision aimed at by the higher clergy and the academic faculties, especially in the course of the theological Enlightenment. This vision insisted on the special form and significance of the education which should be given to pastors, emphasizing the importance of piety and the special tasks of the pastor in instructing the populace. Admittedly, researchers are not agreed about the roots of this tendency for pastors to move closer to temporal, academically educated office holders.[71] Even in a poor and largely rural territory such as the Landgraviate of Hessen-Kassel, the practice of the preachers' seminaries underlines, even if with a certain delay, the consequences of these aims of the theological Enlightenment for the self-image of pastors.[72]

Merchants

Traders and merchants were divided into two main groups, according to economic and social position: small traders and shopkeepers on one hand, and full-scale merchants on the other.[73] Ludovici elevated the 'merchants trading in wholesale, or so-called "Großirer"' above the 'merchants trading in individual items or in retail'. He maintained that the full-scale merchants must be 'titled with the honorific: lord merchants and traders'. He defined 'merchant' as

> everyone who trades or conducts a commerce; that is, buys wares, barters in wares, or has wares manufactured, in order to sell them either in a public shop or vault in the town where he lives, or outside the same, in fairs or yearly markets, or in foreign lands into which he sends them at his own cost.[74]

It must be emphasized that trading in goods also included money and foreign-exchange business.[75] In the 'Allgemeine Landrecht für die Preußischen Staaten' (General Law Code for the Prussian States) of 1794,[76] therefore, the definition of 'merchant' included anyone who 'practised trade in goods, or exchanging, as his main business'.[77] When Ludovici wrote that the merchant under certain circumstances 'had goods manufactured', this gave expression to an additional feature, namely that in the contemporary understanding, the putter-out and the manufactory entrepreneur were included among the merchants. Ludovici distinguished between two 'sorts of merchant', 'in that some re-sell the wares in the same shape and type as they buy them in; others, by contrast, buy in raw wares ... have them processed, and sell them only then.'[78] The 'merchants' of the eighteenth century therefore included wholesale traders, bankers, forwarding agents, shippers, putters-out, and manufactory owners. They can rightly be termed 'Unternehmer' ('entrepreneurs'): the term is found as early as the mid-eighteenth century, and appeared in the General Law Code for the Prussian States in phrases such as 'entrepreneurs of manufactories' and 'manufactory entrepreneurs'.[79]

Early modern entrepreneurs were primarily merchants and putters-out; only to a limited extent did they direct centralized production plants, so-called 'mills', set up mainly to make use of water-power for various purposes. Apart from this, merchants rose to become manufactory entrepreneurs in situations in which centralization of production either favoured rapid adaption to the fluctuations of fashion and the requirements of the emerging consumer society, for instance in calico printing; or where it secured high-value raw materials against embezzlement, for example in the processing of merino wool into fine woollen cloths; or where it eased the production of new types of ware, as in the luxury industries. This is reflected in Ludovici's description of how manufactory entrepreneurs collected 'working people with them in their own houses, so that they could give precise attention to their acts and omissions'. The 'lord and entrepreneur of such manufactories' had to be 'of good invention, in order always to discover something new'. 'Because the frauds of the working people are many' he must 'keep a watchful eye upon them, and know precisely those matters wherein they can defraud'. If 'a batch of goods was hanging around his neck, and the fashion for them changed', he must 'get the same out of his hands the sooner the better'. 'Such a manufacturer, who intends something quite new or something useful for a country, but also to bring something valuable in train', should not petition for privileges, but rather trust in 'his invention and good wares'. He should 'betimes take himself out of the play' when a new product does not succeed, and 'in its place undertake something more useful'.[80] In the eighteenth century, the shift of entrepreneurial activity from commerce into production remained minor on the whole; it was only with factory industrialization in the nineteenth century that this occurred to any substantial degree.

The high esteem which the great merchants already enjoyed before industrialization was essentially based on the fact that, in distinction to the craftsmen and shopkeepers, they enjoyed 'merchant law and merchant rights'. These legal privileges attaching to their estate touched on such various matters as the powers of attorney of factors, managing clerks, and business managers; entitlements to merchant interest-rates and commissions; the ability to engage in exchange business; the regulations governing pledge securities, commercial law cases, and bankruptcy; the credibility of business books as evidence; and the subordination of merchants to a special commercial jurisdiction.[81] In order to enter into enjoyment of these laws and rights, it was necessary to have 'properly learned' or at least to understand commerce, and 'to be included in the register of the merchants and, in any locality where the merchants ... are incorporated into a guild or corporation of any sort, to be admitted to the same'.[82] The relevant provisions of the General Law Code for the Prussian States read, 'Where a merchant guild or corporation is present, a member who is to be admitted to it must adequately perform the requirements of the guild articles, both in observance of the apprenticeship period and in other matters,'[83] and 'in localities where such guilds exist, only he who is admitted to one has the rights of a merchant.'[84] The merchants also enjoyed additional advantages: in individual cases, sometimes for whole branches of industry, the state granted merchant rights outside the merchant guild, in the shape of so-called 'concessions' for industrial concerns, and linked the granting of privileges and monopolies with provision of financial and technical assistance.[85] Not least among those who rose to enjoy merchant rights were the merchants active as putters-out and manufactory owners in the producing industries. The General Law Code for the Prussian States provided that 'the entrepreneurs of the manufactories, in consideration of their operation of the same, and the sales of the wares produced in them, possess merchant rights';[86] the same was conceded to shippers.[87]

The growth observable during the eighteenth century in the economic powers of the full-scale merchants of the classical type, and the expansion of merchants' entrepreneurial activities into putting-out and manufactories, aroused a demand for scholarly systematization of the expertise of the merchant, and the founding of appropriate educational institutions. It was in this context that Ludovici organized the expertise and experience of the merchant into a formal pedagogical edifice.[88] In the centre of this edifice, he placed the 'merchant's main sciences', namely, '1. knowledge of wares, 2. knowledge of trading, and 3. book-keeping'. These were supplemented by 'the merchant's auxiliary sciences' or 'applied merchantry',[89] which included 'the art of reckoning', 'the art of writing', 'knowledge of currencies', 'knowledge of weights and measures', 'commercial geography', 'commercial law', 'instruction in commercial correspondence', 'the knowledge of trade-marks', 'commercial cryptography or the art of secret writing', 'commercial knowledge of languages', and 'the knowledge of manufactories or factories'.[90] At the same time, Ludovici spoke out in favour of the 'establishment of a merchants' academy', 'a place, or a society, wherein the sciences and arts serviceable for commerce are taught systematically, according to a good pedagogical method'.[91] The Leipzig professor advocated that in the universities 'those student youths who are intended at some time to be members of chambers or colleges of commerce, or commercial courts, etc., which are as necessary to a country as they are useful', should obtain an education in 'merchantry', 'commercial policy', and so forth.[92] Such urgings fell on fertile ground. In 1768 the Handlungsakademie (Commercial Academy) was founded in Hamburg, and under its director of many years, Johan Georg Büsch, exerted enormous influence.[93] Büsch continued Ludovici's efforts to develop a systematic science of commerce, and in 1792 published a very broadly conceived 'Theoretical and Practical Description of Commerce in its Manifold Branches of Business'.[94]

Because pre-industrial entrepreneurs were more active in commerce than in production, they exercised managerial functions to only a very limited extent, with the result that they remained dispensable: that is to say, they had free time to spare for public activity. A contributory factor to their dispensability was that fixed capital for the most part played only a very modest role in their concerns compared to circulating capital. This made it possible for them to respond to trade crises by ceasing business activity until better times came. They tended to invest their profits in real estate and financial securities, partly to increase their creditworthiness, but also partly in order to retain a means of surviving as rentiers during periods when they ceased trading. Secured income, dispensability, and education endowed many of them with the rank of men of property. As such, they took an active part in urban government, distinguished themselves through activities for the public good, for example in pious or charitable foundations, and together with the higher office holders, the university-trained professionals, and the well-off nobility, made up 'better society' in German towns. They dwelt in stately burgher's houses situated in the centre of cities, kept large numbers of servants, and entertained their guests as befitted their social estate.[95]

The 'losers' of the eighteenth century: the urban citizens

As late as 1700, there were only ten cities in England with more than 8,000 inhabitants; apart from the world-class city of London, there were only two English cities with more than 15,000 inhabitants. By comparison, the Hessian capital Kassel already had c. 15,000 inhabitants by 1730. With the exception of the metropolis of London, in which every tenth Englishman lived around 1700, England was a rural nation. Apart from the mayor and aldermen of London, the magistrates of the English provincial towns possessed no legal basis at all for administering themselves independently comparable to that enjoyed by German urban governments. In 1654, Nicholas Bacon remarked of Ipswich, 'I perceive few or none of the inhabitants of this towne were acquainted with the true nature of government.'[96] In the Old Empire, by contrast, there were 34 towns with at least 10,000 inhabitants; and, compared to England, these enjoyed a considerable degree of autonomy in self-government and lawmaking. It was not until the end of the eighteenth century that England possessed more inhabitants in cities with over 10,000 inhabitants than the Old Empire.[97] Although the autonomy of the German Free Imperial Cities was increasingly limited in practice by the territorial states, and the German rural towns were largely incorporated into the territorial states,[98] the citizens eligible for town council membership and the guilded craftsmen of these towns were nevertheless important enough to give their name to the expression normally used in German-speaking historiography and research to refer to the middle class: Bürgertum. The following treatment of this particular element of the urban population will not discuss all the inhabitants of early modern German towns, however; and it will also leave out of account those of them who have already been discussed above in other contexts, in their functions as jurists, court preachers, superintendents, and so on.

Only a small portion of urban inhabitants can be included in the Stadt-bürgerschaft (urban bourgeoisie) in the narrow sense of the term. First, only a minority of urban inhabitants were eligible for town council membership. Second, even in smaller towns, such as Nördlingen in Swabia, 6 per cent of the population owned more than 40 per cent of the property recorded in the tax list in the second half of the seventeenth century.[99] At the top of the urban hierarchy stood well-off traders, craftsmen, and innkeepers, as a rule household heads who had been settled in the town for a long time, but to a varying extent 'nouveaux riches' as well.[100] Master craftsmen, depending on their industries, might also be numbered among the better-off families in a town, and those eligible for council membership. In the seventeenth century and up until 1724, only the richest 20 per cent of the inhabitants of Nördlingen ever attained entry to the town council.[101] The numerous urban economic and governmental élites of this sort formed the corporations of the urban bourgeoisies of the Old Empire. As in Nördlingen, they can be more or less sharply distinguished from particular upwardly mobile manufactory owners, merchants, and putters-out. In contrast to the latter, they remained oriented toward their urban surroundings, not to the 'good breeding' of a particular social estate or to territorial office.[102] The shift in urban growth in the eighteenth century, from the old Free Imperial Cities organized around trade and industry to the princely capital cities such as Vienna, Berlin, Dresden, Prague, and Breslau, points to the fact that the classic merchants and craftsmen of the towns, especially those in south-west Germany, were the losers in the great shift in the European trade network from the ancient Mediterranean orientation to the new orientation around the Atlantic.[103] Hamburg and Frankfurt are examples of the successful adaptation of some German free cities to these new circumstances, while Cologne and Aachen provide examples of stagnation. The cities of the German industrial revolution, in the Ruhr district, were without exception wholly unimportant in the early modern period.[104] Apart from the Frankfurt bankers – who for their part operated to a considerable extent with the funds of the territorial princes – and the Hamburg shippers and merchants, the craftsmen and other industrial producers of many sixteenth-century industrial centres were left behind by the economic upswing in other parts of the Central European economy. This fact underlies the soundness of Mack Walker's characterization of these 'Home Towns'.[105] In the Swabian Free Imperial City of Nördlingen (with 7,000 inhabitants) the income of craftsmen declined; the town suffered under military contributions during the wars, both within the Empire and between the Empire and France, which lasted until 1714, and a general impoverishment of the town, particularly of the guilded craftsmen, was the result.[106] In the eighteenth century, the Hessian rural towns (with fewer than 2,000 inhabitants as a rule) were notorious for the dilapidated condition of their houses and the general impoverishment of their *Ackerbürger* ('field citizens', townsmen who also cultivated some land).[107] In the rural town of Hersfeld, the urban upper stratum (with three times the average property listed in the town tax register) declined from 8 per cent of the total population in 1614 to 5.9 per cent in 1747. The share of the Hersfeld lower stratum (with less than half the average property) also declined, from 55.4 per cent in 1614 to 38.6 per cent in 1747. Whereas in 1614 more than one third (36.6 per cent) of the taxable households owned property worth between half the average and three times the average, by 1747 this had risen to more than half (55.5 per cent).

The total value of all property taken together, however, had fallen greatly. At the top of the hierarchy in Hersfeld stood the families eligible for council membership, although they were to some extent still surpassed by the 'learned' princely officials in the town, by the *Samtschultheiß* (the representative of the prince in the town), the town physician, and the Protestant pastor. Around the middle of the eighteenth century two apothecaries, eight millers, five linen-cloth traders, the three innkeepers, the Fulda shipper, and 22 merchants all owned more than 400 *Gulden*-worth of property each.[108] From the analysis carried out on the Frankfurt jurists in the eighteenth century, we know that none of these occupational groups played an important role among the fathers of the jurists. The *Bürgertum* of the rural towns and the jurists of the territorial princes lived in very distinct spheres. For the south-west German towns, the wars between revolutionary France and the Old Empire, and their consequences for the territorial and legal structure of German-speaking Central Europe, brought the final end of what remained of their autonomy.[109]

Conclusions and implications for the 'Bürgertum' of the nineteenth century

As early as 1858, the professor of public law Johan Caspar Bluntschli, referring to the university-trained office holders and professionals on one hand and the entrepreneurs on the other, stated: 'They understand each other easily, get along together comfortably socially, show common character traits, have common basic assumptions, and also have strong common interests in culture and politics.'[110] To this extent, around the mid-nineteenth century, a 'social class' in the sense of Max Weber appears to have arisen, having grown together out of the 'educated *Bürger*' and the 'economic *Bürger*'.[111]

Against this background, public law theorists, historians, and journalists developed the new concept of the *Bürgertum*.[112] Until then, in most of the principalities of the German Federation, the government, the higher levels of administration, the high military officers, and legislation had all remained predominantly the domain of the nobility, and in many towns self-government lay to a greater or lesser extent in the hands of the dominant old patrician families. In this situation, *Bürgertum* became a slogan which was used to support the desires of academics and entrepreneurs to participate in public affairs.

Among the pathbreakers in this use of the term *Bürgertum*, Bluntschli deserves special attention. This jurist, in his *Staatsrecht* (treatise on public law) which appeared in 1852,[113] used as his point of departure the political rights of the 'free *Bürgerstand* (citizenry)' or *Bürgertum* in the 'Athenian democracy'.[114] He pointed out that in Europe in the middle ages 'the *Bürgerschaften* (citizenries) of the towns'[115] – in this context the author used the expressions 'the town *Bürgertum*'[116] and the 'personally free town *Bürgertum*' with similar meaning[117] – ascended 'to the seat of a new *Bürgerfreiheit*' (freedom of the *Bürger*).[118] Bluntschli concluded that in the end the claim to freedom, 'which had come to be widespread among the town *Bürgertum*, was transferred to wider circles of the population of the state at large, and out of the town *Bürgertum* was born the institution of the modern state *Bürgertum*',[119] which exercised 'political rights, and in particular the right to vote in electing the deputies of the people to Parliament'. According to Bluntschli, the modern state *Bürgertum* coincides with the 'Third Estate' (*Dritter Stand*), from which were excluded 'the mass of the members of the populace and the country', as well as the nobles.[120]

Within the state *Bürgertum*, the highest rank was occupied by 'officials, clergy, learned men, lawyers, doctors, and academics of all the faculties'. The next rank was taken by graduates 'who indeed had received not so much an antique classical, but rather instead a modern scientific education', thus 'the officers of the standing army, the engineers, many higher technicians, teachers, and writers'. At the bottom were ranked 'the manufacturers, the artists, the artistic craftsmen, and a mass of medium-sized agriculturalists who are distinguished from the peasants through their education and style of life'. They were to be counted among the *Bürgertum* only in so far as 'urban culture and finer social upbringing' continued to be effective among them.[121]

These quotations make clear that, according to Bluntschli, the fundamental factor which merged together the different occupational groups subsumed under the heading of *Bürgertum* was *Bildung* (education), conceived in the new-humanistic sense of the term, which was developed in the age of the French Revolution as a response to Jacobin egalitarianism. This new-humanistic idea of education was not coloured by social estate, as the characterization of learned men and merchants as members of the well-bred estate (*gesitteter Stand*) had been; instead, it took on quasi-religious traits. The holy nimbus given to *Bildung* was based on the claim of the academics, now called the 'Gebildeten' ('those who are educated'), to exemplify 'through appropriate teaching and properly regulated personal activity the effective and harmonious development of all human powers toward the likeness of God' – according to the definition of 'Bildung' in the eponymous article of the Brockhaus encyclopaedia of 1830; 'gebildet' ('educated') was used to describe anyone who, in the sense of this 'task', had 'already made happy progress toward the general aim of humanity'.[122] Admittedly, the society of learned men of property which was envisaged under the auspices of the new-humanistic idea of *Bildung* remained more vision than reality in nineteenth-century Germany. Not only did the links of intermarriage and social intercourse among the sub-groups of the Bürgertum remain inter-mittent throughout the entire nineteenth century, but, perhaps more im-portantly, no integration was ever achieved with the 'Gebildeten' among the nobles. The nobility largely insisted on frequenting its own exclusive spheres of political and social life.

Admittedly, this reflected the distance between this new concept of Bür-gertum and the nobility. Bluntschli's matter-of-fact references to the city of Athens and the 'personally free town Bürgertum' were clear indications of the orientation of the new concept of Bürgertum toward the town and the urban Bürger, as models of the new society. To early German thinking about the new Bürgertum, the history of the Free Imperial City of Frank-furt, for example,

> with its close relationship with the German Emperors and Kings, as a community which became a Free Imperial City, offered the opportu-nity of a historical legitimization of claims to rights of freedom, with-out discrediting oneself with the French Revolution ... Liberals and conservatives linked their image of the Bürger, even if in differing ways, to Emperor and Empire, and this link left them only the me-dieval town as an object of investigation.[123]

This orientation was compatible with the monarchy as a constitutional form, but it also recognized the existence of the nobility as a power élite of its own, for the time being. It reflected the continuing gulf between Bür-gertum and nobility. To this extent, the invention of the German Bürgertum in the mirror of the medieval city clearly distinguished the German idea of freedom from that underlying the French société des notables or the Eng-lish propertied classes.[124]

Notes

1   'Bürger', in Johann Georg Krünitz, ed., Oeconomische Encyclopädie, oder allgemeines System der Staats-Stadt- Haus- und Landwirthschaft (Brünn, 1787), Part 7, pp. 377–401, pp. 377f, 380f.

2   See Hans-Ulrich Wehler, Deutsche Gesellschaftsgeschichte, i. Vom Feudal-ismus des Alten Reiches bis zur Defensiven Modernisierung der Reformära. 1700–1815 (Munich, 1987) (with exhaustive bibliographical references); Friedrich-Wilhelm Henning, Deutsche Wirtschafts- und Sozialgeschichte im Mittelalter und in der frühen Neuzeit (=Friedrich-Wilhelm Henning, Hand-buch der Wirtschafts- und Sozialgeschichte Deutschlands, i., Paderborn, 1991); Ilja Mieck, ed., Europäische Wirtschafts- und Sozialgeschichte von der Mitte des 17. Jahrhunderts bis zur Mitte des 19. Jahrhunderts (=Wolfram Fischer et al., eds, Handbuch der europäischen Wirtschafts- und Sozialgeschichte, iv. Stuttgart, 1993).

3   Johann Michael von Loen, Der Adel (Ulm, 1752), p. 84.

4   See Abbé Gabriel-François Coyer, *La noblesse commerçante* (London, 1756).
5   In 1756, Johann Heinrich Gottlob von Justi edited Coyer's treatise in a German translation and commented on it approvingly; on this, see Barbara Stollberg-Rilinger, 'Handelsgeist und Adelsethos. Zur Diskusion um das Handelsverbot für den deutschen Adel vom 16. bis zum 18. Jahrhundert', *ZHF* 15 (1988), pp. 273–309.
6   Stollberg-Rilinger, 'Handelsgeist'.
7   Carl Günther Ludovici, *Eröffnete Akademie der Kaufleute: oder vollständiges Kaufmanns-Lexicon, woraus sämmtliche Handlungen und Gewerbe, mit allen ihren Vortheilen, und der Art, sie zu treiben, erlernet werden können* (Leipzig, 1752–6); quotations here from article on 'Handel oder Handlung', Part 3, 1754, cols 122–43, col. 125.
8   Friedrich Gabriel Resewitz, *Die Erziehung des Bürgers zum Gebrauch des gesunden Verstandes, und zur gemeinnützigen Geschäfftigkeit* (Copenhagen, 1773), p. 77.
9   *Ibid.*, p. 54.
10   *Ibid.*, p. 77.
11   'Artists' encompassed non-guilded industrial producers in 'factory and manufactory arts' who 'deliver their products into commerce'; see 'Kunst' in Krünitz, *Encyklopädie*, Part 55 (1793), pp. 91–125, p. 97.
12   Resewitz, *Erziehung*, p. 77.
13   *Ibid.*
14   *Ibid.*
15   *Ibid.*
16   *Ibid.*, p. 2.
17   *Ibid.*, p. 16.
18   *Ibid.*, p. 5.
19   See, to similar effect, the concept of the 'functional estates' in Axel Flügel, 'Wirtschaftsbürger oder Bourgeois? Kaufleute, Verleger und Unternehmer in der Gesellschaft des Ancien Régimes', in Hans-Jürgen Puhle, ed., *Bürger in der Gesellschaft der Neuzeit* (Göttingen, 1991), pp. 107–32, p. 118.
20   Wilhelm Kühlmann, *Gelehrtenrepublik und Fürstenstaat. Entwicklung und Kritik des deutschen Späthumanismus in der Literatur des Barockzeitalters* (Tübingen, 1982); Sebastian Neumeister and Conrad Wiedemann, eds, *Res Publica Litteraria. Die Institutionen der Gelehrsamkeit in der frühen Neuzeit* (2 parts, Wiesbaden, 1987).
21   Mack Walter, *German Home Towns: Community, State, and General Estate, 1648–1871* (Ithaca, NY, 1971).
22   See Gunter E. Grimm, *Literatur und Gelehrtentum in Deutschland. Untersuchungen zum Wandel ihres Verhältnisses vom Humanismus bis zur Frühaufklärung,* (Tübingen, 1983), pp. 314–425.
23   'Pädanterey' in Johann Heinrich Zedler, *Grosses vollständiges Universal-Lexicon aller Wissenschafften und Künste*, xxvi (Leipzig/Halle, 1740), cols 189–92, col. 190; see Kühlmann, *Gelehrtenrepublik*, pp. 288–318.
24   'Galant', in Zedler, *Universal-Lexicon*, x (1735), cols 78f, col. 79.
25   'Politicus', in Zedler, *Universal-Lexicon*, xxviii (1741), cols 1528f, here col. 1528.
26   *Ibid.*, col. 1529.
27   Christine van den Heuvel, *Beamtenschaft und Territorialstaat. Behördenentwicklung und Sozialstruktur der Beamtenschaft im Hochstift Osnabrück. 1550–1800* (Osnabrück, 1984), p. 205, n. 28.
28   See the article under this title in Zedler, *Universal-Lexicon*, xxxv (1743), col. 1546.

29 See Kühlmann, *Gelehrtenrepublik*; Grimm, *Literatur*.

30 Still relevant on the state of research, Filippo Ranieri, 'Vom Stand zum Beruf. Die Professionalisierung des Juristenstandes als Forschungsaufgabe der europäischen Rechtsgeschichte der Neuzeit', *Ius Commune*, 13 (1985), pp. 83–106. The Frankfurt Max-Planck-Institut für Rechtsgeschichte is responsible, with its extensive collections, for the definitive research in this direction.

31 See definitively Karl E. Demandt, 'Amt und Familie. Eine soziologisch-genealogische Studie zur hessischen Verwaltungsgeschichte des 16. Jahrhunderts', *Hessisches Jahrbuch für Landeskunde*, 2 (1952), pp. 79–133; for a more recent summary of the state of research on the late 15th to the early 17th century, and even for this period still pointing out substantial gaps, see Notker Hammerstein, 'Universitäten – Territorialstaaten – Gelehrte Räte', in Roman Schnur, ed., *Die Rolle der Juristen bei der Entstehung des modernen Staates* (Berlin, 1986), pp. 687–736.

32 These few studies include Wolfgang Metz, 'Zur Sozialgeschichte des Beamtentums in der Zentralverwaltung der Landgrafschaft Hessen-Kassel bis zum 18. Jahrhundert', *Zeitschrift des Vereins für Hessische Geschichte und Landeskunde*, 67 (1956), pp. 138–48; Bernd Wunder, 'Die Sozialstruktur der Geheimratskollegien in den süddeutschen protestantischen Fürstentümern (1660–1726)', *Vierteljahrschrift für Sozial- und Wirtschaftsgeschichte*, 58 (1971), pp. 143ff; likewise on Hessen-Kassel, although based on the *Staatskalender* (state calendar) which was published from the mid-18th century on, not only on the councillors but also on the local officials, admittedly (due to documentary availability) only for the period after 1760, Stefan Brakensiek, 'Lokalbehörden und örtliche Amtsträger im Spätabsolutismus. Die Landgrafschaft Hessen-Kassel 1750–1806', in Stefan Brakensiek, Axel Flügel, Werner Freitag, and Robert von Friedeburg, eds, *Kultur und Staat in der Provinz* (Bielefeld, 1992), pp. 129–61; a recent path-breaking work: Barbara Dölemeyer, *Frankfurter Juristen im 17. und 18. Jahrhundert* (Frankfurt, 1993). Dölemeyer relies on the databank on jurists and legal dissertations which has been set up by the Max-Planck-Institut für Rechtsgeschichte in Frankfurt and from which additional informative studies concerning this crucial group of academically educated officials are to be awaited in the near future; on this project, see Ranieri, 'Stand'.

33 On the Reichskammergericht, see Sigrid Jahns, 'Die Personalverfassung des Reichskammergerichts unter Anpassungsdruck – Lösungen im Spannungsfeld zwischen Modernität und Überalterung', in Bernhard Diestelkamp, ed., *Das Reichskammergericht in der deutschen Geschichte. Stand der Forschung, Forschungsperspektiven* (Cologne/Vienna, 1990), pp. 59–109.

34 See e.g. Demandt, 'Amt'; for a summary, see Ranieri, 'Stand', p. 95; even within a single Imperial Knight's domain, without a formally closed territory and with only a few positions for juristically educated specialists, the few offices were repeatedly filled by members of the same group of families; see R. Schmitt, *Frankenberg. Besitz- und Wirtschaftsgeschichte einer reichsritterschaftlichen Herrschaft in Franken 1528–1806/1848* (Ansbach, 1986).

35 Metz, 'Sozialgeschichte', *passim*; Clemens Steinbicker, 'Das Beamtentum in den geistlichen Fürstentümern Nordwestdeutschlands im Zeitraum 1430–1740', in Günther Franz, ed., *Beamtentum und Pfarrerstand 1400–1800* (Limburg, 1972), pp. 121–47, pp. 125ff.

36 This is speculated by Ranieri, 'Stand', p. 99.

37 See the title of the article by Ranieri, 'Vom Stand zum Beruf'.

38 Gerd Heinrich, 'Amtsträgerschaft und Geistlichkeit. Zur Problematik der sekundären Führungsschichten in Brandenburg Preußen 1450–1786', in

Franz, *Beamtentum*, pp. 179–238, pp. 199ff.

39 Ranieri, 'Stand', p. 103.
40 Jürgen Müller, *Von der alten Stadt zur neuen Munizipalität. Die Auswirkungen der Französischen Revolution in den linksrheinischen Städten Speyer und Koblenz* (Koblenz, 1990), p. 56.
41 Dölemeyer, *Frankfurter Juristen*, pp. lxxiiiff.
42 Niklas Freiherr von Schrenck und Notzing, 'Das bayrische Beamtentum 1430–1740', in Franz, *Beamtentum*, pp. 27–50, p. 44.
43 Albrecht Eckhardt, 'Beamtentum und Pfarrerstand in Hessen', in Franz, *Beamtentum*, pp. 81–120, p. 100; Brakensiek, 'Lokalbehörden', *passim*.
44 Harald Schieckel, 'Die Pfarrerschaft und die Beamten in Sachsen-Thüringen', in Franz, *Beamtentum*, pp. 149–78, pp. 160f; Steinbicker, 'Beamtentum', pp. 130–5; Eckhardt, 'Beamtentum', p. 100; Schrenck, 'Bayrische Beamtentum', p. 44.
45 Dölemeyer, *Frankfurter Juristen*, p. lxvi.
46 For Hessen-Kassel see once again Brakensiek, 'Lokalbehörden', *passim*; but also the very enlightening contributions in the collected volume, Franz, *Beamtentum*.
47 Steinbicker, 'Beamtentum', *passim*.
48 Dölemeyer, *Frankfurter Juristen*, p. xxxi.
49 Brakensiek, 'Lokalbehörden', pp. 134ff.
50 *Ibid.*, pp. 152–4.
51 Dölemeyer, *Frankfurter Juristen*, pp. lf; specifically on its development into a discipline, concerning which it is not possible here to go into detail, see Christoph Link, 'Rechtswissenschaft', in Rudolf Vierhaus, ed., *Wissenschaften im Zeitalter der Aufklärung* (Göttingen, 1985), pp. 120–42.
52 H. E. Bödeker, 'Strukturen der Aufklärungsgesellschaft in der Residenzstadt Kassel', in *Mentalitäten und Lebensverhältnisse: Beispiele aus der Geschichte der frühen Neuzeit. Rudolf Vierhaus zum 60. Geburtstag* (Göttingen, 1982), pp. 55–76, pp. 69–70.
53 Winfried Speitkamp, 'Die Landgrafschaft Hessen-Kassel und die französische Revolution', *HessJbLG* 40 (1990), pp. 145–67, pp. 145, 157f; on group consciousness, use must still be made of the letters and memoirs of well-known individuals, e.g., on the Marburg cameralist Jung-Stilling, see Hans W. Panthel, *Johann Heinrich Jung-Stilling. Briefe an Verwandte, Freunde und Fremde aus den Jahren 1787–1816* (Hildesheim, 1976); Johann Heinrich Jung-Stilling, *Lebensgeschichte*, ed. by Gustav Adolf Benrath (Darmstadt, 1976): only here does the significance of the academic education of this social estate, especially its education in the philosophy of Leibniz and Wolff and in Pietism, and the acceptance of the unique patriarchal relationship of the Hessian Landgrave and Elector to his learned men, become clear, see e.g. Jung-Stilling, 'Lehrjahre', in *Lebensgeschichte*, p. 585: 'The Elector, moreover, had from time immemorial much graciousness for Stilling; he will continue to be grateful to him for it for eternity, and his respectful love for this prince, who is great in so many ways, will never disappear'; and his essay 'Untersuchung der Folgen, die aus Empörung der Unterthanen gegen die Obrigkeit entstehen' ('Investigation of the Consequences which Arise from Uprisings of Subjects against the Authorities'), in *Lebensgeschichte*, and especially on pp. 334f. his emphasis that the only path to social improvement was a general 'striving for moral perfection' and 'dispensing with luxury'.
54 This anecdote in W. Demel, *Vom aufgeklärten Reformstaat zum bürokratischen Absolutismus* (Munich, 1993); and Horst Dreitzel, *Absolutismus und ständische Verfassung in Deutschland. Ein Beitrag zur Konti-*

nuität der politischen Theorie in der frühen Neuzeit (Mainz, 1992); specifically on Baden, Helen P. Liebel, 'Enlightened Bureaucracy versus Enlightened Despotism in Baden, 1750–1792', Transactions of the American Philosophical Society, 55/5 (1965), pp. 3–132.

55 Bödeker, 'Strukturen', although on pp. 63f. he points out the sharp division between noble and bourgeois sociability, and on pp. 68f. he discusses the restabilization of the separation between nobility and bourgeoisie in the lodges from the 1780s on; J. Meidenbauer, Aufklärung und Öffentlichkeit. Studien zu den Anfängen der Vereins- und Meinungsbildung in Hessen-Kassel 1770–1806 (Marburg, 1990).

56 Metz, 'Sozialgeschichte', pp. 143–6.

57 Gregory W. Pedlow, The Survival of the Hessian Nobility 1770–1870 (Princeton, 1988), p. 45.

58 Schrenck, 'Bayrische Beamtentum', p. 44.

59 This section discusses only the Protestant clergy.

60 See individual case-studies, such as W. Sommer, Gottesfurcht und Fürstenherrschaft. Studien zum Obrigkeitsverständnis Johann Arndts und lutherischer Hofprediger zur Zeit der altprotestantischen Orthodoxie (Göttingen, 1988); L. Schorn-Schütte, 'Prediger an protestantischen Höfen der Frühneuzeit. Zur politisch-sozialen Stellung einer neuen bürgerlichen Führungsgruppe in der höfischen Gesellschaft des 17. Jahrhunderts, dargestellt am Beispiel von Hessen-Kassel, Hessen-Darmstadt und Braunschweig-Wolfenbüttel', in H. Schilling and H. Diedericks, eds, Städtische Eliten in Deutschland und den Niederlanden vom 16. bis 19. Jahrhundert (Cologne, 1985), pp. 275–336; Monika Hagenmaier, Predigt und Policey. Der Gesellschaftliche Diskurs zwischen Kirche und Obrigkeit in Ulm 1614–1639 (Baden-Baden, 1989).

61 See e.g. Gerd Heinrich, 'Amtsträgerschaft', pp. 203f., 216f.; Johannes Kunisch, 'Die deutschen Führungsschichten im Zeitalter des Absolutismus', in Hanns Hubert Hofmann and Günther Franz, eds., Deutsche Führungsschichten in der Neuzeit. Eine Zwischenbilanz, (Boppard, 1980), pp. 111–42, 137–8; survey in John Michael Stroup, The Struggle for Identity in the Clerical Estate: North West German Protestant Opposition to Absolutist Policy in the 18th Century (Ann Arbor, 1980; Leiden, 1984), cited here according to the Ann Arbor edn, pp. 1–5.

62 On the legal and constitutional background of the relationship between the estates of the Empire and the legal framework of the Imperial Ecclesiastical Law, see Martin Heckel, 'Religionsbann und landesherrliches Kirchenregiment', in Hans-Christoph Rublack, Die lutherische Konfessionalisierung in Deutschland (Gütersloh, 1992), pp. 130–62; C. Link, Die Grundlagen der Kirchenverfassung im lutherischen Konfessionalismus im 19. Jahrhundert (Münster, 1966), pp. 17–37; Georg Ris, Der 'kirchliche Konstitutionalismus' (Tübingen, 1988), pp. 17–47.

63 See recently Oliver Janz, Bürger besonderer Art. Zur Sozialgeschichte der evangelischen Pfarrer in Preußen 1850–1914 (Berlin, 1994).

64 See esp. Schorn-Schütte, 'Prediger' and 'Evangelische Geistlichkeit und katholischer Seelsorgeklerus in Deutschland. Soziale, mentale und herrschaftsfunktionale Aspekte der Entfaltung zweier geistlicher Sozialgruppen vom 17. bis zum Beginn des 19. Jahrhunderts', Paedagogica Historica, 30 (1994), pp. 39–81; Walter Sparn, 'Vernünftiges Christentum', in Vierhaus, Wissenschaften, pp. 18–57; specifically on pastoral theology, Volker Drehsen, Neuzeitliche Konstitutionsbedingungen der praktischen Theologie (Gütersloh, 1988), pp. 222ff.

65 Schorn-Schütte, 'Evangelische Geistlichkeit', pp. 49–54; for the quoted

passage, H. Mitgau, 'Verstädterung und Großstadtschicksal genealogisch gesehen', *Archiv für Bevölkerungswissenschaft*, 11 (1941), pp. 339–64, here p. 355, cited according to Schorn-Schütte, 'Evangelische Geistlichkeit', p. 48; Sigrid Bormann-Heischkeil, 'Die soziale Herkunft der Pfarrer und ihrer Ehefrauen', in Martin Greiffenhagen, ed., *Das evangelische Pfarrhaus* (Zürich, 1984), pp. 149–74, here p. 160ff.; Anthony J. La Vopa, *Grace, Talent and Merit: Poor Students, Clerical Careers, and Professional Ideology in Eighteenth-Century Germany* (Cambridge, 1988), pp. 27–31; Stroup, *Struggle*, pp. 25–31.

66 Schorn-Schütte, 'Evangelische Geistlichkeit', pp. 55–62.

67 *Ibid.*, pp. 129–46; Robert v. Friedeburg, '"Ecclesia renitens". Soziale Stellung und gesellschaftliches Handeln kurhessischer Pfarrer in der ersten Hälfte des 19. Jahrhunderts', in Luise Schorn-Schütte and Walter Sparn, eds, *Evangelische Geistlichkeit. Zur sozialen und politischen Rolle einer bürgerlichen Gruppe in der deutschen Gesellschaft des 18. bis 20. Jahrhunderts* (Göttingen, 1996).

68 Sparn, 'Vernünftiges Christentum', pp. 33–42, quotation from p. 35; Drehsen, *Neuzeitliche Konstitutionsbedingungen*, pp. 85ff., on the distinction which was arising between theology and religion in the theological Enlightenment.

69 On this provisioning, see Schorn-Schütte, 'Evangelische Geistlichkeit', pp. 67–78; Friedeburg, '"Ecclesia renitens"', *passim*; La Vopa, *Grace*, pp. 46–70.

70 Schorn-Schütte, 'Evangelische Geistlichkeit im Alten Reich und in der schweizerischen Eidgenossenschaft. Eine sozialbiographische Skizze zum 17. und 18. Jahrhundert', in Schorn-Schütte and Sparn, *Evangelische Geistlichkeit*; Stroup, *Struggle*, pp. 139ff.

71 See La Vopa, *Grace*, pp. 138–211, on the development of the self-image of the clerical estate in giving increasing value to academic training as a meritocratic honour appropriate to their social estate; see especially p. 185, on the embedding of service and duty into the corporate hierarchy; in contrast, Stroup, *Struggle*, pp. 82ff., places greater emphasis on the self-maintenance of the clerical estate, although under altered auspices.

72 Friedeburg, '"Ecclesia renitens"'.

73 On the development of merchants, putters-out, and manufactory entrepreneurs between the Peace of Westphalia and the end of the Old Empire, see the literature cited in n. 2; see also Wilfried Reininghaus, *Gewerbe in der frühen Neuzeit* (Munich, 1990); Wolfgang Köllmann *et al.*, eds, *Bürgerlichkeit zwischen gewerblicher und industrieller Wirtschaft. Beiträge zum 200. Geburtstag von Friedrich Harkort* (Dortmund, 1994).

74 Article on 'Handelsmann, oder Kaufmann', in Ludovici, *Kaufmanns-Lexicon*, 3 (1754), cols 196–216, col. 196.

75 See article on 'Waaren' in Ludovici, *Kaufmanns-Lexicon*, 5 (1756), cols 543–63.

76 *Allgemeines Landrecht für die Preußischen Staaten*, used according to the edition prepared by Hans Hattenhauer (Frankfurt am Main/Berlin, 1970).

77 Part 2, Titel 8, para. 475: Hattenhauer, ed., *Allgemeines Landrecht*, p. 467.

78 Article on 'Handelsmann, oder Kaufmann', in Ludovici, *Kaufmanns-Lexicon*, 3 (1754), cols 196–216, col. 199.

79 Part 2, Titel 8, paras 407–23: Hattenhauer, ed., *Allgemeines Landrecht*, p. 465.

80 'Fabrik' in Ludovici, *Kaufmanns-Lexicon*, 2 (1753), cols 1406–11, cols 1409–11.

81 See 'Handelsmann, oder Kaufmann' in Ludovici, *Kaufmanns-Lexicon*, x.

'Rechte und Freyheiten der Kaufleute', cols 214–16; in addition, see 'Handelsobligation, Handelsbillet', 3 (1754), cols 216–18; 'Handelsbücher, Bücher der Kaufleute', cols 144–52; 'Handelsgericht, Commerciengericht', cols 174–81; see also the relevant provisions of the 'Allgemeines Landrecht für die Preußischen Staaten', compiled in Peter Raisch, *Die Abgrenzung des Handelsrechts vom Bürgerlichen Recht als Kodifikationsproblem im 19. Jahrhundert* (Stuttgart, 1962), pp. 34–44; and Clemens Wischermann, *Preußischer Staat und westfälische Unternehmer zwischen Spätmerkantilismus und Liberalismus* (Cologne, 1992), pp. 255–73.

82   Article on 'Handelsmann, oder Kaufmann', in Ludovici, *Kaufmanns-Lexicon*, 3 (1754), col. 197.
83   Part 2, Titel 8, para. 479: Hattenhauer, ed., *Allgemeines Landrecht*, p. 467.
84   Part 2, Titel 8, para 480: *ibid.*
85   See 'Allgemeines Landrecht für die Preußischen Staaten', Part 2, Titel 8, para. 481, in Hattenhauer, ed., *Allgemeines Landrecht*, p. 467; see Dietmar Willoweit, 'Gewerbeprivileg und "natürliche" Gewerbefreiheit. Strukturen des preußischen Gewerberechts im 18. Jahrhundert', in Karl Otto Scherner and Dietmar Willoweit, eds, *Vom Gewerbe zum Unternehmen. Studien zum Recht der gewerblichen Wirtschaft im 18. und 19. Jahrhundert* (Darmstadt, 1982), pp. 60–111; Wischermann, *Preußischer Staat*, pp. 255–62.
86   Part 2, Titel 8, para. 483, in Hattenhauer, ed., *Allgemeines Landrecht*, p. 467.
87   *Ibid.*, para. 484.
88   Carl Günther Ludovici, *Grundriß eines vollständigen Kaufmanns-Systems* (Leipzig, 1756).
89   *Ibid.*, para. 7, p. 10.
90   *Ibid.*, paras 9–19, pp. 10–19.
91   *Ibid.*, para. 28, p. 24.
92   *Ibid.*, para. 29, p. 25.
93   See Franklin Kopitzsch, *Grundzüge einer Sozialgeschichte der Aufklärung in Hamburg und Altona* (Hamburg, 1982), pp. 365f., 525.
94   On Büsch see Kopitzsch, *Grundzüge, passim*.
95   See Lothar Gall, *Von der ständischen zur bürgerlichen Gesellschaft* (Munich, 1993); Lothar Gall, *Bürgertum in Deutschland* (Berlin, 1989); Lothar Gall, ed., *Vom alten zum neuen Bürgertum. Die mitteleuropäische Stadt im Umbruch. 1780–1820* (Munich, 1991) and *Stadt und Bürgertum im Übergang von der traditionalen zur modernen Gesellschaft* (Munich, 1993); Hans-Werner Hahn, *Altständisches Bürgertum zwischen Beharrung und Wandel. Wetzlar 1689–1870* (Munich, 1991); Axel Flügel, *Kaufleute und Manufakturen in Bielefeld. Sozialer Wandel und wirtschaftliche Entwicklung im proto-industriellen Leinengewerbe von 1680–1850* (Bielefeld, 1993), section E, 'Auf dem Weg zum gebildeten Stand. Kaufmännische Kultur im 18. Jahrhundert', pp. 205–237.
96   Peter Clark and Paul Slack, 'Introduction', in Peter Clark and Paul Slack, eds, *Crisis and Order in English Towns 1500–1700* (London, 1972), pp. 1–56; Peter Clark and Paul Slack, *English Towns in Transition* (London, 1976), esp. ch. 9, 'The Political Order', pp. 126–140; Peter Clark, ed., *The Transformation of English Provincial Towns* (London, 1984); fundamental on the early modern German town, Heinz Schilling, *Die Stadt der Frühen Neuzeit* (Munich, 1993).
97   Schilling, *Stadt*, p. 5.
98   See Schilling, *Stadt*, on the 'étatist character' of urban development after 1650. On the functional and spatial differentiation of German towns, not considered here, see Schilling, *Stadt*; earlier conceptualization of this urban

bourgeoisie with reference to south-west Germany in Helen P. Liebel, 'The Bourgoisie of Southwestern Germany 1500–1789. A Rising Class?', *International Review of Social History*, 10 (1965), pp. 283–307.

99   Christopher Friedrichs, *Urban Society in an Age of War. Nördlingen 1580–1720* (Princeton, 1979).

100 On the following, Christopher Friedrichs, 'Politik und Sozialstruktur in der deutschen Stadt des 17. Jahrhunderts', in Georg Schmidt, ed., *Stände und Gesellschaft im Alten Reich* (Stuttgart, 1989), pp. 151–70.

101 Friedrichs, *Urban Society*.

102 See Friedrichs, *Urban Society*, on the conflict between the city and the manufactory-owning family Wörner.

103 Schilling, *Stadt*, pp. 24ff.

104 *Ibid.*, p. 28.

105 Mack Walker, *German Home Towns*.

106 Friedrichs, *Urban Society*.

107 U. Möker, 'Entwicklungstheorie und geschichtliche Wirtschaft. Makroökonomische Erklärungen wirtschaftlicher Zustände und Entwicklungen der Landgrafschaft Hessen-Kassel vom 16. bis zum 19.Jahrhundert', (Ph.D. dissertation, Universität Marburg, 1971); K. Greve and K. Krüger, 'Steuerstaat und Sozialstruktur. Finanzsoziologische Auswertung der hessischen Katastervorbeschreibung für Waldkappel 1744 und Herleshausen 1748', *GG* 8 (1982), pp. 295–332.

108 Jörg Witzel, *Hersfeld bis 1525–1756. Wirtschafts-, Sozial- und Verfassungsgeschichte einer mittleren Territorialstadt* (Marburg, 1994), pp. 101–3, 114.

109 See Jürgen Müller, 'Städtische Führungsschichten im Wandel. Die kommunalen Eliten in Speyer und Koblenz vom Ancien Régime zur napoleonischen Zeit', in Karl Otmar von Aretin and Karl Härter, eds, *Revolution und konservatives Beharren. Das alte Reich und die französische Revolution* (Mainz, 1990), pp. 83–93.

110 Bluntschli, 'Dritter Stand', in *Deutsches Staats-Wörterbuch* (Stuttgart/ Leipzig, 1858), iii. pp. 176–82, p. 179.

111 See Max Weber, *Wirtschaft und Gesellschaft* (5th edn, Tübingen, 1980), p. 177.

112 See Manfred Riedel, article on 'Bürger, Staatsbürger, Bürgertum', in *Geschichtliche Grundbegriffe. Historisches Lexikon zur politisch-sozialen Sprache in Deutschland*, i (Stuttgart, 1972), pp. 672–725; Ulrich Engelhardt, '*Bildungsbürgertum*'. *Begriffs- und Dogmengeschichte eines Etiketts* (Stuttgart, 1986); Reinhart Koselleck, Ulrike Spree, and Willibald Steinmetz, 'Drei bürgerliche Welten? Zur vergleichenden Semantik der bürgerlichen Gesellschaft in Deutschland, England und Frankreich', in Hans-Jürgen Puhle, ed., *Bürger in der Gesellschaft der Neuzeit. Wirtschaft – Politik – Kultur* (Göttingen, 1991), pp. 14–58.

113 Johann Caspar Bluntschli, *Allgemeines Staatsrecht, geschichtlich begründet* (Munich, 1852), 6 edns, the 5th edn of 1875 and the 6th edn of 1886 under the title *Lehre vom modernen Staat*; in what follows, quoted according to the first edition.

114 Bluntschli, *Staatsrecht*, pp. 82f.: 'All power of the state was claimed by the bourgeoisie alone, for whom complete equality before the law was seen as the fundamental law' (p. 83).

115 *Ibid.*, p. 88.

116 *Ibid.*, p. 85.

117 *Ibid.*, p. 88.

118 *Ibid.*, p. 84.

119   *Ibid.*, p. 89.
120   *Ibid.*, p. 103.
121   Bluntschli, 'Dritter Stand', *ibid.*, pp. 178f.
122   *Allgemeine deutsche Real-Encyklopädie für die gebildeten Stände* (7th edn, Leipzig, 1830), pp. 899–903, p. 902.
123   Anne Kosfeld, 'Politische Zukunft und historischer Meinungsstreit. Die Stadt des Mittelalters als Leitbild des Frankfurter Bürgertums in der Verfassungs-diskussion der Restaurationszeit', in Reinhart Koselleck and Klaus Schreiner, eds, *Bürgerschaft. Rezeption und Innovation der Begrifflichkeit vom Hohen Mittelalter bis ins 19. Jahrhundert*, (Stuttgart, 1994), pp. 375–454, pp. 450, 449.
124   See Kosfeld, 'Politische Zukunft', pp. 375–79; Anne Kosfeld, *Liberale Ver-fassungsbewegung und alteuropäische Bürgergesellschaft* (Göttingen, forth-coming 1996); on a parallel development in the re-evaluation of Roman Law in legal studies, James Q. Whitman, *The Legacy of the Roman Law in the German Romantic Era: Historical Vision and Legal Change* (Princeton, 1990).

Translated by Sheilagh Ogilvie.

7

The Growth of the Modern State

PAUL MÜNCH

An account of the increase in state power in Germany during the early modern period presents considerable difficulties. To be conceptually correct, for the pre-modern period one should speak neither of the 'state' nor of 'Germany'. Both concepts are problematic because they anachronistically impose modern categories on the early modern period. The concept of the 'state' attained its modern meaning in Germany only gradually from the seventeenth century on,[1] somewhat behind the Romance-language countries. Throughout the entire eighteenth century, the concept of the state in Germany retained a wealth of traditional corporative connotations. However, in so far as it also increasingly referred to 'Herrschaft' (lordship, rule) as exercised by the 'well-regulated princely state', it increasingly lost its old corporative content as time passed.[2] In the meantime, the concept of the 'early modern state' has found its way into German historiography, as a term for describing what developed in the late medieval and early modern period. This concept, it is held, takes account of the special nature of the 'state' form which intervened between the medieval feudal state and the modern national state.[3]

To the semantic problem is added the fact that the state and the political history of Germany in the early modern period can generally only be apprehended in the historiography in a form distorted by ideology, given the background of the Austrian and German national histories which have been following separate paths of development since 1866 and 1871. In a nineteenth-century perspective, the early modern history of Germany – especially after the Thirty Years War – was marred by a politically deficient structure which lacked complete 'Staatlichkeit' ('state-ness', the trait of being like a state).[4] At least in the larger territories, whose own extensive sovereignty had hindered the 'state' development of Germany as a whole, the formation of modern state structures could be detected. Given the background of the Empire as a 'kleindeutsche' union ('little German', referring to the unification of Germany without Austria) dominated by Prussia, reconstructing the history of the state in the early modern period could succeed only in a one-sided way. The non-Prussian territories – with the exception of Habsburg Austria – were largely neglected by the dominant Prussian historiography. This affected the medium-sized and smaller territories of the Empire, especially in the Catholic South, which in Germany has traditionally lain on the historiographical periphery.

Only in the last few decades have historians partially revised these views. Nowadays hardly anyone complains about the deficient 'Staatlichkeit' ('state-ness') of the Old Empire, whose multicentricity is increasingly valued as a positive legacy. The federalist Federal Republic of Germany, with its richly developed regional differences and its cultural diversity, is unthinkable without the long previous history of the Old Empire and its territories. The rejection of old conceptions of states as great powers has also led to an altered view of the Old Empire, as a structure which aimed at maintaining the peace and guaranteeing the law without power politics or expansion at the expense of its neighbours,[5] and which in these respects perhaps might even serve as a model for a future united Europe.

Because Germany achieved unification as a national state only in the nineteenth century, its early modern history has independent and unique contours which can be fitted into the general history of the early modern state only with some difficulty. While in most European states a sovereign and more or less centralized polity had already developed during the early modern period, in Germany the state-building process played itself out with considerable delay and on several different levels. Quite apart from numerous additional differentiation processes, one is always dealing with two quite distinct types of 'state form': first, with the 'Holy Roman Empire of the German Nation' and its institutions; and second, with a large number of more or less autonomous German territories, districts, and cities, which varied widely in size and importance, and whose legal and constitutional status cannot be reduced to a single common denominator. An additional difficulty is posed by the fact that the process of state formation followed contradictory tendencies in the Empire and in the territories. The 'state' development of the Empire, despite scattered centralizing efforts by the Emperor, in effect proceeded centrifugally; by contrast, that of the territories as a rule proceeded centripetally. These divergent constitutional developments were further complicated by the varying importance of the parliamentary estates in different territories, and make it impossible to speak of a unified 'German' development. They also pose difficulties for the comparisons between 'Germany' and western Europe which are so often made; such comparisons inevitably come to very superficial conclusions, since the German situation is comparable only to a limited extent with that of other European states which centralized earlier.

The Empire corresponds to none of the definitions current in the theory of the state; in the seventeenth century, Samuel Pufendorf, in a critical phase of its history, termed it with some justification as an 'irregulare aliquod corpus et monstro simile' ('a somewhat irregular body similar to a monster').[6] However, viewed as a whole, the Empire had an unquestionable political and legal significance, and thus also importance as a 'state', even if it may seem deficient in the light of nineteenth-century definitions of states as great powers. Admittedly, as was already pointed out at the end of the early modern period in the academic discipline of Imperial 'Publicistik' (which taught the public law of the Empire), the Empire was seldom to play more than a defensive role. However, its role in maintaining the peace and guaranteeing the law must not be underestimated.[7] After the Peace of Westphalia no war emanated from the old German Empire for a long time.[8]

By contrast, several of the larger political entities making up the Empire, which for over 300 years were more or less independent, began to transform themselves into modern states (in the sense of great powers). In its basic lineaments, the development of these larger German polities is indeed comparable with that of European national states which were largely organized in a centralized fashion. This is the case despite the fact that under the canopy of the Empire German territories were not fully sovereign states even after the Peace of Westphalia, and internally also retained a dualistic structure in many ways.

The empire and the territories

The 'state' development of the Empire and its territories proceeded in a contradictory fashion and extended over a period of almost 700 years.[9] It reached back well into the middle ages, when the beginnings of princely territorial lordship took shape in complex processes, emerging out of autochthonous noble powers and old immunities. In the end, this princely territorial lordship stole a march on the monarchy during the German state-building process. The inheritability of the *Reichslehen* (Imperial fiefs), on which temporal and ecclesiastical princes could equally rely, combined with their indispensable powers in maintaining the peace in the region and administering justice to form the basis for the emerging territorial powers. With the 'Confoederatio cum principibus ecclesiasticis' (treaty with the ecclesiastical princes) of 1220 and the 'Statutum in favorem principum' (statute in favour of the temporal princes) of 1231–2, the ecclesiastical and temporal territorial lords ('domini terrae') obtained the important 'prerogatives' of customs, coinage, and jurisdiction, which had previously been reserved for the king; in this way, they secured the essential bases for territorial lordship. Of hardly less importance were the *privilegia de non evocando et non appellando* (privileges forbidding appellation and evocation) guaranteed to the Electors by the Golden Bull of 1356, which furthered the process of closing off the politically most important territories against the Empire. A number of additional factors played an essential role in the development of internal territorial supremacy, the beginnings of which had already been attained in the larger German territories during the fourteenth century. Great domain-estates provided the basis for the territorial lord to expand his territorial power, and centralization of criminal jurisdiction in his *Hofgerichten* (central law courts) put the prince in a position to suppress the surviving special ecclesiastical and patrimonial legislation. Primogeniture regulations had secured the impartibility of the Electoral lands as early as the Golden Bull, and came into effect in many other territories in the following period, although this was a lengthy process which in some cases dragged itself out into the eighteenth century. The reception of Roman law appears to have played at least a subsidiary role in the formation of the state in the German territories, although modern research has concluded that the juristic foundation of territorial lordship cannot be traced directly to the Reception.[10] Territorial consolidation measures were supported by the slow development of a functioning territorial administration, centralized in the princely courts, with differentiated structures of offices and agencies, regulated stages of appeal, and a bureaucracy trained in Roman law. The beginnings of a central financial policy laid the basis for tax-raising applied to the entire country, and the 'late medieval regulation of the church by the territorial lords' saw the beginnings of administrative intervention in the Church.[11]

These territorial tendencies toward centralization and consolidation ushered in and accompanied the transformation of *Personenverbandsstaaten* (feudal states characterized by personal loyalty) into *institutionelle Flächenstaaten* ('institutionally and territorially closed states'), in the terms used by Theodor Mayer.[12] However, they must not be overestimated. They did not everywhere lead to the development of modern states in a unilineal, irresistible, and rapid modernization process; most German territories retained their dualistic structure throughout the entire early modern period. Just as on the level of the Empire the estates which convened at the Imperial Diets retained considerable powers, so too in the territories the privileged political estates, meeting at the territorial diet – as a rule, the lower nobility, the clergy, the towns, and in a few cases the peasants as well – maintained their autochtonous powers of lordship against the territorial lord.[13] Only in those territories where princes were able largely to eliminate joint government with the estates (as in Brandenburg and Austria), and in some small and micro-territories where there was no representation at all by estates, could monarchical and absolutist structures begin to establish themselves. Nevertheless, older corporative structures, untouched by absolutist governmental practice, remained in being everywhere on the middle and lower level.[14]

At the beginning of the early modern period the differences in development between Empire and territories deepened. Only in the territories did the centralizing and unifying process of state formation occur relatively successfully; on the level of the Empire, by contrast, despite scattered Imperial initatives, attempts at a comparable intensification of lordship failed. At the end of the fifteenth century, in the sixteenth century, and in the first half of the seventeenth century the Habsburg Emperors took a number of initiatives which attempted to gain dominance over the territories of the Empire. However, the confessional split which began with the Reformation brought all Imperial attempts at dominance to nothing; the constitutional organs of the Empire, especially the Imperial Diet, were increasingly blocked in their operations. This was the case even though – or perhaps precisely because – the confessional parties had negotiated a provisional *modus vivendi* at a comparatively early date, in the Augsburg religious peace of 1555. In the Peace of Prague of 1635 during the Thirty Years War, Emperor Ferdinand II sought to secure his position as monarch in the Empire. However, in doing so he hardly represented any sort of internal 'Imperial absolutism',[15] but rather operated in an older universalist tradition.[16] The opposition of the princes brought these attempts to nothing. The conclusion of the Peace of Westphalia in 1648 spelt the ultimate failure of 'Imperial absolutist' attempts. Article VII.1 of the Peace of Osnabrück finally sealed the defeat of Imperial central power and the victory of corporate *Libertät* (liberty). The territories of the Empire did not attain full sovereignty, but they did obtain a far-reaching supremacy over their subjects ('ius territorii et superioritatis'), and also free right of alliance in so far as it was not directed against Emperor or Empire:

> In this, however, be it provided, so that in future no conflicts arise in the political order, that each and every Elector, prince, and estate of the Roman Empire shall be in their old rights, advantages, freedoms, privileges, and the free exercise of territorial supremacy in both ecclesiastical and temporal matters, in their territories, prerogatives and possession of all of these, by power of this contract, so secured and confirmed, that they cannot and may not ever be disturbed in practice by anyone, under any excuse whatsoever.[17]

Emperor and Empire after 1648

The Peace of Westphalia cemented the dualistic constitutional order of Germany, in which state power was divided between Emperor and territories, and gave it a unique character which endured until the end of the old order in 1803–6.[18] As a whole, the complex Imperial system functioned better than is often believed;[19] its institutions secured – at least in principle – the cohesion of the German territories, and sometimes even exercised an influence on their policies which should not be underestimated. Indeed, the procedurally complicated co-operation of Emperor, Imperial Diet, Imperial Circles, and Circle Associations was even able to defend the integrity of 'Teutschland' (Germany) against external threats, such as French aggression under Louis XIV and the attacks of the Ottomans. Furthermore, in the emerging concert of European powers the Empire played a decidedly peace-maintaining role.

Internally, it was true that the Emperors were no longer really able to build on the earlier beginnings of an Imperial policy; in everyday political life, they were largely reduced to their few *Reservatrechte* (prerogatives). The granting of privileges such as ennoblement might sometimes give them an opportunity to exercise a certain amount of influence over the policy of certain territories, via a clientele loyal to the Empire. Apart from this, however, Imperial power only really counted in a few conflicts involving Imperial Cities. Admittedly, the *Reichshofrat* (Imperial Aulic Council)[20] in Vienna, which was responsible for the granting of fiefs and privileges, retained substantial political importance as the legal instance of appeal – especially for the territorial estates in smaller and medium-sized territories, and for subjects with grievances – and as the highest *Zensurbehörde* (the highest office of censorship for books) until the end of the Old Empire.

Of greater political weight were those Imperial organs which were operated jointly by the Emperor and the Estates of the Empire. The *Reichstag* (Imperial Diet), which from 1663 on convened in Regensburg as a 'perpetual Imperial Diet' or permanent committee,[21] remained one of the most important guarantees of Imperial unity despite its cumbersome procedures. After 1648, because of the confessional division into a 'Corpus Catholicorum' and a 'Corpus Evangelicorum',[22] the Emperor and the estates represented at the Imperial Diet quite often reached an agreement only with difficulty; nevertheless, in the complex system of the Old Empire it retained a significant political role as a clearing-house for peace-making. However, its legislative function, which in many ways created the basis and framework for territorial law-making, encountered barriers, as previously, where the interests of the Empire collided with those of the territories, and the particularistic territorial authorities implemented Imperial laws only in a lax way or not at all. The Imperial Diet was no early stage of the modern parliament, since only the politically and socially privileged estates were represented in its three *Kurien* (curiae) – the *Kurfürstenkollegium* (Council of Electors), the *Reichsfürstenrat* (Council of Princes), and the *Kollegium der Reichsstädte* (Council of the Imperial Cities). Thus only the higher noble and – to a limited extent – bourgeois strata of the population were represented; by contrast, the interests of the lower nobility, the great mass of the (petty) bourgeoisie, and the peasantry were considered either not at all or at most indirectly.

In addition to the Imperial Diet, another institution which retained a stabilizing, supra-territorial function in the political structure of the Empire was the *Reichskammergericht* (Imperial Chamber Court).[23] This body was established in 1495, its members were jointly appointed by the Emperor and the Estates of the Empire, and it had its seat first in Speyer (from 1527 on) and then in Wetzlar (from 1689 until the end of the Old Empire). Despite its sluggish procedures, it constituted a still-recognized body for arbitration and decision in cases of complaints by territorial estates against their territorial lords, in cases where princes were deposed, and especially in the many conflicts between peasants and landlords. The frequency with which it was used provides impressive evidence of the increasing juridification of conflicts within the Empire.

The *Reichskreise* (Imperial Circles) played a political role which cannot be underestimated.[24] These were supra-territorial, geographical sub-divisions of the Empire. They were responsible for publication of Imperial laws, maintenance of the eternal peace among territories of the Empire declared in 1495 requiring settlement of quarrels by judicial means (*ewiger Landfriede*), and defence; and they had supervisory competence in economic matters, taxation, and *Policey* (regulation). The Circles not only gained regional influence (in areas such as Swabia, the Upper Rhine, and Franconia), but to a certain extent took over 'state' functions to do with domestic policy, by carrying out legislative, jurisdictional, and executive tasks (as in the Thirty Years War).[25] The combining of some Imperial Circles into Circle Associations strengthened the political significance of these corporative entities, through which the weaker members of the Empire successfully gave expression to their importance as 'states', especially in military matters.[26]

For the financing of the tasks of Empire,[27] the German kings or Emperors had to resort to funds deriving from their hereditary lands, and (to a lesser extent) to revenues deriving from Imperial lands and prerogatives. The Imperial Estates could be drawn into providing financial support only for the carrying-out of essential Imperial business or in special crises. The Imperial reform, which was decided upon at the Imperial Diet at Worms in 1495,[28] and which effected a certain balance between the Emperor and the Imperial estates, ultimately led (after pre-stages during the Hussite Wars) to the introduction of a general Imperial tax, ('Gemeiner Pfennig', 'Common Penny'). This attempt was justified in terms of financing the Imperial Chamber Court, but soon failed because not all territories paid and because the organizational problems involved in levying the tax were not (yet) soluble. Even the 'Kammerzieler', taxes raised specially for the financing of the Imperial Chamber Court, came in only irregularly. The *Matrikularumlagen* (fixed contributions by the territories) were somewhat more realistically framed: these derived from the estates' obligation to contribute to the king's *Romzug* (procession to Rome), and they ultimately became a sort of extraordinary war tax. In 1521, at the Imperial Diet meeting in Worms, the magnitude of these *Römermonate* (Roman months) was laid down in an Imperial *Matrikel* (Register). Together with other extraordinary taxes, they provided the financial basis for the successful defence of the Empire against the Turks in later periods.[29]

The territories

Even the contrast between the relative political weakness of the Empire and the growing power and autonomous development after 1648 of the large territories, towards which the political centre of gravity shifted, provides only an incomplete portrait of constitutional theory and practice in Germany. Although the most important rights of supremacy were concentrated in the territories, and hence political particularism is unquestionably one of the most important forces favouring continuity in German history, they also continued to be linked into the system of the Empire with varying intensity through Imperial taxes, military obligations, and the possibility for subjects to appeal to the Imperial courts. In the view of Harm Klueting, even after 1648 the 'Holy Roman Empire of the German Nation' was 'no *Bundesstaat* [federal state], because the territories were more than autonomous provinces and the Empire itself lacked a state character'; however, just as little was it a '*Staatenbund* [confederation], because even the large territories were not sovereign, and the numerous small and tiny territories prevented the development of federal forms'.[30] The general situation was so complicated because the territories which made up the Empire varied greatly in size, geographical position, economic structure, legal status, and political significance.[31]

There were fundamental differences between the temporal and ecclesiastical territories. In contrast to the temporal territories, the archbishoprics, bishoprics, princely religious foundations, and abbacies, which were ruled by archbishops, bishops, abbots, and abbesses, were not inheritable. Ecclesiastical rulers were elected for their lifetimes by the Chapters, which were generally recruited from exclusive circles of the nobility. The strength of the Chapters is shown in the 'Wahlkapitulationen' (Electoral Capitulations) which archbishops and bishops often had to swear to upon accession, in the Chapters' exercise of the business of government during vacations of the episcopal see, and in the Chapters' leading positions in the territorial diets (where these existed). Despite the electoral principle, the close interpenetration between nobility and church (because the nobles shared out the ecclesiastical territories among themselves) led to particular families' enjoying regional spheres of influence. Not infrequently, it also gave rise to quasi-dynastic continuities, with doubtful confessional consequences, arising from the institution of the 'Koadjutor' (co-regent and successor),[32] from accumulations of bishoprics, and from ecclesiastical secundogeniture. The most successful strategy in filling bishops' seats was pursued by the Bavarian Wittelsbachs, who for almost 200 years after 1583 succeeded in uniting in a single hand not only the Archbishopric of Cologne, but also (in the eighteenth century under Clemens August of Bavaria) the Westphalian bishoprics of Osnabrück, Münster, Paderborn, and Hildesheim.

The Electorates, which were organized at the Imperial Diets into the *Kurfürstenrat* (Council of Electors),[33] enjoyed a prominent political significance. During the early modern period, they increased in number from the original seven to nine. After the Golden Bull of 1356, they included the archbishoprics of Mainz, Trier, and Cologne; the Kingdom of Bohemia; the margraviate of Brandenburg; Electoral Saxony; and the Electoral Palatinate. In 1648, Bavaria secured the eighth electoral dignity, which had already been transferred to Duke Maximilian in 1623. Finally, in 1692 Hannover obtained the ninth electoral dignity.

The numerous principalities represented in the *Fürstenkolleg* (Council of Princes), and the non-princely ecclesiastical and temporal counties, abbacies, and religious colleges, varied greatly in size, economic significance, and political importance. The smallest of these principalities were not infrequently surpassed in economic strength and political significance by the largest of the fifty-one *Reichsstädte* (Imperial Cities), some of which ruled substantial territories (as in the cases of Nuremberg, Ulm, Rottweil, Aachen, and Dortmund). After 1648, however, they enjoyed very limited voting rights at the Imperial Diet because of the growing political and economic pressure of the larger territorial states; and they increasingly lost their earlier importance. The same was true of the *Reichsritterschaft* (Imperial Knighthood), which after 1577 was divided into four *Ritterkreisen* (Knights' Circles) with 14 cantons, which guaranteed territorial supremacy.[34]

After 1648, apart from the few powers remaining to the Emperor and the Empire, the most important rights of supremacy were concentrated in the territories. In the advanced stages of development toward *institutionelle Flächenstaaten* ('institutionally and territorially closed states'), these rights included legislation, jurisdiction, police powers (including the right of censorship), determination of religious confession (*ius reformandi*), a limited right to form alliances including with foreign powers (*ius foederis*), and in some territories also the right to maintain an army (*ius armorum*) – in each case with a corresponding bureaucracy. 'Standing armies' were maintained not just by the larger ecclesiastical and temporal territories, but also by some medium-sized and smaller territories, such as Münster, Paderborn, Würzburg, Salzburg, Braunschweig-Wolfenbüttel, Hessen-Kassel, Hessen-Darmstadt, Württemberg, and the County of Lippe. In many territories, rulers were able to implement absolutist practices of lordship, concentrate power in the princely court, and considerably reduce the influence of territorial representative assemblies. This was the case in Brandenburg,[35] which served for many territories as a model for imitation, especially under King Friedrich II; but it was also the case in Austria[36] and Hessen-Kassel,[37] to name only a few. Other territories, such as Württemberg, Mecklenburg, Hannover, Electoral Saxony, and East Frisia, by contrast, retained the duality of 'Land und Herrschaft' ('territory and lordship');[38] here, the groups represented in the territorial diets – the clergy, the nobility (lords and knights), and the towns – continued to participate in ruling the territory. Some territorial diets were made up of different combinations of social groups; in some Alpine regions and in northern German marsh regions, even peasants were represented. These intermediate powers defended their corporative constitutions and their right to grant (or deny) taxes against the territorial lord, and in the eighteenth century, after a phase of being threatened by absolutism, were sometimes even able to stabilize their constitutional rights again, with the assistance of the Imperial Courts; this was the case in Lippe, Brauschweig-Wolfenbüttel, Mecklenburg, and Württemberg.[39]

The renaissance of the territorial estates was connected with the growing financial needs of the territories, which were generated by the exorbitantly rising costs of courtly display, bureaucratic administration, and especially the expensive maintenance of standing armies. These expanding financial requirements accelerated the development of German territories into 'Steuerstaaten' ('taxing states').[40] The early modern state in general possessed strong roots in the 'Finanzstaat' ('financial state'),[41] because having cash money at one's disposal was an indispensable prerequisite for rational government. Compared to medieval territorial lordship, with its feudally based revenues largely paid in kind, levying taxes as thoroughly as possible increasingly became of central importance for the early modern state. In contrast to the unsatisfactory fiscal practices in the Empire, in the territories a regular territorial tax was successfully introduced, in some cases at quite early dates. And in contrast to the medieval 'Bede' (derived from 'Bitte', meaning 'petition'), which was levied only on particular occasions, the regular territorial tax represented a combination of tax on land, property, and income. Unlike feudal dues, which were levied on the basis of utilization rights over landholdings, the state levied the territorial tax solely on the basis of the power of supremacy it claimed. The modernity of this financial policy is shown in the fact that as far as possible every inhabitant of the territory began to be taxed as an individual, rather than the units of taxation being larger economic entities such as the family or the peasant farm, as had been the case under feudal conditions.[42] Between the sixteenth and eighteenth centuries the financial demands of princes expanded everywhere, taxes rose correspondingly, and subjects were burdened more heavily. One especially favoured form of cash-collection was the excise tax, an indirect tax on all necessities, which sometimes (as in Brandenburg-Prussia) developed into an indispensable component of state revenue.[43] A special feature of the early modern 'financial state' was that when a territorial lord was unable to pay, the territorial estates leapt into the breach. The estates were customarily the only party which was still creditworthy and able to fend off territorial bankruptcy. As early as the sixteenth century, German territorial estates took over from their territorial lords a burden of debt amounting to more than 17 million *Gulden*, thereby guaranteeing the future payment capacities of their territories.[44] Given the political imponderabilities and crises not infrequently associated with dynastic lordship and its associated inheritance problems, the territorial estates also survived as the load-bearing pillars of continuity and stability in many territories.

Despite all their differences in detail, the territories of the Empire possessed fundamentally similar administrative structures and bureaucratic organizations.[45] Courts and capital cities formed the representative centres of power, and were sometimes very expensively embellished by architects and painters.[46] Everywhere, the dissolution of the older Noble Council (*Adliger Rat*) saw the establishment of a permanent committee of the council, the Court Council (*Hofrat*), filled largely by university-graduated jurists. The financial administration of the territory was carried out by a body known as the *Hofkammer, Amtskammer*, or *Rentkammer*. After the end of the sixteenth century the highest central agency for decision-making ceased to be the *Hofrat* (Court Council) and began to be the *Geheime Rat* (Privy Council), which was responsible for decision-making in matters touching on the Empire and questions of foreign policy. In the age of absolutism, this body in turn was sometimes set aside or transformed into the *Kabinett* (Cabinet). In addition, strong territorial estates possessed an autonomous financial administration of their own. In so far as the territories achieved standing armies,[47] special bureaucratic offices arose to administer them: in Austria the *Hofkriegsrat* (Court War Council), in Brandenburg the *Generalkriegskommissariat* (General War Commissariat). Everywhere, territorial lords and other authorities sought to exercise rule over the Church. In Protestant states and cities,[48] with some differences between the Lutheran and Calvinist confessions, they carried out their *ius circa sacra* (external administration of the Church by the princes) through holding visitations, making appointments to top offices (such as superintendents and inspectors), and controlling certain committees (such as consistories and church councils).[49] In Catholic territories,[50] by contrast, regulation of the Church was not opened up to direct intervention by the territorial lord in the same way – despite the apparent similarity between Protestant and Catholic confessionalization (as discussed in detail in Chapter 10).[51] Nevertheless, most territories developed administrative structures and executive organs which were institutionally comparable: examples are visitations (which were widespread everywhere) and the *Geistliche Rat* (Council of Clergy, which was found in Bavaria, Baden, and some ecclesiastical territories)[52]. However, in Catholic territories, defining the Church's teaching and exercising ecclesiastical jurisdiction remained in general the province of the superordinated ecclesiastical (episcopal and papal) agencies, and hence were removed from direct territorial influence.

Through their regulation of the Church, territorial lords everywhere guaranteed the protection of one of the three confessions recognized in Imperial law in the Peace of Westphalia: the Roman Catholic, the Protestant Lutheran, and the Protestant Calvinist. In addition to supervision over religious teaching, ceremonies, and church property, this *cura religionis* ('care for religion') encompassed responsibility for church and school office-holders, care for the poor, and concern for the everyday morality of the population. It not only aimed at control of religious and moral life in a narrow sense, although in some Protestant territories it could develop into a very strict monitoring of life by the church,[53] but also extended far beyond the narrow ecclesiastical framework, leaving its mark on the political and social mentalities of its subjects.[54] Initially, confessional harmony was everywhere viewed as the most important prerequisite for political and social stability;[55] as a consequence, confession initially formed the most important basis for emerging territorial identities. Only a few territories, such as Brandenburg from the seventeenth century onward, tolerated different denominations in the scattered, confessionally mixed parts of their territory for reasons of state, and thus practised an early form of more or less peaceful coexistence between the confessions.[56] The principle of *Cuius regio, eius religio* (whereby those who possessed the territory could decide on its religion) was also violated in some communities, especially the cities with religious equality ('paritätische Städte'), where the coexistence of the confessions was legally regulated down to the tiniest details.[57] However, highly developed principles of confessional tolerance only began to prevail when the secularizing effects of the Enlightenment began to be felt.[58] Such principles undermined the ideal of the confessionally uniform state, and ultimately, under radically transformed conditions in the nineteenth century, by means of the new paradigms of 'Volk' (people) and 'Nation' (nation), they gave rise to a modern state identity, without thereby losing regional characteristics.

'Policey', absolutism, and cameralism

The path of German territories toward 'Staatlichkeit' ('state-ness'), whose basic law was, in a sense, the Peace of Westphalia, reached its culmination in the epoch after 1648, the age of absolutism. Following on from the developments of the late medieval period, the sixteenth century[59] and then the state-forming Thirty Years War[60] had increased the powers of governmental

authorities in a series of stages.[61] After 1648, these earlier beginnings of territorial concentration were deliberately expanded and systematically consolidated. During this period, each of the more or less independent political
units of the Old Empire – small as well as large – saw the rise of an identity
which was closely bound to the territory or the city. From this time on, anyone speaking in Germany of the 'Vaterland' ('Fatherland') was unlikely to be
referring to the Empire; instead, one usually meant the territory, sometimes
even the city,[62] in which one lived. This territorial and local particularism
was generally combined in a very specific way with the peculiar confessional
characteristics associated with it. It was a particularism based on a gradual
social and cultural standardization of life in each territory, which ultimately
left its unalterable mark on the everyday life and behavioural patterns of the
population. Prohibitions on inter-confessional marriages and attending
extra-territorial ('foreign') schools or universities, together with the obstacles which Catholic territorial lords set up in the eighteenth century even
against pilgrimages into neighbouring areas, increasingly bound subjects to
their own territory. This took place less because of feudal dependencies, as
had been the case previously, than for reasons associated with the deliberate
move toward *institutionelle Flächenstaaten* ('institutionally and territorially
closed states') and the implementation of mercantilistic economic principles.
This is a phenomenon to which we should not be blinded by the special
'Imperial patriotism' which can be observed in some small territories whose
existence was guaranteed by the Empire.

In all German territories, the declared goal was the formation of a uniform mass of subjects which had been levelled out in relation to the territorial lord.[63] But under the conditions of the 'early modern state' it was
not possible to draw out all the theoretical implications of this aim, nor
was it possible to realize it fully in practice.[64] The struggle against all intermediate powers – the Church, the representative assembly of the estates,
the towns, and even the occupational corporations – was supposed to do
away with every form of competition to lordship within the territory. This
process of concentration played itself out on several levels, during which
its theoretical programme and practical political measures often merged
indistinguishably. In many ways, the boundaries between territories had
previously been crossed by feudal ties, dynastic kinship relations, and social
or political clientele relationships. But in the course of these modernizing
measures, for the first time territorial boundaries slowly began to be
defined as geographically accurate and fixed dividing-lines delineating state
territorial lordship, even though their courses did not yet attain modern
precision. Until the end of the Old Empire, ancient supra-territorial structures such as jointly ruled territories (*Kondominien*, 'condominia') cut
across state attempts at rationalization and consolidation.[65]

Territorial lords' growing claim to exercise all-encompassing regulation
over all aspects of life was reflected especially clearly in the theory and practice of *Policey* ('polity' or regulation).[66] Derived from the Greek concept of

'politeia' and the Latin 'politia', *Policey* referred not only to a polity, but also generally to the condition of good order and the ways and means of establishing it. The Empire issued *Polizeiordnungen* ('police ordinances', regulatory ordinances) in 1530, 1548, and 1577, but only the *Polizeiordnungen* of the territories, based on this legislative framework, proved very effective. The content of the *Polizeiordnungen* was directed at regulating a wide array of disparate matters. In modern terms, they dealt with questions of private or civil law, from the regulation of marriage, the family, guardianship, and inheritance, to regulation of property, work, and credit.[67] However, they also covered problems of religion, morality, sociability, and general security, and thus encompassed the 'public' sphere as well.[68] The *Policey* of the authorities was articulated in a very spectacular way in the dress ordinances of the period.[69] With its assistance governments increasingly created their own sphere, in competition with ancient custom and the corporative formation of law handed down from the past; in principle, they put forward a new law which claimed ubiquitous validity within the territory. *Policey* was one of the most important instruments German territorial lords used to extend their emancipation from corporative participation in lordship within their territories. Intervention into almost every area of life was justified in terms of 'necessity of state' (*necessitas* in Latin, *Notturft* in German); the *Policey* legislation of the authorities was portrayed as a public obligation to guarantee and advance the *gemeinen Nutzen* ('common weal') which was justified in transcendent terms. On one hand, in many ways the authorities used the *Policey* ordinances to pursue social goals, combating usury and monopolies, and in particular cases even disregarding differences in social estate in determining punishments. However, on the other hand, especially in the dress and luxury ordinances, they reinforced the hierarchical structure of a corporate society of social estates, with meticulous obsessiveness down to the finest nuances. The attempt to use the theory and practice of *Policey* to create a standardized territorial law emanating from the authorities served primarily to intensify territorial lordship and, connected with this, to suppress traditional intermediate powers.

In the period after the Thirty Years War and during the eighteenth century, *Policey* regulation under the influence of absolutist teaching and Enlightenment welfare programmes was enormously expanded. It was extended far beyond the earlier state tasks of guaranteeing the law and securing the peace, and ultimately encompassed almost the entire sphere of domestic policy (as distinct from the state's external tasks). As early as 1656, Veit Ludwig von Seckendorff[70] had already pragmatically included under the heading of *Policey* not only general regulatory tasks, but also matters concerning the church, schools, and the economy. After the middle of the eighteenth century the notion of *Policey* convered not only traditional matters, but also a wide array of concerns which document in a many-faceted way the regulatory claims of Enlightenment welfare states: from *Kirchenpolizei* (church regulation),[71] which conceived the Church as part of the state administration, to 'Policey der Industrie' (regulation of industry),[72] which aimed at making society in general more diligent, through to medical *Policey*, which concerned itself with the health of the 'Volkskörper' (the 'body of the nation').[73] Everywhere, *Policey* involved regulation of both 'private' and 'public' concerns, indistinguishably. According to Johann Heinrich Gottlob von Justi, the main aim of these wide-ranging domestic tasks was to expand the 'power and happiness of states'.[74]

The slow transformation of German territories into modern states was accompanied by an abundance of legitimizing arguments, which to some extent were intensified into ideological programmes. In addition to the theory and practice of *Policey*, which had been emerging since the end of the middle ages under the influence of humanism, the path toward 'Staatlichkeit' ('state-ness') from the seventeenth century on was also accompanied by the absolutist doctrines of the age, and in a characteristic way strengthened by them.[75] The early and time-tested ideological legitimization of princely and territorial state lordship continued to survive, but the new political theories of the age were not ignored. Everywhere, rulers appealed to transcendent justifications for their governmental activity. They declared that they had come into office not through human power of any kind, but through divine summoning. Theologians equipped the authorities with honorific titles which emphasized their prominent position. A prince was called defender and nourisher of the Church, 'guard of the tables of the Decalogue', shepherd and father of his people.[76] The formula 'by God's mercy' (*Dei gratia*) remained in use in many territories until the end of the Old Empire.

The important theories of absolutism, which had developed since the sixteenth century in Italy, France, and England, exercised only indirect influence on the early modern theory of princely lordship in the German territories. Machiavelli and his teachings were known, and the idea of 'reason of state' also penetrated into Germany toward the end of the sixteenth century; but these theories of government were generally taken over in a milder form, and hence exerted only an indirect and reduced influence. It is striking that an early German translation of Giovanni Botero's classic 1589 work, *Della ragione di Stato libri dieci*, already (in 1596) translated the central concept of 'reason of state' in the title as *gute Policey* ('good polity', 'good regulation'), and thus assigned a subordinate importance to the religious and ethical maxims of the imported concept of *Policey*.[77] Those who went further and, like Theodor Reinkingk in 1653, interpreted 'good *Policey*' as 'biblical *Policey*', and thus designed a 'Politica' out of the Bible,[78] show very clearly indeed how wide the gap could be between German political theory on the one hand, and the teachings of Machiavellianism and 'reason of state' on the other. At best, as in the Bavaria of Maximilian I at the turn of the seventeenth century, there was an acceptance of the doctrines of Justus Lipsius,[79] who defined the concept of 'reason of state' in characteristic wise as *prudentia civilis* (civil prudence). This set clear ethical limits on any approaches toward an unscrupulous rationalization of politics.[80]

Naturally, Jean Bodin and his teaching on sovereignty, which defined the *maiestas* ('majesty') of the monarch in a new way in terms of constitutional law, penetrated to Germany. The theories of Thomas Hobbes were also known; in order to avoid a *bellum omnium contra omnes* ('war of all against all'), Hobbes argued in favour of transferring undivided power to a single sovereign. But these doctrines, which had grown out of situations of confessional civil war, appear to have left their mark only marginally on the political theory of the territorial state in German territories. The conception of office of German princes continued to be coloured by religion until long into the eighteenth century. This conception portrayed princes as devoted *Landesväter* ('fathers of the country'), tirelessly active for the well-being of the *Landeskinder* ('children of the country' or subjects); this endowed indigenous German political theory with an unmistakable patriarchal flavour throughout the entire early modern period.[81] Given the small-scale nature and the low degree of literacy of the German territories, there is a certain plausibility to the great success of this model there. How a *princeps legibus solutus* ('prince above the law') was to be defined was a question reserved for an exclusive circle of learned debaters; but how one was supposed to behave toward a father was not only contained in the Fourth Commandment, which subsumed all superiors under the title of father, but also lay within the sphere of experience of illiterate subjects. It is striking that patriarchal theories of rulership, which until the seventeenth century played an important role in western Europe as well, were there subjected to criticism quite early. In England, John Locke dealt ruthlessly with Robert Filmer's patriarchal theory,[82] and in France Jean Jacques Rousseau banished the patriarchal model from political debate.[83] In Germany, by contrast, where the territorial authorities, as *Landesväter*, governed their polities like large households, the absolutist doctrine could succeed, in the cut-down garb of a narrow patriarchalism weighed down by tradition. This patriarchalism transferred the picture of the father, as developed in the successful *Hausväterliteratur* (literature dealing with the office of the 'house-father') of the age, up to the level of the state.

Admittedly, with the 'Enlightened absolutism' which was emerging in Germany as well from the eighteenth century on, traditional justifications for lordship saw an influx of Enlightenment thinking. The natural-law teaching of Hugo Grotius, Samuel Pufendorf, and Christian Wolff which now came into effect turned the previously untouchable position of the sovereign into a relative one. His position was no longer defined as directly established by God but rather, in a secularized understanding, as the product of a contractual relationship entered into voluntarily. Carl Gottlieb Svarez, one of the authors of the 'General Law for the Prussian States' ('Allgemeines Landrecht für die preußischen Staaten') of 1794, banished from his theory of the ruler the earlier transcendent legitimization, as well as the *Recht des Stärkeren* ('right of the stronger party') so often practised in politics:

> The rights of the leader in a state, or of the ruler, cannot be derived from direct divine consecration, nor from the right of the stronger party, but rather must be derived from a contract, through which the citizens of a state have submitted themselves to the commands of the ruler for the furthering of their own communal happiness.[84]

The main aim of the state was now defined in terms of eudaemonism; the basic maxim of Enlightenment rulers was to guarantee the well-being of their subjects. The ruler no longer identified himself with the state, instead describing himself, like Friedrich II of Prussia, as its 'first servant', or modestly regarding himself, like Leopold of Tuscany, as a 'delegate appointed by the people'.[85] Under the dictates of reason an attempt was made to cleanse the state of the last particularistic intermediate powers which still stood in the way of its rational ordering according to the *mos geometricus* (geometrical method).[86] The basic contradiction of Enlightenment absolutist reasoning was the view that the well-being of the subjects could be guaranteed only by the ruler – 'Alles für das Volk, nichts durch das Volk' ('Everything for the people, nothing by the people'), in the words of Johann Heinrich Gottlob von Justi.[87] Here, natural-law teaching, which assigned every individual basic rights which were also supposed to be respected by the state, came into conflict with the claim which princes seldom relinquished, to exclusive regulation of all things. While in 1762 in his *Contrat social* Jean Jacques Rousseau consistently derived the sovereignty of the people, which ultimately led the way to the Revolution, from natural-law teachings, everywhere in the territories of the Empire appeals were made to princes to put into practice their loudly propagated Enlightenment views through a virtuous and dutiful conduct of office. But reforms were always only pursued as far as it was believed to be possible without endangering one's own position, and without any serious desire to permit one's subjects to exercise personal rights of freedom. Nevertheless, Enlightenment postulates ultimately meant that the picture of the devoted *Landesvater* (father of the country) came under criticism in Germany as well. By the time certain princes attempted to temper their despotic style of lordship into a sort of 'Enlightened patriarchalism', and like Duke Carl Eugen of Württemberg publicly promised to perform their fatherly duties toward the *Landeskinder* ('children of the country', subjects) better than previously, it was already too late; the old justifications had outlived their time, and, faced with rational and objective principles of lordship, the patriarchal model had finally become obsolete even in the territories of the Empire. Immanuel Kant, soon followed by others, criticized patriarchal lordship as the greatest form of despotism conceivable, and regarded it as incapable of being improved. Josef von Sonnenfels rejected the analogy between father and prince as a logically senseless construction: 'The father is there before the son, and gives the son existence. The nation is always in existence before the prince, and the prince obtains his existence from the nation.'[88]

The economic theory of mercantilism was modelled on the absolutist doctrine, and assumed that the state should also enjoy absolute directorial power in the economic sphere.[89] After 1648 this maxim was followed by German territorial authorities, in so far as they were in a position to do so. In this, the Empire played a secondary role. The Imperial Diet issued a large number of economic ordinances, but the territories followed these ordinances only if they served their own advantage. The main aims of mercantilistic policy were a positive balance of trade and as autarkic an economy as possible. The wealth of the state, especially the possession of precious metals and money, were regarded as the necessary prerequisites for political power. As a consequence, economic growth was supposed to be furthered by all possible means. A dirigist system of state support and state control was to be established; all state resources were to be brought into operation for this purpose, and a strict customs policy was to be implemented, favouring imports of raw materials and exports of finished products.

The carefully planned population policy of many states (*Peuplierung*, as it was called) was an especially important aspect of mercantilism. The load-bearing pillars of *Peuplierung* were prohibitions on emigration and deliberate programmes to support immigration. A large population was considered the main prerequisite for political, military, and economic potency: in the words of Friedrich II of Prussia, 'the true strength of a state' was manifested 'in a high population'.[90] For this reason, demographic initiatives and demographic measures were everywhere included among the most important regulatory instruments of mercantilistic policy. Labour, as a factor of production, was also assigned heightened importance, with the ruthless labelling and marginalization of unproductive groups of the population (discussed in detail in Chapter 12). Programmes to make people diligent and to discipline them, which were carried out by confessional, state, and urban institutions, together with attempts to reduce work-free periods of time, were implemented with the aim of exploiting all possible reserves of labour.[91]

Admittedly, while the mercantilist programme was successfully put into practice in France under Louis XIV, in the Empire it could be realized to any extent only in the large territories of Prussia and Austria. The medium-sized and especially the smaller territories and cities were largely unable to pursue an autarkic economic policy. They hardly went any further than to imitate individual measures. The German variant of mercantilism, 'cameralism', whose name derived from the princely *Schatzkammer* (treasury, 'camera' in Latin), was predominantly organized around tax-raising.[92] The relevant knowledge was transmitted through chairs of cameralistics at universities, which were set up first in Prussia, then in all larger territories. Cameralistic teaching proliferated into a wide array of many-faceted variants, depending on the requirements of each territory. In his 1656 book,

Teutscher Fürsten-Staat, Veit Ludwig von Seckendorff, the most influential
early theoretician of the cameralistically organized territorial state, opposed
the outflow of money in so far as it served for the import of luxury goods,
supported the abolition of guilds because their monopolistic activities limited economic growth, and argued for the development of education in
order to train skilled bureaucrats and state servants. At the end of the seventeenth century, the 'Vienna School' of the Austrian cameralists Johann
Joachim Becher, Philipp Wilhelm von Hörnigk, and Wilhelm Schröder put
forward a wide-ranging economic programme which unified all the postulates of mercantilist theory. After the middle of the eighteenth century
cameralism found its most important representatives in Johann Heinrich
Gottlob von Justi and Joseph von Sonnenfels. They combined mercantilist
doctrines with the mechanistic teaching of Enlightened absolutism and the
eudaemonistic theories of the welfare state, in this way laying the intellectual basis for the modernization of the large German territories in the
age of Enlightened absolutism.

The state in everyday life?

Given the state's expanding ambitions as articulated in the concept of
Policey and in absolutist and cameralist doctrines, the following question
arises: how far could political power actually reach in Germany between
the Peace of Westphalia and the end of the Old Empire? International
research on absolutism[93] has begun to widen its purview beyond a pure
étatist perspective to questions of social and economic history. It has also
begun increasingly to investigate the intermediate powers which in many
ways opposed the state, and the social spaces which were hardly or not at
all touched by the authorities' claims to omnipotence. This research has
shown that the absolutist state was only to a very limited degree a first
step towards the modern totalitarian state.[94] However, despite the chasm
between theoretical claims and practical realizability, which was sometimes
quite deep, in many cases the presence of the state in everyday life was
indeed strengthened.

This was especially the case in the years of recovery after the Thirty
Years War, when the areas hardest hit by abandonment of settlements and
loss of population – Württemberg, Franconia, the Palatinate, Thuringia,
Saxony, Mecklenburg, and Pomerania[95] – could only be rebuilt with state
initiatives and state assistance. The reconstruction of the German territories took place by means of a wide array of measures, which together
clearly pointed the way toward the modern state. The financial stimuli
which some territories provided to subjects to encourage reconstruction

already provide evidence of the state's increased willingness to intervene. In contrast to the partial worsening of the position of peasants in areas of *Gutsherrschaft* (the eastern German manorial system, characterized by strong landlord powers), involving the intensification of serfdom, the expropriation of peasant holdings, and unrestricted labour services, in some territories characterized by *Grundherrschaft* (the western German manorial system, characterized by weaker landlord powers) lords reduced financial burdens on their rural subjects in order to accelerate the repair of damages to agriculture caused by the war.[96] Nevertheless, in many places the economic stagnation caused by the Thirty Years War was overcome only in the eighteenth century.

State influence over access to marriage, which was intensified after 1648, was of considerable social and demographic importance.[97] Everywhere, the consent of the household head was required before anyone could marry, and particular groups (bureaucrats, soldiers, students, widows, craft journeymen, and servants), and people without sufficient property, also required marriage permits from the state. After the Thirty Years War, government restrictions on the marriage of servants (whose numbers were regarded as being too low) were introduced in some regions; in the eighteenth century, general and sometimes strict prohibitions on marriage were extended to the growing population of poor people, for reasons of social regulation and military organization. The purpose of all these measures was to permit only those marriages which had a secure economic basis, so as not to burden state and society with welfare cases. In addition, as had already been the case previously, behind all the state regulation of marriage stood the moral aim of restricting sexuality entirely to marriages which had been legitimately concluded.[98]

Programmes to increase population growth were implemented very early on and very directly. Immediately after the Thirty Years War immigrants from Switzerland, The Netherlands, the Tyrol, and even Upper Italy quickly began to make up the severe population losses in areas of *Grundherrschaft* in southern Germany (Württemberg, Baden, the Alsace, and the Palatinate).[99] In areas of *Gutsherrschaft*, immigrants had to be offered extensive privileges to attract them into the country. This succeeded in greater measure after the revocation of the Edict of Nantes by Louis XIV in 1685, which caused more than 200,000 Huguenots and Waldensians to flee from France. The largest contingent which came to Germany found a haven in Brandenburg; others fled to Hesse and Württemberg.[100] The Huguenots brought with them agrarian innovations, new proto-industrial techniques, and special manufacturing expertise. In 1731–2, 22,000 Protestants who were driven out of Salzburg found new homes in Prussia.

The growing concern to promote population growth also accounted for the new measures undertaken by the early modern authorities to protect public health, initially in the towns but by the end of the period in the countryside as well.[101] From the later middle ages on, the cleanliness of streets and wells and more or less well-regulated waste removal began to be a concern. This was mostly for reasons of public order, for there was not yet any clear recognition of the relationship between dirt and infection.[102] Systematic and concerted measures were introduced in the late eighteenth century in the framework of state medical programmes,[103] whose general aim was the maintenance of the health of the *Volkskörper* ('body of the nation').[104] Already at earlier periods in times of great epidemics, especially plague, states had sought to use quarantine and hygiene measures to combat the threat of depopulation of whole stretches of territory. There are many indications that these defensive administrative strategies, which in the eighteenth century were highly differentiated and sometimes even excessive, enjoyed quite decisive success, despite equally significant secondary changes in the rat population. After 1750, the plague finally disappeared from Germany.

Not only the fight against epidemics but also other crisis situations and catastrophes served the emerging state as welcome openings for increasing its power. This can be observed in the great famines of the period,[105] in the beginnings of state regulation of rivers in the aftermath of floods,[106] and in governmental endykement policies. As shown by the events of the great North Sea storm flood of 1717, massive acts of state intervention brought about restrictions on the autonomy of dyke associations; however, without state crisis management, it would probably not have been possible effectively to secure the sea-coasts against future disasters.[107]

In addition to measures directed at increasing population growth, which in a sense formed the basis of all cameralistic programmes, some German states sought to expand the land supply internally to the country. Especially in Brandenburg-Prussia, new, cultivable land was obtained in this way. Friedrich Wilhelm I had the Havelländische Luch (a large marsh) drained. A total of 550 kilometres of drainage canals were built, and *c.* 15,000 hectares of land were thereby obtained. Similarly, under Friedrich II the two marshes of the Oderbruch (in 1743–53) and the Warthebruch (by 1786) were drained. Comparable land improvements (so-called 'Meliorationen') succeeded in Pomerania, the Kurmark and the Altmark, Bavaria, Hannover, and Oldenburg. In addition, from the mid-eighteenth century on, the explosive growth of population in many places brought deserted land under cultivation; many farms carried this out on their own initiative. The planned building of highways, undertaken first in southern Germany, contributed to German territories' being much better covered by transportation networks. The expansion of postal systems, which from the end of the seventeenth century began to carry not only freight but also people, ensured a better penetration of both territories and Empire by administrative techniques and communications.[108]

Hand in hand with internal improvements, there was an increase in the state's hold over 'lordless' land, or land which had been used collectively. This affected fallow land, which in the framework of the reformed agriculture of the eighteenth century was everywhere brought into more intensive utilization. It also affected forests,[109] over which the authorities had already been trying to extend their claims since the end of the middle ages (as they had to the waterways). This development not only conflicted with traditional usufruct rights over common lands, but also ran up against the unrestricted clear-cutting of wood, widespread in proto-industrial regions, which positively demanded state regulations (*Waldordnungung* or 'forest ordinances'). In their regulatory programmes, the concern of the princes was not to protect nature, but rather to exploit the forests economically in a controlled way, and also to secure a feudal prerogative in the shape of princely hunting.[110]

Agrarian reforms and intensification measures, which in the second half of the eighteenth century led to a considerable increase in agricultural production (discussed in detail in Chapter 3), were also generally carried out through state initiatives and Enlightenment enthusiasm. The introduction of the 'improved three-field system', and the spread of alternative crop rotations (which had already long been practised in regions well-suited for agriculture), increased yields; this was urgently needed in order to feed the rapidly growing population. Among the new crop plants which supplemented traditional food supplies, the most important were maize (which spread rapidly in Baden, the Palatinate, and Württemberg) and, above all, the potato.[111] Despite quite considerable resistance, potato cultivation was implemented by the authorities, and greatly benefited regions of the Mittelgebirge unsuited to grain cultivation. Because the potato could easily be cultivated even on infertile soils and under unfavourable climatic conditions, and because during the great failures of the grain harvest in 1770–1 it saved many people from starvation, it soon enjoyed a career as a cheap popular foodstuff.

In the industrial sector (discussed in detail in Chapter 9) state initiatives also expanded under the banner of cameralism. Both Empire and territories sought in many ways to push back the restrictive influence of the guilds, which stood in the way of industrial modernization.[112] The Imperial Craft Ordinance of 1731 prohibited a wide array of guild customs handed down from the past: the arbitrary infliction of punishments, the excessively long training processes, and the widespread cartel agreements. But the Imperial Cities, where the guilds still enjoyed an almost autonomous position in 1800, paid almost no attention to the new regulations. Instead, it was the territories which devoted themselves to modernizing the crafts, with the help of the Imperial laws. They also recruited foreign specialists (such as gun-founders and builders of fortifications), granted privileges to confessional exiles, and sometimes even supported the transfer of technology from abroad for the industries of the future (such as porcelain).

The need to satisfy a growing mass demand, which guilded crafts were no longer able to do, ultimately favoured the development and expansion of early capitalistic forms of proto-industrial production (which had long been in existence);[113] these were often protected by the state. Decentralized putting-out systems, involving a division of labour, became increasingly important in the production of textiles and metal products. Manufactories and factories, where work took place in centralized plants, primarily satisfied the increased demand by princely courts for luxury items such as furniture, coaches, carpets, tapestries, ornaments, mirrors, and porcelain, as well as the military demand for weapons and uniforms. Because manufactories specialized in satisfying the growing state demand for military and luxury goods, they did not threaten the existence of traditional crafts but supplemented them. Frequently, manufactories were combined with putting-out systems, especially in textile industries, where the division of labour came up against natural limits. In this combination, some manufactories employed large numbers of people. The favoured locations for establishing manufactories were barrack-like institutions such as workhouses, poorhouses, orphanages, and foundling-hospitals, which were constructed between 1600 and 1800 in almost all territories, as institutions of punishment and correction for marginalized groups in society.

This is a reminder of the fact that in the framework of their powers of *Policey*, early modern states increasingly also devoted themselves to tasks of social discipline, beginning with the measures they took to combat *landschädliche Leute* ('people harmful to the country') in the later middle ages. Parallel to the entrenchment of the corporate society of social estates which can be observed from the sixteenth century on (discussed in detail in Chapter 5), there occurred a labelling and marginalizing of large social groups, from the begging poor and the travelling people on the roads through to all those who, for an array of different reasons, were no longer regarded as being part of 'good society'.[114] With the assistance of a highly differentiated legal toolkit (such as the process of interrogation) and a body of jurists trained for this purpose,[115] the state everywhere advanced its struggle against criminal elements, and all persons believed to be so. The documents dealing with criminal cases, stored in their thousands in local, regional, and state archives, bear witness to the enormous expansion of state activity in this field in the seventeenth and eighteenth centuries. In this expansion, care and discipline could go hand in hand, as is shown by the incarceration of deviant groups in workhouses and houses of discipline from 1600 on.[116] By contrast, in the case of hunts for robbers[117] and even more for 'gypsies'[118] it was often a question of repression, indeed of elimination – although because of the weakness of the state's 'executive arm', these aims were not always achieved. The role of the state in the witch-hunts of the period is also now regarded as somewhat less important than previously believed. The authorities were involved in all cases arising in this period through their formal conduct of the legal proceedings; but the beginning and course of many of these proceedings provide evidence that the state was not always or everywhere the driving force in the persecutions.[119]

It is impossible to consider the genesis of the early modern state without examining the cultural sector, especially the sphere of education and training. The nourishment of art and scholarship, whose successes reflected back on the patrons of the arts, was an old and traditional princely activity.[120] Even more than the churches, the princely courts succeeded in developing an overwhelming cultural influence during the seventeenth and eighteenth centuries.[121] The universities were given deliberate state support. The loyal services of university graduates, especially bureaucrats in church and government administration, ensured the consolidation of the emerging state (as discussed in Chapter 6). For this reason, states everywhere laid the greatest value on their training. In addition, the expansion and growing concentration of tasks in the hands of the state increasingly furthered the growth of education. After 1648, many territories developed an educational policy, which by the end of the 'pedagogical century' involved all subjects of the state.[122] This had already begun during the sixteenth century under the banner of confessionalism and humanism, and was now differentiated and explicitly furthered in the framework of the cameralist programme. It led to the development of, and concern for, a hierarchically organized school system, and by the end of the eighteenth century achieved considerable success in creating a literate population.

The universities had traditionally stood at the apex of the educational system, and they retained their predominant role as the most important institutions in intellectual and scholarly life.[123] Apart from the Jesuit universities, most universities were subject to state monitoring. After the new foundation of the University of Halle in 1694, whose teachers included Christian Thomasius, August Hermann Francke, and Christian Wolff, teaching began to be modernized, especially through the exemplary combination of *Jus und Historie* ('law and history')[124] and the reform of medicine. The University of Göttingen, founded in 1736 by the Electors of Hannover, also attained a leading position among the German universities. It concentrated on the natural sciences, ancient philology, political theory, and legal studies, disciplines traditionally neglected by academic institutions; and it was distinguished by a freedom of teaching unusual for the period. In contrast to this, the Austrian university reforms under Maria Theresia and Joseph II led to a strictly organized, étatist regulation and supervision of the content and methods of teaching.[125] In comparison to the modernizing universities, the eighteenth-century academy movement provided only a temporary stimulus to intellectual life in Germany.[126] While only a few princes sought to reform the *Gymnasien* (grammar schools), and some (like Joseph II) even closed down grammar schools because of the threat of a 'flood of academics',[127] the expansion of elementary schools and the development of professionalized teacher-training were everywhere included among the most important state pedagogical initiatives. On the model provided by Ernst the Pious of Sachsen-Gotha,[128] and stimulated by Pietism, in 1717 and 1763 Brandenburg-Prussia saw the introduction of general compulsory school attendance, although at first this could be realized only incompletely.[129] The Prussian example was followed after 1774 by Austria under Maria Theresia, to whose reforms other Catholic territories soon oriented themselves.[130] Building on earlier, confessionally motivated successes in literacy, elementary education was furthered everywhere, and this led to clear advances in the gaining of literacy by lower social strata in both town and countryside, even though widespread success was achieved only in the nineteenth century.[131] Support for elementary literacy acquisition from the absolutist state and the Enlightenment campaigns of *Volksaufklärung* ('enlightenment of the people')[132] was on the whole only half-hearted. They aimed to produce useful and obedient subjects, not emancipated citizens. The emergence of a highly differentiated literary market[133] cannot obscure the limitations inherent in the system of governmental tutelage and the survival of censorship.

The continual growth of the state from the later middle ages onward in the territories, and to a limited extent also in the Empire, was highly ambivalent in its effects. On one hand, it unquestionably furthered the modernization of economy and society, decreased the difficulty of everyday life through supporting technical progress and other measures of 'civilization', improved educational opportunities, and ensured the survival of the population better than before. On the other hand, the state's power to define moral norms unquestionably increased, *Policey* developed a ubiquitous system of regulation and social disciplining, the tax burden increased, and the early modern bureaucracy demanded its first victims. In many places the costs of this process led to conflict. In particular, considerable resistance was sometimes directed at the burden of taxation for the maintenance of standing armies, which in the second half of the eighteenth century amounted to between 52 and 57 per cent of state expenditures in Prussia, 48.5 per cent in Austria, and 31.5 per cent in Bavaria.[134] Peasants defended themselves against growing government pressure in many regions, not only in territories such as southern[135] and north-western Germany[136] where they had traditionally participated actively in fiscal, financial, and economy policy, but in all areas where burdens increased. Peasants' reactions did not exclude acts of resistance and revolts, which occurred repeatedly to the end of the Old Empire; but many peasants and communities began increasingly to follow the legal path, bringing prosecutions before the relevant courts, the Imperial Chamber Court, and the Imperial Aulic Council.[137]

This juridification of social conflicts is part of a general process of social pacification and civilization,[138] in which confessional, social, and state powers took equal part.[139] Everywhere it was a question of eliminating from everyday intercourse the agonistic and rabelaisian remnants of the feud, whose surviving legacy appeared obsolete in the light of new and refined ideals of intercourse. To what extent the pedagogical policing campaigns which were propagated on so many levels bore fruit in everyday life has hardly yet been researched. The change in the German 'national character', which in the course of the early modern period was slowly able to shake off its earlier rabelaisian elements, and from the end of the eighteenth century on presented itself in the polished brilliance of bourgeois virtue,[140] is an indication that by the end of the early modern period, at least, the self-perception of the Germans, and their conception of foreigners, had been fundamentally transformed.

The limitations of the early modern state

Between 1648 and the end of the Old Empire the largest of the German territories were on the path toward becoming modern states. Admittedly, as a whole the restructuring of the old corporative *Personenverbandsstaaten* (feudal states characterized by personal loyalty) into *institutionelle Flächenstaaten* ('institutionally and territorially closed states') was still incomplete. The absolutist theory of lordship, and the political, economic, and social measures inspired by it, encountered limitations in the intermediary spheres of lordship which were nowhere wholly suppressed. The less success Enlightened absolutism and patriarchalism enjoyed in fully excluding the traditional corporative or functional élites in town and country (defined by birth as belonging to a particular social estate) from the political and social sphere, the less ability cameralistic dirigism enjoyed in the economic sector to abolish the economic limitations on growth resulting from the feudal mode of production. The agrarian systems of *Grundherrschaft* and *Gutsherrschaft*, with their numerous limitations and negative side-effects, remained largely untouched until the end of the eighteenth century, as did the guild organization of crafts which stood in the way of industrial modernization.

Even putting-out systems and manufactories formed only an apparent exception. The organization and co-ordination of human labour power was increasingly better understood, but at the same time the free development of the forces of production was still hindered: 'The breakthrough to modern economic development required a state-free and legally egalitarian society; under absolutism, given the rootedness of the latter in a corporative and regional social order, it remained impossible.'[141] But the efforts at *Policey* and the strictly organized administrative states which this sought to create also seldom reached the subjects directly. The widely stressed process of 'social disciplining' remained fragmentary.[142] It transformed the 'common man' of the sixteenth century into the 'subject' of the seventeenth and eighteenth centuries,[143] but ultimately failed to create a body of subjects completely adapted to the purposes of the state. Until the emergence of the modern state, which only occurred in the nineteenth century, the modelling of mentalities and the regulation of social behaviour still remained largely in the hands of the churches and of traditional circles of society, and thus remained the responsibility of non-state institutions. Even in Brandenburg-Prussia a totalitarian absolutism never prevailed. And even King Friedrich II was hardly able to break into the sphere of noble self-administration, not to mention the inability of smaller states completely to subordinate their subjects *more geometrico* (according to the 'geometrical method') to state purposes. For this there was lacking not only the executive organs, but also – no less importantly – the requisite dense structure of communications covering the whole country. The twentieth-century experience of totalitarian and bureaucratic systems illuminates very clearly the wide gap between the early modern polity on the one hand and modern states on the other – in Germany in particular. Until the end of the Old Empire, the German territories were on the path toward the modern state; but the 'state on the spot' remained a utopia, even later.[144] In the Holy Roman Empire of the German Nation, in distinction to western Europe, there was a 'continuity between the Enlightened reforming state of the eighteenth century and the bureaucratic state absolutism of the nineteenth century'.[145] This specific German path continued to delay the success of state modernization for a considerable time. However, the 'strategem of reason', with its aim of creating a standardized body of subjects, did begin to level out corporative distinctions, and thus indirectly prepared the way for a democratic society of state citizens based on freedom and equality.

Notes

1 See generally Wolfgang Mager, *Zur Entstehung des modernen Staatsbegriffs* (Mainz, 1968); Paul-Ludwig Weinacht, *Staat. Studien zur Bedeutungsgeschichte des Wortes von den Anfängen bis ins 19. Jahrhundert* (Berlin, 1968); Werner Conze, 'Staat/Souveränität I–II', in Otto Brunner, Werner Conze, and Reinhart Koselleck, eds, *Geschichtliche Grundbegriffe*, vi (Stuttgart, 1990), p. 8.

2 *Ibid.*, p. 18.

3 See Gerhard Oestreich, *Geist und Gestalt des frühmodernen Staates. Ausgewählte Aufsätze* (Berlin, 1969), pp. 5f.; Dieter Wyduckel, *Princeps Legibus Solutus. Eine Untersuchung zur frühmodernen Rechts- und Staatslehre* (Berlin, 1979); Heiner Timmermann, ed., *Die Bildung des frühmodernen Staates. Stände und Konfessionen* (Saarbrücken-Scheidt, 1989).

4 See Karl Biedermann, *Deutschlands trübste Zeit, oder: Der dreißigjährige Krieg in seinen Folgen für das deutsche Culturleben* (Berlin, 1862).

5 On this reappraisal, see, for instance, Friedrich Heinrich Schubert, *Die deutschen Reichstage in der Staatslehre der Frühen Neuzeit* (Göttingen,

1966); Bernd Roeck, *Reichssystem und Reichsherkommen. Die Diskussion über die Staatlichkeit des Reiches in der politischen Publizistik des 17. und 18. Jahrhunderts* (Wiesbaden, 1984); Karl Otmar von Aretin, *Das Reich. Friedensgarantie und europäisches Gleichgewicht 1648–1806* (Stuttgart, 1986).

6 Severini de Monzambano Veronensis, *De statu Imperii Germanici ad Laelium fratrem, Dominum Trezolani, liber unus* (Geneva, 1667), p. vi, §9.

7 Heinz Neuhaus, 'Das Problem der militärischen Exekutive in der Spätphase des Alten Reiches', in Johannes Kunisch, ed., *Staatsverfassung und Heeresverfassung in der europäischen Geschichte der Frühen Neuzeit* (Berlin, 1986), p. 337.

8 Johannes Burkhardt, *Der Dreißigjährige Krieg* (Frankfurt am Main, 1992), p. 123.

9 See on this generally Hermann Conrad, *Der deutsche Staat. Epochen seiner Verfassungsentwicklung (843–1945)* (Frankfurt am Main/Berlin, 1969); Fritz Hartung, *Deutsche Verfassungsgeschichte vom 15. Jahrhundert bis zur Gegenwart* (9th edn, Stuttgart, 1969); Heinrich Mitteis and Heinz Lieberich, *Deutsche Rechtsgeschichte. Ein Studienbuch* (19th edn, Munich, 1992); Karl Kroeschell, *Deutsche Rechtsgeschichte* (7th edn, Opladen, 1989), ii., iii; Gerhard Oestreich, 'Verfassungsgeschichte vom Ende des Mittelalters bis zum Ende des Alten Reiches', in Herbert Grundmann, ed., *Gebhardt – Handbuch der deutschen Geschichte* (9th edn, Stuttgart, 1970), ii, pp. 360–436; Hans Boldt, *Deutsche Verfassungsgeschichte*, i: *Von den Anfängen bis zum Ende des älteren deutschen Reiches 1806* (Munich, 1984); Dietmar Willoweit, *Deutsche Verfassungsgeschichte. Vom Frankenreich bis zur Teilung Deutschlands* (Munich, 1990); Heinz Duchhardt, *Deutsche Verfassungsgeschichte 1495–1806* (Stuttgart, 1991); the most important new survey (with an abundance of bibliographical references for further study) is Kurt G. A. Jeserich, Hans Pohl, and Georg-Christoph von Unruh, eds, *Deutsche Verwaltungsgeschichte*, i: *Vom Spätmittelalter bis zum Ende des Reiches* (Stuttgart, 1983).

10 Dietmar Willoweit, *Rechtsgrundlagen der Territorialgewalt* (Cologne/Vienna, 1975).

11 See e.g. Helmut Rankl, *Das vorreformatorische landesherrliche Kirchenregiment in Bayern (1378–1521)* (Munich, 1971).

12 Theodor Mayer, 'Die Ausbildung der Grundlagen des modernen deutschen Staates im hohen Mittelalter', in Hellmut Kämpf, ed., *Herrschaft und Staat im Mittelalter* (Darmstadt, 1964), pp. 284–331.

13 Peter Blickle, *Landschaften im Alten Reich. Die staatliche Funktion des gemeinen Mannes in Oberdeutschland* (Munich, 1973).

14 Gerhard Oestreich, 'Strukturprobleme des europäischen Absolutismus', in Gerhard Oestreich, *Geist und Gestalt des frühmodernen Staates* (Berlin, 1969), pp. 179–97.

15 Adam Wandruszka, *Reichspatriotismus und Reichspolitik zur Zeit des Prager Friedens von 1635* (Graz/Cologne, 1955); by contrast, see Heiner Haan, *Der Regensburger Kurfürstentag von 1636–1637* (Münster, 1967).

16 Burkhardt, *Dreißigjährige Krieg*, p. 98.

17 Konrad Müller (compiler), *Instrumenta Pacis Westphalicae* (Bern, 1949), Art. viii, §1.

18 Hans Erich Feine, 'Zur Verfassungsentwicklung des Heiligen Römischen Reichs seit dem Westfälischen Frieden', in Friedrich Merzbacher, ed., *Hans Erich Feine: Territorium und Gericht* (Aalen, 1978), pp. 237–305.

19 See on this esp. Volker Press, *Kriege und Krisen. Deutschland 1600–1715* (Munich, 1991).

20 Oswald von Gschliesser, *Der Reichshofrat. Bedeutung und Verfassung,*

Schicksal und Besetzung einer obersten Reichsbehörde von 1559 bis 1806 (Vienna, 1942).

21 Anton Schindling, *Die Anfänge des immerwährenden Reichstags zu Regensburg: Ständevertretung und Staatskunst nach dem Westfälischen Frieden* (Mainz, 1991).

22 Ulrich Belstler, *Die Stellung des Corpus Evangelicorum in der Reichsverfassung* (Bamberg, 1968); Klaus Schlaich, 'Majoritas – protestatio – itio in partes – corpus Evangelicorum', *Zeitschrift für Rechtsgeschichte, kanonistische Abteilung*, 107 (1977), pp. 264–99; 108 (1978), pp. 139–79.

23 Rudolf Smend, *Das Reichskammergericht. Geschichte und Verfassung* (Weimar, 1911).

24 Winfried Dotzauer, *Die deutschen Reichskreise in der Verfassung des Alten Reiches und ihr Eigenleben (1500–1806)* (Darmstadt, 1989).

25 Ferdinand Magen, 'Die Reichskreise in der Epoche des Dreißigjährigen Krieges', *ZHF* 9 (1982), pp. 409–60.

26 See Bernd Wunder, 'Die Kreisassoziationen 1672–1748', *ZGO* 128 (1980), pp. 167–266; Karl Otmar von Aretin, ed., *Der Kurfürst von Mainz und die Kreisassoziation 1648–1746* (Wiesbaden, 1975).

27 Ernst Klein, *Geschichte der öffentlichen Finanzen in Deutschland, 1500–1870* (Wiesbaden, 1974).

28 Heinz Angermeier, *Die Reichsreform 1410–1555* (Munich, 1984).

29 Winfried Schulze, *Reich und Türkengefahr im späten 16. Jahrhundert. Studien zu den politischen und gesellschaftlichen Auswirkungen einer äußeren Bedrohung* (Munich, 1978).

30 Harm Klueting, 'Deutsche Territorien', in Jürgen Ziechmann, ed., *Panorama der Fridericianischen Zeit. Friedrich der Große und seine Epoche* (Bremen, 1985), i. p. 761.

31 Gerhard Köbler, *Historisches Lexikon der deutschen Länder* (4th edn, Munich, 1992).

32 Rudolf Reinhardt, 'Kontinuität und Diskontinuität. Zum Problem der Koadjuterie mit dem Recht der Nachfolge in der neuzeitlichen Germania Sacra', in Johannes Kunisch, ed., *Der dynastische Fürstenstaat* (Berlin, 1982).

33 Winfried Becker, *Der Kurfürstenrat. Grundzüge seiner Entwicklung in der Reichsverfassung und seine Stellung auf dem Westfälischen Friedenskongreß* (Münster, 1973).

34 Volker Press, 'Die Reichritterschaft im Reich der frühen Neuzeit', *Nassauische Annalen*, 87 (1976), pp. 101–22.

35 Hans Rosenberg, *Bureaucracy, Aristocracy and Autocracy: The Prussian Experience 1660–1815* (3rd edn, Cambridge, 1968); Otto Büsch and Wolfgang Neugebauer, eds, *Moderne Preußische Geschichte (1648–1947). Eine Anthologie* (3 vols, Berlin, 1981); Gerd Heinrich, *Geschichte Preußens. Staat und Dynastie* (Frankfurt am Main, 1981).

36 Hugo Hantsch, *Die Geschichte Österreichs* (2 vols: vol. i, 4th edn, Graz, 1959; vol. ii, 3rd edn, Graz, 1962); Erich Zöllner, *Geschichte Österreichs. Von den Anfängen bis zur Gegenwart* (9th edn, Vienna/Munich, 1990).

37 Karl E. Demandt, *Geschichte des Landes Hessen* (2nd edn, Kassel, 1980).

38 Francis L. Carsten, *Princes and Parliaments in Germany: From the Fifteenth to the Eighteenth Century* (Oxford, 1959); Rudolf Vierhaus, 'Ständewesen und Staatsverwaltung in Deutschland im späten 18. Jahrhundert', in Rudolf Vierhaus and Manfred Bötzenhart, eds, *Dauer und Wandel in der Geschichte, Festschrift für Kurt von Raumer* (Münster, 1966), pp. 337–60; Dietrich Gerhard, ed., *Ständische Vertretungen in Europa im 17. und 18. Jahrhundert* (Göttingen, 1969); Peter Baumgart, ed., *Ständetum und Staatsbildung in*

Brandenburg-Preußen (Berlin/New York, 1983), pp. 280–318; Peter Blickle, 'Kommunalismus, Parlamentarismus, Republikanismus', *HZ* 242 (1986), pp. 529–56.

39 See e.g. Walter Grube, *Der Stuttgarter Landtag 1457–1957* (Stuttgart, 1957); Hartmut Lehmann, 'Die württembergischen Landstände im 17. und 18. Jahrhundert', in Dietrich Gerhard, ed., *Ständische Vertretungen im 17. und 18. Jahrhundert* (Göttingen, 1969), pp. 183–207.

40 Uwe Schultz, ed., *Mit dem Zehnten fing es an. Eine Kulturgeschichte der Steuer* (Munich, 1986).

41 Gerhard Oestreich, 'Ständetum und Staatsbildung in Deutschland', in Oestreich, *Geist und Gestalt*, pp. 277–89; Kersten Krüger, *Finanzstaat Hessen 1500–1567. Staatbildung im Übergang vom Domänenstaat zum Steuerstaat* (Marburg, 1980).

42 See Karlheinz Blaschke, 'Finanzwesen und Staatsräson in Kursachsen', in Aldo De Maddalena and Hermann Kellenbenz, eds, *Finanzen und Staatsräson in Italien und Deutschland in der frühen Neuzeit* (Berlin, 1992), p. 177.

43 Adalbert Erler, 'Akzise', in *Handwörterbuch zur deutschen Rechtsgeschichte* (Berlin, 1971), i. col. 87f.

44 Franz Quarthal, 'Öffentliche Armut, Akademikerschwemme und Massenarbeitslosigkeit im Zeitalter des Barock', in Volker Press, Eugen Reinhard, and Hansmartin Schwarzmaier, eds, *Barock am Oberrhein* (Karlsruhe, 1985), p. 162ff.

45 For details see Jeserich, Pohl, and von Unruh, *Deutsche Verwaltungsgeschichte*, with individual references.

46 See Karin Plodeck, *Hofstruktur und Hofzeremoniell in Brandenburg-Ansbach vom 16. bis zum 18. Jahrhundert. Zur Rolle des Herrschaftskultes im absolutistischen Gesellschafts- und Herrschaftssystem* (Ansbach, 1972); Jürgen Freiherr von Kruedener, *Die Rolle des Hofes im Absolutismus* (Stuttgart, 1973); Hubert Christoph Ehalt, *Ausdrucksformen absolutistischer Herrschaft. Der Wiener Hof im 17. und 18. Jahrhundert* (Munich, 1980); Norbert Elias, *Die höfische Gesellschaft* (5th edn, Darmstadt/Neuwied, 1981); August Buck et al., eds, *Europäische Hofkultur im 16. und 17. Jahrhundert* (3 vols, Hamburg 1981); Rudolf Vierhaus, 'Höfe und höfische Gesellschaft in Deutschland im 17. und 18. Jahrhundert', in Klaus Bohnen, Sven-Aage Jorgenson, and Friedrich Schmöe, eds, *Kultur und Gesellschaft in Deutschland von der Reformation bis zur Gegenwart* (Copenhagen, 1981), pp. 36–56; Aloys Winterling, *Der Hof des Kurfürsten von Köln 1688–1794. Eine Fallstudie zur Bedeutung 'absolutistischer' Hofhaltung* (Bonn, 1986).

47 André Corvisier, *Armées et sociétés en Europe de 1494 à 1789* (Paris, 1976); Thomas M. Barker, *Army, Aristocracy, Monarchy: Essays on War, Society and Government in Austria 1618–1780* (New York, 1982); Barbara Stollberg-Rilinger and Johannes Kunisch, eds, *Staatsverfassung und Heeresverfassung in der europäischen Geschichte der frühen Neuzeit* (Berlin, 1986); Geoffrey Parker, *The Military Revolution: Military Innovation and the Rise of the West, 1500–1800* (Cambridge, 1988).

48 Ernst Walter Zeeden, *Konfessionsbildung. Studien zur Reformation, Gegenreformation und katholischen Reform* (Stuttgart, 1985); Heinz Schilling, ed., *Die reformierte Konfessionalisierung in Deutschland. Das Problem der 'Zweiten Reformation'* (Gütersloh, 1986); Hans-Christoph Rublack, ed., *Die lutherische Konfessionalisierung in Deutschland* (Gütersloh, 1992); Heinrich Richard Schmidt, *Konfessionalisierung im 16. Jahrhundert* (Munich, 1992).

49 See e.g. Paul Münch, *Zucht und Ordnung. Reformierte Kirchenverfassungen im 16. und 17. Jahrhundert (Nassau-Dillenburg, Kurpfalz, Hessen-Kassel)* (Stuttgart, 1978).

50 Wolfgang Reinhard, 'Gegenreformation als Modernisierung? Prolegomena zu einer Theorie des konfessionellen Zeitalters', *ARG* 68 (1977), pp. 226–51.

51 Wolfgang Reinhard, 'Zwang zur Konfessionalisierung. Prolegomena zu einer Theorie des konfessionellen Zeitalters', *ZHF* 10 (1983), pp. 257–77.

52 See e.g. Helmut Steigelmann, *Der Geistliche Rat zu Baden-Baden und seine Protokolle von 1577 bis 1584* (Stuttgart, 1962); Herbert Immenkötter, ed., *Die Protokolle des geistlichen Rates in Münster (1601–1612)* (Münster, 1972).

53 See e.g. Paul Münch, 'Kirchenzucht und Nachbarschaft. Zur sozialen Problematik des calvinistischen Seniorats um 1600', in Ernst Walter Zeeden and Peter Thaddäus Lang, eds, *Kirche und Visitation. Beiträge zur Erforschung des frühneuzeitlichen Visitationswesens in Europa* (Stuttgart, 1984), pp. 216–48.

54 Kaspar von Greyerz, ed., *Religion and Society in Early Modern Europe 1500–1800* (London, 1984); Wolfgang Schieder, ed., *Volksreligiosität in der modernen Sozialgeschichte* (Göttingen, 1986); Hansgeorg Molitor and Heribert Smolinsky, eds, *Volksfrömmigkeit in der frühen Neuzeit* (Münster, 1994).

55 Klaus Schreiner, 'Rechtgläubigkeit als "Band der Gesellschaft" und "Grundlage des Staates". Zur eidlichen Verpflichtung von Staats- und Kirchendienern auf die "Formula Concordiae" und das "Konkordienbuch"', in Martin Brecht and Reinhard Schwarz, eds, *Bekenntnis und Einheit der Kirche. Studien zum Konkordienbuch* (Stuttgart, 1980), pp. 351–79.

56 See e.g. Martin Lackner, *Die Kirchenpolitik des Großen Kurfürsten* (Witten, 1973).

57 Paul Warmbrunn, *Zwei Konfessionen in einer Stadt. Das Zusammenleben von Katholiken und Protestanten in den paritätischen Reichsstädten Augsburg, Biberach, Ravensburg und Dinkelsbühl 1548–1648* (Wiesbaden, 1983); exemplarily, see Bernd Roeck, *Eine Stadt in Krieg und Frieden. Studien zur Geschichte der Reichsstadt Augsburg zwischen Kalenderstreit und Westfälischem Frieden* (2 vols, Göttingen, 1989); Etienne François, *Die unsichtbare Grenze. Protestanten und Katholiken in Augsburg 1648–1806* (Sigmaringen, 1991).

58 Helmuth Kiesel, 'Problem und Begründung der Toleranz im 18. Jahrhundert', in Horst Rabe, Hansgeorg Molitor, and Hans-Christoph Rublack, eds, *Festgabe für Ernst Walter Zeeden* (Münster, 1976), pp. 370–85.

59 Winfried Schulze, *Deutsche Geschichte im 16. Jahrhundert* (Frankfurt am Main, 1987), pp. 204–31.

60 See on this generally Burkhardt, *Dreißigjährige Krieg*.

61 Volker Press, 'Soziale Folgen des Dreißigjährigen Krieges', in Winfried Schulze, ed., *Ständische Gesellschaft und soziale Mobilität* (Munich, 1988); Sheilagh C. Ogilvie, 'Germany and the Seventeenth-Century Crisis', *The Historical Journal*, 35 (1992), pp. 417–41.

62 Mack Walker, *German Home Towns. Community, State and General Estate 1648–1871* (Ithaca, NY, 1971); Klaus Gerteis, *Die deutschen Städte in der Frühen Neuzeit* (Darmstadt, 1986).

63 Peter Blickle, *Deutsche Untertanen* (Munich, 1981), p. 87.

64 See on this the fundamental criticism made of the *communis opinio* within German research by Reinhard Blänkner, '"Absolutismus" und "frühmoderner Staat"', in Rudolf Vierhaus *et al.*, eds, *Frühe Neuzeit – Frühe Moderne? Forschungen zur Vielschichtigkeit von Übergangsprozessen* (Göttingen, 1992), pp. 48–74, here esp. pp. 64f.

65 Paul Münch, 'Deutschland 1648 (nach dem Westfälischen Frieden)', in Ernst

Walter Zeeden, ed., *Großer historischer Weltatlas*, iii: *Neuzeit, Erläuterungen* (Munich, 1984), p. 145.

66 Hans Maier, *Die ältere deutsche Staats-und Verwaltungslehre* (2nd edn, Munich, 1980); Jutta Brückner, *Staatswissenschaften, Kameralismus und Naturrecht. Ein Beitrag zur Geschichte der Politischen Wissenschaft im Deutschland des späten 17. und frühen 18. Jahrhunderts* (Munich, 1977); Franz-Ludwig Knemeyer, 'Polizei', in Otto Brunner, Werner Conze, and Reinhart Koselleck, eds, *Geschichtliche Grundbegriffe* (Stuttgart, 1978), iv; Reiner Schulze, *Policey und Gesetzgebungslehre im 18. Jahrhundert* (Berlin, 1982); Peter Preu, *Polizeibegriff und Staatszwecklehre. Die Entwicklung des Polizeibegriffs durch die Rechts- und Staatswissenschaften des 18. Jahrhunderts* (Göttingen, 1983); Marc Raeff, *The Well-Ordered Police State: Social and Institutional Change through Law in the Germanies and Russia, 1600–1800* (New Haven/London, 1983); Michael Stolleis, *Geschichte des öffentlichen Rechts in Deutschland*, i: *Reichspublizistik und Policeywissenschaft 1600–1800* (Munich, 1988).

67 Gustav Klemens Schmelzeisen, *Polizeiordnungen und Privatrecht* (Münster/Cologne, 1955).

68 See the collection of texts in Gustav Klemens Schmelzeisen, ed, *Polizei- und Landesordnungen* (2 vols, Weimar, 1968/69).

69 Liselotte Constanze Eisenbart, *Kleiderordnungen der deutschen Städte zwischen 1350 und 1700* (Göttingen/Frankfurt am Main, 1962); Veronika Baur, *Kleiderordnungen in Bayern vom 14. bis zum 19. Jahrhundert* (Munich, 1975).

70 Veit Ludwig von Seckendorff, *Teutscher Fürstenstaat* (Frankfurt am Main, 1656).

71 See e.g. the relevant works by Johann Heinrich Gottlob von Justi, Johann Heinrich Ludwig Bergius, and Joseph von Sonnenfels; see on this also Christoph Dipper, 'Volksreligiosität und Obrigkeit im 18. Jahrhundert', in Wolfgang Schieder, ed., *Volksreligiosität in der modernen Sozialgeschichte* (Göttingen, 1986), pp. 73–96; Paul Münch, 'Fêtes pour le peuple, rien par le peuple. "Öffentliche" Feste im Programm der Aufklärung', in Dieter Düding, Peter Friedemann, and Paul Münch, eds, *Öffentliche Festkultur. Politische Feste in Deutschland von der Aufklärung bis zum Ersten Weltkrieg* (Reinbek, 1988), pp. 25–45.

72 Philipp Peter Guden, *Polizey der Industrie, oder Abhandlung von den Mitteln, den Fleiß der Einwohner zu ermuntern, welcher die Königl. Groß-Brittannische Societät der Wissenschaften zu Göttingen, i. J. 1766 den Preis zuerkannt hat* (Braunschweig, 1768).

73 See e.g. Johann Peter Frank, *System einer vollständigen medicinischen Polizey* (Mannheim, 1783), iii. p. 785.

74 Johann Heinrich Gottlob von Justi, *Die Grundfeste zu der Macht und Glückseligkeit der Staaten; oder in detaile Vorstellung der gesamten Policey-Wissenschaft* (Königsberg/Leipzig, 1761).

75 Iring Fetscher and Herfried Münkler, eds, *Handbuch der politischen Ideen*, iii: *Neuzeit. Von den Konfessionskriegen bis zur Aufklärung* (Munich, 1985); Hans Fenske, Dieter Mertens, Wolfgang Reinhard, and Klaus Rosen, *Geschichte der politischen Ideen. Von Homer bis zur Gegenwart* (Frankfurt am Main, 1987); see, from the abundance of the general literature on this period: Karl Otmar von Aretin, ed., *Der Aufgeklärte Absolutismus* (Cologne, 1974); Hartmut Lehmann, *Das Zeitalter des Absolutismus. Gottesgnadentum und Kriegsnot* (Stuttgart, 1980); Rudolf Vierhaus, *Staaten und Stände. Vom Westfälischen Frieden bis zum Hubertusburger Frieden 1648–1763* (Berlin, 1984); Horst Möller, *Vernunft und Kritik. Deutsche Aufklärung im 17. und*

18. Jahrhundert (Frankfurt am Main, 1986); Ernst Hinrichs, ed., *Absolutismus* (Frankfurt am Main, 1986); Johannes Kunisch, *Absolutismus. Europäische Geschichte vom Westfälischen Frieden bis zur Krise des Ancien Régime* (Göttingen, 1986); Heinz Schilling, *Höfe und Allianzen. Deutschland 1648–1763* (Berlin, 1989); Heinz Duchhardt, *Das Zeitalter des Absolutismus* (Munich, 1989); Christoph Dipper, *Deutsche Geschichte 1648–1789* (Frankfurt am Main, 1991).

76 See Johannes Heckel, *Cura religionis, Ius in sacra, Ius circa sacra* (2nd edn, Darmstadt, 1962).

77 Giovanni Botero, *Gründlicher Bericht von Anordnung guter Policeyen und Regimente* (Strasbourg, 1596).

78 Theodor Reinkingk, *Biblische Policey* (Frankfurt am Main, 1653).

79 Justus Lipsius, *Politicorum sive civilis doctrinae libri sex, qui ad principatum maxime spectant* (Leiden, 1589).

80 See Heinz Dollinger, 'Zum Problem des Staatsräsondenkens und seiner Differenzierung im 16. und 17. Jahrhundert', in Aldo de Maddalena and Hermann Kellenbenz, *Finanzen und Staatsräson* (Berlin, 1992), pp. 251–68.

81 On what follows, see Paul Münch, 'Die "Obrigkeit im Vaterstand" – Zu Definition und Kritik des "Landesvaters" während der Frühen Neuzeit', *Daphnis*, 11 (1982), pp. 15–40.

82 Gordon A. Schochet, *Patriarchalism in Political Thought: The Authoritarian Family and Attitudes Especially in Seventeenth-Century England* (Oxford, 1975).

83 Münch, '"Obrigkeit"', p. 32.

84 Cited in Georg Lenz, ed., *Deutsches Staatsdenken im 18. Jahrhundert* (Neuwied/Berlin, 1965), pp. 261f.

85 Cited in von Aretin, *Der Aufgeklärte Absolutismus*, p. 15.

86 Barbara Stollberg-Rilinger, *Der Staat als Maschine. Zur politischen Metaphorik des absoluten Fürstenstaates* (Berlin, 1986).

87 Cited in Ilja Mieck, *Europäische Geschichte der Frühen Neuzeit* (Stuttgart, 1970), p. 206.

88 Münch, '"Obrigkeit"', p. 37.

89 Eli F. Heckscher, *Der Merkantilismus* (2 vols, Jena, 1932); Ingomar Bog, *Der Reichsmerkantilismus. Studien zur Wirtschaftspolitik des heiligen Römischen Reiches im 17. und 18. Jahrhundert* (Stuttgart, 1959); Hans Kellenbenz, *Der Merkantilismus in Europa und die soziale Mobilität* (Wiesbaden, 1965); Fritz Blaich, *Die Epoche des Merkantilismus* (Wiesbaden, 1973); Volker Press, ed., *Städtewesen und Merkantilismus in Mitteleuropa* (Cologne/Vienna, 1983).

90 Friedrich der Große, *Die politischen Testamente* (Munich, 1936), p. 135.

91 Focko Eulen, *Vom Gewerbefleiß zur Industrie. Ein Beitrag zur Wirtschaftsgeschichte des 18. Jahrhunderts* (Berlin, 1967); Hubert Treiber and Heinz Steinert, *Die Fabrikation des zuverlässigen Menschen. Über die 'Wahlverwandtschaft' von Kloster- und Fabrikdisziplin* (Munich, 1980); Wolfgang Dreßen, *Die pädagogische Maschine. Zur Geschichte des industrialisierten Bewußtseins in Preußen/Deutschland* (Frankfurt am Main etc., 1982); Paul Münch, ed., *Ordnung, Fleiß und Sparsamkeit. Texte und Dokumente zur Entstehung der 'bürgerlichen Tugenden'* (Munich, 1984).

92 Erhard Dittrich, *Die deutschen und österreichischen Kameralisten* (Darmstadt, 1974).

93 See, for Germany, Gerhard Oestreich, 'Strukturprobleme des europäischen Absolutismus', in Oestreich, *Geist und Gestalt*, pp. 179–97.

94 Heinz Duchhardt, *Das Zeitalter des Absolutismus* (Munich, 1989), esp. pp. 166–71.

95 Günther Franz, *Der Dreißigjährige Krieg und das deutsche Volk* (4th edn, Stuttgart, 1979); Wolfgang von Hippel, 'Bevölkerung und Wirtschaft im Zeitalter des Dreißigjährigen Krieges. Das Beispiel Württemberg', *ZHF 5* (1978), pp. 413–48.

96 Werner Troßbach, *Bauern 1648–1806* (Munich, 1993), pp. 91f.

97 Christian Pfister, *Bevölkerungsgeschichte und historische Demographie 1500–1800* (Munich, 1994), pp. 24ff and 81ff.

98 Christian Simon, *Untertanenverhalten und obrigkeitliche Machtpolitik. Studien zum Verhältnis zwischen Stadt und Land im ausgehenden 18. Jahrhundert am Beispiel Basels* (Basel/Frankfurt am Main, 1981); Richard van Dülmen, *Kultur und Alltag in der Frühen Neuzeit*, i: *Das Haus und seine Menschen* (Munich, 1990); Heide Wunder, *'Er ist die Sonn', sie ist der Mond'. Frauen in der Frühen Neuzeit* (Munich, 1992).

99 Pfister, *Bevölkerungsgeschichte*; Markus Mattmüller, *Bevölkerungsgeschichte der Schweiz*, Part 1: *Die frühe Neuzeit 1500–1700*, i (Basel/Frankfurt am Main, 1987).

100 Jochen Desel and Walter Mogk, *Hugenotten und Waldenser in Hessen–Kassel* (2 vols, Kassel, 1978/1981); Heinz Duchhardt, ed., *Der Exodus der Hugenotten. Die Aufhebung des Edikts von Nantes 1685 als europäisches Ereignis* (Cologne/Vienna, 1985); Rudolf von Thadden and Michelle Magdelaine, eds, *Die Hugenotten 1685–1985* (Munich, 1985); Klaus J. Bade, ed., *Deutsche im Ausland – Fremde in Deutschland. Migration in Geschichte und Gegenwart* (Munich, 1992).

101 Pfister, *Bevölkerungsgeschichte*, pp. 41ff. and 101ff.

102 Bernd Herrmann, ed., *Mensch und Umwelt im Mittelalter* (Stuttgart, 1986); Bernd Herrmann, *Umwelt in der Geschichte* (Göttingen, 1989).

103 Ute Frevert, *Krankheit als politisches Problem 1770–1880. Soziale Unterschichten in Preußen zwischen medizinischer Polizei und staatlicher Sozialversicherung* (Göttingen, 1984); Sabine Sander, *Handwerkschirurgen. Sozialgeschichte einer verdrängten Berufsgruppe* (Göttingen, 1989).

104 See above, pp. 209–10.

105 Wilhelm Abel, *Massenarmut und Hungerkrisen im vorindustriellen Europa. Versuch einer Synopsis* (Hamburg/Berlin, 1974); Ulrich-Christian Pallach, ed., *Hunger. Quellen zu einem Alltagsproblem in Europa und der Dritten Welt 17. bis 20. Jahrhundert* (Munich, 1986).

106 See e.g. Heinz Musall, *Die Entwicklung der Kulturlandschaft der Rheinniederung zwischen Karlsruhe und Speyer vom Ende des 16. bis zum Ende des 19. Jahrhunderts* (Heidelberg, 1969).

107 Manfred Jakubowski-Tiessen, *Sturmflut 1717. Die Bewältigung einer Naturkatastrophe in der Frühen Neuzeit* (Munich, 1992).

108 Paul Münch, *Lebensformen in der frühen Neuzeit 1500–1800* (Frankfurt am Main/Berlin 1992), pp. 486–516.

109 Joachim Radkau, 'Holzverknappung und Krisenbewußtsein im 18. Jahrhundert', *GG 8* (1982), pp. 513–43; Joachim Allman, *Der Wald in der frühen Neuzeit. Eine mentalitäts- und sozialgeschichtliche Untersuchung am Beispiel des Pfälzer Raumes 1500–1800* (Berlin, 1989).

110 Hans Wilhelm Eckhardt, *Herrschaftliche Jagd, Bäuerliche Not und bürgerliche Kritik. Zur Geschichte der fürstlichen und adligen Jagdprivilegien vornehmlich im süddeutschen Raum* (Göttingen, 1976).

111 Helmut Ottenjann and Karl-Heinz Ziessow, eds, *Die Kartoffel. Geschichte und Zukunft einer Kulturpflanze* (Cloppenburg, 1992).

112 Michael Stürmer, ed., *Herbst des Alten Handwerks. Quellen zur Sozialgeschichte des 18. Jahrhunderts* (Munich, 1979); Wilfried Reininghaus, *Gewerbe in der Frühen Neuzeit* (Munich, 1990).

113   Peter Kriedte, Hans Medick, and Jürgen Schlumbohm, *Industrialisierung vor
      der Industrialisierung. Gewerbliche Warenproduktion auf dem Land in der
      Formationsperiode des Kapitalismus* (Göttingen, 1977).

114   Carsten Küther, *Menschen auf der Straße. Vagierende Unterschichten in Bay-
      ern, Franken und Schwaben in der zweiten Hälfte des 18. Jahrhunderts* (Göt-
      tingen, 1983); Franz Irsigler and Arnold Lassotta, *Bettler und Gaukler,
      Dirnen und Henker. Randgruppen und Außenseiter in Köln 1300–1600*
      (Cologne, 1984); Bernd Roeck, *Außenseiter, Randgruppen, Minderheiten*
      (Göttingen, 1993); Robert Jütte, *Poverty and Deviance in Early Modern
      Europe* (Cambridge, 1994).

115   C. Hinckeldey, ed., *Justiz in alter Zeit* (Rothenburg o. d. T., 1984); Richard
      van Dülmen, *Kultur und Alltag in der Frühen Neuzeit*, ii: *Dorf und Stadt*
      (Munich, 1992), pp. 246ff.

116   Ernst Schubert, 'Die Ausgrenzung des fahrenden Volkes', in Winfried Schulze,
      ed., *Ständische Gesellschaft und soziale Mobilität* (Munich, 1988), pp.
      113–64; Hannes Stekl, '"Labore et fame" – Sozialdisziplinierung in Zucht-
      und Arbeitshäusern des 17. und 18. Jahrhunderts', in Christoph Sachße and
      Florian Tennstedt, eds, *Soziale Sicherheit und soziale Disziplinierung.
      Beiträge zu einer historischen Theorie der Sozialpolitik* (Frankfurt am Main,
      1986), pp. 119–47; Adalbert Nagel, *Armut im Barock. Die Bettler und
      Vaganten Oberschwabens* (Weingarten, 1986); Berhard Stier, *Fürsorge und
      Disziplinierung im Zeitalter des Absolutismus. Das Pforzheimer Zucht- und
      Waisenhaus und die badische Sozialpolitik im 18. Jahrhundert* (Sigmaringen,
      1988).

117   Carsten Küther, *Räuber und Gauner in Deutschland. Das organisierte
      Bandenwesen im 18. und frühen 19. Jahrhundert* (Göttingen, 1976); Uwe
      Danker, *Räuberbanden im Alten Reich um 1700. Ein Beitrag zur Geschichte
      von Herrschaft und Kriminalität in der frühen Neuzeit* (2 vols, Frankfurt am
      Main, 1988).

118   Reimer Gronemeyer, ed., *Zigeuner im Spiegel früher Chroniken und Abhand-
      lungen. Quellen vom 15. bis zum 18. Jahrhundert* (Gießen, 1987); Karin
      Bott-Bodenhausen, ed., *Sinti in der Grafschaft Lippe. Studien zur Geschichte
      der 'Zigeuner' im 18. Jahrhundert* (Munich, 1988).

119   Gerhard Schormann, *Hexenprozesse in Deutschland* (2nd edn, Göttingen,
      1986); Wolfgang Behringer, ed., *Hexen und Hexenprozesse in Deutschland*
      (2nd edn, Munich, 1993); Walter Rummel, *Bauern, Herren und Hexen. Stu-
      dien zur Sozialgeschichte sponheimischer und kurtrierischer Hexenprozesse
      1574–1664* (Göttingen, 1991); Rainer Walz, *Hexenglaube und magische
      Kommunikation im Dorf der frühen Neuzeit. Die Verfolgungen in der Graf-
      schaft Lippe* (Paderborn, 1993).

120   Bruce T. Moran, ed., *Patronage and Institutions: Science, Technology, and
      Medicine at the European Court 1500–1750*, (Rochester/Woodbridge, 1991).

121   Bernd Roeck, *Lebenswelt und Kultur des Bürgertums in der Frühen Neuzeit*
      (Munich, 1991), p. 50f.

122   Helmuth Kiesel and Paul Münch, *Gesellschaft und Literatur im 18. Jahrhun-
      dert. Voraussetzungen und Entstehung des literarischen Markts in Deutsch-
      land* (Munich, 1977), pp. 67–76; Anton Schindling, *Bildung und
      Wissenschaft in der Neuzeit 1650–1800* (Munich, 1994).

123   Friedrich Paulsen, *Geschichte des gelehrten Unterrichts auf den deutschen
      Schulen und Universitäten* (2 vols, 3rd edn, Berlin/Leipzig, 1919–21).

124   Notker Hammerstein, *Jus und Historie. Ein Beitrag zur Geschichte des his-
      torischen Denkens an deutschen Universitäten im späten 17. und frühen 18.
      Jahrhundert* (Göttingen, 1972).

125 Grete Klingenstein, 'Despotismus und Wissenschaft. Zur Kritik norddeutscher Aufklärer an der österreichischen Universität 1750–1790', in Friedrich Engel-Janosi, Grete Klingenstein, and Heinrich Lutz, eds, *Formen der europäischen Aufklärung* (Vienna/Munich, 1976), pp. 126–57.

126 Harald Dickerhoff, 'Gelehrte Gesellschaften, Akademien, Ordenstudien und Universitäten. Zur sogenannten "Akademiebewegung" vornehmlich im bayerischen Raum', *ZBLG* 45 (1982), pp. 37–66; Richard van Dülmen, *Die Gesellschaft der Aufklärer* (Frankfurt am Main, 1986).

127 Franz Quarthal, 'Öffentliche Armut, Akademikerschwemme und Massenarbeitslosigkeit im Zeitalter des Barock', in V. Press, E. Reinhard, and H. Schwarzmaier, eds, *Barock am Oberrhein* (Karlsruhe, 1985), pp. 153–88; J. V. H. Melton, *Absolutism and the Eigtheenth-Century Origin of Compulsory Schooling in Prussia and Austria* (Cambridge/New York, 1988).

128 Ludwig Fertig, *Obrigkeit und Schule. Die Schulreform unter Ernst dem Frommen (1601–1675)* (Neuburgweier/Karlsruhe, 1971).

129 Wolfgang Neugebauer, *Absolutistischer Staat und Schulwirklichkeit in Brandenburg-Preußen* (Berlin/New York, 1985).

130 Gerald Grimm, *Die Schulreform Maria Theresias 1747–1775. Das österreichische Gymnasium zwischen Standesschule und allgemeinbildender Lehranstalt* (Frankfurt am Main, 1987).

131 Rolf Engelsing, *Analphabetentum und Lektüre. Zur Sozialgeschichte des Lesens in Deutschland* (Stuttgart, 1973); Rudolf Schenda, *Volk ohne Buch. Studien zur Sozialgeschichte der populären Lesestoffe 1770–1910* (2nd edn, Munich, 1977); Ernst Hinrichs and Wilhelm Norden, *Regionalgeschichte. Probleme und Beispiele* (Hildesheim, 1980); Ernst Hinrichs and Günter Wiegelmann, eds, *Sozialer und kultureller Wandel in der ländlichen Welt des 18. Jahrhunderts* (Wolfenbüttel, 1982); Karl-Heinz Ziessow, *Ländliche Lesekultur im 18. und 19. Jahrhundert. Das Kirchspiel Menslage und seine Lesegesellschaften 1790–1840* (2 vols, Cloppenburg, 1988); Richard van Dülmen, *Kultur und Alltag in der Frühen Neuzeit*, iii: *Religion, Magie, Aufklärung* (Munich, 1994), pp. 152ff.

132 Holger Böning and Reinhart Siegert, eds, *Volksaufklärung. Bibliographisches Handbuch zur Popularisierung aufklärerischen Denkens im deutschen Sprachraum von den Anfängen bis 1850*, i (Stuttgart, 1990).

133 Kiesel and Münch, *Gesellschaft und Literatur*.

134 Werner Troßbach, *Bauern*, p. 18.

135 See esp. Peter Blickle, *Landschaften im Alten Reich*; for a criticism of this, see Volker Press, 'Herrschaft, Landschaft und "Gemeiner Mann" in Oberdeutschland vom 15. bis zum frühen 19. Jahrhundert', in *ZGO* 123 (1975), pp. 169–214.

136 Ulrich Lange, ed., *Landgemeinde und frühmoderner Staat. Beiträge zum Problem der gemeindlichen Selbstverwaltung in Dänemark, Schleswig-Holstein und Niedersachsen in der frühen Neuzeit* (Sigmaringen, 1988).

137 Winfried Schulze, 'Die veränderte Bedeutung sozialer Konflikte im 16. und 17. Jahrhundert', in Hans-Ulrich Wehler, ed., *Der deutsche Bauernkrieg 1524–1526* (Göttingen, 1975), pp. 277–302; Winfried Schulze, *Bäuerlicher Widerstand und feudale Herrschaft in der frühen Neuzeit* (Stuttgart, 1980) and *Aufstände, Revolten, Prozesse. Beiträge zu bäuerlichen Widerstandsbewegungen im frühneuzeitlichen Europa* (Stuttgart, 1983); Werner Troßbach, *Soziale Bewegung und politische Erfahrung. Bäuerlicher Protest in 'hessischen' Territorien 1648–1806* (Weingarten, 1987); Georg Schmidt, 'Agrarkonflikte und Territorialisierung. Beobachtungen zum bäuerlichen Widerstand in einer "hessischen" Region', *JbRegG* 16 (1989), pp. 39–56.

138 Norbert Elias, *Über den Prozeß der Zivilisation* (2 vols, Frankfurt am Main,

1976); Heinrich Heckendorn, *Wandel des Anstands im französischen und im deutschen Sprachgebiet* (Bern, 1970); Karl-Heinz Göttert, *Kommunikationsideale. Untersuchungen zur europäischen Konversationstheorie* (Munich, 1988); Manfred Beetz, *Frühmoderne Höflichkeit. Komplimentierkunst und Gesellschaftsrituale im altdeutschen Sprachraum* (Stuttgart, 1990).

139   See on this Münch, *Lebensformen*, esp. pp. 273–313.

140   Münch, *Ordnung, Fleiß und Sparsamkeit.*

141   Wofgang Mager, 'Absolutistische Wirtschaftsförderung (am Beispiel Frankreichs und Brandenburg-Preußens)', *Sozialwissenschaftliche Informationen*, 4 (1974), pp. 4ff.

142   Gerhard Oestreich, *Strukturprobleme.*

143   Peter Blickle, 'Volk und Untertanen im 17. Jahrhundert', in Wolfgang Brückner, Peter Blickle, and Dieter Breuer, eds, *Literatur und Volk im 17. Jahrhundert. Probleme populärer Kultur in Deutschland* (Wiesbaden, 1985), Part 1, pp. 45–51.

144   Joachim Eibach, *Der Staat vor Ort. Amtmänner und Bürger im 19. Jahrhundert am Beispiel Badens* (Frankfurt/New York, 1994).

145   Walter Demel, *Vom aufgeklärten Reformstaat zum bürokratischen Staatsabsolutismus* (Munich, 1993).

Translated by Sheilagh Ogilvie.

8

War, Economy, and Society

BERNHARD STIER AND WOLFGANG VON HIPPEL

The question of the consequences of war for the economy and for society is a central theme of German history in the seventeenth and eighteenth centuries. Up to now, however, few attempts have been made to provide a differentiated answer to this question, based on detailed empirical research and taking into account the whole range of relevant aspects of the question. As a result, this chapter will turn up more problems than it will supply definite knowledge.

No period in German history was so frequently marked by warfare as the two centuries from the so-called Thirty Years War to the victory of the other European great powers over the France of Napoleon in 1815. Between 1618 and 1815 there was hardly a period of 70 years during which there was peace in all parts of the Holy Roman Empire of the German Nation, or during which at least one of the larger German states was not involved in armed struggle in either Germany or Europe more widely. Soon after the Thirty Years War (1618–48), which had been fought to the point of exhaustion, wars with the France of Louis XIV, and above all the Wars of the Palatine and Spanish Succession (1688–97, 1701–13/14), directly and severely affected large regions of Central Europe. The two 'Northern Wars' (1655–60 and 1700–21), and then the Sweden-Brandenburg War of 1675–79, affected the North and East of Germany. The struggle over the Austrian Succession (1740–8) not only meant that the troops of the largest German estates of the Empire once again took the field against one another, but also, with the two Silesian Wars (1740–2 and 1744–5), there began the phase of hostile dualism between the Habsburg Monarchy and Brandenburg-Prussia which broke out in the Seven Years War (1756–63) and was echoed a few years later – happily without much bloodshed – in the War of the Bavarian Succession (1777–9). In this way, through a series of successful wars, Brandenburg-Prussia rose to become the smallest great power in Europe. In so doing, it followed the Habsburg Monarchy, although in a much more modest way. From an initial purely

defensive stance in its long-standing struggle against the Turks, the
Habsburg Monarchy had built up and extended its position as a European
great power in the Danube region (through the Turkish wars of 1663–4,
1683–99, 1716–18, 1737–9, 1775, 1787–91), despite some reverses.
Moreover, the thoughtless division of Poland among the three 'eastern powers', Russia, Austria, and Prussia, naturally did not occur without military
operations (in 1772, 1793, and 1795). By contrast, the War of the Polish
Succession (1733–5), dominated by the competition between Bourbon and
Habsburg, in the end yielded the Duchy of Lorraine to France, a final great
and lasting territorial gain on France's eastern frontier at the expense of the
German Empire. Finally, at the end of our period, the first Coalition War
against Revolutionary France (1792–5) began a series of severe military
conflicts which until the final defeat of Napoleon at Waterloo (1815) were
particularly burdensome for Central Europe, and which brought in their
wake the irrevocable disintegration of the – by then decrepit – old Imperial
structure.

War and the threat of war, therefore, were means which European states
in the seventeenth and eighteenth centuries frequently and almost unques-
tioningly used in order to implement and maintain their interests and aims.
In the interplay of forces among the great powers, the politically segmented
centre of Europe was very often the place where confrontations occurred:
the route of troop marches, the battlefield, or – at the very least – indirectly
affected through losses of land, population, and money. At best, only the
two German great powers were able to make political gains – certainly not
the Empire as a whole. Moreover, an economic and social cost-benefit
analysis – if it could ever be carried out in anything like a reliable way –
would certainly come out even less favourably. Military decisions, even in
the 'Age of Reason', and despite all invocations of 'reason of state', were
not reached using an account-keeping rationality directed toward considerations of general economic profitability, but according to Machiavellian
power politics, whose aim was to expand, strengthen, and enrich one state
at the expense of others. Then, as now, war generally meant the destruction
of human life, the senseless and ruinous dissipation of valuable labour-
power and scarce economic resources, and a severe burdening of society,
even if individual persons, groups, economic sectors, regions, or states
might profit from it.

However, this does not yet provide an answer to the question of the complex interactions between war, economy, and society in Germany during the
seventeenth and eighteenth centuries. Let us try to dissect it into a series of
more precise questions:[1] firstly, how did war affect population in Central
Europe? Secondly, what economic resources were required – directly and
indirectly – by armaments and war, and in what ways did they influence the
economy? And thirdly, in what ways did war influence the social order of
Central Europe during the seventeenth and eighteenth centuries?

The demographic consequences

There is a long-standing debate about the demographic consequences of warfare, and especially about the effects of the Thirty Years War. Exaggerated estimates of losses of as much as three-quarters of the German population were succeeded by obvious minimizations of the damages, culminating in the opinion of S. H. Steinberg (which is not supported by any detailed confirmation) that the population of Central Europe actually increased during the first half of the seventeenth century, with the number of inhabitants in the Empire rising from *c.* 15–17 million in 1600 to between 16 and 18 million towards the end of the Thirty Years War. Such assessments, which were deliberately directed against the myth of the comprehensive destructive force of the 'Great War', have recently attracted the agreement of H.-U. Wehler.[2] By contrast, the most comprehensive balance-sheet drawn up so far on the demographic effects of the 'Great War', by G. Franz, comes to an assessment which is certainly more accurate and much less favourable.[3] According to this assessment, the events of the war saw a severe overall loss of population, involving a decline of some 40 per cent of the population in the countryside and approximately one-third in the towns. The total population of the Empire decreased from an estimated 15 or 16 million in the pre-war period to about 10 million at the end of the war. That is, the war consumed the entire population growth of the sixteenth century, and this blood-letting was not made good until, at earliest, the beginning of the eighteenth century. These aggregate figures, however, cover widely varying degrees of destruction in different parts of the Empire. A zone in which population losses amounted to at least 30 per cent, and more than 50 per cent in the worst-hit areas (the Palatinate, Württemberg, Thüringen, Saxony, Mecklenburg, and Pomerania), ran from the South-West of the Empire, through Thüringen and Saxony in the middle, up to Brandenburg, Mecklenburg, and Pomerania in the North-East. By contrast, the North-West, the whole Alpine area, and – less distinctively – Silesia, Bohemia, and Moravia were spared this sort of massive demographic infliction.

The mechanisms of war – destruction and plundering, hunger and pestilence, flight and migration – varied a great deal in an economy and society which were still very locally oriented. Nevertheless, all the more recent regional and local studies confirm the basic results of Franz's study. After the Swedish defeat in the Battle of Nördlingen (1634), the misery of war struck the Duchy of Württemberg, for instance, with full fury. According to one set of figures, by 1640 the population had declined to one-quarter of its pre-war level, and in 1645 was still below 30 per cent of that level. These figures may be inexact, but the individual data which survive leave no doubt that the situation was truly catastrophic. The small town of Bietigheim on the Neckar near Stuttgart, for example, had about 1,800 inhabitants in 1634; the plague which appeared in the wake of the war claimed 600 deaths in the following year, and another 200 in each of 1636 and 1637. By 1638, the number of inhabitants in the community had fallen to *c.* 240 people. When Kaiserslautern, in the western Palatinate, which had been occupied by the Swedes, was captured by Imperial troops in the notorious 'Croatian storm' of 1635, some 1,500 persons lost their lives; through siege, capture, military occupation, hunger, and plague, the population slumped from 3,000 ultimately to only 200 inhabitants. Augsburg in Upper Swabia, one of the most populous cities in southern Germany, was especially hard hit: in 1627–8 there raged a pestilence which had been brought in by billeted soldiers, probably bubonic plague and spotted fever; a plague epidemic in 1632–5 was made more severe by the immediate effects of war, especially by the siege of 1635. Whereas in 1600 Augsburg had numbered a good 45,000 inhabitants, according to the census of 1635 it only had about 16,000 inhabitants left.[4]

It was these population losses, combined with the increasing political weakness of the German Empire as a consequence of the Thirty Years War, which first enabled France to obtain the political and military superiority over the centre of Europe necessary to achieve European hegemony – resulting in a series of new and severe wars which continually affected the West and South-West of the Empire in particular. Although general studies of the demographic effects of the wars of the late seventeenth and the eighteenth centuries are lacking, the population loss caused by the direct and indirect effects of war was clearly smaller and less ubiquitous than in the 'Great War', above all because these wars did not generally involve widespread pestilence to such a great extent. But the tendency toward increasing regionalization of the effects of war did not mean that these effects were trivial in the areas directly affected by it. A graphic example is provided by the German South-West, which soon after the end of the Thirty Years War was once again afflicted by warfare under the banner of the so-called 'Reunions' and the European power politics of the 'Sun King'. In the so-called War of the Palatine Succession (1688–97) French armies invaded south-west Germany, systematically laid waste to Baden and especially the Palatinate, and pushed deep into Württemberg territory as well. In accordance with the express command of the French generals, towns and villages went up in flames. The Palatinate on the left and right banks of the Rhine again lost some 30 per cent of its population, but other areas also suffered large population losses. The town of Pforzheim in Baden, afflicted by French troops on four occasions and twice put to the flame, lost more than half its inhabitants within a few years: of the 548 citizens in 1688, only 267 were still alive in 1697; 226 had lost their lives through acts of war, hunger and pestilence, 28 were abroad, and 27 had disappeared. In the town of Bietigheim in Württemberg, mentioned above, the population declined during the Palatine War from the 1,700 inhabitants it had once again attained, to fewer than half that number (750).[5]

In trying to draw up a balance sheet, we must depend to a considerable extent on this sort of local and regional study. But such studies are also the best means of providing deeper knowledge of the causal relationships between the events of war and demographic developments. Numbers of births, marriages, and deaths provide an especially good reflection of what war, with all its consequences, meant for the everyday life of people at the time: a network of mutually causal factors which at worst tended to magnify one another. Siege, occupation, billeting, arson, plundering, destruction and burning of houses, requisitions and forced deliveries of foodstuffs, the impairing of the peasant economy through absence of labour and loss of tools, the hindering and prevention of necessary cultivation of fields and harvest work by the events of war, the intentional laying waste to fields by soldiers, and the seizure of draught animals and seed grains – all of these limited or totally destroyed the food base, and increased people's susceptibility to illness in a situation in which the danger of infection was already intensified by high migration and the rampant 'siege infections' of wartime. The regular deficit in births was not just the consequence of the lower biological fertility to be expected in such a milieu, but was also, like the drastic decline in the number of marriages, socially determined: by the breaking up of families, and even more by the dramatic worsening in people's expectations about the future, and by subjective traumatization resulting from the life-destroying and life-threatening overall experience of war.[6]

In general, it is clear that fewer people fell victim to the direct fighting than to the indirect effects of war, especially pestilence and hunger.[7] For good reasons, G. Franz counted those dying of plague in the 1630s among the victims of the Thirty Years War. The interplay between the classic triad of the Riders of the Apocalypse – War, Hunger, and Pestilence – can be observed in the seventeenth and eighteenth centuries on the local and regional level even after the Thirty Years War. The town of Stockach in Baden, for example, was afflicted in 1693 by a severe mortality crisis, which can be traced to troop movements and billeting during the War of the Palatine Succession; in neighbouring Singen, in 1691, 55 people died out of a total population of 400: nearly every seventh inhabitant. The destruction of Stockach by Bavarian troups during the War of the Spanish Succession in 1705, and renewed billeting in the following year, gave rise to clear incursions in the population statistics. Similarly clear demographic incursions can be seen there during the War of the Austrian Succession decades later, and the Coalition Wars against France in the 1790s. The causes of illness and death known for the end of the century clearly reflect the interrelationship between mortality, pestilence, and infections passed on by soldiers. As a result of the Coalition Wars, in 1798 in Singen, where the population had in the meantime risen to between 700 and 800 inhabitants, 160 people died, one-fifth of the total population.[8]

French troops marched through the area around Gießen in northern

Hesse several times during the Seven Years War; the fortified garrison town of Gießen itself was occupied by the French from mid-1758 to 1763, and in the second half of 1759 it became a direct theatre of war. The vital statistics of the parishes of Gießen and the surrounding villages clearly show a piling-up of severe mortality crises between 1756 and 1763 – the upward leap in mortality in Gießen consumed the entire fertility surplus of the preceding 14 years. The same picture can be seen in the town of Göttingen in Lower Saxony during the Seven Years War: when applied to Göttingen's vital statistics, the events of war, grain prices, and epidemics together explain the severe mortality crises of the 1750s and 1760s. In neighbouring Einbeck, occupied by the French from 1757 to 1761, mortality rose to a rate of 99 deaths per 1,000 inhabitants in 1757, compared to an average of 35 in the preceding years. In Saxony there were 120,000 additional deaths and a reduction in births of 20,000 during the Seven Years War, adding up to a loss of some 8 per cent of the total population (which had been 1.7 million in the last year before the outbreak of war). Neighbouring Brandenburg-Prussia (excluding Silesia) also lost 200,000 people between 1756 and 1763.[9]

The example of Mainz, a strategically important fortress which was consequently an object of conflict in numerous wars, illustrates especially clearly the complex effects of war on population over a period of two centuries.[10] In December 1631 Swedish troops marched in: the war reached the town and drastically worsened the living circumstances of the Mainz population. The harvest of the following year, which was in any case poor, could not be entirely brought in because of the war, and when plague broke out in the autumn of 1632, mortality in Mainz increased by as much as a factor of ten. Between 1632 and 1635, Mainz lost *c.* 8,000 people, amounting to half its inhabitants. This pattern was repeated with oppressive regularity in the wars which followed: the 'Dutch War' (1672–8), the War of the Palatine Succession (1688–97), the War of the Polish Succession (1733–5), and even the Seven Years War. Although the latter did not hit the town directly, the price of rye in the town had doubled by 1762; this immediately resulted in a mortality increase of 40 per cent in 1760–1 over the average for the preceding decade, and a fertility deficit which lasted for several years. During the siege of Mainz in 1792–3 it was less the direct events of the siege that were devastating than the outbreak of dysentery in the summer of 1793, and the scarcity of foodstuffs which arose because 23,000 French soldiers were quartered in the town, while the 55,000-man Prussian Army of the Rhine was foraging between Mainz and Kreuznach. In the single month of August 1793 more than 800 people died in Mainz – more than died in a whole year in peacetime; in the entire year of 1793, a total of 1,800 people died, more than twice the annual average of the period 1783–92. The picture was the same during further sieges by French troops in 1794–5 and 1813–14. After retreating French troops had fortified themselves in the town a devastating epidemic of spotted fever broke out; 2,485 civilians – in a total population of between 21,000 and 25,000 – and more than 17,000 soldiers fell victim to this last great mortality crisis of the 'old style'.

Future research must investigate the migration movements in and after wars more precisely than hitherto, if only because this demographic factor is very important in assessing population losses. Where war endangered survival, people fled; survivors returned, and at the same time new citizens settled – as a rule from regions in which the land was no longer capable of feeding the increased number of people. Especially in the seventeenth century, immigration into areas which had seen great population losses could sometimes be substantial. Thus in the parish of Singen between 1650 and 1675, about half of all marriages were ones in which one or both partners came from outside the community. The largest number of these immigrants had come from Switzerland. After a renewed population decline during the Palatine War, a comparable immigration wave again occurred. After the Peace of Rijwsik (1697) an especially large number of immigrants from Switzerland also settled in the Palatinate, which had been severely affected by the preceding warfare. Confronted with these inflictions of war, many princes in the Empire developed a 'population policy' which aimed to increase the number of their subjects as a guarantee of power and economic well-being.[11]

As a rule, populations recovered surprisingly fast, even after severe losses. Vital statistics for all regions and communities which have been studied show – after the immediate crisis, after the end of struggles, sieges, and epidemics, after the first harvest had been brought in and the famine had slackened – a strong increase in marriages and, with the expected delay, a rise in births. The need to 'catch up', life circumstances which were on the whole more favourable, and especially the temporary disappearance of the tension between population growth and available foodstuffs, all caused recovery to begin swiftly. The people who were left behind thus profited from the deaths caused by war, reacted with higher fertility, and filled up the gaps which had been created.[12] In this sense, war possessed the 'purifying power' which Malthus ascribed to it: forcibly and with terrible costs, it temporarily put the 'Malthusian trap' out of operation. The fact that as early as the mid-seventeenth century a disproportionately strong population growth began in Germany and lasted into the early twentieth century without any great interruptions despite periodic fluctuations may partially be ascribed to the fact that in the seventeenth and eighteenth centuries wars repeatedly opened up 'free spaces' for faster demographic growth. This can hardly be adjudged 'positive'; it did not change the fact that war remained a powerful destroyer of human life.

War and the economy

Just as there is considerable debate about the demographic effects of the Thirty Years War, so too there is disagreement in the literature about the extent of the material damage and losses – or even the gains – which it caused. Small loss of population, no significant damage, and hardly any economic losses: this is how S. H. Steinberg sums up the war's effects in his attempts to counter the 'myth'. The war made itself felt more as a restructuring of economic life, according to Steinberg: in 1648, 'Germany was neither better nor worse off than in 1609, it was simply different from what it had been half a century earlier'. National income, productivity, and standard of living, according to Steinberg, were actually higher than before the outbreak of war.[13] Noticeable negative consequences are supposed to have already been embedded in the long-term trend since the sixteenth century. To evaluate the economic consequences of the Thirty Years War it is indeed important to know the state of the economy in Central Europe before the outbreak of the war. After older attempts to portray the war as a catastrophe which broke over a flourishing economy, nowadays it is generally agreed that symptoms of crisis were already apparent in the early seventeenth century. The economy had reached the 'limits of growth' set by the conditions then prevailing; population pressure made itself felt in a negative way; economic and demographic stagnation and depression made their appearance. That this was a large-scale phenomenon is shown by the debate about the so-called 'crisis of the seventeenth century'. In actuality, the 'Great War' substantially contributed to the crisis during the decades that followed. In any case, in Central Europe the war made the crisis (of whatever variety) more severe and brought it out into the open. The war left behind enormous economic damage and material losses, and destroyed human life, scarce resources, and economic infrastructure – and not only in the immediately affected areas.[14]

Apart from global judgements, still too little is known about the extent of material damage and losses. However, the decline in population could not have left economic life unaffected. More recent regional and local studies document this impressively. The prosperous and densely populated area around Magdeburg and Halberstadt, for example, with its highly developed agriculture, important industrial centres, and far-flung trading relationships, was strongly affected by the war between 1625 and 1647. According to lists of houses and farms, an average of 64 per cent of dwellings were lost through direct combat, dilapidation, plundering, and arson; only one house in six survived the war undamaged. In Württemberg, the Thirty Years War brought in its wake not only the destruction of property, but also enormous indebtedness, especially in agriculture. Around the middle of the seventeenth century indebtedness rose to a level four times that of the pre-war period. In combination with the drastic fall in the prices of houses and land, this burden of debt meant that reconstruction began only gradually. The farms damaged by the war had to raise sums to cover damage which sometimes – as in the Bavarian Landgericht of Schongau – reached eight times the value of the property. The indebtedness of the Free Imperial City of Nürnberg rose from 1.8 million *Gulden* in 1618 to 7.4 million in 1648. Such examples can be multiplied.

Other regions, by contrast, were able to prosper despite the war, or even because of it. Thus the north German Hanseatic cities of Hamburg, Bremen, and Lübeck survived the Great War undamaged – partly through a skilful policy of neutrality, but especially because they were important to the warring parties as centres of trade, finance, and diplomacy. The population of Hamburg grew from *c.* 45,000–54,000 in 1620 to 75,000 in 1660, and the annual revenues of the town rose from 250,000 marks at the end of the sixteenth century to 1.4 million marks in the mid-seventeenth century, a sixfold increase.[15] But this does not mean that what fortunate towns and regions gained from the war came anywhere near to making up for the damage inflicted elsewhere.

However, more recent studies no longer direct attention exclusively to balance sheets of damage and indebtedness, but rather, more comprehensively, to the overall *changes* brought about by the war. They ask how the economy dealt with the effects of war, and inquire into the ways in which it not only caused damage, but also made some economic problems less acute and opened up new opportunities. Thus the Thirty Years War, with all its devastating effects, did relax the pressure of population on food resources, and freed Central European society from the 'Malthusian trap' for about a century. The so-called 'post-war depression' manifested itself in falling grain and land prices, scarcity of labour power, and high wages. The main beneficiaries of this upheaval were the lower strata of the towns and countryside, the small landholders or cottagers, variously termed *Söldner*, *Häusler*, or *Gärtner*. Lower living costs, expansion of their own farming activities, and easier earnings in day-labouring and industrial work, all offered these cottagers opportunities for upward social mobility, or at least for economic improvement. Alongside and precisely by means of the destruction it caused, the Thirty Years War thus also gave rise to processes of economic and social restratification in the medium term. In many parts of Germany the rise in the number of agrarian smallholdings accelerated in the wake of the war, and intensified the transition to partible inheritance in the South and the West. By contrast, in the especially severely desolated areas east of the Elbe, the scarcity of 'human capital' contributed to the nobles being able to extend and intensify 'feudalism' (*Gutsherrschaft*) in the form of the so-called 'second serfdom', in order to make the most profitable use of scarce labour.[16]

A glance at the modes of behaviour and activity of those who were affected by war also reveals how astonishingly quickly the peasant economy, in particular, recovered from its effects. Despite severe demographic and economic losses, it cannot be said that the war lamed the economy for decades afterwards. The Landgericht of Dachau near Munich, for example, was strongly affected by the war, but 79 per cent of farms were already inhabited by 1666, and by 1689 the number of holdings had surpassed the level of 1600. Only in the few areas of Bavaria which had been really catastrophically affected were farms still deserted at the end of the seventeenth century. There was almost the same number of families in Bavaria in the 1690s as in the last decade before the outbreak of the Thirty Years War. In the areas of Bavaria studied by Schlögl, the one and a half decades between the two enemy invasions of 1632–3 and 1646–8 were enough for the food base to recover, for stock levels and grain stores largely to be made good, for damages to houses and farms to be repaired, and for furniture and equipment to be replaced.[17] The peasant economy recovered mainly through its own efforts; it was a regeneration purchased by means of a tightening of belts, harder work, sacrifices of consumption, and self-exploitation by the peasant population. Government policies, by contrast, offered only relatively modest ancillary assistance.

Long-term negative economic consequences were to be observed in terms less of material damage than of structural upheaval and reductions in economic activity. F. Lütge has pointed this out most emphatically, viewing the decisive long-term damage of the Thirty Years War as having resided in 'the breaking apart – often a violent tearing apart – of domestic and international economic relationships, which in most cases were impossible to put back together again'.[18] Local-level studies show how the war was particularly damaging to the trade and industry of the relatively highly developed urban economy, pulling demand, employment, and net production down from a level which had only been achieved with great effort, and creating an economic environment which was fundamentally much less favourable, through blocking routes for provisioning and trade, through the decline which this caused in particular industries, and through an overall regionalization of the economy. The Thirty Years War accelerated the economic decline of the south German towns, in particular, beginning as early as the hyper-inflation of the 'Kipper- und Wipper-Zeit' of 1622–3. Economic regions and trade routes shifted, and the decline in production, consumption, and trade led to a decrease in the revenues from customs and consumption taxes. The result was an increasingly local orientation of south German markets, as is illustrated by the example of the Free Imperial City of Nördlingen. Here the export-orientated clothing sector was especially well-developed, and was thus especially hard hit by the decline in long-distance trade on the routes into Italy. As a consequence, the production and processing of foodstuffs and their distribution into neighbouring regions naturally increased in importance by comparison. But the Thirty Years War not only damaged trade, it also encouraged competition by rural crafts. Many other south German trading and industrial cities shared this fate.

Thus the war was also a cause of the decline of the old Augsburg weaving craft, although it had already shown clear signs of economic weakness in peacetime. Where – as in Nördlingen – economic recovery seemed a possibility, it was ultimately prevented by the Wars of the Palatine and Spanish Succession. The constantly recurring war damages and the lasting economic exhaustion caused by taxes and war contributions deprived the urban economy of its basis.[19]

It is impossible to make any general estimate of the extent of economic damage caused by the wars of the later seventeenth century and the eighteenth century. However, particular examples reveal that the network of causation between war and the economy remained essentially unchanged. Again and again the warring parties demanded substantial portions of the national product via taxes, war contributions, and requisitions; the actions and behaviour of the military destroyed an important part of national wealth, wherever possible destroying the property of the subjects of the enemy. The principle that war must feed itself continued to be valid. Within a very few years, especially for the victims of the events of war, a huge burden of debts and losses piled up. Thus after the end of the Palatine War the Margraviate of Baden-Durlach recorded total costs of more than 9 million *Gulden*, of which 2.7 million were for damage to public and private buildings, and 2.5 million were for losses of property by Baden-Durlach subjects; the remainder chiefly consisted of military contributions and winter-quartering costs for both French and Imperial troops. In the summer of 1730, Elector Max Emanuel of Bavaria, allied with France in the War of the Spanish Succession, occupied the northern Tyrol as far as the Brenner Pass. Although the occupation lasted only a few months, it caused not only some 1.5 million *Gulden* worth of material damages, but also substantial loss of infrastructure and a longer-term disruption of economic life in general, especially trade. Imports and exports from the occupied area stagnated, long-distance trade avoided the region, and revenues from customs and consumption taxes declined drastically. Even a 'small' war, therefore, could enduringly damage the early modern economy, which was in any case always unstable. Similar examples can be provided for each and every one of the wars listed at the beginning of this chapter.[20]

Merely the regular expenses of war laid heavy burdens upon the economic potential of the warring parties – burdens which became increasingly heavy as the armies grew larger. The still relatively small armies of the Thirty Years War already required impressive sums of money. Thus the 10,000 to 15,000 men of the 'Imperial army', set up in 1635 and stationed in the Lower-Rhine-Westfalian Imperial Circle, cost a total of 15 million *Reichstaler* between 1638 and 1649, according to careful estimates.[21] This meant between 100 and 150 *Reichstaler* per man per year, a truly enormous sum – and this did not include the money and services extorted through coercion by enemy troops. In addition to paying the troops, continuing to provision them was one of the greatest problems: it could play a decisive role in the outcome of campaigns, and could sometimes completely ruin an army even without any action of the enemy. Thus in 1644, on the march from Saxony into Holstein and back into the region around Magdeburg, the Imperial army under General Mathias Gallas lost one-third of its cavalry and half of its infantry, without any substantial encounters with the enemy – solely because neither an organized supply system nor enough money was available at that time for short-term purchases of food-stuffs to satisfy the needs of the army.[22] Each campaign required an inge-nious and enormously expensive system of provisioning and supply, and almost inevitably created bottlenecks in markets for foodstuffs. In prepar-ing for campaigns against the Turks, for example, Austria regularly pur-chased grain as far afield as southern Germany – albeit with substantial financial sacrifices and transportation difficulties.[23] The logistics of provi-sioning became increasingly important as armies became larger. The inde-pendent 'military entrepreneurs' of the Thirty Years War, doing business at their own risk, gave way toward the end of the seventeenth century to an emerging military bureaucracy, which maintained the powerful 'war machine' and organized recruitment, armaments, and supplies at state expense. Overcoming the problems posed by massive requirements of weapons, clothing, and foodstuffs was an essential prerequisite for – and itself part of – the 'military revolution' which occurred during the seven-teenth and eighteenth centuries.[24]

For armies were moving forward into hitherto unknown orders of mag-nitude. The establishment of standing armies in fact first took place as a consequence of the Thirty Years War; in place of the so-called *Lands-knechtshaufen* (casually recruited group of mercenaries enlisted for short periods) there appeared the troop of mercenaries or conscripted subjects enlisted for the long term. Around 1780, Prussia maintained an army of *c.* 190,000 men in peacetime, the Habsburg Monarchy nearly 300,000 men, even Bavaria still managed *c.* 35,000, Saxony 30,000, Hannover-Lüneburg 26,000, and so on. For Germany excluding the Habsburg Monarchy, it added up to a total contingent of *c.* 320,000 soldiers, making up almost 2 per cent of the population – and this does not count any sort of 'tail', for many soldiers had wives and children. In Prussia alone, the military made up as much as 3.5 per cent of the population. The 'soldier class' was thus a quantitatively large entity, and the required equipment and provisioning (weapons, food, clothing, and other equipment) meant that armies were also economically significant consumers of mass commodities.

This is the circumstance on which Werner Sombart based his thesis that early modern warfare made a crucial demand-side contribution to 'modern capitalism', by favouring capitalistic forms of production such as manufactories and the putting-out system. Brandenburg-Prussia provides the best supporting evidence for such a view, since the equipping of the military did also further the Prussian domestic economy. The establishment in 1713 of the *Königliches Lagerhaus* ('Royal Storehouse') – a large textile manufactory set up as a model business – and the 1714 *Montierungs-Reglement* of King Friedrich Wilhelm I, which prohibited imports of foreign textiles and ordered that only domestic cloth should be used for production of uniforms, led to an upswing in sheep-raising and woollen-weaving; in the second half of the eighteenth century more than four-fifths of all industrial workers were employed in textile production. In addition, the foundation of the *Spandauer Gewehrfabrik* ('Spandau Weapons Factory') in 1722 and the fact that the Splitgerber and Daun armament firm enjoyed a turnover of four million *Taler* in the penultimate year of the Seven Years War are evidence that war had some partially stimulating effects on the economy, especially on industrial production.[25] But Sombart's thesis has also aroused justified offence. Anglo-Saxon historians in particular, from perspectives opened up by the experience of the Second World War, have accused him of considering only the production of the instruments of war, and not the generally destructive consequences of their use. Even leaving this aside, it must be asked whether an alternative, peaceful use of the resources spent on military purposes might not have stimulated the industrial sector at least equally. In any case, the demand-side effects of the military on industrial production and technological progress in the seventeenth and eighteenth century must not be portrayed as being so very large; they were hardly sufficient for a decisive acceleration in the development of modern 'industrial capitalism'. Even if the desire to obtain greater state revenues in order to finance rising state expenditures and military expenses lent wings to mercantilist efforts to further industry, it remains indisputable that investments in armaments and warfare deprived the economy of already scarce capital and shifted it to a form of consumption which was not very productive.[26] A more precise analysis of military expenditures would show that they outran economic growth: that is, wars became increasingly expensive not only absolutely but also relative to the capacities of the economy. This was equally the case for the great powers and for the smaller territorial states in the heart of Europe. All attempts to resist this development by being economical brought only limited success. The repeated attempts in various states to reactivate in modernized form the notion of 'national defence' by subjects achieved no greater success.[27] On the contrary: the advances in the techniques of war and the changes in tactics and strategy required increasing expenditure. This was especially the case for fortifications, which not only devoured immense sums for building and armaments, but also required labour power from both soldiers and those subjects obliged to render services to the state.[28]

Since the costs of armaments and war could not usually be paid for immediately, there was an increasing tendency to redistribute them onto future generations by taking out large loans. The way in which war could enduringly burden a state budget and could often lead it to the brink of ruin can be seen especially clearly in the financial history of the Habsburg monarchy.[29] The enduring financial demands of the European theatre of war constituted the fundamental reason for Austria's financial disarray in the seventeenth and eighteenth centuries, culminating in its final state bankruptcy in the Napoleonic period. The revenues from princely domain lands, mining and salt-producing privileges, consumption taxes, customs charges, and administration fees hardly covered expenditures on the court and internal administration. The *Contributionale*, which was intended to pay for the army and which was provided from contributions made by the various Habsburg lands, had to be negotiated and granted annually (in Hungary every 3 to 4 years) by the relevant parliamentary body. Ordinary and extraordinary military contributions were raised through taxes on land and buildings, and in the towns also through taxing income from trade and industry. Special taxes, which especially in wartime were increasingly frequently raised even without the consent of parliament, were contrary to the constitution and could only be justified in terms of an emergency situation.

The relative autonomy of the individual parts of the Habsburg monarchy, particularly of Bohemia and Hungary, was an obstacle to the crown's efforts to make more intensive demands on existing financial resources in order to finance the military machine in both peacetime and wartime. As early as 1695, Leopold I sought in vain to introduce a general consumption tax in place of the military contributions; it was not until 1749 that the monarch, Maria Theresia, was able, with the help of Count Haugwitz, to make changes in the financial and tax system favouring the central power. In particular, they were able to impose the principle of general (although still not equal) obligation to pay taxes, thereby including the clergy and nobility more than previously in financial obligations, preventing higher tax revenues from burdening peasants and town-dwellers. Admittedly, not all the crown's dreams were realized. When, in 1789, Joseph II sought to push through his great reform of landholding and taxes based on physiocratic principles, he failed in the face of the concentrated opposition of the nobility in all parts of the monarchy, who would have been hard hit by this attempt at reform.

Faced by chronic financial crisis, the Austrian rulers very early on followed the path of increased borrowing. Domain lands, especially the lucrative mining businesses and mining rights, were sold or mortgaged, and dependency on Jewish court factors increased. The *Wiener Stadtbank* ('Vienna City Bank'), founded in 1706 in imitation of the financially strong Bank of England, could not contain the financial problems caused by the explosion in military expenditures. The War of the Spanish Succession is supposed to have cost the Habsburg monarchy more than 1,000 million *Gulden*, when state revenues in 1700 were only 16 million *Gulden*. In view of this deficit, the 13 million *Gulden* of English subsidies which Austria received were no more than a drop in the ocean. Annual deficits caused the state debt to grow like an avalanche. From *c.* 22 million *Gulden* in 1700, it rose to 54 million by 1714, which, although it is not documented with certitude, is an astonishingly modest figure. After the Turkish war of 1737–9 the state debt rose to 101 million in 1740, and to *c.* 275 million after the Seven Years War. After the Russian-Austrian Turkish War (1788–90) debts had risen to 391 million *Gulden*, and in the following years the costs of war also regularly burst apart the military budget. From 1793 onward, total state revenues were no longer sufficient to cover military expenditures and the servicing of the state debt. The period of the French Revolution and the Napoleonic Wars brought the final collapse of the Austrian financial system. Despite special taxes and currency manipulations, loans, and subsidies – again from England – in the early years of the nineteenth century, a galloping inflation began, and in 1811 the state debt surpassed 1,000 million *Gulden*.[30]

The younger of the two German great powers was much better able than other states to learn a lesson from the experiences of the Thirty Years War, and to orient the state lastingly toward the requirements of the armaments sector.[31] The unexampled rise of Brandenburg-Prussia in the ranks of the European great powers was the result of a consistent military policy; lacking wealth in either population or natural resources, the Prussian regents from the time of the 'Great Elector' Friederich Wilhelm I (1640–88) onward made up for this partly through saving, but above all through entirely orienting their economic and financial policies to the requirements of the army. As early as the Thirty Years War, there arose the military contribution and the excise tax, which became the two basic pillars of the Prussian tax system over the next century and a half. In total contrast to its Austrian competitor, the Prussian central state was able to eliminate parliamentary consent very early on. Only the revenues from the consumption tax which had been imposed since 1641 and the war contributions continuously levied since the 1660s – counter to the opposition of the estates – enabled the 'Great Elector' to expand his standing army from 8,000 men in 1644 to 30,000 in 1688. The yields from war contributions and from the the excise between 1670 and 1688 alone increased from 18,000 to more than 1.6 million *Taler*.

The 'Soldier King', Friedrich Wilhelm I (1713–40), increased the army to 83,000 men and annual state revenues to nearly 7 million *Taler*, partly through extreme economy in administration and court display, but especially through constant exertions on the part of the *Generalkriegskommissariat* ('General War Commissariat') and later the *Generaldirektorium* ('General Directorate'), which in 1722 became the highest office for the military sector and at the same time the central financial office for the whole kingdom. Friedrich II (1740–86) immediately used up in the War of the Austrian Succession the state treasure of 18 million *Taler* which had been collected by his father, and in order to achieve his foreign-policy goals in the years that followed brought the military into action to an unthinkable extent. During his reign, the size and growth of the armaments sector once again dramatically increased; the 'Prussian military machine' equally fascinated and terrified its German and European neighbours. The standing army comprised some 200,000 men at the death of Friedrich, and the share of the state budget devoted to expenditures on armaments increased from nearly 70 per cent in the period of Friedrich Wilhelm I to an average of 83 per cent in the years 1740–56, and as high as 87 per cent in the Seven Years War.[32] Prussia always survived wars better than its opponents. This was due to the total orientation of its economic and financial constitution to the requirements of the military sector; its inconsiderate squeezing of territories occupied during the war (as with Saxony in the Seven Years War); and finally, deliberate depreciations of its currency, and thus a repeated and deep-reaching burdening of its own and foreign subjects. At the end of the eighteenth century, however, even Prussia reached the limits of its capacity to burden its subjects. The state treasure of 55 million *Taler* still in existence at the death of Friedrich II had already been used up in the first Coalition War; the Prussian Peace of Basel (1795) with Revolutionary France can thus be understood as the result of financial exhaustion. In the Napoleonic period Prussia skated very close to financial collapse; in 1818 it evaded state bankruptcy by a hair's breadth.

In the medium-sized and smaller German territorial states, as well, military expenditures developed into a considerable part of their total expenditure – being in many cases, the largest item – without really opening up much room for manœuvre in the foreign policy of these princes. To be reckoned among the 'armed estates of the Empire', however, did nevertheless mean a growth in visible and demonstrable power, for which many princes were willing to pay substantial sums. In this respect, temporal and ecclesiastical states differed very little. In the prince-bishopric of Bamberg, where in the 1670s Prince-Bishop Peter Philipp von Dernbach maintained a standing army of 6,000 men, some 100,000 *Gulden* annually, or more than 40 per cent of total expenditures, flowed into maintaining the army. The necessary sums were raised by a relatively high property tax of 1.33 per cent. After disarmament in 1685 the burden on the subjects decreased, but with the renewed French threat it rose again, with a property tax of 1.5 per cent and additional special taxes for troop-provisioning and winter quartering.[33] In the Duchy of Brauschweig-Wolfenbüttel in the eighteenth century, military expenditures made up about one-third of total state expenditures in peacetime. In the Duchy of Bavaria under the government of Max Emanuel, who had foreign policy ambitions, the deficit in the military budget increased from 440,000 *Gulden* in 1699 to 1.5 million in 1727, as a consequence of entanglement in the War of the Spanish Succession.[34]

The comparatively modest troop contingents of the medium-sized and smaller territories could in any case hardly be brought into action for independent power politics. Nevertheless they could give such rulers the feeling of being able to throw some weight, however modest, into the scales of European politics, especially if they also had functioning fortifications at their disposal. Several princes were able to build up 'playing at soldiers' into 'trading in soldiers', and to operate a quite lucrative business, obtaining large subsidies from foreign powers or hiring out their troops directly to the highest bidder. The landgraves of Hessen-Kassel made a flourishing 'export business' out of this. For more than 40 of the years between 1702 and 1784 their troops were in service with foreign powers, during which period they brought 45 million *Taler* in subsidies (more than 50 per cent of tax revenues) into the treasury of the Landgraviate, thereby enabling the prince to live far beyond the circumstances of his country, and increasing the ratio between military personnel and total population to the highest in Europe, at *c.* 1: 15 (compared to *c.* 1: 30 in Prussia). Braunschweig and Württemberg also exported soldiers in order to reduce the maintenance costs of the army and pay for the luxury requirements of the rulers. The Duchy of Braunschweig received 2 million *Reichstaler* from hiring out troops to the English crown between 1776 and 1786. In Württemberg, Duke Karl Eugen concluded a subsidy contract with France in 1752, whereby he agreed to provide 6,000 soldiers in exchange for 387,000 *Gulden* annually in peacetime and 479,000 in wartime. In the years that followed Karl Eugen brought his army up to 12,000 soldiers, and spent 1.6 million *Gulden* on it annually. The Margraviate of Brandenburg-Ansbach in the mid-eighteenth century maintained a standing 'army' of 500 men and a 180-man guard. In 1777, Margrave Alexander hired these troops out to England for use in the American War of Independence in an attempt to consolidate the state budget, which was in deficit. Thus the war economy could bring measurable financial advantages for individual states – although in many ways at the cost of the soldiers involved, resulting in increasingly severe criticism of this trade in human beings by enlightened public opinion.[35] Nevertheless, because larger German states such as Austria, Prussia, and Bavaria, as well as smaller ones such as the electorates of Cologne and the Palatinate, received significant subsidies, Germany at times became a capital-importing country.[36]

This apparent economic usefulness of the trade in 'war commodities' does not change the fact that the unpleasant business of war could not really be financed from the current revenues of any state, especially since state revenues noticeably shrank during the actual phase of warfare. Even a relatively modest decline of 10 per cent, as in Brauschweig during the Seven Years War, brought the state budget, which in that period was in any case unstable, into serious danger.[37] This made it seem even more important to rulers to raise the required funds by means of regular additional revenues. Thus taxes, originally an extraordinary grant in times of emergency which were only to serve particular purposes, from the Thirty Years War onwards became a fixed component of state financing and a regular additional burden on subjects. This development hardly benefited the German Empire, because territorial lords abused Imperial legislation to enforce tax demands on the population for their own military purposes. Through the Imperial Edict of 1654 the tax obligations of subjects were explicitly extended to covering costs for 'necessary' fortifications, strongholds, and garrisons.

The proliferation of wars in the seventeenth and eighteenth centuries caused taxes to become permanent and to increase almost continually, prevented the burden of state debt inherited from the Thirty Years War from being gradually reduced, and indeed constantly generated new obligations and debts whose interest payments and amortization had to be paid for. The difficulties and opportunities which this could bring have already been shown by the examples of Austrian and Prussian state indebtedness. Only where the central power could lastingly and sufficiently prevail against the parliament did it obtain the necessary room for manœuvre to implement the tool of taxation more effectively; in this respect the two German great powers represent two totally different outcomes in the establishment of central state financial policy. The basic process was, however, similar in all regions and territories. 'Extraordinary' taxes were raised every year at varying levels, as a rule initially on existing property (houses, land, cattle, cash); the higher such demands rose, especially as a result of old and new war burdens, and the more heavily they weighed upon taxpayers, the more important it became to adapt them more precisely to the actual capacity of the economy and to distribute the burden as far as possible onto more shoulders. Thus the development of the system of direct taxation in German states is distinguished by increasing attempts in the larger territories during the eighteenth century to shift to taxation of net proceeds. The *Steuerrektifikation* ('tax rectification') of Maria Theresia in the various parts of the Habsburg monarchy from 1748 onward was the most important instance of such a step, taken by this single European great power before the nineteenth century, to come closer to the principle of more general and more equal direct taxation. From 1785 onward, Maria Theresia's son Joseph II sought to follow this path toward general and equal taxation consistently to the end, but he swiftly failed against the concentrated resistance of the landed nobility.

This experience showed two things. First, rising military burdens in particular were forcing the central power or the territorial prince, if they wanted to obtain higher revenues, to encompass available resources more efficiently, in order to avoid endangering social peace in a society still strongly orientated around the principles of a 'society of corporate estates'. How-ever, this also meant that tax privileges which had been handed down from the past had to be increasingly placed in question, in the unavoidable struggle over distribution.

Secondly, even 'Enlightened absolutism' found it difficult to do away with existing privileges without ceremony, because the entire organization of state and society remained marked through and through by a wide variety of privileges, and continued to be based upon them. Resistance to infringements on existing freedoms from taxation was of course particularly strong, and the argument that these were ancient and customary rights, which could not be questioned without impinging upon the foundations of society, had considerable weight in a society which was still strongly traditionally oriented. However, the urge to obtain higher state revenues for military purposes undoubtedly led to intensified reforming efforts on the part of the state. The reforms to agrarian institutions, which began timidly enough around the middle of the eighteenth century and ultimately issued in the so-called *Bauernbefreiung* ('peasant emancipation') of the first half of the nineteenth century, were also partially an attempt to strengthen the position of the central power in the struggle over scarce economic and financial resources. The agrarian and financial reforms of Stein and Hardenberg in Prussia in 1807–20, in particular, show the sort of pressure for reform which could be exerted by financial emergency in time of war.

How necessary – indeed, unavoidable – it was in the longer term to achieve a juster distribution of the tax burden is shown by data on the increasing level of taxes. In Augsburg, for example, regular taxes rose eightfold during the Swedish period (1632–5) alone; while before the war the average burden of direct and indirect taxes had been about 5–6 *Gulden* per head, in 1635 it was an estimated 20–30 *Gulden*, and in 1646 still approximately 11–12 *Gulden*. In the Electoral Palatinate toward the end of the Thirty Years War, the already-impoverished subjects were burdened with war contributions amounting to between 6 and 9.5 per cent of the value of their property; in 1674 it was still 5 per cent. In Nördlingen the tax rate on land and property rose from 0.5 per cent originally, to 1 per cent in the 1670s, to 3.5 per cent by 1678, because at that time the region was once again afflicted by war and the city had to defray correspondingly high military expenditures. Achilles has estimated that in Braunschweig the total tax burden on a full peasant holding was 7 *Taler* in the period before the Thirty Years War, 13 *Taler* in 1660, and 30 *Taler* by the beginning of the eighteenth century; this growth was for the most part directly caused by war, and in its mechanism of operation was in any case caused by war indirectly.[38] In Bavaria, in 1609–18 state revenues were 1.2 million *Gulden* on average, but between 1659 and 1668 they had already reached nearly 1.8 million – this despite the fact that agricultural production, industry, and trade had declined dangerously during the war. By comparison, in 1770 state revenues amounted to *c.* 4 million *Gulden*. The yield from direct taxation was 247,000 *Gulden* on average in 1621–30; after a drastic decline during the period of the immediate effects of the war, direct taxes developed into the most important source of revenues in the state budget, in particular because the meeting of parliament called in 1669 had reduced the influence of parliamentary representation. In the 1690s, Bavarian subjects already paid a good 750,000 *Gulden* in taxes on possessions and property. In this way, the fiscal and political structures were formed which prevailed for approximately the next century. Into the second half of the eighteenth century, direct taxes made up about 40 per cent of Bavarian state revenues; war thus acted as a 'catalyst and accelerator of Bavarian fiscal policy'.[39] Such incursions into the possessions and property of subjects by means of taxation were in general one of the most serious consequences of the wars of the seventeenth and eighteenth centuries for the economic and financial system as a whole. In every case, the war acted to prepare the way for increasingly ingenious financial policies by the territorial states. In the competition for new financial resources, the central power was as a rule gradually able to prevail against other feudal powers, especially the landed nobility. This meant that the expansion of territorial financial policy, which was caused by war, contributed decisively to the breakthrough of the absolutist state, and ultimately to that of the modern fiscal state as well.

War and the organization of society

Several aspects of the relationship between war and the organization of society have already been mentioned in the two preceding sections. Let us recall them very briefly. The Thirty Years War relaxed the pressure of population on available food resources, at least temporarily. This held out better opportunities, especially to some portions of the lower strata in both town and countryside, to improve their economic and social positions by taking over, or marrying into, niches that had become free, thereby obtaining an economically viable existence to which they would otherwise not so easily have obtained access. Larger farms did not benefit to the same extent from the post-war depression. Declining market prices for grain, increasing labour costs, and the pressure of demands from state and landlords, all pushed family incomes below pre-war levels. The post-war depression made incursions into the substance of market-oriented businesses, although it was still they that were in the best position to lose something in order to survive the phase of contraction.

Increased economic and social mobility was one consequence of this process of social loosening. For about two generations trade in land decisively increased, older landholdings were not infrequently broken up, and there was a much stronger tendency for a stratum of smaller and medium-sized landowners to form below the actual full peasants; in the course of the following century, the number of these new smallholders outstripped that of the peasants in many parts of Germany. Admittedly, there was a different path of development in the area of so-called *Gutsherrschaft* (a manorial system with very strong landlord powers) east of the Elbe. The scarcity of labour which was especially severe there meant that the noble landlords had already earlier noticeably intensified their efforts to submit their subject peasants to estate subjection in the form of the 'second serfdom', and to extend peasants' obligation to perform labour services both themselves and by providing draught animals. The dualism in the agrarian constitution of Central Europe between *Gutsherrschaft* in the East and *Grundherrschaft* (the western German manorial system, with relatively weak seigneurial powers) developed in its full severity only after the Thirty Years War, and must also be viewed as being at least partly a consequence of it.

In addition to increased mobility internal to peasant society, there was also increased mobility from the agricultural sector into the industrial sector. In Saxony, for instance, those active in industry in the countryside increased from 12 per cent of the total population in 1630 to 21 per cent in 1660. This change was especially manifested in the more intensive shift from small peasant farming into industry and rural crafts. Thus, at least for a time, the 'Great War' set free a measure of social dynamism which is difficult to estimate. This was also the case for urban society. In many ways urban wealth had been destroyed; this could weaken the previous great inequality in the distribution of property and offer new opportunities for social elevation, but on the other hand it could also cement and intensify existing social differences in the context of general scarcity. In actuality, the direction of development was not at all uniform. In Oldenburg in northern Germany, severe taxation during the occupation by Imperial troops in 1627–31 consumed considerable economic resources; in these 4 years taxable capital declined from 224,000 to 153,000 *Taler* in total, and from an average of 306 *Taler* per household to only 252. In Augsburg, average tax capacity fell from six *Gulden* per citizen to half this amount, in a context in which the distribution of wealth was highly and lastingly unequal; in the neighbouring princely capital of Munich, by contrast, a clear tendency towards a levelling of property differences can be observed. Apparently, in the trading city of Augsburg with its large lower stratum, the war operated in a different direction than it did in the small princely capital city with a social structure which was in any case more egalitarian. For Nördlingen an actual increase in socio-economic polarization and inequality has been established as an immediate consequence of the Thirty Years War; apparently the better-off were more able than others to maintain their positions, while the middle and lower strata suffered great losses through destruction and exhaustion of their property. Only in the following phase of recovery did the middling sort begin to profit more than proportionally – from the improved chances for the survivors to gain access to niches which had become free. Changes in property distribution clearly reflect this process: in 1646, the wealthiest 2 per cent of the urban population still owned more than 40 per cent of all property, but by 1670 they owned only 22 per cent. However, this change did not remain in existence enduringly. Rather, in the case of Nördlingen the wars of the late seventeenth and early eighteenth century, together with the renewed incursions of Malthusian crisis mechanisms, led once more to intensified social polarization; by 1720 the old pattern of wealth had been restored to exactly the situation which had prevailed before and during the Thirty Years War. The old encrustation of the social pyramid entrenched itself anew; war still operated at best as an accelerator of decline.[40]

In any case, it must be stressed that the increased social mobility resulting from the Thirty Years War was essentially a process of filling up niches, which occurred at relatively low levels of wealth. The Thirty Years War changed the basic mechanisms of the economy and society as little as it changed the social framework. The authorities were wholly bent upon re-establishing the old order in all areas of life. Structures of government changed little, even though the 'Great War' itself had clearly shown how unstable state ordering of affairs could be.[41] On the other hand, the (larger) territorial state emerged as the true and long-term winner of the Thirty Years War and the conflicts that followed. It was able to increase its sphere of responsibility at the expense of the Imperial state, and in the following decades was able to build up this position – not least in war and by means of war. This can be seen as a basic 'achievement' of the war. The central administrative state was increasingly able to gain ground against parliamentary participation in government, and to strengthen its hold on subjects and their property (as discussed in detail in Chapter 7). In particular, this was expressed in the type and extent of state financing, which in turn substantially served to establish and extend standing armies. The building-up of a ruler's own military organization not only enabled him to extend the state's claims to power in jurisdiction and administration, but also contributed to creating the absolutist state. The power and reputation of a state within the German Empire was especially measured by whether or not it belonged among the 'armed estates of the Empire'. In the concert of German and European powers, in which war represented the continuation of politics by other means, only the 'armed' state could obtain attention and respect as a serious participant.[42]

The 'military state' of Brandenburg-Prussia was a unique phenomenon in early modern Europe.[43] Nowhere else were state, economy, and society instrumentalized for the purposes of monarchical power politics to the extent they were here. Armaments and the military here actually first created the absolutist state: the establishment and extension of the standing army beginning in the 1640s and 1650s were accompanied by the disempowerment of parliament, the obtaining of sources of finance (such as the land tax and excise) without being obliged to gain the consent of parliament, the rise of a central administration which itself was orientated towards the needs of the military, and the integration of the various territories of the electorate. On the basis created by the 'Great Elector', a comprehensive 'social militarization' developed in the eighteenth century, beginning in the reign of the 'Soldier King' Friedrich Wilhelm I (1713–40). The *Kantonreglement* ('Canton Regulation') of 1733 brought order into the problems of recruitment, by a more-or-less frictionless unification of the feudal system and compulsory military service, making it possible to employ the state's subjects in military service with an intensity unknown elsewhere. After initial resistance, Prussian nobles found their way into the officer corps and there obtained a substitute for their loss of functions in other domains of life. The Prussian system of social estates – nobility, urban

Bürger, and peasants – was fundamentally oriented around the requirements of the army, and the feudal lord and the peasant confronted each other in the regiment again as officer and soldier. As Frederick the Great demanded in his Political Testament of 1752, the King of Prussia had to maintain the 'equilibrium' between nobility and peasants by means of their respective military services to the state. The agreement between the war constitution and the state constitution provided a sound basis for the striking power of the Prussian army, but also constituted the terrifying feature of the Prussian 'military state'. In addition to imposing compulsory military service to an extent unknown elsewhere, it placed heavy financial burdens on its subjects to pay for the excessively large army. Toward the end of the seventeenth century, the tax burden per inhabitant in Prussia was already double that in France.[44] But the Prussian crown was unable to refrain from recruiting mercenaries, and did not desire to so refrain: at the death of Frederick the Great, about half the Prussian army consisted of 'foreigners'.

The orientation of all of life around the requirements of the army had far-reaching consequences for the structure of society, for everyday life, and for the mentality of the population in the Prussian state, and created a doubtfully exemplary 'disciplined society'. No other German state achieved such a 'rationalization of organized violence'. At no period was the Habsburg monarchy able to perfect the state's utilization of power to the extent displayed by its Prussian rival to the eyes of all of Europe. In particular, the parliamentary right of consent, and the extensive autonomy enjoyed by the individual countries of the monarchy, made it impossible to establish and extend the military organization to the extent possible in Prussia.

The larger German territorial states, at least, could not and did not want to deviate from this trend toward militarization. Here, too, the result was a standing army. But nowhere outside Prussia did the military became a really central element of the social order. To a considerable extent, the nobility of the officer corps came from abroad; the 'soldier estate', mostly consisting of enlisted mercenaries with usually doubtful pasts, formed a sub-group among the lower orders with a low social reputation, and was separated by occupation, an independent jurisdiction, and increasingly by the construction of barracks, from the normal life of 'citizens', remaining subject to the most severe discipline and penalties. But even in the Free Imperial Cities, where the citizens' militia was a basic component of the urban constitution, the government increasingly made use of the modern 'miles perpetuus'. The rivalry which this evoked between the 'town military' and the citizens' militia reflected the power struggle between citizenry and ruling oligarchy, and a permanent tug-of-war developed over the right to grant military expenditures, like the one that developed between estates and central power in territorial states. Ecclesiastical principalities, too, found it difficult to abstain from the trend toward militarization. Thus a series of prince-bishops in the prince-bishopric of Bamberg embarked on their own military policy – as a defence against the perpetual French menace, as a means to support Imperial and Austrian policies, and not least as a way of strengthening the reputation of the prince-bishop in the circle of his equals and his power against the cathedral chapter. In the 1670s, in the prince-bishoprics of Bamberg and Würzburg which were ruled in personal union, there was a standing army of 6,000, and its expense surpassed by several multiples the prince-bishop's obligation to contribute 800 men to the collective defence system of the Franconian Circle.[45]

These remarks still do not provide an exhaustive answer to the question about the causal interrelationships between war and society. The references made earlier to some sort of increase in opportunities for social elevation must not make us forget the extent to which the Thirty Years War in particular, but the other wars of this period as well, uprooted people socially by destroying the basis on which they had hitherto survived. The number of vagrants, beggars, robbers, pillaging mercenaries, and 'veterans' was regularly pushed up to high levels by the inclemencies of war. Recurring warfare meant the loss of calculable perspectives for the future, and this cannot have had a favourable effect on the 'work ethic' of the affected population. Together with the destruction caused by war, and the huge expenditure of scarce resources for military purposes, this contributed to the encrustation of social and economic relationships, and reduced possibilities for greater economic dynamism. On the other hand, it must be emphasized that the economic backwardness of Germany in the seventeenth and eighteenth century compared to the more advanced western European states, which to this day is readily traced to the Thirty Years War and its consequences, was not so great that it could not be made up for in a few decades in the nineteenth century.

The conviction that war is 'merely a continuation of politics by other means' (in the famous words of Clausewitz) perfectly expresses the thoughts and actions of the statesmen of the *ancien régime*. In so far as politics, in the calculations involved in the so-called 'cabinet wars', endeavoured to make use of this means as economically as possible, and as long as a 'balance of powers' was achieved which minimized the possibility of victory and certain gains, enlightened contemporaries in the late eighteenth century could hope that 'eternal peace' would be attainable in the foreseeable future. The reality turned out differently. The French Revolution very soon developed into an all-encompassing declaration of war against the pre-revolutionary order in Europe as a whole; the 'nation in arms' and the 'people's army' unfolded a hitherto unknown, strongly ideological, and emotionally supported penetrating power, and Napoleon was able to make use of this new power to change the map of Europe – not least Central Europe – enduringly. The new era of European wars ultimately meant a decisive breakthrough to 'modernity' in the resolution of conflicts by force; it was also to place the inherited economic and social order of the *ancien régime* fundamentally in question, ultimately generating far-reaching changes in the old order.

Notes

1   The present essay is based mainly on more recent studies in economic and social history. On more specific questions of military and war history, see: *Handbuch zur deutschen Militärgeschichte 1648–1939* (Munich, 1979), i; Carl Hans Hermann, *Deutsche Militärgeschichte* (Frankfurt am Main, 1966); S. Fiedler, *Grundriß der Militär- und Kriegsgeschichte 1640–1789* (Munich, 1972). For research studies, see: Ernst Willi Hansen, 'Zur Problematik einer Sozialgeschichte des deutschen Militärs im 17. und 18. Jahrhundert', *ZHF* 6 (1979), pp. 425–60; Bernhard R. Kroener, 'Vom "extraordinari Kriegsvolck" zum "miles perpetuus". Zur Rolle der bewaffneten Macht in der europäischen Geschichte der Frühen Neuzeit', *Militärgeschichtliche Mitteilungen*, 43 (1988), pp. 141–88. For studies in English: Michael Howard, *War in European History* (Oxford, 1976); William H. McNeill, *The Pursuit of Power: Technology, Armed Force and Society since A. D. 1000* (Chicago, 1982); Jeremy Black, ed., *The Origins of War in Early Modern Europe* (Edinburgh, 1987); Geoffrey Parker, *The Military Revolution: Military Innovation and the Rise of the West, 1500–1800* (Cambridge, 1988); Matthew S. Anderson, *War and Society in Early Modern Europe* (London, 1988); Jeremy Black, *A Military Revolution? Military Change and European Society, 1550–1800* (Basingstoke, 1991). For a survey of the literature, see Denis E. Showalter, *German Military History, 1648–1982. A Critical Bibliography* (New York, 1984).

2   Sigfrid Heinrich Steinberg, *The 'Thirty Years' War' and the Conflict for European Hegemony 1600–1660* (London, 1966), p. 107 (German version: *Der Dreißigjährige Krieg und der Kampf um die Vorherrschaft in Europa 1600–1660* (Göttingen, 1976)); Sigfrid Heinrich Steinberg, 'Der Dreißigjährige Krieg: Eine neue Interpretation', in Hans U. Rudolf, ed., *Der Dreißigjährige Krieg: Perspektiven und Strukturen* (Darmstadt, 1977), pp. 51–67 (English version 1947); Hans-Ulrich Wehler, *Deutsche Gesellschaftsgeschichte*, i: *Vom Feudalismus des Alten Reiches bis zur defensiven Modernisierung der Reformära, 1700–1815* (Munich, 1987), pp. 53ff; Wehler gives a population figure for the Empire of 15 million for 1600 and some 15 to 16 million for the period around 1650; for the most recent survey of overall estimates of population development, see Christoph Dipper, *Deutsche Geschichte 1618–1789* (Frankfurt am Main, 1991), p. 44.

3   Günther Franz, *Der Dreißigjährige Krieg und das deutsche Volk. Untersuchungen zu Bevölkerungs- und Agrargeschichte* (Jena, 1940; 4th edn, revised and expanded, Stuttgart/New York, 1979).

4   On Württemberg, see Wolfgang von Hippel, 'Bevölkerung und Wirtschaft im Zeitalter des Dreißigjährigen Krieges. Das Beispiel Württemberg', *ZHF* 5 (1978), pp. 413–45; on Bietigheim, see *Bietigheim 789–1989. Beiträge zur Geschichte von Siedlung, Dorf und Stadt* (Bietigheim-Bissingen, 1989), p. 328; on Kaiserslautern, see Karl Moersch, *Geschichte der Pfalz. Von den Anfängen bis zur Gegenwart* (Landau, 1987), pp. 348f.; on Augsburg, see Bernd Roeck, *Eine Stadt in Krieg und Frieden. Studien zur Geschichte der Reichsstadt Augsburg zwischen Kalenderstreit und Parität* (Munich, 1989), i. pp. 301ff.; ii.

pp. 630ff., 742f.; in *ibid.*, pp. 880f., can be found further figures on the population losses in south German regions and towns, e.g. for Nuremberg (a loss of 50 per cent), Munich (60 per cent), and Kaufbeuren (75 per cent).

5 On Pforzheim: Hans-Peter Becht and Gerhard Fouquet, 'Pforzheim im Pfälzischen Krieg 1688–1697. Ein Beitrag zur Geschichte und Topographie der Stadt am Ende des 17. Jahrhunderts', in Hans-Peter Becht, ed., *Pforzheim in der Frühen Neuzeit. Beiträge zur Stadtgeschichte des 16. bis 18. Jahrhunderts* (Sigmaringen, 1989), pp. 81–116; on Bietigheim: *Bietigheim 789–1989*, p. 381; on the Palatinate: H. Musall and H. Scheuerbrandt, 'Die Kriege im Zeitalter Ludwigs XIV. und ihre Auswirkungen auf die Siedlungs-, Bevölkerungs- und Wirtschaftsstruktur der Oberrheinlande', in Horst Eichler and Heinz Musall, eds, *Festschrift Hans Graul* (Heidelberg, 1974), p. 369.

6 Fundamental on the causal relationships between war and population: Arthur Imhof and Øivind Larsen, *Sozialgeschichte und Medizin. Probleme der quantifizierenden Quellenbearbeitung in der Sozial- und Medizingeschichte* (Oslo/Stuttgart, 1975), pp. 125ff. (based on the example of the Swedish-Finnish war against Russia in 1741–3); Myron P. Gutmann, *War and Rural Life in the Early Modern Low Countries* (Assen, 1980), based on the example of the Niedermaas area between Liège and Maastricht; typical for a core area of the Empire: Arthur E. Imhof, ed., *Historische Demographie als Sozialgeschichte. Gießen und Umgebung vom 17. zum 19. Jahrhundert* (Darmstadt/Marburg, 1975), i. pp. 234, 255ff.; on the instructive example of northern Hesse: Arthur E. Imhof, *Die verlorenen Welten. Alltagsbewältigung durch unsere Vorfahren und weshalb wir uns heute so schwer damit tun* (Munich, 1984), pp. 91ff., 118ff.

7 For a summary of the direct losses, in terms of the numbers of dead and wounded on the battlefields: Boris Zesarewitsch Urlanis, *Bilanz der Kriege. Die Menschenverluste Europas vom 17. Jahrhundert bis zu Gegewart* (Russian version, 1960; Berlin, GDR, 1965).

8 Reinhard Brosig, 'Die Pest als Krisenzeit. Die Bevölkerung des Hegaus im Dreißigjährigen Krieg', in Frank Göttman and Jörn Sieglerschmidt, eds, *Vermischtes zu neueren Sozial-, Bevölkerungs und Wirtschaftsgeschichte des Bodenseeraumes. Horst Rabe zum 60. Geburtstag* (Konstanz, 1990), pp. 46–74; Peter Bohl, 'Die Stadt Stockach im 17. und 18. Jahrhundert. Strukturen und Funktionen einer Oberamtsstadt. Verwaltung – Wirtschaft – Gesellschaft – Bevölkerung' (Ph.D. dissertation, Univ. of Konstanz, 1987); Peter Bohl, 'Aspekte der Bevölkerungsentwicklung Singens im 17. und 18. Jahrhundert', in Herbert Berner, ed., *Singen – Dorf und Herrschaft. Singener Stadtgeschichte* (Konstanz, 1990), ii. pp. 310–29.

9 Imhof, *Historische Demographie*, i. pp. 93ff., 122ff., 232ff.; Wieland Sachse, *Göttingen im 18. und 19. Jahrhundert. Zur Bevölkerungs- und Sozialstruktur einer deutschen Universitätsstadt* (Göttingen, 1987), pp. 91ff.; Hubert Walter, *Bevölkerungsgeschichte der Stadt Einbeck* (Hildesheim, 1960), pp. 19, 34f.; on Saxony: Karlheinz Blaschke, *Bevölkerungsgeschichte von Sachsen bis zur Industriellen Revolution* (Weimar, 1967), pp. 125f.; on Brandenburg-Prussia: Dipper, *Deutsche Geschichte*, p. 60.

10 Walter G. Rödel, *Mainz und seine Bevölkerung im 17. und 18. Jahrhundert. Demographische Entwicklung, Lebensverhältnisse und soziale Strukturen in einer geistlichen Residenzstadt* (Wiesbaden, 1985), pp. 119ff., 228ff., 246ff., 249; see also: Walter G. Rödel, *Bevölkerungsbewegung und soziale Strukturen in Mainz zur Zeit des Pfälzischen Krieges (1680–1700). Eine historisch-demographische Fallstudie* (Wiesbaden, 1978).

11 On Singen: Bohl, 'Aspekte', p. 323; on the Palatinate: Musall and Scheuerbrandt, 'Kriege', pp. 370f.; on the problem of migration see Franz,

Dreißigjähriges Krieg, pp. 2ff.; Wehler, *Deutsche Gesellschaftsgeschichte*, p. 54; on immigration and 'Peuplierungspolitik' ('population policy'): Rudolf Vierhaus, *Deutschland im Zeitalter des Absolutismus 1648–1763* (Göttingen, 1978), pp. 29f.; Hermann Aubin and Wolfgang Zorn, eds, *Handbuch der deutschen Wirtschafts- und Sozialgeschichte* (Munich, 1971), i. pp. 628ff.

12 Fundamental on the course and elasticity of population growth after demographic crises: Markus Mattmüller, *Bevölkerungsgeschichte der Schweiz* (Basel, 1987), i. pp. 249ff.

13 Steinberg, '*Thirty Years' War*', p. 3; the same opinion is also expressed by Wehler, *Deutsche Gesellschaftsgeschichte*; for orientation on the Thirty Years' War, see: Geoffrey Parker, *The Thirty Years' War* (London, 1984); for a survey of research: Heinrich Lutz, *Reformation und Gegenreformation* (Munich, 1979; 2nd edn, 1982), pp. 179ff.

14 Friedrich Lütge, 'Die wirtschaftliche Lage Deutschlands vor Ausbruch des Dreißigjährigen Krieges', *Jahrbücher für Nationalökonomie und Statistik*, 170 (1958), pp. 43–99; reprinted in Hans U. Rudolf, ed., *Der Dreißigjährige Krieg. Perspektiven und Strukturen* (Darmstadt, 1977), pp. 458–539; Wolfgang von Hippel, 'Zum Problem der wirtschaftlichen Auswirkungen des Dreißigjährigen Krieges im Deutschen Reich', in Wolfgang Brückner *et al.*, eds, *Literatur und Volk im 17. Jahrhundert. Probleme populärer Kultur in Deutschland* (Wiesbaden, 1985), pp. 111–25. On the debate about the 'crisis of the seventeenth century', see Geoffrey Parker and Leslie Smith, eds, *The General Crisis of the Seventeenth Century* (London, 1978), as well as the survey of research in Heinz Duchardt, *Das Zeitalter des Absolutismus* (Munich, 1989), pp. 155ff.; Sheilagh C. Ogilvie, 'Germany and the Seventeenth-Century Crisis', *Historical Journal*, 35 (1992), pp. 417–41.

15 On Magdeburg and Halberstadt: Lutz Miehe, 'Materielle Verluste und Bevölkerungsrückgang in den Städten der Stifte Magdeburg und Halberstadt während des Dreißigjährigen Krieges' (Ph.D. dissertation, Univ. of Magdeburg, 1985); Lutz Miehe, 'Zerstörungen durch den Dreißigjährigen Krieg in westelbischen Städten des Erzbistums Magdeburg und des Hochstifts Halberstadt', *JbWG* 4 (1990), pp. 31–48; on Württemberg: Hippel, 'Bevölkerung'; on Schongau: Rudolf Schlögl, *Bauern, Krieg und Staat. Oberbayerische Bauernwirtschaft und frühmoderner Staat im 17. Jahrhundert* (Göttingen, 1988), p. 66; on Nürnberg: Matthew S. Anderson, *War and Society in Europe of the Old Regime* (London, 1988), p. 73; on Hamburg: Stephan Michael Schröder, 'Hamburg und Schweden im Dreißigjährigen Krieg. Vom potentiellen Bündnispartner zum Zentrum der Kriegsfinanzierung', *Vierteljahrsschrift für Sozial- und Wirtschaftsgeschichte*, 76 (1989), pp. 305–31.

16 See the summary in Franz, *Dreißigjähriges Krieg*, pp. 115ff.

17 Schlögl, *Bauern*, pp. 59ff., 80, 113.

18 Lütge, 'Wirtschaftliche Lage', p. 539 (cited from 1977 edn).

19 On Nördlingen: Christopher R. Friedrichs, *Urban Society in an Age of War: Nördlingen, 1580–1720* (Princeton, 1979), pp. 78f., 82ff., 84ff.; on Augsburg: Roeck, *Stadt*, ii. pp. 914ff.

20 On Pforzheim and Baden-Durlach: Becht, *Pforzheim*, pp. 108ff.; on the Tyrol: Franz Mathis, *Die Auswirkungen des bayerisch-französischen Einfalls von 1703 auf Bevölkerung und Wirtschaft Nordtirols* (Innsbruck, 1975).

21 Hubert Salm, *Armeefinanzierung im Dreißigjährigen Krieg. Der niederrheinisch-westfälische Reichskreis 1635–1650* (Münster, 1990).

22 *Ibid.*, pp. 42ff.

23 Ingomar Bog, 'Türkenkrieg und Agrarwirtschaft', in Othmar Pickl, ed., *Die wirtschaftlichen Auswirkungen der Türkenkriege* (Graz, 1971), pp. 13–26.

24 Fritz Redlich, *The German Military Enterpriser and his Work Force. A Study*

in European Economic and Social history (2 vols, Wiesbaden, 1964–5); on the logistics of provisioning as a part of the 'military revolution': Geoffrey Parker, *The Military Revolution: Military Innovation and the Rise of the West, 1500–1800* (Cambridge, 1988), pp. 45ff.; Anderson, *War*, pp. 139ff.; G. Perjés, 'Army Provisioning, Logistics and Strategy in the Second Half of the Seventeenth Century', *Acta Historica: Journal of the Hungarian Academy of Sciences*, 16 (1970), pp. 1–52; see also: Pickl, *Wirtschaftliche Auswirkungen*; Martin L. van Creveld, *Supplying War: Logistics from Wallenstein to Patton* (Cambridge, 1977); additionally, the exhaustive article from a contemporary perspective in Johann Georg Krünitz, *Oekonomisch-technologische Enzyklopädie, oder Allgemeines System der Staats-, Stadt-, Haus- und Landwirthschaft*, 49–53 (Berlin, 1790–1), above all on 'Kriegs- oder Feldbäckerey' (49, pp. 673ff.), 'Kriegs-Etat' (50, pp. 213ff.), 'Kriegs-Heer' (pp. 642ff.), 'Kriegs- oder Feld-Magazin- und Proviantwesen' (60, pp. 516ff.), and 'Kriegs-Waffen und Kleidung' (52, pp. 562ff.).

25   On Prussian economic and military policy, see Gerhard Oestreich, *Friedrich Wilhelm I. Preußischer Absolutismus, Merkantilismus, Militarismus* (Göttingen, 1977), pp. 63f., 85f.

26   Werner Sombart, *Krieg und Kapitalismus* (Munich/Leipzig, 1913); on the Sombart thesis, see J. M. Winter, 'The Economic and Social History of War', in J. M. Winter, ed., *War and Economic Development: Essays in Memory of David Joslin* (Cambridge, 1975), pp. 1–10; Anderson, *War*, pp. 155f. On the dimensions of demand and its effects on proto-industries: Bernhard R. Kroener, 'Die materiellen Grundlagen österreichischer und preußischer Kriegsanstrengungen 1756–1763', in Bernhard R. Kroener, ed., *Europa im Zeitalter Friedrichs des Großen. Wirtschaft, Gesellschaft, Kriege* (Munich, 1989), pp. 47–78; Peter Kriedte, Hans Medick, and Jürgen Schlumbohm, *Industrialisierung vor der Industrialisierung. Gewerbliche Warenproduktion auf dem Land in der Formationsperiode des Kapitalismus* (Göttingen, 1977), pp. 256ff.

27   Helmut Schnitter, *Volk und Landesdefension. Volksaufgebote, Defensionswerke, Landmilizen in den deutschen Territorien vom 15. bis zum 18. Jahrhundert* (Berlin, GDR, 1977); Helmut Schnitter, 'Söldnerheer und Landesdefension. Militärische Alternativentwicklungen im 16. und 17. Jahrhundert in Territorien des deutschen Feudalreiches', *Zeitschrift für Geschichtswissenschaft*, 35 (1987), pp. 708–16.

28   On the building of fortifications see Henning Eichberg, *Militär und Technik. Schwedenfestungen des 17. Jahrhunderts in den Herzogtümern Bremen und Verden* (Düsseldorf, 1976); Henning Eichberg, *Festung, Zentralmacht und Sozialgeometrie. Kriegsingenieurwesen des 17. Jahrhunderts in den Herzogtümern Bremen und Verden* (Cologne/Vienna, 1988); Hans-Walter Herrman and Franz Irsigler, eds, *Beiträge zur Geschichte der frühneuzeitlichen Garnisons- und Festungsstadt* (Saarbrücken, 1983); Christopher Duffy, *Siege Warfare*, ii: *The Fortress in the Age of Vauban and Frederick the Great, 1666–1789* (London, 1985); Parker, *Military Revolution*, pp. 6ff.

29   Ernst Klein, *Geschichte der öffentlichen Finanzen in Deutschland (1500–1800)* (Wiesbaden, 1974), pp. 24ff.; Gustav Otruba and Michael Weiss, *Beiträge zur Finanzgeschichte Österreichs 1740–1840* (Linz, 1986); Brigitte Holl, *Hofkammerpräsident Gundaker Thomas Graf v. Starhemberg und die österreichische Finanzpolitik der Barockzeit (1705–1715)* (Vienna, 1976); Peter G. M. Dickson, *Finance and Government under Maria Theresia 1740–1780* (2 vols, Oxford, 1987).

30   For a survey on war costs and state indebtedness, see Otruba and Weiss, *Beiträge*, pp. 54f.

31 On what follows, see: Klein, *Geschichte*, pp. 41ff.; Rudolf Braun, 'Taxation, Sociopolitical Structure and State-Building: Great Britain and Brandenburg-Prussia', in C. Tilly, ed., *The Formation of National States in Western Europe* (Princeton, 1975), pp. 268ff.

32 Adelheid Simsch, 'Armee, Wirtschaft und Gesellschaft. Preußens Kampf auf der "inneren Linie"', in Kroener, *Europa*, pp. 35–46.

33 Hermann Caspary, *Staat, Finanzen, Wirtschaft und Heerwesen im Hochstift Bamberg (1672–1693)* (Bamberg, 1976), pp. 171ff., 355ff.

34 On Braunschweig: Walter Achilles, *Die steuerliche Belastung der braunschweigischen Landwirtschaft und ihr Beitrag zu den Staatseinnahmen im 17. und 18. Jahrhundert* (Hildesheim, 1972), pp. 193ff.; on Bavaria: Klein, *Geschichte*, pp. 63ff.; Peter Claus Hartmann, 'Die Schuldenlast Bayerns von Kurfürst Max Emanuel bis Ludwig I.', in Andreas Kraus, ed., *Land und Reich – Stamm und Nation. Probleme und Perspektiven bayerischer Geschichte. Festschrift Max Spindler zum 90. Geburtstag* (Munich, 1984), i. pp. 369–82.

35 On Hessen-Kassel: Charles Ingrao, *The Hessian Mercenary State: Ideas, Institutions and Reform under Frederick II, 1760–1785* (Cambridge, 1987); Charles Ingrao, 'Kameralismus und Militarismus im deutschen Polizeistaat: Der hessische Söldnerstaat', in Winfried Schulze, ed., *Ständische Gesellschaft und soziale Mobilität* (Munich, 1988), pp. 171–86; on Brauschweig: Achilles, *Steuerliche Belastung*, pp. 137ff., pp. 142; on Württemberg: Klein, *Öffentliche Finanzen*, pp. 72ff.; on Ansbach: Bernhard Sicken, 'Truppenstärke und Militäretat des Fürstentums Ansbach um 1730', *Jahrbuch des Historischen Vereins für Mittelfranken*, 84 (1967/68), pp. 60–83; Günter Schuhmann, 'Residenzen der fränkischen Hohenzollern', *BdLG* 123 (1987), pp. 74f.

36 For a survey: Aubin and Zorn, *Handbuch*, i. p. 569; on Bavaria, the Palatinate, and Cologne: Peter Claus Hartmann, *Geld als Instrument europäischer Machtpolitik im Zeitalter des Merkantilismus. Studien zu den finanziellen und politischen Beziehungen der Wittelsbacher Territorien Kurbayern, Kurpfalz und Kurköln mit Frankreich und dem Kaiser von 1715 bis 1740* (Munich, 1978); Peter Claus Hartmann, 'Die Finanz- und Subsidienpolitik des Kurfürsten Max Emanuel von Bayern und der kurbayerische Gesandte in Paris Comte d'Albert – Fürst Grimberghen' (Ph.D. dissertation, Univ. of Munich, 1967); on Austria: Jean Bérenger, *Finances et absolutisme autrichien dans la séconde moitié du XVII siècle* (Paris, 1965); Holl, *Hofkammerpräsident*; Gustav Otruba, 'Die Bedeutung englischer Subsidien und Antizipationen für die Finanzen Österreichs 1701–1748', *Vierteljahrsschrift für Sozial- und Wirtschaftsgeschichte*, 51 (1964), 192–234; Dickson, *Finance*, ii. pp. 157ff.

37 Achilles, *Steuerliche Belastung*, p. 95.

38 On Augsburg: Roeck, *Stadt*, ii. pp. 583f., 601f.; on the Palatinate: Volker Sellin, *Die Finanzpolitik Karl Ludwigs von der Pfalz. Staatswirtschaft und Wiederaufbau nach dem Dreißigjährigen Krieg* (Stuttgart, 1978), pp. 161ff.; on Nördlingen: Friedrichs, *Urban Society*, pp. 158ff.; on Braunschweig: Achilles, *Steuerliche Belastung*, pp. 167, 169f.

39 Schlögl, *Bauern*, pp. 198ff., 230, 240, 362, 386f.

40 On Saxony: Volkmar Weiss, 'Sozialstruktur und soziale Mobilität der Landbevölkerung: Das Beispiel Sachsen 1550–1880', *ZAgrarGAgrarSoz* 39 (1991), pp. 24–43; on Oldenburg: Kersten Krüger, ed., *Sozialstruktur der Stadt Oldenburg 1630 und 1678. Analysen zur historischen Finanzsoziologie anhand staatlicher Steuerregister* (Oldenburg, 1986), p. 117; on Augsburg: Roeck, *Stadt*, ii. pp. 905ff., 975; on Munich, Roeck, 'Bayern im Dreißigjährigen Krieg. Demographische, wirtschaftliche und soziale Auswirkungen am Beispiel Münchens', *GG* 17 (1991), pp. 434–58; on Nördlingen: Friedrichs, *Urban Society*, pp. 95ff.

41 Roeck, *Stadt*, ii. p. 931; Friedrichs, *Urban Society*, p. 294; in general on the consequences of the Thirty Years War for various social groups, Volker Press, 'Soziale Folgen des Dreißigjährigen Krieges', in Schulze, *Ständische Gesellschaft*, pp. 239–68.

42 Gerhard Oestreich, 'Zur Heeresverfassung der deutschen Territorien von 1500 bis 1800. Ein Versuch vergleichender Betrachtung', in *Forschungen zu Staat und Verfassung. Festgabe für Fritz Hartung* (Berlin, 1958), pp. 419–39, repr. in Gerhard Oestreich, *Geist und Gestalt des frühmodernen Staates* (Berlin, 1969), pp. 290–310; Samuel E. Finer, 'State and Nation-Building in Europe: The Role of the Military', in Charles Tilly, ed., *The Formation of National States in Western Europe* (Princeton, 1975), pp. 84–163.

43 On this, the basic works are: Otto Büsch, *Militärsystem und Sozialleben im alten Preußen 1713–1807. Die Anfänge der sozialen Militarisierung der preußisch-deutschen Gesellschaft* (Berlin, 1962; 2nd edn, 1981); Otto Büsch, 'Die Militarisierung von Staat und Gesellschaft im alten Preußen', in Manfred Schlenke, ed., *Preußen. Beiträge zu einer politischen Kultur* (Reinbek, 1981), pp. 45–60; Finer, 'State', pp. 134ff.

44 Finer, 'State', p. 140.

45 In general on the social history of the military population: Reinhard Baumann, *Landsknechte. Ihre Geschichte und Kultur vom späten Mittelalter bis zum Dreißigjährigen Krieg* (Munich, 1994); Peter Burschel, *Söldner im Nordwestdeutschland des 16. und 17. Jahrhunderts. Sozialgeschichtliche Studien* (Göttingen, 1994); on the Free Imperial Cities' military, based on the example of Lübeck: Thomas Schwark, *Lübecks Stadtmilitär im 17. und 18. Jahrhundert. Untersuchungen zur Sozialgeschichte einer reichsstädtischen Berufsgruppe* (Lübeck, 1990); on Augsburg: Jürgen Kraus, *Das Militärwesen der Reichsstadt Augsburg 1548–1806. Vergleichende Untersuchungen über städtische Militäreinrichtungen in Deutschland vom 16. – 18. Jahrhundert* (Augsburg, 1980); on Hamburg: Joachim Ehlers, *Die Wehrverfassung der Stadt Hamburg im 17. und 18. Jahrhundert* (Boppard, 1966); on Göttingen: Ralf Pröve, *Stehendes Heer und städtische Gesellschaft im 18. Jahrhundert. Göttingen und seine Militärbevölkerung* (Munich, 1994); on Bamberg and Würzburg: Caspary, *Staat*, pp. 291, 304; see also Reinhard Weber, *Würzburg und Bamberg im Dreißigjährigen Krieg. Die Regierungszeit des Bischofs Franz v. Hatzfeld 1631–1642* (Würzburg, 1979). There is some debate concerning the degree of militarization of ecclesiastical states and the importance of military power for their self-image, see on this: Peter Hersche, 'Intendierte Rückständigkeit. Zur Charakteristik des geistlichen Staates im Alten Reich', in Georg Schmidt, ed., *Stände und Gesellschaft im Alten Reich* (Stuttgart, 1989), pp. 133–49.

Translated by Sheilagh Ogilvie

|9|

The Beginnings of Industrialization

SHEILAGH OGILVIE

Germany and industrialization

It may seem curious to speak of industrialization as beginning around 1600. Industrialization is often regarded as synonymous with the rise of mechanized manufacturing in centralized factories, and this did not occur even in England until 1760–80, and in Germany not until 1830–50. But machines and factories were only late landmarks – albeit important ones – in a much longer process of industrial growth in Europe, dating back to at least 1500. This long-term industrialization was based almost wholly on decentralized work in producers' own houses, using domestic labour and a simple, slowly changing technology. Yet it was responsible for a gradual expansion in the proportion of the labour-force working in industry and the share of the total output of the economy represented by manufactures. It was also responsible for the emergence, between about 1500 and about 1800, of what German historians have called *Gewerbelandschaften*, 'industrial regions', in which an above-average proportion of people worked in industry and a substantial share of what they produced was exported beyond the region.[1] Important as factory industrialization was, many of its seeds were sown long before, during the slow and dispersed industrialization of many regions of early modern Europe.

This early modern industrial growth was part of a wider process of *regional specialization*, which began slowly in the late medieval period, but accelerated decisively during the sixteenth century. During this process many more European regions than ever before began to specialize in particular forms of agriculture, as well as particular branches of industry, producing surpluses for export and importing what they did not produce for themselves. Thus regional self-sufficiency declined, and inter-regional trade grew. For the first time, large volumes of non-luxury goods began to be traded not only among households and communities, but also among regions. By the end of the sixteenth century specialized regions had arisen all over Europe, producing surpluses of grain, livestock, industrial raw materials, and manufactured products, and exporting them. Without increases in agricultural production and improvements in trade, those specializing in industry would have lacked food, and those specializing in the production of food would not have provided markets for industry – and hence the specialization and growth of industry could not have occurred. The early beginnings of industrialization were thus part of a wider process of regional specialization, in which the growth of agriculture and trade played essential roles.[2]

Germany took part fully in the regional specialization and economic growth of the sixteenth century. As early as 1500, the Upper German region around Nuremberg and Ulm was one of the three most important manufacturing regions of Europe, alongside Upper and Central Italy and The Netherlands. By 1600, building on this base, some of the most vigorous industrial and trading areas in Europe were located in German-speaking Central Europe. Mining and metal production, in particular, had seen important technological innovations and enormous growth. In 1500, the Holy Roman Empire was already producing half the iron in Europe; the sixteenth century saw an estimated doubling of output, and the rise and growth of metal-producing regions in the Rhineland, Hesse, the Harz, Upper Saxony, and the Thuringian Forest. In textile production, the 'leading sector' of early modern industry, Germany was less advanced. In the woollen branch, English and Dutch imports were generally cheaper and better than German products, but the sixteenth century saw the expansion of German sheep herds, the introduction by Dutch religious refugees of the more saleable 'new draperies' or worsteds, and the rise of German fine woollen industries. Wide expanses of Germany were well suited to flax cultivation, and during the sixteenth century flourishing linen regions developed beyond the traditional German linen area in Upper Germany, to the Rhineland, Westphalia, Saxony, and Silesia. Cotton had begun to be imported in large quantities as early as the fifteenth century by the great south German Imperial Cities, where it was turned into fustian (a linen-cotton mix). Turnover of dyed fustian in Augsburg increased by a factor of twenty in the course of the sixteenth century, peaking at 410,000 pieces annually in the decade after 1600.[3]

Commercially, too, Germany occupied an advantageous position in 1600. During most of the sixteenth century, the economic centre of gravity of Europe still clearly lay in the Mediterranean world, and the flourishing south German Imperial Cities functioned as important links between the Mediterranean and northern Europe. Yet the centre of gravity of the European economy was gradually shifting to the north Atlantic, with which Germany also had numerous important ties.[4] The Rhineland and Westphalia were already supplying textiles to Dutch markets and competing with The Netherlands and England through lower labour costs. Saxony and Silesia were supplying linens and metals to the Atlantic trade. North-eastern Germany was supplying grain to the growing consumer markets of The Netherlands and England. The Hanseatic cities (particularly Hamburg) and the great fair centres of Leipzig and Frankfurt an der Oder functioned as important commercial channels for raw materials from eastern Europe to feed the growing demand of the Atlantic economies. Through its multiple connections with the Mediterranean and Atlantic worlds, Germany occupied a central position in the growing European economy of the sixteenth century.

It is therefore all the more striking that by 1800 Germany as a whole had become relatively backward compared to much of western Europe – especially England and Flanders, but also Switzerland and France. The relative retardation of German agriculture and trade, discussed in Chapters 3 and 4 of this volume, were paralleled in German industry by the late eighteenth century. While England had begun to industrialize in the 1760s, and Belgium, Switzerland, and France followed over the next few decades, Germany would not see industrial take-off until the 1840s. One or two very advanced German regions, in the Rhineland and Saxony, experienced what has been called 'pre-industrialization' from the late 1780s onward, with the scattered introduction of factories and machines, but even they did not see true factory industrialization until after about 1810. Westphalia did not industrialize until the 1850s, Württemberg and Baden not until the 1870s, Bavaria and much of the Prussian East not until the very end of the nineteenth century. By 1800, therefore, German industrial development was characterized by two striking features: overall relative backwardness (even in the most advanced regions), and enormous regional variation.[5]

How was Germany transformed from the dynamic and advanced economy of the sixteenth century into the relatively stagnant and conservative backwater of 1800? This question underlies any account of the growth which did take place in German industry between 1600 and 1800. The two answers most often proposed emphasize external shocks, one at the beginning of Germany's long relative decline – the Thirty Years War – and one at the end, in the competition from foreign (especially British) cotton, factories, and machines. However, there are some problems with such exogenous explanations of German industrial development.

It is certainly true that the 'great war' devastated many areas of Germany between 1620 and 1650. But, as discussed in Chapter 8 of this volume, most of the direct demographic and economic depredations of this war were made good quite rapidly. According to the thorough survey by Karl-Heinrich Kaufhold, most German industrial regions which were hit hard by the Thirty Years War recovered astonishingly quickly.[6] In a number of German regions there had already been signs of downturn by the end of the sixteenth century, a generation before the war began, at the beginning of the 'crisis of the seventeenth century' which afflicted many parts of Europe.[7] The severity of the Thirty Years War was not geographically correlated with subsequent industrial backwardness. Rather, a number of regions hard hit by the war were subsequently among the most industrialized in Germany: the linen and worsted regions of depopulated and devastated Württemberg; much of the Rhineland, which had been a corridor for troop movements; and the linen regions of Saxony and Silesia.[8] Historians generally agree that the most profound and enduring effects of the war were indirect: not the immediate loss of labour or capital, nor even the disruption of trade routes, but rather the ratchet-like growth in the powers of the state, and the proliferation of privileges granted to favoured social groups by princes concerned to ensure fiscal and political support during military crises.[9] These indirect effects were influenced by social and political institutions, which varied widely from one German territory to the next. What mattered for industry was not the war itself, but how each German society responded to it; and that depended on its internal characteristics.

The relative backwardness of German industries is also sometimes explained in terms of competition from English factories after 1760. But this explanation encounters similar problems. Many German industries were already falling behind non-factory industries in England, Flanders, and Switzerland as early as the seventeenth century, long before the first factories. Moreover, the proliferation of factories in England itself was quite slow: only a very small percentage of English industry mechanized until around 1820, and the replacement of linen by cotton in the European textile sector took at least 50 years (from 1780 to 1830). The continental European economies had a long time to adjust; and different economies did so in different ways. Belgium and Switzerland responded by shifting from linen to cotton and introducing mechanized production; so, more hesitantly, did Saxony and the Rhineland. But other German linen regions (in Silesia, Württemberg, and Westphalia) obstinately resisted cotton and machines for many generations. The effect of factory competition thus varied widely according to the ability and willingness of different German societies to adapt to the challenge.[10]

The theory of proto-industrialization

If German industrial development in the seventeenth and eighteenth centuries cannot be explained in terms of exogenous factors, such as war or foreign competition, how can it be explained? A major contender for the role of explaining industrial development, not just in Germany but throughout Europe in the early modern period, is the 'theory of proto-industrialization'. 'Proto-industrialization' is a term invented in 1972 by a historian of Flanders, Franklin Mendels, to describe the growth of export-orientated rural industries which took place in many parts of Europe between about 1600 and about 1800. According to Mendels, these 'proto-industries' were responsible for generating the population growth, labour, capital, entrepreneurship, commercial agriculture, and consumer markets ultimately required for factory industrialization.[11] Mendels' hypotheses were extended in 1977 when three German historians, Peter Kriedte, Hans Medick and Jürgen Schlumbohm, argued that proto-industrialization played a major role in the European transition from 'feudalism' to 'capitalism'.[12]

How are 'proto-industries' supposed to have transformed European societies so fundamentally?[13] For one thing, they are supposed to have changed people's demographic behaviour. Before proto-industries, it is argued, population growth was slow, because it was carefully adjusted to slow economic growth, through late marriage (in the mid- to late twenties) and high celibacy (10–15 per cent of people never marrying). Proto-industries are supposed to have freed marriage from waiting on inheritance, enabling universal marriage at an early age. Early and universal marriage, combined with the increased value of child labour in proto-industrial work, increased fertility, leading to a 'population explosion'. This population growth created an unlimited supply of cheap industrial labour for the first factories and also, according to Kriedte, Medick, and Schlumbohm, helped to break down the structures of traditional 'feudal' society.[14]

Proto-industries are also supposed to have changed society and the economy directly, through transforming social institutions. Because proto-industries arose in the countryside, it is argued, they circumvented town privileges, craft guilds, and merchant companies, causing these traditional urban institutions to break down. Because they brought in their train population growth, non-agricultural livelihoods, continual expansion in production, and new economic and social practices, they also helped break down traditional rural institutions such as village communities and manorial systems. In place of 'feudal' institutions – privileged towns, guilds, merchant associations, peasant communities, and manorial systems – proto-industries introduced what was to become the central institution of 'capitalist' society: the market.[15]

Finally, proto-industries are supposed to have generated the inputs necessary for factory industrialization. According to the theorists, they stimulated production of the food surpluses and industrial raw materials needed for factories by encouraging the rise of regions specializing in commercial agriculture. They created the cheap industrial labour which would ultimately be recruited into the factories; they accumulated the capital necessary for investing in the first factories through the profits they made for merchants and putters-out; finally, they created the consumer markets, both at home and abroad, which would subsequently buy the output of the first factories.[16]

The *terms* 'proto-industry' and 'proto-industrialization' have been widely adopted by historians of Germany seeking a concise way of referring to the industrial component of the regional specialization which took place here, as elsewhere in Europe, during the early modern period.[17] But how useful is the *theory* of proto-industrialization in explaining the development of industry in Germany between 1600 and 1800? Since the original hypotheses about proto-industrialization were put forward in the 1970s, there has been an outpouring of research on early modern export industries all over Europe, including Germany. This rich new body of empirical work, much of it directly stimulated by the theory of proto-industrialization, has revealed a number of fundamental drawbacks to the original hypotheses.

The systematic changes which the growth of rural export industries are supposed to have wrought in demographic behaviour have failed to materialize. Instead, a very wide variety of demographic patterns can be observed in different proto-industrial regions; this is reflected by considerable demographic variation among different German industrial regions before 1800.[18] The replacement of traditional social institutions by markets shows little geographical or chronological association with the rise of rural export industries; in Germany, as we will see below, traditional institutions survived in many industrial regions. The commercialization of agriculture appears to have begun in many places before, and independently of, the rise of proto-industries; urban centres already provided a substantial pool of demand for agricultural surpluses, even without rural industrial regions. Indeed, the neglect of the role of towns and cities in early modern industrialization is widely recognized as a major gap in the theory. Finally, it has proved difficult to establish clear links between proto-industrialization and factory industrialization: the labour, capital, skills, food supplies, raw materials, and consumer markets for the early factories did not necessarily derive from proto-industries; and although some proto-industrial regions successfully made the transition to machines and factories, others remained proto-industrial, and still others shifted back to agriculture.[19]

To sum up: the growth of rural export industries, although indeed widespread in early modern Europe, had widely varying demographic, social, and economic effects. Indeed, this regional variation is itself one of the most striking findings to emerge from the last 20 years of empirical research on proto-industrialization. Rather than attempting to force all early modern European industries into the straitjacket of a single pattern of development, the 'second generation' of proto-industrialization studies is now focusing on explaining the *variation* among industries and regions, as a more promising approach to explaining the sources of economic change and development.[20]

This is particularly relevant in the German context, since the theories of proto-industrialization assume that all of Europe responded in much the same way to the economic changes of the early modern period. They do not even address – let alone answer – the question of why some European economies with numerous 'proto-industries' (such as Germany) grew and industrialized more slowly than others (such as England, Flanders, Switzerland, or France). Nor do the theories of proto-industrialization concern themselves with why certain early modern industrial regions (such as those in Saxony or the Rhineland) experienced rapid economic, social, and demographic development between 1600 and 1800, while others (such as those in Westphalia, Württemberg, or Silesia) remained extraordinarily resistant to change for centuries.[21] How, then, might historians provide a satisfactory account of the industrial development of different parts of early modern Germany?

Early modern German industrial regions

One approach has been to try to put together a complete empirical picture of German industries before 1800. Although there is a rich older literature, most of it is oriented toward specific industries, *Landesgeschichte* (the history of particular German territories), or the teleological perspectives of German factory industrialization in the nineteenth century.[22] As a consequence the state of research on early modern Germany industry is fragmentary, with plenty of case studies but few general perspectives, and no complete account of what happened to industry in Germany as a whole in the course of the early modern period. In an attempt to remedy this unsatisfactory state of affairs, in 1986 Karl-Heinrich Kaufhold undertook the heroic task of providing a thorough survey of German industries between 1650 and 1800. Eschewing the term 'proto-industry' as too restrictive, he focused on *Gewerbelandschaften* (industrial regions), which he defined as regions with an above-average density of industrial employment and a large proportion of output sold beyond the region.[23] On the basis of the scattered and uneven existing literature, he identified no fewer than thirty-nine industrial regions in Germany before 1800. These are listed in Table 9.1, and their general locations are shown in Fig. 9.1. Kaufhold's survey provides historians with a much better picture than before of the characteristics of early industrialization in Germany which any satisfactory theory about it must explain.

As can be seen from Table 9.1, there were wide expanses of Germany with no industrial regions. In the far North and East – Schleswig-Holstein, Mecklenburg, and the eastern and central provinces of Prussia (Pomerania, East and West Prussia, Lithuania, the Netze District (Noteć), Neumark, Kurmark, Magdeburg, and Halberstadt) – there was little rural industry, and even the densest urban industries (as in Berlin) were oriented primarily to the local market.[24] Industrial regions were also absent from parts of

Table 9.1 German industrial regions *c.* 1800: a provisional survey[a]

Industrial region	Most important products and branches of industry[b]
Upper Lusatia (Saxony)	Linen yarn and linen cloth
Chemnitz and area (Saxony)	Cotton yarn and cloths, stockings, gloves, caps, etc., calico-printing
Erzgebirge (Ore Mountains) (Saxony)	Silver, cobalt, tin, dyes; iron and iron wares; lace-making, trimmings-making, embroidery; straw-plaiting, toys
Vogtland (Saxony)	Cotton yarn and cotton cloth; embroidery; lace-making; stockings, caps; musical instruments
Region of Schmalkalden, Zella, Mehlis, and Suhl (Thuringia)	Iron, steel; iron and steel wares, especially weapons
Meininger Oberland (esp. Kreis Sonneberg) (Thuringia)	Toys; wooden wares; slates and slate-pencils
Schwarzburgische Oberherrschaften (Thuringia)	Wooden and iron wares; medicaments
Reuß principalities (Thuringia)	Woollens and worsteds; cotton cloths, stockings
Duchy of Weimar (Thuringia)	Stockings
Obereichsfeld (Thuringia)	Worsteds; linen cloth
Lower Silesian mountains (Silesia)	Linen yarn and linen cloth
Upper Silesian mining area (Silesia)	Iron, lead, silver, tin, mineral coal
Area around Nuremberg (Principality of Ansbach) (Franconia)	Cotton cloths and cotton wares; stockings; needles; mirrors; Lyon wire
Area around Bayreuth (Franconia)	Cotton yarn and cotton cloth
Area around Hof (Franconia)	Cotton yarn and cotton cloth
Upper Palatinate	Iron; glass; linen cloth
Allgäu (Swabia)	Linen yarn and linen cloth; embroidery; cotton cloth
Ulm and area (Swabia)	Linen yarn and linen cloth
Swabian Jura (Heidenheim-Urach-Münsingen-Blaubeuren) (Württemberg)	Linen yarn and linen cloth
Eastern Black Forest and its eastern foothills (Württemberg)	Worsteds
Southern Black Forest (Baden, Anterior Austria, etc.)	Embroidery; cotton yarn and cotton cloth
High Black Forest (Todtnau, Triberg, Furtwangen, Neustadt) (Baden, Anterior Austria, etc.)	Clocks; music-boxes; straw-plaiting, brushes, spoons
Saar area (Middle Rhineland)	Mineral coal, iron; glass

Table 9.1 *cont.*

Neuwieder Becken with Westerwald (Middle Rhineland)	Iron; furniture; pottery
Nordeifel (North Rhineland)	Iron, lead; fine woollens; sole-leather
Aachen-Stolberg-Düren (North Rhineland)	Mineral coal, brass; woollens; iron and iron wares; paper; needles
Krefeld-Gladbach-Rheidt and area (North Rhineland)	Silk wares; linen yarn and linen cloth; cotton cloth
Siegerland and Principality of Nassau-Dillenburg (North Rhineland)	Iron, steel, lead, silver, copper; linen cloth; cotton cloth; sole-leather
County of Mark (North Rhineland)	Iron, steel; iron and steel wares; wire; needles; brass wares; woollens; cotton cloth
Duchy of Berg, 'upper' half (North Rhineland)	Steel; iron and steel wares, esp. cutlery and small iron wares; cotton yarn and cotton cloth; woollens
Duchy of Berg, 'lower' half (North Rhineland)	Yarn-bleaching; ribbons, cords, braid; linen cloth; cotton yarn and cotton cloth; dyeing; silk wares
Tecklenburg (Westphalia)	Linen yarn and linen cloth
Minden-Ravensburg (Westphalia)	Linen yarn and linen cloth
Western Münsterland (Westphalia)	Linen cloth
Lippe-Detmold (Westphalia)	Linen yarn and linen cloth
Prince-Bishopric of Osnabrück (Westphalia)	Linen yarn and linen cloth
Harz (Lower Saxony)	Silver, lead, copper, iron
Central and southern Lower Saxony	Linen yarn and linen cloth
North Hesse	Linen yarn and linen cloth

[a] 'Industrial regions' are defined as being areas in which there was an above-average density of industry (measured according to number employed in industry per 1,000 inhabitants) and where the industries involved sold a considerable proportion of their output beyond the local area.

[b] The order of appearance is not identical to the order of importance (which cannot be estimated because of lack of adequate empirical information).

Source: K.-H. Kaufhold, 'Gewerbelandschaften in der frühen Neuzeit', in H. Pohl, ed., *Gewerbe- und Industrielandschaften vom Spätmittelalter bis ins 20. Jahrhundert* (Stuttgart, 1986), pp. 112–202, this table on pp. 171–3; definition of industrial region on pp. 114–15.

the German South: Bavaria and most of present-day Baden except for the Black Forest had a high general density of locally oriented rural crafts, but no concentrated and export-oriented industrial regions.[25] At the other end of the spectrum, there were four large geographical agglomerations within Germany which together accounted for more than three-quarters of the industrial regions identified by Kaufhold: Saxony-Thuringia (containing more than one-quarter of all German industrial regions), the Rhineland (with more than one-fifth), south-west Germany, and Westphalia-Lower Saxony.[26] Industry was distributed across Germany very unevenly.

Early modern German industrial production was also concentrated into

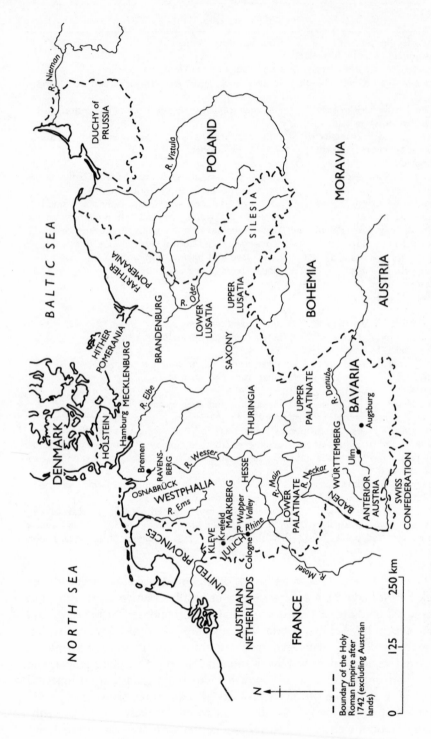

Fig. 9.1 Map of the Holy Roman Empire of the German Nation after 1742 (excluding Austrian Lands)

Boundary of the Holy
Roman Empire after
1742 (excluding Austrian
lands)

0   125   250 km

certain sectors. Two-thirds of the industrial regions identified by Kaufhold were 'monostructured' (dominated by a single industry). The vast majority concentrated on textiles: in nine out of ten monostructured regions the single industry was a textile one, and in two-thirds of 'polystructured' regions textiles played an important role. All metal industries taken together came a long way behind. Linen was by far the most important single industry: half of the monostructured textile regions, and between a quarter and a third of all German industrial regions, produced linen only.[27]

Within German industrial regions, rural production played an important role, but by no means an exclusive one. In most cases, industry formed a rural–urban conglomeration, with some production stages located in the countryside, others in the towns, and others split between the two types of location. Some of the most vigorous and successful industrial regions, those in Saxony and the Rhineland, largely lacked the strong town–country dichotomy found elsewhere in Germany.[28]

Industry was organized into a wide variety of forms of enterprise. The original theories of proto-industrialization emphasized a universal and uni-lineal transition towards domestic industry in production and the putting-out system in finance and marketing. Kaufhold found that these two organizational forms did make an appearance in most German industrial regions between 1650 and 1800. However, his analysis revealed a more complicated picture than can be accounted for by a stage-like progression to domestic industry and putting-out: more often than not, different forms of enterprise existed side by side in the same industry. Thus it was not uncommon to find an industry in which some production occurred as craft work (with a workforce of masters, journeymen, and apprentices, producing in a craft workshop), others in domestic industry (with a family workforce, producing in the dwelling), and still others in a centralized manufactory (with a hired workforce, producing in a central 'proto-factory'). Similarly, a single industry might see all three systems of early modern industrial finance and marketing: a *Kaufsystem* (artisanal system), where independent producers procured their own raw materials, owned their own tools, and sold their output to merchants; a *Verlagssystem* (putting-out system), where merchants advanced raw materials and sometimes tools to producers, who turned them into finished products in exchange for a small fee per item; and a manufactory system, in which capital and marketing were supplied to some or all stages of production in a central plant. Which organizational form was dominant, in either production or finance and marketing, varied within the same industry, across different stages of production and different points in time.[29]

On the basis of these findings, Kaufhold comes to the interesting, if negative, conclusion, that in Germany between 1650 and 1800,

> The development of the industrial region was not determined by any single branch of production (not even linen, despite its importance),

nor by urban or rural industry alone (despite the importance of the latter), nor by any particular form of enterprise (not even domestic industry or putting-out, despite the fact that they were very widespread). When they became sufficiently widespread – and not alone, but in typical combinations – these factors influenced the development of particular regions or groups of regions, sometimes considerably, but they did not become general causes of development.[30]

The theory of proto-industrialization, with its stress on rural domestic industry and a unilineal progression toward the putting-out system, offers 'a too one-sided and short-sighted explanation'.[31]

But when it comes to formulating a 'typology' or positive explanation to account for why industrial regions arose in certain parts of Germany but not in others, or why some grew and others declined, Kaufhold is much more hesitant. His empirical survey leads him to conclude that three 'location factors' were essential: labour supply, raw materials, and market outlets. Capital, technology, and state industrial policies were much less important.[32] However, he finds that no general conclusions can be drawn about which regions of Germany could be expected to supply such 'location factors' in the requisite amounts, or why. Industrial labour supply was affected by population growth, agriculture, social stratification, and entry restrictions (such as guild rules).[33] Raw materials were sometimes produced within German industrial regions, but often imported.[34] Markets for German manufactures were created through growing domestic demand, European outlets, the growth of overseas colonies, improvements in transportation, and the entrepreneurial activities of merchants.[35] In short, Kaufhold's survey provides enormously useful empirical generalizations, but no explanation for why German industries were located where they were, and why they developed as they did. Must we content ourselves with empirical descriptions, or are there more general explanatory tools available which can help to make sense of the heterogeneity in early modern German industrial development?

There is, in fact, a single general concept underlying all the 'location factors' one meets in descriptive accounts of early modern industries. This is *opportunity cost*, the central idea behind the economic theory of supply, and thus the fundamental explanation for why certain European regions and not others supplied industrial goods in the early modern period. All forms of production require inputs of resources – labour, capital, land, raw materials. Because each of these resources could be used in other ways, it has what economists call an 'opportunity cost' – a cost in terms of the next-best alternative use for it. 'Opportunity cost' is a more useful way of thinking about costs than simple money costs, because it takes into account costs which are not traded in markets or expressed in money terms. In early modern Europe many goods were not formally traded in markets and thus did not have money prices; this was especially the case for labour, the most important input for early modern industry. But all inputs had opportunity costs: labour which a household allocated to weaving could not simultaneously be used for farming; land used for growing flax could not simultaneously be used for growing grain;[36] capital invested in wool or looms could not be used to buy cattle or build a barn. So, for example, opportunity costs explain why industries often arose in barren, mountainous regions: the opportunity cost of allocating labour, land, and capital to industry was very low in terms of foregone agricultural income.

An important component of opportunity costs is *transactions costs*: costs incurred in all the transactions connected with obtaining inputs, moving the product along from one stage of production to the next, and selling it to the final customer. Transactions costs include costs of transportation, negotiation, information, contract enforcement, protection from coercion, and so on. Chapter 4 of this volume illustrates the enormous addition to the final price to customers caused simply by two of the most easily quantified transactions costs, those of transportation fees and customs charges. Other transactions costs, such as those incurred in preventing embezzlement of raw materials or conveying information about changes in demand from potential customers to producers, are harder to quantify but no less important.

Thinking about the 'location factors' for early modern industries in terms of costs gives us a powerful tool for understanding why industries arose in certain regions of Germany rather than others, and why different industries responded to changing circumstances in different ways. An industry was more likely to arise in a region where its particular mix of inputs and transactions was least costly. Once in existence, an industry organized production so as to minimize costs within the constraints imposed by the natural and social characteristics of the region. This did not even require conscious calculation on the part of producers: the grim realities of survival meant that if you produced at higher cost than spinners, weavers, or metal-workers in a neighbouring region, your products went unsold on export markets, your family went hungry, and you were not be able to go on producing. Even the protectionist legislation of cities and princes created only regional or, at most, national monopolies, and could not protect producers from cost competition on international export markets.[37] Poverty and scarcity alone ensured that cost mattered. What, then, determined the costs – and thus the location and development – of industries in early modern Germany?

Industry and nature

Early modern industries were generally more dependent on nature than industries are nowadays. Because agriculture made up most of the economy, the opportunity cost of using resources in industry was strongly affected by the costs of using them in agriculture, and these in turn were powerfully affected by natural factors such as soil and climate. Because trade was still costly and primitive, industries were still very reliant on local inputs, and thus strongly affected by the natural endowments of the local region. In most early modern industries, relatively immobile inputs (such as raw materials and labour) made up a larger percentage of costs than mobile inputs (such as capital, technology, and knowhow); again, this made industries more dependent on local resource endowments. As a result, the costs of industrial production in a particular region were affected by the region's natural endowments – its climate, soil, natural resources, energy supplies, topographical barriers to transportation, location near trade routes, and so on.[38] The effect of local natural endowments on industrial cost may even have been higher in early modern Germany than in many other parts of western Europe, because trade faced more obstacles in Germany than elsewhere, and the geographical mobility of labour was often institutionally restricted (by ties of serfdom in the East, for example, or by community citizenship restrictions in the South). That is, the extent to which natural endowments influenced industry depended very much on the extent to which social arrangements increased (or reduced) the costs of moving raw materials and labour away from the place where they occurred 'naturally'.

Perhaps the most important way in which natural endowments affected the opportunity costs of industry, and thus its location and development, was through their influence on agriculture. Where soil and climate were such as to favour agriculture, this increased the opportunity costs of using any resource – labour, capital, or land – for industry instead. This accounts for Kaufhold's finding that German industrial regions, with a few exceptions, did not tend to be located in the fertile plains: eight of the nine great ranges of hills in Germany – the Swabian Jura, the Black Forest, the Eifel, the Sauerland, the Harz, the Sudeten, the Erzgebirge, and the Thuringian Forest – contained one or more industrial regions.[39] The less fertile soils and lower temperatures common at higher altitudes reduced potential agrarian yields, thereby lowering industrial opportunity costs. But a hilly location was not sufficient for the emergence of an industrial region, as is shown by the example of the non-industrialized Bohemian Forest in Bavaria. Nor was it necessary, as is shown by the location of some of the most important industrial regions in Germany in the fertile plains: the vigorous linen and silk region around Krefeld, Gladbach, and Rheydt in the

Rhineland; the important linen industry of the western Münsterland of Westphalia; and the linen region in Lower Saxony. This is not surprising, since there were many factors other than agricultural infertility which influenced the costs of industry.

Nature also clearly affected industrial costs through raw materials. Where nature provided existing deposits of raw materials (such as iron ore or wood), or favoured their cultivation (as with flax or wool), they would tend to be cheaper. Holding other factors constant, this would favour the rise of industries which used these materials. However, other factors, such as the cost of labour, were not always held constant. This made it profitable to sell natural raw materials to areas with low labour costs or other advantages instead of using them in industry locally. The existence of trade meant that natural endowments of raw materials were seldom sufficient in themselves to give rise to an industry.[40]

But they were very important for industries such as metals and glass, which used large volumes of heavy raw materials or fuels which were costly to transport from their 'natural' location.[41] Fuels became even more important for the iron industry during the sixteenth century with the spread of the 'indirect process', which required much higher heat levels, consuming more than 250 kilograms of charcoal to produce 100 kilograms of raw iron.[42] Accordingly, the German iron industries did arise in close proximity to ore deposits and/or forests: in the Thuringian Forest, the Harz, Upper Saxony, Upper Silesia, the Upper Palatinate, the Saar and Neuwieder Becken in the central Rhineland, and in several areas of the northern Rhineland.[43] The inexorable rise in costs triggered by exhaustion of ore or wood deposits led to the decline of many of the great sixteenth-century German iron regions (such as the Upper Palatinate) around 1600, and the emergence of new centres (such as the Harz and Silesia) in the course of the seventeenth and eighteenth centuries.[44] Iron-processing was often very dependent on water-power to drive the forge-hammers, and thus smithies tended to be located along waterways. As Reininghaus observes, this prevented iron-goods industries from arising in the north German plains, where the waterways were too slow to drive hammers; wind power did not provide an adequate substitute.[45] Glass, too, required large quantities of three heavy raw materials: lime, siliceous earth or quartz sand, and wood for potash and (especially) fuel. The scarcity of these materials meant that the glass industry was even more 'mobile' than the iron industry: as the example of Hesse shows, glass areas were worked out very quickly indeed. As a consequence, glass alone rarely determined the emergence or survival of an industrial region.[46]

As the early modern period progressed, however, even the metal and glass industries depended less on local raw materials and more on imports. As early as the sixteenth century, many German iron-*producing* regions were supplying raw and half-finished iron and steel to separate iron-*processing* regions, and this tendency had become almost ubiquitous by the eighteenth century. The iron-processing regions of Mark and Berg in the Rhineland, for instance, obtained raw iron and steel and half-finished goods from separate (although not very distant) regions in the Siegerland and the principality of Nassau-Dillenburg. Glass, too, was transported from its production areas (like those in the Upper Palatinate) to separate nearby centres of polishing and mirror production (in Nuremberg and Fürth). Charcoal was increasingly imported into iron-smelting areas: in the eighteenth century, as they ran out of wood, the Harz imported charcoal from the Solling, and the Siegerland from the Sauerland of Westphalia.[47] Social arrangements could help make up for natural scarcity: thus the Siegerland managed to sustain an expanding metal industry between 1650 and 1800 despite scarcity of charcoal, through the *Haubergwirtschaft*, a system of collective administration and rational cultivation of forests.[48] In a number of German territories, governments and communities re-planted the native deciduous trees with faster-growing conifers to replace fuel supplies more rapidly (as discussed in Chapter 1 of this volume). Thus not only natural endowments but also trade and the social organization of resource exploitation affected the costs of raw materials and fuels, and thus the location of industry.

Natural endowments were less important for textile industries, which used lighter and more easily tradeable raw materials, and little if any fuel. Silk and cotton could not in any case be economically cultivated in Germany; it was only the costs of flax, hemp, and wool which could be affected by natural variations among German regions.[49] Linen production did arise in those areas of Germany with the soils (lime and sand) and climate (cool and wet) required for growing flax and hemp: on a band running through northern Central Europe from the lower Rhineland through Westphalia, Saxony, northern Bohemia, and Silesia; and a smaller area in Swabia in the South.[50] Yet the Saxon Vogtland, although 'no less endowed with a favourable climate for flax culture . . . never developed a linen business of commercial significance' (although it did develop many other industries).[51] That is, natural endowments were not sufficient to bring a linen region into existence. Nor were they necessary to create one: during the early modern period, linen yarn began to be exported in huge volumes from regions where flax was cultivated and spun, to others which specialized in weaving, bleaching, lace-making, stocking-knitting, or producing any number of other fancy goods. Before 1600, Swabia was importing linen yarn from Austria, Bohemia, and Silesia, and by 1700 it was exporting yarn in bulk to Switzerland. The Wupper Valley and the county of Mark in the Rhineland imported yarn from Westphalia, Lower Saxony, Hesse, and Silesia, and sent their own woven and bleached goods to France for further processing into luxury items. Silesia imported low-quality yarn from Bohemia, Moravia, and Saxony, and exported high-quality *Lothgarn* to The Netherlands for lace-making. Upper Lusatia exported its own high-quality yarn to Holland and England, while its own weavers imported lower-quality yarn from Bohemia.[52] This enormous trade in linen yarn reduced the importance of natural endowments in determining the location and development of German linen regions in the longer run.

The German woollen industries, too, initially grew up (during the fifteenth and sixteenth centuries) on the basis of indigenous sheep herds. The loss of many of these herds during the Thirty Years War is supposed to have been the cause of the decline of the German woollen industry. Certainly, those few German woollen regions which survived increasingly relied on imports of raw materials.[53] Thus Monschau in the Eifel area of the northern Rhineland became famed for producing some of the finest woollens in Europe, using imports of Spanish Merino wool.[54] The production of worsteds, lighter and cheaper cloths made of long-stranded combed wool rather than the shorter carded wool used for woollens, also initially established itself in areas with indigenous supplies of wool: in the Württemberg Black Forest from c. 1560 onward, and in Gera and the Obereichsfeld in Thuringia in the later seventeenth century. However, all three main German worsted regions increasingly depended on raw-wool imports, the Württemberg Black Forest from as early as 1600.[55]

Because industrial regions, being export-orientated, depended on trade to sell their output and obtain foodstuffs, and also increasingly imported raw materials, their costs were affected by geographical location. Ease of transportation or proximity to trade routes or trade fairs meant lower transactions costs. This was more important for goods in which transport and other transactions costs made up a higher proportion of the final price at which the wares could be sold: transactions costs thus mattered much more for cheap mass-market wares than for expensive luxury products, and more for heavy goods (such as metals) than for light wares (such as textiles). The enormously lower costs of water transportation ought to have given advantages to those German regions located along the short northern coastline and on the five great rivers (the Rhine, the Danube, the Weser, the Elbe, and the Oder). But the location and development of German industrial regions does not clearly follow the availability of water transportation. The North Sea coast and neighbouring territories were among the least industrialized parts of Germany. The Elbe flowed through highly industrialized Saxony, but also through almost completely non-industrialized Brandenburg. The Rhine flowed through the highly industrialized Rhineland, but also through the non-industrialized areas of Baden and Anterior Austria in the far South-West. Württemberg did not extend as far as the Danube, and during most of the early modern period the Württemberg stretch of the Neckar was not navigable.[56] Nevertheless, Württemberg was more highly industrialized than neighbouring Bavaria (with the Danube) or Baden (with the Rhine). The Westphalian county of Ravensberg became and remained an important linen region despite the fact that its distance from trade routes made food imports too costly, so that it had to produce its own grain supply.[57] The Monschau woollen industry became 'the first and most renowned in Europe', despite the extraordinarily high transport costs caused by its

difficult location; admittedly, this was partly due to the fact that it produced very high-quality cloths, for which transportation costs comprised a
relatively low share of the (high) final price which could be charged to customers.[58] The stimulus which trade provided to industry appears to have
depended as much on reduction in transactions costs through the activities
of merchants – their seeking out of low-cost transportation and market
links, their transmission of information from customer to producer, their
financing of the delay between production and sales – as on that engendered by natural location. Based on the geographical distribution of
German industrial regions, Kaufhold concludes that 'the great trade routes
oriented themselves to the main locations of industry, more than the other
way around'.[59]

Germany's natural resource endowments did contribute to the location
and development of its industries before 1800. But their influence was circumscribed. Natural resources were more important for industries requiring large volumes of heavy raw materials and fuels than for those with
lighter and easily traded inputs. They were more important for earlier
stages of production (such as smelting or spinning) than for later ones (such
as smithing or weaving). Above all, the influence of nature in a given case
depended on social arrangements, especially trade. As trade became less
costly and more widespread, local endowments declined in importance relative to other influences on costs. Thus industries arose between 1600 and
1800 in areas of Germany without obvious natural advantages, while other
areas endowed with cheap raw materials, good energy supplies, favourable
location on waterways, and infertile soils for agriculture failed to develop
into industrial regions. Nature alone was neither necessary nor sufficient to
cause industries to arise in particular regions or develop in specific ways.

This should not be surprising. People make economic decisions within a
framework defined not just by nature but by society. That is, the costs of
any economic activity – including industry – are affected by the *social* and
institutional framework governing the transactions through which inputs
are obtained, production is organized, and output is sold. It is sometimes
assumed that markets are the most important social institutions governing
economic activity. But in most societies markets operate within the constraints imposed by other social institutions. This was certainly the case in
early modern Germany. Markets in labour, land, capital, raw materials,
foodstuffs, and industrial output – and thus the costs of all these goods –
were constrained by a variety of non-market institutions. In the countryside, where a great deal of German industrial production occurred before
1800, markets were regulated by village communities and manorial systems
with powerful landlords. In towns and cities, where most trade and a good
share of industrial production still took place, markets were constrained by
the powers and privileges of the towns themselves and their constituent
craft guilds and merchant companies. In both town and countryside, markets were increasingly regulated by the expanding early modern state. In

Germany territorial fragmentation meant that social institutions evolved differently, and varied enormously, over short distances.[60] The ways in which markets were formally and informally regulated by other social institutions affected the costs, and thus the location and development, of most industries in early modern Germany.

Industry and rural society

By 1800 a larger share of industrial production was taking place in the countryside than had been the case in 1600, partly because of urban decline and partly because of faster rural growth.[61] Rural economic activity was regulated by landlords within the manorial system, and by village communities. Although formally organized around agrarian production, these institutions, because they regulated the use of labour, land, and capital in agriculture, inevitably affected the opportunity cost of these inputs in industry. Landlords and communities remained powerful in most parts of Germany until the later eighteenth century, to a much later date than, for example, in Flanders or in England.[62] But the precise ways in which they regulated the rural economy varied enormously from one German territory to the next, in a way which cannot be reduced merely to the distinction between the two ideal-typical German agrarian systems, the eastern *Gutsherrschaft* (with powerful landlords, strong ties of serfdom, heavy labour dues, and large demesne operations) and the western *Grundherrschaft* (with weak landlords, few ties of serfdom, rents in cash or kind, and little demesne activity).

This is illustrated by the relationship between early industrialization and *Gutsherrschaft*. It is often argued that *Gutsherrschaft* – or indeed any agrarian system which gave substantial powers to landlords – was incompatible with the expansion of early modern industry.[63] It is certainly true that institutional powers could enable landlords, if they desired, to prevent rural people from engaging in industry. In many parts of northern and eastern Germany, landlords did precisely this. These were fertile regions offering high returns to agriculture; thus when peasants sought to shift to industry, it was not because it was more productive than agriculture but because it was less subject to landlord extortion. High agrarian productivity meant landlords had little incentive to incur the costs of redefining their manorial powers to enable them to extort dues from peasants' industrial work. But in less fertile regions the incentives were different. Here, people really did produce more valuable output working in industry than in agriculture, and as long as landlords could extend their powers to profit from it, they had an incentive to let their rural subjects shift to industry. The requisite widening of landlords' powers was ensured during the so-called 'second serfdom' – the state-supported expansion in landlord powers in most areas of *Gutsherrschaft* from the later sixteenth century on. This combination of agricultural infertility and 'second serfdom' permitted the rise of export-orientated industrial regions under conditions of *Gutsherrschaft* in many parts of eastern and Central Europe: in Silesia (ruled by Austria until annexed by Prussia in 1740–2), Bohemia, Moravia, Poland, Bulgaria, and parts of Russia.[64]

Originally it was argued that these 'feudal proto-industries' arose only where there was a weakening or deviation from 'classic' *Gutsherrschaft*, characterized by relations of serfdom defined according to strict legal criteria, and by large demesne farms specializing in grain production.[65] Empirical studies, however, suggest that the only 'deviation' from *Gutsherrschaft* in proto-industrial regions of Central and eastern Europe was that landlords exploited their institutional powers in the industrial sector instead of (or as well as) in agriculture. The *Gutswirtschaft* (demesne economy) did not disappear, but rather expanded to include other rural activities (in addition to the classic grain farming): mining, smelting, glass-making, flax-growing, spinning, and weaving, whether in putting-out systems or in manufactories or 'proto-factories' on the feudal estate. Landlords were no weaker in industrial than in agrarian regions of *Gutsherrschaft*. On the contrary, they permitted industries to arise precisely because their expanding extra-economic powers enabled them to extract revenues from them: through loom fees, selling monopoly rights over peasants' output to foreign merchants, compelling workers to buy demesne flax at above-market prices, encouraging their rural subjects to shift to industry by restricting access to land, levying labour dues in the form of transporting ores and fuels and even sometimes spinning flax, using ties of serfdom to recruit 'forced wage-labour' at below-market wages, and many other strategies.[66] It was precisely their low labour costs, forcibly maintained through landlords' extra-economic powers, which made the export industries in areas such as Silesia and Bohemia so competitive internationally. What mattered for industry was not whether landlords were strong or not, but the precise powers they had and how they used them, and these varied from one region of *Gutsherrschaft* to the next.

It was only in the longer term that the powers of landlords under *Gutsherrschaft*, which in Silesia, for instance, kept flax and labour costs so low and the region's yarn and linen exports so competitive, became an obstacle to industrial development. Beginning in the 1770s, the challenge of English cotton and mechanized production could not be met by cheap flax and labour alone, but required technical adaptation, skill, and capital. But technological changes in linen production were opposed by Silesian landlords concerned to maintain the revenue stream from their serf weavers; the Prussian state instituted legal prohibitions on new practices. Capital flowed into landownership rather than industrial machines, because of the enormous legal privileges associated with it under *Gutsherrschaft*. In the last decades of the eighteenth century, as the Saxon and Rhenish linen industries began – however gradually – to shift to cotton and machines, the greatest German linen industry of all, that of Silesia, slid inexorably into crisis and ultimate de-industrialization.[67] In the words of Herbert Kisch:

> In many ways the Silesian linen trades corroborate the contention … that domestic industry was not always, as might be generalized from the English case, an agent of progress; rather, where domestic trades have been appendices of the feudal order they have had the opposite effect.68

Strong landlord powers were not incompatible with export-oriented domestic industry, but they were incompatible with long-term economic growth.

The more limited landlord powers characteristic of *Grundherrschaft* in Germany west of the Elbe could not artificially lower labour costs, but they permitted (or were associated with) other cost advantages: labour markets not constrained by serfdom, more flexible land use, less incentive for capital to flow into landholding, livelier commerce, and more open rural markets. The rise of export-orientated industries in areas such as Saxony, the Rhineland, and Württemberg benefited from the relatively limited powers of landlords there to regulate rural society. Peter Kriedte finds that silk processing tended to arise in those villages around Krefeld in the Rhineland where landlords were least restrictive, a pattern also observed in parts of England and Switzerland.[69] But there were also areas of *Grundherrschaft*, such as Westphalia, where although landlord powers did not altogether prevent the rise of export-orientated linen production, they did exercise a limiting influence on it. Thus in parts of Westphalia, landlords continued to exercise significant influence over land use and expansion of the rural industrial labour force, at least until the abolition of the *Acker-Marken-Wirtschaft* (the collective system of regulating agriculture, which often involved important powers for landlords as well as peasant communities). The *Acker-Marken-Wirtschaft* was not abolished until the 1770s in the Prussian-ruled county of Ravensberg, and not until around 1810 in the neighbouring prince-bishopric of Osnabrück. Wolfgang Mager ascribes Ravensberg's ultimately successful factory industrialization in the nineteenth century, while most other Westphalian linen districts de-industrialized, partly to the early breakdown of the Ravensberg *Acker-Marken-Wirtschaft*.[70] Thus even west of the Elbe landlord powers, while not preventing the rise of export-oriented industries, did constrain their growth in some regions until the last decades of the Old Empire, and set certain regions on divergent paths of industrialization.

The other main social institution regulating the rural economy was the village community. Originally it was argued that export-orientated rural industries only arose where communities were weak.[71] This seemed to be borne out by early research showing proto-industries arising in weak communities in preference to strong ones, in parts of England and Switzerland.[72] But later research has shown that although strong community institutions did increase the costs of industries, it did not prevent them from arising in regions with other cost advantages.[73] Communities, too, varied in strength from one German territory to the next, depending on the local institutional legacy, as well as the changing powers of landlords and princes. With regional exceptions, they tended to be weaker in areas of *Gutsherrschaft* or effective absolutism, and strong where landlords were weak or princes supported local village powers in exchange for fiscal and administrative support.[74]

The cost advantages of weak communities are shown by the concentration and vigour of industry in Saxony and the Rhineland, where village institutions were often as weak as in England or the Low Countries. In many parts of Saxony village communities began to weaken in the early sixteenth century, and received little support from the state: settlement and rural factor markets began to operate relatively freely, and rural export industries proliferated.[75] In many areas of the Rhineland, as well, village communities appear to have been relatively powerless even before rural industries arose in the sixteenth century.[76] But in this, as in other aspects of their social organization, the Rhineland and Saxony were exceptional.

In other German industrial regions, village institutions were on the whole much stronger. Although they did not wholly prevent the rise of export industries, they imposed costs which had enduring effects. Thus in the linen region of Ravensberg in Westphalia, Wolfgang Mager identifies 'the effectiveness of the communal *Markenwirtschaft*' as one of 'the two basic factors of economic and social retardation', which 'lasted until the late eighteenth or early nineteenth century'.[77] The *Markenwirtschaft* was a communally organized agrarian system imposing a close regulation of land and labour markets as well as many other economic practices; and it was only gradually, in the course of the eighteenth century, that the Prussian state begin to permit infringements on it in Ravensberg. The forcible abolition of communal controls in the 1770s unleashed rapid industrial growth, creating a proletarianized labour force before international linen demand fell, and giving Ravensberg the industrial momentum to survive until mechanization became possible in the 1850s. In the neighbouring linen region of Osnabrück, by contrast, the prince-bishops maintained the *Markenwirtschaft* until *c.* 1810; this constrained industrial growth and, in the view of both Wolfgang Mager and Jürgen Schlumbohm, helped to set Osnabrück on the path to de-industrialization.[78]

In the German South, communities were notoriously strong until well into the nineteenth century, restricting marriage and settlement, regulating markets in most commodities, and enforcing the privileges of rural guilds.[79] Although these constraints increased costs and reduced flexibility, they did not altogether exclude the growth of domestic industries where other local advantages were present. In Württemberg, for instance, partible inheritance generated plentiful labour, manorial restrictions were weak, and the great south German trading cities were near. Consequently, the Swabian Jura (with favourable conditions for flax cultivation) developed into a linen region, while the margins of the eastern Black Forest (with infertile soils, indigenous sheep-raising, plentiful water-power, and a tradition of woollen manufacturing) became a dense centre of worsted exports. Village communities remained strong, and it was not until the later eighteenth century that their rigidities – among others – began to weigh heavily on the two great Württemberg industrial regions, contributing to industrial stagnation, technological backwardness, and a failure to adapt to the challenges of cotton and mechanization.[80] In many regions of Germany, therefore, the powers of rural communities, like the powers of landlords, did not prevent the rise of export industries between 1600 and 1800, but did constrain their development.

Industry and urban society

Although rural industry grew enormously in significance between 1600 and 1800 towns retained a variety of important industrial functions, something not always recognized in the theories of proto-industrialization, which tend to regard towns as simply the location of the merchants who organized the rural putting-out systems.[81] Towns certainly did play the dominant role in organizing the trade in industrial raw materials, food for the industrial population, and the products they manufactured, as well as in supplying the capital to finance the gap between purchasing inputs and selling outputs. This was especially the case in Germany, where, although rural industrial traders did arise, in most territories until the late eighteenth century their illegal status limited their operations (as we will see below). But towns were also where *production* took place, especially for certain industries and stages of manufacturing: for processes involving expensive raw materials, such as silk, urban location reduced embezzlement; for those requiring a highly skilled labour-force, such as weaving fine woollens, towns facilitated training and monitoring; for those requiring rapid response to changes in fashion, such as dyeing and finishing textiles, towns eased information transmission; and for those using large pieces of capital equipment, such as calico printing, towns provided a central location. Finally, they functioned as wealthy and concentrated pools of consumption and demand, and thus as important markets for rural production. Because towns played this range of essential roles in early modern industry, urban institutions affected industrial costs.

Originally, based on the examples of England and the Low Countries, it was argued that proto-industrialization led to the breakdown of urban industrial institutions: the powers of towns over the countryside, and the legal privileges of guilds and merchant companies.[82] But subsequent research has shown that the English and Low Countries pattern whereby urban institutions broke down at the same time as industrial regions emerged in the sixteenth century was the exception, not the rule.[83] The only areas of Germany in which the industrial privileges of towns, guilds, and merchant companies played as little role as in the Low Countries and England were parts of the northern Rhineland, especially the county of Moers (around Krefeld) and the duchy of Jülich. The enormously successful linen and silk city of Krefeld had no institutional powers over the country-side, and its industrial producers and merchants enjoyed no corporate privileges. This was partly because of Krefeld's quasi-village origins (with a population of only about 600 in 1650), and partly because it was ruled by the Dutch princes of Orange according to *laissez-faire* economic policies until 1702. Krefeld merchants only began to obtain monopolies and privileges during Prussian rule in the eighteenth century.[84] The nearby duchy of Jülich had a constitutional tradition of *Gewerbefreiheit* (freedom from guilds), which attracted entrepreneurial Protestant refugees to Monschau in the sixteenth century, turning it into the foremost fine woollen centre in Germany. Not until the mid-eighteenth century did producers seek to establish guilds; the merchants responded by establishing the so-called *Feine Gewandschaft*, a corporate group which opposed the producers, lobbied the state, and tried to limit entry to the trade.[85]

But this relative lack of urban industrial regulations and corporate privileges was exceptional, even for the Rhineland. The woollen industry of Aachen stagnated in the eighteenth century until guild restrictions on production were removed in 1798, while neighbouring Burtscheid, whose guilds had declined in the seventeenth century, flourished.[86] In the Wupper Valley, the dukes of Berg in 1527 granted state privileges over bleaching and trading linens to a powerful merchant company, the notorious Wuppertaler Garnnahrung, which was still regulating the regional textile industry in its own interests in the late eighteenth century. So effective and so onerous were the Garnnahrung privileges that the rural linen-weavers set up their own rural guild in 1738, which attempted to regulate the industry in its members' interests until abolished in 1783 through Garnnahrung opposition and army intervention.[87] Similar rural guilds were established elsewhere in the duchy of Berg, by producers of cutlery, scythes, and small iron wares in Solingen and Remscheid; new guilds were still being formed as late as the 1750s.[88]

It is sometimes argued that guilds in reality often failed to impose effective economic regulations: that they admitted outsiders freely, did not impose low wages on their employees, did not place constraints on the work of women or youths, did not restrict output or impose high prices on customers, and did not resist new techniques and new production practices. Sometimes it is even claimed that guilds positively benefited the economy, through overcoming capital-market imperfections, maintaining quality standards, defending intellectual property rights, guiding and supervising the production process, and providing a low-cost framework for industrial conflict resolution.[89] Theoretical speculations such as these, about the neutral or even beneficial economic effects of guilds, can only be investigated through concrete, micro-level empirical research into the activities of particular guilds in particular industries. Such research has, as a rule, not yet been carried out.

Available studies of German industrial regions, however, do provide certain indications that the net effect of guilds and merchant companies, even in the relatively 'liberal' Rhineland industries, was often far from positive. Thus, for instance, the Remscheid scythe smiths' guild successfully resisted the introduction of water-driven scythe hammers in the eighteenth century.[90] The Solingen cutlery-makers' guild resisted new techniques, resulting in technological backwardness compared to western European competitors; bitter corporate conflicts further contributed to its stagnation toward the end of the eighteenth century.[91] Attempts by Brügelmann, a Wupper Valley merchant, to set up the first English-style spinning mill in Germany in 1782 confronted huge opposition from the Wuppertaler Garnnahrung and the rural weavers' guild; eventually he obtained a state monopoly concession, but built the mill outside the Wupper Valley. As late as 1792, the Garnnahrung was prosecuting one of its members who tried to set up a ribbon manufactory in Alsace.[92] Thus the continuing importance of corporate privileges during both 'proto-industrialization' and early factory industrialization probably did contribute to the industrial backwardness of even this most 'advanced' of German industrial regions in 1800.

In Saxony, too, urban and corporate privileges dogged the expansion of industry between 1600 and 1800. Until the Thirty Years War, linen-weaving was in many areas an urban monopoly; most linen was sold through collective *Zünftkäufe* ('guild purchases') made by foreign merchant-houses, particularly those of Nuremberg. Only in the course of the seventeenth century did Saxon linen production shift decisively to the countryside.[93] Even then, towns and guilds successfully asserted control over many aspects of production, not only for linen-weaving but also for lace- and trimmings-making, ribbon-weaving, and the emerging cotton industry. Thus new regional guilds were formed among the makers of trimmings and lace in the Erzgebirge-Vogtland in the late seventeenth and early eighteenth centuries.[94] The urban ribbon-makers' guilds of Lusatia obtained a state ban on ribbon mills, so strictly enforced that its repeal in 1765 was followed by a boom in rural production; again, this suggests that the guild regulations had exercised real – and negative – economic effects on rural production.[95] The emerging Vogtland cotton industry permitted rural spinners, but retained weaving as a closely regulated urban monopoly throughout much of the eighteenth century, so that as late as 1786 two-thirds of muslin workers in the region around Plauen were still guilded.[96]

But it was the trade in industrial output that was particularly closely monopolized in Saxony by cities and guilds. Rural producers were legally obliged to sell their output through the towns and the urban merchant guilds in most Saxon industrial regions until the early nineteenth century; although illegal rural traders naturally emerged, their operations were limited by the risks and penalties of having to trade in the 'informal sector'.[97] Yet it was not the privileged urban merchants of Zittau and Löbau but illegal village traders who in the 1770s 'promoted the shift away from linen work to cotton' in Lusatia, and after 1800 'ventured into mechanical cotton spinning'.[98] In the Vogtland, rival guilds of cotton 'merchants' and 'manufacturers' were founded in 1764, bitterly contested all changes in the industry for the next 50 years, and retained valuable privileges until the 1840s. A state monopoly was still in force in 1805, and it was not until after 1817 that the structure of corporate privileges in the Vogtland cotton industry began gradually to be dismantled, permitting successful adaptation to English competition.[99]

In neighbouring Thuringia, in which a number of industrial regions arose between 1600 and 1800, towns were less powerful than in Saxony, but rural guilds appear to have been more widespread. Until the later eighteenth century, guild organizations dominated some or all stages of production among the small-iron-goods-makers in the principality of Schmalkalden,[100] the gun-builders of Suhl,[101] the knife-smiths of Ruhla in the Thuringian Forest,[102] the toymakers and slatemakers in the Meininger Oberland,[103] the stocking-knitters in the duchy of Weimar,[104] and the worsted-weavers in the Obereichsfeld.[105] Thuringian merchants also formed companies which enjoyed monopolies and other state privileges over export industries, such as the company formed in 1710 in the weapon-making industry of Zella and Mehlis in the Thuringian Forest,[106] or that formed with a ducal privilege in 1789 over the toymaking industry of the Meininger Oberland.[107] Again, these corporate organizations had real economic effects. Far from providing a framework for rapid resolution of costly economic conflicts, guilds themselves generated bitter struggles within industries: guild conflicts, for instance, contributed to the decline of the stocking-knitting industry of the duchy of Weimar between 1740 and 1760.[108] Far from failing to enforce restrictions on entry into practice or volume of output, the Obereichsfeld linen-weavers' guild constrained growth, as is shown by the fact that linen-weaving expanded in the Obereichsfeld only when the guild monopoly was removed in 1780.[109] Given this long survival of town, guild, and company privileges, it is not surprising that even in comparatively 'advanced' Saxony and Thuringia industry was less developed in 1800 than it was in western Europe.

In the Westphalian linen regions, too, the privileges of towns and urban merchants cast a long shadow over industrial development. The urban linen-weavers' guilds lost their monopolies in the late seventeenth or early eighteenth century, and rural guilds did not arise.[110] But rural spinners and weavers were obliged by law to sell yarn and wool through *Leggen* (inspection offices) in the towns. This turned the linen export trade into a legal monopoly of urban merchants; in some towns, such as Bielefeld, the linen merchants established a privileged company.[111] Most of the Westphalian *Leggen* were strengthened by princes in the 1770s, and survived into the nineteenth century.[112] Although there was some rural smuggling, Schlumbohm has estimated that the majority of linen produced between the 1770s and the mid-nineteenth century in the prince-bishopric of Osnabrück, for instance, passed through the *Legge*.[113] The successful transition to factory industry in the county of Ravensberg around 1850, while other Westphalian linen regions (such as Osnabrück) de-industrialized, is ascribed partly to the less thorough enforcement of the *Legge*, permitting black-market operations by illegal rural traders.[114] Even so, the privileged company of linen merchants in Bielefeld delayed mechanization for decades, and boycotted the first spinning mill in 1852; the second mill was established in 1856 only with state assistance and foreign managers.[115]

In Württemberg, urban privileges took a different form: towns had few powers over the countryside, but privileged merchant companies and 'regional' (urban-rural) guilds exercised monopolies over both urban and rural industry. In the Württemberg Black Forest, worsted weavers were organized into district-level guilds with equal jurisdiction over both town and village producers, which closely regulated every aspect of production and were not abolished until long into the nineteenth century. From 1650 until 1797, weavers were obliged to sell all their cloths to a privileged company of merchant-dyers, the famous Calwer Zeughandlungskompagnie, at fixed quotas and prices. Bitter corporate conflicts attest to the real economic effectiveness of both guilds and company, and to the fact that they did not provide a framework for peaceful conflict resolution; if anything, they may have increased industrial conflict by creating monopoly rents for different groups to struggle over.[116] Further east, on the Swabian Jura, the linen-weavers in the districts of Urach, Heidenheim, and Blaubeuren were also organized into rural guilds until 1828, and until the 1790s were obliged to sell to privileged merchant companies under similar conditions to those prevailing in the Black Forest worsted industry.[117] Although territorial fragmentation and the proximity of Ulm facilitated smuggling, the economic impact of the company monopolies is shown not only by the generations of bitter conflict they evoked, but also by the fact that the Urach and Heidenheim companies were able to maintain clear price differentials relative to the 'free-market' prices in Ulm.[118] In the Black Forest, both guilds and merchant company controlled entry, output, employment, product selection, prices, and wages, and concertedly resisted competition and new techniques, resulting in the decline of worsted production after about 1800 and a late and difficult transition to factory production.[119] In the

Swabian Jura, company monopolies and state regulation prevented either privileged company merchants or illegal rural traders from amassing the physical or human capital to become the agents of factory industrialization; thus, far from overcoming capital market imperfections, corporate organizations helped to sustain them. The region of Urach failed to shift to cotton or mechanize production, and was only industrialized in the 1860s by outside entrepreneurs.[120] Only in the district of Heidenheim, where company regulation had begun to break down in the 1760s because of repeated bankruptcies, was flexibility sufficient for a gradual shift into cotton in the 1790s, and to mechanical production in the 1830s; even here, the linen-weavers' guild initially violently opposed the shift to cotton.[121] To an even greater extent than in other areas of Germany, therefore, industry in Württemberg was stagnating by 1800 partly because of the late survival of guild and merchant privileges.[122]

Industry and the state in Germany

German industry was also affected by the state. Traditionally, two diametrically opposed views have prevailed about the role of the state in the growth of industry in early modern Europe. One view has been to take mercantilistic industrial policies at face value, and assume that the growing tendency for early modern princes to establish manufactories, subsidize industries, institute protectionist legislation, and set up elaborate structures of industrial regulation successfully encouraged industrialization between 1600 and 1800. In reaction against the many weaknesses of this view many economic historians, including the theorists of proto-industrialization, have almost totally ignored the state, restricting its role to guaranteeing market transactions and occasionally helping merchants coerce producers.[123] Neither view is wholly satisfactory. While early modern German princes' direct support of industry saw very mixed success, their indirect role, particularly in supporting (or breaking down) other institutions, was substantial.

Traditionally, accounts of the role of the state in early modern German industry have focused on the attempts made by many German princes to support specific industries directly, in accordance with the principles of cameralism (the German variant of mercantilism). Where such protectionist legislation freed industrial producers from taxation or conscription, granted them subsidies, or enforced lower-than-market prices for their labour or raw materials, it could lower their costs relative to those of less favoured producers, and enhance their ability to compete, at least in the short term. But in most cases, such cost-reducing privileges were combined with others which increased costs: monopolies (leading to output restrictions and higher prices); restrictive practices (entry barriers, labour-market regulations, prohibitions on women's work); and resistance to (or outright prohibitions on) new techniques, new products, or new production practices.

The net effect of state support varied from industry to industry in Germany. On the whole, however, the vast majority of these attempts were costly failures, and many damaged other economic endeavours.[124] The Prussian princes in particular are famous for their persistent and expensive attempts to establish and protect luxury industries, especially in Berlin and Potsdam. However, deeper research reveals the many costs these policies imposed on other local economic activities and on Prussia's own Rhineland possessions, and the inefficiencies and corruption they fostered within the protected industries.[125] Their success was minimal: not a single industrial region developed in the central and eastern provinces of Prussia before 1800, and by the end of the eighteenth century it was cotton, the one branch almost wholly neglected by the state, which dominated Berlin's textile sector.[126] So notorious was the long, expensive, and futile record of royal support for the Berlin silk industry that the Comte de Mirabeau wrote in the 1790s, referring to the successful silk factories of Krefeld in the Rhineland, 'Unhappy those [factories] if ever a Prussian king should love them.'[127] The Prussian pattern was repeated elsewhere. In Baden, state foundations of privileged 'proto-factories' in Pforzheim and elsewhere failed to flourish, while the neighbouring Black Forest, neglected by the state, developed by 1800 into 'one of the most important German industrial regions'.[128] The Thuringian Forest was one of the most important glass-smelting regions of Germany, if not of Europe, yet new glassworks established with princely support in the early eighteenth century almost all failed because they were set up without considering fuel supplies.[129] Based on his survey of German industrial regions before 1800, Kaufhold concludes:

> When the different industrial regions are inspected, it quickly emerges that the influence exerted on their development by cameralistic support for industry was generally not high. ... [In] several regions there was state support for industry, but although this strengthened the position of industry, it did not decisively influence it. Above all, however, absence of state support did not have a negative effect on industry – if anything, the converse was the case. Several of the most important German industrial regions, such as those in the duchy of Berg, on the left bank of the lower Rhine, in the county of Mark, and almost all the linen regions, developed without state assistance, or with very little. In summary, it must be stressed that if one subtracts the state components from the picture of early modern German industrial regions ... its basic lineaments remain unchanged.[130]

But although purposeful state intervention in industry seldom succeeded, state activity for non-economic purposes had massive indirect repercussions on many German industries. The annexation of Silesia by Prussia in 1740–2 set in motion a re-equilibration of the linen industry not just in Silesia itself, but also in neighbouring Saxony and Bohemia, with lasting repercussions for the whole 'linen triangle'.[131] The industries of the northern Rhineland were similarly disrupted in the 1790s, when much of the left bank came under French administration.[132] Most important of all, however, was state reinforcement or weakening of other social institutions. Especially from the Thirty Years War onward, government was impossible in most parts of Germany without the co-operation of other institutions: the central state granted and enforced the privileges of landlords, village communities, towns, guilds, and merchant companies in tacit exchange for their co-operation in taxation, state borrowing, conscription, regulation, and suppression of domestic discontent.[133]

The role of German princes in sustaining and shaping the powers of landlords and village communities is evident in the development of many German regions. In the central and eastern Prussian provinces, the landlord powers under *Gutsherrschaft*, which prevented the rural population from engaging in industrial activity, derived their strength and longevity from state support. The control of the Silesian linen industry by feudal landlords, endowing it with its extraordinarily low and competitive labour costs, was only possible because of state support for *Gutsherrschaft* during and after the 'second serfdom'. From the 1760s on, the *Landschaft* (a state credit institution) channelled almost all available capital in Silesia to the feudal landlords, thereby depriving industry of investment funds. The Hohenzollerns also prohibited linen mechanization in order to protect the profits landlords derived from their feudal powers over serf weavers.[134] The stance of the prince was also important for the powers of landlords and peasant communities under *Grundherrschaft*. In Westphalia the differing policies of the Hohenzollerns and the prince-bishops of Osnabrück toward manorial controls and the communal *Acker-Marken-Wirtschaft* led to divergent agrarian developments in Ravensberg and Osnabrück, with enduring repercussions for their linen industries.[135] In Württemberg, it was their symbiotic relationship with the state that sustained the powerful local communities well into the nineteenth century.[136]

Urban and corporate institutions, too, could exercise more effective internal regulation of industries with state support, even while their external powers were being surpassed by those of the state.[137] Guilds and merchant companies were increasingly concerned during the early modern period to gain state charters and government enforcement, and in return delivered taxes, loans, bribes, political support, and fiscally useful surveillance of industrial output and trade. In Württemberg, the guilds and merchant companies which monopolized different stages of the export-orientated linen and worsted industries expended enormous resources over a period of centuries in lobbying the state to enforce and extend their privileges; when the merchant companies became unprofitable in the 1790s and sought to dissolve themselves, they encountered enormous state opposition.[138] In the Wupper Valley of the Rhineland, the state issued and enforced the privileges of both the Wuppertaler Garnnahrung and the rural linen-weavers' guild; government support for corporatism did not begin to wane until the 1780s.[139] The *Leggen* and urban merchant privileges in the Westphalian linen industries, and the privileges of Saxon merchant guilds over industrial exports, also relied heavily on state enforcement: where, as in Westphalia, the state supported these privileges, they were effectively enforced until the mid-nineteenth century; where, as in Saxony, it sought to reduce them, rural black-market trading became a source of entrepreneurial flexibility which favoured factory industrialization from the 1780s onwards.

In most Germany territories the state did not become powerful enough to begin to dispense with the support of traditional institutions – landlords, communities, privileged towns, guilds, and merchant companies – until, at earliest, the last decades of the eighteenth century. In Saxony, for instance, it was the growth of central state power which made possible the gradual withdrawal of state support for town and guild privileges. In the Vogtland it was not until 1817 that the government began to remove 'the prohibitions, monopoly rights and restrictions' which had hobbled competition and mechanization in the cotton industry. It was not until the 1840s that it became politically possible in Saxony to neutralize the guilds.[140] In Westphalia it was the strength of the Prussian state which enabled the agrarian reforms in the county of Ravensberg in the 1770s, which in turn created the industrial momentum for the regional linen industry to achieve factory industrialization in the 1850s. Less powerful states, such as – in very different ways – the prince-bishopric of Osnabrück in Westphalia or the duchy of Württemberg in the South remained more dependent on local interests into the nineteenth century, and traditional institutions did not begin to break down until after 1800.

The growth of the early modern state also led to rising public expenditures, making the state a major source of demand. In theory this could have had two effects on industry. On one hand, the demand pull of state expenditures could have drawn idle resources (unemployed labour, hoarded capital) into productive use. But this would only have occurred if the resources used for armies, fortifications, and princely courts were previously lying unused. If not, then state demand simply took away resources already being used in other productive activities; the sectors deprived of these resources would have been harmed rather than stimulated.[141] Both mechanisms are theoretically possible. Which one predominated in early modern Germany can only be answered empirically.

What would one expect to observe empirically, if the demand of the growing German states did mobilize idle resources rather than crowding out existing uses for them, and thus did contribute to industrial growth? Most state spending was for military purposes, so one might expect the most highly militarized German territories to have had the liveliest industries. Accordingly, Brandenburg-Prussia provides most of the examples adduced in support of the view that state demand stimulated early industry: the *Königliches Lagerhaus*, a large textile manufactory established to supply the army in 1713; the *Montierungs-Reglement* of 1714, which stimulated raw-wool production and heavy-woollen-weaving by ordering that only domestic cloth should be used for military uniforms; the hugely profitable Prussian armaments firms.[142] But, as we have already seen, Brandenburg-Prussia, by far the most highly militarized German territory, was one of the least industrialized. Either military spending simply crowded out other, more productive uses for resources; or, even if there was a demand pull, it was not powerful enough to do more than foster a few, isolated manufactories producing directly for the army.

But perhaps military (or court) spending by large states such as Prussia provided a market for industries in other German territories? This seems unlikely, judging by the sectoral distribution of industrial growth in early modern Germany. If military demand played a stimulating role, one would expect to observe growth in the iron sector, weapons manufacturing, and heavy woollen textiles for uniforms. However, as can be seen in Table 9.1, only one of the 39 German industrial regions identified by Kaufhold (the area around Zella, Mehlis, and Suhl in the Thuringian Forest) depended on weapons production. Iron regions, part of whose output may have been exported to manufacture armaments elsewhere, made up a minority of German industrial regions. Much of the output of the most successful iron regions (such as those in the Rhineland) consisted of small metal goods for household use. Heavy woollen cloths, which might have been used for military uniforms, were produced only in three German industrial regions (the Reuß region of Thuringia, and Mark and Berg in the Rhineland), and even there were merely part of a broad palette of products. The same is true of court demand. If princely courts provided a crucial demand pull for early industry, one would expect to observe growth in luxury textiles (fine woollens and silk) and furnishings (porcelain, glass, mirrors, clocks, music boxes, and musical instruments). But comparatively few German industrial regions were based on such luxury products. Instead, the greatest industrial growth in early modern Germany was in cheap, light textiles (linen, worsteds, and cottons), and an enormous variety of smaller items (stockings, gloves, caps, lace, trimmings, cord, braid, embroidery, straw hats, toys, slates, needles, wire, brushes, spoons, pottery, cutlery, and small iron household goods) – which addressed neither military nor court demand, but the mass consumer market.

If demand did play an autonomous role in stimulating industry in early modern Germany, therefore, it came not from the state but from mass consumer markets, whether at home or abroad. There is a certain amount of evidence that from the mid-seventeenth century onward people in parts of Europe (particularly England and the Low Countries) were indeed consuming more market-produced goods. This tendency can also be observed in Germany, although it appears to have accelerated only in the eighteenth century (as discussed in Chapters 4 and 11 of this volume). There is also evidence that more German people were engaging in market-orientated production, although a large proportion of agrarian and industrial production (particularly east of the Elbe) continued to be absorbed by the household, the community, and the feudal economy, and not to reach the market (as discussed in Chapter 3); when it did reach the market, the many barriers to trade quickly made many wares too expensive for the budgets of ordinary Germans.[143] But the causal connection between the growth in market-orientated consumption and the growth in market-orientated production is still obscure: did production grow because consumer demand grew (i.e., because of changing tastes), or because producers and merchants could supply ordinary consumers more cheaply with desirable goods (i.e., because of changing technology and prices)?[144] Much better empirical knowledge of the links between industrial production and consumption in early modern Germany, and Europe more widely, will be needed before we can begin to answer this question. It seems fairly clear, however, that in so far as demand did play any autonomous role, it emanated from ordinary consumers, especially those further down the social scale. There is little evidence that the state – whether the army or the court – played more than a peripheral role in providing markets for early modern German industries. If anything, state expenditures, by requiring high taxation, reduced the disposable income of ordinary consumers, thereby diminishing their ability to provide markets for industrial wares.

In German industry between 1600 and 1800, therefore, the state played a range of roles. Among these, probably the least important was its intentional, though not often effective, intervention to encourage industrial enterprises. State expenditures grew enormously, but provided no more than isolated demand stimuli for German industries, which depended much more on growing consumer markets at home and abroad. German states in this period were perpetually engaged in making war, taxing, capturing and losing territory, and enforcing customs barriers, and all of these activities shaped the international markets within which early export industries operated. But the principal way in which early modern German states affected industry was by helping to maintain and shape the various traditional institutions which had such a wide-ranging impact on most German industries. When these institutions did gradually become weaker at the end of the eighteenth century, it was often through the growth of the state rather than that of the market. In more cases than not, industrial producers merely exchanged the monopolies, privileges, and regulations of traditional social institutions for a different set of non-market institutional constraints laid down by the state; the thoroughgoing state regulation of industry remained a distinguishing characteristic of the German path to factory industrialization in the nineteenth century.[145]

Conclusion

The beginnings of industrialization in Germany, as elsewhere in Europe, are to be found not in the machines and factories of the industrial revolution, but in the busy landscapes of small-scale workers in textiles, metals, wood, and glass which sprang up throughout the continent after about 1500. Indeed, the origins of industry must be sought more widely still, in the proliferation of market-orientated farmers producing food surpluses, and the inventive diligence of small traders and large merchants in creating markets linking consumers with producers of food and manufactured wares in specialized regions otherwise unknown to one another. This process of regional specialization continued and accelerated during the early modern period throughout Europe, including in most parts of German-speaking Central Europe. Yet, while in the sixteenth century German industries had been vigorous and important, by 1800 Germany as a whole was an industrial backwater. Some historians ascribe this to the depredations of the Thirty Years War, others to foreign factory competition at the end of the eighteenth century. But the widely differing responses to these challenges in different parts of Germany suggest that internal factors may have been more important. This is borne out by the German experience of 'proto-industrialization', which did not follow a unilineal development path, but rather showed enormous regional variation.

Early modern industrial growth was distributed very unevenly across early modern Germany. On one hand there were very high concentrations of industry in Saxony-Thuringia, the Rhineland, south-west Germany, and Westphalia-Lower Saxony. On the other, there were wide expanses of Germany which were almost completely non-industrialized – in the far North and East (especially the central and eastern Prussian provinces) and in Bavaria. The crucial question is 'Why?'. Empirical surveys reveal a number of 'location factors' which had to be present for an industrial region to emerge. But they yield little by way of a general explanation for the location and development of industries in different parts of early modern Germany. A more promising approach is offered by consideration of the costs of the inputs and transactions required by industries, which were determined by varying natural and social features.

Germany was by no means under-endowed with natural features favouring industry. It had very significant metal ore deposits; considerable expanses of forest for fuel; some of the largest coal deposits in Europe (in

1800 still all but untapped); and favourable conditions for growing flax and hemp. Although its coastline was restricted, it had five great navigable inland rivers, and a number of partly usable lesser waterways. The southern Imperial Cities lay on the great overland trade routes from the Mediterranean, and Leipzig and Frankfurt an der Oder mediated trade from eastern to western Europe. Germany's industrial backwardness in 1800 cannot be ascribed, therefore, to lack of natural cost advantages. Moreover, as the early modern period progressed and trade expanded, German industries became increasingly independent of local natural-resource endowments.

But industrial costs were also strongly affected by social institutions. Owing to political fragmentation these varied greatly from one German region to the next; but as a general rule, traditional institutions – manorial systems with powerful landlords, village communities, privileged towns, guilds, and merchant companies – survived in Germany for a long time after they had broken down in other parts of western Europe. Partly, this was owing to the 'institutional hothouse' of the Thirty Years War (and the century of almost continual warfare that followed), during which repeated military crises forced German princes to grant and enforce privileges to powerful institutions and groups within their societies in exchange for fiscal, military, and political support. A large number of studies show that the costs and flexibility of industries in most parts of Germany were profoundly affected by the privileges of traditional institutions to the very end of the Old Empire. Even in the most 'advanced' areas – Saxony and the Rhineland – traditional institutions did not begin to break down until the late eighteenth century. Even then, they tended to be replaced not by markets, but by a framework of state regulation. Elsewhere, they lasted long into the nineteenth century, delaying industrialization in Westphalia until the 1850s, and in Württemberg and Silesia until the 1870s. In Bavaria and most parts of Prussia the social institutions which had prevented the emergence of industries in the period between 1600 and 1800 delayed factory industrialization until the very end of the nineteenth century. As a consequence, the characteristics of German industry in the early modern period – its relative retardation, its regional variation, and its pervasive regulation by corporate and state institutions – were mirrored, often in intensified form, during German factory industrialization of the nineteenth century.[146]

Notes

I should like to thank André Carus, Dietrich Ebeling, Jeremy Edwards, Wolfgang Mager, Hamish Scott, Tom Scott, and Bob Scribner, who kindly read and commented upon an earlier version of this chapter and made many useful and stimulating suggestions.

1   'Above-average' refers to the average for Germany in 1800; for a more detailed discussion of the concept of *Gewerbelandschaften* (translated in this chapter as 'industrial regions', but elsewhere sometimes as 'industrial countrysides' or 'industrial landscapes'), see Karl-Heinrich Kaufhold, 'Gewerbelandschaften in der frühen Neuzeit (1650–1800)', in H. Pohl, ed., *Gewerbe- und Industrielandschaften vom Spätmittelalter bis ins 20. Jahrhundert* (Stuttgart, 1986), pp. 112–202, here pp. 112ff.; and Wolfgang Mager, 'Proto-industrialization and Proto-industry: The Uses and Drawbacks of Two Concepts', *Continuity and Change*, 8/2 (1993), pp. 181–216, here pp. 181ff. Approaches toward the concept of *Gewerbelandschaften* can be found in the concept of 'rustikalisierte Industrie' ('ruralized industry') developed by Werner Sombart, *Der moderne Kapitalismus*, ii: *Das europäische Wirtschaftsleben im Zeitalter des Frühkapitalismus, vornehmlich im 16., 17. und 18. Jahrhundert* (2nd edn, Berlin, 1916), esp. chs 47 and 54, as well as by other members of the German Historical School of Political Economy.

2   See the account of these processes in Jan de Vries, *The Economy of Europe in an Age of Crisis, 1600–1750* (Cambridge, 1976), esp. pp. 33ff., 94ff., 149ff.; and Peter Kriedte, *Peasants, Landlords and Merchant Capitalists: Europe and the World Economy, 1500–1800* (Leamington Spa, 1983).

3   Wilfried Reininghaus, *Gewerbe in der frühen Neuzeit* (Munich, 1990), pp. 18–29; Kriedte, *Peasants*, pp. 32–9. W. Fischer *et al.*, eds, *Handbuch der europäischen Wirtschafts- und Sozialgeschichte* (4 vols, Stuttgart, 1993), vols. iii and iv, provide basic surveys on this subject and the relevant literature, as does F.-W. Henning, *Handbuch der Wirtschafts- und Sozialgeschichte Deutschlands*, i: *Deutsche Wirtschafts- und Sozialgeschichte im Mittelalter und in der frühen Neuzeit* (Paderborn, 1991).

4   On the key role of the Upper German Free Imperial Cities in the trade between Mediterranean and northern Europe, see Hermann Kellenbenz, 'Le déclin de Venise et les relations économiques de Venise avec les marchés au nord des Alpes', in F. Braudel *et al.*, eds, *Aspetti e cause della decadenza economica veneziana nel secolo XVII* (Venice, 1961), here esp. pp. 135–6. On the shift of the economic centre of gravity of Europe from Mediterranean to north Atlantic, see in general de Vries, *Economy*, pp. 113ff.; and Kriedte, *Peasants*, pp. 32–3, 70ff.

5   On the timing of German industrialization relative to that of other parts of Europe, and its variation among different German regions, see R. H. Tilly, 'Soll und Haben II: Wiederbegegnung mit der deutschen Wirtschafts- und Sozialgeschichte', in R. H. Tilly, *Kapital, Staat und sozialer Protest in der deutschen Industrialisierung* (Göttingen, 1980), pp. 228–51, here pp. 233–4; F. B. Tipton, *Regional Variations in the Economic Development of Germany during the Nineteenth Century* (Middletown, Conn., 1976); W. R. Lee, 'Economic Development and the State in Nineteenth-Century Germany', *EcHR* 2nd ser. 41 (1988), pp. 346–67, here pp. 347–50; A. S. Milward and S. B. Saul, *The Economic Development of Continental Europe, 1780–1870* (London, 1973), esp. pp. 365ff.

6   Kaufhold, 'Gewerbelandschaften', p. 173.

7   See e.g. H. Kamen, 'The Economic and Social Consequences of the Thirty Years War', *JMH* 29 (1968), pp. 44–61; F. L. Carsten, 'Was There an Economic Decline in Germany before the Thirty Years War?', *English Historical Review*, 71 (1956), pp. 240–7.

8   K. H. Wolff, 'Guildmaster into Millhand: The Industrialization of Linen and Cotton in Germany to 1850', *Textile History*, 10 (1979), pp. 7–74, pp. 18–20.

9   For a discussion of the workings of this process on the regional and local level, see S. C. Ogilvie, 'Germany and the Seventeenth-Century Crisis', *Historical Journal*, 35 (1992), 417–41; specifically on its agrarian aspects, see Kamen, 'Consequences', pp. 52ff.; on the indirect consequences of the war for German society and the growth of the power of the princes, see Chapters 5, 7 and 8 in this volume.

10   On responses to competition from cotton and mechanization in Germany, with some comparisons with Switzerland, see Wolff, 'Guildmaster', esp. pp. 60–2; see also Tipton, *Regional Variations*, *passim*.

11   Mendels invented the concept in his 1970 doctoral dissertation, later published as F. F. Mendels, *Industrialization and Population Pressure in Eighteenth-Century Flanders* (New York, 1981). A first version of the concept was proposed in a seminal article, F. F. Mendels, 'Proto-industrialization: The First Phase of the Industrialization Process', *Journal of Economic History*, 32 (1972), 241–61. It was further elaborated in F. F. Mendels, 'Proto-industrialization: Theory and Reality, General Report', in *Eighth International Economic History Congress, Budapest 1982, 'A' Themes* (Budapest, 1982), pp. 69–107, published in a revised and expanded French version as F. F. Mendels, 'Des industries rurales à la protoindustrialisation: Historique d'un changement de perspective', *Annales E.S.C.*, 39 (1984), 977–1008.

12   P. Kriedte, H. Medick, and J. Schlumbohm, *Industrialization before Industrialization: Rural Industry in the Genesis of Capitalism* (Cambridge, 1981), translation of the German original, P. Kriedte, H. Medick, and J. Schlumbohm, *Industrialisierung vor der Industrialisierung. Gewerbliche Warenproduktion auf dem Land in der Formationsperiode des Kapitalismus* (Göttingen, 1977).

13   For summaries of the various theories of proto-industrialization and the ensuing debate, see S. C. Ogilvie, 'Proto-industrialization in Europe', *Continuity and Change*, 8 (1993), pp. 159–79, pp. 159–62; and S. C. Ogilvie and M. Cerman, 'The Theories of Proto-industrialization', in S. C. Ogilvie and M. Cerman, eds, *European Proto-industrialization* (Cambridge, 1996), pp. 1–11.

14   On the demographic ramifications of proto-industrialization, see Mendels, 'Proto-industrialization', pp. 249–53 and *passim*; and Kriedte, Medick, and Schlumbohm, *Industrialization*, pp. 38–93.

15   On the breakdown of traditional institutions and their replacement by markets, see Mendels, *Industrialization*, pp. 16, 26; Mendels, 'Theory and Reality', p. 80; and Kriedte, Medick, and Schlumbohm, *Industrialization*, pp. 7–8, 13, 16–17, 22, 40, 106, 115, and 128.

16   Mendels, 'Proto-industrialization'; Mendels, 'Theory and Reality'; Kriedte, Medick, and Schlumbohm, *Industrialization*.

17   Although see the early criticisms of the concept of proto-industrialization by historians from both Germanies after the publication of Kriedte, Medick, and Schlumbohm, *Industrialisierung*, in 1977. From the former German Democratic Republic: J. Kuczynski, *Geschichte des Alltags des deutschen Volkes* (4 vols, Berlin, 1981), ii, esp. pp. 97ff., 105, 119ff.; Helga Schultz, '"Proto-industrialisierung" in der Manufakturperiode: Der Gegensatz von Theorie und Empirie', *JbWG* (1979), p. 4, pp. 187–95; Helga Schultz, 'Die Ausweitung des Landhandwerks vor der industriellen Revolution. Begünstigende Faktoren und Bedeutung für die "Protoindustrialisierung"', *JbWG* (1982), p. 3, pp. 79–90; Helga Schultz, '"Protoindustrialisierung" und Übergangsepoche vom Feudalismus zum Kapitalismus', *Zeitschrift für Geschichtswissenschaft*, 31 (1983), pp. 1079–91. From the Federal Republic

of Germany: H. Linde, 'Proto-Industrialisierung: zur Justierung eines neuen Leitbegriffs der sozialgeschichtlichen Forschung', *GG* 6 (1980), pp. 103–24; E. Schremmer, 'Industrialisierung vor der Industrialisierung. Anmerkungen zu einem Konzept der Protoindustrialisierung,' *GG* 6 (1980), pp. 420–48; E. Schremmer, 'Proto-industrialisation: A Step Towards Industrialisation?', *JEEH* 10 (1981), pp. 653–70. See also the scepticism about the theories of proto-industrialization expressed by Kaufhold, 'Gewerbelandschaften', esp. pp. 187, 196, 202; and by Mager, 'Proto-industrialization', pp. 181–8.

18 For a summary of research on demographic behaviour in German proto-industrial regions, see S. C. Ogilvie, 'Proto-industrialization in Germany', in Ogilvie and Cerman, eds, *European Proto-industrialization*, pp. 118–36, here pp. 126–9.

19 For a recent survey of the criticisms of the theories of proto-industrialization, see Ogilvie, 'Proto-industrialization in Europe', pp. 160–2; Ogilvie and Cerman, 'Theories', pp. 7–11; and S. C. Ogilvie and M. Cerman, 'Proto-industrialization, Economic Development and Social Change in Early Modern Europe', in Ogilvie and Cerman, eds, *European Proto-industrialization*, pp. 227–39. One example of a German region which continued to be proto-industrial is the area around Nuremberg (which remained a 'proto-industrial region' for more than four centuries); see e.g. Wolfgang von Stromer, 'Gewerbereviere und Protoindustrien in Spätmittelalter und Frühneuzeit', in Hans Pohl, ed., *Gewerbe- und Industrielandschaften vom Spätmittelalter bis ins 20. Jahrhundert* (Stuttgart, 1986), pp. 39–111.

20 See Ogilvie, 'Proto-industrialization in Europe', p. 176.

21 Regional variation in German proto-industrialization is discussed in detail in Ogilvie, 'Proto-industrialization in Germany'.

22 These are identified by Kaufhold, 'Gewerbelandschaften', pp. 113–14, as causes for the 'unsatisfactory' state of research on early modern German industry.

23 *Ibid.*, pp. 114–16.

24 *Ibid.*, pp. 119–124.

25 *Ibid.*, pp. 142–3, 148.

26 *Ibid.*, p. 176.

27 *Ibid.*, p. 174–5.

28 *Ibid.*, pp. 175–8.

29 *Ibid.*, p. 179–81; the same finding emerges from case studies of German proto-industrialization, as summarized in Ogilvie, 'Proto-industrialization in Germany', p. 131, and – for the 16th century – from the recent survey of putting-out systems and large industrial concerns in Germany by Rudolf Holbach, *Frühformen von Verlag und Grossbetrieb in der Gewerblichen Produktion (13.-16. Jahrhundert)* (Stuttgart, 1994).

30 Kaufhold, 'Gewerbelandschaften', pp. 186–7.

31 *Ibid.*, p. 187.

32 *Ibid.*

33 *Ibid.*, pp. 188–90.

34 *Ibid.*, pp. 191–3.

35 *Ibid.*, pp. 191–6.

36 Although land could be switched from one crop to the other in a complementary fashion, as in the Westphalian county of Ravensberg, where farmers cultivated both grain for food and flax for the local linen industry; see W. Mager, 'Protoindustrialisierung und agrarisch-heimgewerbliche Verflechtung in Ravensberg während der Frühen Neuzeit. Studien zu einer Gesellschaftsformation im Übergang', *GG* 8 (1982), 435–74.

37 Protectionist legislation could sometimes reduce costs, in so far as it provided tax breaks, subsidies, state loans, or regulations keeping input costs artificially low. However, in so far as it established and supported monopolistic privileges, protectionist legislation increased costs by enabling existing producers to restrict output, maintain higher prices, prevent the employment of women, youths, and new entrants, and block the use of new techniques and production practices. For a detailed discussion of these issues, and an assessment of the net effect on industrial costs and development, see pp. 290–6 below.

38 The dependence of early modern industries on nature is discussed in Reininghaus, *Gewerbe*, pp. 11ff. One of the most important German contributions to the proto-industrialization debate also stresses the technical requirements of different industries, products, and operations, and the influence these exerted on the location, organization, and development of proto-industries: see Mager, 'Proto-industrialization', pp. 188ff.

39 Kaufhold, 'Gewerbelandschaften', pp. 175–6.

40 This is also the conclusion reached by Kaufhold, 'Gewerbelandschaften', p. 193, where he points out that although some German industrial regions were raw-material-oriented, as time passed a substantial trade in raw materials, fuels, and half-finished products developed among different German regions.

41 See H. Kellenbenz, 'Europäisches Eisen. Produktion – Verarbeitung – Handel (vom Ende des Mittelalters bis ins 18. Jahrhundert)', in H. Kellenbenz, ed., *Schwerpunkte der Eisengewinnung und Eisenverarbeitung in Europa, 1500–1650* (Cologne/Vienna, 1974), pp. 397–452; the importance of fuels in particular is emphasized by Mager, 'Proto-industrialization', p. 199.

42 Reininghaus, *Gewerbe*, p. 20.

43 Kellenbenz, 'Europäisches Eisen'; Kaufhold, 'Gewerbelandschaften', pp. 171–3; Reininghaus, *Gewerbe*, pp. 11, 18–20.

44 Kellenbenz, 'Europäisches Eisen'; R. Stahlschmidt, 'Eisenverarbeitende Gewerbe in Süd- und Westdeutschland. Ein Forschungsbericht', in W. Kroker and E. Westermann, *Montanwirtschaft Mitteleuropas vom 12. bis 17. Jahrhundert. Stand, Wege und Aufgaben der Forschung* (Bochum, 1984); Reininghaus, *Gewerbe*, p. 19; Kaufhold, 'Gewerbelandschaften', pp. 131, 140–1.

45 Reininghaus, *Gewerbe*, p. 11.

46 *Ibid.*, pp. 11, 43–4; F. Lerner, *Geschichte des deutschen Glaserhandwerks* (2nd edn., Schorndorf, 1981).

47 Kaufhold, 'Gewerbelandschaften', pp. 182, 192.

48 Fritz Schulte, *Die Entwicklung der gewerblichen Wirtschaft in Rheinland-Westfalen im 18. Jahrhundert* (Cologne, 1959), pp. 25f.; Kaufhold, 'Gewerbelandschaften', p. 156.

49 Despite the costly Prussian state policy of encouraging the cultivation of mulberry trees and the breeding of silkworms, so little raw silk was produced in Germany that it was wholly without economic significance; see Kaufhold, 'Gewerbelandschaften', p. 193 n. 358.

50 Reininghaus, *Gewerbe*, p. 27; Wolff, 'Guildmaster', pp. 15–18, esp. maps on pp. 16–17.

51 *Ibid.*, p. 36.

52 E. Harder-Gersdorff, 'Leinen-Regionen im Vorfeld und im Verlauf der Industrialisierung (1780–1914)', in Pohl, ed., *Gewerbe- und Industrielandschaften*, pp. 203–53; A. J. Warden, *The Linen Trade, Ancient and Modern* (London, 1864; repr. London, 1967); Kaufhold,

'Gewerbelandschaften', pp. 124, 182; Reininghaus, *Gewerbe*, pp. 27–8; Mager, 'Proto-industrialization', p. 189.

53 Reininghaus, *Gewerbe*, pp. 23–6.

54 W. Barkhausen, *Die Tuchindustrie in Montjoie, ihr Aufstieg und Niedergang* (Aachen, 1925); H. Kisch, *Hausindustrie und Textilgewerbe am Niederrhein vor der Industriellen Revolution. Von der ursprünglichen zur kapitalistischen Akkumulation* (Göttingen, 1981), pp. 280–96.

55 Reininghaus, *Gewerbe*, p. 25; Kaufhold, 'Gewerbelandschaften', p. 136; on the Württemberg Black Forest industry, and its dependence almost from the beginning on raw wool imports, see Walter Troeltsch, *Die Calwer Zeughandlungskompagnie und ihre Arbeiter* (Jena, 1897), pp. 35, 38, 47, 98–102, 153–6.

56 On Württemberg's difficulties with respect to river transportation, see Wilhelm Söll, 'Die staatliche Wirtschaftspolitik in Württemberg im 17. und 18. Jahrhundert' (Ph.D. diss., Univ. of Tübingen, 1934), pp. 11–12, 72–4, 98.

57 Mager, 'Verflechtung', pp. 442, 444–6, 465.

58 Kisch, *Hausindustriellen Textilegewerbe*, pp. 281–2; quotation from Joachim Kermann, *Die Manufakturen im Rheinland 1750–1833* (Bonn, 1972), p. 145.

59 Kaufhold, 'Gewerbelandschaften', p. 195.

60 Before 1804, the Holy Roman Empire consisted of some 384 separate sovereign jurisdictions, excluding the *c.* 1,500 sovereign estates of Free Imperial Knights: see the recent survey of the structure of the Empire in John G. Gagliardo, *Germany under the Old Regime, 1600–1790* (London, 1991).

61 This was strongly emphasized for Europe as a whole by Mendels, 'Proto-industrialization', and Kriedte, Medick, and Schlumbohm, *Industrialization*; for a systematic criticism of the under-emphasis of theories of proto-industrialization on urban centres, see M. Cerman, 'Proto-industrialization in an Urban Environment: Vienna, 1750–1857', *Continuity and Change*, 8/2 (1993), pp. 281–320, esp. pp. 281–7. While Kaufhold, 'Gewerbelandschaften', confirms the growing importance of rural industries in Germany between 1650 and 1800 (p. 185), he also warns against too narrow an emphasis on the rural at the expense of the urban location of industry (p. 187).

62 For a useful introductory account of the agrarian systems of different early modern European societies, see De Vries, *Economy*, pp. 47–82, on Germany esp. pp. 55–7 and 59–63.

63 Mendels, 'Theory and Reality', p. 80; Kriedte, Medick, and Schlumbohm, *Industrialization*, pp. 8, 16–17, 40; Kaufhold, 'Gewerbelandschaften', pp. 188–9.

64 See G. Aubin and A. Kunze, *Leinenerzeugung und Leinenabsatz im östlichen Mitteldeutschland zur Zeit der Zunftkäufe. Ein Beitrag zu industriellen Kolonisation des deutschen Ostens* (Stuttgart, 1940); H. Aubin, 'Die Anfänge der grossen schlesischen Leinenweberei und -handlung', *VSWG* 35 (1942), pp. 103–78; H. Kisch, 'The Textile Industries of Silesia and the Rhineland: A Comparative Study of Industrialization,' in Kriedte, Medick, and Schlumbohm, *Industrialization*, pp. 178–200. For recent surveys of 'feudal proto-industries' in central and eastern Europe, see Milan Myška, 'Proto-industrialization in Bohemia, Moravia and Silesia', in Ogilvie and Cerman, *European Proto-industrialization*, pp. 188–207; and S. C. Ogilvie, 'Social Institutions and Proto-industrialization', in Ogilvie and Cerman, *European Proto-industrialization*, pp. 23–37, here pp. 28–30.

65 For this view in general, see Kriedte, Medick, and Schlumbohm, *Industrialization*, pp. 18ff., 29; on Silesia in particular, see U. Lewald, 'Die Entwicklung der ländlichen Textilindustrie im Rheinland und in Schlesien', *Zeitschrift für Ostforschung*, 10 (1961), pp. 601–31, here esp. 606–9.

66 For details of the various ways in which 'feudal proto-industries' depended on the strength, not the weakness, of landlord powers, see Kisch, 'Silesia and the Rhineland', pp. 179, 180–3, 185, 198 (explicitly taking issue with the arguments of Lewald); Myška, 'Proto-industrialization'.

67 Kisch, 'Silesia and the Rhineland', pp. 182–7; Tipton, *Regional Variations*, pp. 18–20; Wolff, 'Guildmaster', pp. 20–3.

68 Kisch, 'Silesia and the Rhineland', p. 187.

69 On Krefeld, see Peter Kriedte, 'Proto-Industrialisierung und großes Kapital. Das Seidengewerbe in Krefeld und seinem Umland bis zum Ende des Ancien Regime', *Archiv für Sozialgeschichte*, 23 (1983), 219–66, here pp. 257–8; on two villages in Leicestershire in England, see David Levine, *Family Formation in an Age of Nascent Capitalism* (New York/London, 1977); on Switzerland, see A. Tanner, 'Arbeit, Haushalt und Familie in Appenzell-Außerrhoden. Veränderungen in einem ländlichen Industriegebiet im 18. und 19. Jahrhundert', in J. Ehmer and M. Mitterauer, eds, *Familienstruktur und Arbeitsorganisation in ländlichen Gesellschaften* (Vienna, 1986), 449–94.

70 Mager, 'Verflechtung', pp. 443, 447–9; W. Mager, 'Spenge vom frühen 18. Jahrhundert bis zur Mitte des 19. Jahrhunderts', in W. Mager, ed., *Geschichte der Stadt Spenge* (Spenge, 1984), pp. 162–3. The same contrasts are drawn by Schlumbohm in his comparison of Ravensberg and neighbouring Osnabrück: see J. Schlumbohm, 'Agrarische Besitzklassen und gewerbliche Produktionsverhältnisse: Großbauern, Kleinbesitzer und Landlose als Leinenproduzenten im Umland von Osnabrück und Bielefeld während des frühen 19. Jahrhunderts', in *Mentalitäten und Lebensverhältnisse. Rudolf Vierhaus zum 60. Geburtstag* (Göttingen, 1982), 315–34, here p. 334; J. Schlumbohm, 'Seasonal Fluctuations and Social Division of Labour: Rural Linen Production in the Osnabrück and Bielefeld Regions and the Urban Woollen Industry in the Niederlausitz, ca. 1700 – ca. 1850', in M. Berg, P. Hudson, and M. Sonenscher, eds, *Manufacture in Town and Country before the Factory* (Cambridge, 1983), pp. 92–123, here p. 121; J. Schlumbohm, 'From Peasant Society to Class Society: Some Aspects of Family and Class in a Northwest German Proto-industrial Parish, 17th–19th Centuries', *Journal of Family History*, 17 (1992), pp. 183–99, here pp. 187, 197. A definitive work on the whole process of the breakdown of the *Acker-Marken-Wirtschaft* is Stefan Brakensiek, *Agrarreform und ländliche Gesellschaft. Die Privatisierung der Marken in Nordwestdeutschland, 1750–1850* (Paderborn, 1991), summarized in Stefan Brakensiek, 'Agrarian Individualism in North-Western Germany, 1770–1870', *German History*, 12 (1994), pp. 137–79, esp. pp. 157–61 on the interpenetration between landlord powers and the *Markverfassung* in parts of Westphalia (particularly ecclesiastical territories such as Osnabrück).

71 Mendels, 'Theory and Reality', p. 80; Kriedte, Medick, and Schlumbohm, *Industrialization*, pp. 8, 16–17, 40.

72 On England, see Levine, *Family Formation*; on the Swiss canton of Zürich, see R. Braun, 'Early Industrialization and Demographic Change in the Canton of Zürich', in C. Tilly, ed., *Historical Studies of Changing Fertility* (Princeton, 1978), pp. 289–334, pp. 299, 307, although see also the evidence that industry arose in some villages in the canton of Zürich in which strong community institutions survived, presented in U. Pfister, 'Proto-industrialization and Demographic Change. The Canton of Zürich Revisited',

JEEH 18 (1989), 629–62, here p. 635 with n. 14, and esp. pp. 653–9.

73 See the discussion in Ogilvie, 'Proto-industrialization in Europe', pp. 166–7; Ogilvie, 'Social Institutions', 27–8, 30.

74 See the discussion of the relationship between state and local community in Mack Walker, *German Home Towns: Community, State, and General Estate 1648–1871* (Ithaca, NY, 1971), and the discussion of the mechanisms by which the German symbiosis between community and state arose in the early modern period in Ogilvie, 'Crisis', 432f.

75 E. Gröllich, *Die Baumwollweberei der sächsischen Oberlausitz und ihre Entwicklung zum Grossbetrieb* (Leipzig, 1911); A. Kunze 'Der Weg zur kapitalistischen Produktionsweise in der Oberlausitzer Leineweberei im ausgehenden 17. und zu Beginn des 18. Jahrhunderts', in E. Winter, ed., *E. W. von Tschirnhaus und die Frühaufklärung in Mittel- und Osteuropa* (Berlin, 1960).

76 H. Kisch, 'From Monopoly to Laissez-faire: The Early Growth of the Wupper Valley Textile Trades', *JEEH* 1 (1972), pp. 298–407, pp. 299–304; Kisch, *Hausindustriellen Textilgewerbe*, pp. 94–6; Kriedte, 'Großes Kapital', p. 225.

77 Mager, 'Spenge', pp. 162–3; Mager, 'Verflechtung', pp. 443, 447–9.

78 Mager, 'Verflechtung', pp. 441; W. Mager, 'Die Rolle des Staates bei der gewerblichen Entwicklung Ravensbergs in vorindustrieller Zeit', in K. Düwell and W. Köllmann, eds., *Rheinland-Westfalen im Industriezeitalter*, i: *Von der Entstehung der Provinzen bis zur Reichsgründung* (Wuppertal, 1983), pp. 61–72, p. 71; J. Schlumbohm, 'Agrarische Besitzklassen und gewerbliche Produktionsverhältnisse: Großbauern, Kleinbesitzer und Landlose als Leinenproduzenten im Umland von Osnabrück und Bielefeld während des frühen 19. Jahrhunderts', in *Mentalitäten und Lebensverhältnisse* (Göttingen, 1982), pp. 315–34, pp. 330–34; Schlumbohm, 'Peasant society', pp. 187, 197.

79 Walker, *German Home Towns*; for a detailed examination of what this meant on the local level in an industrial region of the duchy of Württemberg, see S. C. Ogilvie, 'Coming of Age in a Corporate Society: Capitalism, Pietism and Family Authority in Rural Württemberg 1590–1740', *Continuity and Change*, 1 (1986), 279–331, and S. C. Ogilvie, 'Institutions and Economic Development in Early Modern Central Europe', *Transactions of the Royal Historical Society*, 6th ser., 5 (1995), pp. 221–50; on the survival of strong communities into the nineteenth century in many parts of the German south, and their impact on factory industrialization, see Tipton, *Regional Variations*.

80 On the Black Forest worsted industry, see Troeltsch, *Calwer Zeughandlungskompagnie*; and Ogilvie, 'Institutions and Economic Development'; for a comparison of the Black Forest worsted industry and the linen industry in the district of Heidenheim, see R. Flik, *Die Textilindustrie in Calw und in Heidenheim 1705–1870. Eine regional vergleichende Untersuchung zur Geschichte der Frühindustrialisierung und Industriepolitik in Württemberg* (Stuttgart, 1990); for a detailed examination of certain aspects of the linen industry in the district of Urach, see Hans Medick, '"Freihandel für die Zunft": Ein Kapitel aus der Geschichte der Preiskämpfe im württembergischen Leinengewerbe des 18. Jahrhunderts', in *Mentalitäten und Lebensverhältnisse*, pp. 277–94; and Hans Medick, 'Privilegiertes Handelskapital und "kleine Industrie". Produktion und Produktionsverhältnisse im Leinengewerbe des alt-württembergischen Oberamts Urach im 18. Jahrhundert', *Archiv für Sozialgeschichte*, 23 (1983), pp. 267–310.

81 This aspect of the theory of proto-industrialization is criticized by Carlo Poni, 'Proto-industrialization, Rural and Urban', *Review*, 9 (1985), pp. 305–14, and by Cerman, 'Proto-industrialization', pp. 281–7.

82 Mendels, *Industrialization*, pp. 16, 26; Kriedte, Medick, Schlumbohm, *Industrialization*, pp. 7, 13, 22, 106, 115, 128.

83 Poni, 'Proto-industrialization'; Cerman, 'Proto-industrialization', pp. 281–7; Ogilvie, 'Proto-industrialization in Europe', pp. 169–71.

84 Kisch, *Hausindustriellen Textilgewerbe*, pp. 100–3, 116, 130–1, 140; Kriedte, 'Großes Kapital', pp. 221, 225, 241, 246, 249, 258; Peter Kriedte, 'Demographic and Economic Rhythms: The Rise of the Silk Industry in Krefeld', *JEEH* 15 (1986), pp. 259–89, here pp. 260–1.

85 See Kisch, *Die Hausindustriellen Textilgewerbe*, pp. 280–92; Barkhausen, *Tuchindustrie in Montjoie*.

86 Kaufhold, 'Gewerbelandschaften', p. 152; Kisch, *Hausindustriellen Textilgewerbe*, pp. 273–316; Joachim Kermann, *Die Manufakturen im Rheinland 1750–1833* (Bonn, 1972), pp. 118–30, 132ff.

87 Kisch, 'Monopoly', pp. 307, 351–3, 400, 403–7.

88 Kaufhold, 'Gewerbelandschaften', p. 160; Alphons Thun, *Die Industrie am Niederrhein und ihre Arbeiter*, ii: *Die Industrie des bergischen Landes (Solingen, Remscheid und Elberfeld-Barmen)* (Leipzig, 1879), pp. 109–22.

89 See e.g. the arguments put forward in Charles R. Hickson and Earl A. Thomson, 'A New Theory of Guilds and European Economic Development', *Explorations in Economic History*, 28 (1991), pp. 127–68.

90 W. Engels and P. Legers, *Aus der Geschichte der Remscheider und bergischen Werkzeug- und Eisenindustrie* (Remscheid, 1928), i. pp. 131–9.

91 Kaufhold, 'Gewerbelandschaften', p. 160; Thun, *Industrie am Niederrhein*, ii. pp. 16–19, 32ff., 57–9.

92 Kisch, 'Monopoly', pp. 394–401.

93 Aubin and Kunze, *Leinenerzeugung*; Aubin, 'Anfänge'; Kisch, 'Silesia and the Rhineland'; Kaufhold, 'Gewerbelandschaften', p. 125. In some areas, the beginnings of rural linen production are already observable in the early 16th century: see e.g. Gerhard Heitz, *Ländliche Leinenproduktion in Sachsen (1470–1555)* (Berlin, 1961).

94 B. Schöne, 'Kultur und Lebensweise Lausitzer und erzgebirgischer Textilproduzenten sowie von Keramikproduzenten im Manufakturkapitalismus und in der Periode der Industriellen Revolution', in H. Zwahr, ed., *Die Konstituierung der deutschen Arbeiterklasse von den dreißiger bis zu den siebziger Jahren des 19. Jahrhunderts* (Berlin, 1981), pp. 446–67; B. Schöne, 'Posamentierer – Strumpfwirker – Spitzenklöpplerinnen. Zu Kultur und Lebensweise von Textilproduzenten im Erzgebirge und im Vogtland während der Periode des Übergangs vom Feudalismus zum Kapitalismus (1750–1850)', in R. Weinhold, ed., *Volksleben zwischen Zunft und Fabrik. Studien zu Kultur und Lebensweise werktätiger Klassen und Schichten während des Übergangs vom Feudalismus zum Kapitalismus* (Berlin/GDR, 1982), pp. 107–64; Wolff, 'Guildmaster', pp. 33–5; Kaufhold, 'Gewerbelandschaften', p. 128.

95 B. Schöne, 'Lausitzer Bandweberei vom Zunfthandwerk zur Manufaktur und zur frühen Fabrik,' in *Internationales Handwerksgeschichtliches Symposium Veszprém 20–24.11.1978* (Veszprém, 1979), pp. 176–81, pp. 178–9.

96 Kaufhold, 'Gewerbelandschaften', p. 129; Albin König, *Die Sächsische Baumwollindustrie am Ende des vorigen Jahrhunderts und während der Kontinentalsperre* (Leipzig, 1899), pp. 148ff.; Tipton, *Regional Variations*, p. 32.

97 Wolff, 'Guildmaster', pp. 33–5, 38.

98 *Ibid.*, p. 35.

99 Tipton, *Regional Variations*, p. 32.

100 Hans Lohse, *Schmalkalder Bergbau, Hüttenwesen und Eisenhandwerk* (Schmalkalden, 1955), pp. 45–67.

101 P. Rotschky, 'Die Waffenindustrie in Suhl, ihre Entwicklung und Lage' (Jur. D. diss., Univ. of Jena, 1933), pp. 26–33.

102 Emanuel Sax, *Die Hausindustrie in Thüringen*, ii: *Ruhla und das Eisenacher Oberland* (Jena, 1884), pp. 5–37.

103 Emanuel Sax, *Die Hausindustrie in Thüringen*, i: *Das Meininger Oberland* (2nd edn, Jena, 1885), pp. 11ff., 138–50.

104 Walter Schneider, *Die Apoldaer Wirkwarenindustrie bis zum Jahre 1914* (Jena, 1922) and Hans Eberhardt, *Goethes Umwelt. Forschungen zur gesellschaftlichen Struktur Thüringens* (Weimar, 1951), pp. 67–85.

105 Johann Peter Baum, 'Die wirtschaftlicher Entwicklung des Obereichsfeldes in der Neuzeit, mit besonderer Berücksichtigen der Hausindustrie' (Ph.D. diss., Univ. of Berlin, 1903).

106 Hans Patze and Walter Schlesinger, eds, *Geschichte Thüringens* (5 vols, Cologne, 1982), here vol. v, pt 1, p. 421.

107 Sax, *Hausindustrie in Thüringen*, i: *Das Meininger Oberland*, pp. 11ff.

108 Schneider, *Apoldaer Wirkwarenindustrie*; Eberhardt, *Goethes Umwelt*, pp. 67–85.

109 Baum, 'Die wirtschaftliche Entwicklung'.

110 Mager, 'Verflechtung', p. 444.

111 See the detailed examination of the company of the Bielefeld linen merchants in A. Flügel, *Kaufleute und Manufakturen in Bielefeld: Sozialer Wandel und wirtschaftliche Entwicklung im proto-industriellen Leinengewerbe von 1680 bis 1850* (Bielefeld, 1993).

112 On the *Legge* in the county of Ravensberg, see Mager, 'Verflechtung', pp. 452ff.; on Ravensberg and the prince-bishopric of Osnabrück, see Schlumbohm, 'Seasonal fluctuations'; on the county of Tecklenburg, see Stephanie Reekers, 'Beiträge zur statistischen Darstellung der gewerblichen Wirtschaft Westfalens um 1800, T. 3 Tecklenburg-Lingen', *Westfälische Forschungen*, 19 (1966), pp. 34ff.

113 Mager, 'Rolle des Staates', p. 67; Schlumbohm, 'Seasonal fluctuations', p. 94.

114 Schlumbohm, 'Agrarische Besitzklassen', p. 330.

115 J. Mooser, 'Der Weg vom proto-industriellen zum fabrik-industriellen Gewerbe in Ravensberg, 1830–1914', in K. Düwell and W. Köllmann, eds, *Rheinland-Westfalen im Industriezeitalter*, i: *Von der Entstehung der Provinzen bis zur Reichsgründung* (Wuppertal, 1983), pp. 73–95, pp. 75–82; Schlumbohm, 'Agrarische Besitzklassen', p. 330; Wolff, 'Guildmaster', pp. 30–3.

116 On the worsted weavers' guilds, see Ogilvie, 'Coming of Age'; Ogilvie, 'Institutions'; on the Calw merchant company, see Troeltsch, *Calwer Zeughandlungskompagnie*.

117 On the guilds of the linen weavers, see Medick, '"Freihandel"'; on the Heidenheim merchant company, see Flik, *Textilindustrie*; on the Urach company, see Medick, 'Privilegiertes Handelskapital'.

118 *Ibid.*, p. 301; Flik, *Textilindustrie*, pp. 92–3.

119 Ogilvie, 'Institutions'; Flik, *Textilindustrie*.

120 Medick, 'Privilegiertes Handelskapital', pp. 306–10.

121 Flik, *Textilindustrie*, pp. 117ff., 142–3.

122 For detailed examples of how guilds continued to constrain growth in many

parts of 19th-century Germany during industrialization, see Tipton, *Regional Variations*, pp. 26–7, 30, 52–3, 59, 71, 72–76.

123   At best, the state is allocated a part share in a nine-page 'excursus' on 'The political and institutional framework of proto-industrialization' in Kriedte, Medick, and Schlumbohm, *Industrialization*, pp. 126–34.

124   See the summary in Reininghaus, *Gewerbe*, p. 18: 'With many, if not all, foundations of manufactories by the state, the yield must be estimated as being small. Few of these manufactories worked economically in the longer term.'

125   See e.g. Herbert Kisch, 'Prussian Mercantilism and the Rise of the Krefeld Silk Industry: Variations upon an Eighteenth-Century Theme', *Transactions of the American Philosophical Society*, NS 58 (1968), part 7, 1–50, pp. 1–15.

126   Kaufhold, 'Gewerbelandschaften', pp. 122–4.

127   Quoted in Kisch, 'Prussian Mercantilism', p. 15, n. 1.

128   Eberhard Gothein, *Wirtschaftsgeschichte des Schwarzwaldes und der angrenzenden Landschaften*, i: *Städte- und Gewerbegeschichte* (Strasbourg, 1892), quotation from p. 449; Wolfram Fischer, *Der Staat und die Anfänge der Industrialisierung in Baden 1800 bis 1850*, i: *Staatliche Gewerbepolitik* (Berlin, 1962).

129   Herbert Kühnert, *Unkundenbuch zu thüringischen Glashüttengeschichte und Aufsätze zu thüringischen Glashüttengeschichte* (Wiesbaden, 1973), pp. 21–7; Hans Patze and Walter Schlesinger, eds, *Geschichte Thüringens* (5 vols, Cologne/Vienna, 1982), i, section 1, pp. 198–231, 422, 478, 509–10, 516, 534.

130   Kaufhold, 'Gewerbelandschaften', pp. 197–8.

131   *Ibid.*, p. 137; Wolff, 'Guildmaster', pp. 15–26, 33–36; Alfred Zimmermann, *Blüthe und Verfall des Leinengewerbes in Schlesien* (Breslau, 1885), p. 76.

132   Kaufhold, 'Gewerbelandschaften', pp. 150–1; Clemens Brückner, *Zur Wirtschaftsgeschichte des Regierungsbezirks Aachen* (Cologne, 1976), p. 322.

133   On this, see e.g. the literature surveyed in Ogilvie, 'Crisis', 434–5.

134   Kisch, 'Silesia and the Rhineland', 184–5.

135   Mooser, *Bäuerliche Gesellschaft*, p. 166; Mager, 'Verflechtung', p. 441; Mager, 'Rolle des Staates', p. 71; Schlumbohm, 'Agrarische Besitzklassen', pp. 330–4; Schlumbohm, 'Peasant Society', pp. 187, 197.

136   W. Grube, *Vogteien, Ämter, Landkreise in der Geschichte Südwestdeutschlands* (2nd edn., Stuttgart, 1960), esp. pp. 18–41; J. A. Vann, *The Making of a State: Württemberg, 1593–1793* (Ithaca, NY, 1984), pp. 51, 295, and *passim*; D. W. Sabean, *Property, Production and Family in Neckarhausen, 1700–1870* (Cambridge, 1990), esp. pp. 66–87.

137   See Ogilvie, 'Crisis', where the process by which this symbiotic relationship between corporate groups and the German state developed is explored in greater detail; an illustration of how this was seen from the perspective of the state bureaucracy is provided by the persistently corporatist (and extremely influential) recommendations of the mercantilist Johann Joachim Becher, chronicled in H. Hassinger, *Johann Joachim Becher 1635–1682: Ein Beitrag zur Geschichte des Mercantilismus* (Vienna, 1951).

138   Troeltsch, *Calwer Zeughandlungskompagnie*, p. 327; Medick, 'Privilegiertes Handelskapital', pp. 306–8; Flik, *Textilindustrie*, pp. 99–101, 105–7; Ogilvie, 'Institutions'.

139   Kisch, 'Monopoly', pp. 307–8, 316, 323, 345, 355, 372, 386.

140   Wolff, 'Guildmaster', pp. 39–41; Tipton, *Regional Variations*, pp. 30ff.

141 For a recent survey of the role of demand in European industrial growth, see Jan de Vries, 'Between Purchasing Power and the World of Goods: Understanding the Household Economy in Early Modern Europe', in John Brewer and Roy Porter, eds, *Consumption and the World of Goods* (London/New York, 1993), pp. 85–132, esp. 85–9. See also the brief but enlightening discussion of the possible role of state demand in stimulating and/or inducing crises in particular economic sectors, in N. Steensgaard, 'The Seventeenth-Century Crisis', in N. G. Parker and L. M. Smith, eds, *The General Crisis of the Seventeenth Century* (London, 1978), pp. 36–42. For the view that high military spending stimulated industry in early modern Europe, see Werner Sombart, *Luxus und Kapitalismus* (Munich, 1913); F. Braudel, *The Mediterranean and the Mediterranean World in the Age of Philip II* (2 vols, London, 1972), i. pp. 409–10.

142 Werner Sombart, *Krieg und Kapitalismus* (Munich/Leipzig, 1913); see also Gerhard Oestreich, *Friedrich Wilhelm I. Preußischer Absolutismus, Merkantilismus, Militarismus* (Göttingen etc., 1977), pp. 63f., 85f. For a discussion of Sombart's views on war as a demand-side stimulus to industry, see J. M. Winter, 'The Economic and Social History of War', in J. M. Winter, ed., *War and Economic Development: Essays in Memory of David Joslin* (Cambridge, 1975), pp. 1–10.

143 On the general growth in consumer demand in early modern Europe, see e.g. de Vries, 'Purchasing Power', and the other essays in Brewer and Porter, eds, *Consumption*. Studies of the growth of consumption in German-speaking Europe are still not numerous, although there are important exceptions: see e.g. Roman Sandgruber, *Die Anfänge der Konsumgesellschaft: Konsumgüterverbrauch, Lebensstandard und Alltagskultur in Österreich im 18. und 19. Jahrhundert* (Vienna, 1982); and Ruth Mohrmann, *Alltagswelt im Land Braunschweig: Stadt und ländliche Wohnkultur vom 16. bis zum frühen 20. Jahrhundert* (Münster, 1990). A growth in market-orientated consumption and production in a Württemberg village from about 1750 onward is described by Sabean, *Property*.

144 In the most important recent contribution to this debate, Jan de Vries argues that demand for market goods led households in many parts of Europe from the mid-seventeenth century onward to re-allocate time from leisure and 'consumption-preparing' activities to 'income-earning' work; thus consumer demand drew previously 'idle' household labour into market production: see de Vries, 'Purchasing Power', esp. 107–21, and Jan de Vries, 'The Industrial Revolution and the Industrious Revolution,' *Journal of Economic History*, 54 (1994), 249–71. However, while de Vries brilliantly illuminates a possible mechanism by which demand could have drawn idle resources into productive use, he leaves unresolved the question of what caused the initial growth of consumer demand, merely mentioning that it may have derived either from changing tastes or from changing relative prices – e.g. from greater availability of cheap, attractive market wares (*Ibid.*, p. 257).

145 Lee, 'Economic Development'; F. B. Tipton, 'Government Policy and Economic Development in Germany and Japan: A Skeptical Reevaluation', *Journal of Economic History*, 41 (1981), pp. 139–50; W. Fischer, 'Government Activity and Industrialization in Germany 1815–70', in W. W. Rostow, ed., *The Economics of Take-off into Sustained Growth* (London, 1963).

146 The widening regional disparities within Germany during 19th-century industrialization are emphasized by Tipton, *Regional Variations*.

|10|

Confession as a Social and Economic Factor

KASPAR VON GREYERZ

Some 40 years ago, in the wake of the disaster of the Third Reich, when German historians looked for points of reorientation, Dietrich Gerhard, among many others, took exception to the 'genetic principle' inherent in German historicism, because it was misleading scholars into seeking in the past solely what mattered in the present, without appreciating at all the past forces that had managed to survive innovation and renewal.[1] The role of religion and confession – a term I shall use throughout in the sense of the German *Konfession* – in early modern Germany was too crucial to be gauged exclusively from the vantage-point of secularized modernity, as is done, to cite only one example, in a recent and otherwise important study on the social and economic history of late eighteenth- and nineteenth-century Germany.[2] In dealing with early modern religion and confession and their significance in the life of German peasants, burghers, nobles, and princes, we must not only seek to explain their impact on historical change; we are under an obligation, at the same time, to understand their role as causes or aspects of historical continuity or, indeed, as moments of inertia.

Introduction

A crucial element in Germany's history in the seventeenth and eighteenth centuries was the formation of the territorial state and the consolidation of princely rule (discussed in detail in Chapter 7 of this volume). The state became ever more present in the lives of Germans. Its mandates and organs progressively overruled local laws and exemptions and transformed the common man into a regular taxpayer and soldier, and, thus, into a subject (*Untertan*) encompassed by the government's *Polizey* (common wel-

fare policy) and by the episcopal courts, consistories, *Konvente*, and pres-
byteries of the church.[3] In the territorial states of Germany the drive
towards absolutism gained an initial momentum during the last decades
of the sixteenth century. It was enhanced from the start by the simultaneous process of confessionalization, which covered the entire Empire within
the space of only a couple of decades.[4] Given the fact that the establishment of government control over religious life and the territorial church
was an important part of the consolidation of princely rule, the growth of
territorial absolutism and the process of confessionalization were inextricably intertwined from their beginning.

The official ecclesiastical basis of confessionalization was provided by
written statements of creed whose number steadily increased from 1530,
when Philip Melanchthon and his close associates drafted the Augsburg
confession, the first 'official' confessional statement of German Lutheranism. It was followed in 1577 by the Formula of Concord and, in 1580, by
the Book of Concord, which incorporated all major Lutheran statements of
creed. The Heidelberg catechism of 1563 was the authoritative German
articulation of Calvinist dogma, while the decrees of the Council of Trent of
1564 and the *Catechismus Romanus* initiated the Catholic Counter-Reformation.

Confessional pluralism, occasionally even within one and the same community, was a basic factor in Germany's early modern history. Nonetheless,
the great majority of Germans believed, well into the seventeenth century,
that there was nothing permanent about the split between different
churches and creeds created by the Reformation. Thus, although the
Reformation had brought about ecclesiastical and doctrinal pluralism, each
of the three Christian groups claimed to represent the traditional unity of
the church and, as a result, found itself in competition with the other two
churches. In fact, the propagation of printed formulations of creed helped
to inaugurate a new era of narrow-minded confessionalism, of which the
clergy became the most vociferous agents. In Lutheranism and Calvinism
this led, from the last decades of the sixteenth century onward, to the formation of theological schools of orthodoxy, which, in the course of the seventeenth century, progressively came to dominate much of the life of these
churches. While the centres of Reformed (Calvinist) orthodoxy formed outside the confines of the German Empire, as at Basel, Geneva, and Leiden,
the universities of Leipzig and Wittenberg became watchtowers of Lutheran
orthodoxy.

Although Lutheranism and Calvinism likewise experienced a period of
theological orthodoxy, they otherwise differed in crucial respects, not least
in their respective doctrines of predestination and of the Lord's Supper and,
most visibly, in the form of public worship, in whose reform John Calvin
and his successors had been considerably more radical than Martin Luther
and his followers. The clearest difference between the two branches of
Protestantism, however, consisted in the organization of the church. In

Calvinist churches the ultimate authority, at least in theory, did not rest with those entrusted with a public function (*Amt*), as in Lutheranism, but with the congregation as a corporate body. Through its consistory or presbytery, composed of pastors and elders, the congregation exercised moral control, including matrimonial jurisdiction, among the parishioners. However, where Calvinism made inroads into German territories between the 1560s and the beginning of the Thirty Years War, this model was rarely institutionalized in pure form, because the German princes who adopted the Reformed faith were just as eager to preserve their authority in ecclesiastical matters as their Lutheran counterparts.[5] Despite such similarities, there was a stronger emphasis in German Calvinism on the reform of congregational life as a corollary of doctrinal reform. As a result, Calvinism's urge to suppress all forms of traditional popular culture and religion which looked like 'papal superstitions' was clearly more marked.[6]

Before the advent of Pietism and the early Enlightenment towards the end of the seventeenth century, confessionalism was very strenuously advocated by a good number of Protestant and Catholic clergymen. It frequently encapsulated a message of disdain and occasionally of confessional hatred. Not all lay people, however, accepted this message at face value. In December 1610 we find Johann Morhard, the Lutheran town physician of Schwäbisch Hall, enraged about a pastor's vilification of a deceased friend of his, on account of the latter's conversion to Catholicism.[7]

In late sixteenth- and early seventeenth-century Augsburg, Kaufbeuren, Dinkelsbühl, Ravensburg, and Biberach, bi-confessional Imperial Cities of southern Germany, where co-operation on a daily basis between Lutherans and Catholics was necessary, the social climate among lay people was marked to a certain extent by toleration. The subsequent growth of corporate exclusiveness on both sides in these cities, and more particularly in Augsburg, remains a matter of interpretation. While Bernd Roeck suggests that it was in the long run unavoidable, Etienne François tends to highlight that which kept uniting the adherents of both confessions in spite of their tendency to develop social and economic traits specific to each group.[8] In tri-confessional Oppenheim there seems to have reigned a similar pragmatic spirit of co-operation throughout the eighteenth century. The only question which repeatedly led to conflict was the confessional adherence of the local midwife.[9] On the whole, however, as is shown by the confessionally motivated cruelties of the Thirty Years War, as well as by the popular resistance against 'enlightened' hymn-books at the turn of the eighteenth century, these were cases of toleration born out of necessity rather than conviction. The common people of the period considered here gained much of their confessional identity from the vilification of the confessional 'other', and to this extent the corresponding campaign of the clergy was, in the long run, largely successful.

Confessionalization, as we have already seen, was a process inextricably linked to the formation of the early modern state and thus to the corresponding attempt to create a new society of disciplined subjects. It was a fundamental process of change touching on various aspects of contemporary life.[10] But it has justly been pointed out that it would be wrong 'to describe confessionalization only as a historical process generated by the bureaucratic and intellectual élites and imposed on the rest of society'.[11] We should not overlook the active role played by local agents, such as teachers, urban magistrates, merchants, and the upper echelons of village society. At all times in this process the church and the state could count on the support of such local 'middlemen', who co-operated in the attempt to establish confessional uniformity. During the periods between visitations of the local church, by which the progress of this uniformity was measured, these agents tried to make sure that church ordinances and corresponding mandates of the state were being heeded and that recalcitrant persons met their punishment.

It would be misleading, however, to view confessionalization exclusively as a vehicle for the establishment of *doctrinal* uniformity by means of catechism lessons and ecclesiastical visitations. Generally, it also entailed the enhancement of state control over the local administration of church and poor relief and, most importantly, the imposition of *Kirchenzucht* and *Sittenzucht*, of congregational and communal moral discipline. This could go well beyond ecclesiastical matters in the strict sense of the term. It could encompass excessive drinking, playing dice, idleness, prostitution, matrimonial matters, blasphemy, disobedience of children to their parents, in short the entire spectrum of possible social behaviour. The state's police ordinances are a case in point. They were concerned, *inter alia*, with the suppression of concubinage and fornication, carnivalesque traditions which were considered excessive, public brawls, extravagant baptismal and wedding celebrations, and overdone luxury at funeral receptions.

Church discipline and the state's moral regime went hand in hand. The process of confessionalization thus was an intrinsic part of 'social disciplining' (*Sozialdisziplinierung*), which Gerhard Oestreich has shown to have been an important component of the consolidation of early modern absolutist rule.[12] For this reason it is frequently impossible to determine with any precision whether individual measures enforcing moral discipline should be attributed to confessionalization or instead to secular *Polizey*.

Whereas confessionalization was a result of the reform movements of the sixteenth century, the origins of the state's moral regime went back to the fifteenth century. The duchies of Bavaria and Württemberg are cases in point. It would thus clearly be wrong to attribute early modern social disciplining exclusively to the lasting influence of the Protestant and Catholic reforms of the sixteenth century.[13] Important secular motives were involved as well. Conversely, we should not overestimate the effect of religion and *Konfession* as instruments of social control.

On account of the concatenation of church and state measures, the process of confessionalization contained from the beginning the seeds of secularization. In the words of a well-known historical sociologist, secularization 'is that dialectical process, in the course of which Christian religion favours the rise of modern entrepreneurial capitalism, the modern bureaucratic state, and modern experimental science, and is itself weakened by these powers'.[14] Hand in hand with the state's claim to moral social control, confessional pluralism progressively contributed to an erosion of the erstwhile monopoly of church and religion in providing the essential norms for collective and individual behaviour. The revalorization of norms this brought about encouraged the secularization of state policy: in the course of the eighteenth century the German princes ceased to consider it their duty to uphold confessional uniformity. Confessionalization had turned into purely secular moral *Polizey*. This notion has nothing in common with the idea of modern police enforcement; it rather encapsulated a campaign of safeguarding, by way of princely mandates and edicts, the traditional social order. Parallel to this occurred an increasing shift from the guidelines of religion to those of secular morality in public attempts to regulate individual behaviour.[15]

In the Protestant states of Germany, confessionalization began during the 1560s. The Palatine Electorate with Heidelberg as its centre took the lead in the Reformed camp, while the Duchy of Württemberg, followed shortly by electoral Saxony, was heading the drive among the Lutheran states. Within a relatively short period of time the process had reached all Calvinist and Lutheran territories of Germany. About a decade later, confessionalization also began in Catholic territories, strongly encouraged by the papal curia. During the 1570s and 1580s a new generation of Tridentine bishops and suffragans was instituted in the bishoprics of Würzburg, Hildesheim, Cologne, and Münster, albeit with varying results. Soon confessionalization had become a concern in a majority of German Catholic states and bishoprics, from Bavaria and the Tyrol in the South to Hildesheim and Münster in the North. In most German territories there began a period of enforcing doctrinal and moral uniformity in domestic matters, coupled with an increasingly confessionalist stance towards the outside, for instance in Imperial politics.

Catholic and Protestant confessionalization are inherently comparable historical phenomena. Both gave an important impetus to the political, administrative, and social reform and renewal of church and state.[16] Within the Catholic church, authority was consolidated in the hands of the parish clergy and the bishops. A series of parish registers for baptisms, weddings, and funerals, including a *Kommunikantenregister* keeping track of those who partook in the eucharist, henceforth were to permit an effective control of the ecclesiastical life of lay people. Regular synods and visitations were to complement this control. At the same time, similar measures were taken in Protestant parishes. Everywhere they greatly increased the possibilities not only of improved administrative control, but also of a new moral control, over the mass of parishioners.[17]

In Lutheran territories complementary measures of reform were implemented by consistory courts and, in Württemberg from the mid-seventeenth century onwards, by the local *Kirchenkonvente*, as well as by regular parish visitations. In Calvinist states similar functions were assured by presbyters and preachers on the local level, as well as by synodal, provincial, and class meetings of the ministers. In Catholic states the central ecclesiastical council and frequent episcopal visitations were instruments for enforcing uniformity and discipline over and above that which was already done at the parish level.

The new doctrinal and moral policy in question aimed likewise at a transformation of society *and* culture. In this connection, I shall use the terms 'popular culture' and 'popular religion' in order to pay heed to the fact that in many respects the culture of the common people was not identical with the culture of the bureaucratic and ecclesiastical élites which initiated the campaign of 'confessionalizing' the German people. This is not to imply, of course, that the common people reacted to this campaign uniformly in the same way. As we shall see, their reactions ranged, in fact, from active support via passive acquiescence to simple ignorance and open resistance.[18]

Politics and society

Agents

The principal agents of confessionalization were the territorial state, the confessional churches and, to some extent, their local supporters.

Most German states of the early modern period were marked to varying degrees by the political dualism of prince and estates. The latter periodically convened at a territorial diet, chiefly to vote on taxation. In the majority of territories, however, the political influence of the estates had been considerably reduced by about the middle of the seventeenth century. A notable exception was East Frisia. Elsewhere, the state and the central administration were almost relentlessly on the advance. Thus, by the eighteenth century, open conflicts between princes and estates had become rare. Considerable and prolonged conflicts took place, however, in Württemberg and Mecklenburg, which ended in 1770 and 1755 respectively.[19]

In Württemberg the eighteenth-century conflict between the dukes Karl Alexander and Karl Eugen and the estates had much to do with confessional matters, although the central issues at stake were the traditional rights and privileges of the territorial diet, which the dukes sought to minimize. The adherence to Pietism of a number of the leaders of the opposition helped to sustain the resistance against the princely campaign.[20]

A particularly close connection between confessionalization and the dualism of ruler and estates can be observed in seventeenth-century Habsburg Austria, most clearly in Bohemia following the Protestant disaster in the Battle of the White Mountain of 1620, and in Hungary in the wake of the defeat and the withdrawal of the Ottoman army in 1683; although it must be added that the Viennese court ultimately failed to break the power of the Calvinist Hungarian magnates. A systematic and rigidly enforced policy of Catholic reform amongst a nobility which at the turn of the sixteenth century strongly sympathized with Protestantism, decisively weakened the power of the estates in Austria, and, at least partially, in Hungary too. In Bohemia a considerable number of Protestant noblemen were simply sent into exile in the course of the Thirty Years War. These measures assured the state of the renewed support of an important, formerly estranged section of its political élite. What has been called *pietas Austriaca*, a specific form of officially encouraged, patriotic Catholic piety, played a critical role in Habsburg state-building.[21]

After Maria Theresia acceded to the Habsburg throne in 1740, it was once again a religious current which assisted the government in a wholesale revision of its traditional confessional policy. As the Vienna government initiated a series of badly needed reforms from 1740 onwards, it was the growing influence of Late Jansenism within the political élite, inside as well as outside court, which considerably helped to loosen the once-welcome ties between state and Catholic church, which had now become an obstacle to political change. At the end of this estrangement stood the triumph of secular absolutism, culminating in Joseph II's radical (and partly abortive) reforms of ecclesiastical life in the 1780s.[22]

The Habsburgs did not, however, assume leadership in the early stages of the Counter-Reformation in the Holy Roman Empire. This role was played by the dukes of Bavaria. In this duchy, too, the advance of confessionalization followed upon the suppression of Protestant sympathies among the nobility and a concomitant weakening of the estates. As elsewhere, the vanguard of the renewal were the Jesuits, who established a number of Bavarian colleges from 1556 onwards. But the church was by no means autonomous in these endeavours. It was the clerical council (*Geistlicher Rat*) established at the Munich court in 1570 which was instrumental in co-ordinating the Tridentine reform of the clergy, as well as in enforcing confessional uniformity among the political élite.[23]

A similar pattern appears in the Bishopric of Würzburg, where Julius Echter von Mespelbrunn (1573–1617), founder of the University of Würzburg in 1582, made himself the first Counter-Reformation bishop in Germany. At Würzburg, too, the newly created clerical council played a decisive role in the establishment of confessional uniformity, which included the expulsion of about 600 Protestants in 1586 and a call extended to the Jesuits. Extensive visitations served to gauge the gradual success of the reform of the clergy.[24]

Nonetheless, these early examples should not lead us to assume that the Counter-Reformation everywhere took root overnight. The moral and educational reform of the Catholic clergy, the basis of any further renewal, was, on the whole, a rather slow process. It was generally slower in the North-West than in the South of Germany. In the bishopric of Münster, for example, the largest ecclesiastical state in the Empire, it was only really completed after the end of the Thirty Years War, under Bishop Christoph Bernhard von Galen (r. 1650–78).

Among the major German territorial states during this period a singular and special role was played by Brandenburg-Prussia – chiefly for two reasons.

At Christmas in 1613 Prince Elector Johann Sigismund (r. 1608–19) solemnly converted from Lutheranism to Calvinism without, however, expecting his subjects to follow him down the same path.[25] During the ensuing decades the Calvinist court-preachers managed none the less to build up among the noble and courtly élite of the country a loyal group of Calvinists (examples were the counts of Dohna), who, reliable and dedicated to their task, were to become instrumental in the consolidation of Prussian absolutism. The Calvinist faith of Johann Sigismund, and of his successors and their closer entourage, made a measure of tolerance an indispensable ingredient of domestic politics in otherwise largely Lutheran Brandenburg-Prussia. This enabled the Great Elector, Friedrich Wilhelm (1640–88), as well as King Friedrich Wilhelm I (1713–40), to open their country to religious refugees from the Low Countries immediately following the end of the Thirty Years War, from France after the Revocation of the Edict of Nantes in 1685, and from the prince-bishopric of Salzburg in 1731, and to profit from these economically beneficial measures.[26]

Secondly, unlike the gradual establishment of absolutist rule in other German territories and in France, state-building in Brandenburg-Prussia did not rely to any significant extent on the integrative socio-cultural and political role of the court. The domestication of the nobility, as well as the consolidation of state authority as a whole, were primarily achieved through the establishment of a large army composed mostly of Prussian subjects and of its concomitant recruitment and training system.[27] This was one of the more important reasons why Friedrich I (1688–1713) could allow an alliance to form between the court and the Pietist movement, which was to come to full fruition in the first half of the eighteenth century. Halle, particularly its orphanage and university, became the centre of the Pietist movement, under the leadership of August Hermann Francke (1663–1727). In their wide-ranging endeavours, including extensive international trade and substantial printing geared to finance Pietist activities, Francke and his associates could count on the Prussian court's essential support. Under Friedrich Wilhelm I (1713–40), Pietism became a kind of 'Prussian state religion' (Carl Hinrichs) and, as such, an important ideological foundation for the administrative renewal of government. During those years the king's proximity to Pietism indirectly contributed to a further weakening of the political independence of the nobility. Next to Francke, another founding father of the Pietist movement also found an abode and new employment in Brandenburg-Prussia. This was Philipp Jakob Spener (1635–1705), who became a provost and member of the consistory in Brandenburg in 1691.[28]

In Brandenburg-Prussia the social life of the village or manorial demesne was clearly dominated by the Junker and the parson. As in most other Protestant states of Germany, confessionalization made the clergy into local agents of the state's central administration. The Lutheran pastor, as Ronnie Hsia put it, 'stood at the frontier of the confessional territorial state, expanding the boundary of discipline, morality, piety, obedience and sobriety'.[29] Originally of urban descent and generally representing the values and norms of the urban bourgeoisie, Lutheran ministers tended to found 'dynasties' of pastors and thus to become a partially self-co-opting caste. In eighteenth-century Württemberg 44 per cent of all Lutheran clergy came from such clerical families. In Pomerania, during the same period, 55 per cent of pastors and as many as 64 per cent of their wives had grown up in a parsonage. The latter became an important outpost of the culture of the urban middle and upper classes. Hundreds of luminaries of Germany's eighteenth- and nineteenth-century intellectual life came from this milieu, such as Andreas Gryphius, Lessing, Matthias Claudius, Schleiermacher, Wilhelm Mommsen, and Gustav Droysen, to name only a few.

On the side of Catholicism the major clerical force behind the renewal was the order of the Jesuits, established in Cologne and elsewhere in Germany from 1544 onwards. During the ensuing decades the first Jesuit colleges were founded in Vienna, Cologne, Ingolstadt, Prague, Munich, Trier, Innsbruck, and Dillingen. From 1573, the Jesuits were likewise entrusted with the reorganization of the German College in Rome, where the élite of priests, who were to implement the Tridentine reform throughout Germany, were henceforth given their training. These priests were to become a spiritual as well as a social élite. By 1600, 41 per cent of the alumni of this college were of noble descent, and this percentage steadily increased during the next two centuries, reaching 75 per cent by 1740. Other Counter-Reformation orders, such as the Capuchins, important in remoter areas where the influence of the Jesuits did not reach, were of a less élitist complexion, it is true; but the Jesuits were by far the most important in Germany.[30]

The spread of the new religious and moral discipline was no one-way street. The confessional and moral regime propagated by church and state also found lay support at the local level. Elders and deacons, lawyers, teachers and professors, sextons, sacristans, and curators typically found themselves in this role. But as yet we lack a sufficient number of case studies on the function of these local agents in the process of confessionalization.

Chronology

In terms of the effect of confessionalization on the social and economic life of Germans of the seventeenth and eighteenth centuries, that is, in accordance with the chronological division between the volumes of this handbook, we can distinguish roughly six different phases of development.[31]

In the first phase (1580–1620) the Catholic church and territorial states during the 1580s and 1590s joined ranks with the Protestant states, among which the Calvinist Palatine Electorate and Lutheran Württemberg had initiated the process of confessionalization during the 1560s. From Bavaria, Inner Austria, and Salzburg, where the Tridentine renewal set in at about the same time, the reform movement spread to Würzburg and Bamberg and hence to Fulda and the Eichsfeld, as well as to Trier and the dioceses of Constance, Basel, and Strasbourg. The occupation of the see of Cologne by a representative of the Bavarian Wittelsbachs in 1583 assured the eventual success of the further spread of Tridentine reform in the ecclesiastical territories of north-west Germany, albeit at a rather slow pace. On all sides, confessionalization during this phase was accompanied by a growing readiness to put peace at risk, as became apparent in the increasing paralysis on account of confessional tensions of the Imperial Chamber Court (*Reichskammergericht*) and the Imperial Diet. The centenary celebrations of the Reformation in 1617 confirmed the formidable extent to which confessionalism had got hold of the Protestant churches and of the Empire's political and social climate more generally.[32]

In its second phase (1620–50) the process of confessionalization reached its zenith, while the horrors of the Thirty Years War, as well as plagues and epidemics, provided a frequently almost apocalyptic scenery. While Calvinism decisively lost its political leverage, although it made its headway inside Brandenburg-Prussia's élite, Catholicism was able to regain a lot of lost ground. During the 1630s, with Sweden's and France's entry into the war, the Thirty Years War quickly began to lose its initial confessionalist momentum. From then onwards religion and politics began to separate, and it was secular political pragmatism which was ultimately to determine the outcome of the peace negotiations held at Münster and Osnabrück, which in 1648 culminated in the final drafting of the Peace of Westphalia.[33] This is not to say, of course, that confessional strife and antagonism in politics and theology ended abruptly in 1648; but they did lose some of their previous vehemence and venom after that date. This is why German histori-

ans conventionally regard 1648 as the end of the confessional era
(*Konfessionelles Zeitalter*), commonly dated 1555–1648. There are also
good reasons for thinking that, by the mid-seventeenth century, confessionalization had likewise spent most of its energy at the grassroots level as
well, even though, as we have seen, in some Catholic territories Tridentine
reform reached its completion only after that date.[34]

The third phase (1650–80) witnessed the beginning of the full
épanouissement of Baroque Catholicism, most remarkably in the bishopric
of Würzburg and the archdiocese of Mainz, where, during about a century
after 1650, a number of notable representatives of the Franconian family of
the Schönborns brought the Baroque culture and art of the Catholic court
to their fullest bloom and splendour. The first of the Schönborn bishops,
Johann Philipp (1605–73), bishop of Würzburg from 1642 and archbishop
of Mainz from 1647, signalled through his relatively moderate and even
irenic confessional policy that outright confessionalism had decisively spent
its lease of life. Renewed Catholic devotion was everywhere in its heyday –
well beyond 1680, although the latter date also heralded the beginning of
the end of the implementation of an actively confessional policy by the territorial state. Between about 1680 and 1740 what was left of confessionalization in politics in most major states of the Holy Roman Empire became a
part of the state's moral regime of purely secular *Polizey*.

The beginning of the fourth phase (1680–1740) marks a caesura not so
much regarding changes in Catholicism as in German Protestantism. The
beginning of the Lutheran Pietist movement in Germany is conventionally
dated to 1675, when the publication of Philipp Jacob Spener's *Pia
Desideria* gave Pietism its programme: the reform and revitalization of
ecclesiastical life through an intensification of practical and devotional
piety and the eschatologically saturated 'hope for better times', as well as
the implementation of Christian social reforms, notably in education and
welfare.[35] As a reform movement comprising professional men of the
church as well as lay people, Pietism had roots that went back as far as
Johann Arndt's first publication of his immensely popular and influential
Vier Bücher vom wahren Christentum in 1605–10.[36] The actual 'fathers' of
Pietism were the pastor and theologian Philipp Jacob Spener, consecutively
Lutheran pastor in Frankfurt am Main, Dresden, and Brandenburg, and
August Hermann Francke, professor of oriental languages (and later also of
theology) at the newly founded University of Halle, founder of the famous
orphanage at Halle, and indefatigable organizer of the Pietist entrepreneurial and missionary effort. Outside Brandenburg-Prussia a second strong-
hold of Pietism formed early on in Württemberg, where a close friend of
Spener's and Francke's, Johann Andreas Hochstetter (1637–1720), became
its first leader and spokesman.

Within a short period of time Pietism managed to establish itself as a
powerful reform movement within German Lutheranism. The spread of
this movement was accompanied by the unfolding of all the splendour of

Baroque Catholicism in Franconia and on the Rhine, where the Catholic élite gradually rediscovered the church's Erasmian heritage, that is, a relatively 'ecumenical' outlook, the roots of which can be traced back to the Christian humanism of the early sixteenth century. Notwithstanding these irenical tendencies, confessionalism of the worst kind manifested itself for the last time in the banishment of thousands of Protestant peasants from the archbishopric of Salzburg in 1731.

The fifth period (1740–89) was marked by the rise of Enlightened absolutism in Germany. The major German princes were trying increasingly to legitimate their authority in ways compatible with the principles championed by the Enlightenment. The Enlightenment's critical stance toward the traditions of church and religiosity created a growing distance between state and church in some Catholic territories, particularly in the Austria of Maria Theresia. Nonetheless the German Enlightenment, unlike some currents of thought among the French *philosophes*, was an essentially Christian intellectual movement.[37] Notwithstanding this qualification, the new status accorded by the Enlightenment to reason as opposed to tradition became an important source of secular thought, drawing many educated people away from the church and traditional forms of religiosity. This tendency was to manifest itself in the educated bourgeoisie (*Bildungsbürgertum*), which began to rise to social and political prominence towards the very end of the period considered here. The Enlightenment also left its imprint on Pietism. Among Pietists the influence of the new rationality, as well as, more generally speaking, the gradual change of the intellectual climate and *mentalité* surrounding them, helped to transform religious self-scrutiny into more secular forms of self-observation. The development of Pietist autobiography, from August Hermann Francke via Adam Bernd to Karl Philipp Moritz's autobiographical novel *Anton Reiser*, first published in instalments between 1785 and 1790, is a case in point.[38]

The German Enlightenment remained throughout the concern of an élite, which tried to impose its new standards of rationality on popular culture and religion. This was the case especially during the last decades of the eighteenth century. The aims of this campaign were twofold. First, rural dwellers were to be taught some elementary skills (such as reading, writing, and reckoning) and a measure of moral and religious education. Secondly, the peasantry was to receive professional instruction in order to improve its contribution to the agrarian economy of the day.[39] Peasants and rural dwellers were to become better subjects as well as better Christians. On the level of religious practice and belief this included a systematic onslaught against that which the Enlightened reformers condemned as superstition. In Catholic territories this campaign converged with the ecclesiastical and religious reforms initiated by Joseph II. The latter aimed at the submission of the Catholic church to the state and at a transformation of ecclesiastical and religious life according to the principles of Enlightened rationality. Monastic life was a particular target of Josephinism. But its propagators also turned against pilgrimages, liturgy which was considered excessive, the cult of saints, and many other aspects of Baroque Catholic piety.[40]

The joint effort of *Volksaufklärung* and *Josephinismus* abated during the sixth and last phase of confessional development (1789 to 1800 and beyond) that we want to consider. Following the outbreak of the French Revolution it not only became clear that Enlightened thought could have dangerous political consequences, but in Catholic territories it also became gradually more evident that the official encouragement of traditional forms of devotion could be used as a bulwark against the ideological advance of the French Revolution.[41] At the same time, the period after 1789 witnessed a first considerable wave of secularization in all areas of political, social, and economic life. Secularization gradually began to affect the daily life of all social groups, although this was a slow and not always linear process continuing well into the nineteenth century, notwithstanding the fact that a kind of endemic secularization was an intrinsic aspect of the process of confessionalization from the sixteenth century onward.[42]

It should be clear that we have looked chiefly at the 'official' timetable of the changes confession underwent as a political and social factor in Germany in the course of the seventeenth and eighteenth centuries, at transitions mainly experienced by the middle and upper classes. Changes in the religion of the common people followed a slower rhythm, as we shall see below by examining the limits of confessionalization.

Social aspects

Calvinism came to Germany at a time when the cities had long ceased to play their role as pacemakers of the Reformation. Although originally an urban movement, Calvinism in Germany was largely a territorial phenomenon. It was adopted in the Palatine Electorate by the Prince Elector of Brandenburg-Prussia and his closer courtly entourage, as well as in a number of lesser territories, chiefly of the Wetterau and Rhineland regions.[43] Where it made inroads into urban society, as in Aachen and Cologne, the Reformed confession was able to attract mainly a numerically small commercial and professional élite. Bremen and Colmar were the only Imperial Cities whose Protestant churches came to adhere semi-officially to the Reformed faith at the turn of the sixteenth century.[44] Almost everywhere Calvinist sympathies were above all an attribute of academic, civic, and administrative élites.

Not unlike the late intrusion of Calvinism into German territories, the

Catholic Counter-Reformation was very much a renewal imposed from above: hence the great importance attached by the Church of Rome to conversions of princes and other high-ranking Protestants.[45] The German Jesuits' main recruiting ground consisted of the middling and patrician ranks of urban society. It was from the cities that the Catholic renewal spread across the country.[46]

However, Baroque Catholicism was by no means as much an 'urban religion' as Lutheranism, which, in the course of the seventeenth and eighteenth centuries, became the almost quintessential expression of burgher society and its cultural values. The considerable embourgeoisement of the Lutheran clergy referred to above was part and parcel of this process. The Lutheran pastor in the countryside was an influential emissary of urban culture and values.

Nonetheless, whatever its cultural importance, it was not the city that primarily produced the impulses that led to confessional and religious change during the period considered here. This role was played above all by the state. It was to the territorial and confessional state that the entrepreneurial and educated bourgeoisie, which gained shape as distinct social groups towards the end of the eighteenth century, owed their existence (these groups are discussed in detail in Chapter 6 of this volume).

Without state protection, ethnic and religious minority groups, such as Jews, Huguenots, Mennonites, and Calvinists, especially along the Rhine and Lower Main, as well as in Brandenburg-Prussia, could not have become a small but entrepreneurial class in the way they did during the eighteenth century. On the whole, it was not the cities with their corporate organization of trade and commerce which generally proved hostile to large-scale innovation, but the princes, who accorded these groups the commercial freedom necessary for the accumulation of entrepreneurial capital.

The educated bourgeoisie (*Bildungsbürgertum*) owed its rise to the confessional state in so far as it was originally a primarily Protestant phenomenon, with some exceptions to this rule, it is true, such as the Catholic duchy of Baden in the eighteenth century.[47] It was composed of university-trained officials, pastors, professors, and lawyers. Most of them owed their position to the territorial state and, by way of the eighteenth-century bureaucratization of the state, eventually assumed the role of a kind of intelligentsia. As such, the *Bildungsbürgertum* of the late eighteenth and nineteenth centuries was an exclusively Central European phenomenon.[48]

Family and gender[49]

From the 1560s onward, the celibacy of the Catholic priest and Protestant clerical marriage became distinctive marks of confessional division. The Council of Trent clearly raised the value of priestly celibacy, while Protestantism – especially the Lutheran persuasion – imparted to marriage a new kind of day-to-day dignity.[50] However, regardless of these and other differences, like that concerning the sacramental nature of marriage, all three confessions, during the entire early modern period, strove with considerable success to bring the act of marriage gradually under ecclesiastical control.[51] At the end of the period considered here, marriage had become an exclusive preserve of the church, whereas previously, on the eve of the Reformation and Trent, the 'pre-marital' (in the modern sense) exchange of nuptial vows was generally considered to be the legally binding act. The wedding in church still played a secondary role. Sexual contact between men and women following a promise of marriage was not considered an offence.[52]

It was only logical, therefore, that the campaign of the churches to control marriage should go hand in hand with an attempt to suppress clandestine betrothals and premarital sex. The effect of this endeavour is mirrored by the distinctive increase in cases of broken marriage promises brought before the Calvinist presbytery of Emden in the course of the seventeenth and the early decades of the eighteenth centuries.[53] Likewise, during the years 1551–1620, the Catholic *Offizialat* of Constance turned from a marital into a pre-marital court, 'with the vast majority of its cases involving marital agreements before consecration and consummation'.[54]

However, we should not underestimate the extent of popular resistance against the authority of marital courts, especially among the lower classes, such as those of the duchy of Holstein. The peasants of Hohenlohe are another case in point. Neither should we overlook the extent to which the presence of an episcopal court in marital matters could simply be ignored.[55] The fact that a number of Constance court cases linked the problem of an unkept marriage promise with that of the loss of virginity indicates that marriage was still an entirely public event, very unlike its modern private nature.

The material aspects of an early modern marriage agreement should thus by no means be underestimated. A daughter's virginity, because it was an indispensable part of a family's reputation and honour, was an important constituent of a family's 'symbolic capital', especially in rural areas.[56] This is why village communities were not necessarily opposed to the campaign of the churches concerning marriage, for clandestine weddings without the previous consent of parents, premarital sex, and cases of illegitimacy could upset the social and economic balance of village society. There were control mechanisms at work on this social level, which were hardly imposed 'from above'; and they did not necessarily change overnight or break down with the advent of proto-industrialization from the later seventeenth century onwards.[57]

The interpretation of the rate of illegitimacy shows that we are still in need of more broadly based research. According to Peter Zschunke's research, illegitimacy differed among the three confessional groups. In eighteenth-century Oppenheim, a small town on the Rhine between Mainz and Worms, it amounted to an average 3.0 per cent among Catholics and to only 0.9 per cent among the better-off Reformed population. The Lutheran community assumed a middle position (2.4 per cent). In Augsburg, however, the Lutheran and Catholic rates were very similar during the first half of the eighteenth century while there was even a slight surplus of illegitimate baptisms on the Lutheran side (5.7 per cent as compared to 5.1 per cent) during the second half of the century.[58]

There are other contentious areas of demographic interpretation, too, notably regarding the fertility of women in the three confessional groups. Zschunke assumes that Oppenheim's Protestants probably practised birth control from the late seventeenth century onward.[59] However, such assumptions leave much open to speculation, as has been demonstrated recently regarding the demographic behaviour of the Huguenots of seventeenth century France.[60] Although Etienne François shows for Augsburg during the years 1648–1806 that Catholics and Lutherans developed specific forms of demographic behaviour, he hesitates to attribute this only to religious and confessional influence and prefers to suggest that 'confessional adherence had a much more indirect than direct influence on demographic behaviour'.[61]

This caveat also applies to the observation that infant mortality differed between the three confessional groups. In eighteenth-century Oppenheim it was clearly higher among Catholics than among Protestants. This has been attributed to confessionally specific conditions of *mentalité*, in so far as the death of an infant may have been less resignedly accepted among Protestants, but it probably also had to do – for social and confessional reasons – with the improved standards of hygiene in Protestant families.[62]

The Protestant Reformation did not strengthen traditional patriarchy alone; it also enhanced the social prestige of parenthood.[63] It should none the less be clear that men and women could, and often did, experience the religious and confessional changes of the age in a manner specific to their gender. The result of the growing exposure of religious belief and piety to currents of secularization from the late seventeenth century onward is a case in point. While religious practice in general underwent a gradual transition from the public to the private sphere, piety (*Frömmigkeit*) as an expression of Christian conduct became increasingly associated with the social role of women.[64] Already during earlier periods women had frequently been assigned a different relationship to the supernatural (or preternatural) than men, most visibly in the persecution of witches from the second half of the sixteenth century onward: the average witch, who could do harm to neighbours by magical means, was a woman.[65]

Confessional culture

Where confessionalization worked by persuasion rather than force, it deeply influenced the culture of the age.[66] It affected the theatre, for example, which the Jesuits came to use with great skill as a popular means of moral and religious instruction.[67] It drew music within its orbit, the singing of psalms by Calvinists and Lutherans, the magnificent painting tradition of the Baroque period beginning with the Prague school under Rudolf II, and Baroque architecture. We are dealing with a vast field, and there is no space here to discuss every individual aspect of contemporary culture, which gave expression to, or reflected in one way or other, the influence of the confessional and moral policy of church and state.[68] The culture thus 'authorized' was dominated by the princely court, and the latter in turn also reflected confessional preferences. The Catholic courts of southern and western Germany tended to follow the fashions *en vogue* at the Imperial court of Vienna, while the Protestant courts of central and northern Germany looked to the Prussian court in Berlin for similar inspiration.[69]

On a more popular level, a common cultural trait of the Catholic and Protestant confessions was the different expressions of a belief in the miraculous. Before the eighteenth century, when educated people in increasing numbers came to adopt a more rational world view, such expressions were very widespread socially. The Catholic *Mirakelbücher* pointing to miracles performed at saints' shrines, as well as the Protestant prognostics recording extraordinary phenomena observed in nature, which were interpreted as divine signs and thought to enjoin moral and religious improvement, are cases in point.[70] Another example for this is provided by the many dozens of seventeenth century printed reports on comets. The latter were seen as God's most eloquent warnings to sinful mankind, threatening individuals as well as communities which had swerved from the path of rectitude. This literature, too, seems to have appealed to members of all social classes before learned pamphlets on comets started to differ visibly from more pious tracts on the same theme from about the mid-seventeenth century onward.[71] In Protestant circles the concern for prognostics and divine signs could take on an apocalyptic urgency, especially during the Thirty Years War, such as in a warning expressed by the Württemberg theologian Johann Valentin Andreae against the sinfully luxurious life of the Stuttgart court 'dazing its conscience with entertainment'. It was prompted by miraculous signs seen in 1640. 'With such leaders', Andreae wrote about the courtiers, 'we are fast approaching the abyss.'[72]

Obvious limits on the efficacy of confessionalization reveal themselves when we consider the fact that the pre-Reformation veneration of saints found its continuation in German Lutheranism in the cult of its founder. Stories from the seventeenth and eighteenth centuries reveal that images of Luther were on occasion held to be incombustible, just as were saints' relics in popular Catholicism.[73] The frequent attacks of Protestant churchmen against the Catholic belief in the miraculous thus cannot really be taken at face value.

There can be no doubt, however, that Tridentine Catholicism was more successful than Protestantism in appealing to the popular belief in magic, as well as in quenching lay people's thirst for the miraculous. The pilgrimages revived in the course of the seventeenth and eighteenth centuries testify to this.[74] The pilgrimage to the bleeding-host shrine of Walldürn in the Odenwald came to assume the form of a kind of 'religious industry' by the mid-eighteenth century.[75] In Bavaria in particular, the Tridentine church strongly encouraged the growth and intensification of pilgrimage to Marian shrines, such as those of Altötting and Mariahilf at Passau.

Education

When Wolfgang Reinhard wrote his seminal essay in 1977 on the Counter-Reformation as modernization, in which he highlighted the basic similarities between Catholic and Protestant confessionalization, he specifically singled out literacy as an area in which early modern Protestantism stayed well ahead of the Catholic renewal.[76] It is still difficult, to discuss this thesis in any depth, given the fact that German research on early modern literacy, owing to the lack of good sources, very much lags behind modern French and British research on literacy. The following must necessarily remain sketchy.

The number of people able to read in late-fifteenth-century Germany has been estimated at only about 3 to 4 per cent of the entire population.[77] The Reformation seems to have initiated a significant boost in literacy. Circumstantial evidence from the sixteenth century suggests that 'a good proportion even of rural parishioners were presumed literate enough to study the catechism. In towns and cities expectations were even higher.'[78] The percentage probably exceeded the mere 20 to 30 per cent of sixteenth-century Germans who are thought to have been able to read. However, the level of literacy stagnated or even receded during the Thirty Years War, and real progress was made only from the mid-eighteenth century. The number of readers during this period has been estimated at 15 per cent in 1770 and 25 per cent in 1800. If Roger Schofield's theory that only about half of those able to read could also write is applicable here, this would leave us with a mere 13 per cent of Germans able to write in about 1800.[79] More recent research would indicate that these figures are probably too low.

For the Protestant Duchy of Oldenburg, Ernst Hinrichs has been in a position to calculate the considerably higher literacy rate of 83 per cent of men and 42 per cent of women for the period 1760–5 to 1811–14. This is based on a study of marriage signatures in registers introduced in the Protestant Duchy of Oldenburg during the Napoleonic occupation.[80] Etienne François has analysed the same kind of source material for Catholic Koblenz and the Mosel area. His findings are just as surprising: 87 per cent of literate men and 60 per cent of literate women. They apply to couples married between 1798 and 1802, and suggest that the quality of schooling and the degree of literacy in Catholic areas may have been considerably underrated in the past.[81]

It is risky to draw general conclusions from the Oldenburg and Koblenz material. What we really need for comparative purposes are similar quantitative studies on other German territories, because it is questionable, for example, whether literacy was as widespread in east-Elbian regions as in central and south-west Germany. The evidence unearthed by Hinrichs and François, however, does lend authority to the assumption that the degree of literacy in Germany during the last decades of the eighteenth century may well have been noticeably higher than hitherto assumed.

The Protestant Reformation of the sixteenth century doubtless had an important impact on the rise of literacy, but we should be careful not to look for monocausal explanations. For seventeenth-century England, at any rate, David Cressy's research has convincingly established that changes in literacy were caused by a variety of factors and not by religious causes alone.[82] Notwithstanding this caveat, it is safe to say that Tridentine Catholicism, and notably the Jesuit order, were more concerned with the schooling of an élite than with the education of the common people. At least for the first decades of the seventeenth century, if not for the entire century, it must be clear that Lutheran primary education excelled the quality of Catholic schooling on the same level, as is demonstrated by the cases of Augsburg and Bavaria.[83] Although Calvinist primary education was superior to its Lutheran counterpart in the duchies of Cleves and Berg at the end of the period considered here, there are no indications that this may have been the case as early as the beginning of the seventeenth century, and subsequent development remains obscure.[84]

During the initial phase of confessionalization considerably more attention was paid to the Calvinist *Gymnasien* and academies founded at Herborn in 1584, Bremen in 1585, Burgsteinfurt in 1588–91, and Hanau in 1607. Before the Thirty Years War these schools enjoyed excellent connections with the international network of late humanism. Reforms on this level of education were an intrinsic part of confessionalization from the 1530s and 1540s onwards, when Strasbourg founded its famous *Gymnasium* (to become a *Hochschule* under Johann Sturm's guidance in 1566) and the prince elector of Saxony made himself the patron of the three new élite schools of Grimma, Pforta, and Meissen in 1543.[85]

In Catholic territories the success of similar reforms, launched from the mid-sixteenth century on at the same level of education, was assured by the rapid creation of a network of Jesuit colleges, of which nine were founded in Bavaria alone between 1556 and 1631. In the important archbishopric of Mainz, colleges were founded between 1561 and 1621 in Mainz, Heiligenstadt, Aschaffenburg, and Erfurt. On the Lower Rhine and in Westphalia, the network spread outward from Cologne, where the Jesuits were entrusted with the direction of the *Gymnasium Tricoronatum* in 1556. It eventually reached as far as Hildesheim, whose cathedral school came under Jesuit control in 1595.[86]

As far as we know to date, there was a marked improvement in elementary schooling only from about the middle of the eighteenth century, when the problem increasingly came into the purview of cameralist reformers of the state's *Polizei*, and when enlightened reformers became concerned with the education of the common people. Unlike earlier educational reforms, this had purely secular motives and was pursued in Protestant and Catholic states alike. A modicum of education, it was thought, would enable the common people to become better and economically more productive subjects.[87]

The first decades of the sixteenth century witnessed a rapid decline of German universities. It was therefore incumbent on the Protestant territorial authorities to reform and reorganize their universities if the growing demand for trained clergy and administrators was to be met. This led to the reorganization of theological faculties and to the foundation of a number of Protestant universities and academies, mainly along the lines proposed by Philip Melanchthon. Marburg (1529) was the first of these foundations. The last new university to be created on a Melanchthonian basis was Lutheran Helmstedt (1576).[88]

Rather than humanist learning, theological orthodoxy was henceforth to dominate university life. The creation of the Hessian University of Giessen in 1607 is a case in point. In the eyes of the landgrave of Hessen-Darmstadt, it was to counterbalance the impact of Marburg, which had turned Calvinist on account of the conversion of Landgrave Moritz of Hessen-Kassel.[89] The more confessionalization held sway over universities, the more their traditional corporate autonomy was undermined by the princes, a fact explicitly recognized for the first time in the Imperial university privileges issued on 19 October 1693 for the new foundation of Halle.[90]

In the Catholic territories of Germany, where the impact of the Reformation likewise had left the universities in a state of disarray, the move toward a reform of higher learning was spearheaded by the Jesuits, beginning with their control over the University of Dillingen, which the prince-bishop of Augsburg entrusted to the Society of Jesus in 1563 shortly after its foundation. Ingolstadt and Würzburg were to become additional Jesuit strongholds, as well as the universities of Graz and Innsbruck.[91]

During the decades following the end of the Thirty Years War there was a marked diversification of the subject matter on offer at *Gymnasium* and university level, as mirrored notably by the contemporary revalorization of natural science and mathematics. From the turn of the century at the latest, orthodox theology was gradually losing its pre-eminence in higher education.[92]

The Lutheran University of Halle, founded by the Great Elector of Brandenburg in 1694, initiated the badly needed reform of Germany's universities on the eve of the Enlightenment. Halle became a model for subsequent reform of higher learning in other places – including the seminal foundation of the University of Göttingen in 1737 – not so much on account of its important impact as a centre of the Pietist movement, but rather as a result of the exemplary reform of legal studies (and, thus, of the training of state officials) by Christian Thomasius (1655–1728) and his colleagues.[93]

Book ownership

What did partially or entirely literate Germany read during the two centuries under consideration? The choice of reading was much influenced by religious concerns and by confessional choice. However, church and state did not leave this choice entirely up to chance. Well into the eighteenth century, even up to its very end, censorship was used by most sizeable territorial states in order to ensure confessional uniformity; at the same time, it was applied in order to keep out politically subversive literature. From the 1740s onward it was this purpose, rather than any attempt to maintain confessional uniformity, which in Brandenburg-Prussia, Austria, and other major states remained the chief reason for maintaining censorship.[94]

However, the effect of state control should not be overestimated. Bible ownership in German Lutheran households of the eighteenth century was based on real 'demand' rather than on the frequent incitements in contemporary state ordinances encouraging the common people to own Bibles.[95] This convincingly challenges the thesis that Bible ownership only became widespread in German Lutheran households in the course of the eighteenth century owing to the influence of Halle Pietism on German Protestant school ordinances issued between about 1725 and 1775.[96] The Bible was above all a book of spiritual edification and comfort. But it was also used among German Protestants in attempts to predict the future by using God's word in order to harness, as it were, His providence, or for magical purposes.

Protestant culture, as Thomas Nipperdey has written, 'is a culture of the ear, not of the eye. Books and writings are not the concern of the priest alone but the concern of all.'[97] Ronnie Hsia has recently confirmed this view, albeit only indirectly, by referring to 'the poverty of Catholic bourgeois literature'. Book ownership in Bavaria, for example, was largely the preserve of the monasteries with their substantial libraries.[98] However, the lack of specific modern research may yet hide from us variations in this picture.

Seventeenth- and eighteenth-century book ownership by the urban middle and lower middle classes as well as rural dwellers was dominated by religious and spiritual literature. A study of book-ownership in the villages of the Salzgitter area during the 1750s informs us that the hymn-book and the Bible were the most frequently encountered books. In terms of frequency, they were followed by a series of treatises for family edification, whose authors belong to the forerunners of Pietism.[99] A more broadly based investigation of the Swabian village of Laichingen in the years 1748–1820 has yielded very similar results: the percentage of books of a secular content owned by Laichingers during those years was practically nil (1.3 per cent of all titles examined), and considerably lower than the ownership of secular books in Speyer during the period 1780–6 (20 per cent) or in nearby Tübingen in the years 1800–10 (22 per cent). What is more, during the period in question the Laichingers owned more books on average than the burghers of Tübingen. In Laichingen, books of meditation, prayer, and spiritual edification amounted to almost 50 per cent of the volumes examined, and the majority of these were of a Pietist complexion.[100]

We must of course pay heed to the fact that the overwhelming majority of the book-owners referred to above were non-academics, peasants, artisans, and even day-labourers. The eighteenth-century book-ownership of these classes reveals few traces of secularization. But the popularity of pre-Pietist and Pietist authors in Salzgitter and Laichingen indicates that for many of the book-owners in question the blind confessionalism of earlier generations had become a thing of the past.

It was chiefly among the educated classes, and above all within the new *Bildungsbürgertum*, that the secular thought of the eighteenth century found its adherents. This finds its expression in contemporaneous book production, which brought fourth a new bourgeois literature.[101] Figures from the Leipzig book fair from the years 1740 to 1800 indicate that the production of novels, plays, books of poetry, and those of *Trivialliteratur* increased from 6 to 21 per cent of the entire turnover. At the same time, the literature on education grew from 0.5 to 5 per cent and even learned treatises on agriculture from 1 to 8 per cent. Meanwhile, theology clearly lost ground at Leipzig compared to this new kind of literature: it declined dramatically from 39 to 14 per cent.

Taken together, the various figures on book ownership discussed here indicate that between about 1740 and 1800 secularized thought was the almost exclusive province of the learned and administrative élite.

Economy

After the end of the Thirty Years War the force and vitality which the German economy had demonstrated in the course of the preceding century were largely spent. The reorientation of the world market from the Mediterranean to the north Atlantic on the eve of the Thirty Years War left Germany stranded in the backwaters of the new Atlantic trade, and, with the exception of Hamburg, left the German states excluded from direct participation in the expanding colonial and world market, which proved to become an important avenue toward social and economic modernity in the case of Britain.

When Max Weber published his seminal essay on 'Protestantism and the spirit of capitalism' in 1904–5 there were good reasons, therefore, why he concentrated his analytical effort mainly on locating the roots of the capitalist spirit in the history of English and western European Protestantism.[102] There is no need to rehearse Weber's well-known argument in great detail. His aim was to demonstrate an inner connection – not a causal relationship, but rather an elective affinity – between the ethic of ascetic Protestantism and the spirit of early entrepreneurial capitalism. As he saw it, the classic representation of ascetic Protestantism was English Puritanism as mirrored mainly in the pastoral works of Richard Baxter. However, he did not entirely exclude from his purview other forms of strict Protestantism, such as the Quakers and Mennonites, for example, who likewise combined a strict methodicalness of individual life with the 'most intensive development of business acumen'. And Weber added the following observations:

> The part which the former have played in England and North America fell to the latter in Germany and the Netherlands. That in East Prussia Frederick William I tolerated the Mennonites as indispensable to industry, in spite of their absolute refusal to perform military service, is only one of numerous well-known cases which illustrate the fact, though, considering the character

of that monarch, it is one of the most striking. Finally, that this combination of intense piety with just as strong a development of business acumen, was also characteristic of the Pietists, is common knowledge. It is only necessary to think of the Rhine country and of Calw.[103]

Elsewhere, however, Weber thought that Calvinism rather than Pietism (although both were forms of what he calls ascetic Protestantism) shared the closest affinity with the spirit of capitalism, in so far as it advocated the sanctification of the self in one's profession, while the Lutheran way to seek God's grace – inherent in German Pietism – was primarily one of seeking forgiveness of sins.[104] Despite this differentiation, Weber left no doubt that he was convinced that the ethic of ascetic Protestantism in general, particularly that of Puritanism, but also that of the Quakers, Mennonites, and Pietists, stood at the cradle of modern *homo œconomicus*.

It cannot be the task of this chapter to do justice to the lively discussion and debate which Weber's thesis has generated from 1905 down to this day.[105] Let us rather look in more detail at the economic role of the Mennonites in Germany, and, in particular, at the economic activity of ascetic Protestants in the Rhineland and Calw.

Owing to their persecution by most confessional churches and states of early modern Germany, a considerable number of Dutch and German Mennonites emigrated to eastern and south-eastern Europe from the mid-sixteenth century onwards. In Central Europe they could only find an abode where the mercantilist policy of princes allowed them to settle. This was the case in Brandenburg-Prussia, and, notably in the Lower Rhenish County of Moers, where William of Orange gave shelter to Mennonite refugees for the first time in 1583. Before this County was inherited by Friedrich I of Brandenburg-Prussia in 1702, the Mennonite colony in Krefeld experienced a continuous economic rise and became an important centre of the proto-industrial production of linen and of silk manufactory.[106] Not too far up the Rhine, the Counts of Neuwied allowed Mennonites to stay in the town of Neuwied in the later seventeenth century. In 1770 there were 23 Mennonite families out of a total of 490 households. They had been joined in the meantime by a small group of 'inspired' Protestant separatists (*Inspirierte*) and a number of Moravian brethren. The latter, as well as the Mennonites, deployed some significant commercial activity at Neuwied, which included the superb furniture-making trade of the Roentgen family.[107]

It was above all the mercantile interest of greater and lesser princes of all three confessions concerned, which – particularly on the Lower Rhine – allowed Mennonite, Reformed, and other religious exiles progressively to ignore the restrictions inherent in local guild regulations or else to step entirely outside the corporate protection afforded by the urban environment in order to be able to operate in a much less regulated market. From these beginnings in the late sixteenth and seventeenth centuries, there began to develop in the course of the eighteenth century a well-to-do entrepreneurial bourgeoisie, which owed its existence chiefly to the mercantilist policy of the territorial state. Like the new educated bourgeoisie, which was to surface on a broader scale at the very end of the eighteenth century, this new entrepreneurial bourgeoisie was not in any significant way tied to the traditions of the society of estates of the past. Although it may be tempting to exaggerate their significance for eighteenth-century Germany, both types of new bourgeoisie did herald the new *Bürgertum* of the nineteenth century, albeit to an initially rather modest extent.[108]

The Imperial City of Aachen is a good case in point. In the sixteenth century, Reformed immigrant families from the Low Countries quickly rose to social prominence. Their rise created political turmoil whose eventual outcome was that the Catholic authorities firmly resumed their position for generations to come. Reformed merchants, henceforward cut off from political rule, soon established themselves as important entrepreneurs in Aachen's hinterland on account of princely protection extended to them. Their commercial activity extended from textile production, which was gradually transformed in this area into a proto-industrial putting-out system, to iron and metal mining and manufacture.[109]

Another instructive example is the *Lindfabrique*, the manufacture of linen ribbons in the Wuppertal, particularly in Barmen and Elberfeld, where the so-called *Garnnahrung* enjoyed princely privilege. During the seventeenth and eighteenth centuries this was in the hands of Calvinist families in the midst of an otherwise largely Catholic environment. As their production rapidly expanded in the course of the eighteenth century they turned to putting-out linen for spinning, thus gradually employing the rural population of an extended area.[110]

A similar corporation also formed at Calw in Württemberg in 1650, the *Calwer Färber- und Zeughaus-Compagnie*, a commercial organization producing and dyeing worsted cloths and engaged in banking. From the 1680s the families involved in this endeavour gradually came under the influence of Pietism, and as Pietist entrepreneurial families they put out a significant amount of work to the rural population of the adjoining regions. The Calw company, referred to by Max Weber in the passage cited above, was an exemplar of efficiency, clearly a result of the zeal, dedication, and optimal use of time of its members.

However, as Hartmut Lehmann has demonstrated, it would be misleading to view the Pietist work ethic as an exclusive cause of the success of the Calw company, for the corporation was founded and became successful before Pietism began to have its particular impact on its members. All we can claim, therefore, is that 'here, as elsewhere, Pietism encouraged zeal, care, and plain-dealing', virtues, in short, whose economic advantage is undeniable.[111] But it would be wrong to conclude that the Pietist ethic was a specific cause of the Calw variety of the spirit of capitalism. And it would be just as misleading to view the Calw Pietists, as well as the Lower Rhenish entrepreneurs referred to above, as heralds of the bourgeois individualism of the nineteenth-century entrepreneurial class. Economic individualism, which Max Weber sees as an expression of ascetic Protestantism, had yet to come, for we should not overlook how closely the Calw, Aachen, and Barmen families discussed here were interwoven by family and corporate ties, which, taken together, almost amounted to a system of risk-sharing.[112]

On a slightly different level of discussion, the examination of corporate structures in the Nagold valley, where the Calw merchants put out their *Zeugmacherei* (worsted weaving) to a small army of rural and urban weavers, has led Sheilagh Ogilvie to argue that proto-industry in this area of Württemberg, unlike the suggestions made by the proponents of the theory of proto-industrialization, did not lead to the dissolution of traditional social ties or of traditional matrimonial and sexual habits. As a result, Ogilvie highlights Pietism 'as the *expression* of the prevailing structure. The organs of strict Protestantism', she adds, 'often enforced the socializing norms of the corporate community or the guild in which the commercial ethos of the unregulated market transaction associated by intellectual historians with "early capitalism" is conspicuously absent.'[113]

Likewise it has been argued that Prussian Pietism centred on Halle was marked not by an individualistic but by an altruistic professional and economic ethic. Unlike in Calw, where evidence to this effect is conspicuously lacking, the considerable profits which resulted from the broad commercial activities and the particular business acumen of the Halle Pietists were used for poor relief and in education.[114]

In the case of the economic success of the Mennonites and Reformed exiles in Neuwied, Krefeld, Aachen, and Barmen, we should not overlook the fact that the professional ethic was not the only cause of achievement. Princely protection as well as the particular conditions of exile likewise played their role. Religious exiles were frequently 'condemned' to seek commercial success simply for lack of other economic options, and in order to establish themselves in a new environment in which they frequently enjoyed only a limited franchise.

A number of German princes were aware of this and were willing to profit where the opportunity to give shelter to religious exiles arose. They did so mainly out of mercantile considerations; genuine religious toleration played no part in their decisions. This applies in particular to Brandenburg-Prussia, where religious exiles repeatedly found a new abode during the seventeenth and eighteenth centuries, notably several thousand Huguenot refugees in the wake of the Revocation of the Edict of Nantes in 1685. Many of these Huguenots settled in Berlin, completely transforming its social and cultural complexion. Smaller communities formed at Prenzlau, Frankfurt an der Oder, Stendal, Magdeburg, Halle, and Halberstadt. They were instrumental in modernizing Brandenburg's textile production, especially in silk-weaving, hat-making, weaving of stockings and gloves, as well as in introducing new ways of producing worsted draperies (*Zeug-druckerei*). They also brought with them essential knowhow in the manufacturing of gold and silver wire.[115]

For all the nuances in economic behaviour between the various groups of early modern Protestants, it should none the less remain clear that the most obvious differences in this respect can be observed between Catholics and Protestants. This is demonstrated, for example, by Peter Zschunke's study of tri-confessional Oppenheim in the late seventeenth and eighteenth centuries. His findings show that while Catholics concentrated almost exclusively on the here and now in their economic behaviour, Protestants were more farsighted, most visibly in the fact that they stored noticeably greater provisions of corn as seed and nutritional reserve for bad times.[116] However, Zschunke's work also leads us to assume that the differences between the socio-economic behaviour of Lutherans and Calvinists were in general not as marked as Max Weber would like us to expect. This is supported by the findings from Etienne François's analysis of Augsburg's tax registers from the late seventeenth and eighteenth centuries, which reveals a relatively even distribution of property between Catholics and Lutherans.[117]

To what extent did the common people of the period in question identify themselves with and adapt to the norms and standards of behaviour recommended and inculcated by the confessional church and state? This will be looked at in the last section of this chapter.

Limits of confessionalization and *Polizey*

The consolidation of absolutist rule in German territories not only was a gradual process; the degree of its achievement also differed between one state and the other, and everywhere there was a gap between the theory of absolute princely sovereignty and the practical results of its establishment on the regional and local level. Likewise, the thrust of confessionalization and, in particular, its acceptance by the common people varied not only over time, but also from one town and region to the next.

The most commonly used indicators for measuring the impact of confessionalization at the grass-roots level are visitation records and the study of baptismal names. The following remarks are based chiefly on examinations of such sources.

A visitation held in the bishopric of Speyer in 1583 revealed that the great majority of the people were satisfied with the Catholic church and that there was no particular hiatus separating lay people from the clergy.[118]

However, the visitation also made clear

> that the villagers and the authorities had different ideas of how priests
> should behave. The Church wanted a sober, educated and celibate
> élite. The villagers wanted the priests to perform their duties and to
> obey the rules of the community. In the traditional Church the parish
> priests behaved as the villagers wanted.[119]

Local social and cultural interest could thus well develop into a barrier
against the advance of Tridentine Catholicism. This was the case, for example, in the bishopric of Osnabrück, where the visitation of 1624–5 revealed
the deep inroads Protestantism had made in this diocese, as well as the desolate state of the Catholic clergy, many of whom 'had succeeded their
fathers in their parish livings'. The church hierarchy's attempt to mend
these deficiencies and to imbue the common people with a sense of Catholic
confessional identity – sorely lacking in 1624–5 – met with stiff resistance.[120] Likewise, in villages of Upper Austria, where Protestantism had
won considerable support at the local level, the introduction of Tridentine
norms was a long-term endeavour with only limited success, as is shown by
a study of the change in baptismal names in the late sixteenth and seventeenth centuries. A similar situation also prevailed in Augsburg.[121]

Although the success of a number of measures of Catholic reform on the
local level should by no means be underrated, as is demonstrated by the
consistently high level of church attendance reached in the Electorate of
Cologne from the later seventeenth century onwards, it was, to all appear-
ances, impossible to generate a broadly based climate of *active* participation in the celebration of the mass.[122]

How do we explain this reticence of the common people? We should primarily be aware of the fact that Tridentine reform of worship was essentially directed against traditional forms of popular religion which did not
blend easily with the new, more hierarchical forms of worship.[123] These traditional forms of popular religion gave expression to the communal social
and cultural concerns referred to above.[124] During the period considered
here, they were more resilient against change in the countryside, while confessional renewal conversely had a better chance of taking root in cities and
towns.[125] The latter clearly served as points of departure as well as strongholds of Catholic reform, as centres for missions in the countryside.

The same claim could be made for Protestant confessionalization,
although in this case, too, it should be clear that rural communities did take
over important aspects of Protestant doctrine on their own terms:
'Christocentric language is used in more than a formulaic way in wills;
Psalms and hymns are sung at times of trial; family prayers are said; the
consistory is appealed to for the settling of quarrels in reformed areas.'[126]
On the other hand, evidence from the late-sixteenth and early-seventeenth
century Palatinate leads us to assume that the impact of reform was considerably more efficacious among town and village élites than among the great

majority of lay people, who were deeply rooted in traditional forms of popular religious belief and practice, including the frequent resort to therapeu-
tic forms of magic, which the established Protestant churches largely fought
in vain.[127]

Next to the resort to magic, it was particularly the widespread belief in
judicial astrology which gave assurance in times of particular insecurity.
Well into the second half of the seventeenth century, when upper-class
defection set in, this was largely shared even by the upper strata of contemporary society, as was the belief in the miraculous nature of comets. Lower
down the social scale, judicial astrology lost none of its enduring fascina-
tion, as can be seen in the fact that the rural population in the area of Fulda
boycotted a calendar for 1768, which, as ordered by the prince-abbot of
Fulda, had appeared without the traditional lists of propitious days for
bloodletting.[128]

Small wonder that Bernd Roeck is able to advance the thesis that the
number of soothsayers, crystal-gazers, chiromantists, and wizards in
Augsburg during the first half of the seventeenth century must have been
'astonishingly high', considering the fact that court records most probably
only reveal the tip of the iceberg in this matter. At the same time he makes
clear, however, that the countryside continued to provide the cultural breeding ground in which such professions developed, whereas by the seventeenth century cities of the size of Augsburg had ceased to play this role.[129]
The criticism of wise women voiced by the seventeenth-century Catholic
preacher Prokop von Templin, whom he seemed to oppose primarily as
unwanted competition, confirms this picture.[130] It has been pointed out –
correctly, to my mind – that among lay people of the seventeenth century
there was little awareness of a conflict between officially sanctioned religion and the resort to magic and sorcery, despite the campaign of the
churches, especially the Protestant ones, against what they perceived as
'superstition'.[131] However, as long as representatives of the established
churches continued to advocate the persecution of witches, which had its
heyday in Germany between the 1590s and the mid-seventeenth century, it
was difficult for the average lay person to recognize this conflict.[132]

Among the common people of the countryside the doctrines and new
ecclesiastical institutions of the confessional church and state were often
accepted and used only selectively, as is shown by the case of the peasants
of Hohenlohe, or by the early-modern worship of Martin Luther as a kind
of saint, particularly widespread in Saxony and Thuringia.[133] While in
German Protestantism some forms of traditional Catholic belief and religious practice thus managed to survive for a long time, the success of the
Catholic Counter-Reformation in suppressing currents of Protestantism
varied from region to region. In Bavaria a kind of 'Crypto-Protestantism'
held on tenaciously, especially in areas bordering on the bishopric of
Salzburg.[134] In the latter territory, as perhaps in Bavaria, too, the real problem 'was popular religion, not Protestantism. At issue was the power of the

state versus the rural communes.'[135] The state won, of course, and the
result was the great wave of expulsion of Salzburg peasants in 1731, many
of whom found refuge in East Prussia and Lithuania.[136]

Although this was the last attempt within the Holy Roman Empire by a
territorial prince to impose confessional uniformity, the relationship
between popular religion on the local level and the state's secular *Polizey*
was no less tenuous, especially when enlightened administrators turned
toward improving the culture and religion of the rural population during
the last decades of the eighteenth century. This came to light especially in
Catholic areas, as secular as well as ecclesiastical authorities went about
reducing the number of holidays and days of rest. These measures were
greeted with considerable resistance, notably on the part of the lower
classes and of young people, who stood to lose a number of hitherto popular festive occasions.[137]

Similarly, the new hymn books introduced throughout Protestant Germany during the last couple of decades of the eighteenth century, reorganized along guidelines provided by the reforming spirit of the
Enlightenment, provoked protracted acts of open resistance on the part of
the common people in various parts of the country. While in towns this was
expressed chiefly by the middle and lower-middle classes, there was wholesale rejection of the new hymn book by entire village communities in the
countryside.[138] A recent survey of the controversy rightly emphasizes its religious and cultural aspects and shows the extent to which the elements of
confessionalization wholeheartedly accepted by the common people, such as
the hymns, had in time become elements of a popular cultural tradition of
which rural communities were not prepared to let go because they encapsulated a part of their cultural as well as confessional identity.[139] In a rather
strange reversal of roles, the population of the countryside had thus become
the standard-bearer of its own version of confessionalization at a time when
the attempt to impose confessional uniformity and discipline in state and
ecclesiastical policy had long since given way to purely secular *Polizey*.

Notes

I should like to thank Roland E. Hofer, Manfred Jakubowski-Tiessen, Ulrich Pfister,
and Dominik Sieber for having read and commented on an earlier draft of this
chapter. The manuscript was essentially completed in June, 1992. More recent
books and articles are referred to only very selectively in the appropriate places.
Material on early modern Switzerland, *de facto* a separate state from the
Reformation period onwards, has been excluded throughout.

1   Dietrich Gerhard, 'Regionalismus und ständisches Wesen als ein Grundthema
    europäischer Geschichte', *HZ* 147 (1952), esp. pp. 308ff.

2   Hans-Ulrich Wehler, *Deutsche Gesellschaftsgeschichte* (Munich, 1987), i. esp. pp. 270 and 278–9.

3   See e.g. Peter Blickle, 'Untertanen in der Frühneuzeit: Zur Rekonstruktion der politischen Kultur und der sozialen Wirklichkeit Deutschlands im 17. Jahrhundert', *Vierteljahrsschrift für Sozial- und Wirtschaftsgeschichte*, 70 (1983), pp. 483–522. See also Peter Blickle, *Deutsche Untertanen: Ein Widerspruch* (Munich, 1981).

4   For detailed accounts of several aspects of the following, which appeared after the completion of the manuscript for this chapter, see Heinrich R. Schmidt, *Konfessionalisierung im 16. Jahrhundert* (Munich, 1992); Hans-Christoph Rublack, ed., *Konfessionalisierung im Luthertum: Wissenschaftliches Symposion des Vereins für Reformationsgeschichte . . .* (Gütersloh, 1992); Heinz Schilling, ed., *Kirchenzucht und Sozialdisziplinierung im frühneuzeitlichen Europa* (Berlin, 1994). Reliable regional accounts for the period up to 1650 can be found in Anton Schindling and Walter Ziegler, eds, *Die Territorien des Reiches im Zeitalter der Reformation und der Konfessionalisierung: Land und Konfession, 1500–1650*, i: *Der Südosten* (Münster, 1989); ii: *Der Nordosten* (Münster, 1990); iii: *Der Nordwesten* (Münster, 1991); iv: *Mittleres Deutschland* (Münster, 1992); v: *Der Südwesten* (Münster, 1994). See also n. 65 below.

5   See Heinz Schilling, ed., *Die reformierte Konfessionalisierung in Deutschland – Das Problem der 'Zweiten Reformation'* (Gütersloh, 1986).

6   Paul Münch, 'Volkskultur und Calvinismus. Zu Theorie und Praxis der "reformatio vitae" während der "Zweiten Reformation"', in Schilling, *Die reformierte Konfessionalisierung*, pp. 291–307.

7   Johann Morhard, *Haller Haus-Chronik* (Schwäbisch Hall, 1962), p. 97.

8   See Paul Warmbrunn, *Zwei Konfessionen in einer Stadt: Das Zusammenleben von Katholiken und Protestanten in den paritätischen Reichsstädten Augsburg, Biberach, Ravensburg und Dinkelsbühl von 1548 bis 1648* (Wiesbaden, 1983), and Bernd Roeck, *Eine Stadt in Krieg und Frieden: Studien zur Geschichte der Reichsstadt Augsburg zwischen Kalenderstreit und Parität* (2 parts, Göttingen, 1987), i. pp. 20, 93–94; ii. pp. 844–69; Etienne François, *Die unsichtbare Grenze: Protestanten und Katholiken in Augsburg 1648–1806* (Sigmaringen, 1991), esp. pp. 110–11, 133, and 140–1. See also Etienne François, 'De l'uniformité à la tolérance: Confession et société urbaine en Allemagne, 1650–1800', *Annales*, 37 (1982), pp. 783–9; and the forthcoming study by Peter Wallace, *Communities and Conflict in Early Modern Colmar, 1600–1730* (Atlantic Highlands, NJ, 1995).

9   Peter Zschunke, *Konfession und Alltag in Oppenheim: Beiträge zur Geschichte von Bevölkerung und Gesellschaft einer gemischtkonfessionellen Kleinstadt der frühen Neuzeit* (Wiesbaden, 1984), pp. 100–2.

10 Heinz Schilling, 'Die Konfessionalisierung im Reich: Religiöser und gesellschaftlicher Wandel in Deutschland zwischen 1555 und 1620', *HZ* 246 (1988), pp. 1–45, esp. p. 6.

11 Ronnie Po-chia Hsia, *Social Discipline in the Reformation: Central Europe, 1550–1750* (London, 1989), p. 143.

12 Gerhard Oestreich, 'Strukturprobleme des europäischen Absolutismus', in Gerhard Oestreich, *Geist und Gestalt des frühmodernen Staates: Ausgewählte Aufsätze* (Berlin 1969), pp. 179–97. See also Winfried Schulze, 'Gerhard Oestreichs Begriff der Sozialdisziplinierung', *ZHF* 14 (1987), pp. 265–302, and Stefan Breuer, 'Sozialdisziplinierung. Probleme und Problemverlagerungen eines Konzepts bei Max Weber, Gerhard Oestreich und Michel Foucault', in Christoph Sachße and Florian Tennstedt, eds,

Soziale Sicherheit und soziale Disziplinierung (Frankfurt am Main, 1986), pp. 45–69.

13 Münch, 'Volkskultur und Calvinismus', p. 305.

14 Wolfgang Schluchter, 'Die Zukunft der Religionen', *Kölner Zeitschrift für Soziologie und Sozialpsychologie*, 33 (1981), pp. 605–22, esp. p. 608 (the translation is mine).

15 Heinz Schilling, 'Konfessionalisierung als gesellschaftlicher Umbruch: Inhaltliche Perspektiven und massenmediale Darstellung', in Sigfried Quandt, ed., *Luther, die Reformation und die Deutschen: Wie erzählen wir unsere Geschichte?* (Paderborn, 1982), pp. 35–51, Section 8; Richard van Dülmen, 'Reformation und Neuzeit: Ein Versuch', *ZHF* 14 (1987), pp. 1–25, esp. pp. 24–5.

16 Wolfgang Reinhard, 'Gegenreformation als Modernisierung? Prolegomena zu einer Theorie des konfessionellen Zeitalters', *ARG* 68 (1977), pp. 226–52; Wolfgang Reinhard, 'Zwang zur Konfessionalisierung? Prolegomena zu einer Theorie des konfessionellen Zeitalters', in *ZHF* 10 (1983), pp. 257–77; Schilling, 'Konfessionalisierung im Reich'.

17 See e.g. Harm Klueting, *Das Konfessionelle Zeitalter, 1525–1648* (Stuttgart, 1989), pp. 150–1. See also Gottfried Maron, 'Katholische Reform und Gegenreformation', in *Theologische Realenzyklopädie* (Berlin, 1989), vol. xviii, pp. 45–72.

18 See pp. 335–8 below.

19 See Rudolf Vierhaus, *Deutschland im Zeitalter des Absolutismus (1648–1763)* (Göttingen, 1978), pp. 130–3; Gerhard Oestreich, *Verfassungsgeschichte vom Ende des Mittelalters bis zum Ende des alten Reiches* (Stuttgart, 1970), esp. pp. 77–83; Volker Press, 'Formen des Ständewesens in den deutschen Territorialstaaten des 16. und 17. Jahrhunderts', in Peter Baumgart, ed., *Ständetum und Staatsbildung in Brandenburg-Preußen* (Berlin, 1983), pp. 280–318; see also Volker Press, *Krieg und Krisen: Deutschland 1600–1715* (Munich, 1991), pp. 110–23.

20 Mary Fulbrook, *Piety and Politics: Religion and the Rise of Absolutism in England, Württemberg and Prussia* (Cambridge, 1983); Hans Medick, 'Von der Bürgerherrschaft zur Staatsbürgerlichen Gesellschaft: Württemberg zwischen Ancien Régime und Vormärz', in Lutz Niethammer, Ute Frevert, Hans Medick, *et al.*, eds, *Bürgerliche Gesellschaft in Deutschland: Historische Einblicke, Fragen, Perspektiven* (Frankfurt am Main, 1990), pp. 52–79.

21 R. J. W. Evans, *The Making of the Habsburg Monarchy, 1550–1700* (Oxford, 1979); Heinz Schilling, *Höfe und Allianzen: Deutschland 1648–1763* (Berlin, 1989), pp. 310–23; Karin MacHardy, 'Der Einfluß von Status, Konfession und Besitz auf das politische Verhalten des niederösterreichischen Ritterstandes 1580–1620', in Grete Klingenstein and Heinrich Lutz, eds, *Spezialforschung und Gesamtgeschichte* (Munich, 1982), pp. 56–83.

22 Peter Hersche, *Der Spätjansenismus in Österreich* (Vienna, 1977); Elisabeth Kovács, ed., *Katholische Aufklärung und Josephinismus* (Munich, 1979).

23 Heinrich Lutz, 'Das konfessionelle Zeitalter, Erster Teil: Die Herzöge Wilhelm IV. und Albrecht V.', in Max Spindler, ed., *Handbuch der Bayerischen Geschichte* (Munich, 1966), ii. pp. 297–350, esp. pp. 335–50.

24 See Hans Eugen Specker, 'Die Reformtätigkeit der Würzburger Fürstbischöfe Friedrich von Wirsberg (1558–1573) und Julius Echter von Mespelbrunn (1573–1617)', *Würzburger Diözesan-Geschichtsblätter*, 27 (1965), pp. 29–125; Johannes Meier, 'Die katholische Erneuerung des Würzburger Landkapitels Karlstadt im Spiegel der Landkapitelsversammlungen und Pfarreivisitationen 1579 bis 1624', *Würzburger Diözesan-Geschichtsblätter*,

33 (1971), pp. 51–125; Hans-Christoph Rublack, *Gescheiterte Reformation: Frühreformatorische und protestantische Bewegungen in süd- und west-deutschen geistlichen Residenzen* (Stuttgart, 1978), pp. 50–75.

25 Bodo Nischan, *Prince, People, and Confession: The Second Reformation in Brandenburg* (Philadelphia, 1994).

26 See, *inter alia*, Rudolf von Thadden, *Die Brandenburgisch-Preussischen Hofprediger im 17. und 18. Jahrhundert: Ein Beitrag zur Geschichte des absolutistischen Staatsgesellschaft in Brandenburg-Preussen* (Berlin, 1959); Rudolf von Thadden and Michelle Magdelaine, eds, *Die Hugenotten, 1685–1985* (Munich, 1985); Heinz Duchhardt, ed., *Der Exodus der Hugenotten: Die Aufhebung des Edikts von Nantes als europäisches Ereignis* (Cologne, 1985).

27 Peter Lundgreen, 'Gegensatz und Verschmelzung von *alter* und *neuer* Bürokratie im Ancien Régime: Ein Vergleich von Frankreich und Preußen', in Ernst Hinrichs, ed., *Absolutismus* (Frankfurt am Main, 1986), pp. 162–80; Hans Rosenberg, *Bureaucracy, Aristocracy, and Autocracy: The Prussian Experience, 1660–1815* (Boston, 1966), esp. pp. 27–45.

28 Carl Hinrichs, 'Die universalen Zielsetzungen des Halleschen Pietismus', in Carl Hinrichs, *Preußentum und Pietismus: Der Pietismus in Brandenburg-Preußen als religiös-soziale Reformbewegung* (Göttingen, 1971), pp. 1–125; Klaus Deppermann, *Der hallesche Pietismus und der preußische Staat unter Friedrich III. (I.)* (Göttingen, 1961); Fulbrook, *Piety and Politics*.

29 On this and the following see Hsia, *Social Discipline*, pp. 14–21 (citation from p. 20); see also Otto Hintze, 'Der Absolutismus im Kirchenregiment und die Entstehung einer preußischen Landeskirche (Territorialismus)', first published in 1906, in Hinrichs, *Absolutismus*, pp. 361–76; Hans-Christoph Rublack, 'Der "Wohlgeplagte Priester": Vom Selbstverständnis lutherischer Geistlichkeit im Zeitalter der Orthodoxie', *ZHF* 16 (1989), pp. 1–30.

30 Peter Schmidt, *Das Collegium Germanicum in Rom und die Germaniker: Zur Funktion eines römischen Ausländerseminars (1522–1914)* (Tübingen, 1914).

31 For a necessarily different chronology of confessionalization owing to its concentration on the 16th century, see Schmidt, *Konfessionalisierung*.

32 See e.g. Jürgen Schönstädt, *Antichrist, Weltheilsgeschehen und Gottes Werkzeug: Römische Kirche, Reformation und Luther im Spiegel des Reformationsjubiläums 1617* (Wiesbaden, 1978).

33 Ernst Walter Zeeden, *Das Zeitalter der Glaubenskämpfe, 1555–1648* (Stuttgart 1970), pp. 104–5.

34 Klueting, *Das Konfessionelle Zeitalter*, pp. 26–7; Rainer Beck, 'Der Pfarrer und das Dorf: Konformismus und Eigensinn im katholischen Bayern des 17./18. Jahrhunderts', in Richard van Dülmen, ed., *Armut, Liebe, Ehre: Studien zur historischen Kulturforschung* (Frankfurt am Main, 1988), pp. 107–43, esp. p. 136. See also Rainer Beck, *Unterfinning: Ländliche Welt vor Anbruch der Moderne* (Munich, 1993).

35 See e.g. Hartmut Lehmann, *Das Zeitalter des Absolutismus: Gottesgnadentum und Kriegsnot* (Stuttgart, 1980), esp. pp. 83–93, and Hartmut Lehmann, '"Absonderung" und "Gemeinschaft" im frühen Pietismus: Allgemeinhistorische und sozialpsychologische Überlegungen zur Entstehung und Entwicklung des Pietismus', *Pietismus und Neuzeit*, 4 (1979), pp. 54–82. Manfred Jakubowski-Tiessen and Hartmut Lehmann, 'Der Pietismus', in Verein für Schleswig-Holsteinische Kirchengeschichte, ed., *Schleswig-Holsteinische Kirchengeschichte* (Neumünster, 1984), iv. pp. 269–334, esp. pp. 304–05, provide a good regional example of the spread of Pietist social reform. For recent general accounts, see W. R. Ward, *The*

Protestant Evangelical Awakening (Cambridge, 1992); Martin Brecht, ed., *Der Pietismus vom 17. bis zum frühen 18. Jahrhundert* (Göttingen, 1993); Richard L. Gawthrop, *Pietism and the Making of Eighteenth-Century Prussia* (Cambridge, 1993).

36 Johannes Wallmann, 'Die Anfänge des Pietismus', *Pietismus und Neuzeit*, 4 (1979), pp. 11–53.

37 See e.g. Horst Möller, *Vernunft und Kritik: Deutsche Aufklärung im 17. und 18. Jahrhundert* (Frankfurt am Main, 1986), pp. 81 and 99 *et passim*.

38 Robert Minder, *Glaube, Skepsis und Rationalismus: Dargestellt aufgrund der autobiographischen Schriften von Karl Philipp Moritz* (Frankfurt am Main, 1974); Hans-Jürgen Schings, *Melancholie und Aufklärung: Melancholiker und ihre Kritiker in Erfahrungsseelenkunde und Literatur des 18. Jahrhunderts* (Stuttgart, 1977), pp. 97–121; Günter Niggl, *Geschichte der deutschen Autobiographie im 18. Jahrhundert: Theoretische Grundlegung und literarische Entfaltung* (Stuttgart, 1977), pp. 62–75.

39 Jürgen Voss, 'Der Gemeine Mann und die Volksaufklärung im späten 18. Jahrhundert', in Hans Mommsen and Winfried Schulze, eds, *Vom Elend der Handarbeit: Probleme historischer Unterschichtenforschung* (Stuttgart, 1981), pp. 208–33, esp. p. 210.

40 See n. 21 above.

41 Christof Dipper, 'Volksreligiosität und Obrigkeit im 18. Jahrhundert', in Wolfgang Schieder, ed., *Volksreligiosität in der modernen Sozialgeschichte* (Göttingen, 1986), pp. 73–96, esp. pp. 92–3.

42 Hartmut Lehmann, 'Neupietismus und Säkularisierung: Beobachtungen zum sozialen Umfeld und politischen Hintergrund von Erweckungsbewegung und Gemeinschaftsbewegung', *Pietismus und Neuzeit*, 15 (1989), pp. 40–58, esp. pp. 40–1; Richard J. Evans, 'Religion and Society in Modern Germany', *European Studies Review*, 12 (1982), pp. 249–88, esp. p. 273.

43 Henry J. Cohn, 'The Territorial Princes in Germany's Second Reformation, 1559–1622', in Menna Prestwich, ed., *International Calvinism 1541–1715* (Oxford, 1985), pp. 135–65; J. F. Gerhard Goeters, 'Genesis, Formen und Hauptthemen des reformierten Bekenntnisses in Deutschland: Eine Übersicht', in Schilling, *Die reformierte Konfessionalisierung*, pp. 44–59.

44 Jürgen Moltmann, *Christoph Pezel (1539–1604) und der Calvinismus in Bremen* (Bremen, 1958); Kaspar von Greyerz, *The Late City Reformation in Germany: The Case of Colmar, 1522–1628* (Wiesbaden, 1980), esp. pp. 124–54.

45 Hsia, *Social Discipline*, pp. 44–5.

46 Wolfgang Brückner, 'Zum Wandel der religiösen Kultur im 18. Jahrhundert: Einkreisungsversuche des "Barockfrommen" zwischen Mittelalter und Massenmissionierung', in Ernst Hinrichs and Günter Wiegelmann, eds, *Sozialer und kultureller Wandel in der ländlichen Welt des 18. Jahrhunderts* (Wolfenbüttel, 1982), pp. 65–83, esp. p. 70.

47 Klaus Gerteis, *Bürgerliche Absolutismuskritik im Südwesten des Alten Reiches vor der Französischen Revolution* (Trier, 1986), p. 93 *et passim*.

48 Wehler, *Deutsche Gesellschaftsgeschichte*, i. pp. 206–12; Rosenberg, *Bureaucracy*, pp. 159–65; Medick, 'Von der Bürgerherrschaft', esp. pp. 75–9. See also Wolfgang Ruppert, *Bürgerlicher Wandel: Die Geburt der modernen deutschen Gesellschaft im 18. Jahrhundert* (Frankfurt am Main, 1983), esp. pp. 36–42.

49 Important studies on the role of gender in early modern Germany which have appeared since the completion of the manuscript for this chapter are Heide Wunder, *'Er ist die Sonn, sie ist der Mond': Frauen in der Frühen Neuzeit* (Munich, 1992); Lyndal Roper, *Oedipus and the Devil: Witchcraft,*

Sexuality and Religion in Early Modern Europe (London, 1994); Claudia Ulbrich, 'Frauen- und Geschlechtergeschichte, Teil I: Renaissance, Humanismus und Reformation', in *Geschichte in Wissenschaft und Unterricht*, 45 (1994), pp. 108–20 (a review article).

50 Luise Schorn-Schütte, ' "Gefährtin" und "Mitregentin": Zur Sozialgeschichte der evangelischen Pfarrfrau in der Frühen Neuzeit', in Heide Wunder and Christina Vanja, eds, *Wandel der Geschlechterbeziehungen zu Beginn der Neuzeit* (Frankfurt am Main, 1991), pp. 109–53, esp. pp. 110 and 116–17.

51 Richard van Dülmen, 'Fest der Liebe: Heirat und Ehe in der frühen Neuzeit', in Richard van Dülmen, ed., *Armut, Liebe, Ehre: Studien zur historischen Kulturforschung* (Frankfurt am Main, 1988), pp. 67–106, and Richard van Dülmen, *Kultur und Alltag in der Frühen Neuzeit: Das Haus und seine Menschen* (Munich, 1990), pp. 157–72; see also Meier, 'Die katholische Erneuerung', p. 98.

52 See e.g. Stefan Breit, *"Leichtfertigkeit" und ländliche Gesellschaft: Voreheliche Sexualität in der frühen Neuzeit* (Munich, 1991).

53 Heinz Schilling, 'Sündenzucht und frühneuzeitliche Sozialdisziplinierung: Die calvinistisch-presbyteriale Kirchenzucht in Emden vom 16. bis 19. Jahrhundert', in Georg Schmidt, ed., *Stände und Gesellschaft im Alten Reich* (Stuttgart, 1989), pp. 265–302, esp. pp. 277 and 294–7.

54 Thomas Max Safley, 'Marital Litigation in the Diocese of Constance, 1551–1620', *The Sixteenth Century Journal*, 12 (1981), pp. 61–77 (citation from p. 65). See also Thomas Max Safley, *Let No Man Put Asunder: The Control of Marriage in the German Southwest, A Comparative Study, 1550–1600* (Kirksville, Mo., 1984).

55 Karl-Sigismund Kramer, *Volksleben in Holstein (1550–1800)* (Kiel, 1987), p. 114; Thomas Robisheaux, 'Peasants and Pastors: Rural Youth Control and the Reformation in Hohenlohe, 1540–1680', *Social History*, 6 (1981), pp. 281–300; Safley, *Let No Man Put Asunder*, p. 77.

56 David Sabean, 'Unehelichkeit: Ein Aspekt sozialer Reproduktion kleinbäuerlicher Produzenten. Zu einer Analyse dörflicher Quellen um 1800', in Robert Berdahl, *et al.*, eds, *Klassen und Kultur: Sozialanthropologische Perspektiven in der Geschichtsschreibung* (Frankfurt am Main, 1982), pp. 54–76, esp. p. 62. See also David Sabean, *Property, Production and Family in Neckarhausen, 1700–1870* (Cambridge, 1990); Jürgen Schlumbohm, *Lebensläufe, Familien, Höfe: Die Bauern und Heuerleute des Osnabrückischen Kirchspiels Belm in protoindustrieller Zeit, 1650–1860* (Göttingen, 1994).

57 Sheilagh C. Ogilvie, 'Coming of Age in a Corporate Society: Capitalism, Pietism and Family Authority in Rural Württemberg, 1590–1740', *Continuity and Change*, 1 (1986), pp. 279–331. See also Thomas Robisheaux, *Rural Society and the Search for Order in Early Modern Germany* (Cambridge, 1989).

58 Zschunke, *Konfession und Alltag*, pp. 149; François, *Die unsichtbare Grenze*, pp. 42 and 65–66. For a general discussion of this and the following, see Hans-Christoph Rublack, 'Konfession als demographischer Faktor?', in Horst Rabe *et al.*, eds, *Festgabe für Ernst Walter Zeeden zum 60. Geburtstag* (Münster, 1976), pp. 62–96.

59 Zschunke, *Konfession und Alltag*, pp. 193–226.

60 Philip Benedict, 'The Huguenot Population of France, 1600–1685: The Demographic Fate and Customs of a Religious Minority', *Transactions of the American Philosophical Society*, 81/5 (1991), pp. 19–20. But see also Ulrich Pfister, 'Die Anfänge der Geburtenbeschränkung in Europa: Wege zu einer umfassenden Analyse', in Peter Borscheid and Hans J. Teuteberg, eds, *Ehe,*

Liebe, Tod. Zum Wandel der Familie ... in der Neuzeit (Münster, 1983), pp. 213–32; and Christian Pfister, *Bevölkerungsgeschichte und Historische Demographie, 1500–1800* (Munich, 1994), pp. 91–4.

61 François, *Die unsichtbare Grenze*, p. 72.

62 For the former thesis, see Zschunke, *Konfession und Alltag*, pp. 168–71; on early modern infant mortality more generally, see Dülmen, *Kultur und Alltag*, pp. 87–101. Regarding hygiene, see Peter Hersche, 'Die protestantische Laus und der katholische Floh: Konfessionsspezifische Aspekte der Hygiene', in Benedikt Bietenhard, ed., *Ansichten von der rechten Ordnung: Bilder über Normen und Normenverletzung in der Geschichte; Festschrift für Beatrix Mesmer* (Bern/Stuttgart, 1991), pp. 43–60. On Halle Pietism and hygiene, see Hinrichs, 'Die universalen Zielsetzungen', p. 21. See also Alfons Labitsch, *Homo Hygienicus: Gesundheit und Medizin in der Neuzeit* (Frankfurt am Main, 1992), esp. pp. 60–104.

63 Schorn-Schütte, ' "Gefährtin" und "Mitregentin" ', p. 153.

64 Heide Wunder, 'Von der *frumkeit* zur *Frömmigkeit*: Ein Beitrag zur Genese bürgerlicher Weiblichkeit (15.–17. Jahrhundert)', in Ursula A. J. Becher and Jörn Rüsen, eds, *Weiblichkeit in geschichtlicher Perspektive: Fallstudien und Reflexionen zu Grundproblemen der historischen Frauenforschung* (Frankfurt am Main, 1988), pp. 174–88.

65 See e.g. Ingrid Ahrendt-Schulte, 'Schadenzauber und Konflikte: Sozialgeschichte von Frauen im Spiegel der Hexenprozesse des 16. Jahrhunderts in der Grafschaft Lippe', in Heide Wunder und Christina Vanja, eds, *Wandel der Geschlechterbeziehungen zu Beginn der Neuzeit* (Frankfurt am Main, 1991), pp. 198–228; Gerhard Schormann, *Hexenprozesse in Deutschland* (Göttingen, 1981), p. 118. See also Wolfgang Behringer, *Hexenverfolgung in Bayern: Volksmagie, Glaubenseifer und Staatsräson in der Frühen Neuzeit* (Munich, 1987); the special issue of *GG* 16/1 (1990), on the persecution of witches in rural society; Rainer Walz, *Hexenglaube und magische Kommunikation im Dorf. Frühneuzeitliche Hexenverfolgungen in der Grafschaft Lippe* (Paderborn, 1993); Harald Siebenmorgen, ed., *Hexen und Hexenverfolgung im deutschen Südwesten* (2 vols., Ostfildern, 1994); Roper, *Oedipus and the Devil*, esp. part III. See also below, n. 131.

66 For general information, see Richard van Dülmen, *Kultur und Alltag in der frühen Neuzeit*, iii: *Religion, Magie, Aufklärung, 16.-18. Jahrhundert* (Munich, 1994); Hansgeorg Molitor and Herbert Smolinsky, eds, *Volksfrömmigkeit in der Frühen Neuzeit* (Münster, 1994). See also Paul Münch, *Lebensformen in der Frühen Neuzeit* (Frankfurt am Main/Berlin, 1992); Norbert Schindler, *Widerspenstige Leute. Studien zur Volkskultur der frühen Neuzeit* (Frankfurt am Main, 1992), and the discussion of this work in *Historische Anthropologie*, 1 (1993), pp. 294–312.

67 Jean-Marie Valentin, *Theatrum Catholicum, XVIe-XVIIe siècles: Les Jésuites et la scène en Allemagne au XVIe et au XVIIe siècles* (Nancy, 1990).

68 An excellent summary of the various aspects of this theme can be found in Hsia, *Social Discipline*, pp. 89–121. On music and singing, see particularly Patrice Veit, 'Das Gesangbuch in der Praxis Pietatis der Lutheraner', in Hans-Christoph Rublack, ed., *Die lutherische Konfessionalisierung in Deutschland* (Gütersloh, 1992), pp. 435–54, 455–9 (discussion), and earlier publications by this author.

69 Schilling, *Höfe und Allianzen*, pp. 25–6. See also Horst Rabe, *Reich und Glaubensspaltung: Deutschland 1500–1600* (Munich, 1989), pp. 420–1.

70 Rebekka Habermas, 'Wunder, Wunderliches, Wunderbares: Zur Profanisierung eines Deutungsmusters in der Frühen Neuzeit', in van

Dülmen, *Armut, Liebe, Ehre*, pp. 38–66. See also Wolfgang Brückner, 'Erneuerung als selektive Tradition: Kontinuitätsfragen im 16. und 17. Jahrhundert aus dem Bereich der konfessionellen Kultur', in *Der Übergang zur Neuzeit und die Wirkung von Traditionen* (Hamburg, 1978) [Veröffentlichungen der Joachim Jungius-Gesellschaft der Wissenschaften, vol. 32], pp. 55–78, esp. p. 73.

71 Hartmut Lehmann, 'Die Kometenflugschriften des 17. Jahrhunderts als historische Quelle', in Wolfgang Brückner, Peter Blickle, and Dieter Breuer, eds, *Literatur und Volk im 17. Jahrhundert: Probleme populärer Kultur in Deutschland* (Wiesbaden, 1985), ii. pp. 683–700.

72 Johann Valentin Andreae, *Selbstbiographie*, ed. and transl. David Christoph Seybold, in David Christoph Seybold, ed., *Selbstbiographien berühmter Männer* (Winterthur, 1977), ii, pp. 220–1.

73 R. W. Scribner, 'Incombustible Luther: The Image of the Reformer in Early Modern Germany', *P&P* 90 (1986), pp. 38–68; now also in R. W. Scribner, *Popular Culture and Popular Movements in Reformation Germany* (London, 1987), pp. 323–53.

74 See, *inter alia*, Werner Freitag, *Volks- und Elitenfrömmigkeit in der Frühen Neuzeit: Marienwallfahrten im Fürstbistum Münster* (Paderborn, 1991); Rebekka Habermas, *Wallfahrt und Aufruhr: Zur Geschichte des Wunderglaubens in der Frühen Neuzeit* (Frankfurt am Main, 1991).

75 Wolfgang Brückner, *Die Verehrung des Heiligen Blutes in Walldürn: Volkskundlich-soziologische Untersuchung zum Strukturwandel barocker Wallfahrten* (Aschaffenburg, 1958).

76 Reinhard, 'Gegenreformation', p. 236.

77 Rudolf Engelsing, *Analphabetentum und Lektüre: Zur Sozialgeschichte des Lesens in Deutschland zwischen feudaler und industrieller Gesellschaft* (Stuttgart, 1973), p. 20.

78 Gerald Strauss, *Luther's House of Learning: Indoctrination of the Young in the German Reformation* (Baltimore, 1978), pp. 127–8.

79 See Engelsing, *Analphabetentum*, pp. 61–2; Roger Schofield, 'Dimension of Illiteracy in England, 1750–1850', in Harvey J. Graff, ed., *Literacy and Social Development in the West* (1973; Cambridge edn, 1981), p. 203.

80 Ernst Hinrichs, 'Zum Alphabetisierungsstand in Norddeutschland um 1800: Erhebungen zur Signierfähigkeit in zwölf oldenburgischen Gemeinden', in Ernst Hinrichs and Günter Wiegelmann, eds, *Sozialer und kultureller Wandel in der ländlichen Welt des 18. Jahrhunderts* (Wolfenbüttel, 1982), pp. 21–42. See also Ernst Hinrichs, 'Lesen, Schulbesuch und Kirchenzucht: Eine Fallstudie zum Prozeß der Alphabetisierung in Norddeutschland', in *Mentalitäten und Lebensverhältnisse: Beispiele aus der Sozialgeschichte der Neuzeit. Festschrift für Rudolf Vierhaus* (Göttingen, 1982), pp. 15–33.

81 Etienne François, 'Die Volksbildung am Mittelrhein im ausgehenden 18. Jahrhundert: Eine Untersuchung über den vermeintlichen "Bildungsrückstand" der katholischen Bevölkerung Deutschlands im Ancien Régime', *Jahrbuch für westdeutsche Landesgeschichte*, 3 (1977), pp. 277–304. See also Voss, 'Der Gemeine Mann', pp. 221–32.

82 David Cressy, *Literacy and the Social Order: Reading and Writing in Tudor and Stuart England* (Cambridge, 1980), p. 96; see also Richard Gawthrop and Gerald Strauss, 'Protestantism and Literacy in Early Modern Germany', *P&P* 104 (1984), pp. 32–41.

83 Hsia, *Social Discipline*, pp. 114–15.

84 Gerhard Schormann, 'Zweite Reformation und Bildungswesen am Beispiel der Elementarschulen', in Schilling, *Die reformierte Konfessionalisierung*, pp. 308–16.

85 Anton Schindling, *Humanistische Hochschule und Freie Reichsstadt: Gymnasium und Akademie in Strassburg 1538–1621* (Wiesbaden, 1977); Friedrich Paulsen, *Geschichte des gelehrten Unterrichts auf den deutschen Schulen und Universitäten vom Ausgang des Mittelalters bis zur Gegenwart* (Leipzig, 1919; 3rd edn., Berlin, 1965), i. pp. 276–325.

86 Paulsen, *Geschichte des gelehrten Unterrichts*, pp. 387–443.

87 See Dipper, 'Volksreligiosität'; and Wehler, *Deutsche Gesellschaftsgeschichte*, i. pp. 285–6.

88 Paulsen, *Geschichte*, i. pp. 216–55.

89 Manfred Rudersdorf, 'Der Weg zur Universitätsgründung in Gießen: Das geistige und politische Erbe Landgraf Ludwigs von Hessen-Marburg', in Peter Moraw and Volker Press, eds, *Academia Gissensis: Beiträge zur älteren Gießener Universitätsgeschichte* (Marburg, 1982), pp. 45–82; see also Paulsen, *Geschichte des gelehrten Unterrichts*, p. 307.

90 Notker Hammerstein, 'Zur Geschichte der deutschen Universität im Zeitalter der Aufklärung', in Hellmuth Rössler and Günther Franz, eds, *Universität und Gelehrtenstand, 1400–1800* (Limburg/Lahn, 1970), pp. 145–82, esp. p. 152.

91 Ernst Schubert, 'Zur Typologie gegenreformatorischer Universitätsugründungen: Jesuiten in Fulda, Würzburg, Ingolstadt und Dillingen', in Rössler and Franz, *Universität und Gelehrtenstand*, pp. 85–105; Paulsen, *Geschichte des gelehrten Unterrichts*, i. p. 412.

92 *Ibid.*, pp. 495–7 and 512–24.

93 Hammerstein, 'Zur Geschichte', pp. 162–6.

94 Engelsing, *Analphabetentum*, p. 64; see also Schilling, *Höfe und Allianzen*, p. 315.

95 Etienne François, 'Les Protestants allemands et la Bible: Diffusion et pratiques', in Yvon Belaval and Dominique Bourel, eds, *Le siècle des Lumières et la Bible* (Paris, 1986), pp. 47–58, esp. p. 52.

96 Gawthrop and Strauss, 'Protestantism and Literacy', pp. 43–50.

97 Thomas Nipperdey, 'The Reformation and the Modern World', in E. I. Kouri and Tom Scott, eds, *Politics and Society in Reformation Europe: Essays for Sir Geoffrey Elton on his Sixty-Fifth Birthday* (London, 1987), pp. 535–52, esp. p. 543.

98 Hsia, *Social Discipline*, p. 99.

99 Mechthild Wiswe, 'Bücherbesitz und Leseinteresse Braunschweiger Bauern im 18. Jahrhundert', *ZAgrarGAgrarSoz* 23 (1975), pp. 210–15.

100 Hans Medick, 'Buchkultur auf dem Lande: Laichingen 1748–1820. Ein Beitrag zur Geschichte der protestantischen Volksfrömmigkeit in Altwürttemberg', in Hans Erich Bödeker, Gérald Chaix, and Patrice Veit, eds, *Der Umgang mit dem religiösen Buch. Studien zur Geschichte des religiösen Buches in Deutschland und Frankreich in der frühen Neuzeit* (Göttingen, 1991), pp. 156–79; Etienne François, 'Buch, Konfession und städtische Gesellschaft im 18. Jahrhundert: Das Beispiel Speyers', in *Mentalitäten und Lebensverhältnisse*, pp. 34–55, esp. p. 37. Erdmann Weyrauch, 'Die Illiteraten und ihre Literatur', in Brückner, Blickle, and Breuer, eds, *Literatur und Volk*, ii. pp. 465–74, on book ownership by non-academics in Braunschweig and Kitzingen between 1600 and 1660, confirms these findings.

101 On this and the following see Ruppert, *Bürgerlicher Wandel*, p. 126. See also Ursula A. J. Becher, 'Religiöse Erfahrung und weibliches Lesen – Zu einigen Beispielen des 18. Jahrhunderts', in Hans Erich Bödeker, Gerald Chaix, and Patrice Veit, eds., *Der Umgang mit dem religiösen Buch: Studien zur Geschichte des religiösen Buches in Deutschland und Frankreich in der*

frühen Neuzeit (Göttingen, 1991), pp. 316–34, esp. pp. 324–5.

102 Max Weber, 'Die protestantische Ethik und der Geist des Kapitalismus', in Max Weber, *Die protestantische Ethik: Eine Aufsatzsammlung*, ed. Johannes Winckelmann (7th edn, Gütersloh, 1984), i. pp. 27–277. For a translation which unfortunately lacks accuracy in details, see Max Weber, *The Protestant Ethic and the Spirit of Capitalism*, transl. and ed. by Talcott Parsons (New York, 1958).

103 Weber, 'Die protestantische Ethik', p. 37; the citations are from Weber, *The Protestant Ethic*, p. 44.

104 Weber, 'Die protestantische Ethik', p. 151; or Weber, *The Protestant Ethic*, pp. 137–38.

105 For recent summaries of the debate, see Hartmut Lehmann, 'Asketischer Protestantismus und ökonomischer Rationalismus: Die Weber-These nach zwei Generationen', in Wolfgang Schluchter, ed., *Max Webers Sicht des okzidentalen Christentums: Interpretation und Kritik* (Frankfurt am Main, 1988), pp. 529–53; Richard van Dülmen, 'Weber's Thesis in Light of Recent Social History', *Telos*, 78 (1989), pp. 71–80. See also Hartmut Lehmann and Guenther Roth, eds, *Weber's Protestant Ethic: Origins, Evidence, Contexts* (Cambridge, 1993).

106 Herbert Kisch, *Die hausindustriellen Textilgewerbe am Niederrhein vor der industriellen Revolution: Von der ursprünglichen zur kapitalistischen Akkumulation* (Göttingen, 1981), esp. pp. 130–52.

107 Walter Grossmann, 'Städtisches Wachstum und religiöse Toleranzpolitik am Beispiel Neuwied', *Archiv für Kulturgeschichte*, 62/63 (1980/81), pp. 207–32; Michael Stürmer, *Handwerk und höfische Kultur: Europäische Möbelkunst im 18. Jahrhundert* (Munich, 1982), pp. 240–75.

108 See Heinz Schilling, 'Wandlungs- und Differenzierungs-prozesse innerhalb der bürgerlichen Oberschichten West- und Nordwestdeutschlands im 16. und 17. Jahrhundert', in Marian Biskup and Klaus Zernack, eds, *Schichtung und Entwicklung der Gesellschaft in Polen und Deutschland im 16. und 17. Jahrhundert* (Wiesbaden, 1982), pp. 121–73, esp. pp. 159–63. See also above, pp. 320, 322.

109 See, *inter alia*, Heinz Schilling, 'Bürgerkämpfe in Aachen zu Beginn des 17. Jahrhunderts: Konflikte im Rahmen der alteuropäischen Stadtgesellschaft', *ZHF* 1 (1974), pp. 175–231; Herbert von Asten, 'Religiöse und wirtschaftliche Antriebe im niederrheinischen Montangewerbe des 16. und 17. Jahrhunderts', *Rheinische Vierteljahrsblätter* 28 (1963), pp. 62–83; Kisch, *Textilgewerbe*, pp. 258–316.

110 Walter Dietz, *Die Wuppertaler Garnnahrung: Geschichte der Industrie und des Handels von Elberfeld und Barmen, 1400 bis 1801* (Neustadt an der Aisch, 1957); see also Kisch, *Textilgewerbe*, pp. 162–257, and Stephanie Reekers, 'Das Baumwollgewerbe in Westfalen von den Anfängen im 16. Jahrhundert bis zum Beginn des 19. Jahrhunderts', *Westfälische Forschungen*, 37 (1987), pp. 105–34, esp. pp. 122–5.

111 Hartmut Lehmann, 'Pietismus und Wirtschaft in Calw am Anfang des 18. Jahrhunderts: Ein lokalhistorischer Beitrag zu einer universalhistorischen These von Max Weber', *ZWLG* 31 (1972), pp. 249–77; the citation is from p. 273 (translation mine).

112 See Asten, 'Religiöse und wirtschaftliche Antriebe', p. 75.

113 Ogilvie, 'Coming of Age'; the citation is from p. 322.

114 Hinrichs, 'Die universalen Zielsetzungen', pp. 12 and 74; Deppermann, *Der hallesche Pietismus*, pp. 177–9. See also Carl Hinrichs, 'Pietismus und Frühkapitalismus in Preußen', in Carl Hinrichs, *Preußentum und Pietismus*, pp. 301–51, esp. pp. 320–4.

115	See esp. Stefi Jersch-Wenzel, 'Ein importiertes Ersatzbürgertum? Die Bedeutung der Hugenotten für die Wirtschaft Brandenburg-Preußens', in Thadden and Magdelaine, *Die Hugenotten*, pp. 160–71.

116	Zschunke, *Konfession und Alltag*, p. 124. In a revisionist reappraisal, Peter Hersche has recently pointed to what he considers to be the basic virtues of eighteenth century Catholic 'backwardness', in Peter Hersche 'Intendierte Rückständigkeit: Zur Charakteristik des geistlichen Staates im alten Reich', in Schmidt, *Stände und Gesellschaft*, pp. 133–49.

117	François, *Die unsichtbare Grenze*, pp. 101–7.

118	Marc R. Forster, *The Counter-Reformation in the Villages: Religion and Reform in the Bishopric of Speyer, 1560–1720* (Ithaca, NY, 1992).

119	Forster, *The Counter-Reformation in the Villages*, p. 30.

120	Hsia, *Social Discipline*, pp. 132–5. The citation is from p. 132.

121	Hans Krawarick, 'Neue Methoden zur Erforschung konfessioneller Strukturen der Frühen Neuzeit', *Archiv für Kulturgeschichte*, 70 (1988), pp. 375–410; François, *Die unsichtbare Grenze*, pp. 168–72.

122	Thomas Paul Becker, *Konfessionalisierung in Kurköln: Untersuchungen zur Durchsetzung der katholischen Reform in den Dekanaten Ahrgau und Bonn anhand von Visitationsprotokollen 1583–1761* (Bonn, 1989), pp. 157–60; see also Meier, 'Die katholische Erneuerung', pp. 93–5.

123	Becker, *Konfessionalisierung*, p. 151. On the notions of 'popular culture' and 'popular religion', see, *inter alia*, Norbert Schindler, 'Spuren in die Geschichte der "anderen" Zivilisation: Probleme und Perspektiven einer historischen Volkskulturforschung', in Richard van Dülmen and Norbert Schindler, eds, *Volkskultur: Zur Wiederentdeckung des vergessenen Alltags (16.–20. Jahrhundert)* (Frankfurt am Main, 1984), pp. 13–77, and R. W. Scribner, 'Ritual and Popular Religion in Catholic Germany at the Time of the Reformation', in Scribner, *Popular Culture and Popular Movements*, pp. 17–47.

124	See also Hermann Hörger, 'Dorfreligion und bäuerliche Mentalité im Wandel ihrer ideologischen Grundlagen', *ZBLG* 38 (1975), pp. 244–316.

125	See e.g. Becker, *Konfessionalisierung*, pp. 181–225, on the Tridentine reform of confraternities and pilgrimages in the Electorate of Cologne. See also Roeck, *Eine Stadt*, i. pp. 81 and 447, on the cultural background of the soothsayers, wise women, and sorcerers of Augsburg.

126	Natalie Z. Davis, 'From "Popular Religion" to Religious Cultures', in Steven Ozment, ed., *Reformation Europe: A Guide to Research* (St. Louis, Mo., 1982), pp. 321–41; the citation is from p. 330.

127	Bernard Vogler, 'Die Entstehung der protestantischen Volksfrömmigkeit in der rheinischen Pfalz zwischen 1555 und 1619', *ARG* 72 (1981), pp. 193–5.

128	Ludwig Andreas Veit and Ludwig Lenhart, *Kirche und Volksfrömmigkeit im Zeitalter des Barock* (Freiburg im Breisgau, 1956), p. 30.

129	Roeck, *Eine Stadt*, i. p. 81. See also Vogler, 'Entstehung', p. 161, on the prominent role of wise women in the early 17th-century Palatinate.

130	Veit and Lenhart, *Kirche und Volksfrömmigkeit*, pp. 237–8.

131	Roeck, *Eine Stadt*, i. pp. 107–8.

132	The best overview in monographic form still is Gerhard Schormann, *Hexenprozesse in Deutschland* (Göttingen, 1981). See also Hartmut Lehmann, 'Hexenverfolgungen und Hexenprozesse im Alten Reich zwischen Reformation und Aufklärung', *Jahrbuch des Instituts für Deutsche Geschichte*, 7 (1978), pp. 13–70; H. C. Erik Midelfort, *Witch Hunting in Southwestern Germany, 1562–1684* (Stanford, Calif., 1972); Wolfgang Behringer, *Hexenverfolgung in Bayern: Volksmagie, Glaubenseifer und Staatsräson in der Frühen Neuzeit* (Munich, 1987); Norbert Schindler, 'Die

Entstehung der Unbarmherzigkeit: Zur Kultur und Lebensweise der Salzburger Bettler am Ende des 17. Jahrhunderts', *Bayerisches Jahrbuch für Volkskunde* (1988), pp. 61–130 (a study of the Salzburg trials of 1675–90, one of the last major cases of witch hunting in the Holy Roman Empire). See also n. 64 above.

133 Thomas Robisheaux, 'Peasants and Pastors: Rural Youth Control and the Reformation in Hohenlohe, 1540–1680', *Social History*, 6 (1981), pp. 281–300; Scribner, 'Incombustible Luther'.

134 Hermann Hörger, *Kirche, Dorfreligion und bäuerliche Gesellschaft: Strukturanalysen zur gesellschaftsgebundenen Religiosität ländlicher Unterschichten des 17. bis 19. Jahrhunderts, aufgezeigt an bayerischen Beispielen* (Munich, 1978), i. pp. 156–7.

135 Hsia, *Social Discipline*, p. 65.

136 Mack Walker, *The Salzburg Transaction: Expulsion and Redemption in Eighteenth-Century Germany* (Ithaca, NY, 1992).

137 Peter Hersche, 'Wider "Müssiggang" und "Ausschweifung": Feiertage und ihre Reduktion im katholischen Europa, namentlich im deutschsprachigen Raum zwischen 1750 und 1800', *Innsbrucker Historische Studien*, 12/13 (1990), pp. 97–122.

138 See esp. Hartmut Lehmann, 'Der politische Widerstand gegen die Einführung des neuen Gesangbuches von 1791 in Württemberg: Ein Beitrag zum Verhältnis von Kirchen- und Sozialgeschichte', *Blätter für württembergische Kirchengeschichte*, 66/67 (1966/67), pp. 247–63; Heinrich Schmidt, 'Aufgeklärte Gesangbuch-Reform und ländliche Gemeinde: Zum Widerstand gegen die Einführung neuer Gesangbücher im Herzogtum Oldenburg und der Herrschaft Jever am Ende des 18. Jahrhunderts', in Hinrichs and Wiegelmann, *Sozialer und kultureller Wandel*, pp. 85–115.

139 See Catherine Maurer, 'Aufgeklärte Gesangbücher und "gemeine Leute": Äußerungen und Inhalte der Gesangbuchstreite des ausgehenden 18. Jahrhunderts im protestantischen Deutschland', in Bödeker, Chaix, and Veit, *Der Umgang mit dem religiösen Buch*, pp. 269–88.

|11|

Daily Life, Consumption, and Material Culture

ERNST SCHUBERT

The conditions of everyday life in the German world in 1700, and indirectly also in 1800, were determined by the consequences of the Thirty Years War. This is more than a question of demography: by 1720 at latest the population losses of the war had been made up; after that, the population doubled within three generations; and from about 1750 on, over-population fuelled a huge emigration to south-east Europe and the beginning of the exodus to North America.[1] The effects of the Thirty Years War on centuries of daily life in Germany arose instead from the nature of the reconstruction which took place in all German territories after it. The usual consequence of wars and raging epidemics, that of a change in social structure, largely failed to occur after 1648.

The Great War had not left behind destruction and desolation everywhere.[2] There were regions which had survived the terrible end-phase of the war almost undamaged: Lower Saxony, Holstein, parts of eastern Germany, East and West Prussia, Austria. But even in the centre of the areas of the great troop movements, where brush now grew over former fields, one thing remained in existence: the rights, fixed in writing, which were claimed by the landlords. In town and countryside, the post-war reconstruction took the form of a restoration of old legal relationships. No irrational conglomeration in the corporate village fields was dissolved; burned districts of the town were not rebuilt according to new ideas of planning. (The geometrical ground-plan, the grid square of the ideal town proposed in the Renaissance, was realized only around 1700 in the newly founded Huguenot towns – Erlangen (Christian-Erlang) and Karlshafen.)

The effect of the 'great war' which characterized everyday life was thus the juridification of all relationships, a restoration according to legal structures handed down from the past. One example is the 1654 decree of the Imperial Diet, which prescribed that old debt certificates dating from the time before the Great War were to be valid even if the originals had been lost and the only surviving evidence was provided by copies in official registers. Like the whole post-war restoration, this sort of provision bene-fited those – especially the rulers – who still possessed a partially intact archive, namely the large monasteries and foundations which before the Thirty Years War had functioned as lenders of capital, especially to the temporal nobility. They presented the old debt certificates to the astonished heirs, and after long and weary legal proceedings lasting for between 30 and 60 years they managed to implement their claims on the basis of the 1654 decree of the Imperial Diet. At a stroke, cash money flowed into monastery exchequers: the material basis of the south German Baroque.

Like any restoration, the one after the 'great war' failed to do anything to improve actual life.[3] It was typical that only Saxony, Hannover, and Prussia attempted with greater or lesser success to create a territorially unified sys-tem of weights and measures in place of the highly various units which had grown up historically. The power of the past was shown by the failure of similar attempts by the House of Orange in its German possessions in the 1680s. From place to place, the ell remained a different length. The metric system was only implemented in the Napoleonic period. The persistence of the old weights and measures was linked to the restoration of legal relation-ships, not least seigneurial relationships. For these were the same weights and measures as had already been listed in late-medieval estate registers and with which the peasant of the eighteenth century also had to conform. But although pre-war seigneurial relationships were restored, pre-war economic relations were not. The thoroughly profitable German mining industry, a system of dovetailed production centres, basically did not survive the Thirty Years War. Hammer mills fell into decay or were transformed into grain mills, and flooded tunnels were not pumped out. Even where mines were brought back into operation they no longer formed crystallization points for a wide palette of industrial production. In the Erzgebirge, a mining area still flourishing in the sixteenth century, after the closing down of the min-ing industry simple people earned their livings with lace-making, trim-mings-making, straw-plaiting, and producing wooden toys. The fate of the mining industry is an important indicator of a hidden but at the same time very deep-reaching consequence of the 'great war'. Capital no longer sought out risky, but for that reason also profitable, investments in early industrial enterprises, but rather merely sought the security offered by land rents. The successors of the once-adventurous Nuremberg merchants took their ease on landed estates, consuming the rents of their inherited wealth. The re-agrarianization of many German territories was caused by the fact that hardly any investment capital was available, and that big money sought out secure land rents, so that the prices of knightly estates tripled in the course of the eighteenth century. The economic behaviour of the upper strata intensified the tendencies toward restoration.

What distinguished the economic behaviour of the upper strata was that new economic forms, the factory and the manufactory, were for a long time the realm of outsiders. For example, in Berlin it was the Jews who in 1769 had the largest proportion of the new large industrial concerns, owning 40 per cent of the manufactories with more than 100 employees. To some extent, they were compelled by the king to take over poorly conducted state enterprises, velvet and silk manufactories facing bankruptcy. The well-off bourgeoisie remained in the grip of a way of thinking in which the primary principle was security of *Nahrung* (literally 'nourishment', livelihood): this group could not be attracted into adventurous entrepreneurship.

An additional direct and indirect consequence of the Thirty Years War was an absence of vertical mobility: a society labouring under the weight of a restoration of legal relationships, in which capital exerted no pressure for change, placed limitations on opportunities to rise in life. To an extent never seen before, many-branched kinship systems developed: dynasties of university professors, district officials, even foresters. The state administration, in so far as it has been genealogically investigated, has revealed itself to have been a system of interlinked kinship circles. The Württemberg *Ehrbarkeit* ('notability') and the Hannoverian *hübsche Familien* ('nice families') are only the best-known examples of the connection between genealogy and state administration.[4] Crafts were also organized according to the same principle of marriage and kinship circles; the exclusionary tendencies of the guilds, which had already been established previously, now came to fullest fruition. Even a recommendation from a prince could not sway a guild to admit as a master a journeyman who had the requisite abilities but did not belong to its own kinship circle. Social inbreeding was rife. Even hangmen formed supra-territorial kinship circles and dynasties. And even among them, genealogical exclusionism appeared to have been the response to pressure from below. After all, a hangman managed a medium-sized business, employing flayers and *Wasenmeister* (knackers), people who were similarly excluded from society but who had no opportunity to rise into one of the materially lucrative hangman's positions. Where social elevation was possible, it was for clear reasons: thus when Upper Swabian peasants' sons, as monks in an Imperial Abbacy, were ultimately able to become abbots and thus princes of the Empire, it was because the nobility no longer accepted the monastic way of life. That is, a bourgeoisification, indeed a peasantification of the Imperial church in its monastic form was taking place.

Research into everyday life cannot leave out of account the economic and social framework as it was specifically shaped in Germany as a direct or indirect consequence of the 'great war'. Everyday life was very different for the mass of the population, which had no chance of upward social mobility, and for the upper stratum, hierarchized into various ranks, whose way of life was determined by the kinship network. But for both high and low – albeit in quite different ways – a wholly new degree of state power defined the framework of their lives (as is discussed in detail in Chapter 7 of this volume). Through the new phenomenon of the territorial tax, through its exhaustion of the low cash reserves in both town and countryside, the state, although itself deeply indebted, had become the greatest source of capital in the region. Members of the upper stratum experienced the state because they lived off it, whether directly or indirectly, while simple people might experience it in the shape of taxes, or possibly in the shape of the brutal saltpetrer who ruthlessly ripped up the rotting planks of their floors, in order – with a privilege from the territorial prince – to scrape out saltpetre deposits; they experienced the state in the recruiting of soldiers for the standing army which the prince, as a further consequence of war, had in the meantime established.

Social inbreeding, lack of credit, consequent under-capitalization of peasant and town economies, and finally an increasingly intense presence of the state – these were the factors which determined everyday life and consumption in Germany in the period after the 'great war'.

Space and time

The road network had not changed decisively since the later middle ages: only the highway building of the second half of the eighteenth century brought a decisive innovation, albeit one which initially only benefited the princely capital city. Nevertheless, roads had become wider. It was now possible to drive in a carriage and pair, indeed on some stretches even with a carriage and four, whereas previously the horses had to be harnessed one behind another. But this was largely based on a road development which had occurred over a space of centuries; only in exceptional cases did it represent purposeful planning. However, people's travelling behaviour had changed.[5] Coaches, already achieving a speed of 8 kilometres an hour, had become prevalent as the chosen means of transportation of the upper strata. The first regular traffic rhythms arose: for instance, beginning in 1720, a ship travelled regularly between Minden and Bremen, transporting passengers and packages. However, it must be remembered that in river traffic – highly important for trade – ships seldom had capacities above 15 tons. There was a regulated system of passenger travel and transportation: the post. The monopoly position of the princes of Thurn and Taxis in the postal sector in the Empire was not seriously endangered, despite some attempts at competition from the territorial princes.

The spatial experience of travelling now involved a new factor, typical of the intensified presence of the state, namely frontier guards and customs barriers on the main roads leading into a territory and, ultimately becoming prevalent around 1700, the legitimization document for travellers, the passport. Mobility and new experiences of frontiers were also characterized by the fact that only now did princes begin to mark their territories, mount their coats of arms on all the access roads, and erect 'gypsy poles' which were supposed to frighten travelling people off from entering the area. (The first evidence of this sort of warning pole, with a gallows pictured upon it, dates from 1708.) Frontier controls were burdensome for travellers of high social standing – edicts of territorial princes repeatedly warned that 'the commerces' should not be hindered by overly strict inspections – but for the wanderer of lower standing, who came on foot, they were discriminatory, particularly since his legitimation generally consisted of a passport issued by his home community, which had been worn out by handling at many checkpoints.

Even for people of high standing, travelling was not without its dangers. In little-travelled forested areas there was the threat of being waylaid (although the official post took protective measures against this); and the frequent breakdowns of axles and wheels could lead to serious injuries when the carriage suddenly tumbled forward. Nevertheless, for people of high social standing travelling was no longer an adventure in the medieval sense, but rather merely the bridging of the distance between two settled points. (The word and meaning of 'adventure' was discovered by Germany only at the end of the eighteenth century, from English literature.) Finally, from about 1600 on – not dramatically interrupted by the Thirty Years War – a graduated system of inns had developed, which in every well-known town offered an elegant hostelry for the better-off.

While carters and carriers still favoured the old system of rest-places, which were often small road-junctions, more distinguished travellers stayed the night in larger cities, for example in Schaffhausen instead of (as the carrier did) in Diessenhofen, in Hameln instead of in Coppenbrügge. The wandering craft journeyman, finally, sought his sleeping place as his road offered it, not even scorning barns. He was happy when he reached a larger city where a frugally equipped hostel was available for journeymen of his guild.

Travelling options and hence people's experiences of spatial relationships varied according to social status, therefore. The only thing they had in common was that travelling had become regulated, that not only routes but also ordinances had become more firmly established. In the last analysis, this constituted the great difference between the period after 1648 and that even as late as the sixteenth century. Travelling was now perceived as an interruption in the condition of being settled in one place. Mobility itself no longer constituted a way of life of its own.

The wandering behaviour of the journeymen illustrates the ways in which society, which had become more sedentary in the course of the post-war restoration, altered travelling behaviour, and thus constricted opportunities for mobility. On one hand, journeymen were required to 'go on the tramp' as a way of preventing them from demanding upward mobility (strikingly, masters' sons were exempt from the obligation to wander as journeymen); on the other hand, the wandering craft-journeyman was subject to suspicion as a tramp and was prohibited from *Fechten* ('scroung-

ing'), the customary begging of the wanderer. The obligation for journeymen to 'go on the tramp' became an instrument of repression by master and
guild, and the old notion of the exchange of craft knowledge fell into dis-
use.

Typical of a society which had become sedentary, and which could now
conceive of mobility as a way of life only as a deviation from the norm, was
the intellectualization of the idea of space. In place of the old milestones, a
practical aid to travel which gave the distances from one town to another,
around 1700 there arose the map of the country, the most important drawn
up in the Homann Offizin in Nuremberg, which now portrayed each small
region according to who governed it. The Homann maps were still illustra-
tive representations of space: they still did not encompass physical geography, a favourite field of study in the eighteenth century. Thus the
eye-catching aspects of these maps are the vignettes, containing allegorical
figures and the coats of arms of the reigning princely houses on the particular map section being shown, generally held by tumbling angels or putti.[6]

The new experience of spatial relationships was also a theme of the military. In the course of the eighteenth century – also touching on the conditions for highway building – a cartographic description of the country was
increasingly frequently recognized as a precondition for national defence.
Although these used advances in cartography, they were treated as a state
secret. It was a great achievement of the electoral state of Hannover, which
had become linked with England in personal union, that it made its
national map (interestingly, inaugurated by the military) publicly accessible.
This was an early and daring example of the later transition from the concept of spatial relationships to the first beginnings of spatial planning, the
cartographical fixing of a governed area.[7]

Spatial experiences, journeys within a fundamentally sedentary society,
changed mentalities: only at the end of the eighteenth century did the word
Landschaft (the German word meaning both 'parliamentary Estates' and
'landscape') gain its present-day content. What was earlier a legal term
referring to those gathered together at the national diet now became,
as a condensed travel experience, a term for a natural space, a geographical
area. In the same period, too, *Heimat* ('home', 'native place'), made
its way into ordinary use and gained its emotional associations (as
discussed in Chapter 2 of this volume). Both sentiment and picturing of
landscape were united in the widely read travel books. In these, towns
could lie in a 'very fine and cheerful area', while hills by contrast could
work 'very mournfully' on the mood.[8] Friedrich Nicolai admired in the
German South-West 'the great herds of sheep and horned cattle, which
make the landscape even more picturesque'.[9] Travel books reflect a change
in mentality in the experience of spatial relationships. In the second half of
the eighteenth century, the era was past in which the new enterprise, the
Hessen-Kassel spa of Schlangenbad, could be advertised (in 1721) as admittedly lying in a desolate and unfriendly area, but as having been made into

a pleasant sojourning place for spa guests through artistic geometric planta-
tions. The disciplining of nature according to geometric systems – 'systema'
was a favourite term of the Baroque – was no longer fascinating in the second half of the eighteenth century, when elemental landscapes began to be
seen as exciting, and the Alps became the embodiment of a wild and thus
fascinating Godly Creation. In general, the English garden began to prevail
only in the second half of the eighteenth century. In 1757, the French model
was still viewed as compulsory in the Baden princely capital of Karlsruhe.
The replacement of the French garden by the English was much more than
a change in garden fashions: it reflected changes in mentalities. In this connection, it must be remembered that after 1700 the ornamental garden
(usually embellished with an intimate garden pavilion) replaced the old
kitchen garden among the bourgeois upper stratum as well.

Like experiences of space, experiences of time varied according to social
status. To mention only the extremes of the social spectrum: the tramp who
was eyed mistrustfully by the authorities, the wandering tinker, or the mole-
catcher measured time according to the characteristics of his livelihood ('at
the time of the cherry harvest'); the traveller of high social standing had a
pocket watch and a calendar.

By around 1700, every merchant required a calendar, if only to be able to
calculate the various dates of the Catholic and Protestant market centres, in
order to know in Protestant Schweinfurt on what day in his calendar the
festival of Kiliani would be celebrated in Catholic Würzburg. It was such
obstacles to trade, here only hinted at, which in 1700 compelled even those
governments characterized by Lutheran orthodoxy to accept the modern
Gregorian calendar of the Catholics.

But the September 1699 Regensburg Edict of the Imperial Diet, which
provided for the abolition, beginning on 1 March 1700, of the difference
between the old and new calendars (which had in the meantime mounted
up to 11 days), initially only attempted a half-hearted unification. Although
the leap-year rule was adopted, the reckoning of Easter according to the
Gregorian calendar was not: instead, use was made of the tables of the
Protestant astronomer Johannes Kepler – even though he himself had
argued in favour of the Gregorian Reform – which made it possible to
avoid the name of the Pope and instead to speak of the 'improved Imperial
calendar'. As a consequence of this, dates for Easter in 1724 and 1744 differed across territories, and this led Frederick the Great to introduce the
Gregorian reckoning of Easter into his lands in 1775. Here in Prussia, a
learned society had been expressly formed in 1700 to implement the calendar reform; this then developed into the Prussian Academy of Sciences, but
throughout the entire eighteenth century its budget was essentially covered
by the calendar trade over which it enjoyed a royal monopoly.

In the eighteenth century calendars became popular reading-matter.
Although they still contained lists of the times propitious or unpropitious
for bloodletting, in other ways their popularization prepared the way for a

change in the eighteenth-century calendar calculated for a learned public. The 'unlucky days', knowledge of which had previously been so important, and which had been marked with black signs (hence the expression 'black day'), were now noted – if at all – only shamefacedly. The clumsy historical examples were abbreviated, the complicated astrological calculations were reduced to a simple weather forecast, and household hints – for example, of the times when vinegar should best be prepared – took up more and more room. In place of the previous bloodletting mannekin, now the small and large multiplication tables and the tables of interest rates covered a calendar. At the end of the century, calendars began to be used as sources of enlightenment for the populace, for the 'moral improvement of the nation's people'. However, despite their altered shape, these popular writings show how intensely everyday life was shaped by seasonal rhythms.

In dividing up the day, the trend toward privatization of time measurement had already become unmistakable around 1700. Pocket watches were expensive status symbols, but they generated so much admiration that even craft-journeymen sought, with great material sacrifices, to obtain watches. Almost all private clocks were pocket watches; the hall clock is found in house inventories only among the upper stratum.

Whoever saw a clock thought, in a world strongly stamped by the church, of his life clock. Life expectancy was on average 60 years for women and 55 years for men.[10] Naturally, these averages obscure large variations and deviations. The average age at marriage was about 25 years, which meant that the youthful unmarried phase ended only when almost half, or at least two-fifths, of life was over.[11] And this life played itself out in a world in which, for simple people, mobility was no longer a social opportunity – in which, to use the words of Annette Droste-Hülshoff, just a trip to the capital city made a peasant's son into a Ulysses; that is, in a world in which living in one place became a life's destiny.

Living conditions

Residence and work were in the eighteenth century still assigned, as a single unit, to the house.[12] In towns, the cellars of craftsmen's houses contained the workshops, unhealthful and musty; the house, with counter and storerooms, was the focus of the merchant firm. In the countryside, especially among the smaller-scale peasants, stable and farm formed a single building, the *Wohnstallhaus* ('dwelling- and stable-house'). The workers, whether serving-maids, craft-journeymen or farm servants, slept several to a room, often in partioned-off hutches under the roof, in any case under conditions which provided no individualized private dwelling, indeed not even intimacy.

The close relationship between residence and work, and thus the spatial division of the house, provided individuals with few opportunities to create a private sphere. Only the household heads had their own bedroom; the head's children were treated the same as the servants. The four-poster bed had since the Renaissance been a symbol of a high standard of comfort and had been reserved for the couple heading the household; it had not only provided protection against vermin falling from the ceiling, but had also for the first time created an intimate space within the house for the couple heading the household (since several groups of family members often slept in the same room). But in the course of the eighteenth century, the four-poster bed fell from fashion, as the bedroom as a whole (rather than just the bed) developed into a new intimate space, where the domestic altar was often located. The privy, by contrast, was not yet an intimate space: it still recognizably stood in the tradition of the medieval *Sprachhaus* ('speaking house', later to become 'secret speaking house', and then 'privy'). Even in the town, the privy was not integrated into the burgher's house, but rather was recognizable as an oriel-like outbuilding or annexe.

In both town and country, building was subject to the norms and laws of the neighbourhood, as far as the height of the eaves, the position on the street, and the shape of the back yard were concerned. Even where individualized building was attempted, it was restricted to the shape of the façade. But even this was to a considerable degree dictated by the height of the storeys and the structure of the windows. Within this narrow framework, there developed regional and local building styles whose functional background was often ignored. For example, in a town in which brewing privileges were enjoyed by each individual citizen, house doors became disproportionately large in order to be able to transport the urban brewers' coppers into the houses.

In the building of a house, the most important man was the carpenter (architects were to develop only gradually in the second half of the nineteenth century); for wood was the decisive building material, and bore the load of the whole structure of the building. The mason – not, interestingly, a guilded occupation – was responsible only for the building of the basement storey and, more in towns than in villages, for filling up with masonry the individual 'compartments' in the half-timbered house.

Where wood was the most important building material, the danger of fire was great, particularly given that roofing with stone shingles, or at least wood shingles, instead of the old straw roofs, had begun to prevail only in the town and not yet in the countryside. The emergence and rapid spread of fire insurance in the last third of the eighteenth century removed a great source of anxiety: for the latent threat of fire was a threat to life. The house was the most important part of the property of a town burgher or a peasant.

The forms of house which were handed down from the past in incalcu-lable variety (despite all normative neighbourhood pressures), as well as the differing modes of building between rich and poor, can be classified at least approximately by beginning with the central element in all dwellings, the fireplace. Within the houses of the poor in the countryside – which were the simplest sort of *Ständerblockbauten* (houses where the load rested on the four external posts), without cellars, and with their entrances at ground level – there was no separation of hearth from oven, even as late as 1800. The open fireplace which marked the centre of the house and whose smoke stained the straw roof was the cooking place as well as the source of warmth. In the houses of the better-off from the lower middle stratum upwards, although the separation of hearth and oven had taken place, gen-erally only one room, the parlour, was heatable. Chimneys were less com-mon in both town and countryside than one assumes: the chimney sweep exercised a wandering trade because as a settled man he would have had too few customers.

The mention of heated parlours leads to consideration of the fact that the rise of the bourgeois living-room had already begun in the seventeenth cen-tury. Now the cupboard became the most important piece of furniture – in the dwellings of the upper social strata, chests declined in importance. The chest of drawers began its career as a new piece of furniture. With the sepa-rate living room, in the early nineteenth century the *Cannapé* (sofa) came into fashion, as in general did the proliferation of seating furniture which characterized the new residential arrangements. Chairs, which in earlier periods were only infrequently listed in house inventories (people sat on benches), now changed decisively in style as well. The stiff upright chairs, which had enforced an uncomfortable although elegant seating posture, now turned into movable pieces of furniture on which one could sit *sans gêne*. This also broke down the former social symmetry of the communal room, in which a special seating-place had been reserved for the household head, in a *Herrenwinkel* ('lord's nook') or on the front side of the room.

In bourgeois circles, rooms for purposes of display were fitted with car-pets. Only the high nobility could yet afford velvet coverings. Printed linen with impasto colours covered the walls. Wood panelling was at most reserved for the ceiling. As soon as he came into the house, the guest could tell whether he was visiting truly elegant people: that is, if the light fell through high sash windows framed by heavy woollen or silken curtains draped at the side. (The bulk of the population lived in low rooms at most two metres in height.) The eye-catcher, however, was the mirror with its expensively carved frame. This was the item of house decoration which penetrated most quickly into the lower strata. Simple mirrors of a value of one *Gulden* were found even among small peasants by the end of the cen-tury. Only in the houses of the leading social strata, by contrast, was it pos-sible to adopt the technique used in constructing palaces, in which the highly embellished oven was heated from behind, as a so-called 'breech loader', outside the dwelling area, so that the unavoidable soot and dirt – wood was the most important heating material – could not settle on the furniture as a fine dust. Here, too, as smaller versions of the grand halls of the court, first the boudoir arose, and then the salon.

It might seem that the salon, already part of residential arrangements for large sections of the bourgeois strata by around 1800, was only an urban variant on the peasant parlour, as an eating and communal room furnished in such a way as to favour the head of the house. But the salon was quite different from the peasant parlour: it was not oriented around the community of people residing in the household, but rather around the guests. The central, organizing concept of most Enlightenment writings, the instruction of 'the public', was made concrete in the salon of the upper stratum.

The furnishing of houses was, despite all variations, functional. Outside the salon, aesthetic perspectives were only secondary considerations. Pieces of furniture were precious objects which for the mass of the population were not subject to changes in fashion, but rather were passed on by inheritance wherever possible. The clothes cupboard had not yet become widespread, because people in any case owned little more clothing than that which they wore on their bodies. A chest for underwear sufficed. Nevertheless, the peasant farm also began to fill up with furniture, and the village joiner appeared as a new rural craft. In peasant houses there were now at least stools as movable seats. They were needed for squatting by the hearth, in winter the only source of warmth. In the peasant world, the seating hierarchy still remained in being. It was always the weakest member of the community, the youngest manservant, the youngest child, who had the worst place, facing the house or hall door.

However different the living situations of poor and rich, they were affected by the same plagues of insects. As in earlier centuries, the flea, the 'night friend', was the most loyal companion to human beings. In the upper stratum, people defended themselves with flea traps, some made of ivory; in their hands or under their clothes, ladies carried 'flea furs' made from the pelts of martens or fitchets, which were supposed to attract the insects and keep them away from the human body. Insect plagues were connected as much with living conditions as with those of hygiene. But they also had to do with the fact that there still existed no publicly guaranteed cleanliness. Although one no longer waded ankle-deep in mud in towns during rainy periods, nevertheless dirt belonged to both town and country. After all, the stables were still part of the house of the well-off urban citizen. Sewage was taken away from houses by open drains in the streets.

Clothing and personal grooming

After the decline of the late medieval culture of bathing – where the sauna-like public baths survived this period, they began to attract the disapprobation of well-intentioned Enlightenment figures – it was not the dictates of fashion, but rather sheer necessity, which made women cover pustules and pimples on their skin with beauty patches. The cleansing of the whole body was unusual. In 1790, the well-known physician Hufeland wrote a 'Necessary Reminder Concerning Baths and their Re-introduction into Germany'.[13] The wash-basins used for cleaning face and hands were often astonishingly small, at most no larger than eating bowls. This was caused by the fact that alcohol, especially wine, was used to clean the skin. In any case, in a short period between 1745 and 1749 the work of Johann Siegemund Hahn, entitled 'Instruction in the Strength and Operation of Fresh Water' went through three editions.[14] In this work, Hahn explained to his contemporaries what 'strength for cleansing and washing' water possessed, 'when used externally'.[15] Water appears to have gained general prevalence in the course of the eighteenth century – poor people could not afford alcohol for cleaning their bodies anyway – but soap was by no means in everyday use; it was more a question of smell, of perfumes, than of soap.[16]

Where there was only one heatable room in a house, the need for warm clothing was great. This is a factor which must not be overlooked behind all the fashion changes between 1680 and 1800. The transformations in fashionable style affected the outside of the clothing. Among women of the upper stratum, the décolleté was stressed; around 1760, this lost its geometric angularity through firm corsetry at the middle of the bosom, and instead, with the favouring of flowing silk cloths, pushed forward both breasts. Since the upper social stratum determined fashion, this gave rise to the hidden drama of the silk kerchief: the lower strata formally imitated the free décolleté, but to serve modesty wrapped a silk kerchief around the neck. The traditional costume, as the dress for public purposes, favoured the high, closed ruff. From the waist downward, however, clothing remained long, puffed out, and distant from the body, permitting fashionable variations only in the shape of the folds. As far as men's clothing was concerned, the second half of the eighteenth century saw a trend toward greater decency, toward greater restraint in the decorative elements which until then had dominated, but which were now only permitted in the embellishment of edgings and buttons. However, unlike with women's clothing, trousers and stockings emphasized the body. The legs, with the calves clad in closely clinging stockings, were a sign of physicality. Interestingly for the internalization of sexual morality, the male breast was ornamentally encased, stressing the sexually least interesting part of the man.

Fashion was a concern primarily of the upper stratum. Among the middle strata only gradually did a separation between working and ordinary clothing become prevalent; until then, the only distinction had been between everyday and festival dress. As we will also see with eating habits, the clothing fashions of the upper strata formed styles among the lower strata, naturally limited by economic forces. The so-called *Trachten* – traditional peasant costumes – are nothing more than a conservation of a state of affairs attained around 1780. These costumes did not arise out of peasant needs. The impressive peasant festival-costumes found around the Tegernsee were actually invented by the court tailor in Madrid: after all, Spanish court ceremonial prevailed at the Munich court. The conservation of a fashion of clothing specific to a particular period initially occurred only because peasants retained for longest the custom of passing clothes on through inheritance.[17]

Traditional costume thus arose through the coincidence of two developments. First, there was the old custom, to a considerable extent resistant to fashion (if only for economic reasons), of retaining the costly Sunday dress as long as it held together, and even passing it on through inheritance. Second, there was the new principle of fashion, which now demanded a change in clothing at ever-shorter intervals. The latter could be achieved by the poorer strata only to a limited degree. However, changes in fashion demanded a growth in textile production. (Quite apart from the fact that in the eighteenth century the trade in old clothes, mostly practised as a wandering trade, formed a new occupation.) The expansion in textile production during the eighteenth century, from yarn production to specialized manufactory-organized braid-making and domestic-industrial stocking-knitting, is only understandable in terms of the growth in consumption which became necessary because of the dictates of fashion.

Despite all the changes in clothing style, and all the regional specialities in working clothes, one piece of clothing was worn everywhere, in both North and South, among both the lower and the middling strata: *Lederhosen* (leather trousers), the jeans of the eighteenth century, worn with coloured stockings and bound together below the knee.

From head to toe, the lower strata sought to imitate the clothing of fashion-determining better society. Naturally the shoe buckles were not as expensive, naturally the wigs were not produced in the precisely fitting shapes and as artfully as corresponded to the requirements of the salon, but he who could at all afford it made efforts, at least on Sunday, to wear a wig.

Shoe buckles and wigs, when worn by the lower strata, show a trend toward non-functional clothing. Physical labour, although traditionally and repeatedly lauded by preachers and in contemporary form by Enlightenment publicists as well, was no more highly regarded than in earlier centuries: otherwise, the working population would not have felt it necessary to adopt the external pretence of carrying other than their own social status. That which could not be hidden at the midday table must at least not be externally visible on the streeet: namely, that the necessity of earning one's living through physical labour meant precisely what was referred to in the German proverb, 'living from hand to mouth'.

Eating and drinking

The cuisine of the simplest people in the eighteenth century remained what it had always been: uninventive and meatless. Economic forces operated at the stove. Grain made up the main component of solid nourishment. Although meat was relatively good value compared to grain, the small difference in price constituted an insurmountable financial hurdle for poor people. (A 2-year-old pig had a weight of merely some 40 kilograms.) It already counted as a feast when millet (widespread in fertile areas by about 1700) made up the main component of the gruel. Otherwise the norm was oat gruel or, when by about 1700 buckwheat showed itself to be a resistant crop on meagre soil, buckwheat porridge. Bread, mostly baked with any possible supplement (such as chestnut meal) to stretch the grain, often served as a substitute for spoons.[18]

The simple man ate what was grown around where he lived. In pastoral areas, milk and milk soups formed the basis of nourishment. The comparatively small cows, which could mostly be nourished only poorly on the meagre pastures with their low hay yields, brought an average milk yield of only 750 litres, and in wintertime did not provide any milk at all. Cheesemaking was a typical summer industry. In poor areas foods made of flour predominated. Mediterranean fruits, which were hawked around by peddlars, could only be afforded by the richer farm-owners. Where fruit appeared on the table, it was mostly in dried form. The monotony of the menu was interrupted only twice a year, at the church dedication day or *Kermesse*, which was the main festival of the village, and at Christmas. The mass of the population lived constantly at the margin of undernourishment. Even in normal times, necessary calorie intake was not guaranteed. In times of high prices and dearth, the mortality rate rose steeply.

However difficult it is to define the *Bürgertum* (bourgeoisie), as discussed in Chapter 6 of this volume, nevertheless it ought to be possible to circumscribe the 'middle stratum' as a basis for the *Bürgertum* by the fact that the people belonging to this group had enough to eat. This stratum was distinguished at its bottom end by the fact that nourishment was not the main question of every day, and at its top end by the plainness of its meals. The town was responsible for making menus more refined. Culture followed trade.[19] In north-west Germany the influence of English cuisine was already recognizable around 1700. Here as everywhere in that period, however, French recipes were regarded as the best models: cutlets and ragouts were known as dishes served for purposes of display, even among the upper bourgeoisie. On the French model, a separate dining-room also came into fashion among the upper strata. In this area, even among the middle strata, salads were already appearing on the table at the appropriate season; here the expression *Gemüse* ('vegetables') changed its meaning, from a collective term referring to everything cooked together, to a word meaning side dish or trimmings, mostly of horse-beans *(vicia faba)* and later of peas.

Finally, the court, with its requirements for dishes served for purposes of display, ensured that cultural exchange also made itself felt in the kitchen. The era of the great exhibitionary feasts of the late Renaissance was over. Spices no longer obscured the taste of the dishes themselves. The Mannerist style of cooking had by around 1700 passed its era at German princely courts, and quails were now allowed to taste like quails again. However, the need for variety, and at the same time the informal system of the court within a supra-regional cultural and social network, also enabled new, foreign dishes to find their way onto the princely table. Through imitation of court society in the houses of bureaucrats, princely capital cities became mediators of new recipes. Even if *Wiener Schnitzel* had not yet made its triumphal progress, nevertheless the Imperial capital city of Vienna became the decisive mediator through which Italian cuisine with its pasta was able to spread into southern Germany. A comparable role was played in central Germany by the Dresden court, while in northern Germany the great Hanseatic cities became influential. The influence of the court was also shown in an expansion in the code of table manners alongside the growing refinement in meals themselves.

For the simple man, drinking habits had changed much more than food habits, except for the fact that now, as ever, water was still basic. Around 1700, the wine-growing frontier had decisively pulled back, and even in the classic wine-growing regions with their specially favourable climates the harvest failures of the 1790s are supposed to have changed the landscape. To a considerable extent beer had displaced wine as the drink of the masses; the market was dominated by wheat beers with a low alcohol content. The frequent complaints made in travel accounts written by elegant people about the miserable beer served in rural inns sound almost topical.

For the majority of the population in the countryside, for whom a separate kitchen was a luxury, nature delivered a variety of dishes which seem strange to us. In Alpine regions, for example, marmots were still consumed. In the impoverished regions of the German Mittelgebirge the wealth of animals in the forests was used as a nutritional reserve; even jackdaws were eaten. But tasty game, even hares, could only be poached at great risk. Hunting was reserved for the lord. However, songbirds were not forgotten by the poor, but rather sold in town-markets as tidbits (larks in particular counted as delicacies).

The contraction in the wine-growing area around 1800 had significant consequences. It must not be forgotten that this occurrence hit hard the survival of the quasi-proletarian lower stratum of the *Häcker*, the small-scale owners and workers of vineyards. Only now did the various distinct varieties of wine, with their differentiated locational designations, become prevalent; previously, except for a few top locations about which the connoisseur had naturally always known, the wines of the most various locations had been thoughtlessly mixed. Indeed, in the individual vineyards themselves vines of different varieties had grown side by side. At the same time, on the abandoned terraces of now unprofitable vineyards, fruit-growing became prevalent. Cherries, for example, were still a very rare fruit in the eighteenth century. In general, this century did not do a great deal for the improvement of fruit-growing.

By way of the kitchens of the refined, a new drink penetrated into further circles of the population from the second half of the eighteenth century on: coffee. Its path shows in exemplary fashion the wide variety of factors which could help shape eating customs. Maritime trade, and in particular the influence of English merchants, caused the first coffee-house in Hamburg to be set up in 1679. The turn of the tide in the wars against the Turks created the mental preconditions in Upper Germany for the adoption of cultural practices from the old 'arch-enemy of Christendom'. As early as 1683 there is evidence of a coffee-house in Vienna, and in 1686 in Nuremberg and Regensburg as well. Baptized Turks were the first operators of this quite new type of restaurant, which rapidly became widespread. In Augsburg in 1720, there were eight coffee-houses, four Protestant and four Catholic.

At first, only well-off people could afford coffee, which was very expensive. Only around 1750, with the fall in the price of the product through more efficient trade routes, did the stratum of coffee consumers expand. Interestingly, it was at this point that the (ineffective) prohibitions against coffee began to be issued. In the countryside, as well, the new luxury made headway. Peddlars with coffee-mills were able to sell their products in villages. Certainly, it was only a weak drink which the simple man could afford (stretched with surrogates such as chestnuts, rye, and wheat), but nevertheless it provided a warming drink, and this explains its rapid spread. However, the expensive chocolate drunk by refined people could be afforded by hardly anyone else, and the third of the new drinks, tea, was rendered so expensive in the interior of Germany by internal customs charges that it was widespread among simple people only in the north German area.

Coffee, tea, and chocolate required new drinking vessels. The tin, clay, and especially wooden bowls handed down from the past were not suited to the new drinks. The triumphal advance of porcelain was linked with the change in drinking customs. The porcelain manufactory founded in Meißen in 1710 had by the mid-eighteenth century already found numerous successors, mostly state-owned enterprises. The most important man both in these foundations and in the faïence manufactories which must be set beside them was the so-called 'arcanist', who prepared the special recipes. Porcelain and faïence enabled the cup to emerge as a new drinking vessel. Its original form, the handleless 'cuplet', remained the simplest form of porcelain in ordinary use until the end of the century. More refined people used under-bowls as well, which also served as drinking vessels and only later developed into saucers. In the salons, coffee-cups and tea-cups were combined into the 'service', which began to develop its own shapes and designs. In the painting of porcelain, flower decorations were favoured, and later also paintings of birds, and, in the reception of antique bucolicism (not as a social reminder), generic peasant scenes. Of such luxuries simple people could only dream. When they could afford it, they bought the new drinking vessels from a wandering porcelain peddlar; these, however, were very coarse wares, or sometimes outright fakes. Interestingly, the porcelain peddlar occupied the lowest rank in the hierarchy of wandering traders.

In the eighteenth century *Branntwein* ('brandy spirit'), previously only known in the town, became a drink of the people; it should be envisaged as a cheap rotgut, a grain spirit. After harvest failures, the territorial authorities almost always prohibited the distilling of spirits. The meagrely harvested corn was to be reserved for solid nourishment. Spirit-drinking was repeatedly attacked by pastors and 'enlighteners of the populace', ignoring the fact that simple people, even if they did drink spirits in the morning, were only obtaining the necessary calorie intake for their hard labour. Alcoholism was not a problem of the masses.

Despite all the innovations and modifications which occurred, nourishment remained bound to tradition; and this only changed with the real revolution of the introduction of the potato. That by about 1800 this dominated the menu for the mass of the population was owed to sheer necessity, the catastrophic famines which peaked in 1770 and 1771-2. Until then, the potato had been cultivated almost everywhere only as a cash crop, suitable only as swine fodder. It had not yet made headway as human nourishment, since it effected such a radical change in the bodily economy that even the poor (and surely not fastidious) peasants of the Rhone area complained of a queasiness which lasted for weeks. The emergency of the famine years, however, implemented this enormous change in the menu. It had emerged that the potato was more resistant to the spring frosts and wet summers which spoiled grain. The former cash crop now became the dominant field crop. Nor was the distilling of potato spirit absent.

Transformations in human intercourse and relationships with the written word

The only successful book which the copious writer Adolph Freiherr von Knigge ever wrote bore the title 'Concerning Dealings with People' (1788).[20] This work was no collection of rules of conduct, but rather a philosophical reflection on the ways in which human beings interacted with one another. There was great interest in a work such as this because the inflexible obligations which had regulated interpersonal intercourse were increasingly weakened in the course of the eighteenth century. Admittedly, the addiction to titles survived: only a simple person might be addressed by his name, otherwise only addressing someone with his or her title counted as proper, and women were addressed with the titles of their husbands. The external transformation in forms of intercourse, the tendency toward less regulated sociability, created irritations, and this explains the success of Knigge's book. The tension between good breeding and etiquette became a daily dissonance, to which the young Goethe gave expression not only in Werther but also as a supplementary motif in various poems.

The coexistence of various styles of intercourse was reflected in the history of dance. Around 1700, the Baroque suite dance (such as the minuet) was competing with the more recent *Kontratanz* or country dance (such as the cotillion and the anglaise), and the beginnings of the relaxed couple dance, of which the waltz was to become the most well-known example. The suite dance, with its geometric pattern and its reverences toward those present, especially toward those of highest rank in the room, was still the expression of an older, more hierarchical, and more systematizing etiquette. The country dance, which originated in England, developed a much greater wealth of steps, dissolved the symmetry, and replaced the reverence with a community-forming effect. The emerging couple-dance completely dissolved the formations; each couple danced for itself independently. That around 1700 the *Allemande* became the favourite dance in Paris shows the trend which was expressing itself in dance towards a more relaxed sociability.[21] In Don Giovanni, Mozart represented the social contradictions of the protagonists by means of the juxtaposition of different styles of dance. The high nobility, Don Ottavio and Donna Anna, celebrate a minuet; with Cerlina, Don Giovanni dances the bourgeois country dance; while Masetto and Leporello move in three-four time to the typical rhythm of the *Schleifermelodie* (slide melody).[22]

The history of dance reveals the transformation in mentalities by which good breeding began to be defined as the expression of turn of mind. Behind this, there also stands a hitherto unrecognized transformation in constitutional history. The style of princes became plainer, and although court ceremonial remained formally in being it was restricted to special occasions. The era of the martial-horseman portraits of princes was past. At the end of the eighteenth century even the pictures on coins no longer represented the prince in his trappings of authority, but rather as a private man.

The shift from etiquette to good breeding is an especially important event in social history, one which affected intercourse both within and between social strata. The despised peasant now became the *Landmann* ('country-man'), with associations of simplicity and plainness, the characteristics of the new mentalities. Beating a peasant, which a local district official could still afford to do around 1700, now counted as a serious failing. When in 1806 the Prussian military abolished whipping as a punishment, this 'free-dom of the back' had already been introduced for the simple man in the preceding generation. Areas where the landlord whipped his peasants, such the lands east of the Elbe, counted as backward.

The fact that by the end of the eighteenth century the simple man was taken more seriously by the upper stratum than previously also influenced a great transformation in the history of reading. In the course of the eigh-teenth century, knowledge of reading and writing, and reckoning as well, had become more widespread, although the exact percentages involved can-not be estimated. However, the fact (for which there is considerable evi-dence) that around 1700 in a village only the pastor was in a position to be able to conduct the community accounts, or that applicants for state posi-tions boasted that they could count up to 200, by 1800 belonged to the past. The expansion in literacy can be seen in the spread of songbooks, which in the second half of the eighteenth century territorial lords some-times distributed in the villages at their own expense. But even if village society itself became more accustomed to reading (special religious commu-nities characterized by Pietism had already achieved a quite astonishing level of literacy by around 1700), nevertheless writing remained a practice which was to a considerable extent foreign to the peasant world. Reading and writing were still, as in the middle ages, learnt as two distinct skills. The peasant upper stratum, however, was thoroughly accustomed to writ-ing, as is shown by the so-called *Anschreibebücher* (account books), a type of household book, at the end of the century.

The countervailing tendencies which constituted obstacles to the acquir-ing of literacy are illustrated by the autobiography of Ulrich Bräker. When in 1776 Bräker desired to be admitted to the reading society in Lichtensteig, this at first caused difficulties: not only did reading and fine society still belong together, but also Bräker's step evoked head-shaking among his neighbours; his wife went so far as to lament that he was neglecting his work for reading. What was unusual in Bräker's step, however, was that his autobiography was able to appear at all in 1789 (with Orell, Geßner, and Füßli in Zürich).[23] Admittedly, it was not initially recognized as the most important German-language life description of the eighteenth century, but rather as the life utterances of a 'child of nature'; nevertheless it showed that even the educated 'public' had some feeling for the spiritual efforts of the simple man.

Behind the growing literacy of village society stood, naturally, the school. This, still supervised by the pastor, was largely a winter school, since in summer time the children were needed for work in the fields. The schoolmaster was proverbially poor, and frequently exercised his office only as a by-employment to a village craft. In town and countryside, this lower level of schooling, although not legally prescribed, was nevertheless widely made use of, and was not divided by sex. 'Teaching in the trivia' was dispensed in the countryside to girls and boys together, although separate girls' schools developed in the towns (they were already known in the large cities in the fifteenth century).

Together with the increasing literacy of the population, reading matter became a desired economic item.[24] Although obtaining books remained largely restricted to the social strata from the upper-middle stratum upwards, as is shown by lists of book-subscribers as late as 1800, pamphlets reporting remarkable or sensational occurrences, frightful murders, great natural occurrences, and wars in foreign lands, and especially calendars with practical hints for the overcoming of everyday problems, were widely purchased in town and countryside even by simple people. A separate market for popular literature began to form,[25] in which wandering traders were responsible for the spread of the products. This market, like the whole progress in the acquisition of partial literacy, is an indicator of a much more deep-reaching process, announcing the gradual severing of the agrarian world from the fetters of tradition.

Not only among simple people can a change in reading habits be observed, but also within the higher social estates. Reading societies arose everywhere in the last third of the eighteenth century. They were a branch of a movement which had turned the age of the late Enlightenment in Germany into a 'sociable century'.[26] This 'society movement' generated, in addition to the traditional learned society, literary and economic societies as well. In contrast to the *Verein* (association) of the nineteenth century, here it was a question of a sort of mutual social insurance – as can be seen most clearly among the Freemasons. These societies naturally manifested the most various shadings: a society could just as easily (as with the Freemasons) be an artificial kinship network as an association of kindred spirits (as was the case with the many 'economic' societies). Even a federation for purely economic purposes could conceal itself behind the façade of the 'closed reading society' of Elberfeld businessmen established in 1775. At centre stage in these societies, even when they were not 'reading societies', stands the book; for in order to realize the purposive rationalism of the spirit of the age, it was important for an economic society, for instance, to turn with books to the wider so-called 'public'.

The gradual transformation of the world from the mid-eighteenth century onward

At latest from the mid-eighteenth century onwards, it was no longer possible to ignore the fact that population growth in the countryside was creating substantial social problems. While the size of the population in the towns, as a consequence of very restrictive admissions policies for citizens, was stagnating (although in the suburbs and garden towns in front of the town walls, an early proletariat of married journeymen and day-labourers dwelt in makeshift huts, providing a labour-reserve always available for work peaks), the countryside had to bear the main burden of population growth, and high child mortality hardly put a brake on this. The corporate fields of a village could be increased only to a limited extent, by 5 or at most 10 per cent, even through clearing hitherto unutilized areas. As a consequence, the number of people living from work as small-scale peasants or sub-peasants rose dramatically. With stagnating wages precluding any real social opportunities, they lived at the subsistence minimum, excluded from any cultural progress. Given this mass misery, traditional representations of poverty as God's will were no longer convincing. Anyone who wanted to take the Enlightenment seriously had to regard poverty as a scandal. In particular, as can be observed in all German territories at this time, this represented a challenge for the authorities. With relatively few regional differences, they made a twofold response to the problem: first, they attempted to prohibit the marriage of 'people without means', 'so that the country will not be overrun with beggars'; and second, they tried to create new jobs in the country, in order to increase national well-being. Both efforts affected everyday life.

Prohibitions and restrictions on marriage were only a continuation, albeit with different intentions, of the mandates and edicts issued by the state to regulate its subjects since the 'age of confessionalism'. The aggregation of many scattered observations, however, suggests that it was only around 1700 that this legislation, which went further than discriminating against women bearing illegitimate children, experienced any success. This sort of mandate reflected a shift from a model according to which the state was already pleasing to God, to one in which the state was viewed as a machine, and calculations were entered into 'for the welfare of the country'; however, the continuation of this sort of mandate failed in its intentions. The number of poor people was not reduced: even where the marriage prohibitions were not in any case circumvented, the number of illegitimate births and thus the number of people without social opportunities continued to rise.

The second princely measure against poverty in the late Enlightenment also had its precursors; it represented the late phase of mercantilism of manufactory foundations, state-owned enterprises which failed, like their precursors, even when they were not subjected to fiscal compulsion as was still the case in 1700. That state-financed employment was expensive had already been remarked by governments in their 'houses of discipline'. These were to some extent planned as state-owned industrial enterprises, and correspondingly condemned to fail. Even privatization, which was frequently attempted, helped not at all: the entrepreneurs in question soon went bankrupt. The workhouses, which were linked to the houses of discipline, and which were supposed to be used to combat idleness and provide the diligent with the opportunity to earn a livelihood independently, everywhere fell into decay. Despite all the high-sounding intentions expressed in the foundation documents, what were left were only institutions concentrating on the notion of punishment. This took place despite all the intentions which a prince might originally have had for his house of discipline, as an institution to be shown off and proudly displayed to his guests. Government measures ultimately failed because of lack of money, and more particularly because of a lack of readiness to invest money over long periods; apart from edicts, princes had little to offer their countries.

Certainly the measures of the authorities failed. But in their failure they had consequences: the presence of the state in social policy was taken to absurd lengths. The sigh heaved by the Würzburg bishop, Franz Ludwig von Erthal, 'It is not as easy as one thinks to become master over begging', is a sign of the retreat of the prince out of the paternalistic role of the father. As usual, failures were covered up. But the repeal, observed generally from the 1780s on, of all the paternalistic social measures taken by princes as 'fathers of the country' which had failed to master the problems of poverty, was one of the basic preconditions for economic liberalization or, more precisely, the transfer of social problems to a self-organizing economy. (Admittedly, princes did not yet dare to rattle at the privileges of the guilds.)

Essentially, what has been called 'proto-industrialization' (discussed in detail in Chapter 9 of this volume) was a consequence of the crisis in the countryside: it was a form of self-organization created to deal with poverty.[27] It built on a structural change in the village which had been taking place since the later middle ages: since the fifteenth century the village had been not only an agrarian settlement, but also characterized by crafts. This was observed to the highest degree in south-west Germany and then the Lower Rhine, with (respectively) 60 and 40 masters per 1,000 inhabitants in the mid-eighteenth century. The theme of proto-industrialization is a differentiation and an expansion of crafts. It transferred the techniques and products of the age of manufactures into the village, even if often incompletely. Rural crafts, domestic industries, and proto-industrialization went hand in hand, especially in textile production, but also (with a large delay) in the pottery industry. In regions rich in forests – most significantly in the Thuringian Forest – glass production attained the status of a leading industry.

Domestic industry in villages must be seen in connection with a new phase in the pre-industrial foundation of manufactories, which were located above all in small towns and in villages with functions as 'central places' for their surrounding areas. This phase of industrialization has been neglected for so long because it did not take place in large cities. While the famous *Ansbacher Fayence-Manufactur* (Ansbach Faïence Manufactory), for example, employed only between 10 and 12 people, in 1780 in the smaller community of Schwabach 700 people lived from a calico manufactory and the production of needles. The workers in such manufactories worked for day-wages, which yielded very meagre livings. For the worker, as contemporaries knew, this sort of work generated 'only a very scanty bread'.[28]

In connection with proto-industrialization in the countryside and the new manufacturing centres in small towns and market centres, there also arose a new stratum of merchants in the second half of the eighteenth century, which replaced the earlier 'outsiders' who had dominated the ranks of the manufactory operators. However, it must not be overlooked that this was a new social stratum which was highly dependent on economic fluctuations: despite the yawning gap in wealth between it and the poor workers whom it employed, for the most part the new stratum of entrepreneurs could not, themselves, earn a secure living, while the higher bourgeoisie in the towns took for granted an inherited material fall-back. Furthermore, it was not only in their production conditions that these early manufactories were characterized by an opposition between poor and rich, but also in their market opportunities. For what was produced was either cheap mass wares for sale to a clientele with low purchasing power, or expensive luxury goods. Finally, the range of products remained correspondingly small, consisting essentially of textiles and (with a big gap) metal goods.

But all the indisputable changes caused by proto-industrialization would not have had any effect, and would not have been able to temper the harshness of population growth, if a change in agrarian structure had not at the same time ensured greater productivity, as discussed in Chapter 3 of this volume.

In the corporate fields of villages in all German territories (although with a clear delay in eastern Germany), it became clear around 1800 that the situation on the land was beginning to change. It was not so much the legal conditions which were affected, for the attention-arousing measures of the authorities, the spectacularly advertised abolition of serfdom, had a greater effect on the educated 'public' than in reality: these were calculated acts taken by princes who were now supposed to be renowned for their social consciences. Thus, the fact is generally ignored that in 1765 serfdom had been abolished in the Hohenlohe principality of Langenburg because of the small volume of revenues resulting from it. Frederick the Great's abolition of serfdom on the royal domains, therefore, which had such an impact on the public, was not much more than an abolition of compulsory servant work by peasants' children, which the king could well afford given the over-population of the country. Moreover, this measure affected only the royal domains, which meant only some 4 per cent of the agriculturally utilized area outside East Prussia.

What began to change was the situation in the stable, in the pasture, and in the corporate fields of the village. In this context, it must be remembered that the peasant had always operated under twofold coercion: that of the soil and that of the authorities. Thus the 'agrarian improvements' which were introduced from the second half of the eighteenth century on were adopted by the peasants with some delay, and gradually began to be implemented around 1800; this took place with the introduction of clover cultivation on the fallow, which simultaneously generated a cheap fodder enabling an expansion of cattle raising. Up until now, the number of animals (especially beef cattle) which could be kept had been determined by the availability of pasture land. Now, however, this dependence could be loosened through stall-feeding. Stall-feeding, like so many other agrarian improvements, also meant the beginning of individualized cultivation. Pasture land had generally been 'common land' and therefore subject to corporative regulation by the community and thus by the peasant upper stratum which held sway in the community. Now, however, the peasant could himself decide on the number of cattle that could be kept, based on his individual economic opportunities. No longer was he confronted with the quota system laid down by the village community.

A decisive change had also come about in sheep-raising. It had proved possible to introduce Merino sheep from Spain into Germany, and thus to increase wool yields by a factor of three. Admittedly, this measure mainly benefited the nobility, since most sheep were kept by the demesne sheep-raising enterprises in the possession of noble landlords. But indirectly, these breeding successes were also important for the common man: the increased production of wool for the first time permitted the expansion of woollen-cloth production and of stocking-knitting as domestic industries and bases for proto-industrialization.

In the corporate fields of the village, the beginnings of great changes in the world could be observed. We will select two examples of this, tobacco and hemp cultivation. Around 1700, tobacco was still a 'medicinal' plant which had to be obtained from an apothecary. From the first third of the eighteenth century on, however, tobacco, which flourished on sandy soils which until then had been barren, was cultivated to an ever-increasing extent as an earning opportunity for simple people, for the younger sons of small peasants of the Eichsfeld, and for discharged soldiers in the Mark Brandenburg. Tobacco was especially consumed among the lower strata. While the higher social estates persisted in the more refined snuff-taking, around 1800 the pipe belonged to the manservant and the peasant, the soldier and the craftsman. Smoking had become a mass phenomenon, which led the authorities to attempt concerned but ineffectual intervention, and to issue the prohibitions against smoking in the open street which can be met with everywhere after about 1770.

A decisive change in the visual appearance of the corporate fields of the village was brought about by hemp and flax. Small peasants, in particular, cultivated these plants to an ever-increasing extent; for in every eighteenth-century village spinning was practised by both men and women. Admittedly, despite all improvements, a wheel-spinner could only spin about eight grams of medium cotton yarn per hour, but this nevertheless provided supplementary earnings. Spinning and knitting were explicitly prized by all governments as new forms of earnings, especially as a remedy for so-called idleness, to disguise the real prevailing mass unemployment. Domestic industries arose in villages – proto-industrialization. In Germany, as well, proto-industrialization was a pacemaker for new economic forms. While in Elberfeld, for example, a typical textile countryside, the number of linen-weaving masters rose from 300 in 1740 to 1,100 in 1781, signifying a substantial decline in the status of the industry, the textile putter-out could rise to become an entrepreneur trading like a merchant. This is the economic background to the 'closed reading society' of the Elberfeld businessmen, already mentioned above, in which the membership contribution paid by the merchant was equivalent to 2 years' wages for a weaver.[29]

The history of agrarian improvements – we can only hint at the whole catalogue of measures – shows the great difficulties in the dialogue between upper-stratum and common man. For the great stimulators of the reform measures were bourgeois people, learned men, and pastors. What they recommended, what they published in their prize writings for learned societies, what then was recommended in government edicts to the – as one said at that time – 'countryman', was only reluctantly adopted by the peasants, even when it concerned central problems such as improvements in manuring. For the government which recommended such measures was the same government which had hitherto only been known by the peasant as a coercive and penalizing authority, as an institution which extorted taxes and enforced laws in the countryside, and which was often regarded as implementing senseless and restrictive regulations, as with the prohibition against keeping doves. The resistance of the common man, above all the common man living in the countryside, against measures by the authorities, which reached deep into the struggle against crime, had important consequences for the history of agrarian improvements. Basically it meant – as already evidenced by the history of the most important of all innovations, the introduction of the potato – that the practical sense of the countryman primarily sought to separate out the numerous senseless recommendations from the sensible ones, with the result that their implementation was ultimately forced by sheer necessity.

As far as the conditions of daily life were concerned, in German territories the period between the Peace of Westphalia and the French Revolution may appear to have been a quite unified epoch both in its external framework and in its legal and political constitution; but in its ways of life it showed itself to be a world susceptible to change, containing tendencies toward deep-reaching transformations.

Notes

1 Klaus J. Bade, ed., *Deutsche im Ausland – Fremde in Deutschland. Migration in Geschichte und Gegenwart* (Munich, 1992); Wolfgang von Hippel, *Auswanderung aus Südwestdeutschland. Studien zur württembergischen Auswanderung und Auswanderungspolitik im 18. und 19. Jahrhundert* (Stuttgart, 1984).

2 Günther Franz, *Der Dreißigjährige Krieg und das deutsche Volk* (4th edn, Stuttgart, 1979).

3 An outstanding survey of the industrial situation is offered by Karl-Heinrich Kaufhold, 'Gewerbelandschaften in der frühen Neuzeit', in Hans Pohl, ed., *Gewerbe- und Industrielandschaften vom Spätmittelalter bis ins 20. Jahrhundert* (Wiesbaden, 1986), pp. 112–202.

4 Standard works: Joachim Lampe, *Aristokratie, Hofadel und Staatspatriziat in Kurhannover. Die Lebenskreise der höheren Beamten an den kurhannoverschen Zentralbehörden 1714–1760* (2 vols, Göttingen, 1963); Hanns Hubert Hofmann and Günther Franz, eds, *Deutsche Führungsschichten in der Neuzeit. Eine Zwischenbilanz* (Boppard, 1980).

5 Wolfgang Griep and Hans-Wolf Jäger, *Reise und soziale Realität am Ende des 18. Jahrhunderts* (Heidelberg, 1983).

6 Wilhelm Bonacker, *Kartenmacher aller Länder und Zeiten* (Stuttgart, 1966). A survey of German political geography around 1700 is offered by the too-often-neglected work of Konrad Kretschmer, *Historische Geographie von Mitteleuropa* (Munich, 1904), pp. 551ff.

7 Niedersächsisches Landesverwaltungsamt – Landesvermessung, ed., *Kurhannoversche Landesaufnahme des 18. Jahrhunderts (1764–1786). 1:25.000* (Hannover, 1959). See Franz Engel, *Die Kurhannoversche Landesaufnahme des 18. Jahrhunderts* (2nd edn, Hannover, 1978).

8 Friedrich Nicolai, *Beschreibung einer Reise durch Deutschland und die Schweiz im Jahre 1781. Nebst Bemerkungen über Gelehrsamkeit, Industrie, Religion und Sitten* (2 vols, Berlin, 1783), i. p. 73.

9 Nicolai, *Beschreibung*, p. 114.

10 Christian Pfister, *Bevölkerungsgeschichte und historische Demographie 1500–1800* (Munich, 1994), arrives at different figures for life expectancies on pp. 35ff. and 95ff.

11 Arthur E. Imhof, 'Unsere Lebensuhr – Phasenverschiebungen im Verlauf der Neuzeit', in Peter Burscheid and Hans J. Teuteberg, eds, *Ehe, Liebe, Tod* (Münster, 1983), pp. 170ff.

12 Richard van Dülmen, *Kultur und Alltag in der frühen Neuzeit, i: Das Haus und seine Menschen 16.–18. Jahrhundert* (Munich, 1990), pp. 12ff.; Hans-Jürgen Teuteberg, 'Beobachtungen zu einer Geschichte des Wohnens', in Hans-Jürgen Teuteberg, ed., *Homo habitans. Zur Sozialgeschichte des ländlichen und städtischen Wohnens in der Neuzeit* (Münster, 1985), pp. 1ff.

13 Christoph Wilhelm Hufeland, *Nöthige Erinnerung an die Bäder und ihre Wiedereinführung in Teutschland* (Weimar, 1801).

14	Johann Siegemund Hahn, *Unterricht von Krafft und Würckung des frischen Wassers* (3rd edn, Breslau, 1749).

15	Hahn, *Unterricht*, p. 65.

16	Gisela Reineking von Bock, ed., *Bäder, Duft und Seife. Kunstgewerbemuseum der Stadt Köln* (Cologne, 1976).

17	Helmut Ottenjann, ed., 'Mode, Tracht, regionale Identität. Historische Kleidungsforschung heute', *Referate des internationalen Symposions im Museumsdorf Cloppenburg* (Cloppenburg, 1985).

18	Ernst Schubert, *Arme Leute, Bettler und Gauner im Franken des 18. Jahrhunderts* (2nd edn, Neustadt, 1990).

19	Günter Wiegelmann, *Alltags- und Festspeisen. Wandel und gegenwärtige Stellung* (Marburg, 1967).

20	Adolph Freiherr von Knigge, *Über den Umgang mit Menschen* (Hannover, 1788).

21	Volker Saftien, 'Von der höfischen Tanzkultur zum Tanzgeschmack des Biedermeier – der Umbruch sozioökonomischer Werke', in Württembergisches Landesmuseum Stuttgart, ed., *Baden und Württemberg im Zeitalter Napoleons*, ii: *Aufsätze* (Stuttgart, 1987), pp. 599ff.

22	Paul Nettl, *Mozart und der Tanz. Zur Geschichte des Balletts und Gesellschaftstanzes* (Zürich, 1960), p. 50.

23	Werner Günther, ed., *Ulrich Bräker, Lebensgeschichte und natürliche Ebenteuer des Armen Mannes im Tockenburg* (Stuttgart, 1965), pp. 174ff.

24	Reinhart Siegert, *Aufklärung und Volkslektüre. Exemplarisch dargestellt an Rudolf Zacharias Becker und seinem 'Noth- und Hülfsbüchlein'. Mit einer Bibliographie zum Gesamtthema* (Frankfurt, 1978).

25	Rudolf Engelsing, 'Die Perioden der Lesegeschichte in der Neuzeit', in Rudolf Engelsing, ed., *Zur Sozialgeschichte deutscher Mittel- und Unterschichten* (Göttingen, 1973), pp. 112–54; Rudolf Engelsing, 'Dienstbotenlektüre im 18. und 19. Jahrhundert', in Engelsing, ed., *Sozialgeschichte*, pp. 180–224.

26	Ulrich Im Hof, *Das gesellige Jahrhundert. Gesellschaft und Gesellschaften im Zeitalter der Aufklärung* (Munich, 1982).

27	See Peter Kriedte, Hans Medick, and Jürgen Schlumbohm, 'Die Proto-Industrialisierung auf dem Prüfstand der historischen Zunft', *GG* 9 (1983), pp. 87–105.

28	Johann Bernhard Fischer, *Statistisch topographische Beschreibung des Burggraftums Nürnberg unter dem Gebirg oder Fürstenthums Brandenburg-Anspach* (2 vols, Ansbach, 1787), ii. p. 240.

29	Herbert Kisch, *Die hausindustriellen Textilgewerbe am Niederrhein vor der industriellen Revolution* (Göttingen, 1981).

Translated by Sheilagh Ogilvie.

|12|

Poverty and Poor Relief

ROBERT JÜTTE

The causes of poverty: the European context

Since the end of the middle ages, urban and rural communities and the developing nation states of western Europe have been confronted with the ubiquitous and perennial problem of poverty. The problems of economic insecurity were similar in all those countries which experienced the diffi-cult shift from an agrarian to an industrialized society. A comparative study would reveal the common nature of the social and economic questions that are involved in the development of poor-relief schemes and welfare pro-grammes as well as pointing out the different responses to the challenge of destitution and poverty in different environments and political and reli-gious frameworks.

Poverty had many faces in pre-industrial society. Several factors con-tributed to the problem of poverty and vagrancy, varying in importance, however, from country to country, from area to area, and from decade to decade. The following list is not intended to be a comprehensive enumera-tion of the various causes of poverty. Its purpose is merely to indicate broadly the major forces which generated mass impoverishment not only in early modern Germany but elsewhere as well. Poverty was experienced at many social levels, although the lower classes were prone to life-threatening deprivation. Not only day-labourers, smallholders, and wage earners but also artisans and middle-ranking peasants were at risk. Anyone could fall victim to ill fortune (illness, accident, premature death of breadwinners, etc.), from which recovery in an age in which social security was not guar-anteed was difficult, and which therefore in many cases led to impoverish-ment or even destitution.

Accidental causes

Although early modern European governments varied in their approaches to the problems of indigency, we always find acceptance of the role of sickness in poverty. This is manifest not only in the legislation which in one way or another provided more medical care to the indigent, but primarily in the basic tenet which was restated from time to time, to wit: that sickness and its consequences were a distinctive feature of the 'deserving' poor. Although the importance of sickness as a causal element in poverty had been indicated since the later middle ages, we do not find until the middle of the nineteenth century any real attempt to measure the extent to which sickness was responsible for poverty. However, from recent studies on poor relief in early modern Germany we learn that between 10 and 25 per cent of persons relying on outdoor relief were sick; and furthermore, that old age or permanent disability was the cause of destitution in more than one-half of the persons described as ill. Table 12.1 reflects the importance of disabilities of various kinds as a factor in dependency in that period.

However, one has to be careful not to generalize such data. From these limited observations it should be clear that the problem of the interrelationship between disease and poverty must be considered, as Ciocco and Perrott have shown, 'in terms of the two major variables involved – the pre-disease economic status of the individual and the nature of the disease itself'.[1] The impact of disease was not the same for different socio-economic groups, even if lower-class people made up for lacking financial resources by accumulating 'social capital'. But the difference depended also on the nature of the disease, as a social history of the plague will clearly demonstrate.[2]

Warfare was another major cause of poverty. The major wars that accompanied the 'iron century' (the Peasants' War, the Thirty Years War, the War of the Palatinate 1688–97, and the various Turkish Wars, whose effects are discussed in detail in Chapter 8) further increased the number of the destitute. The direct negative effects of warfare (loss of goods and chattels, death of the breadwinner, financial ruin by levies and taxes) were less significant than its indirect effects, which included famine, the spread of disease, and subsistence migration. While there are a few studies on early modern Germany which tell us how the Thirty Years War, for example, brought about a decline in wealth and economic status,[3] we have hardly any investigations providing basic data on the question of the extent to which the war uprooted people and forced them to require assistance from the community. Titz-Matuszak,[4] for example, examined the causes for almsgiving in Lower Saxony in the seventeenth and eighteenth centuries and found out that 1,726 persons had fled from the atrocities committed by the French army during the War of the Palatinate (1688–97). For 1,165 of

Table 12.1 Disease conditions of foreign recipients of alms in Lower Saxony in the seventeenth and eighteenth centuries

Lame	192
Maimed (soldiers)	187
Sick (not specified)	103
Frail	96
Blind	71
Epileptic	44
Fractured or missing limbs	26
Insane	22
Deaf and/or dumb	19
Without tongue	12
Crippled	10
Cancer	6
Pox	2
Dropsy	2
Other illnesses	5
Sick persons (total)	797
Total number of recipients	9,418

Source: Ingeborg Titz-Matuszak, 'Mobilität der Armut – Das Almosenwesen im 17. und 18. Jahrhundert im südniedersächsischen Raum', *Plesse-Archiv*, 24 (1988), pp. 9–338, here pp. 66ff.

these refugees or displaced persons we have data which allows us to differentiate between three major groups of recipients: 47 per cent of them were male, 46 per cent were female, and 7 per cent were children, in which case no gender was given. The evidence seems to be conclusive that the war affected not only men and women but whole families. However, not only innocent civilians were pauperized when a full-fledged war ravaged towns and countryside; often the numbers of the poor were also increased by demobilized soldiers. Among the identifiable types of vagrants, wandering soldiers seeking employment as mercenaries made up by far the most fearsome single group, as Robert Scribner has shown.[5] Among the demobilized soldiers were many maimed soldiers (according to data from Lower Saxony more than 58 per cent) who at that time had no other means to secure their livelihoods than by begging.

Cyclical causes

The steadily rising population – a trend which was interrupted only by the demographic impact of the Thirty Years War – led to increasing pressure on limited resources that failed to grow as quickly and therefore brought about a steady rise in prices for foodstuffs. A sample made up of several German towns shows that grain prices rose 3.3 to 3.6 times, on average, in the period 1501–1625, while the prices of other basic commodities 'only' doubled. Wages did not keep up with the rapid development of prices. At the beginning of the seventeenth century weavers and carpenters earned twice as much as at the beginning of the sixteenth century, while the price of food had almost tripled. The studies by Wilhelm Abel[6] and other economic historians have made quite clear that the purchasing power of wages declined by almost 50 per cent on average in major German cities between 1500 and 1700 (see Fig. 12.1). Only in the eighteenth century does there seem to have been a small improvement in at least some cities, but even then the real wages did not reach again the level they had at the beginning of the early modern period. What these bare statistical facts meant for the subsistence of an average household in early modern Augsburg has been made clear by Wilhelm Abel. Around 1500 a building worker could buy with his annual wage 1.5 times the quantity of commodities needed by a household consisting of five members. At the beginning of the seventeenth century his income covered no more than 75 per cent of his household expenses. If starvation was to be ávoided, this household had to find additional sources of income. It does not come as a surprise, therefore, that in times of soaring food prices the lower-income groups often had no other choice than to supplement their wages through private charity or public poor-relief. In the city of Trier, for example, about 20 per cent of recipients of outdoor poor-relief only appear once in the account books of the 'Almosenamt' ('alms office'), which indicates that in most of these cases poor-relief must have been granted in a momentary situation of economic and financial distress.[7]

Rather than to look for the correlation between rising grain-prices and demographic growth, it is preferable to concentrate on obvious years of dearth caused by harvest failures. For evidence of purer crises of subsistence we can turn the pioneering research of Wilhelm Abel and his school. In a normal crisis the consequence of high food prices was not starvation but general impoverishment. However, there were crisis years in the sixteenth and seventeenth centuries, when grain prices rose to staggering heights and contemporaries complained that poverty and hunger were mounting in quantity and intensity. Such crises of subsistence occurred when there were several bad harvests in a row, as, for example, in Germany in 1527–34, 1556–7, 1571–4, 1624–5, 1637–9, 1691–3, 1739–41, and 1771–4. Bad harvests, however, were never the only cause of impoverishment and its concomitant, mortality crisis. Besides malnutrition there were other factors which influenced the mortality rate. One of these exogenous determinants of mortality crises was epidemic disease such as plague and influenza.[8]

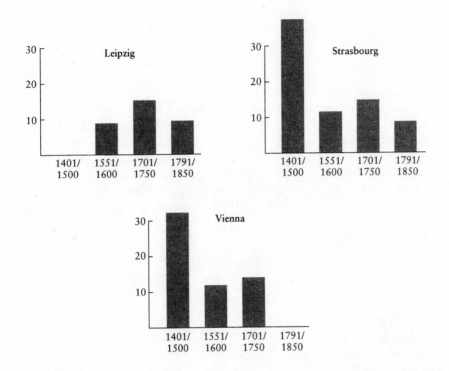

Fig. 12.1 The decline in the purchasing power of the wages of building workers (masons and carpenters) in selected German cities, 1401–1850 (day wages in kilograms of grain) (*Source:* Wilhelm Abel, *Massenarmut und Hungerkrisen im vorindustrielle Europa* (Hamburg/Berlin, 1974), p. 63)

Structural Causes

The fact that impoverishment was to a greater exent caused by 'cyclical' than by 'structural' factors has directed historical attention toward the causes rather than the condition of poverty. In order to understand what poverty in a pre-industrial society was about, one has to look at household structure. The life cycle, too, was no less important in establishing a borderline between independence and indigence in early modern Germany. The age structure of poor households thus tells us a lot about the causes and likely frequency of the decline into dependent poverty, as can be seen in Table 12.2

Recipients of poor relief in early modern German towns, as well as in other European cities, differed in their household structure from that of the overall urban population. Poor households were usually very small and rarely made up of complete nuclear families with a married couple at their head. More than half of the households consisted of single persons, usually widows, and some of the rest were also headed by women. This also accounts for the sex ratio among recipients of poor relief, as shown in Table 12.3.

If the normal household of the period contained a married couple, children, and servants, then the poor household was a radical departure from it. Family structure among the urban poor (and even more so among vagrants) is a story of fragments. The disintegration of the families took many forms, but a classic one was death of one of the marriage partners. However, there were also cases in which either husband or wife left their families and became vagrants. Desertion by the male partner occurred, as Robert Scribner has shown for sixteenth-century Württemberg, because of debts, family disputes, impressment, and adultery.[9] Death or prolonged

Table 12.2 The structure of poor households in a German and an English town in the sixteenth century

	Strasbourg (1523)	Worcester (1557)
Mean household size	2.3	2.4
Households with married heads	44.0%	34.4%
Households with female heads	11.5%	41.4%
Households consisting of solitary persons	36.9%	50.2%
Households with children	38.5%	38.6%
Children per household, where present	2.7	2.7

Source: Paul Slack, *Poverty and Policy in Tudor and Stuart England* (London/New York, 1988), p. 76; Thomas Fischer, *Städtische Armut und Armenfürsorge im 15. und 16. Jahrhundert* (Göttingen, 1979), pp. 130f.

Table 12.3 The sex ratio of poor-relief recipients

	Strasbourg 1523		Trier 1591–1650		Würzburg 1791	
	No.	%	No.	%	No.	%
Male	81	31	–	ø 26	143	18
Female	182	69	–	ø 63	658	82
Not known	–	–	–	ø 11	–	–

Note: ø = average

Source: Thomas Fischer, *Städtische Armut und Armenfürsorge im 15. und 16. Jahrhundert* (Göttingen, 1979), pp. 128f; Maria Ackels, 'Das Trierer städtische Almosenamt im 16. und 17. Jahrhundert: Ein Beitrag zur Analyse sozialer Unterschichten', *Kurtrierisches Jahrbuch*, 24 (1984), pp. 75–103, p. 95; Hans-Christoph Rublack, *Gescheiterte Reformation* (Stuttgart, 1978), p. 153.

absence of the breadwinner plunged many families into desperate poverty. Widowhood, as shown in Fig. 12.2, meant a considerable loss of income for all social groups, but hit the lower classes in particular; because of their limited resources they could hardly cope with such decline.

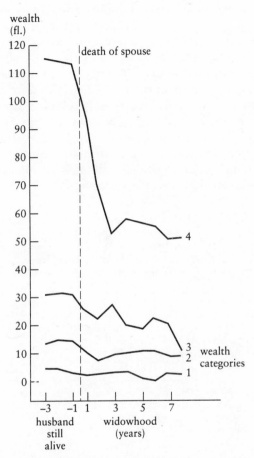

Fig. 12.2 Decline of economic assets in case of widowhood in early modern Lemgo, *c.* 1500 (*Source:* Heinrich Rüthing, *Höxter um 1500. Analyse einer Stadtgesellschaft* (Paderborn, 1986), p. 364)

The pressures toward dissolution or fragmentation varied according to the development cycle of these families. People were more or less liable to slide beneath subsistence to dependence on charity at different stages in their lives. Although – unlike Italy or England, for example – there are no censuses of the poor before the eighteenth century in early modern Germany which give details on the age of the recipients, we can assume from the frequent mentioning of children and widows in the account books that there was a heavy incidence of poverty among the very old and the very young, but that people in the prime of their life between the ages of 30 and 60 were also affected.[10]

To turn from size of the household and its age structure to the relationship between low-income professions and poverty allows us to identify more precisely the differences and relative weaknesses of the family structures. Within the pre-industrial economy, the distribution of earnings was markedly unequal, reflecting not only the sexual division of labour and the life-cycle of the individuals, but also the unequal distribution of wealth among occupational groups. No weaver in Augsburg, for example, could earn as much as a butcher or taverner. The distribution of occupational groups among poor-relief recipients displays in almost classic fashion the profile of a pre-industrial urban economy (as can be seen in Table 12.4). In most cases, individual occupations were highly stratified, but there were some occupations which almost invariably implied a certain wealth level: obviously, merchants were almost all near the top, and weavers and textile workers almost always near the bottom.

Table 12.4 Distribution of poverty among male citizens in major occupational groups (percentage of poor-relief recipients)

	Trier 1591–1650	Augsburg 1622
Textile and clothing crafts	17.7	44.6
Leather and fur crafts	6.1	13.8
Construction	12.2	5.0
Metal wares	5.8	1.7
Food and drink trades	10.1	3.8
Commerce and retailing	14.6	3.0
Other	33.5	28.1

Source: Maria Ackels, 'Das Trierer städtische Almosenamt im 16. und 17. Jahrhundert: Ein Beitrag zur Analyse sozialer Unterschichten', *Kurtrierisches Jahrbuch*, 24 (1984), pp. 75–103, here p. 95; Bernd Roeck, *Eine Stadt in Krieg und Frieden. Studien zur Geschichte der Reichsstadt Augsburg zwischen Kalenderstreit und Parität* (2 vols, Göttingen, 1989), ii. p. 525.

However, one has to bear in mind the relative importance of different causes of poverty. Families and individuals often had more than one disadvantage to contend with. But the chief misfortunes and the proportion of persons affected by them (shown in Fig. 12.3) tell us something about the origins of poverty and their proportional weight in one concrete instance, that of late-eighteenth-century Würzburg.

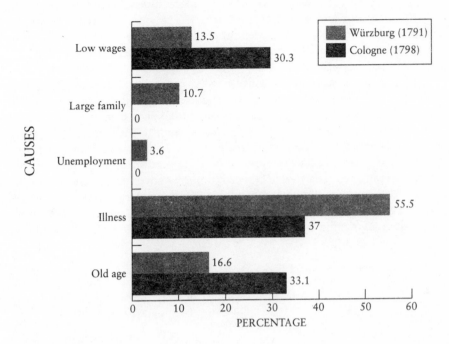

Fig. 12.3 The causes of poverty in Würzburg (1791) and Cologne (1798) (percentage of poor families) (*Source:* Robert Jütte, *Poverty and Deviance in Early Modern Europe* (Cambridge, 1994), p. 41)

The extent of the problem: spatial and temporal variations

Problems of definition and measurement

Those who wrote about 'the poor' or distributed alms in the sixteenth and seventeenth centuries did not worry about the fact that the term was an elastic one, used in different ways in changing political and social contexts. The relative nature of poverty makes it impossible to define a poverty threshold which has universal validity. In recent studies on poverty in early modern England we find the distinction between 'shallow' and 'deep' poverty. However, these still rather vague criteria for the intensity of poverty were not used by contemporary authors dealing with this paramount social problem. At this point one must keep in mind how fundamentally different pre-industrial societies are from industrial ones and how difficult it is to apply sociological concepts such as 'absolute' or 'relative' deprivation to phenomena which were judged differently by people living in the sixteenth and seventeenth centuries. The sources present us with a number of people who have been labelled 'poor' according to criteria that are often vague and that vary according to the people, the institution, the period, and the place.

In order to quantify the extent of poverty in the past, historians have used tax records. However, the data and figures produced for the poor from those studies are so varied, even confusing, that such evidence is not at all adequate. Even if we disregard the problems of different criteria used by tax authorities and the lack of standardization, we still have no answer to the important question of how representative the poor mentioned in these documents really are. The people labelled 'poor' by government officials are the so-called 'fiscal poor', which means that taxation records do not provide us with an exact measure of the economic condition of the poor, but rather include quite a range of wealth within their exempt categories. Nevertheless

Table 12.5 'Fiscal poor' in early modern German tax records

	Year	Number of taxable persons	Exempted persons or households belonging to bottom category	
			no.	%
Frankfurt am Main	1495	2,492	1,081	43.3
	1556	2,111	208	9.9
Freiburg im Breisgau	1530	1,065	303	26.9
Würzburg	1547	2,230	696	31.2
	1564	1,790	529	29.6
Schmalkalden	1576	615	131	21.4
Nördlingen	1579	1,541	415	1.6
Cologne	1582	4,062	189	4.7
Augsburg	1618		4,240	48.5
	1646		1,570	37.2

Source: Bernd Roeck, *Eine Stadt in Krieg und Frieden. Studien zur Geschichte der Reichsstadt Augsburg zwischen Kalenderstreit und Parität* (2 vols, Göttingen, 1989); Christopher R. Friedrichs, *Urban Society in an Age of War, Nördlingen, 1580–1720* (Princeton, NJ, 1979); Hans-Christoph Rublack, *Gescheiterte Reformation* (Stuttgart, 1978); Robert Jütte, *Obrigkeitliche Armenfürsorge in deutschen Reichsstädten der frühen Neuzeit* (Cologne/Vienna, 1985); Wieland Held, 'Die Vermögens- und Sozialstruktur Schmalkaldens unter Berücksichtigung der Vorstädte', *Jahrbuch für Regionalgeschichte*, 9 (1982), pp. 235–54.

registers concerning direct personal taxation have also been studied for several early modern German towns. The results give figures ranging between 1 per cent and 50 per cent of the persons or households liable to pay taxes. It emerges from Table 12.5 that even within the space of only a few years the differences in one and the same place or community are considerable.

A study of the extent of poverty must cover the welfare policies of the authorities and the almsgiving of the better-off. The institutional measures as well as the individual position with regard to donations can also be a valuable guideline for any attempt at quantification. In practice, it was the administrative or personal distinction imposed by the selective and inconsistent hand of poor-relief agents or private individuals which distinguished 'paupers' from the poor in general. This is also in line with the modern definition of who is to be considered poor, formulated by the German sociologist Georg Simmel.[11]

The extent of poverty

Inadequate as these almsgiving bodies or charity institutions were, their records do show something of the scale of poverty in the early modern period. The weight of evidence from various German towns suggests that 4 or 5 per cent was commonly the proportion of urban populations to be granted poor-relief in the period between 1500 and 1800, as can be seen in Table 12.6. In years of crisis (e.g. during the Thirty Years War) or in towns with particular economic problems, however, the number of poor-relief recipients was considerably higher. The figures for early modern German towns are not much different from those for English and other European cities for which we have similar quantitative studies. The available figures suggest that 5 per cent was the normal level of poverty in pre-industrial urban societies, and around 15 to 20 per cent was the potential crisis level.

The same economic and demographic pressures were felt to a lesser degree, and from a later date, in the countryside. In most regions of the Holy Roman Empire of the German Nation, the first signs of massive rural poverty appeared in the last third of the sixteenth century. By that time, the rural economy had become prone to more subsistence crises; the larger population of the late sixteenth century did not have the land or the material resources to survive easily in times of dearth. A substantial part of the rural population could no longer acquire land, and became cottars who had no fields to provide for their subsistence needs and who earned their livelihoods from wage labour. The growth of a new squatter and labouring population in the countryside was not restricted to certain regions, although

Table 12.6 Poor-relief recipients in selected German towns

Place	Date	Poor-relief recipients	Recipients as proportion of total population (%)
Frankenberg	1533–42	91	4.2
Augsburg	1550–74	1,260	3.6
Trier	1591–2	95	8.0
	1618–19	359	30.4
Würzburg	1791	791	4.5
	1794	778	4.3

Source: William J. Wright, 'A Closer Look at House Poor Relief through the Common Chest and Indigence in Sixteenth Century Hesse', *Archiv für Reformationsgeschichte*, 70 (1979), pp. 225–7; Claus-Peter Clasen, 'Armenfürsorge in Augsburg vor dem Dreißigjährigen Kriege', *Zeitschrift des Historischen Vereins für Schwaben*, 78 (1984), pp. 65–115; Maria Ackels, 'Das Trierer städtische Almosenamt im 16. und 17. Jahrhundert: Ein Beitrag zur Analyse sozialer Unterschichten', *Kurtrierisches Jahrbuch*, 24 (1984), pp. 75–103; Hans-Christoph Rublack, *Gescheiterte Reformation* (Stuttgart, 1978), pp. 134–6.

the extent of the problem varied from area to area. In Saxony, for instance, the number of cottars increased from 20,000 in 1550 to 310,000 in 1750.[12] In the same period, the population rose by 183 per cent. Compared to eastern German territories where the percentage of cottars among the rural population was already high in the later sixteenth century (e.g. in the district of Muskau near Cottbus, in 1552, 56 per cent of the population were farmers and 32 per cent cottars), the number of cottars in south-west Germany was still rather low. In the Langenburg district of the county of Hohenlohe, for example, no more than 10 per cent of the labouring population belonged to this group. How close the cottars were to the brink of destitution was explained by one of them, Hans Hanselmann the younger, who owned only a cottage and few tiny plots of land near Unterregenbach, a small village in south-west Germany: 'I shall be completely destitute unless I get several fields which, along with my day-labour, might help me to feed my small children.'[13] In quantitative terms alone, the increasing numbers of cottars and farm servants were disturbing, since they represented a substantial slice of the rural population in early modern Germany. The threat of an escalating number of paupers was thus sharply perceived in the countryside, in particular in the eighteenth century, and it did not come only from 'masterless men', wandering soldiers, rogues, and fake beggars thronging the roads, villages, and markets of rural Germany, but also from the respectable labouring classes who no longer had access to a plot of land.

The extent of rural poverty can be seen still more clearly if one looks at various censuses of the rural poor in the early eighteenth century. These listings show that a contemporary Franconian newspaper only slightly exaggerated in saying that one rich person had to support more than twenty poor householders.[14] In Allfeld, one of the rural parishes under the rule of the City of Nuremberg, in 1700, 75 households were able to contribute to the common chest while 79 were considered to be too poor to pay the poor tax. The overseers of Allfeld and the neighbouring villages also listed the groups of poor-relief recipients by name: there were six impotent and aged poor, nine begging children, and 15 able-bodied poor not able to maintain themselves and their families by their labour. In the parish of Kansberg the situation was worse still: the parish had only 252 taxpaying households and 280 households exempted from the poor tax. A minority of the village households thus had to finance an expensive poor-relief scheme providing alms for 116 destitute members of the parish. At the top of the social scale were the 40 to 60 per cent of the householders who were ratepayers, none of them in imminent danger of destitution. At the bottom were those receiving poor relief. But in between was a vaguely defined group of householders who hovered around the poverty line and who might fall below it when the harvest failed, when sickness hit the chief breadwinner, or when employment opportunities for wives and children in rural industries contracted.

The discourse on poverty

The medieval tradition

In the middle ages the common view, drawing on the biblical verse 'the poor you have with you always', was that poverty was perennial and divinely willed. The poor were seen as a natural part of a Christian commonwealth. They were valued and esteemed by the rich because almsgiving was considered to be an act of justice and mercy which wiped away sin. However, charity was never regarded as a remedy for poverty, and its long-term results were at best a slight amelioration of the condition of the poor. Despite a certain mainstream theological conception of poverty, there were already many strands of thinking about the hoary question of whether Christ's teaching really encourages the almsgiver to think only of self-advantage and thus to give indiscriminately to the poor. There was already some criticism of the poor both in theological tracts and in popular literature.[15] Already in the fourteenth century one can find phrases such as 'modest paupers' or 'shame-faced poor' which anticipate the mainly sixteenth-century distinction between deserving and undeserving poor. Since the fourteenth and fifteenth centuries, the admirers of poverty had been losing ground within the church and among the literate laity. However, the traditional attitude toward the poor was still predominant, and can be found in the poems as well as the tracts of the later middle ages. Hans Folz, the famous Meistersinger of Nuremberg, for example, writing in 1480, still shows some sympathy for the old virtue of poverty and almsgiving: 'So mich got arm hat an gesehen / Wie mag mir ymmer pas gscheen / Ich drag mein armut willecleich / Und nem dar umb das himelreich' ('As God has considered me poor / What better could ever have happened to me / I gladly bear my poverty / And I gain heaven by it'). The same idea, but theologically much more elaborated, was advocated by a doctor of divinity and professor at the University of Tübingen, Gabriel Biel (1410–1495). He idealized the poor and declared that moral judgements should be excluded entirely from acts of mercy. The Strasbourg preacher Geiler von Kayserberg (1445–1510) also could not free himself from such scholastic thinking. With typical intellectual complexity, he not only showed sympathy for the traditional teaching of the Church on acts of mercy, but at the same time suggested a more pragmatic attitude toward almsgiving, advising donors that, in giving alms, they should take into account their own resources, the qualities and needs of the recipients, and the effects of the alms on the pauper. In his memorandum for the City of Strasbourg, the famous 'XXI Articles', he made radical suggestions about the rights as well as the duties of the poor. A new scheme for the relief of the poor ought, in his view, to be worked out by the municipal authorities and put into practice. The guiding principles of his reform programme were the obligation of the able-bodied poor to work and the confident identification of the deserving poor by taking into account their condition. Geiler von Kaysersberg, unlike most other churchmen of this time, firmly believed that the secular authorities played a paramount role in providing relief for the poor and that the government had a certain social responsibility.

The humanists' initiative

The sixteenth century witnessed the full emergence of the fundamental and age-old distinction between deserving and undeserving poor as well as an increase in state intervention (which also had medieval roots) in matters of poor relief and social welfare. These harsher attitudes cannot be ascribed to purely intellectual developments. There can be no doubt that they were strongly influenced by the pressing economic and social problems on the eve of the Reformation period. The growing numbers of traditional vagrants and of shiftless, sturdy beggars wakened the curiosity as much as the fear of contemporaries. German humanists such as Sebastian Brant (1458–1521), Heinrich Bebel (1472–1518), and Thomas Murner (*c.* 1475–1537), and the anonymous author of the 'Liber vagatorum' (*c.* 1510), portrayed the evil practices, shameless customs, and ungodly life of fake beggars and their fellow travellers. Those writers with their extremely successful works had a substantial share in the development of the social stereotype of the 'fake beggar' which provided the ideological underpinning for Protestant as well as Catholic poor-relief reform plans.[16] The growing fears about foreign wandering beggars and the social as well as political dangers of unrelieved poverty were accompanied by humanist concerns to improve the conditions of men. Many humanists, in Germany and elsewhere, proposed means to alleviate need and to counter vagabondage. Erasmus of Rotterdam (1469–1536), for example, suggested that municipal authorities should take strong measures against idle beggars and the swelling armies of the poor. Heinrich Cornelius Agrippa of Nettesheim (1486–1535) wrote that one should not pity the poor, but despise beggars and vagabonds instead. However, among the very few European humanists who really grasped the problem and composed a detailed reform programme was the Spanish writer Juan Luis Vives (1492–1540), who published at Bruges the most famous sixteenth-century tract on poor relief, 'De subventione pauperum' (1526). It was quickly translated from Latin into French, Italian, English, and German.[17] Its contents not only were very much debated in circles of theologians but invoked government response all over Europe. Vives's main thesis was that the state should act directly in alleviating poverty by offering employment opportunities for the jobless, building centres for the support of the needy (such as hospitals and orphanages) and aiding poor families in their homes. He favoured a paternalistic approach to social policy:

> Just as it is disgraceful for the father of the family to allow any member to suffer hunger, nakedness, or the embarrassment of wearing rags, so it follows that in a wealthy city, it is unjust that magistrates permit any of its citizens to be pressed down by hunger and misery.

Vives's proposals influenced in one way or another the reforms undertaken in Nuremberg, Strasbourg, Mons, Ypres, Lille, Brussels, Oudendarde, and Valenciennes. Among the sixteenth-century authors who referred to Vives' 'De subventione pauperum' are Conrad Wimpina, theological adviser of Joachim I of Brandenburg, Christian Cellarius, Peter Papäus, Domingo de Soto, Aegidius Wystius, and Laurentio Villavicentio.[18]

Protestant reform

Religious reformers were equally concerned with poverty during the early modern period. However much Luther, Zwingli, Karlstadt, Bugenhagen, Hyperius, and Bucer differed, they agreed that poverty was neither virtuous nor sanctifying.[19] Protestant reformers saw labour as an alternative to poverty. Idleness of any kind was frowned upon; its opposite, work, was cherished. Luther established a 'work ethic' which was not completely new but gathered momentum in the course of the Reformation period.[20] Labour thus became the new medicine for poverty in many cities, not only in Germany, but in many other European countries as well. Begging was considered by these Protestant reformers to be on a par with idleness. Nobody was really unable to work. Even the blind, for example, were able to gain their livelihoods by performing minor jobs. The theological and ethical justification of work and the condemnation of idleness and its concomitant, begging, gave secular authorities the opportunity to act and to develop a social policy based on two principles: the strict prohibition of begging, and the duty of the sturdy and able-bodied poor to work. All Protestant schemes of poor-relief had certain points in common. The most distinctive feature was the idea of a 'common chest',[21] which was filled with funds that were taken from the formerly Catholic hospitals and charitable institutions, from monastic properties, from gifts and endowments, and from current collections in the church. Such 'chests' were administered by certain elected citizens of the community. However, the idea of centralizing funds had one flaw: the money which went into the 'common chest' was used for a variety of church activities, from paying pastors and preachers and the upkeep of church buildings to – last but not least – providing relief for the poor.

The obsolescence of acts of mercy and traditional charity was not only preached but also put into practice by Protestant reformers. In 1523 Luther helped in the reorganization of poor-relief in the Saxon town of Leisnig; three years later Zwingli proposed a plan for the reform of public welfare in Zürich. Bugenhagen projected the church ordinance and poor-relief schemes of Braunschweig (1528), Hamburg (1529), Lübeck (1531), and Pomerania (1534). Theological works by less prominent Protestant theologians such as Hyperius and Bucer proved to be helpful not only for German magistrates but also for the lawgivers in Elizabethan England.[22] Calvin, to name another outstanding Church reformer of the sixteenth century, set up a distinctive 'Protestant' poor-relief scheme in the church ordinance which he drew up for Geneva in 1541. Although the above-mentioned reformers differed on numerous points in the actual conformation of their welfare programmes, the principles proclaimed and approved by almost all of them followed the same general lines: (1) recognizing the serious nature of poverty and its threat to social order; (2) providing a theological justification for the prohibition of begging; (3) denying that almsgiving was a merit; (4) promoting the esteem of labour and advocating compulsory work for the able-bodied paupers; (5) proposing a centralized administration of poor-relief; and (6) suggesting a poor-relief scheme on a congregational basis under secular control. The impact which Luther and the new Protestant theology had on the reorganization of poor relief in the sixteenth century was certainly less than Ernst Troeltsch and other nineteenth- and early twentieth-century church historians thought.[23] Research on poor relief in Catholic countries has demonstrated that centralization, bureaucratization, and communalization of welfare was by no means a Protestant prerogative. Even if Reformation theology was not a necessary factor in the acceptance of welfare reform in the Holy Roman Empire of the German Nation, it was nevertheless an important stimulus or challenge for theologians and politicians alike.

The Catholic response to new social needs

While the bulk of nineteenth- and early twentieth-century historiographical work on poor relief deals with the variations in attitude toward the poor taken by Protestant and Catholic governments in the age of reformation, recent historical writing has emphasized that the actual welfare policy cut across religious boundaries and followed a pattern which was adjusted to local circumstances. The 'ubiquity of disease, crime, and crisis',[24] to quote Brian Pullan, caused magistrates and territorial rulers to respond in a similar way. As we now know, Protestant and Catholic governments and legislators discriminated in a broadly similar way between different categories of poor. Members of both religions approved of the establishment of centralized municipal relief agencies. Catholic confraternities were no less interested in ameliorating the condition of the poor than were Protestant welfare officials and deacons. There are even comparative studies, especially on sixteenth- and seventeenth-century German towns such as Cologne, Strasbourg, Frankfurt am Main, and Freiburg im Breisgau, which suggest that there was a sort of secularization of poor relief on either side of the confessional frontier. One should therefore dismiss the idea which can still be found in some dictionaries and handbooks that the care of the poor in Catholic communities was essentially casual, ineffective, and haphazard.

Although we have tried to refute traditional arguments and to warn against unrefined contrasts, the question remains whether there was anything distinctive in the practice of poor-relief in Catholic territories. Brian

Pullan, for example, believes that there were a certain number of pronounced characteristics of Catholic theory and practice to be found all over
Europe. He draws our attention to the fact that the presence of discriminating measures in Catholic territories 'should not cause us to deduce that
the quest in them for merit and self-sanctification had altogether ceased'.[25]
And he quotes from a tract written by the eminent Bavarian Jesuit, Jeremias
Drexel, which expresses this ambivalent approach to almsgiving and acts of
mercy: 'The poor are not, as we shall see, to be subjected to too much pry-
ing curiosity. Nonetheless one must consider where the benefit can best be
bestowed and where the need presses with greatest weight.'[26] Another distinguishing feature of Catholic poor relief was the importance of action, not
by the individual and not by the state or the religious community as a whole,
but by the confraternities. In most cases the old fraternities survived and
were multiplied and modified by being tied more securely into the structure
of the Church through being pegged to the parish and the diocese.[27]

It was in Catholic territories, especially in those German states ruled by
ecclesiastical princes, that acts of mercy retained their traditional functions
as channels of grace. The traditional view of the poor and feeble as representatives of Christ persisted longer in these societies. Catholic welfare was
on the whole decentralized and embraced a variety of needs, showing a relatively high level of social tolerance. Its major aim was to give a helping
hand to various groups of the population in general, and to reform the
moral habits of the population through compassion, almsgiving, and religious instruction. In Germany, as elsewhere in early modern Europe, the
Counter-Reformation was a campaign for the conquest of the soul. The
beggar dying in the street was a lost soul because he died without the benefit of the sacraments, and the idle vagrant lived in permanent danger of hell.
Poor relief in the eyes of Catholic reformers was therefore more than just
'corporal' relief; it involved, in fact, a total moral transformation of the
receiver. Prince Bishop Julius Echter of Mespelbrunn (1547–1617), for
example, proclaimed an ordinance for the City of Würzburg in which the
recipients of poor relief were subjected to a stricter church discipline and
moral control than they had experienced in the past. Before he was given
alms, the recipient had to prove that he attended mass regularly and that he
lived decently and according to Christian values.[28] Thus the poor became
not only objects but also instruments of large-scale ecclesiastical and moral
reform. Catholic rulers were aware of the fact that centralized poor-relief
gave both religious and civil authorities greater control over the private
lives of their subjects. The movement to centralize hospitals and outdoor
poor-relief institutions was very strong in Catholic territories, although the
battle between the adherents of public and private relief was not always an
easy one. In the city of Würzburg, for example, Bishop Julius Echter's plan
to centralize hospitals and charitable foundation encountered serious obstacles when brought to the attention of the magistrates. At the outset the city
council was prepared to block the reform. The magistrates were, however,

by no means opposed to centralization. The important question for them was who would be in charge of the centralized poor-relief: the bishop himself or the city council. Such sixteenth-century developments as the collection of alms by civil officers, a stricter regulation of begging, and the reallocation and centralization of funds were in no way opposed to the aims of the church hierarchy and Catholic rulers. On the contrary, these measures were in line with Tridentine charity legislation and with attempts by the Catholic church to get rid of the inadequacies of unregulated charitable activities while at the same time saving as much of the spirit of traditional Christian charity as possible.[29] The Council of Trent provided an ideological means by which Catholic communities across Germany, and indeed across Europe, developed similar expressions of welfare assistance.

The growth of social welfare

In the last 10 years especially, social historians of Germany have carried out valuable primary research in the field of poor relief. Some have concentrated on one particular urban society, but have, for one reason or another, shrunk from making comparisons with developments in other cities of a similar or contrasting character. Others have dealt with particular types of institution common to many German towns, including hospitals, workhouses, and confraternities, but have seldom explored the contribution of these organizations to the growth of social welfare in a particular urban environment. But what is even more deplorable is the fact that as far as rural poverty and the attempts by territorial rulers to alleviate it are concerned, we hardly have any modern study based on primary research.[30] It is difficult, therefore, to try to construct a framework within which the developments of formal, organized, and regulated charity in early modern Germany may be studied over a long stretch of time, extending from the late fifteenth to the eighteenth century, and crossing the crucial periods of Protestant reform and Catholic Counter-Reformation but stopping short of the Enlightenment.[31] As there was almost no nationwide legislation in the Holy Roman Empire of the German Nation (with the exception of some police ordinances of the sixteenth century which forbade all forms of begging but left the detailed regulations to local governments), we have no other choice than to compare developments in some of the German cities, each endowed with its own distinctive economic, social, religious, and political structure: Augsburg, Frankfurt am Main, Münster, and Cologne. Cologne and Augsburg were among the largest cities in the Holy Roman Empire, while Frankfurt and Münster had populations of some 10,000 to 15,000 in the sixteenth and early seventeenth centuries. Cologne and Frankfurt provide striking examples of important trade centres, while Münster shows the characteristic economy of a typical German 'home town', especially in the decades after the Thirty Years War. Augsburg's economy was distinguished, especially in the sixteenth century, by international banking and trading as well as by extensive textile industries. Throughout our period, Cologne, Augsburg, and Frankfurt am Main were Imperial towns; only Münster was a territorial capital under the rule of the bishops of Münster, who in most cases were recruited from the Wittelsbach dynasty.

Clearly, such a survey can pretend only to offer a sketch of municipal poor-relief and does not touch on rural poverty and the relieving of it. However, it was one of the functions of towns in the early modern period to provide charity to adjacent rural areas, as can be seen from the geographical and social pattern of municipal poor-relief.[32]

In these four cities, there was some form of shift from casual late-medieval charity to a rational approach to poor relief in the sixteenth century. However, this shift was straightforward in Protestant cities (e.g. Frankfurt), and less visible in those cities which either remained Catholic (Cologne) or became more or less bi-confessional (Augsburg and Münster). Initiatives to organize poor-relief in German towns passed almost completely, irrespective of confessional alliance, from ecclesiastical into lay hands. Short of establishing a central bureau of poor relief, similar to the 'Almosenamt' or 'Gemeiner Kasten' in Augsburg (1522) and Frankfurt am Main (1530), the magistrates in the Catholic cities of our sample nevertheless exercised tight control over the dispensing of alms to the poor. In Münster as well as in Cologne and other towns ruled by a Catholic majority, there existed, in fact, two systems of poor relief. The dominant one was the official system of welfare, consisting of prohibitions against foreign beggars, the registration of welfare recipients, a more efficient use of limited funds, and the communalization or even centralization of hospitals. Parallel to this public domain of poor relief was private charity. Of all the various sorts of philanthropy, we know most about endowed charities. The study of charitable bequests made by will in Münster between 1530 and 1618 shows the rising quantity and changing quality of private benefactions for charitable purposes in a post-Reformation city (see Table 12.7).[33] Out of 1,235 wills, 691 (56 per cent) contain clauses of almsgiving. The figures show that the restoration of Catholicism had some impact on charity, with legacies to the poor increasing after 1560. Aside from renewed Catholic piety, the rise in charitable donations also resulted from two major developments: first, rising prosperity and the greater willingness to give, after Münster had recovered from economic setbacks caused by the Anabaptist rebellion; and second, the increasing numbers of the poor, among them many refugees. The pattern of distribution demonstrates, as R. Po-chia Hsia has shown, that poor relief in Münster was primarily a civic act of charity and that there was a significant difference between men and women regarding donations to institutions of poor relief. Women obviously

Table 12.7 Distribution of charitable legacies in Münster, 1530–1618

	To institutions			To poor directly			To *Elende*			Total
	C	M	F	C	M	F	C	M	F	
pre-1530	–	1	1	–	–	1	–	–	–	= 3
1530–39	–	5	3	1	3	2	–	–	–	= 14
1540–49	1	6	9	2	3	7	–	–	1	= 29
1550–59	2	2	13	4	7	10	1	–	1	= 40
1560–69	2	–	6	7	3	5	1	–	–	= 24
1570–79	7	8	19	12	12	22	2	–	4	= 86
1580–89	4	7	13	24	22	31	1	–	–	= 102
1590–99	19	9	22	42	19	26	–	4	3	= 144
1600–09	25	11	25	50	30	49	–	–	1	= 191
1610–18	15	11	26	37	19	45	–	–	4	= 157
	272 (34.4%)			494 (62.6%)			23 (3%) = 789			(100%)

Note: C = couple; M = men; W = women
The numbers refer to clauses of poor-relief donations; multiple clauses of donations in a single will are quite common.
Source: R. Po-chia Hsia, 'Civic Wills As Sources For The Study of Piety in Muenster 1530–1618', *Sixteenth Century Journal*, 14 (1983), pp. 321–48, Table 2, p. 342.

preferred to give to hospitals and poorhouses in which widows and old women constituted the largest group among the inmates.

Protestants, too, gave to the poor as an expression of their evangelical faith. However, they were urged to bequeath money not to the various charitable institutions still in existence but to the 'common chest'. In Frankfurt am Main,[34] for example, members of the Protestant middle class, who identified the modest fortunes of their families with the fate of their city, expressed good neighbourliness and civic consciousness by giving relative small amounts of money to the 'common chest'. The decisive upturn began in the 1590s, when the rising number of charitable legacies indicates that the less-wealthy citizens were no longer concerned with their livelihoods but had small sums of money to spare. The average of the bequeathed sums remained significantly small throughout the period. The low level of testamentary bequests (in terms of money) might suggest widespread indifference among the wealthy citizens who perhaps wished their benefactions to create personal memorials, and memorials which were both locally conspicuous and socially worthy. It seems that centralized poor-relief no longer had the same incentives to offer to many rich benefactors who wished to perpetuate their names by founding hospitals or similar charitable institutions. The magistrates in Protestant cities knew about this reticence, and encouraged large-scale liberality by offering tax exemptions for those who bequeathed their money to the 'common chest'.[35] But this financial incentive was obviously not enough. People were to be exposed to moral persuasion by preachers and gentle admonitions by notaries and physicians, according to a decision made by the aldermen of the City of Augsburg in the year 1527.

Similar appeals can be found in other Protestant cities throughout the sixteenth and seventeenth centuries. At least for the first decades of the Reformation we have ample evidence (e.g. for Frankfurt and Augsburg) that
many citizens turned a deaf ear to this request.

Much more spontaneous, however, and much less discriminatory, even in
Protestant communities, were straightforward gifts to beggars – in the
street, outside church, in the yards of inns. There can be no doubt that
throughout our period this uncontrolled form of almsgiving was far from
being eradicated but was still proliferating, despite all attempts to outlaw
begging from the sixteenth century onwards. And it is only a guess that in
Protestant cities the massive condemnation of mendicancy and the availability of alternative forms of poor relief had some effect on individual
almsgiving in the long run. In Catholic cities, however, there was – according to some well-known travellers' reports of the eighteenth century – a
vast number of beggars in the street, and they would not have been there if
there had been no response from passers-by.[36] Nevertheless, we should not
take this evidence at face value. There are also sources which indicate that
even in Catholic communities citizens gradually became fed up with distributing alms to beggars who went from door to door, although they were
aware of the fact that mendicancy filled some gaps in welfare provision.

At least for early modern Germany it is almost impossible to measure the
growth of public poor-relief after the emergence of a social policy in the sixteenth century. The most useful quantitative indicator is perhaps the total
payments on public poor relief in selected German towns, measured in relation to population size. Fig. 12.4 shows estimated expenditure per thousand
people at various dates in some of the towns already mentioned. Although
limited by deficiencies in the records, and in some cases based on population estimates, this figure gives a suggestive picture of the importance of
public poor-relief in early modern German towns. Public expenditure on the
poor increased, with an initial leap at the end of the sixteenth century, and
then a more gradual increase over the following centuries. The figure also
shows that even in towns which had been rather reticent in introducing
schemes for public welfare before the late eighteenth century, the financial
outlay doubled between the beginning and the end of our period.

From this necessarily tentative statistical picture there emerges the
impression that gradually social welfare became a rather important feature
in the provision for the poor in most German urban centres during the early
modern period. However, some towns, like Augsburg, could obviously
afford to be more generous to the poor than others.

So far we have been concerned with outdoor relief, the kind envisaged by
welfare reformers as it applied to the deserving poor. Now we shall finally
look at the way in which institutions were developed as a means of obeying
the injunction to employ the poor and to deal with sturdy beggars. In some
European countries (such as England and The Netherlands) attempts were
made in the second half of the sixteenth century to shut away in carceral

Expenditure per 1000 inhabitants

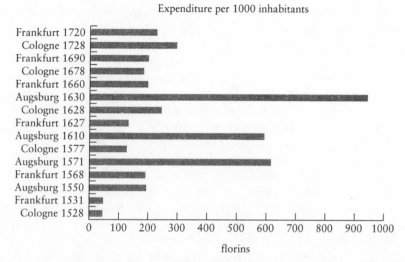

florins

Fig. 12.4 Expenditure on public poor relief in selected German towns, 1528–1720 (Source: Robert Jütte, *Poverty and Deviance in Early Modern Europe* (Cambridge, 1994), p. 141)

institutions those groups which in the eyes of contemporary thinkers and rulers constituted a threat to society. These institutions, part houses of correction and part workhouses, aimed at disciplining all those groups of society supposed to be most inclined towards idleness and disorder, especially beggars and vagabonds. The Dutch 'tuchthuizen' in particular directly or indirectly provided examples for German magistrates.[37] Four German towns founded similar 'Zuchthäuser' at the beginning of the seventeenth century: Bremen (1609 to 1613), Lübeck (1613), Hamburg (1614 to 1622), and Danzig (1629). All these institutions fulfilled from the beginning the combined functions of house of correction and workhouse. Towards the end of the seventeenth century the example of the Dutch and north German cities was followed by Breslau (1668), Vienna (1670), Leipzig and Berlin (1671), Lüneburg (1676), Braunschweig (1678), Frankfurt am Main (1679), Munich (1682), Spandau and Magdeburg (1687), Königsberg (1691), and Cologne (1696). Augsburg and other major German cities had no such institutions until the middle of the eighteenth century. The main strongholds of the German workhouse movement were the northern trading centres. As far as Brandenburg-Prussia is concerned, for example, there can be little doubt that by the middle of the eighteenth century the urban community of market-town size or above which had no workhouse was a rarity.[38] What is also quite obvious is that this idea of putting the able-bodied poor to work was spreading outwards from this area in the late seventeenth and early eighteenth centuries and finally reached the mainly Catholic regions of southern Germany.

The inmates lists show women (young, deserted, unmarried, and widowed) as the largest group in most workhouses. Able-bodied males rarely found their way into the workhouse. The case of the 'Armenhaus' in Cologne makes it quite clear that the majority of the inmates were sick or otherwise handicapped.[39] Not only in England but also in Germany the workhouses were homes for the most needy of the deserving poor: the children, the sick, the insane, and the elderly, those with no homes of their own and no relatives to nurse and to care for them. This much-cherished institution thus failed to employ significant numbers of able-bodied beggars; and the picture of the able-bodied poor as rarely entering the workhouse, but receiving alms and pensions to tide them over periods of temporary necessity, contrasts sharply with the system of relief seventeenth- and eighteenth-century German pamphleteers and magistrates had in mind when they opted for institutions to combat begging and vagabondage. The high hopes for workhouses as well as for houses of correction were largely dashed, mainly because of bad management.[40] When one considers the administrative problems and the economic difficulties facing so many governors of workhouses, one is impressed less by the many abuses and by the high number of insolvencies which occurred than by the unbroken will and determination to continue this experiment.

Conclusion

It is difficult to ascertain whether the centralized relief programmes of Protestant communities, designed to allocate resources efficiently, provided for the poor better than the basically decentralized system of Catholic towns. In any case, neither system was intended to do more than alleviate the worst ills of poverty. While historians have been aware of the shift in policy in the sixteenth century, they have not – as far as the history of poverty and poor relief in German territories is concerned – studied long-term developments. There can be little doubt that expenditure on poor relief rose tremendously in most German urban communities in the seventeenth and eighteenth centuries, outstripping price inflation and population growth. At least in the urban centres of early modern Germany, poor relief was a powerful element in controlling disorder among the needy and enforcing social discipline. Town-council records show that local government could often cope successfully with short crises such as harvest failures, trade slumps, and epidemics. In addition to poor relief, other forms of government action dampened begging and vagrancy. However, in the countryside the situation was quite different. The traditional forms of poor relief in rural settlements were overburdened and thus could not prevent beggary and vagrancy. In order to cope with the situation, the local authorities saw no other solution than to remove the transient pauper to his place of origin where – at least in theory if not in reality – he was supposed to receive statutory relief. This system of passing on paupers without additional punishment was an expensive and time-consuming business; but only towards the end of the eighteenth century did local authorities lose interest in it. It was a vagrancy policy which was not only inhumane and repressive, but which also failed in its purpose. Although investigation of the nature of nineteenth- and twentieth-century welfare policy falls outside the scope of this chapter, it is essential to draw attention to the fact that the economic growth of Germany after 1750 did not prevent mass pauperization, but helped to introduce new forms of poor relief, known collectively as the 'Elberfeld System'.[41]

Notes

1 See Antonio Ciocco and Dorothy Perrott, 'Statistics on Sickness as Cause of Poverty: An Historical Review of U. S. and English Data', *Journal of the History of Medicine and Allied Sciences*, 12 (1957), pp. 42–60, quotation from p. 59.

2 For an excellent analysis of the social topography of epidemics in early modern Augsburg, see Bernd Roeck, *Eine Stadt in Krieg und Frieden. Studien zur Geschichte der Reichsstadt Augsburg zwischen Kalenderstreit und Parität* (2 vols, Göttingen, 1989), esp. ii. pp. 630ff.

3 For the countryside, see e.g. Fritz Kaphahn, *Die wirtschaftlichen Folgen des 30jährigen Krieges für die Altmark* (Gotha, 1911); Manfred Lasch, *Untersuchungen über Bevölkerung und Wirtschaft der Landgrafschaft Hessen-Kassel und der Stadt Kassel vom 30jährigen Krieg bis zum Tode Landgraf Karls 1730* (Kassel, 1969). For the economic and demographic impact of the Thirty Years War on various German cities, see e.g. Christopher R. Friedrichs, *Urban Society in an Age of War, Nördlingen, 1580–1720* (Princeton, 1979); Roeck, *Krieg und Frieden, passim;* Wolfgang Sannwald, *Spitäler in Pest und Krieg. Untersuchungen zur Wirtschafts- und Sozialgeschichte südwestdeutscher Spitäler im 17. Jahrhundert* (Gomaringen, 1993); as well as Chapter 8 of the present volume.

4 Ingeborg Titz-Matuszak, 'Mobilität der Armut – Das Almosenwesen im 17. und 18. Jahrhundert im südniedersächsischen Raum', *Plesse-Archiv*, 24 (1988), pp. 9–338.

5 Robert W. Scribner, 'Mobility: Voluntary or Enforced? Vagrants in Württemberg in the Sixteenth Century', in G. Jaritz and A. Müller, eds, *Migration in der Feudalgesellschaft* (Frankfurt am Main, 1988), pp. 65–88. See Ernst Schubert, 'Mobilität ohne Chance: Die Ausgrenzung des fahrenden Volkes', in Winfried Schulze, ed., *Ständische Gesellschaft und soziale Mobilität* (Munich, 1988), pp. 113–64.

6 Wilhelm Abel, *Massenarmut und Hungerkrisen im vorindustriellen Europa* (Hamburg/Berlin, 1974); Wilhelm Abel, *Agricultural Fluctuations in Europe:*

From The Thirteenth to the Twentieth Centuries (New York, 1980); Wilhelm Abel, *Massenarmut und Hungerkrisen im vorindustriellen Deutschland* (Göttingen, 1972).

7 See Maria Ackels, 'Das Trierer städtische Almosenamt im 16. und 17. Jahrhundert: Ein Beitrag zur Analyse sozialer Unterschichten', *Kurtrierisches Jahrbuch*, 24 (1984), pp. 75–103.

8 See e.g. the important case studies by Walter G. Rödel, *Mainz und seine Bevölkerung im 17. und 18. Jahrhundert* (Stuttgart, 1985); and Peter Zschunke, *Konfession und Alltag in Oppenheim* (Stuttgart, 1984).

9 See Scribner, 'Mobility', pp. 65ff. For the family background of begging children in seventeenth-century Salzburg, see Norbert Schindler, 'Die Entstehung der Unbarmherzigkeit. Zur Kultur und Lebensweise der Salzburger Bettler am Ende des 17. Jahrhunderts', *Bayerisches Jahrbuch für Volkskunde* (1988), pp. 61–130.

10 See e.g. the census of the poor in Würzburg in 1791, which allows a precise analysis of the age structure, in Hans-Christoph Rublack, *Gescheiterte Reformation* (Stuttgart, 1978), p. 151.

11 Georg Simmel, *Soziologie. Untersuchungen über die Formen der Vergesellschaftung*, ed. Otthein Rammstedt (Frankfurt am Main, 1992), p. 553.

12 See Karlheinz Blaschke, *Bevölkerungsgeschichte von Sachsen bis zur industriellen Revolution* (Weimar, 1967), p. 190.

13 Quoted by Thomas Robisheaux, *Rural Society and the Search for Order in Early Modern Germany* (Cambridge, 1989), p. 76.

14 Quoted in Ernst Schubert, *Arme Leute, Bettler und Gauner im Franken des 18. Jahrhunderts* (Neustadt a. d. Aisch, 1983), p. 93. The following figures on the extent of rural poverty are also taken from Schubert, *Bettler*, p. 99. For other studies on urban and rural poverty in early modern Germany, see e.g. Claus Kappl, *Die Not der kleinen Leute* (Bamberg, 1984); Claudia Schott, *Armenfürsorge, Bettelwesen und Vagantenbekämpfung in der Reichsabtei Salem* (Bühl, Baden, 1978); Ingomar Bog, 'Über Arme und Armenfürsorge in Oberdeutschland und in der Eidgenossenschaft im 15. und 16. Jahrhundert', *JbfränkLF* 34/35 (1974/75), pp. 983–1001; Hannelore Dreves, *Das Armenwesen der Stadt Goslar. Eine Einzeluntersuchung zur städtischen Armut und Armenfürsorge im 15. und 16. Jahrhundert* (Goslar, 1992); Annette Boldt, *Das Fürsorgewesen der Stadt Braunschweig in Spätmittelalter und Früher Neuzeit* (Braunschweig, 1988).

15 Still the best summary of medieval and early modern theories on poverty and charity available in German is Hans Scherpner, *Theorie der Fürsorge* (Göttingen, 1962). For a brief account of medieval theories, see Otto Gerhard Oexle, 'Armut, Armutsbegriff und Armenfürsorge im Mittelalter', in Christoph Sachsse and Florian Tennstedt, eds, *Soziale Sicherheit und soziale Disziplinierung* (Frankfurt am Main, 1986), pp. 73–100.

16 For the origins of the stereotype of the 'fake beggar' see Robert Jütte, *Abbild und soziale Wirklichkeit des Bettler- und Gaunertums zu Beginn der Neuzeit* (Cologne, 1988).

17 See Wilhelm Weitzmann, *Die soziale Bedeutung des Humanisten Vives* (Borna, 1905). See also A. A. Alves, 'The Christian Social Organism and Social Welfare: The Case of Vives, Calvin, and Loyola', *Sixteenth Century Journal*, 20 (1989), pp. 3–22.

18 See Carl R. Steinbicker, *Poor Relief in the Sixteenth Century* (Washington DC, 1937), p. 16.

19 See e.g. Harold J. Grimm, 'Luther's Contribution to Sixteenth Century Organization of Poor Relief', *ARG* 61 (1970), pp. 222–34; Carter Lindberg,

'There Should Be No Beggars Among Christians: Karlstadt, Luther and the Origins of Protestant Poor Relief', *Church History*, 46 (1977), 313–34; William Wright, Jr, 'Reformation Contributions to the Development of Public Welfare Policy in Hesse', *JMH* [on-demand supplement] 49 (1977), pp. D1145–79.

20 See Ferdinand Seibt, 'Vom Lob der Handarbeit', in Hans Mommsen and Winfried Schulze, eds, *Vom Elend der Handarbeit* (Stuttgart, 1981), pp. 158–81; and Conrad Wiedemann, *Arbeit und Bürgertum* (Heidelberg, 1979).

21 For the history of the 'common chest', see Wilhelm Maurer, 'Die hessischen Kastenordnungen', *Jahrbuch der hessischen Kirchengeschichtlichen Vereinigung*, 4 (1953), pp. 1–37; Ursula Rotzoll, 'Kastenordnungen der Reformationszeit' (Ph.D. diss., Univ. of Marburg, 1969); Otto Winckelmann, 'Über die ältesten Armenordnungen der Reformationszeit (1522–1525)', *Historische Vierteljahrschrift*, 17 (1914/15), pp. 187–228, 361–400.

22 See Robert Jütte, 'Andreas Hyperius (1511–1564) und die Reform des frühneuzeitlichen Armenwesens', *ARG* 75 (1984), pp. 113–38.

23 The most extensive 19th-century work with a distinct Protestant bias is by Gerhard Uhlhorn, *Die christliche Liebesthätigkeit in der alten Kirche* (3 vols, Stuttgart, 1882–90).

24 See Brian Pullan, 'Catholics and the Poor in Early Modern Europe', *Transactions of the Royal Historical Society*, 5th ser., 26 (1976), pp. 15–34.

25 Pullan, 'Catholics', p. 28.

26 Jeremias Drexel, *Gazophylacium Christi*, in *Opera Omnia III* (Lyon, 1647), pp. 141–211, original Latin quotation, p. 167; English transl. by Pullan, 'Catholics', p. 28.

27 For the contribution of fraternities to public welfare in sixteenth- and seventeenth-century Cologne, see Arnold Lassotta, 'Formen der Armut im späten Mittelalter und zu Beginn der Neuzeit' (Ph. D. diss., Univ. of Freiburg im Breisgau, 1984).

28 See Rublack, *Reformation*, pp. 134–6.

29 See e.g. the similar social policy of Catholic towns such as Cologne and Münster: Jütte, *Armenfürsorge*, pp. 294–318; and Alwin Hanschmidt, 'Zur Armenpolizei der Stadt Münster im ausgehenden 16. Jahrhundert', in Helmut Jäger *et al.*, eds, *Civitatum Communitatis* (2 vols, Cologne, 1984), ii. pp. 655–82.

30 The very few studies on the relief of rural poverty concentrate on territorial legislation or the history of hospitals, e.g. Reinhold A. Dorwart, *The Prussian Welfare State before 1740* (Cambridge, Mass., 1971); Karl Otto Scherner, 'Arme und Bettler in der Rechtstheorie des 17. Jahrhunderts', *Zeitschrift für neuere Rechtsgeschichte*, 10 (1988), pp. 129–50; Karl E. Demandt, 'Die Anfänge der staatlichen Armen- und Elendenfürsorge in Hessen', *HessJbLG* 30 (1980), pp. 176–235.

31 The only modern synthesis is Christoph Sachsse and Florian Tennstedt, *Geschichte der Armenfürsorge in Deutschland. Vom Spätmittelalter bis zum 1. Weltkrieg* (Stuttgart, 1980). Wolfram Fischer, *Armut in der Geschichte* (Göttingen, 1982), and Robert Jütte, *Poverty and Deviance in Early Modern Europe* (Cambridge, 1994), deal with poverty in European context but draw heavily on German studies. A shorter period is covered by Rudolf Endres, 'Das Armenproblem im Zeitalter des Absolutismus', in Franklin Kopitzsch, ed., *Aufklärung, Absolutismus und Bürgertum in Deutschland* (Munich, 1976), pp. 220–41.

32 See e.g. the chapters on the geographical origins of poor relief recipients, in Jütte, *Armenfürsorge*, pp. 146–8; Ackels, 'Almosenamt', pp. 96–8; Titz-Matuszak, 'Mobilität', pp. 64ff.

33   In other Catholic cities there was also a rise in charitable bequests in the late 16th century. For e.g. Cologne, see Lassotta, *Armut*, p. 186 and Fig. IV.4.

34   See Jütte, *Armenfürsorge*, pp. 155–60.

35   See e.g. Max Bisle, *Die öffentliche Armenpflege der Reichsstadt Augsburg mit Berücksichtigung der einschlägigen Verhältnisse in anderen Reichsstädten Süddeutschlands* (Paderborn, 1904), p. 44.

36   For Cologne, see the contemporary sources cited by Dietrich Ebeling, *Bürgertum und Pöbel* (Cologne, 1987), pp. 133ff.

37   See e.g. Christian Marzahn, *Das Zucht- und Arbeitshaus. Die Kerninstitution frühbürgerlicher Sozialpolitik* (Bremen, no date); Hannes Stekl, '"Labore et fame" – Sozialdisziplinierung in Zucht- und Arbeitshäusern des 17. und 18. Jahrhunderts', in Christoph Sachsse and Florian Tennstedt, eds, *Soziale Sicherheit und soziale Disziplinierung* (Frankfurt am Main, 1986), pp. 119–47.

38   See Helga Eichler, 'Zucht- und Arbeitshäuser in den mittleren und östlichen Provinzen Brandenburg-Preußens', *JbWG* (1970), especially pp. 146f.

39   See the statistics provided by Norbert Finzsch, *Obrigkeit und Unterschichten* (Stuttgart, 1990), p. 127ff.

40   For case studies, see Marlene Sothmann, *Das Armen-, Zucht- und Werkhaus in Nürnberg bis 1806* (Nürnberg, 1970); Bernhard Stier, *Fürsorge und Disziplinierung im Zeitalter des Absolutismus. Das Pforzheimer Zucht- und Waisenhaus und die badische Sozialpolitik* (Sigmaringen, 1988).

41   For the 19th-century social policy of a German state before the introduction of the 'Elberfeld-System', see e.g. Peter Blum, *Staatliche Armenfürsorge im Herzogtum Nassau 1806–1866* (Wiesbaden, 1987).

General Index

Aachen 333
absolutism 207, 209, 210–12, 214
  and confessionalism 310, 315, 320
Acker-Marken-Wirtschaft 283, 292
Ackerbürger 68
Ackerbürgerstädte 68
advertisements 108
Agrarverfassungsverträge 78
agriculture 16–21, 22–3
  agrarian system 71–7
  commercialization and intensifica-
    tion 84–7
  eighteenth-century reforms 87–91
  framework 66–71
  and nature 5, 6, 8–9, 276
  questions and methodological
    problems 63-6
  social change 78–84
  tasks of 4
  yields 10–11
Agrippa, Heinrich Cornelius 391
alcoholism 366
Alexander, Margrave of Brandenburg-
  Ansbach 249
Allgemeine Landrecht für die
  Preußischen Staaten (General
  National Law Code for the Prussian
  States) 142, 146, 180, 181
altitude
  and climate 7
  and harvest yields 10–11
  and soil quality 9
Amsterdam 119, 122
Amt 175

Amtmann 175
Andreae, Johann Valentin 325–6
animal husbandry 22, 30
  yields from 5
annual markets 105, 106
Antwerp 117
arable land 19, 67
arcanist 366
armaments 245
armies 204, 206, 220, 243–4
Arndt, Johann 319
astrology 337
Augsburg, Peace of (1555) 200
August, Count of Sayn-Wittgenstein 81
aurochs 21

Bacon, Nicholas 183
balance of trade 112, 115–16
Bankhaus Gebrüder Bethmann 111
banks 111
barley 16
bathing 361
Bauernschutz (peasant protection) 82
Baxter, Richard 331
beans 17
beaver 21
Becher, Johann Joachim 214, 307 n.137
beds 358
beech 11, 12
beer 364
beggars 154–5, 398–9
Berlin
  Academy of Sciences 90
  social structure 149

Bernd, Adam 320
Bestallung 175
Bible ownership 329–30
Biel, Gabriel 390
bills of exchange 111
birch 12
Black Forest 16, 269, 271
black market 289, 293
blade production 24
Bluntschli, Johan Caspar 185–7, 194, 195
Bodin, Jean 164, 211
books 105, 329–31
Botero, Giovanni 210, 228
bourgeoisie 141, 145–51, 158
    see also *Bürgertum*
Bräker, Ulrich 368–9
Brandenburg-Prussia 140–3, 269, 291, 294
brandy 366
brass 24
breastfeeding 56–7
breeding of animals 5, 25–6
Bremen 119, 120, 122
Brenner Pass 31, 32
Bromberg Canal 32
brown bear 21
Brunn, F. L. 34 n.8
buckwheat 16–17
Bugenhagen 392
bureaucracy 89–90
Bürgertum 185–7
    definitions and concepts 164–8
    learned men 168–79
    merchants 180–5
Büsch, Johan Georg 182
bustard 21

cabinet 206
calendars 356–7
Calvin, John 392
Calvinism 206, 207, 310–11, 314, 316, 318, 321, 327, 332, 335
Calw 289, 333–4
cameralism 90, 123, 213–14, 217, 290
canals 32, 69, 102–3
Cannabich, J. G. F. 34, 36, 37, 38
capitalism 244–5, 267, 331
carriage post 105
cartography 355

cash crops 50, 78
Catholicism
    administration 206–7
    confession 310–11, 313-14, 317–29, 335–8
    and poverty 393-5, 396, 398
cattle 22, 70
celibacy 323
censorship 220, 329
chairs 359
chamois 21
Chapters, cathedral 203
charcoal 277, 278
charities 396–7
chests of drawers 359
chicory 17, 26
chimneys 359
chocolate drink 365
Circle Associations 202
citizenship 146
civil prudence 210
class society 136–7, 148, 185
Clemens August, Elector of Bavaria, 204
climatic characteristics 7–9
    and agriculture 5, 11, 66–7
    and forests 12
    and transportation 104
clocks 27, 357
clothing 7, 360, 361–2
coaches 103, 353
coal 6, 15, 24, 25
Cochlaeus, Johannes 2, 4
coffee 120, 365
collective identity 4
Cologne 112–13, 117
comets 325
commercialization 101
    of agriculture 84–7, 263–4
commission trade 110
common chests 392, 397
Common Penny 202
commons 74, 86, 88, 217
communication networks 105, 216
communities, and industry 283–5
companies, merchant 286–90
competition 108, 242, 266
concessions, merchant 181
Concord, Book of 310
Concord, Formula of 310

confession, religious 4, 207, 309–14
  and culture 325–31
  and economy 331–5
  limits and *Polizey* 335–8
  politics and society 314–25
coniferous forests 15, 16, 278
consignment warehouses 109–10
constitutional law 2, 3-4
contraception *see* family planning
copper 24
cornhouses 71
corporate groups 3
corporate orders 135, 148
corporations 135
corporative ties 4
corvée 76
cottage industry 56
cottagers 83, 84, 153
cotton 25, 26, 264, 288, 290, 291
Council of Clergy 206
Council of Electors 204
Council of Princes 204
Court Council 206
Court War Council 206
Coyer, Abbé Gabriel-Françoise 188
craftsmen 108, 146, 149–50
credit 111
crises, trade 122–3
crop rotation 20, 50, 67
cultural sector 219
culture, confessional 325–31
cupboards 359
customs barriers 69, 104, 353
customs wars 122

dance 367
debt 240–1, 243, 247, 350–1
deciduous forests 15, 16, 278
décolleté 361
demand 294–5
demesne economy 79–82, 85, 282
demographic consequences of war
  235–9
depot trade 109, 110
Dernbach, Peter Philipp von 248
desertion 382
devaluation of money 111
discipline 218, 221
  church 312
dislocation 39

Donaumoos 83
dowries 48
draught animals 70
Drexel, Jeremias 394, 403
drinking 364–6
Droste-Hülshoff, Annette 357
dye plants 18
dynastic associations 148
dynastic policy 2–3

eating 363–4, 366
ecclesiastical territories 203
Echter, Bishop Julius of Mespelbrunn
  315, 394
economic *Bürger* 164, 165, 180–5, 322
economic dominion
  (*Wirtschaftsherrschaft*) 75
economy
  and confession 331–5
  and war 240–52
educated *Bürger* 150, 164, 165, 168–9
  jurists 169–77
  pastors 177–9
education 219–20, 326–9, 369
Eider Canal 32
Eigenwirtschaft 176
Einlieger 84
Elberfeld System 401
elementary schools 219, 220
elk 21
emigration 46, 47
enclosure 20, 86, 88
endykement 20, 216
energy 5–6, 12–15, 23
England 143–4, 151, 183, 266
ennoblement 201
entrepreneurial *Bürger* 150, 180–1,
  333
Erasmus of Rotterdam 391
Erbuntertänigkeit (hereditary serfdom)
  78
Erthal, Franz Ludwig von 371
eudaemonism 212, 214
excise tax 205–6

faïence 366
fallow land 19, 67, 88, 216–17
family
  and confession 4, 323–4
  structure 156–7

family planning 54, 324
  and confession 4
family reconstitution 41–2
famines 8, 17, 216, 366
fashion 362
Feine Gewandschaft 286
fens 83
Ferdinand II, Emperor 200
fertility
  and confession 324
  control 54
  natural 53–4, 57
  rates 56–7
feudal constitution 2
feudal noble estates 20
feudalism 4, 241, 267
Filmer, Robert 211
Finow Canal 30
fir 11
fire 358
firearms 24
fireplaces 359
fiscal poor 386
Fischer, Johann Bernhard 376
fish 21
flax 17, 25, 26, 264, 278
fleas 360
floods 9, 216
fluitschips 33, 103–4
Flurzwang 94 n.45
Folz, Hans 390
food 363–4, 366
forest
  and climatic conditions 12
  coverage 12–16
  ordinances 217
  usage 67
  yields and altitude 11
fortifications 245
four-poster beds 358
fragmentation, territorial 135
France 144, 151–2
Francke, August Hermann 316–17, 319, 320
Franckenstein, Philipp Ludwig von, Free Imperial Knight 81
Frank, Johann Peter 227
Frankfurt
  Bürgertum 173-4, 184
  trade 117

Frederick the Great of Prussia 255, 356, 372–3
Freemasons 369
French Revolution 2, 256
Friederich Wilhelm I of Prussia ('Great Elector', 1640–88) 247, 254, 316
Friedrich I of Prussia 316
Friedrich II of Prussia 90, 102, 122, 123, 141, 154, 205, 212, 213, 216, 222, 247–8
Friedrich Wilhelm I of Prussia ('Soldier King', 1713–40) 86, 216, 245, 247, 248, 254, 316, 317
Friedrich Wilhelm Canal 32
Fritsch, Thomas von 123
frontier controls 353, 354
frontiers, German 2, 7
fruit 17, 365
fur animals 21
furlongs (*Gewanne*) 19
furnishings 360
fustian 25, 26, 122, 264

Gädike, Johann Christian 105
Galen, Christoph Bernhard von 316
Gallas, General Mathias 244
game 21, 81
ganzes Haus (whole household) 4, 156–7
gardens 356
Gaspari, A. C. 25, 34, 36, 37, 38
gender
  and confession 323–5
  and poverty 382
General National Law Code for the Prussian States 142, 146, 180, 181
General War Commissariat 206
geological characteristics 7
Gerichtsstand 171
Gewanne (furlongs) 19
Gewerbefreiheit 286
glass 26, 277, 278, 291
Goethe, J. W. von 169
gold 26–7
Golden Bull (1356) 198–9, 204
golden eagle 21
Göttingen, University of 219, 329
grain 16, 17
  intensive cultivation 19
  monoculture 18

grain *cont.*
  saleable 71
  storage 71
  trade 113, 121
  transportation 23, 70
  yields and altitude 11, 18
grammar schools 219
grand tour 30
Gregorian calendar 356
Grotius, Hugo 211
Grundherrschaft 75, 79, 81, 113
  and industry 281, 283, 292
  and modern state 215, 221
  and social structure 138, 158
  and war 252
Guden, Philipp Peter 227
guilds 47, 286–90, 292–3
  restrictive influence 217
guns 24
Gutsherrschaft 75, 79, 81, 113
  and industry 281–3, 284, 292
  and modern state 215, 221
  and war 252
Gutswirtschaft 81, 84
  and industry 282
  and social structure 138, 141, 142,
    152, 153, 158
gypsy poles 353–4

Hahn, Johann Siegemund 361, 376
hail 9
Halle, University of 219, 329
Hamburg
  Handlungsakademie 182
  social structure 147–8
  trade 118–20, 122
  urban growth 184
Hamburgische Bank 111
hammer mills 6, 351
Hanseatic League 118
Hanselmann, Hans, the younger 388
Hassel, G. 34, 36, 37, 38
Haugwitz, Count 246
Havelländer Luch 20, 83, 216
hawkers (*Tödden*) 108
health 215–16
Heimat 40–1, 355
hemp 17, 278, 374
hereditary serfdom 78
Hersfeld 184–5

Hessen-Kassel 174
Hildt, Johann Adolph 105
Hobbes, Thomas 211
Hochstetter, Johann Andreas 319
Hofgerichten 199
Hohenlohe oxen 22
Holstein Canal 32
Holy Roman Empire
  dissolution of 2
  frontiers 2, 3
  structure 40, 135
  towns 67
hops 17
Hörnigk, Philipp Wilhelm von 214
horse post 105
horses 5, 22
housing 7, 357–60
Hufeland, Christoph Wilhelm 376
Huguenots 334–5
humidity 11
hunting 81, 217
Hüpeden, C. L. P. 114
hygiene 7
hymn books 338

ibex 21
illegitimacy rates 52–3, 324
impartible inheritance 45–8
Imperial Circles 202
Imperial Craft Ordinance 217
Imperial Diet 201
Imperial Edict (1654) 249
Imperial Knighthood 204
Imperial postal system 105
imperialism 3, 4
inbreeding 55, 352
individualization in economic activity
    91
industrial production 5–6, 22–7
industrialization 263–6, 296–7
  early modern German industrial
    regions 269–75
  and nature 276–81
  proto-industrialization 266–9
  and rural society 281–5
  and the state 290–6
  and urban society 285–90
infant mortality 7, 56, 324
infections 7
inflation 111, 380

inheritance 41, 43, 77
  impartible 45–8
  partible 48–51
innovations 88
inns 354
Insten 154
insurance 110
intensification of agriculture 84–7
intensive farming 5
iron 6, 23–4, 264, 277–8, 294

Johann Sigismund, Elector of
  Brandenberg-Prussia, 316
jointly ruled territories 208
Joseph II, Emperor 154, 219, 246,
  250, 315, 320–1
journeymen 30, 47, 354–5
Jung-Stilling, J. H. 190
jurists, learned 169–77
Justi, Johann Heinrich Gottlob von
  210, 212, 214

Kant, Immanuel 212
Karl Alexander, Duke of Württemberg
  314
Karl Eugen, Duke of Württemberg
  212, 249, 314
Kassel 174, 175, 177, 183
Kaufsystem 107
Kayserberg, Geiler von 390
Kepler, Johannes 356
kinship systems 352
Kleefeld, Schubart von 90
knife production 24
Knigge, Adolph Freiherr von 367, 376
Knights' Circles 204
Krünitz, Johann Georg 36, 164, 165,
  260

labour rents 75–6
Landesscharwerk 76
landless peasants 153
landlords
  changes in economy of domination
    78–82
  and industry 281–3
Landschaft 292
laudemia 79
lead 24–5
learned men 165, 168–9

jurists 169–77
pastors 177–9
Lederhosen 362
Leipzig 117–18, 121
lentils 17
Leopold I, Emperor 246
Leopold of Tuscany 212
life expectancy 7, 357
linen 25, 26
  and confession 333
  exports 114, 115
  industrialization 264, 273, 278–9,
    282–3, 286, 287, 289–90, 292
  markets 107
  middlemen 110
Lipsius, Justus 210, 228
literacy 4, 219, 220, 326–7, 368–9
'Little Ice Age' 66
living standards 44, 357–60
Locke, John 211
Loen, J. M. von 166
long-term property rights 77
Louis XIV of France 42, 144, 201,
  213, 215
loyalty 34 n.8
Lübeck 107–8, 118, 119–20, 122
Ludovici, C. G. 166, 180–1, 182, 192,
  193
Lüneburg 15–16
Luther, Martin 392, 393
Lutheranism
  administration 206, 207
  confession 310–11, 314, 317–30,
    332, 335
lynx 21

madder 18
magic 337
maize 17, 217
manufacturing
  nature, dependence on 5
  and population 55
  and warfare 44
manure 18, 19, 50
maps 355
marginal social groups 154–5
Maria Theresia, Empress 154, 219,
  220, 246, 250, 315
Markenwirtschaft 284
market principle 100

market relations 85–6
markets 105–6, 107, 108
marriage 30
    age at 51, 54, 56, 57–8, 357
    and confession 323
    flexibility 52–3
    and inheritance 49
    jurists 176, 177
    and proto-industrialization 267
    restrictions 370
    state influence 215
    and warfare 43
marsh farmers 81
Marxist theory 136
Max Emanuel, Elector of Bavaria 243, 248
Maximilian III Joseph, Elector of Bavaria 102
meadows 11, 19
Melanchthon, Philip 310, 328
Meliorationen 216
Mennonites 332
mercantilism 213, 214
mercenaries 47, 379
merchants 109–10, 165–6, 180–5, 292–3
    social structure 146
merino sheep 32, 85, 279, 373
middlemen 110
migration 148, 239
militarization 255–6
millet 16–17
mining regions 24
Mirabeau, Comte de 291
miracles 235–6
mirrors 359
modern state, growth of 196–8
    Emperor and Empire after 1648 200–3
    Empire and territories 198–200
    everyday life 214–21
    limitations 221–2
    Policey, absolutism and cameralism 207–14
    territories 203-7
money 110–11
money rents 75–6
morality 312
Morhard, Johann 311
Moritz, Karl Philipp 320

Moser, C. von 173
Müllroser Kanal 103
municipal framework 40–2
muscle-power 5

Nantes, Edict of 215
Napoleon I of France 2, 256
natural law 211, 212
nature
    dependence on 5–6, 7
    and industry 276–81
needles 24
Neolithic Revolution 1
Netzebruch 20, 83
newspapers 105
Nicolai, Friedrich 117, 375
Nipperdey, T. 330
nobility 139–45, 156, 166
Noble Council 206
Nördlingen 183-4
nucleated villages 48
Nuremberg 12
Nuremberger Banco Publico 111
nutrition 6–7, 66, 67
nuts 18

oak 11, 12
oats 16
Oderbruch 20, 83, 216
oil plants 17–18
oils 18
Oker 103
opportunity costs 274–5, 276
Ortssippenbücher 42
Osnabrück, Peace of 200
Ottoman attacks 201
oxen 22, 113, 122

pack carriers 109, 114
Palatine Succession, War of the 236, 243
Papenburg Canal 32
paper production 6, 26
parish registers 41, 42
partible inheritance 48–51
particularism 208
passenger posts 103
passenger traffic 103
pastors 177–9
pasturage rights 74

pasture 19
patriarchalism 211
patriotism 4
paupers 155, 387
peas 17
peasant freight carriers 104
peasant protection (*Bauernschutz*) 82, 154
Peasants' War 71, 78
peddling 108–9
perquisites 175, 176
personal grooming 361
Pietism 315, 316–17, 319–20, 330, 332, 333-4
pigs 22
pilgrimages 30, 326
pine 12
plague 216
    settlement patterns 83
    and war 12, 236, 237, 238
Plauen Canal 32
pocket watches 357
Pohl, H. 35n.17
Policey 208–10, 218, 313, 335–8
political élites 147
Polizeiordnungen 209
poorhouses 155
population 12, 16, 39–40
    and agriculture 67, 82–3
    density 28–30
    municipal framework 40–2
    and peasant labour services 76–7
    policy 213, 215, 239
    problems 370
    and proto-industrialization 267, 268
    prudential check 51, 52, 54–5
    regional diversity 56
    urban and rural 101, 151
    and warfare 43, 235–9, 241
porcelain 27, 365–6
post carts 103
post coaches 103
postal system 103, 105, 216, 353
potatoes 17, 217, 366
poverty 150, 155, 370, 400–1
    causes 377–85
    discourse on 389–95
    extent 385–9
    social welfare, growth of 395–400
Prague, Peace of (1635) 200

precipitation 7, 8, 9, 10
pre-industrialization 265
primogeniture 199
printed matter 27
privatization 371
privy 358
Privy Council 206
property rights 77
Protestantism
    administration 206
    confession 310–11, 313–15, 318–20, 323–7, 329–38
    pastors 177–9
    poverty 392–3, 397–8
    writing and literacy 4
proto-industrialization 165, 266–9, 273, 274, 371–2
provisioning 244
public spending 293–4
Pufendorf, Samuel von 2, 34 n.4, 197–8, 211
pulses 17
putting-out 166, 218

rafts 33
railways 32, 33
Rantzau, Count 20
rape 52
reading 368–9
reconstruction 214–15, 241
reference works 105
Regensburg Edict (1699) 356
regional diversity 56–8
regional specialization 263–4
Reichshofrat 170, 201
Reichskammergericht 170, 202
Reichskreise 202
Reichslehen 198
Reichstag 201
Reinkingk, Theodor 210, 228
religion
    administration 206–7
    pastors 177–9
    poverty 392–5
    see also confession
remarriage 43
Rentmeister 175
rents, peasant 75–6
Resewitz, F. G. 166–7
resident retailing 108

Reunion Wars 82
Rhine Canal 32
rivers 32–3
roads 30–2, 69, 102–3, 216, 353
root vegetables 11, 17
Rousseau, Jean Jacques 211, 212
Rudolf II, Emperor 325
rural society 151–4, 281–5
rusticalized industry 165
rye 16, 121–2

Sabbatini, Angelo 111
salons 360
salt 25
sand peasants 81
Schleswig-Holsteinische Kanal 103
Schlözer, A. L. 130
Schniggen 104
Schönborn family 139
schools 219–20, 327–9, 369
Schröder, Wilhelm 214
scientific instruments 27
scientific revolution 1
scissors production 24
scythes 24
seating 359, 360
Seckendorff, Veit Ludwig von 209,
    214, 227
secularization 313, 321
selling practices 108
serfdom 80–1, 154
    abolition 372–3
    'second' 282
servants 153-4
settlement patterns 11–12, 15, 19–20,
    27–30
    agriculture 82–3
    impartible inheritance 46–7
    partible inheritance 48
Seven Years War
    trade 122, 123
sewage disposal 7, 360
sexual harassment 52
sexual intercourse 323
sharecropping 77
shareholding shipping 110
sheep 22, 25–6, 85, 279, 373
ship shares 110
shipping companies 110
ships 32–3, 103–4, 119–20, 353

shoe buckles 362
shopkeepers 108
short-term property rights 77
sickles 24
sickness and poverty 378, 379
silk 115, 283, 291
silver 24, 26–7
Skontration 111
smacks 104
smallholders 153
Smith, Adam 90
smoking 373–4
smuggling 289
social estate 136, 136, 148, 254–5
    well-bred 167, 179
social intercourse 367–9
social structure 134–9
    bourgeoisie 145–51
    ganzes Haus and family 156–7
    marginal social groups 154–5
    nobility 139–45
    rural society 151–4
    transformation as long-term
        phenomenon 157–8
social welfare, growth of 395–400
sofas 359
soil
    cultivation 16
    and forests 12
    quality and altitude 9–11, 67
solar energy 5
soldier estate 255
Sonnenfels, Josef von 212–13, 214
space 355–6
Spanish Succession, War of the 247
specialization, regional 263-4
Spener, Philipp Jakob 317, 319
spices 116
spirits 366
splintered family 43
Sporteln 175, 176
spruce 11, 12
stability 39
standards of living *see* living standards
standing armies 204, 206, 220, 244
staple and warehousing obligation
    107, 108
state and industry 290–6
'state-ness' (*Staatlichkeit*) 196–7, 207,
    210

steel 24, 278
storehouses 71, 109
storms 9
Sturm, Johann 328
Svarez, Carl Gottlieb 211–12

table manners 364
tanning 6
tavern-keepers 108
taxes
  and land use 20
  modern state, growth of 202, 205–6,
    220
  territorial 352–3
  territorial lords 78
  wartime 246, 247, 248, 249–51, 253
tea 365
technical revolution 1
temperatures 7, 8–9
Templin, Prokop von 337
temporal territories 203
territorial lords 78–82, 198–9
textile production 25–6
  exports 115
  and fashion 362
  industrialization 264, 273, 278
  and population 55
Thaer, Albrecht Daniel 4
thermal energy 5, 12–15
Thirty Years War
  confessionalism 318
  deaths 43
  demesne economy 80
  demographic consequences 235, 236
  economy 121, 123, 240, 241, 242,
    243, 250, 256
  effects 350–2
  industrial centres 114
  and industrialization 265–6
  and organization of society 252–4
  parish registers 42
  Peace of Prague (1635) 200
  settlement patterns 12, 20, 82, 83
  social structure 152
  standing armies 244
Thomasius, Christian 168, 329
three-field system 19, 20, 50, 74
time 356–7
tin 24
titles 367

tjalks 104
tobacco 17, 26, 373-4
Tödden (hawkers) 108
towns 27–8, 67–8
toys 27
Trachten 362
trade
  general preconditions 100–2
  localities, agents and means of
    105–11
  objects, directions, and centres of
    112–21
  role in transitional phase 124–5
  transportation and communication
    102–5
  trends and fluctuations 121–3
trade fairs 105, 106–7, 109, 117–18, 121
transactions costs 275, 279–80
transportation
  and agriculture 69–71
  and climate 9
  forms 31, 32–3
  and industrialization 279–80
  location of industry 23
  muscle-power 5
  and trade 102–4
travel 30–1, 353–4
Trent, Council of 323
turf 15, 25
turnips 17
tutelage 220

Ulm 23
universities 168–70, 176
  and confession 328–9
  state support 219
urban society and industry 285–90
Utrecht, Treaty of 42

vagrants 154–5
vegetables 11, 17
vegetation 11
Veronensis, Severini de Monzambano
  223
vetch 17
Vienna City Bank 246
village communities 284, 285
viniculture 17, 18
visitations 206, 335–6
Vives, Juan Luis 391

wages 380, 381
  and population level 44
warehouses 109–10
warfare 233–4
  demographic consequences 235–9
  and economy 44–5, 240–52
  illegitimacy rates 52–3
  and population 43
  and poverty 378–9
  and society 252–7
  and trade 122
Warthebruch 20, 83, 216
watches 357
water-power 5, 6, 277
water supplies 7, 12
weather *see* climatic conditions
weaving 55
weekly markets 105–6
weights and measures 351
weld 18
Westphalia, Peace of (1648) 198, 200,
  207, 318
wheat 16
whipping 368
white turnips 17
whole household (*ganzes Haus*) 4,
  156–7
wholesale trade 109–10
widows and widowers 43, 382, 383
wigs 362
wind-power 5
wine 364–5
wine-grapes 17

winter spelt 16
wire mills 24
Wirtschaftsherrschaft (economic
  dominion) 75
witches 218, 325, 337
woad 18
Wolff, Christian 211
wolves 21
women
  impartible inheritance 45, 46, 47
  partible inheritance 48, 49, 50
  warfare 52
wood
  house-building 358
  importance 5, 6, 12–16
  needs 67
  trade 116
  uses 25
wool 25–6, 85
  industrialization 264, 279–80
  production 373
  trade 115
workhouses 155, 371, 399–400
worsted 289, 290
writing 4, 368
written word 367–9
Wuppertaler Garnnahrung 286, 287,
  293

Zedler, J. H. 188
Zelge 19
zinc 24
Zwingli, Ulrich 392

Index of Modern Authors

Achilles, W. 36, 65, 91, 95, 97, 99, 251, 261
Ackels, M. 402
Ahrendt-Schulte, I. 344
Albrecht, P. 125, 126, 127, 128
Allmann, J. 36, 229
Alves, A. A. 402
Anderson, M. S. 257, 259, 260
Andorka, R. 62
Andreae, J. V. 345
Angermeier, H. 224
Applegate, C. 58
Aretin, K. O. von 194, 223, 224, 227, 228
Ashton, T. S. 162
Asten, H. von 347
Aubin, G. 302, 305
Aubin, H. 125, 128, 130, 162, 259, 261, 302
Augel, J. 128

Baasch, E. 127, 128
Backmann, G. 60
Bade, K. J. 229, 375
Bader, K. S. 98
Bairoch, P. 58
Balazs-Kovács, S. 62
Barker, T. M. 225
Barkhausen, W. 302, 305
Baszanowski, J. 130
Bátori, I. 159, 161
Batou, J. 58
Bauer, E. 96
Baulant, M. 59
Baum, J. P. 306

Baumann, R. 262
Baumann, W.-R. 130–1
Baumgart, P. 224, 340
Baumgarten, K. 94
Baur, V. 227
Beall, K. F. 128
Becht, H.-P. 258, 259
Beck, R. 92, 94, 95, 97, 341
Becker, L. 132
Becker, T. P. 348
Becker, U. A. J. 344, 346
Becker, W. 224
Beetz, M. 232
Behringer, W. 127, 230, 344, 348
Belaval, Y. 346
Belstler, U. 224
Benedict, P. 343
Benrath, G. A. 190
Bentzien, U. 94
Benz, E. 59
Berdahl, R. 343
Berding, H. 162
Bérenger, J. 261
Berg, M. 303
Berkner, L. 60
Berner, H. 258
Berthold, R. 35, 37, 93
Beutin, L. 128
Beyer, P. 127, 131
Beyrer, K. 126
Biedermann, K. 222
Bietenhard, B. 344
Biskup, M. 161, 347
Bisle, M. 404
Black, J. 257

Blaich, F. 228
Blankner, R. 226
Blaschke, K. 126, 225, 258, 402
Blickle, P. 95, 161, 223, 224, 226, 231, 232, 339, 345, 346
Blickle, R. 95
Blum, J. 58
Blum, P. 404
Bock, G. R. von 376
Bödeker, H. E. 190, 191, 346, 349
Boelcke, W.A. 95, 96
Boetticher, M. v. 96, 97
Bog, I. 98, 228, 259, 402
Bohannan, P. 100, 125
Bohl, P. 258, 259
Böhme, H. 161
Bohnen, K. 225
Boldt, A. 402
Boldt, H. 159, 223
Bölts, J. 127, 130
Bonacker, W. 375
Böning, H. 231
Bormann-Heischkeil, S. 192
Born, M. 36, 37, 96
Borscheid, P. 343
Boserup, E. 60
Bott-Bodenhausen, K. 230
Bötzenhart, M. 224
Bouniatian, M. 122, 132
Bourel, D. 346
Brakensiek, S. 92, 98, 189, 190, 203, 303
Braudel, F. 109, 124, 125, 128, 298, 308
Braun, R. 61, 261, 303
Brecht, M. 226, 342
Brednich, R. W. 128
Breit, S. 343
Brenner, P. S. 37
Brenner, R. 60
Breuer, D. 232
Breuer, S. 339, 345, 346
Brewer, J. 125, 308
Briggs, R. 160, 162
Brimblecmbe, P. 37
Brosig, R. 38, 258
Brosius, D. 132
Brübach, N. 127, 128, 129, 131
Brück, T. 126
Brückner, C. 307

Brückner, J. 227
Brückner, W. 232, 259, 342, 345, 346
Brunner, H. 96
Brunner, O. 4, 34, 160, 162, 163, 222, 227
Bruns, F. 38
Buck, A. 225
Burkhardt, J. 223, 226
Burscheid, P. 375
Burschel, P. 262
Büsch, J. G. 123, 132
Büsch, O. 224, 262
Butel, P. 132

Carrière, C. 101, 104, 111, 125, 126, 129
Carsten, F. L. 224, 298
Caspary, H. 261, 262
Cerman, M. 299, 300, 302, 305
Chaix, G. 346, 349
Chapman, S. D. 110
Chartres, J. A. 125
Chèvre, P. 58
Chrisman, M. U. 161
Christaller, W. 33
Ciocco, A. 378, 401
Ciriacono, S. 130
Clark, P. 163, 193
Cohn, H. J. 342
Coleman, D. C. 132
Conrad, H. 34, 223
Conze, W. 34, 160, 162, 163, 222, 227
Corvisier, A. 225
Cressy, D. 327, 345
Creveld, M. L. van 260

Dahlmann-Waitz 125
Dalton, G. 100, 125
Danker, U. 230
Dann, D. 34
Davis, N. 348
Degn, C. 126
Deike, I. 99
Deike, L. 99
Demandt, K. E. 189, 224, 403
Demel, W. 190, 232
Dengler, D. 36
Denzel, M. A. 129
Deppermann, K. 341
Desel, J. 229

Dettmering, E. 127
Deyon, P. 132
Dickerhoff, H. 231
Dickson, P. G. M. 260, 261
Diederiks, H. 161, 191
Diestelkamp, B. 161, 189
Dietz, A. 117, 126, 127, 131
Dietz, W. 347
Dinges, M. 160
Dipper, C. 94, 98, 125, 227, 228, 257, 258, 342, 346
Dittrich, E. 228
Dölemeyer, B. 189, 190
Dollinger, H. 228
Dollinger, P. 131
Dorwart, R. A. 403
Dotzauer, W. 224
Drehsen, V. 191, 192
Dreitzel, H. 190
Dreßen, W. 228
Dreves, H. 402
Droege, G. 94
Duchardt, S. C. 259
Duchhardt, H. 160, 223, 228, 229, 259, 341
Düding, D. 227
Duffy, C. 260
Dülmen, R. van 229, 230, 231, 340, 341, 343, 344, 345, 347, 348, 375
Dupâquier, J. 59
Düwell, K. 304, 306

Eaton, J. 61
Ebel, W. 160
Ebeling, D. 126, 128, 131, 132, 404
Eberhardt, H. 306
Eckhardt, A. 190
Eckhardt, H. W. 229
Edlin-Thième, M. 129
Ehalt, H. C. 160, 225
Ehlers, J. 262
Ehmer, J. 303
Ehrenberg, R. 131
Eibach, J. 232
Eichberg, H. 260
Eichler, H. 258, 404
Eisenbart, L. C. 160, 227
Elias, N. 144, 160, 225, 231
Elsner, G. V. 35
Elton, G. R. 160

Enders, L. 80–1, 92, 94, 95, 96, 97
Endres, R. 95, 96, 97, 160, 162, 403
Engel, F. 375
Engel-Janosi, F. 231
Engelbrecht, T. H. 36, 37
Engelhardt, U. 194
Engels, F. 155, 305
Engels, W. 305
Engelsing, R. 231, 345, 346, 376
Ennen, E. 91, 93
Erler, A. 225
Eulen, F. 228
Evans, J. 98
Evans, R. J. W. 340, 342
Eversley, D. 60

Faber, J. A. 132
Fassl, P. 131
Fedorowicz, J. K. 95
Fehn, K. 36, 37
Feine, H. E. 223
Feldenkirchen, W. P. 127, 130
Fels, E. 13–14, 36
Fenske, H. 227
Fertig, L. 231
Fetscher, I. 227
Fiedler, S. 257
Filzer, P. 11, 35
Finer, S. E. 262
Finzsch, N. 404
Fischer, W. 130, 187, 298, 307, 308, 403
Fleury, M. 59
Flik, R. 304, 307
Flohn, H. 35
Flügel, A. 127, 188, 189, 193, 306
Fontaine, L. 128
Forster, M. R. 348
Forster, R. 59
Fouquet, G. 93, 258
Fout, J. 60
Fox, T. 127
François, E. 162, 226, 311, 324, 327, 335, 339, 344, 345, 346, 348
Frankenberg, P. 35
Franz, G. 34, 59, 91, 98, 189, 190, 191, 228, 235, 237, 257, 259, 346, 375
Freitag, W. 189, 345
Freudenburger, H. 166

Frevert, U. 162, 229, 340
Friedeburg, R. von 189, 192
Friedemann, P. 227
Friedrichs, C. R. 161, 194, 259, 261,
  262, 401
Fritze, K. 131
Fulbrook, M. 340

Gaenschalz, E. 93, 94
Gagliardo, J. G. 302
Gall, L. 159, 193
Gascon, R. 131
Gawthrop, R. L. 342, 345, 346
Gensicke, H. 96
Gerhard, D. 159, 224, 225, 309, 338
Gerteis, K. 93, 97, 127, 226, 342
Giesen, B. 34
Glaser, R. 35
Glass, D. 60
Gleitsmann, R.-J. 36
Goeters, J. F. G. 342
Goldstein, A. 59
Gönnenwein, O. 127
Goody, J. 60
Gothein, E. 128, 307
Göttert, K.-H. 231
Gottlieb, G. 131
Göttmann, F. 36, 38, 127, 130, 132,
  258
Graff, H. J. 345
Gramulia, G. S. 128, 129, 130, 131
Gras, N. S. B. 36
Grees, H. 37, 97
Greiffenhagen, M. 192
Grenz, R. 127
Greve, K. 93, 194
Greyerz, K. von 159, 226, 342
Griep, W. 375
Griffeth, R. 161
Grimm, G. E. 188, 231
Grimm, H. J. 403
Gröllich, E. 304
Gronemeyer, R. 230
Grossman, W. 347
Grube, W. 225, 307
Gründler, O. 161
Grundmann, H. 159, 162, 223
Gschliesser, O. von 223
Gudd, M. 93
Gunst, P. 93

Günther, W. 376
Gutmann, M. P. 38, 258
Gyimesi, S. 96

Haan, H. 95, 132, 223
Häberle, E. J. 126
Habermas, R. 344, 345
Hagedorn, B. 126
Hagenah, U. 98
Hagenmaier, M. 191
Hahn, A. 97
Hahn, H.-W. 193
Hajnal, J. 60
Hammerstein, N. 189, 230, 346
Hanschmidt, A. 403
Hanschmidt, H. 97
Hansen, E. W. 257
Hantsch, H. 224
Harder-Gersdorff, E. 131, 301
Harnisch, H. 91, 92, 97, 98, 99, 130
Härter, K. 194
Hartinger, W. 97
Hartmann, P. C. 261
Hartung, F. 223
Hasse, E. 127
Hassinger, H. 307
Hattenhauer, H. 192, 193
Hauptmeyer, D.-H. 99
Heckel, J. 228
Heckel, M. 191
Heckendorn, H. 231
Heckscher, E. F. 228
Heinrich, G. 189, 191, 224
Heitz, G. 91, 97, 99, 305
Hélin, E. 59
Helleiner, K. F. 98
Heller, H. 97
Hellmann, G. 35
Henderson, W. O. 132
Henning, F.-W. 37, 72, 91, 95, 125,
  126, 130, 187, 298
Henry, L. 59, 61
Henze, H. 35
Hermann, C. H. 257
Herrmann, B. 229
Herrmann, F. 92
Herrmann, H.-W. 260
Herrmann, K. 99
Hersche, P. 262, 340, 344, 348, 349
Hertner, P. 127

Herzfeld, E. 97
Heumann, G. D. 128
Heuvel, C. van den 188
Hickson, C. R. 305
Hildebrandt, H. 93
Hinckeldey, C. 230
Hinrichs, E. 95, 97, 227, 231, 327,
  341, 342, 344, 345, 347, 349
Hintze, O. 341
Hippel, W. von 94, 95, 228, 257, 259,
  375
Hobsbawm, E. 59
Hof, U. I. 376
Hoffmann, T. 93
Hofmann, D. 60
Hofmann, H. H. 34, 191, 375
Hofmann, W. 102, 125
Holbach, R. 300
Holl, B. 260
Homburg, H. 128
Hoock, J. 127
Hörger, H. 348, 349
Houdaille, J. 59, 61
Howard, M. 257
Howell, N. 61
Hroch, M. 162
Hsia, R. 317, 330, 339, 341, 342, 344,
  345, 346, 348, 349, 396
Hudson, P. 303
Hüpeden, C. L. P. 130
Huppertz, B. 97

Imhof, A. E. 59, 258, 375
Immenkötter, H. 226
Ingrao, C. 261
Irsigler, F. 93, 132, 230, 260
Isenmann, E. 93, 161
Israel, J. I. 131

Jäger, H. 34, 375, 403
Jahns, S. 189
Jakubowski-Tiessen, M. 35, 229, 341
Janczak, J. 128
Janssen, W. 91
Janz, O. 191
Jaritz, G. 401
Jeannin, P. 119, 120, 127, 128, 131,
  132
Jersch-Wenzel, S. 348
Jeserich, K. G. A. 223, 225

Johansen, H. C. 130
Jorgenson, S.-A. 225
Jütte, R. 230, 402, 403, 404

Kadell, F.-A. 126
Kahlert, H. 128
Kamen, H. 298, 299
Kampf, H. 223
Kaphahn, F. 401
Kappl, C. 402
Kaufhold, K.-H. 37, 91, 98, 130, 265,
  269, 271, 273–4, 276, 280, 291–2,
  298, 300, 301, 302, 305, 307, 375
Kellenbenz, H. 36, 38, 94, 98, 116,
  125, 128, 129, 130, 131, 225, 228,
  298, 301
Kellner, S. 95
Kermann, J. 302, 305
Kerschbaumer, D. 96, 97
Keyer, E. 93
Keyser, E. 27–8, 37
Kiesel, H. 226, 230, 231
Kießling, R. 94
Kintner, H. 62
Kirchner, J. 127
Kisch, H. 283, 302, 303, 304, 305,
  307, 308, 347, 376
Kiss, I. N. 130
Klein, E. 129, 224, 260, 261
Kliche, W. 126
Klingenstein, G. 96, 230–1, 340
Klose, O. 126
Klueting, H. 159, 203, 224, 340, 341
Knemeyer, F.-L. 227
Knittler, H. 79, 96, 125
Knoch, K. 35
Knodel, J. 59, 61, 62
Köbler, G. 224
Kohl, W. 97
Köllmann, W. 192, 304, 306
König, A. 305
Kopitzsch, F. 161, 162, 193, 404
Körber-Grohne, U. 36–7
Koselleck, R. 34, 98, 160, 162, 163,
  194, 195, 222, 227
Kosfeld, A. 195
Kötzschke, R. 33
Kouri, E. I. 346
Kovács, E. 340
Kramer, K.-S. 343

Kraus, A. 261, 262
Kravis, I. B. 102, 125
Krawarick, H. 348
Kresse, W. 126, 129, 132
Kretschmer, K. 375
Kriedte, P. 61, 130, 131, 132, 229,
    260, 267, 283, 298, 299, 302, 303,
    304, 305, 307, 376
Krimpenfort, W. 93
Kroener, B. R. 257, 260, 261
Kroeschell, K. 223
Kroker, W. 36, 301
Kruedner, J. F. von 160, 225
Krüger, H. 133
Krüger, K. 93, 194, 225, 261
Ksoll, M. 93, 95, 97
Kuchenbuch, L. 99
Kuczynski, J. 299
Kühlmann, W. 188, 189
Kühn, S. 127, 128, 132
Kuhn, W. 93
Kühnert, H. 307
Kulischer, J. 162
Kullen, S. 38
Kunisch, J. 191, 223, 224, 225, 227
Kunze, A. 128, 130, 302, 304, 305
Kuske, B. 104, 126
Küther, C. 162, 230
Kutz, M. 130, 131

Labitsch, A. 344
Labrousse, E. 125
Lackner, M. 226
Lampe, J. 375
Lang, P. T. 226
Lange, U. 231
Langosch, K. 34
Larsen, Ø. 258
Lasch, M. 401
Laslett, P. 59
Lassotta, A. 230, 403, 404
Lauer, W. 35
Lee, Robert 59, 60
Lee, Ronald 60
Lee, W. R. 98, 298, 308
Legers, P. 305
Lehe, E. von 127
Lehmann, H. 225, 227, 333, 341, 342,
    345, 347, 348, 349
Lehmann, R. 97

Lenhart, L. 348
Lenz, G. 228
Léon, P. 101, 104, 125, 126
Lerch, H. 95, 96
Lerner, F. 301
Levine, D. 59, 61–2, 303
Lewald, U. 303
Liebel, H. P. 191, 194
Lieberich, H. 223
Lindberg, C. 403
Linde, H. 300
Lindgren, U. 38
Link, C. 190, 191
Livi-Bacci, M. 59
Lohse, H. 306
Looz-Corswarem, C. G. von 127
Lorenzen-Schmidt, K.-J. 93
Lösch, A. 1, 33
Lundgreen, P. 341
Lütge, F. 74–5, 94, 95, 131, 162, 242,
    259
Lutz, H. 96, 231, 259, 340
Lutz, J. 35
Lynch, K. 59

MacHardy, K. 340
Maddalena, A. de 225, 228
Magdelaine, M. 229, 341, 348
Magen, F. 224
Mager, F. 98
Mager, W. 222, 232, 283, 284, 298,
    300, 301, 302, 303, 304, 306, 307
Magnusson, L. 132
Mai, E. 126
Maier, H. 227
Malthus, T. 60, 239
Mandrou, R. 160
Manegold, K.-H. 126
Margairaz, D. 128
Maron, G. 340
Marx, K. 100, 124, 125, 133, 155
Marzahn, C. 404
Mathieu, J. 92
Mathis, F. 160, 259
Matis, F. 130
Matis, H. 125
Mattmüller, M. 259
Maurer, C. 349
Maurer, W. 403
Mayer, A. 61

Mayer, T. 199, 223
McKendrick, N. 125
McNeill, W. H. 257
Meckseper, C. 93
Medick, H. 60, 61, 128, 130, 132,
　229, 260, 267, 299, 302, 303, 304,
　306, 307, 340, 342, 346, 376
Meidenbauer, J. 191
Meier, J. 340, 348
Meister, A. 34
Melton, J. V. H. 231
Mendels, F. 60, 266–7, 299, 302, 303,
　304, 305
Merkle, W. 128
Mertens, D. 227
Merzbacher, F. 223
Metz, R. 129
Metz, W. 189, 191
Meyer-Stoll, C. 128, 129
Midelfort, H. C. 348
Mieck, I. 34, 187, 228
Miehe, L. 259
Milward, A. S. 298
Minder, R. 342
Mitgau, H. 192
Mitteis, H. 223
Mittenzwei, I. 97, 99, 133
Mitterauer, M. 163, 303
Moersch, K. 257
Mogk, W. 229
Mohrmann, R. 308
Möker, U. 194
Molitor, H. 34, 226, 344
Möller, H. 58, 159, 160, 161, 162,
　227, 342
Möller, P. 94
Moltmann, J. 342
Mommsen, H. 342, 403
Mommsen, W. J. 159
Mooser, J. 91, 97, 98, 127, 306, 307
Moran, B. T. 230
Moraw, P. 159, 346
Morhard, J. 339
Mörke, O. 159, 161
Möser, J. 108, 109, 114, 128, 130, 169
Mui, H.-C. 128
Mui, L. H. 128
Müller, A. 401
Müller, H.-H. 98, 99, 132
Müller, J. 190, 194

Müller, K. 223
Münch, P. 34, 225, 226, 227, 228,
　229, 230, 231, 232, 339, 340, 344
Münkler, H. 227
Musall, H. 229, 258, 259
Myška, M. 302, 303

Nagel, A. 230
Naudé, W. 94, 130
Netting, R. 62
Nettl, P. 376
Neugebauer, W. 224, 231
Neuhaus, H. 223
Neumeister, S. 188
Niethammer, L. 340
Niggl, G. 342
Nipperdey, T. 346
Nischan, B. 341
Norden, W. 231
North, M. 94, 95, 96, 97, 98, 129

Oeppen, J. 61
Oestreich, G. 159, 222, 223, 225, 228,
　232, 260, 262, 308, 339, 340
Oexle, O. G. 34, 402
Ogilvie, S. 226, 259, 299, 300, 302,
　304, 305, 306, 307, 308, 334, 343,
　347
Ohlin, G. 61
Olechnowitz, K.-F. 126, 131
Otremba, E. 35
Otruba, G. 260, 261
Ottenjann, H. 92, 229, 376
Ozment, S. 348

Pallach, C. 130
Pallach, U.-C. 229
Panthel, H. W. 190
Pardoe, M. 61
Parker, G. 225, 257, 259, 260
Parker, N. G. 308
Parsons, T. 347
Patze, H. 306, 307
Paulinyi, A. 37
Paulsen, F. 230, 346
Pedlow, G. W. 191
Perjés, G. 260
Perrott, D. 378, 401
Peters, J. 92, 95, 97
Peters, L. F. 129, 131

Petersen, E. L. 130
Petřán, J. 162
Petri, F. 94
Petzina, D. 128
Pfister, C. 35, 36, 37, 58, 59, 60, 93, 229, 344, 375
Pfister, U. 304, 343
Phayer, M. 61
Pickl, O. 259, 260
Pierenkemper, T. 91, 98
Plodeck, K. 225
Plumb, J. H. 125
Pohl, H. 37, 126, 129, 131, 132, 223, 225, 271, 298, 300, 301, 375
Poni, C. 305
Porter, R. 308
Prange, R. 129
Prange, W. 98
Press, V. 93, 159, 223, 224, 225, 226, 228, 231, 262, 340, 346
Prestwich, M. 342
Preu, P. 227
Pröve, R. 262
Puhle, H.-J. 188, 194
Pullan, B. 393–4, 403

Quandt, S. 340
Quarthal, F. 225, 231

Rabe, H. 34, 35, 226, 343, 344
Radkau, J. 37, 38, 229
Raeff, M. 227
Raisch, P. 193
Ranieri, F. 189, 190
Rankl, H. 223
Ranum, O. 59
Rauch, G. 159
Rausch, W. 161
Rebel, H. 60
Redich, F. 166, 260
Reekers, S. 306, 347
Reinhard, E. 225, 231
Reinhard, W. 225–6, 227, 326, 340, 345
Reinhardt, R. 224
Reinhold, J. 128, 131, 132, 133
Reininghaus, W. 128, 192, 229, 277, 298, 301, 302, 307
Reißmann, M. 129
Rey, M. v. 93

Riedel, M. 160, 194
Riedmann, J. 130
Ris, G. 191
Ritterband, P. 59
Rittmann, H. 129
Robisheaux, T. 35, 59, 92, 97, 343, 349, 402
Rödel, W. G. 258, 402
Roeck, B. 94, 127, 131, 132, 162, 163, 222, 226, 230, 257, 259, 261–2, 311, 337, 339, 348, 401
Röhlk, F. 126, 132
Romano, R. 133
Roper, L. 342, 344
Rosen, K. 227
Rosenbaum, H. 163
Rosenberg, H. 91, 224, 341, 342
Rössler, H. 346
Rostow, W. W. 308
Roth, G. 347
Roth, J. L. 98
Rothe, H. 97
Rotschky, P. 306
Rotzoll, U. 403
Rublack, H.-C. 35, 159, 161, 191, 225, 226, 339, 341, 343, 344, 402, 403
Rudolf, H. U. 257, 259
Rudersdorf, M. 346
Rummel, W. 230
Ruppert, W. 162, 342, 346
Rüsen, J. 344
· Rüthing, H. 93, 383

Saalfeld, D. 95, 96, 97
Sabean, D. 59, 60, 61, 92, 97, 307, 308, 343
Sachse, W. 258
Sachße, C. 230, 258, 339, 402, 403, 404
Safley, T. M. 343
Saftien, V. 376
Salm, H. 259
Sander, S. 229
Sandgruber, R. 308
Saul, S. B. 298
Sax, E. 306
Schenda, R. 231
Scherner, K. O. 193, 403
Scherpner, H. 402

Scheuerbrandt, H. 258, 259
Schieckel, H. 190
Schieder, W. 226, 227, 342
Schildhauer, J. 131
Schilling, H. 131, 159, 160, 161, 162,
    191, 193, 194, 225, 228, 339, 340,
    342, 343, 344, 345, 346, 347
Schindler, N. 344, 348, 349, 402
Schindling, A. 224, 230, 339, 346
Schings, H.-J. 342
Schissler, H. 98
Schlaich, K. 224
Schlechte, H. 133
Schlenke, M. 262
Schlesinger, W. 306, 307
Schlögl, R. 92, 95, 97, 98, 259, 261
Schluchter, W. 340, 347
Schlumbohm, J. 61, 96, 97, 130, 132,
    229, 260, 267, 284, 289, 299, 302,
    303, 304, 305, 306, 307, 343, 376
Schmelzeisen, G. K. 227
Schmidt, G. 194, 231, 262, 343
Schmidt, H. R. 225, 339, 349
Schmidt, P. 341, 348
Schmise, F. 225
Schmitt, R. 109
Schmitt, S. 95
Schmöe, F. 225
Schmoller, G. 94
Schnee, H. 94
Schneider, J. 129
Schneider, W. 226, 306
Schnelbögl, F. 94
Schnelzer, P. 129
Schnitter, H. 260
Schnur, R. 189
Schnyder-Burghartz, A. 92
Schochet, G. A. 228
Schöck, H. 92
Schofield, R. 62, 327, 345
Schöne, B. 305
Schönstädt, J. 341
Schormann, G. 230, 344, 345, 348
Schorn-Schütte, L. 162, 191, 192, 343,
    344
Schott, C. 402
Schreiner, K. 195, 226
Schremmer, E. 95, 97, 125, 126, 127,
    128, 129, 130, 131, 300
Schrenck, N. F. von 190, 191

Schröder, H.-C. 143–4, 160
Schröder, S. M. 259
Schröder-Lembke, G. 99
Schubert, E. 35, 38, 230, 346, 402
Schubert, F. H. 222
Schubnell, H. 60
Schuhmann, G. 261
Schulte, F. 301
Schultz, H. 93, 161, 299–300
Schultz, U. 225
Schultze, B. 125–6
Schulze, H. K. 94
Schulze, R. 227
Schulze, W. 224, 226, 230, 231, 261,
    262, 339, 342, 402, 403
Schumpeter, E. B. 132
Schwab, D. 163
Schwark, T. 262
Schwarz, R. 226
Schwarzer, O. 129
Schwarzmaier, H. 225, 231
Scott, T. 346
Scribner, R. 379, 345, 348, 349, 382,
    401, 402
Segalen, M. 59
Seibold, G. 128
Seibt, F. 403
Sellin, V. 261
Seybold, D. C. 345
Sharlin, A. 60
Shlaich, K. 224
Shorter, E. 59, 60–1
Showalter, D. E. 257
Sicken, B. 261
Siebenmorgen, H. 344
Sieder, R. 163
Sieferle, R. P. 37
Siegert, R. 231, 376
Sieglerschmidt, J. 34, 38, 258
Simmel, G. 387, 402
Simon, C. 229
Simsch, A. 261
Skalweit, A. 99, 130, 132
Slack, P. 193
Smend, R. 224
Smith, L. 259, 308
Smolinsky, H. 226, 344
Soenke, J. 96
Soergel, T. 60
Sogner, S. 59

Soliday, G. L. 161
Söll, W. 302
Sombart, W. 108, 109, 125, 128, 165, 244–5, 260, 298, 308
Sommer, W. 191
Sonenscher, M. 303
Sonnenfels, J. von 102
Sothmann, M. 404
Sparn, W. 191, 192
Specker, H. E. 340
Speitkamp, W. 98, 190
Spindler, M. 340
Spree, U. 194
Sprenger, B. 129
Stahlschmidt, R. 301
Stark, W. 131
Steensgard, N. 131, 308
Stehl, H. 230, 404
Steigelmann, H. 226
Stein, R. 98
Steinberg, H. G. 34
Steinberg, S. H. 240, 257, 259
Steinbicker, C. 189, 190, 403
Steinert, H. 228
Steinmetz, W. 194
Stekl, H. 230
Stier, B. 230, 404
Stollberg-Rilinger, B. 188, 225, 228
Stolleis, M. 227
Strauss, G. 345, 346
Stoob, H. 37, 93
Stromer, W. von 35, 36, 37, 300
Stroup, J. M. 191, 192
Stürmer, M. 162, 229, 347
Sundhausen, H. 96
Swart, F. 97

Tanner, A. 303
Tennstedt, F. 230, 339, 402, 403, 404
Teuteberg, H.-J. 35, 38, 93, 343, 375
Thadden, R. von 229, 341, 348
Thirsk, J. 60, 125
Thomas, C. G. 161
Thompson, E. 60
Thomson, E. A. 305
Thünen, J. H. von 33, 112
Thunn, A. 305
Tilly, C. 60, 61, 261, 262, 303
Tilly, R. H. 298
Timmermann, H. 222

Tipton, F. B. 298, 299, 303, 304, 306, 307, 308
Titz-Matuszaki, I. 378–9, 401, 404
Topolski, J. 95
Treiber, H. 228
Treue, W. 162
Troeltsch, E. 302, 304, 306, 307, 393
Troitzsch, U. 37, 38
Troßbach, W. 65, 91, 92, 94, 96, 97, 160, 162, 163, 229, 231
Turner, B.L. 36

Uhlhorn, G. 403
Ulbrich, C. 95, 343
Ulbricht, O. 98
Ullmann, H.-P. 162
Unger, W. S. 130
Unruh, G.-C. von 223, 225
Urlanis, B. Z. 258

Valentin, J.-M. 344
Vanja, C. 343, 344
Vann, J. A. 307
Vári, A. 96
Veit, L. A. 348, 349
Veit, P. 344, 346
Vierhaus, R. 162, 190, 191, 224, 225, 226, 227, 259, 340
Vogel, B. 98
Vogel, W. 132
Vögele, J. 36
Vogler, B. 348
Volz, G. B. 132
Vopa, A. J. La 192
Vos, S. D. 62
Voss, J. 342, 345
Vries, J. de 101, 125, 162, 298, 302, 308

Wake, C. H. H. 131
Walker, M. 58, 97, 149, 161, 184, 188, 194, 226, 304, 349
Wallace, P. 339
Walle, E. van de. 62
Wallerstein, I. 165
Wallmann, J. 342
Walter, H. 258
Walter, R. 126, 127
Walz, R. 230, 344
Wandruszka, A. 223

Ward, W. R. 341
Warden, A. J. 302
Warmbrunn, P. 226, 339
Weber, M. 106, 127, 137, 159, 185, 194, 331–2, 333, 334, 347
Weber, R. 262
Weczerka, H. 38
Wehler, H.-U. 154, 159, 160, 161, 162, 187, 231, 235, 257, 259, 339, 342, 346
Weigelmann, G. 35
Weinacht, P.-L. 222
Weinhold, R. 305
Weis, E. 162
Weise, C. 168
Weiß, H. 92, 94
Weiss, M. 260, 261
Weiss, V. 61, 261
Weitzmann, W. 402
Westermann, E. 36, 94, 127, 130, 301
Weyrauch, E. 346
Whaley, J. 161
Whitman, J. Q. 195
Wied, W. 96, 97
Wiedemann, C. 188, 403
Wiegelmann, G. 92, 93, 95, 97, 231, 342, 345, 349, 376
Wiese, H. 127, 130
Wiese-Schorn, L. 161
Willerding, U. 93
Williams, M. 36
Willoweit, W. 193, 223
Wilson, C. 61
Winckelmann, J. 347
Winckelmann, O. 403

Winkel, H. 99
Winter, E. 304
Winter, J. M. 260, 308
Winterling, A. 160, 225
Wischermann, C. 193
Wiswe, M. 346
Witthöft, H. 36, 126
Witzel, J. 194
Witzendorff, H. J. von 132
Wolff, K. H. 299, 301, 303, 305, 306, 307, 308
Wright, W. 403
Wrigley, E. A. 59, 61, 62
Wulfert, H. 99
Wunder, B. 189, 224
Wunder, H. 94, 95, 97, 229, 342, 343, 344
Wyduckel, D. 222

Zeeden, E. W. 225, 226, 341
Zeile, C. 98
Zellfelder, F. 129
Zernack, K. 161, 347
Ziechmann, J. 224
Ziegler, W. 339
Ziekursch, J. 99
Ziessow, K. H. 229, 231
Zimmermann, A. 307
Zimmermann, C. 97, 99
Zöllner, E. 224
Zorn, W. 98, 125, 130, 131, 162, 259, 261
Zschunke, P. 59, 61, 324, 335, 339, 343, 344, 348, 402
Zwahr, H. 305